AF785342

Advances in Infectious Diseases and Clinical Microbiology during the COVID-19 Pandemic

Advances in Infectious Diseases and Clinical Microbiology during the COVID-19 Pandemic

Editors

Yusra Habib Khan
Tauqeer Hussain Mallhi
Tahir Mehmood Khan
Muhammad Salman

MDPI

Basel • Beijing • Wuhan • Barcelona • Belgrade • Novi Sad • Cluj • Manchester

Editors
Yusra Habib Khan
Jouf University
Sakaka, Saudi Arabia

Tauqeer Hussain Mallhi
Jouf University
Sakaka, Saudi Arabia

Tahir Mehmood Khan
University of Veterinary & Animal Sciences
Lahore, Pakistan

Muhammad Salman
Lahore College for Women University
Lahore, Pakistan

Editorial Office
MDPI
St. Alban-Anlage 66
4052 Basel, Switzerland

This is a reprint of articles from the Special Issue published online in the open access journal *Medicina* (ISSN 1648-9144) (available at: https://www.mdpi.com/journal/medicina/special_issues/B6ANN35B26).

For citation purposes, cite each article independently as indicated on the article page online and as indicated below:

Lastname, A.A.; Lastname, B.B. Article Title. *Journal Name* **Year**, *Volume Number*, Page Range.

ISBN 978-3-0365-9468-2 (Hbk)
ISBN 978-3-0365-9469-9 (PDF)
doi.org/10.3390/books978-3-0365-9469-9

© 2023 by the authors. Articles in this book are Open Access and distributed under the Creative Commons Attribution (CC BY) license. The book as a whole is distributed by MDPI under the terms and conditions of the Creative Commons Attribution-NonCommercial-NoDerivs (CC BY-NC-ND) license.

Contents

About the Editors

Yusra Habib Khan

Dr. Yusra Habib Khan is an assistant professor at the Department of Clinical Pharmacy at Jouf University, Saudi Arabia. She received her Ph.D. in Clinical Pharmacy from Universiti Sains Malaysia (USM). Dr Yusra's research expertise include vaccine hesitancy, clinical outcomes among chronic kidney disease patients, pharmaceutical care, pharmacoepidemiology, pharmacovigilance, and viral infections, the latter of which can be observed in her recent articles published on COVID-19. Dr Yusra's current research has significantly contributed to ascertaining the atypical complications, particularly nephropathies, of various infectious diseases. Dr. Yusra has published more than 140 scholarly articles in well-reputed scientific journals, and her work has been cited more than 1500 times with a h-index of 21. She has also published one book entitled: "Expanded Dengue Syndrome" and various chapters with reputable publishers. Dr. Yusra has gained teaching experience in Malaysia, Pakistan, and Saudi Arabia and is responsible for the supervision of postgraduate students. She leads various funded projects in the field of health sciences, and based on her significant scientific contributions to the field of pharmaceutical and medical sciences, she has been awarded several awards (Best Researcher and Best Presenter).

Tauqeer Hussain Mallhi

Dr. Tauqeer Hussain Mallhi holds a doctoral degree in Clinical Pharmacy from Universiti Sains Malaysia (USM), Malaysia. He currently works as an assistant professor at the Department of Clinical Pharmacy, College of Pharmacy at Jouf University (JU), Kingdom of Saudi Arabia. Previously, he served as an assistant professor and coordinator of the Department of Pharmacy Practice at GC University Faisalabad, Pakistan. He has also worked as a research officer in the Chronic Kidney Disease (CKD) Resource Center, Hospital Universiti Sains Malaysia (HUSM), Malaysia. Dr. Mallhi's work broadly concentrates on the epidemiology of dengue infection and explores the burden of acute kidney injury (AKI) and subsequent renal recovery among dengue patients surviving an episode of AKI. His current research plan is centered around atypical manifestations of infectious disease, vaccine hesitancy, pharmaceutical care, pharmacist outreach in public and psychological health, the rational use of drugs, drug safety, health policy, and drug therapy-related problems. Dr. Mallhi has published more than 150 articles in internationally recognized and peer-reviewed ISI-indexed journals; he has also published one authored book entitled "Expanded Dengue Syndrome". He has also published several book chapters with international publishers. Dr. Mallhi also serves as an editorial board member of various peer-reviewed journals related to infectious diseases, pharmaceutical science, and healthcare.

Tahir Mehmood Khan

Tahir Mehmood Khan is the Director Institute of Pharmaceutical Sciences, University of Veterinary & Animal Sciences, Pakistan. His prime area of interest is evidence-based pharmacotherapy, systematic reviews, and meta-analyses. He is also Editor-in-Chief of the journal *Archives of Pharmacy Practice.*

Muhammad Salman

Muhammad Salman holds a doctoral degree in Clinical Pharmacy from Universiti Sains Malaysia (USM), Malaysia. He currently works as an assistant professor at the Institute of Pharmacy, Faculty of Pharmaceutical and Allied Health Sciences at Lahore College for Women University, Pakistan. Previously, he served as an assistant professor and as the Coordinator of the Department of Pharmacy Practice at the University of Lahore, Pakistan. His work broadly concentrates on chronic kidney disease, atypical manifestations of infectious disease, vaccine hesitancy, pharmaceutical care, pharmacist outreach in public and psychological health, the rational use of drugs, drug safety, health policy, and drug therapy-related problems. Dr. Salman has published numerous articles in internationally recognized and peer-reviewed ISI-indexed journals. He has also published several book chapters with reputed publishers. Dr. Salman also serves as an editorial board member of various peer-reviewed journals related to infectious diseases, pharmaceutical science, and healthcare.

medicina

Editorial

Advances in Infectious Diseases and Clinical Microbiology during the COVID-19 Pandemic

Yusra Habib Khan [1,*], Tauqeer Hussain Mallhi [1,*], Tahir Mehmood Khan [2] and Muhammad Salman [3]

1 Department of Clinical Pharmacy, College of Pharmacy, Jouf University, Sakaka 72341, Saudi Arabia
2 Institute of Pharmaceutical Sciences, University of Veterinary & Animal Sciences, Lahore 54000, Pakistan
3 Institute of Pharmacy, Faculty of Pharmaceutical and Allied Health Sciences, Lahore College for Women University, Lahore 54000, Pakistan
* Correspondence: yhkhan@ju.edu.sa (Y.H.K.); thhussain@ju.edu.sa (T.H.M.)

Infectious diseases pose substantial challenges to the healthcare system and are associated with significant morbidity and mortality. The COVID-19 pandemic has necessitated considerable public health maneuvers across the globe [1]. Changes in the patterns of various infectious diseases were observed during the pandemic. A growing body of evidence indicates the decline in influenza virus circulation during the COVID-19 pandemic in various regions around the world that is primarily related to several controlling measures and non-pharmaceutical interventions employed to curb the growing encumbrance of SARS-CoV-2 [2]. However, the COVID-19 pandemic has caused disruptions in reporting of other infectious diseases, such as dengue, sexually transmitted diseases, and other coronavirus infections [3]. Likewise, this pandemic has also disrupted various routine immunization campaigns [4]. Other infections such as HIV/AIDS, tuberculosis, and hepatitis carry equivalent health risks to the global population. The reduction in the reporting of these infections due to an overwhelmed healthcare system during the COVID-19 pandemic remained a significant concern for health authorities. Understanding the transmission patterns of other infectious diseases during the COVID-19 pandemic is of utmost importance for designing and implementing mitigating strategies for public health. However, there is a dearth of investigations on this topic. Ascertaining the impact of the COVID-19 pandemic on the incidence of other infectious diseases will improve the responsiveness of health authorities during disease outbreaks in future. It is pertinent to mention that the COVID-19 pandemic also resulted in improved healthcare metrics for other infectious diseases, i.e., improved influenza vaccination rate during the pandemic. On the other hand, the implications, scope, and relevance of clinical microbiology have gained invaluable appreciation during this pandemic [5]. Clinical microbiologists played an aggressive role during the pandemic through the provision of various expert services such as the identification of viral structure, differential diagnosis, and optimized sterilization and disinfection processes. The COVID-19 pandemic has initiated new horizons for infectious disease research, control, funding acquisitions, administrative assistance, and health promotion. This issue emphasizes various aspects of the advancements and progress in infectious diseases and clinical microbiology during the ongoing COVID-19 pandemic. Potential topics include, but are not limited to, the following:

- Impact of the COVID-19 pandemic on the reporting of infectious diseases;
- Emerging atypical complications during the disease course of COVID-19;
- Clinical and laboratory characteristics and outcomes among COVID-19 patients with co-infections;
- The burden of common and major infectious diseases before, during, and after the COVID-19 pandemic;
- Challenges in the clinical management of serious and neglected tropical infections;

Citation: Khan, Y.H.; Mallhi, T.H.; Khan, T.M.; Salman, M. Advances in Infectious Diseases and Clinical Microbiology during the COVID-19 Pandemic. *Medicina* **2022**, *58*, 1362. https://doi.org/10.3390/medicina58101362

Received: 16 September 2022
Accepted: 25 September 2022
Published: 28 September 2022

Publisher's Note: MDPI stays neutral with regard to jurisdictional claims in published maps and institutional affiliations.

Copyright: © 2022 by the authors. Licensee MDPI, Basel, Switzerland. This article is an open access article distributed under the terms and conditions of the Creative Commons Attribution (CC BY) license (https://creativecommons.org/licenses/by/4.0/).

- Impact of the COVID-19 pandemic on the development and repurposing of drugs against SARS-CoV-2;
- Changes in vaccination patterns for other infectious diseases during the COVID-19 pandemic;
- Correlation of COVID-19 vaccination campaigns with routine immunization programs;
- Challenges in the management of infectious diseases during the COVID-19 pandemic;
- Disruptions in preventive measures or services for vaccine-preventable diseases (VPDs) during the COVID-19 pandemic;
- Evolution of Scope of Clinical Microbiology in response to the rapid spread of COVID-19;
- Implications of knowledge related to Clinical Microbiology in the identification and screening of SARS-CoV-2;
- Variations in response of health authorities to the challenges during the pandemic, i.e., conspiracy beliefs or theories, control measures and mandates;
- Epidemiological variations in infectious diseases during the COVID-19 pandemic, more specifically during the period of lockdowns;
- Implications of information technology for screening, identification, and control of SARS-CoV-2.

This Special Issue welcomes submissions ranging from original, clinical, and translational articles to reviews in the field of Clinical Microbiology and Infectious Diseases during the COVID-19 Pandemic.

Author Contributions: Y.H.K. and T.H.M. substantially contributed to the concept and design of the article, T.M.K. and M.S. revised the article critically and approved the version to be published. All authors have read and agreed to the published version of the manuscript.

Funding: This research received no funding.

Institutional Review Board Statement: Not applicable.

Informed Consent Statement: Not applicable.

Data Availability Statement: Not applicable.

Conflicts of Interest: The authors declare no conflict of interest.

References

1. Amar, S.; Avni, Y.S.; O'Rourke, N.; Michael, T. Prevalence of common infectious diseases after COVID-19 vaccination and easing of pandemic restrictions in Israel. *JAMA Netw. Open* **2022**, *5*, e2146175. [CrossRef] [PubMed]
2. Khanolkar, R.A.; Trajkovski, A.; Agarwal, A.; Pauls, M.A.; Lang, E.S. Emerging evidence for non-pharmacologic interventions in reducing the burden of respiratory illnesses. *Intern. Emerg. Med.* **2022**, *17*, 639–644. [CrossRef] [PubMed]
3. Chen, Y.; Li, N.; Lourenço, J.; Wang, L.; Cazelles, B.; Dong, L.; Li, B.; Liu, Y.; Jit, M.; Bosse, N.I.; et al. Measuring the effects of COVID-19-related disruption on dengue transmission in southeast Asia and Latin America: A statistical modelling study. *Lancet Infect. Dis.* **2022**, *22*, 657–667. [CrossRef]
4. Ota, M.O.C.; Badur, S.; Romano-Mazzotti, L.; Friedland, L.R. Impact of COVID-19 pandemic on routine immunization. *Ann. Med.* **2021**, *53*, 2286–2297. [CrossRef] [PubMed]
5. Dunbar, S.; Babady, E.; Das, S.; Moore, C. Impact of COVID-19 on the clinical microbiology laboratory: Preparing for the next pandemic. *Front. Cell. Infect. Microbiol.* **2022**, *12*, 1031436. [CrossRef]

medicina

MDPI

Article

Analysis of Prior Aspirin Treatment on in-Hospital Outcome of Geriatric COVID-19 Infected Patients

Khaoula Zekri-Nechar [1], José Barberán [2], José J. Zamorano-León [3,*], María Durbán [4], Alcira Andrés-Castillo [1], Carlos Navarro-Cuellar [5], Antonio López-Farré [1], Ana López-de-Andrés [3], Rodrigo Jiménez-García [3] and Carlos H. Martínez-Martínez [1]

1 Medicine Department, School of Medicine, Universidad Complutense de Madrid, 28040 Madrid, Spain
2 Internal Medicine Department HM Hospital, 28250 Madrid, Spain
3 Public Health and Maternal and Child Health Department, School of Medicine, Universidad Complutense de Madrid, IdISSC, 28040 Madrid, Spain
4 Statistics Department, Universidad Carlos III, 28903 Madrid, Spain
5 Maxillofacial Surgery Department, Hospital General Universitario Gregorio Marañón, 28007 Madrid, Spain
* Correspondence: jjzamorano@ucm.es; Tel.: +34-91-394-1523

Abstract: *Background and Objectives*: Aspirin (ASA) is a commonly used antithrombotic drug that has been demonstrated to reduce venous thromboembolism. The aim was to analyze if geriatric COVID-19 patients undergoing a 100 mg/day Aspirin (ASA) treatment prior to hospitalization differ in hospital outcome compared to patients without previous ASA therapy. *Materials and Methods*: An observational retrospective study was carried out using an anonymized database including geriatric COVID-19 patients (March to April 2020) admitted to Madrid Hospitals Group. A group of COVID-19 patients were treated with low ASA (100 mg/day) prior to COVID-19 infection. *Results*: Geriatric ASA-treated patients were older (mean age over 70 years; $n = 41$), had higher frequency of hypertension and hyperlipidemia, and upon admission had higher D-dimer levels than non-ASA-treated patients (mean age over 73 years; $n = 160$). However, patients under ASA treatment did not show more frequent pulmonary thromboembolism (PE) than non-ASA-treated patients. ASA-treated geriatric COVID-19-infected patients in-hospital < 30 days all-cause mortality was more frequent than in non-ASA-treated COVID-19 patients. In ASA-treated COVID-19-infected geriatric patients, anticoagulant therapy with low molecular weight heparin (LMWH) significantly reduced need of ICU care, but tended to increase in-hospital < 30 days all-cause mortality. *Conclusions*: Prior treatment with a low dose of ASA in COVID-19-infected geriatric patients increased frequency of in-hospital < 30 days all-cause mortality, although it seemed to not increase PE frequency despite D-dimer levels upon admission being higher than in non-ASA users. In ASA-treated geriatric COVID-19-infected patients, addition of LMWH therapy reduced frequency of ICU care, but tended to increase in-hospital < 30 days all-cause mortality.

Keywords: aspirin; COVID-19; elderly population; low molecular weight heparin; pulmonary thromboembolism; mortality; hospital stay

Citation: Zekri-Nechar, K.; Barberán, J.; Zamorano-León, J.J.; Durbán, M.; Andrés-Castillo, A.; Navarro-Cuellar, C.; López-Farré, A.; López-de-Andrés, A.; Jiménez-García, R.; Martínez-Martínez, C.H. Analysis of Prior Aspirin Treatment on in-Hospital Outcome of Geriatric COVID-19 Infected Patients. *Medicina* **2022**, *58*, 1649. https://doi.org/10.3390/medicina58111649

Academic Editors: Yusra Habib Khan, Tauqeer Hussain Mallhi, Tahir Mehmood Khan and Muhammad Salman

Received: 6 October 2022
Accepted: 10 November 2022
Published: 15 November 2022

Publisher's Note: MDPI stays neutral with regard to jurisdictional claims in published maps and institutional affiliations.

Copyright: © 2022 by the authors. Licensee MDPI, Basel, Switzerland. This article is an open access article distributed under the terms and conditions of the Creative Commons Attribution (CC BY) license (https://creativecommons.org/licenses/by/4.0/).

1. Introduction

Thrombotic complications and a hypercoagulable state are frequent in SAR-CoV-2 (COVID-19), strongly contributing to mortality. Venous thrombotic embolisms (VTE) have been observed in patients who were otherwise asymptomatic and in hospitalized COVID-19-infected patients in whom up 20% to 30% of critically ill patients could develop VTE [1]. Moreover, published retrospective series of cases of COVID-19 patients have shown frequent elevation of D-dimer, which has been related to acute pulmonary thrombosis, dramatically worsened the prognosis [2].

Several reports have shown that older people were at a higher risk of COVID-19 complications, with higher rates of hospitalization, intensive care unit admissions, and death [3,4]. Among other proposed hypotheses to explain the higher vulnerability of older people to worse COVID-19 prognosis and higher frequency of hospitalization there have been a weaker immune response, obesity, fragility, etc. [5]. At present, it is evident that age of people infected by COVID-19 has decreased, probably because a greater number of older people have already received their vaccination. However, at present, it is difficult to predict the future ability of vaccines to prevent possible new mutations in the virus that may confer them immunity escape and increased infectivity. Therefore, it is important to not stop analyzing effects and impact of currently used antithrombotic drugs.

Aspirin (ASA) is without doubt the main antithrombotic drug in the world to prevent thrombotic events including venous thrombosis. For example, the multinational and prospective Pulmonary Embolism Prevention (PEP) study, where patients undergo surgery for hip fracture or elective arthroplasty, found that 160 mg of ASA daily reduced the risk of symptomatic VTE by ~36% when compared with placebo [6]. Other studies as Warfarin and Aspirin (WARFASA) and the Aspirin to Prevent Recurrent Venous Thromboembolism (ASPIRE) trials, in which patients underwent initial anticoagulation therapy before randomly being assigned to low-dose ASA or placebo, also demonstrated significant reduction in VTE recurrence with ASA [7,8].

ASA is often prescribed for secondary prevention in patients with cardiovascular diseases and other comorbidities that, in older patients with COVID-19, might be associated with higher mortality [9]. However, to our knowledge, there are very few studies analyzing the effect of ASA on the outcome of COVID-19-infected patients, and even less in the older population. Moreover, in most of the studies, ASA was added as in-hospital active treatment against COVID-19. In this regard, for example, a work carried out in critically ill COVID-19 patients analyzed the effects of in-hospital treatment of ASA combined with low molecular weight heparin (LMWH) [10]. Paradoxically, this study concluded higher incidence of VTE and worse in-hospital outcome after combined treatment of ASA with a therapeutic dose of LMWH [10]. Another study also suggested that there was no significant difference in terms of mortality under ASA treatment of COVID-19-infected patients [11]. The study did not clearly report whether the use of ASA was an active prescription or a history of exposure [11]. Moreover, the possible influence of ASA in the older population infected by COVID-19 was not previously analyzed.

Therefore, the main aim of the present study is to retrospectively analyze if geriatric COVID-19 patients taking daily low ASA (100 mg/day) doses prior to hospitalization have their <30 days in-hospital outcome affected compared to non-ASA-treated geriatric patients.

2. Materials and Methods

2.1. Included Patients

This retrospective study was carried out using an anonymized database provided by Madrid Hospitals Group. Data are from COVID-19-infected patients admitted to their hospital net who kindly made available their medical information to some Spanish researchers within the program: COVID-19 data saves lives in Spain.

The study included 201 consecutive patients aged 60 admitted for hospitalization between 7 March and 4 April, 2020 (initiation of the first COVID-19 wave in Spain) with clinical and radiological data compatible with COVID-19 (On 25 March the Spanish Health Secretary recommended not to confirm COVID-19 infection by reverse transcriptase polymerase chain reaction (RT-PCR) when clinical and radiological presentation was typical). Therefore, only in patients included before these data or patients without the typical clinical and radiological presentation COVID-19 infection was confirmed by RT-PCR.

Exclusion criteria were hospital stays >30 days and admission platelet count lower than 25 × 109 platelets/L. These criteria were based on guidelines recommendation of prophylactic dose of LMWH in COVID-19 patients and the follow-up of patients with short hospitalization stay [12,13].

As clinical outcomes, parameters considered included <30 days in-hospital all-cause mortality, requirement of admission to intensive care unit (ICU), diagnosis of pulmonary embolism (PE), length of hospital stay 30 days longer. PE was assessed by pulmonary computed tomography (CPTA). Upon admission, C-reactive protein and D-dimer levels were also considered.

COVID-19-infected patients admitted for hospitalization were considered and divided into two groups: 1. COVID-19-infected patients who were taking cardiovascular doses of ASA (100 mg/day) prior to COVID-19 infection and 2. COVID-19-infected patients without prior ASA treatment. Only the patients who were taking ASA before hospital admission continued receiving 100 mg/day ASA during hospitalization.

From admission and during hospitalization some patients received LMWH (bemiparin sodium, Rovi Lab. Madrid. Spain. 2.500–10.000 UI). Patients who, upon admission, had not been treated with LMWH did not receive anticoagulating therapy during their hospitalization course.

The study was approved by the local Ethical Committee (Code: 21/084-E. Approval date: 17 February 2021) and conducted in accordance with the Declaration of Helsinki.

2.2. *Statistical Analysis*

Categorical variables were expressed as frequency and percentage and compared by Chi-square test. Continuous variables were expressed as mean $\pm$ standard error of mean (S.E.M). Student t-test was used to compare quantitative variables. A p value < 0.05 was considered significant. The statistical analysis was performed with the SPSS software version 25.0.

3. Results

3.1. *Comparison among Patients under ASA Treatment before Hospital Admission*

The mean age of the studied COVID-19 patients was over 73 years old (Table 1). COVID-19 patients under ASA treatment before hospital admission were slightly but statistically significantly older than the patients who were not undergoing ASA treatment prior hospitalization (Table 1). Gender was not different among analyzed geriatric COVID-19 patients that were or were not taking ASA (Table 1).

Upon admission, geriatric COVID-19 patients under ASA treatment more frequently had hypertension or dyslipidemia compared to geriatric patients without previous ASA therapy (Table 1). There was a similar frequency of diabetic mellitus patients between the two analyzed groups.

In the in-hospital follow up, patients taking ASA prior to hospitalization had a higher frequency of <30 days all-cause mortality than patients without ASA treatment (Table 1). The other analyzed parameters such as need of ICU care, PE development, and length of hospital stay were not different among the geriatric COVID-19-infected patients that were or were not taking ASA before hospitalization (Table 1).

Upon admission, D-dimer levels, but not C-reactive protein, were significantly higher in COVID-19 patients taking ASA than in those without ASA (Table 1). It was noteworthy that in patients with prior ASA treatment, upon-admission D dimer levels were similar among patients discharged alive and those who died in <30 days of follow up (D-dimer upon admission µg/L: ASA-treated dead patients: 2.18 ± 0.63; ASA-treated discharged patients: 1.97 ± 0.48, $p = 0.494$). Moreover, in the group of ASA-treated COVID-19 patients, in-hospital < 30 days all-cause mortality was more frequently observed in patients showing higher C-reactive protein levels upon admission (C-reactive protein upon admission (mg/L): ASA-treated < 30 days dead patients: 139.02 ± 26.12; discharged patients: 83.73 ± 16.11, $p = 0.033$).

3.2. *Effect of LMWH Therapy in Geriatric Patients Who Were Taking ASA before Hospitalization*

A number of geriatric patients ($n = 32$) taking ASA before hospitalization were treated with LMWH upon admission (Table 2). As Table 2 shows, these LMWH-treated geriatric ASA patients were of similar age and gender compared to those ASA patients who were not treated with LMWH (Table 2). It should be pointed out that the patients who, upon admission, were not treated with LMWH never received LMWH during hospitalization follow up. Moreover, four patients taking ASA were from admission treated with therapeutic doses of LMWH (5.000–10.000 IU) continuing this dosage during the follow-up. In addition, 28 of the 32 analyzed ASA-treated patients, upon admission received prophylactic dosage of LMWH (2.500–3.500 IU) but during in-hospital follow up in 6 of them LMWH dosage was increased reaching therapeutic LMWH dose.

Table 1. Effect of previous Aspirin treatment on in-hospital outcome of geriatric COVID-19-infected patients.

Variables			Previous Aspirin Treatment		
			Not *n* = 160 (%)	Yes *n* = 41 (%)	*p* Value
Age (years)			73.54 ± 0.63	76.05 ± 1.11	0.041
Gender	Men		99 (61.9)	26 (63.4)	0.856
	Women		61 (38.1)	15 (36.6)	
Diseases	Hypertension	No	96 (60.0)	17 (41.5)	0.033
		Yes	64 (40.0)	24 (58.5)	
	Hyperlipidaemia	No	105 (65.6)	17 (41.5)	<0.001
		Yes	55 (34.4)	24 (58.5)	
	Diabetes mellitus	No	144 (90.0)	34 (82.9)	0.204
		Yes	16 (10.0)	7 (17.1)	
ICU	No		113 (70.6)	27 (65.9)	0.553
	Yes		47 (29.4)	14 (34.1)	
Length of Hospital Stays (days)			11.64 ± 0.53	11.05 ± 1.02	0.623
PE	No		119 (74.4)	32 (78.0)	0.627
	Yes		41 (25.6)	9 (22.0)	
Mortality	Survivals		113 (70.6)	27 (65.9)	0.014
	Death		47 (29.4)	14 (34.1)	
D-Dimer (µg/mL)			1.66 ± 0.24	2.02 ± 0.37	0.011
C-Reactive Protein (mg/L)			111.68 ± 8.48	106.46 ± 14.28	0.871

Age, length of hospital stays, D-dimer, and C-reactive protein values are expressed as mean ± SE.

In addition, with the aim of identifying the possible additional effect of anticoagulant treatment, closely associated with antiplatelet treatment with ASA, on <30 days in-hospital outcome, it was analyzed potential effect of LMWH treatment on hospital admission in geriatric COVID-19-infected patients taken daily Aspirin (100 mg/day) (Table 2). Geriatric COVID-19 patients taking ASA who received LMWH therapy less frequency required ICU care than patients taking ASA who did not receive LMWH (Table 2). Length hospital stay was similar between the geriatric COVID-19 patients taking ASA treated or no with LMWH. Frequency of PE tended to be slightly higher in the patients taking ASA that were treated with LMWH although it did not reach statistical significance (Table 2). Among geriatric COVID-19 ASA patients, <30 days all-cause in-hospital mortality almost reached statistics significant as comparing those who were treated or not with LMWH. In fact, ASA patients who did not receive LMWH tended to show less frequency of <30 days all-cause mortality that patients taking ASA who received LMWH therapy (Table 2).

Upon admission D-dimer and C-reactive protein levels were similar among patients taking ASA who were treated or not with LMWH (Table 2).

Two geriatric COVID-19 patients taking ASA undergoing to LMWH treatment had a hemorrhagic event (drop in hemoglobin levels > 5 g/dL but without clinical hemorrhage sign).

Table 2. Effect of LMWH treatment on hospital admission in geriatric COVID-19-infected patients taken daily Aspirin (100 mg/day).

Variables			LMWH Administration on Hospital Admission: Not $n = 9$ (%)	LMWH Administration on Hospital Admission: Yes $n = 32$ (%)	p Value
Age (years)			74.11 ± 2.413	76.59 ± 1.25	0.360
Gender	Men		3 (33.3)	12 (37.5)	0.819
	Women		6 (66.7)	20 (62.5)	
Diseases	Hypertension	No	6 (66.7)	11 (34.4)	0.082
		Yes	3 (33.3)	21 (65.6)	
	Hyperlipidaemia	No	4 (44.4)	13 (40.6)	0.837
		Yes	5 (55.6)	19 (59.4)	
	Diabetes mellitus	No	8 (88.9)	26 (81.3)	0.591
		Yes	1 (11.1)	6 (18.8)	
ICU	No		1 (11.1)	26 (81.3)	<0.001
	Yes		8 (88.9)	6 (18.7)	
Length Hospital Stays (days)			9.4 ± 1.4	11.50 ± 1.25	0.670
PE	No		9 (100)	23 (71.9)	0.072
	Yes		0 (0)	9 (28.1)	
Mortality	Survivals		8 (88.9)	17 (53.1)	0.052
	Death		1 (11.1)	15 (46.9)	
D-Dimer (μg/mL)			1.41 ± 0.25	1.94 ± 0.40	0.565
C Reactive protein (mg/L)			68.42 ± 15.73	114.93 ± 17.80	0.312

Age, Length hospital stays, D-dimer and C-reactive protein values are expressed as mean ± SEM. may have a footer.

4. Discussion

This retrospective study suggested that geriatric patients who were taking a low daily ASA dose (100 mg/day) prior to COVID-19 infection and during hospitalization showed higher frequency of <30 days all-cause mortality than those geriatric COVID-19 patients not taking ASA before or during the hospitalization course. As compared with COVID-19-infected geriatric patients not previously treated with ASA, patients under ASA treatment showed higher D-dimer levels upon admission. However, the incidence frequency of PE was not different among them.

The World Health Organization reported that over 95 % of fatalities caused by COVID-19 in Europe had been individuals aged over 60 [14]. In Spain, during the most critical period of the first wave of COVID-19 disease, older age was the main risk factor for severity of COVID-19 disease [15]. Although mean age of infected patients in the following COVID-19 waves was significantly lower, probably because a larger proportion of older people were vaccinated, it is not possible to discard that COVID-19 mutations may favor the infection of these particular special vulnerable population. Therefore, while waiting for new specific drugs against COVID-19 to be developed, it is important to continue to study more "classic" commonly used drugs that may have a certain effect against the deleterious effects of COVID-19 infection.

It is recognized that viral infections, as COVID-19 infections, are commonly accompanied by platelet activation and aggregation [16]. In this regard, it was reported that ASA had an impact on both DNA and RNA viruses, although, certainly, these studies were carried out in vitro and using high ASA doses [17,18].

The elderly population has a high frequency of use of ASA within their daily treatments. However, to our knowledge, in the elderly population, possible associations between prior use of low-dose ASA and in-hospital progression of COVID-19 infection were not analyzed. In fact, the reported studies about effects of ASA on COVID-19-infected patients were carried out in critically ill COVID-19 patients of a wide range of ages, suggesting that patients under ASA treatment had higher VTE incidence and mortality [19]. However, a meta-analysis of six eligible studies which included patients of all ages concluded that use of low-dose ASA was independent of reduced mortality of COVID-19 patients [20].

In the present study, geriatric COVID-19 patients taking ASA (100 mg/day) prior to hospital admission, with the daily ASA treatment continuing during hospitalization follow up, had higher <30 days in-hospital all-causes mortality than those patients not taking ASA. Contrarily, different studies reported that active prescription of low-dose aspirin during or prior to hospitalization was associated with reduced risk of mortality among patients with COVID-19 [20,21]. These apparently paradoxical results could be related to difference in age of population and/or difference in the prevalence of cardiovascular comorbidities, which have been widely associated with worse COVID-19 outcome [22,23]. Following the same line of evidence, in COVID-19 patients with coronary artery disease no differences in <30 days all-cause mortality was found among those taking low dose ASA and those without ASA treatment [24].

COVID-19 disease has been associated with increased risk of VTE [25]. COVID-19-infected geriatric patients under ASA treatment showed higher D-dimer levels upon admission than those without ASA treatment. However, PE frequency was similar among them. It could be related to evidence showing low dose ASA may reduce VTE [26].

Guidelines recommend a prophylactic dose of LMWH as treatment for all COVID-19 patients requiring hospitalization, in the absence of any contraindications such as active bleeding and platelet count lower than 25×109 platelets/L [12]. Interestingly, a recent report has identified heparan sulfate, a glycosaminoglycan molecule like heparin, as coreceptor for COVID-19, further supporting that exogenous heparin may provide therapeutic benefits for patients with COVID-19 infection [27]. Moreover, as mentioned above, the WARFASA and ASPIRE trials demonstrated that, in patients under anticoagulant therapy, low-dose ASA led to a significant reduction in VTE [7,8]. Therefore, we analyzed if early addition of LMWH to ASA-treated geriatric COVID-19-infected patients may improve their hospital outcome.

In geriatric patients taking ASA, anticoagulant treatment was significantly associated only with reduced frequency of ICU care as compared with ASA-treated patients who did not receive LMWH. In LMWH-treated patients taking ASA, >30 days all-cause mortality tended to be higher than in those ASA patients who did not receive LMWH therapy, although it did not reach statistical significance probably due to the limited sample size. In this regard, there are many discrepancies in the results of COVID-19 patients treated with anticoagulation with respect to promotion of changes in mortality risk. Previous studies which included all ages of COVID-19-infected patients have reported reduction of in-hospital mortality as a result of anticoagulant therapy, particularly in patients with severe disease [28]. However, other reports have found no differences in mortality between heparin users and nonusers, and there was an observed mortality reduction in critically ill patients [29], although, even in these critical COVID-19 populations treated with prophylatic or therapeutic dose LMWH, controversial results were reported [30,31]. In addition, it was analyzed if the effect of LMWH treatment on the mortality may be based on the condition of patients (ICU care or not ICU care). Results revealed that mortality significantly decreased in patients who took LMWH without ICU care (76% vs. 24%); however, this reduction was not observed in those patients under LMWH who needed ICU care (48% vs. 52%). This interesting finding was supported by previous studies [32,33].

In this regard, authors suggest that D-dimer levels should guide more aggressive thromboprophylaxis regimens using higher doses of heparin, although studies have also reported that the mortality rate of patients from both prophylactic and therapeutic LMWH-treated groups was similar when patients were classified according to D-dimer results [31]. In our study, D-dimer levels upon admission were similar among geriatric patients taking ASA prior to COVID-19 infection who were treated or not with LMW during hospitalization.

Study Limitations and Comments

The present study has some limitations and the results should be interpreted with caution. As mentioned, data was obtained from an anonymized database made freely available to some researchers by the Madrid Hospital Group and, therefore, recruitment of new data to increase sample size was not possible. Therefore, sample size is a limiting factor for the result interpretation. In addition, confounding factors may exist that were not included in the database. In this regard, patients subjected to aspirin treatment usually have, as a main indication, the involvement of peripheral, coronary, neurologic, or renal arteriosclerosis. Therefore, it would be plausible to find higher mortality in those patients who were not taking aspirin prior to hospital admission. In addition, several factors influencing death in patients with COVID-19 were not considered. However, it would be plausible to consider the admissions to ICU as approximation of severity of COVID-19 and, therefore, of factors influencing death in patients with COVID-19. Relative to the patients taking ASA, a study limitation is that we did not know how long they were under the antithrombotic treatment prior to hospitalization for COVID-19 and their compliance to the therapeutic regimen. However, all these patients were taking daily ASA before being infected with COVID-19. Moreover, we could not assess if the platelets of all the included ASA-treated patients responded to ASA. In this regard, it is demonstrated that patients with ASA-resistant platelets have higher incidence of thrombotic events than patients with ASA-sensitive platelets [34]. Being aware of these limitations, there is no doubt about the need to carry out specific studies in one of the populations most vulnerable to COVID-19, the elderly population.

5. Conclusions

To conclude, geriatric COVID-19 patients who underwent prior antiplatelet treatment with ASA had a higher frequency of in-hospital < 30 days all-cause mortality than non-ASA-treated patients. It could be probably related to higher frequency of comorbidities associated with worse prognosis of COVID-19. Moreover, despite ASA-treated patients having higher D-dimer levels upon admission, they showed similar frequency of PE compared to COVID-19-infected geriatric patients who were not taking ASA, despite the fact that the latter had lower D-dimer levels upon hospital admission. Administration of LMWH to geriatric COVID-19-infected patients taking ASA before hospitalization reduced the frequency of ICU care, but tended to increase < 30 days all-cause mortality with respect to patients taking ASA and who, during hospitalization, never received LMWH therapy.

Author Contributions: Conceptualization, K.Z.-N., J.B., J.J.Z.-L. and A.L.-F.; methodology, J.B. and M.D.; formal analysis, K.Z.-N., J.J.Z.-L., A.L.-d.-A. and R.J.-G.; writing—original draft preparation, K.Z.-N. and J.J.Z.-L.; writing—review and editing, C.H.M.-M., A.A.-C. and C.N.-C. All authors have read and agreed to the published version of the manuscript.

Funding: This research received no external funding.

Institutional Review Board Statement: The study was approved by the local Ethical Committee (Code:21/084-E. Approval date 17 February 2021) and conducted in accordance with the Declaration of Helsinki.

Informed Consent Statement: Not applicable.

Data Availability Statement: This study was carried out using an anonymized database provided by Madrid Hospitals Group. Data are from COVID-19-infected patients admitted in their hospital net that they made kindly available to some Spanish researchers within the program: COVID-19 data saves lives in Spain.

Acknowledgments: This work was supported by the GenObIA Consortium (S2017/BMD-3773) of the Community of Madrid, Spain. We thank HM Hospitals group for kindly making your COVID-19 patient database available to us. This study is a part of the "Grupo de Investigación en Biomedicina Predictiva e Investigación Traslacional de las Enfermedades Respiratorias, Cardiovasculares y Metabólicas (Code 970793) of the Complutense University from Madrid, Spain. Authors also want to thank Begoña Larrea for her editorial assistance.

Conflicts of Interest: The authors declare that they have no conflict of interest.

References

1. Gratz, J.; Wiegele, M.; Maleczek, M.; Herkner, H.; Schöchl, H.; Chwala, E.; Knoebl, P.; Schaden, E. Risk of Clinically Relevant Venous Thromboembolism in Critically Ill Patients With COVID-19: A Systematic Review and Meta-Analysis. *Front. Med.* **2021**, *8*, 647917. [CrossRef] [PubMed]
2. Chen, N.; Zhou, M.; Dong, X.; Qu, J.; Gong, F.; Han, Y.; Qiu, Y.; Wang, J.; Liu, Y.; Wei, Y.; et al. Epidemiological and clinical characteristics of 99 cases of 2019 novel coronavirus pneumonia in Wuhan, China: A descriptive study. *Lancet* **2020**, *395*, 507–513. [CrossRef]
3. Richardson, S.; Hirsch, J.S.; Narasimhan, M.; Crawford, J.M.; McGinn, T.; Davidson, K.W.; the Northwell COVID-19 Research Consortium. Presenting Characteristics, Comorbidities, and Outcomes Among 5700 Patients Hospitalized with COVID-19 in the New York City Area. *JAMA* **2020**, *323*, 2052–2059. [CrossRef] [PubMed]
4. Nikolich-Zugich, J.; Knox, K.S.; Rios, C.T.; Natt, B.; Bhattacharya, D.; Fain, M.J. SARS-CoV-2 and COVID-19 in older adults: What we may expect regarding pathogenesis, immune responses, and outcomes. *Geroscience* **2020**, *42*, 505–514. [CrossRef] [PubMed]
5. Sattar, N.; McInnes, I.B.; McMurray, J.J.V. Obesity Is a Risk Factor for Severe COVID-19 Infection: Multiple Potential Mechanisms. *Circulation* **2020**, *142*, 4–6. [CrossRef]
6. O'Brien, J.; Duncan, H.; Kirsh, G.; Allen, V.; King, P.; Hargraves, R.; Mendes, L.; Perera, T.; Catto, P.; Schofield, S.; et al. Prevention of pulmonary embolism and deep vein thrombosis with low dose aspirin: Pulmonary Embolism Prevention (PEP) trial. *Lancet* **2000**, *355*, 1295–1302.
7. Becattini, C.; Agnelli, G.; Schenone, A.; Eichinger, S.; Bucherini, E.; Silingardi, M.; Bianchi, M.; Moia, M.; Ageno, W.; Vandelli, M.R.; et al. WARFASA Investigators. Aspirin for preventing the recurrence of venous thromboembolism. *N. Engl. J. Med.* **2012**, *366*, 1959–1967. [CrossRef]
8. Brighton, T.A.; Eikelboom, J.W.; Mann, K.; Mister, R.; Gallus, A.; Ockelford, P.; Gibbs, H.; Hague, W.; Xavier, D.; Diaz, R.; et al. Low-dose aspirin for preventing recurrent venous thromboembolism. *N. Engl. J. Med.* **2012**, *367*, 1979–1987. [CrossRef]
9. Pranata, R.; Huang, I.; Lim, M.A.; Wahjoepramono, E.J.; July, J. Impact of cerebrovascular and cardiovascular diseases on mortality and severity of COVID-19-systematic review, meta-analysis, and meta-regression. *J. Stroke Cerebrovasc. Dis.* **2020**, *29*, 104949. [CrossRef]
10. Pavoni, V.; Gianesello, L.; Pazzi, M.; Stera, C.; Meconi, T.; Frigieri, F.C. Venous thromboembolism and bleeding in critically ill COVID-19 patients treated with higher than standard low molecular weight heparin doses and aspirin: A call to action. *Thromb. Res.* **2020**, *196*, 313–317. [CrossRef]
11. Alamdari, N.M.; Afaghi, S.; Rahimi, F.S.; Tarki, F.E.; Tavana, S.; Zali, A.; Fathi, M.; Besharat, S.; Bagheri, L.; Pourmotahari, F.; et al. Mortality Risk Factors among Hospitalized COVID-19 Patients in a Major Referral Center in Iran. *Tohoku J. Exp. Med.* **2020**, *252*, 73–84. [CrossRef] [PubMed]
12. Thachil, J.; Tang, N.; Gando, S.; Falanga, A.; Cattaneo, M.; Levi, M.; Clark, C.; Iba, T. ISTH interim guidance on recognition and management of coagulopathy in COVID-19. *J. Thromb. Haemost.* **2020**, *18*, 1023–1026. [CrossRef] [PubMed]
13. Signes-Costa, J.; Núñez-Gil, I.J.; Soriano, J.B.; Arroyo-Espliguero, R.; Eid, C.M.; Romero, R.; Uribarri, A.; Fernández-Rozas, I.; Aguado, M.G.; Becerra-Muñoz, V.M.; et al. Prevalence and 30-Day Mortality in Hospitalized Patients with COVID-19 and Prior Lung Diseases. *Arch. Bronconeumol.* **2021**, *57*, 13–20. [CrossRef] [PubMed]
14. World Health Organization. Coronavirus Disease (COVID-19) Outbreak. Regional Office for Europe. Available online: https://www.euro.who.int/en/health-topics/health-emergencies/coronavirus-covid-19/statements/statement-older-people-are-at-highest-risk-from-covid-19,-but-all-must-act-to-prevent-community-spread (accessed on 10 July 2022).
15. Berenguer, J.; Ryan, P.; Rodríguez-Baño, J.; Jarrín, I.; Carratalà, J.; Pachón, J.; Yllescas, M.; Arriba, J.R.; for the COVID-19@Spain Study. Characteristics and predictors of death among 4035 consecutively hospitalized patients with COVID-19 in Spain. *Clin. Microbiol. Infect.* **2020**, *26*, 1525–1536. [CrossRef] [PubMed]
16. Assinger, A. Platelets and infection—An emerging role of platelets in viral infection. *Front. Immunol.* **2014**, *5*, 649. [CrossRef]
17. Glatthaar-Saalmüller, B.; Mair, K.H.; Saalmüller, A. Antiviral activity of aspirin against RNA viruses of the respiratory tract-an in vitro study. *Influenza Other Respir. Viruses* **2016**, *11*, 85–92. [CrossRef]
18. Walz-Cicconi, M.A.; Weller, T.H. Dose-related effect of acetylsalicylic acid on replication of varicella zoster virus in vitro. *Proc. Natl. Acad. Sci. USA* **1984**, *81*, 5223–5226. [CrossRef]
19. Speir, E.; Yu, Z.X.; Ferrans, V.J.; Huang, E.S.; Epstein, S.E. Aspirin attenuates cytomegalovirus infectivity and gene expression mediated by cyclooxygenase-2 in coronary artery smooth muscle cells. *Circ. Res.* **1998**, *83*, 210–216. [CrossRef]
20. Martha, J.W.; Pranata, R.; Lim, M.A.; Wibowo, A.; Akbar, M.R. Active prescription of low-dose aspirin during or prior to hospitalization and mortality in COVID-19: A systematic review and meta-analysis of adjusted effect estimates. *Int. J. Infect. Dis.* **2021**, *108*, 6–12. [CrossRef]

21. Wijaya, I.; Andhika, R.; Huang, I.; Purwiga, A.; Budiman, K.Y. The effects of aspirin on the outcome of COVID-19: A systematic review and meta-analysis. *Clin. Epidemiol. Glob. Health* **2021**, *12*, 100883. [CrossRef]
22. Kulkarni, S.; Jenner, B.L.; Wilkinson, I. COVID-19 and hypertension. *J. Renin. Angiotensin Aldosterone Syst.* **2020**, *21*. [CrossRef] [PubMed]
23. Choi, G.J.; Kim, H.M.; Kang, H. The Potential Role of Dyslipidemia in COVID-19 Severity: An Umbrella Review of Systematic Reviews. *J. Lipid Atheroscler.* **2020**, *9*, 435–448. [CrossRef] [PubMed]
24. Yuan, S.; Chen, P.; Li, H.; Chen, C.; Wang, F.; Wang, D.W. Mortality and pre-hospitalization use of low-dose aspirin in COVID-19 patients with coronary artery disease. *J. Cell. Mol. Med.* **2021**, *25*, 1263–1273. [CrossRef] [PubMed]
25. Malas, M.B.; Naazie, I.N.; Elsayed, N.; Mathlouthi, A.; Marmor, R.; Clary, B. Thromboembolism risk of COVID-19 is high and associated with a higher risk of mortality: A systematic review and meta-analysis. *EClinicalMedicine* **2020**, *29*, 100639. [CrossRef]
26. Simes, J.; Becattini, C.; Agnelli, G.; Eikelboom, J.W.; Kirby, A.C.; Mister, R.; Simes, J.; Becattini, C.; Agnelli, G.; Eikelboom, J.W.; et al. INSPIRE Study Investigators (International Collaboration of Aspirin Trials for Recurrent Venous Thromboembolism). Aspirin for the prevention of recurrent venous thromboembolism: The INSPIRE collaboration. *Circulation* **2014**, *130*, 1062–1071. [CrossRef]
27. Clausen, T.M.; Sandoval, D.R.; Spliid, C.B.; Pihl, J.; Perrett, H.R.; Painter, C.D.; Narayanan, A.; Majowicz, S.A.; Kwong, E.M.; McVicar, R.N.; et al. SARS-CoV-2 Infection Depends on Cellular Heparan Sulfate and ACE2. *Cell* **2020**, *183*, 1043–1057. [CrossRef]
28. Qin, W.; Dong, F.; Zhang, Z.; Hu, B.; Chen, S.; Zhu, Z.; Li, F.; Wang, X.; Zhang, Y.; Wang, Y.; et al. Low molecular weight heparin and 28-day mortality among patients with coronavirus disease 2019: A cohort study in the early epidemic era. *Thromb. Res.* **2020**, *198*, 19–22. [CrossRef]
29. Tang, N.; Bai, H.; Chen, X.; Gong, J.; Li, D.; Sun, Z. Anticoagulant treatment is associated with decreased mortality in severe coronavirus disease 2019 patients with coagulopathy. *J. Thromb. Haemost.* **2020**, *18*, 1094–1099. [CrossRef]
30. Leentjens, J.; van Haaps, T.F.; Wessels, P.F.; Schutgens, R.E.G.; Middeldorp, S. COVID-19-associated coagulopathy and antithrombotic agents-lessons after 1 year. *Lancet Haematol.* **2021**, *8*, e524–e533. [CrossRef]
31. Canoglu, K.; Saylan, B. Therapeutic dosing of low-molecular-weight heparin may decrease mortality in patients with severe COVID-19 infection. *Ann. Saudi Med.* **2020**, *40*, 462–468. [CrossRef]
32. Goligher, E.C.; Bradbury, C.A.; McVerry, B.J.; Lawler, P.R.; Berger, J.S.; Gong, M.N.; Carrier, M.; Reynolds, H.R.; Kumar, A.; Turgeon, A.F.; et al. Therapeutic Anticoagulation with Heparin in Critically Ill Patients with COVID-19. *N. Engl. J. Med.* **2021**, *385*, 777–789.
33. Lawler, P.R.; Goligher, E.C.; Berger, J.S.; Neal, M.D.; McVerry, B.J.; Nicolau, J.C.; Gong, M.N.; Carrier, M.; Rosenson, R.S.; Reynolds, H.R.; et al. Therapeutic Anticoagulation with Heparin in Noncritically Ill Patients with COVID-19. *N. Engl. J. Med.* **2021**, *385*, 790–802. [PubMed]
34. Eikelboom, J.W.; Hirsh, J.; Weitz, J.I.; Johnston, M.; Yi, Q.; Yusuf, S. Aspirin-resistant thromboxane biosynthesis and the risk of myocardial infarction, stroke, or cardiovascular death in patients at high risk for cardiovascular events. *Circulation* **2002**, *105*, 1650–1655. [CrossRef] [PubMed]

medicina MDPI

Article

Surveillance of Side Effects after Two Doses of COVID-19 Vaccines among Patients with Comorbid Conditions: A Sub-Cohort Analysis from Saudi Arabia

Tauqeer Hussain Mallhi [1,2,*], Yusra Habib Khan [1,*], Muhammad Hammad Butt [3], Muhammad Salman [4], Nida Tanveer [5], Nasser Hadal Alotaibi [1], Abdulaziz Ibrahim Alzarea [1] and Abdullah Salah Alanazi [1,2]

1 Department of Clinical Pharmacy, College of Pharmacy, Jouf University, Sakaka 72388, Saudi Arabia
2 Health Sciences Research Unit, Jouf University, Sakaka 72388, Saudi Arabia
3 Department of Medicinal Chemistry, Faculty of Pharmacy, Uppsala University, 75123 Uppsala, Sweden
4 Institute of Pharmacy, Faculty of Pharmaceutical and Allied Health Sciences, Lahore College for Women University, Lahore 54000, Pakistan
5 Institute of Molecular Cardiology, University of Louisville, Louisville, KY 40202, USA
* Correspondence: thhussain@ju.edu.sa or tauqeer.tauqeer.hussain.mallhi@hotmail.com (T.H.M.); yusrahabib@ymail.com or yhkhan@ju.edu.sa (Y.H.K.)

Abstract: *Background*: Individuals with underlying chronic illnesses have demonstrated considerable hesitancy towards COVID-19 vaccines. These concerns are primarily attributed to their concerns over the safety profile. Real-world data on the safety profile among COVID-19 vaccinees with comorbid conditions are scarce. This study aimed to ascertain the side-effects profile after two doses of COVID-19 vaccines among chronic-disease patients. *Methodology*: A cross-sectional questionnaire-based study was conducted among faculty members with comorbid conditions at a public educational institute in Saudi Arabia. A 20-item questionnaire recorded the demographics and side effects after the two doses of COVID-19 vaccines. The frequency of side effects was recorded following each dose of vaccine, and the association of the side-effects score with the demographics was ascertained through appropriate statistics. *Results*: A total of 204 patients with at least one comorbid condition were included in this study. A total of 24 side effects were reported after the first dose and 22 after second dose of the COVID-19 vaccine. The incidence of at least one side effect was 88.7% and 95.1% after the first and second doses of the vaccine, respectively. The frequent side effects after the first dose were pain at the injection site (63.2%), fatigue (58.8%), fever (47.5%), muscle and joint pain (38.7%), and headache (36.3%). However, pain at the injection site (71.1%), muscle and joint pain (62.7%), headache (49.5%), fever (45.6%), and stress (33.3%) were frequent after the second dose. The average side-effects score was 4.41 ± 4.18 (median: 3, IQR: 1, 6) and 4.79 ± 3.54 (median 4, IQR: 2, 6) after the first and second dose, respectively. Female gender, diabetes mellitus, hypertension, hyperlipidemia, comorbidity > 2, family history of COVID-19, and the AstraZeneca vaccine were significantly associated with higher side-effect scores. Only 35.8% of study participants were satisfied with the safety of COVID-19 vaccines. *Conclusions*: Our analysis showed a high proportion of transient and short-lived side effects of Pfizer and AstraZeneca vaccines among individuals with chronic illnesses. However, the side-effects profile was comparable with the safety reports of phase 3 clinical trials of these vaccines. The frequency of side effects was found to be associated with certain demographics, necessitating the need for further investigations to establish a causal relationship. The current study's findings will help instill confidence in the COVID-19 vaccines among people living with chronic conditions, overcome vaccine hesitancy, and increase vaccine coverage in this population.

Keywords: COVID-19; side effects; safety; vaccine hesitancy; comorbidities; hypertension; diabetes mellitus; hyperlipidemia; pharmacovigilance

Citation: Mallhi, T.H.; Khan, Y.H.; Butt, M.H.; Salman, M.; Tanveer, N.; Alotaibi, N.H.; Alzarea, A.I.; Alanazi, A.S. Surveillance of Side Effects after Two Doses of COVID-19 Vaccines among Patients with Comorbid Conditions: A Sub-Cohort Analysis from Saudi Arabia. *Medicina* **2022**, *58*, 1799. https://doi.org/10.3390/medicina58121799

Academic Editor: Pierpaolo Di Micco

Received: 31 October 2022
Accepted: 25 November 2022
Published: 6 December 2022

Publisher's Note: MDPI stays neutral with regard to jurisdictional claims in published maps and institutional affiliations.

Copyright: © 2022 by the authors. Licensee MDPI, Basel, Switzerland. This article is an open access article distributed under the terms and conditions of the Creative Commons Attribution (CC BY) license (https://creativecommons.org/licenses/by/4.0/).

1. Introduction

The first case of coronavirus disease (COVID-19) was identified in December 2019 in Wuhan, China. The mortality rate of COVID-19 is lower than that of other coronaviruses such as severe acute respiratory syndrome (SARS) and Middle East respiratory syndrome (MERS). However, its causative pathogen, "severe acute respiratory syndrome coronavirus 2 (SARS-CoV-2)" is considered more contagious than other coronaviruses causing SARS and MERS [1]. Initially, patients with COVID-19 presented with typical manifestations such as fever, fatigue, and respiratory symptoms. However, the rapid distribution of COVID-19 across the globe resulted in several atypical intricacies in various organ systems during the disease course of COVID-19 [2]. Immediate prevention and control measures were taken to curtail the epidemic across the globe. The phenomena of social distancing [3], drug repurposing for the management of patients [4], and the development of vaccines proved to be effective maneuvers to combat the growing encumbrance of COVID-19.

The COVID-19 vaccination is one of the effective preventive measures to curb the encumbrance of the ongoing pandemic [5]. Various health authorities around the globe have endorsed herd immunity as a potential tool against the COVID-19 outbreak. Vaccination against COVID-19 is an essential driver of herd immunity. Despite aggressive and continuous maneuvers to increase vaccine coverage, vaccine hesitancy is still a prominent phenomenon that may impact the process of mass immunization against COVID-19. However, the fear of side effects of the COVID-19 vaccines is considered a dominant factor in vaccine hesitancy [6,7]. The safety of COVID-19 vaccines is of great public health concern and is crucial to neutralize vaccine hesitancy. There has been widespread speculations of serious post-vaccination adverse events. In addition, the safety of these vaccines became a priority concern immediately after a few reports of blood clotting [8], Bell's palsy [9], and myocarditis [10] following the administration of specific vaccines.

Healthcare researchers around the globe responded swiftly to the safety profile of the COVID-19 vaccines and conducted various post-marketing real-world surveillance studies of side effects among vaccinees [11–14]. However, there is a dearth of investigations into post-vaccination side-effects of COVID-19 vaccines among recipients with underlying comorbid conditions. In addition, there are also increased safety concerns regarding the vaccination of people living with underlying chronic conditions [15]. The use of more than one medication and the co-occurrence of multiple health conditions among chronic-disease patients may increase the frequency and severity of the post-vaccination side effects [15,16]. It is pertinent to mention that most of the clinical trials on vaccines have included only stable chronic-disease patients. Moreover, this population accounted for only 15% to 42% of total participants in these trials [17]. Most chronic-disease patients remain reluctant to adopt any therapeutic intervention except the medications they are already receiving. Yi et al. reported that most of the patients with rheumatic diseases were reluctant to receive COVID-19 vaccines due to the fear of side effects and disease flare [18]. These findings are alarming, as patients with rheumatic diseases are at high risk of COVID-19 infection attributed to their compromised immune systems [19]. However, recent investigations have demonstrated satisfactory immunogenicity and an acceptable safety profile of the COVID-19 vaccines among patients with autoimmune inflammatory rheumatic diseases (AIIRDs) [20,21]. The findings of Li et al. also encourage COVID-19 vaccination among rheumatic-disease patients. The authors have reported a satisfactory safety profile of COVID-19 vaccines among individuals with various rheumatic diseases, and indicated that immunosuppressive therapy was not associated with the frequency of side effects [21]. Educating these patients regarding the benefits and safety of COVID-19 vaccines will ensure optimal coverage. Similar results have also been observed in a study conducted on the Saudi population, where adults with chronic conditions demonstrated a low willingness to receive the COVID-19 vaccination [22]. It is expected that people with chronic health conditions will hesitate to receive COVID-19 vaccines, most probably due to fear of side effects. In this context, there is an impetus to inform this population regarding safety profile of the COVID-19 vaccines. Cautious pharmacovigilance is indeed warranted for people with one or more chronic illnesses. This study aimed to ascertain the prevalence of side effects after the first and second doses of COVID-19 vaccines among chronic-disease patients. Moreover, this study determined the relationship between the frequency of side effects and the demographics. The findings may serve to inform the general community regarding the safety of COVID-19 vaccines among individuals with underlying medical conditions.

2. Materials and Methods

2.1. Ethics Statement

The study protocol was approved by the Local Committee of Bioethics (LCBE) at Jouf University, KSA (Reference: 05-05-43). Informed consent was obtained from all the participants and data were anonymized before analysis.

2.2. Study Design, Population, and Location

This study is a sub-cohort analysis of an ongoing project on the pharmacovigilance of the COVID-19 vaccines. This project aimed to collect data on the side effects of COVID-19 vaccines from university students, faculty members, and the general population. Since the side-effects profile of COVID-19 vaccines among chronic-disease patients is lacking in the literature, a sub-group analysis on vaccinees with chronic disease was performed. Considering the dire need for a rapid report on the safety profile of the COVID-19 vaccines among chronic-disease patients, data on faculty members of Jouf University, Saudi Arabia were readily available for analysis. The participants who had received at least two doses of the COVID-19 vaccines, had at least one chronic condition, and consented to participate were included in this study, or otherwise excluded.

2.3. Validation and Reliability of Study Instrument

A 20-item questionnaire comprising three sections was constructed by a team of physicians and hospital/community pharmacists. Following the face and content validity, the study instrument was administered to a small sample of 30 participants. The internal consistency of the study tool was estimated through Cronbach's alpha at 0.821, indicating the suitability and reliability of the study instrument.

2.4. Components of Study Instrument

The study instrument was specifically designed to evaluate the safety profile of COVID-19 vaccines. The questionnaire was initially designed in English. The English version was translated into Arabic with the help of native Arabic speakers using forward–backward translation. The study questionnaire consisted of four sections. Section 1 collected information on demographics including age, gender, marital status, nationality, and education. Section 2 inquired about the chronic conditions present among the study participants. Section 3 evaluated the safety profile of vaccines such as the type of side effect after each dose of vaccine, the onset and duration of side effects, and their management. Section 4 had two questions inquiring about the satisfaction and recommendation of the COVID-19 vaccines among study participants. The list of side effects included all common events reported in clinical trials of vaccines as well as in the previous literature. Moreover, participants were also encouraged to document any other side effect that was not present in the list. All the participants were asked to respond against each side effect on a scale of "Yes" and "No". The option "Yes" was scored "1", otherwise "zero". A cumulative side-effect score of each participant was estimated by adding the total number of side effects. The mean side-effects scores were also estimated after the first and second doses of COVID-19 vaccines. The total number of side effects after the first and second dose was estimated. This resulted in a cumulative side-effect score (CSES) (the presence of each side effect was scored 1). The average side-effect score (ASES) was also estimated after each dose (ASES = (CSES-Dose 1 + CSES-Dose 2)/2). The reported side effects were further stratified into four categories i.e., common (side effects indicated by >50% of the study population), moderately common (30–50%), uncommon (10% to <30%), and rare (<10%). The respondents were also asked to rate the severity of side effects from mild to moderate or severe.

2.5. Data Collection

Using a convenient sampling technique, the questionnaire was distributed among the staff of the Jouf University via official emails with regular reminders at predefined intervals. A brief overview of the study was given to the participants. Subsequently, the participants were asked about their volunteer participation in this study and an online consent was obtained with the statement "I agree to participate in this study". If the participants did not agree, the form was submitted without recording their responses. All questionnaires were checked for completeness and transferred to a Microsoft spreadsheet for cleaning purposes. Initially, all the data were collected but only responses meeting the inclusion criteria were included in the analysis.

2.6. Statistical Analysis

All the data were subjected to analysis by Statistical Package for Social Sciences (IBM-SPSS version 25). The data were descriptively presented as the frequency with proportion and mean with standard deviation. The categorical data were compared with the Chi-square test i.e., the comparison of side effects across demographics and types of the COVID-19 vaccine. The independent Student's t-test and one-way ANOVA compared the mean score between two or more than two groups, respectively. Pearson correlation was used to estimate the relationship between the number of side effects and comorbidities. The coefficient of determination was also estimated through linear regression. A significance level of $p < 0.05$ value was adjusted in all analyses.

3. Results

3.1. Demographics

A total of 204 patients with at least one comorbid condition were included in the analysis. The age of the participants ranged from 30 to 49 years. The most common comorbid condition was diabetes mellitus (41.2%) followed by hypertension (31.9%) and hyperlipidemia (30.4%). Almost a quarter of the participants (23.5%) had a history of COVID-19 infection. Most of the participants (62.3%) had received two doses of Pfizer vaccine (BioNTech, BNT162b2), and only 17.2% had received two doses of Astra-Zeneca (Oxford, AZD1222). A homologous vaccine regime was used in 79.9% of participants, while 20.1% of participants received a heterologous regime. The post-vaccination COVID-19 infection rate was only 2% in this study (Table 1).

Table 1. Demographics of study participants.

Variables	Frequency	Percentage
Age		
18–29 Years	24	11.8
30–49 Years	105	51.5
≥50 Years	75	36.8
Gender		
Male	91	44.6
Female	113	55.4
Marital status		
Single	41	20.1
Married	158	77.5
Divorced	2	1.0
Widowed	3	1.5

Table 1. *Cont.*

Variables	Frequency	Percentage
Comorbidities		
Diabetes mellitus	84	41.2
Hypertension	65	31.9
Hyperlipidemia	62	30.4
Asthma	56	27.5
Anemia	3	1.5
Hypothyroidism	12	5.9
Hyperthyroidism	6	2.9
Gout	2	1.0
Seasonal allergy	11	5.4
Peptic ulcer	5	2.5
Congestive heart failure	8	3.9
Eczema	2	1.0
Comorbidities > 2		
Yes	38	18.6
No	166	81.4
Allergic to any vaccine		
Yes	9	4.4
No	195	95.6
COVID-19 infection before vaccination		
Yes	48	23.5
No	156	76.5
COVID-19 infection in family before vaccination		
Yes	138	67.6
No	66	32.4
COVID-19 infection in acquaintance before vaccination		
Yes	161	78.9
No	43	21.1
COVID-19 vaccination regime		
Astra-Zeneca (two doses)	36	17.6
Pfizer (two doses)	127	62.3
Pfizer and Astra-Zeneca	41	20.1
Type of vaccine during 1st dose		
Pfizer	168	82.4
Astra-Zeneca	36	17.6
Type of vaccine during 2nd dose		
Pfizer	127	62.3
Astra-Zeneca	77	37.7
Combination of vaccine		
Homologous regime	163	79.9
Heterologous regime	41	20.1
COVID-19 infection after vaccination		
Yes	4	2.0
No	200	98.0

3.2. Incidence of Side Effects after COVID-19 Vaccines

The incidence of at least one side effect was 88.7% and 95.1% after the first and second doses of the vaccine, respectively. Pain at the injection site and fatigue were common side effects after the first dose, while pain at the injection site and muscle or joint pain were common side effects after the second dose. The frequent side effects after the first dose were pain at the injection site (63.2%), fatigue (58.8%), fever (47.5%), muscle and joint pain (38.7%), and headache (36.3%). However, pain at the injection site (71.1%), muscle and joint pain (62.7%), headache (49.5%), fever (45.6%), and stress (33.3%) were frequent after the second dose. Most of these side effects occurred within the 6 h following the first dose (45.1%) and second dose (28.4%). Most of the side effects (61.3%) lasted for 48 h among the study participants (Table 2).

Table 2. Frequency of side effects after two doses of COVID-19 vaccines.

	First Dose		Second Dose	
	Frequency	**Percentage**	**Frequency**	**Percentage**
Pain at injection site	129	63.2	145	71.1
Swelling at injection site	51	25.0	30	14.7
Redness at injection site	35	17.2	20	9.8
Headache	74	36.3	101	49.5
Muscle and joint pain	79	38.7	128	62.7
Fatigue	120	58.8	64	31.4
Fever	97	47.5	93	45.6
Stress	78	38.2	68	33.3
Malaise (feeling sick)	42	20.6	12	5.9
Chills	41	20.1	47	23.0
Nausea/vomiting	21	10.3	30	14.7
Diarrhea	22	10.8	31	15.2
Cough	18	8.8	42	20.6
Sore throat	15	7.4	21	10.3
Flu-like symptoms	15	7.4	21	10.3
Loss of smell	11	5.4	25	12.3
Loss of taste	10	4.9	33	16.2
Shortness of breath	17	8.3	50	24.5
Menstrual problems	2	1.0	3	1.5
Chest pain	1	0.5	-	-
Palpitations	1	0.5	-	-
Hair loss	3	1.5	3	1.5
Insomnia	10	4.9	8	3.9
Lymph-node swelling	2	1.0	2	1.0
Onset of side effects				
Immediately	26	12.7	9	4.4
Within 6 h	92	45.1	58	28.4
Within 6–12 h	15	7.4	37	18.1
Within 12–24 h	21	10.3	25	12.3
After 24 h	19	9.3	21	10.3
Immediately	26	12.7	9	4.4

3.3. Side-Effect Score and its Association with Demographics

A total of 24 side effects were reported after the 1st dose, and 22 after the 2nd dose of the COVID-19 vaccines. The average -effects score was 4.41 ± 4.18 (median: 3, IQR: 1, 6) and 4.79 ± 3.54 (median 4, IQR: 2, 6) after the first and second dose, respectively. However, the cumulative side-effect score after both doses was 4.60 ± 2.93 (median: 4.2, IQR: 2.5, 6.5). The number of comorbidities was found to be positively correlated with side-effects score after the first dose (r = 0.345, R2 = 0.125, $p < 0.001$), second dose (r = 0.230, R2 = 0.053, $p < 0.001$), and both doses (r = 0.390, R2 = 0.152, $p < 0.001$). Female gender, diabetes mellitus, hypertension, hyperlipidemia, comorbidity count more than 2, family history of COVID-19 infection, and the Astra-Zeneca vaccine were significantly associated with higher side-effect scores following the first dose. On the other hand, participants aged 30–49 years, >2 comorbidities, family history of COVID-19 infection, and those who received Pfizer had significantly higher side-effect scores after the second dose (Table 3). It is pertinent to mention that homologous and heterologous vaccine regimes were not associated with the SES (score: 4.83 versus 4.61, $p = 0.717$) (Table 3). Tables 4 and 5 show that the occurrence of certain side effects (common and moderately common) was statistically associated with various demographic features.

Table 3. Relationship of demographics with side-effects score.

Variables	First Dose			Second Dose		
	Mean	SD	*p* Value	Mean	SD	*p* Values
Age			0.070			**0.004**
18–29 Years	3.75	4.235	24	3.63	2.856	
30–49 Years	5.07	4.091	105	5.56	3.648	
≥50 Years	3.71	4.194	75	4.08	3.356	
Gender			**<0.001**			0.729
Male	3.24	3.331		4.89	4.416	
Female	5.35	4.555		4.71	2.641	
Marital status			0.939			
Single	4.32	4.077		4.51	3.399	
Married	4.47	4.238		4.92	3.601	
Divorced	4.00	5.657		3.50	3.536	
Widowed	3.00	3.464		2.67	1.528	
Comorbidities						
Diabetes mellitus			**<0.001**			0.249
No	3.16	3.483		4.55	3.793	
Yes	6.20	4.453		5.13	3.123	
Hypertension			**0.036**		0.084	
No	139	3.99		4.50	3.431	
Yes	65	5.31		5.42	3.699	
Hyperlipidemia			**0.003**			0.064
No	3.75	3.416		4.49	3.459	
Yes	5.94	5.272		5.48	3.638	
Asthma			0.813			0.730
No	4.36	3.393		4.74	3.329	
Yes	4.55	5.806		4.93	4.062	
Anemia			0.916			0.698
No	4.41	4.192		4.80	3.555	
Yes	4.67	4.041		4.00	2.000	

Table 3. *Cont.*

Variables	First Dose			Second Dose		
Hypothyroidism			0.726			0.704
No	4.44	4.160		4.77	3.575	
Yes	4.00	4.671		5.17	2.949	
Hyperthyroidism			**<0.001**			**<0.001**
No	4.52	4.200		4.63	3.469	
Yes	1.00	0.000		10.00	0.000	
Gout			0.658			0.187
No	4.41	4.199		4.82	3.538	
Yes	5.00	1.414		1.50	0.707	
Seasonal allergy			0.319			0.955
No	4.34	4.169		4.79	3.619	
Yes	5.64	4.388		4.82	1.537	
Peptic ulcer			0.441			0.995
No	4.43	4.216		4.79	3.537	
Yes	3.80	2.588		4.80	3.899	
Congestive heart failure			0.080			0.178
No	4.52	4.207		4.81	3.605	
Yes	1.88	2.475		4.38	0.518	
Eczema			0.517			0.263
No	4.43	4.194		4.82	3.541	
Yes	2.50	2.121		2.00	1.414	
Comorbidities > 2			**0.007**			**<0.001**
Yes	6.63	5.630		6.66	3.052	
No	3.90	3.605		4.36	3.508	
Allergic to any vaccine			0.279			0.766
Yes	5.89	5.302		4.44	2.242	
No	4.34	4.126		4.81	3.587	
COVID-19 infection before vaccination			0.141			0.117
Yes	3.75	3.219		4.54	3.246	
No	4.62	4.423		5.60	4.286	
COVID-19 infection in family before vaccination			**0.012**			**0.009**
Yes	138	3.80		138	5.21	
No	66	5.68		66	3.91	
COVID-19 infection in acquaintance before vaccination			**0.046**			**0.003**
Yes	161	3.96		161	4.76	
No	43	6.09		43	4.91	
COVID-19 vaccination regime			**0.005**			0.593
Astra-Zeneca (two doses)	6.44	3.308		5.33	3.033	
Pfizer (two doses)	3.96	4.571		4.69	3.802	
Pfizer and Astra-Zeneca	4.02	2.962		4.61	3.089	
Type of vaccine during 1st dose			**0.001**			-
Pfizer	3.98	4.227		-	-	
Astra-Zeneca	6.44	3.308		-	-	

Table 3. *Cont.*

Variables	First Dose		Second Dose		
Type of vaccine during 2nd dose					**0.047**
Pfizer	-	-	3.96	4.571	
Astra-Zeneca	-	-	5.16	3.337	
Combination of vaccine					0.717
Homologous regime	-	-	4.83	3.647	
Heterologous regime	-	-	4.61	3.089	

The **bold** values represent statistical significance.

Table 4. Distribution of common and moderately common side effects across demographic features after 1st dose of COVID-19 vaccine.

Variable	Sub-variable	Headache		Injection-Site Pain		Fatigue		Bone-Joint Pain		Stress		Fever	
		No	Yes	No	Yes	No	Yes	No	Yes	No	Yes	No	Yes
		%	%	%	%	%	%	%	%	%	%	%	%
Gender	Male	52.0	31.0	5.0	40.0	57.0	35.0	50.0	35.0	4.0	42.0	52.0	36.0
	Female	47.0	68.0	4.0	59.0	42.0	64.0	49.0	64.0	5.0	57.0	47.0	63.0
	p-value	0.003 *		0.1		0.003 *		0.036 *		0.6		0.020 *	
Age	18–29 Years	13.0	9.0	13.0	10.0	15.0	9.0	1.0	11.0	11.0	12.0	1.0	8.0
	30–49 years	5.0	54.0	54.0	49.0	35.0	62.0	4.0	5.0	41.0	67.0	43.0	59.0
	>50 Years	36.0	36.0	3.0	39.0	48.0	28.0	4.0	31.0	47.0	19.0	41.0	3.0
	p-value	0.7		0.5		0.001 *		0.4		<0.001 *		0.1	
Marital status	Single	22.0	16.0	2.0	17.0	20.0	2.0	19.0	21.0	20.0	19.0	19.0	20.0
	Married	73.0	83.0	74.0	79.0	76.0	78.0	78.0	75.0	7.0	78.0	77.0	77.0
	Divorced	1.0		1.0	0.0	1.0	0.0	0.0	1.0	0.0	1.0	0.0	
	Widowed	2.0			2.0	2.0	0.0	1.0	1.0	1.0	1.0	1.0	
	p-value	0.2		0.4		0.8		1.0		1.0		1.0	
Allergic to vaccine	No	95.0	95.0	9.0	95.0	96.0	9.0	95.0	96.0	9.0	94.0	97.0	93.0
	Yes	4.0	4.0		4.0	3.0		4.0	3.0		5.0	2.0	6.0
	p-value	0.9		0.8		0.6		0.7		0.7		0.2	
COVID-19-infected	No	70.0	86.0	81.0	73.0	78.0	7.0	77.0	74.0	75.0	78.0	7.0	82.0
	Yes	29.0	13.0	18.0	26.0	21.0	2.0	22.0	25.0	24.0	21.0	2.0	17.0
	p-value	0.011 *		0.2		0.6		0.6		0.6		0.1	
Family member infected with COVID-19	No	25.0	44.0	29.0	34.0	3.0	33.0	25.0	4.0	30.0	35.0	29.0	35.0
	Yes	74.0	55.0	70.0	65.0	6.0	66.0	74.0	5.0	69.0	64.0	70.0	64.0
	p-value	0.005 *		0.5		0.7		0.010 *		0.4		0.4	
Friends infected with COVID-19	No	21.0	20.0	2.0	17.0	20.0	21.0	20.0	21.0	2.0	17.0	1.0	27.0
	Yes	78.0	79.0	7.0	82.0	79.0	78.0	79.0	78.0	7.0	82.0	8.0	72.0
	p-value	0.8		0.1		0.8		0.9		0.4		0.024 *	
COVID-19 infection after vaccinations	No	97.0	98.0	98.0	97.0	98.0	97.0	10.0	94.0	99.0	96.0	98.0	97.0
	Yes	2.0	1.0	1.0	2.0	1.0	2.0		5.0	0.0	3.0	1.0	2.0
	p-value	0.6		0.6		0.5		0.011 *		0.1		0.9	

Table 4. *Cont.*

Variable	Sub-variable	Headache		Injection-Site Pain		Fatigue		Bone-Joint Pain		Stress		Fever	
		No	Yes	No	Yes	No	Yes	No	Yes	No	Yes	No	Yes
		%	%	%	%	%	%	%	%	%	%	%	%
Vaccine type	AZ two doses	11.0	28.0	1.0	18.0	9.0	23.0	9.0	30.0	18.0	16.0		37.0
	Pfizer two doses	67.0	52.0	6.0	61.0	71.0	55.0	70.0	49.0	66.0	55.0	78.0	44.0
	Pfizer and AZ	20.0	18.0	2.0	20.0	1.0	20.0	2.0	20.0	15.0	28.0	21.0	18.0
	p-value	0.009 *		0.9		0.025 *		<0.001 *		0.1		<0.001 *	

* Statistical significance.

Table 5. Distribution of common and moderately common side effects across demographic features after 2nd dose of COVID-19 vaccine.

Variable	Sub-Variable	Headache		Injection-Site Pain		Fatigue		Bone-Joint Pain		Stress		Fever	
		No	Yes	No	Yes	No	Yes	No	Yes	No	Yes	No	Yes
Gender	Male	50.5	38.6	69.5	34.5	46.1	43.8	48.6	35.9	41.9	50	45.9	43
	Female	49.5	61.4	30.5	65.5	53.9	56.3	51.4	64.1	58.1	50	54.1	57
	p-value	0.088		<0.001 *		0.092		0.749		0.273		0.674	
Age	18-29 Years	14.6	8.9	0	16.6	15.8	9.4	15.7	3.1	12.5	10.3	17.1	5.4
	30–49 Years	51.5	51.5	30.5	60	43.4	56.3	51.4	51.6	49.3	55.9	45.9	58.1
	>50 Years	34	39.6	69.5	23.4	40.8	34.4	32.9	45.3	38.2	33.8	36.9	36.6
	p-value	0.402		<0.001 *		0.021 *		0.155		0.666		0.025 *	
Marital status	Single	24.3	15.8	0	28.3	23.7	18	22.1	15.6	20.6	19.1	24.3	15.1
	Married	73.8	81.2	98.3	69	72.4	80.5	74.3	84.4	76.5	79.4	72.1	83.9
	Divorced	1	1	0	1.4	1.3	0.8	1.4	0	1.5	0	0.9	1.1
	Widowed	1	2	1.7	1.4	2.6	0.8	2.1	0	1.5	1.5	2.7	0
	p-value	0.472		<0.001 *		0.285		0.488		0.777		0.133	
Allergic to vaccine	No	93.2	98	98.3	94.5	97.4	94.5	95	96.9	94.9	97.1	96.4	94.6
	Yes	6.8	2	1.7	5.5	2.6	5.5	5	3.1	5.1	2.9	3.6	5.4
	p-value	0.094		0.228		0.545		0.34		0.47		0.539	
COVID-19-infected	No	74.8	78.2	74.6	77.2	72.4	78.9	81.4	65.6	100	29.4	73	80.6
	Yes	25.2	21.8	25.4	22.8	27.6	21.1	18.6	34.4	0	70.6	27	19.4
	p-value	0.56		0.684		0.014 *		0.287		<0.001 *		0.198	
Family member infected with COVID-19	No	34	30.7	39	29.7	48.7	22.7	33.6	29.7	46.3	4.4	25.2	40.9
	Yes	66	69.3	61	70.3	51.3	77.3	66.4	70.3	53.7	95.6	74.8	59.1
	p-value	0.616		0.197		0.582		<0.001 *		<0.001 *		0.017 *	
Friends infected with COVID-19	No	22.3	19.8	22	20.7	25	18.8	16.4	31.3	27.2	8.8	16.2	26.9
	Yes	77.7	80.2	78	79.3	75	81.3	83.6	68.8	72.8	91.2	83.8	73.1
	p-value	0.658		0.831		0.016 *		0.29		0.002 *		0.063	
COVID-19 infection after vaccinations	No	98.1	98	100	97.2	98.7	97.7	97.9	98.4	99.3	95.6	99.1	96.8
	Yes	1.9	2	0	2.8	1.3	2.3	2.1	1.6	0.7	4.4	0.9	3.2
	p-value	0.984		0.198		0.781		0.609		0.074		0.233	

Table 5. *Cont.*

Variable	Sub-Variable	Headache		Injection-Site Pain		Fatigue		Bone-Joint Pain		Stress		Fever	
		No	Yes	No	Yes	No	Yes	No	Yes	No	Yes	No	Yes
Vaccine type	AZ two doses	17.5	17.8	15.3	18.6	15.8	18.8	17.9	17.2	22.8	7.4	0	38.7
	Pfizer two doses	55.3	69.3	55.9	64.8	73.7	55.5	60	67.2	58.1	70.6	75.7	46.2
	Pfizer and AZ	27.2	12.9	28.8	16.6	10.5	25.8	22.1	15.6	19.1	22.1	24.3	15.1
	p-value	0.033 *		0.139		0.521		0.016 *		0.024 *		<0.001 *	

* Statistical significance.

3.4. Self-Reported Side Effects Severity and Medication Recommendations

Around 7% of participants reported that the side effects were severe after both doses, while 4.4% and 6.9% indicated the severe nature of side effects after the first and second doses, respectively. Paracetamol was recommended to 44.1% of study participants. However, vitamin C along with paracetamol was recommended in 5.4% of vaccine recipients. Medical consultation was sought by 5.4% of vaccinees due to severe side effects, and such consultation was more frequent after the first dose (3.4%). Only 2% of participants reported healthcare consultation after both doses.

3.5. Perception of Respondents towards Safety of Vaccination

Only 35.8% of vaccinated individuals considered the COVID-19 vaccines safe, while 9.3% suggested that they are not safe and 54.9% were not sure about their safety. However, three-fourths (75.5%) of the study population indicated that they recommend vaccines to their family members and friends.

4. Discussion

To the best of our knowledge, this is the first study to assess the side-effects profile following two doses of COVID-19 vaccines among individuals with comorbid illnesses in the Northern Region of Saudi Arabia. Given the rapid development of COVID-19 vaccines, the safety and efficacy of these vaccines remain an area of concern [23]. Such concerns are even more profound for patients with comorbid conditions due to the high prevalence of polypharmacy and vaccine hesitancy in this population [15–17,22]. Our analysis showed that the safety profile of COVID-19 vaccines among chronic-disease patients is comparable to healthy individuals, and these findings are aligned with the existing claims [24,25]. However, the incidence of at least one side effect was higher in individuals with comorbidities when compared to those without any underlying medical conditions. This result is aligned with the findings of Alemayehu et al. where authors reported that the magnitude of COVID-19 vaccine adverse effects was comparatively higher among participants with comorbid conditions [26]. Considering the higher risks of disease progression or death during COVID-19, the benefits of the COVID-19 vaccination outweigh the risks among patients with underline medical conditions.

Various clinical trials on vaccine development have included 20% to 30% of individuals with underlying medical conditions. The trials on Pfizer [27] and Moderna [28] vaccines showed that the protective effects were similar across the study participants with and without comorbidities [25]. However, the trials on Astra-Zeneca [29,30] and Janssen [31] showed better protective effects among participants without any comorbid condition than those with comorbidities, but the difference was statistically insignificant. It is important to note that mortality was not associated with any vaccine among participants with and without comorbid conditions. Based on these results, The Advisory Committee on Immunization Practices (ACIP) in the USA, The Joint Committee on Vaccination and immunization (JCVI) in the UK, and the WHO Strategic Advisory Group of Experts on Immunization (SAGE) recommend the vaccination for individuals with high-risk comorbidities [25].

Most of the participants in our study experienced at least one side effect following both doses of COVID-19 vaccines. These findings are in concordance with the results of a large surveillance report from the United Arab Emirates (UAE), where participants with comorbidities experienced more side effects than those without any comorbid condition [32]. Other studies among Arab population have also demonstrated significant association of chronic diseases with the development [33], as well as frequency and severity, of postvaccination side effects [34]. However, another study of Turkish healthcare workers revealed no association of chronic illness with the emergence and intensity of side effects following the Sinovac vaccine [35]. This inconsistency in results might be attributed to the differences in the study population and type of vaccines. Moreover, the existing evidence suggests a lower frequency of side effects after Sinovac than the Pfizer and Astra-Zeneca vaccines. Elnaem et al. reported that the frequency of side effects among recipients of the Sinovac vaccine was significantly lower than Pfizer-BioNTech and Oxford-Astra-Zeneca recipients [36]. This might be a contributing factor to a high prevalence of side effects, as all the participants in our study received either Pfizer or Astra-Zeneca vaccines. These findings suggest the relationship between the type of vaccine and the frequency of side effects. He et al. reviewed the comparative efficacy and safety of various COVID-19 vaccines and reported a high prevalence of local and systemic side effects after mRNA (Pfizer) and adenovirus-based (Astra-Zeneca) vaccines [37], and these results are aligned with our findings. Interestingly, the frequency of side effects was slightly higher after the second dose and these findings are in agreement with other investigations [38–40]. However, these findings are contradicted by the results of some other studies [41,42] where the proportion of side effects was more profound after the first dose. It is pertinent to mention that these contradictions might be attributed to the variation in the study population, the types of vaccines, and the status of chronic illnesses among participants. Taken together, our analysis confirms the high proportion of side effects among Pfizer and Astra-Zeneca recipients with chronic diseases, particularly in those with diabetes mellitus, hypertension, and hyperlipidemia. Moreover, the frequency of side effects was more among patients with >2 comorbid conditions. These results necessitate the need for more investigations on the correlation of type and number of comorbidities with the safety profile of the COVID-19 vaccines.

The distribution of side effects was similar to that reported in other studies [24,43], where the most commonly reported complaints were pain at the injection site, headache, muscle/joint pain, and fever. Most of these symptoms were reported within 6 h following the jab. The recipients of Astra-Zeneca experienced more side effects as compared to Pfizer vaccinees. Likewise, the participants who received two doses of Pfizer had an average of four side effects while recipients of two doses of Astra-Zeneca had an average of six side effects). These findings corroborate the results of other studies [24,43,44] comparing the frequencies of side effects across the types of vaccines. However, it is important to note that a conclusion on the association of the frequency of side effects with the type of vaccine should not be established, as this such association is markedly affected by the recipient's demographics. A recent meta-analysis has indicated a higher incidence of side effects following the administration of the Sputnik vaccine [45]. Since these side effects are self-reported by the vaccinees, several covariates must also be considered while interpreting the results. Considering the relationship of demographics with side-effects score, only gender and age were associated with the incidence of side effects after the first and second dose, respectively. Our analysis showed a higher frequency of side effects among females after the first dose as compared to males. These results are in contrast with the findings of Al Bahrani et al. [46] but in agreement with other investigations [24,47]. The higher frequency of side effects among females is well explained by biological mechanisms such as stronger antibody, innate, and adaptive immune responses among females [48]. It is pertinent to mention that the side-effects score was higher among males after the second dose, but the difference was not significant. Similar to other studies [24], our analysis showed that the side effects were more common among the adult population. These results indicate that the pattern of side effects reported among individuals with chronic conditions was similar to that reported among the healthy population.

In this study, 7% of the study population reported that the side effects were severe after both doses, while 6.9% reported more severe side effects after the second dose. Similar results have been reported by Kang et al. [40], where authors indicated the higher severity of adverse events after the second vaccination dose. However, only 5% of the study participants sought medical consultation due to severe side effects. The severity of side effects was self-reported in our study and might be associated with perceived severity among study participants. Nevertheless, most of the study participants used only paracetamol, indicating the mild nature of side effects. These findings necessitate the need for further investigations on the severity of side effects based on clinicians' observations among patients with chronic illnesses.

It is worth mentioning that only one-third of the study population reported that the COVID-19 vaccines are safe. Although the recommendation of the vaccines to family and friends was high in our study, the widespread concerns over the safety of COVID-19 vaccines among this population were considerable. The data from various countries have indicated that concerns about side effects are the main reason for hesitancy toward COVID-19 vaccines [49,50]. Established evidence has suggested widespread speculation on the safety profile of COVID-19 vaccines among individuals living with comorbidities and endorsed the prioritized measures to tackle vaccine hesitancy and to improve vaccine uptake in this population [15,51,52]. The side effects reported in our study were self-limiting and were primarily linked with the provocation of the immune system by the vaccines. The public sharing of these findings may enhance the confidence of individuals with comorbidities in the safety profile of the COVID-19 vaccines. This may result in the acceleration of the vaccine-coverage process. The side effects after the second dose of COVID-19 vaccines can interfere with booster dose uptake [53]. In this context, educating the population on the safety profile will be of paramount importance. Given the progression of the disease, odds of mortality, and complications linked with COVID-19 infection among chronic-disease patients, the vaccination of this population against COVID-19 holds an instrumental position in mass-vaccination campaigns. In this context, the confidence of this population in the vaccines is a major factor leveraging the vaccination success.

Study Limitations and Strengths

The findings of the current study should be interpreted in light of a few shortcomings. Demerits of convenient sampling, and information bias such as reporting bias and recall bias cannot be disregarded in this study. Since the side effects were self-reported, there is a possibility of incorrect blame, as the study population was also using several medications, and some complaints may have been associated with the use of drugs. The patients with diabetes mellitus, hypertension, hyperlipidemia, and asthma represented most of the study population; therefore, the implications of the findings for patients with other comorbid conditions are limited. The long-term impact of these side effects was not determined in this study, necessitating the need for further investigations in this particular population. Moreover, this study does not provide information on the status of comorbidities, as unstable patients may exaggerate the symptoms after vaccination. Since the safety profile of booster doses of COVID-19 vaccines has been investigated [54], our study does not provide any pharmacovigilance data following the booster dose among chronic-disease patients. Considering the limited number of participants in our analysis, replication and verification of our findings by a larger cohort are warranted. Despite these limitations, our findings are strengthened by a detailed analysis of the side-effect profile of the two doses of COVID-19 vaccines among people having diverse chronic conditions. Since various strong evidence suggests the increased risk of COVID-19, breakthrough infection, and waning vaccine effectiveness among people living with various health conditions [55], optimal vaccination coverage is direly needed in this population. In this context, the findings of the current study will help instill confidence in the COVID-19 vaccines and subsequently increase vaccine coverage in this population. Nevertheless, this study confirms the safety of the COVID-19 vaccines, and its findings can be utilized in creating awareness among this vulnerable population with vaccine hesitancy and ambivalence.

5. Conclusions

This study indicated a high proportion of transient and short-lived side effects of Pfizer and Astra-Zeneca vaccines among individuals with chronic illnesses. Pain at the injection site was a common side effect after the first and second doses. Fatigue and muscle or joint pain were the second-most-common side effects after the first and second dose, respectively. Most of these side effects occurred after 6 h of vaccine administration and lasted for 48 h. The number of comorbid conditions was found to be positively correlated with the side-effect score after the first and second doses. Only a few participants reported that the side effects were severe in nature. Although three-fourths of the study population indicated the recommendation of vaccines to their family members, only one-quarter of vaccinees endorsed COVID-19 vaccines as safe. The side-effects profile reported in this study was comparable with the safety reports of phase 3 clinical trials of these vaccines. It is important to note that the side effects reported in this study require further validation, verification, and replication through active pharmacovigilance or qualitative studies. A larger study with random sampling would likely detect the relationship of side effects between demographics, type and severity of comorbid illness, and the type of vaccine. The results of this study may help in solving the ongoing challenge of vaccine hesitancy in this vulnerable population that is nurtured by widespread concerns over safety profile.

Author Contributions: Conceptualization, T.H.M., Y.H.K., N.H.A. and A.S.A.; formal analysis, M.H.B. and N.T.; funding acquisition, T.H.M. and Y.H.K.; investigation, M.H.B., M.S. and N.T.; methodology, T.H.M., Y.H.K., M.H.B., M.S. and A.I.A.; project administration, T.H.M., Y.H.K., N.H.A. and A.S.A.; resources, M.S. and A.I.A.; software, M.H.B. and M.S.; supervision, T.H.M., N.T., N.H.A., A.I.A. and A.S.A.; validation, N.T., N.H.A. and A.I.A.; visualization, M.S.; writing—original draft, T.H.M., M.H.B. and M.S.; writing—review and editing, Y.H.K., N.T., N.H.A., A.I.A. and A.S.A. All authors have read and agreed to the published version of the manuscript.

Funding: This research was funded by the Deanship of Scientific Research at Jouf University under grant number: DSR-2021-01-0335.

Institutional Review Board Statement: The study was conducted in accordance with the Declaration of Helsinki and approved by the Local Committee of Bioethics (LCBE) at Jouf University, KSA (Reference: 05-05-43).

Informed Consent Statement: Informed consent was obtained from all subjects involved in the study.

Data Availability Statement: Not applicable.

Conflicts of Interest: The authors declare no conflict of interest.

References

1. Alsharif, W.; Qurashi, A. Effectiveness of COVID-19 diagnosis and management tools: A review. *Radiography* **2021**, *27*, 682–687. [CrossRef]
2. Mallhi, T.H.; Khan, Y.H.; Alzarea, A.I.; Khan, F.U.; Alotaibi, N.H.; Alanazi, A.S.; Butt, M.H.; Alatawi, A.D.; Salman, M.; Alzarea, S.I. Incidence, risk factors and outcomes of acute kidney injury among COVID-19 patients: A systematic review of systematic reviews. *Front. Med.* **2022**, *9*, 973030. [CrossRef]
3. Daghriri, T.; Ozmen, O. Quantifying the Effects of Social Distancing on the Spread of COVID-19. *Int. J. Environ. Res. Public Health* **2021**, *18*, 5566. [CrossRef]
4. Mallhi, T.H.; Khan, Y.H.; Alotaibi, N.H.; Alzarea, A.I.; Alanazi, A.S.; Qasim, S.; Iqbal, M.S.; Tanveer, N. Drug repurposing for COVID-19: A potential threat of self-medication and controlling measures. *Postgrad. Med. J.* **2021**, *97*, 742–743. [CrossRef]
5. Aouissi, H.A.; Kechebar, M.S.A.; Ababsa, M.; Roufayel, R.; Neji, B.; Petrisor, A.-I.; Hamimes, A.; Epelboin, L.; Ohmagari, N. The importance of behavioral and native factors on COVID-19 infection and severity: Insights from a preliminary cross-sectional study. *Healthcare* **2022**, *10*, 1341. [CrossRef] [PubMed]

6. Khan, Y.H.; Mallhi, T.H.; Alotaibi, N.H.; Alzarea, A.I.; Alanazi, A.S.; Tanveer, N.; Hashmi, F.K. Threat of COVID-19 vaccine hesitancy in Pakistan: The need for measures to neutralize misleading narratives. *Am. J. Trop. Med. Hyg.* **2020**, *103*, 603. [CrossRef]
7. Misbah, S.; Ahmad, A.; Butt, M.H.; Khan, Y.H.; Alotaibi, N.H.; Mallhi, T.H. A systematic analysis of studies on corona virus disease 19 (COVID-19) from viral emergence to treatment. *J. Coll. Physicians Surg. Pak.* **2020**, *30*, 9–18. [PubMed]
8. Østergaard, S.D.; Schmidt, M.; Horváth-Puhó, E.; Thomsen, R.W.; Sørensen, H.T. Thromboembolism and the Oxford–AstraZeneca COVID-19 vaccine: Side-effect or coincidence? *Lancet* **2021**, *397*, 1441–1443. [CrossRef] [PubMed]
9. Wan, E.Y.F.; Chui, C.S.L.; Lai, F.T.T.; Chan, E.W.Y.; Li, X.; Yan, V.K.C.; Gao, L.; Yu, Q.; Lam, I.C.H.; Chun, R.K.C. Bell's palsy following vaccination with mRNA (BNT162b2) and inactivated (CoronaVac) SARS-CoV-2 vaccines: A case series and nested case-control study. *Lancet Infect. Dis.* **2022**, *22*, 64–72. [CrossRef] [PubMed]
10. Salah, H.M.; Mehta, J.L. COVID-19 vaccine and myocarditis. *Am. J. Cardiol.* **2021**, *157*, 146–148. [CrossRef] [PubMed]
11. Manning, M.L.; Gerolamo, A.M.; Marino, M.A.; Hanson-Zalot, M.E.; Pogorzelska-Maziarz, M. COVID-19 vaccination readiness among nurse faculty and student nurses. *Nurs. Outlook* **2021**, *69*, 565–573. [CrossRef]
12. Riad, A.; Pokorná, A.; Attia, S.; Klugarová, J.; Koščík, M.; Klugar, M. Prevalence of COVID-19 vaccine side effects among healthcare workers in the Czech Republic. *J. Clin. Med.* **2021**, *10*, 1428. [CrossRef]
13. Lucia, V.C.; Kelekar, A.; Afonso, N.M. COVID-19 vaccine hesitancy among medical students. *J. Public Health* **2021**, *43*, 445–449. [CrossRef]
14. Lu, L.; Xiong, W.; Mu, J.; Zhang, Q.; Zhang, H.; Zou, L.; Li, W.; He, L.; Sander, J.W.; Zhou, D. The potential neurological effect of the COVID-19 vaccines: A review. *Acta Neurol. Scand.* **2021**, *144*, 3–12. [CrossRef]
15. Lai, F.T.T.; Huang, L.; Chui, C.S.L.; Wan, E.Y.F.; Li, X.; Wong, C.K.H.; Chan, E.W.W.; Ma, T.; Lum, D.H.; Leung, J.C.N. Multimorbidity and adverse events of special interest associated with COVID-19 vaccines in Hong Kong. *Nat. Commun.* **2022**, *13*, 411. [CrossRef]
16. Hanlon, P.; Nicholl, B.I.; Jani, B.D.; McQueenie, R.; Lee, D.; Gallacher, K.I.; Mair, F.S. Examining patterns of multimorbidity, polypharmacy and risk of adverse drug reactions in chronic obstructive pulmonary disease: A cross-sectional UK Biobank study. *BMJ Open* **2018**, *8*, e018404. [CrossRef] [PubMed]
17. Incalzi, R.A.; Trevisan, C.; Del Signore, S.; Volpato, S.; Fumagalli, S.; Monzani, F.; Bellelli, G.; Gareri, P.; Mossello, E.; Malara, A. Are vaccines against COVID-19 tailored to the most vulnerable people? *Vaccine* **2021**, *39*, 2325–2327. [CrossRef]
18. Yi, Z.; Yao, Z.; Xu, D.; Xu, C.; Fang, W.; Guo, Z.; Wang, Y.; Huang, J.; Li, Q.; Zhang, H. Attitudes toward COVID-19 Vaccination: A Survey of Chinese Patients with Rheumatic Diseases. *Vaccines* **2022**, *10*, 1604. [CrossRef] [PubMed]
19. Aouissi, H.A.; Belhaouchet, I. What about rheumatic diseases and COVID-19? *New Microbes New Infect.* **2021**, *41*, 100846. [CrossRef]
20. Furer, V.; Eviatar, T.; Zisman, D.; Peleg, H.; Paran, D.; Levartovsky, D.; Zisapel, M.; Elalouf, O.; Kaufman, I.; Meidan, R. Immunogenicity and safety of the BNT162b2 mRNA COVID-19 vaccine in adult patients with autoimmune inflammatory rheumatic diseases and in the general population: A multicentre study. *Ann. Rheum. Dis.* **2021**, *80*, 1330–1338. [CrossRef] [PubMed]
21. Li, Y.K.; Lui, M.P.K.; Yam, L.L.; Cheng, C.S.; Tsang, T.H.T.; Kwok, W.S.; Chung, H.Y. COVID-19 vaccination in patients with rheumatic diseases: Vaccination rates, patient perspectives, and side effects. *Immun. Inflamm. Dis.* **2022**, *10*, e589. [CrossRef] [PubMed]
22. Al-Hanawi, M.K.; Ahmad, K.; Haque, R.; Keramat, S.A. Willingness to receive COVID-19 vaccination among adults with chronic diseases in the Kingdom of Saudi Arabia. *J. Infect. Public Health* **2021**, *14*, 1489–1496. [CrossRef] [PubMed]
23. Al-Zalfawi, S.M.; Rabbani, S.I.; Asdaq, S.M.B.; Alamri, A.S.; Alsanie, W.F.; Alhomrani, M.; Mohzari, Y.; Alrashed, A.A.; AlRifdah, A.H.; Almagrabe, T. Public knowledge, attitude, and perception towards COVID-19 vaccination in Saudi Arabia. *Int. J. Environ. Res. Public Health* **2021**, *18*, 10081. [CrossRef]
24. Alzarea, A.I.; Khan, Y.H.; Alatawi, A.D.; Alanazi, A.S.; Alzarea, S.I.; Butt, M.H.; Almalki, Z.S.; Alahmari, A.K.; Mallhi, T.H. Surveillance of Post-Vaccination Side Effects of COVID-19 Vaccines among Saudi Population: A Real-World Estimation of Safety Profile. *Vaccines* **2022**, *10*, 924. [CrossRef] [PubMed]
25. Choi, W.S.; Cheong, H.J. COVID-19 vaccination for people with comorbidities. *Infect. Chemother.* **2021**, *53*, 155. [CrossRef] [PubMed]
26. Alemayehu, A.; Demissie, A.; Yusuf, M.; Abdullahi, Y.; Abdulwehab, R.; Oljira, L.; Feleke, D. COVID-19 vaccine side effect: Age and gender disparity in adverse effects following the first dose of AstraZeneca COVID-19 vaccine among the vaccinated population in Eastern Ethiopia: A community-based study. *SAGE Open Med.* **2022**, *10*, 20503121221108616. [CrossRef]
27. Food and Drug Administration. Vaccines and Related Biological Products Advisory Committee Meeting December 10, 2020: FDA Briefing Document, Pfizer-BioNTech COVID-19 Vaccine. 2020. Available online: https://www.fda.gov/advisory-committees/advisory-committee-calendar/vaccines-and-related-biological-products-advisory-committee-december-10-2020-meeting-announcement (accessed on 30 October 2022).
28. Oliver, S.E.; Gargano, J.W.; Marin, M.; Wallace, M.; Curran, K.G.; Chamberland, M.; McClung, N.; Campos-Outcalt, D.; Morgan, R.L.; Mbaeyi, S. The advisory committee on immunization practices' interim recommendation for use of moderna COVID-19 vaccine—United States, December 2020. *Morb. Mortal. Wkly. Rep.* **2021**, *69*, 1653. [CrossRef] [PubMed]

29. Committee for Medicinal Products for Human Use (CHMP). COVID-19 Vaccine AstraZeneca. Product Information as Approved by the CHMP on 29 January 2021, Pending Endorsement by the European Commission. 2021. Available online: https://www.ema.europa.eu/en/documents/product-information/covid-19-vaccine-astrazeneca-product-information-approved-chmp-29-january-2021-pending-endorsement_en.pdf (accessed on 30 October 2022).
30. Voysey, M.; Clemens, S.A.C.; Madhi, S.A.; Weckx, L.Y.; Folegatti, P.M.; Aley, P.K.; Angus, B.; Baillie, V.L.; Barnabas, S.L.; Bhorat, Q.E. Safety and efficacy of the ChAdOx1 nCoV-19 vaccine (AZD1222) against SARS-CoV-2: An interim analysis of four randomised controlled trials in Brazil, South Africa, and the UK. *Lancet* **2021**, *397*, 99–111. [CrossRef] [PubMed]
31. Vaccines and Related Biological Products Advisory Committee Meeting. FDA Briefing Document. Janssen Ad26.COV2.S Vaccine for the Prevention of COVID-19. Available online: https://www.fda.gov/media/146217/download (accessed on 30 October 2022).
32. Ganesan, S.; Al Ketbi, L.M.B.; Al Kaabi, N.; Al Mansoori, M.; Al Maskari, N.N.; Al Shamsi, M.S.; Alderei, A.S.; El Eissaee, H.N.; Al Ketbi, R.M.; Al Shamsi, N.S. Vaccine Side Effects Following COVID-19 Vaccination Among the Residents of the UAE—An Observational Study. *Front. Public Health* **2022**, *10*, 876336. [CrossRef]
33. Alghamdi, A.N.; Alotaibi, M.I.; Alqahtani, A.S.; Al Aboud, D.; Abdel-Moneim, A.S. BNT162b2 and ChAdOx1 SARS-CoV-2 post-vaccination side-effects among Saudi vaccinees. *Front. Med.* **2021**, *8*, 760047. [CrossRef] [PubMed]
34. Hatmal, M.m.M.; Al-Hatamleh, M.A.I.; Olaimat, A.N.; Mohamud, R.; Fawaz, M.; Kateeb, E.T.; Alkhairy, O.K.; Tayyem, R.; Lounis, M.; Al-Raeei, M. Reported adverse effects and attitudes among Arab populations following COVID-19 vaccination: A large-scale multinational study implementing machine learning tools in predicting post-vaccination adverse effects based on predisposing factors. *Vaccines* **2022**, *10*, 366. [CrossRef] [PubMed]
35. Riad, A.; Sağıroğlu, D.; Üstün, B.; Pokorná, A.; Klugarová, J.; Attia, S.; Klugar, M. Prevalence and risk factors of CoronaVac side effects: An independent cross-sectional study among healthcare workers in Turkey. *J. Clin. Med.* **2021**, *10*, 2629. [CrossRef] [PubMed]
36. Elnaem, M.H.; Mohd Taufek, N.H.; Ab Rahman, N.S.; Mohd Nazar, N.I.; Zin, C.S.; Nuffer, W.; Turner, C.J. COVID-19 Vaccination Attitudes, Perceptions, and Side Effect Experiences in Malaysia: Do Age, Gender, and Vaccine Type Matter? *Vaccines* **2021**, *9*, 1156. [CrossRef] [PubMed]
37. He, Q.; Mao, Q.; Zhang, J.; Bian, L.; Gao, F.; Wang, J.; Xu, M.; Liang, Z. COVID-19 vaccines: Current understanding on immunogenicity, safety, and further considerations. *Front. Immunol.* **2021**, *12*, 669339. [CrossRef]
38. Polack, F.P.; Thomas, S.J.; Kitchin, N.; Absalon, J.; Gurtman, A.; Lockhart, S.; Perez, J.L.; Marc, G.P.; Moreira, E.D.; Zerbini, C. Safety and efficacy of the BNT162b2 mRNA COVID-19 vaccine. *N. Engl. J. Med.* **2020**, *383*, 2603–2615. [CrossRef]
39. El-Shitany, N.A.; Harakeh, S.; Badr-Eldin, S.M.; Bagher, A.M.; Eid, B.; Almukadi, H.; Alghamdi, B.S.; Alahmadi, A.A.; Hassan, N.A.; Sindi, N. Minor to moderate side effects of Pfizer-BioNTech COVID-19 vaccine among Saudi residents: A retrospective cross-sectional study. *Int. J. Gen. Med.* **2021**, *14*, 1389. [CrossRef]
40. Kang, Y.M.; Lim, J.; Choe, K.-W.; Lee, K.-D.; Jo, D.H.; Kim, M.J.; Kim, J.M.; Kim, K.N. Reactogenicity after the first and second doses of BNT162b2 mRNA coronavirus disease vaccine: A single-center study. *Clin. Exp. Vaccine Res.* **2021**, *10*, 282. [CrossRef]
41. Desalegn, M.; Garoma, G.; Tamrat, H.; Desta, A.; Prakash, A. The prevalence of AstraZeneca COVID-19 vaccine side effects among Nigist Eleni Mohammed memorial comprehensive specialized hospital health workers. Cross sectional survey. *PLoS ONE* **2022**, *17*, e0265140. [CrossRef]
42. Omeish, H.; Najadat, A.; Al-Azzam, S.; Tarabin, N.; Abu Hameed, A.; Al-Gallab, N.; Abbas, H.; Rababah, L.; Rabadi, M.; Karasneh, R. Reported COVID-19 vaccines side effects among Jordanian population: A cross sectional study. *Hum. Vaccines Immunother.* **2022**, *18*, 1981086. [CrossRef]
43. Rahman, M.; Masum, M.; Ullah, H.; Wajed, S.; Talukder, A. A comprehensive review on COVID-19 vaccines: Development, effectiveness, adverse effects, distribution and challenges. *Virusdisease* **2022**, *33*, 1–22. [CrossRef]
44. Amer, F.H.I.; Alzayyat, R.; Alzayyat, N.; Alomran, S.; Wafai, S.; Alabssi, H.; Alsultan, D. Side Effects of COVID-19 Vaccines (Pfizer, AstraZeneca) in Saudi Arabia, Eastern Province. *Cureus* **2022**, *14*, e27297.
45. Liu, Q.; Qin, C.; Liu, M.; Liu, J. Effectiveness and safety of SARS-CoV-2 vaccine in real-world studies: A systematic review and meta-analysis. *Infect. Dis. Poverty* **2021**, *10*, 132. [PubMed]
46. Al Bahrani, S.; Albarrak, A.; Alghamdi, O.A.; Alghamdi, M.A.; Hakami, F.H.; Al Abaadi, A.K.; Alkhrashi, S.A.; Alghamdi, M.Y.; Almershad, M.M.; Alenazi, M.M. Safety and reactogenicity of the ChAdOx1 (AZD1222) COVID-19 vaccine in Saudi Arabia. *Int. J. Infect. Dis.* **2021**, *110*, 359–362. [CrossRef] [PubMed]
47. Ahsan, W.; Syed, N.K.; Alsraeya, A.A.; Alhazmi, H.A.; Najmi, A.; Bratty, M.A.; Javed, S.; Makeen, H.A.; Meraya, A.M.; Albarraq, A.A. Post-vaccination survey for monitoring the side effects associated with COVID-19 vaccines among healthcare professionals of Jazan province, Saudi Arabia. *Saudi Med. J.* **2021**, *42*, 1341–1352. [CrossRef]
48. Jensen, A.; Stromme, M.; Moyassari, S.; Chadha, A.S.; Tartaglia, M.C.; Szoeke, C.; Ferretti, M.T. COVID-19 vaccines: Considering sex differences in efficacy and safety. *Contemp. Clin. Trials* **2022**, *115*, 106700. [CrossRef]
49. Solís Arce, J.S.; Warren, S.S.; Meriggi, N.F.; Scacco, A.; McMurry, N.; Voors, M.; Syunyaev, G.; Malik, A.A.; Aboutajdine, S.; Adeojo, O. COVID-19 vaccine acceptance and hesitancy in low-and middle-income countries. *Nat. Med.* **2021**, *27*, 1385–1394. [CrossRef]
50. Qunaibi, E.; Basheti, I.; Soudy, M.; Sultan, I. Hesitancy of Arab healthcare workers towards COVID-19 vaccination: A large-scale multinational study. *Vaccines* **2021**, *9*, 446. [CrossRef]

51. Tsai, R.; Hervey, J.; Hoffman, K.; Wood, J.; Johnson, J.; Deighton, D.; Clermont, D.; Loew, B.; Goldberg, S.L. COVID-19 vaccine hesitancy and acceptance among individuals with cancer, autoimmune diseases, or other serious comorbid conditions: Cross-sectional, internet-based survey. *JMIR Public Health Surveill.* **2022**, *8*, e29872. [CrossRef]
52. Alghamdi, A.A.; Aldosari, M.S.; Alsaeed, R.A. Acceptance and barriers of COVID-19 vaccination among people with chronic diseases in Saudi Arabia. *J. Infect. Dev. Ctries.* **2021**, *15*, 1646–1652. [CrossRef]
53. Alshahrani, N.Z.; Alsabaani, A.A.; Ridda, I.; Rashid, H.; Alzahrani, F.; Almutairi, T.H.; Alzahrani, B.A.S.; Albeshri, A.S.S. Uptake of COVID-19 Booster Dose among Saudi Arabian Population. *Medicina* **2022**, *58*, 972. [CrossRef]
54. Lounis, M.; Aouissi, H.A.; Abdelhadi, S.; Rais, M.A.; Belkessa, S.; Bencherit, D. Short-Term Adverse Effects Following Booster Dose of Inactivated-Virus vs. Adenoviral-Vector COVID-19 Vaccines in Algeria: A Cross-Sectional Study of the General Population. *Vaccines* **2022**, *10*, 1781. [CrossRef] [PubMed]
55. Adab, P.; Haroon, S.; O'Hara, M.E.; Jordan, R.E. Comorbidities and COVID-19. *BMJ* **2022**, *377*, o1431. [CrossRef] [PubMed]

medicina

MDPI

Article

Prevalence of Latent Tuberculosis Infection among Patients Undergoing Regular Hemodialysis in Disenfranchised Communities: A Multicenter Study during COVID-19 Pandemic

Mohamad Bachar Ismail [1,2], Nesrine Zarriaa [1], Marwan Osman [3,4,*], Safa Helfawi [1], Nabil Kabbara [5], Abdel Nasser Chatah [6], Ahmad Kamaleddine [7], Rashad Alameddine [7], Fouad Dabboussi [1] and Monzer Hamze [1]

1 Laboratoire Microbiologie, Santé et Environnement (LMSE), Doctoral School of Sciences and Technology, Faculty of Public Health, Lebanese University, Tripoli 1300, Lebanon
2 Faculty of Science, Lebanese University, Tripoli 1300, Lebanon
3 Cornell Atkinson Center for Sustainability, Cornell University, Ithaca, NY 14853, USA
4 Department of Public and Ecosystem Health, College of Veterinary Medicine, Cornell University, Ithaca, NY 14853, USA
5 Nini Hospital, Tripoli 1300, Lebanon
6 Dar Al-Chifae Hospital, Tripoli 1300, Lebanon
7 Orange Nassau Hospital, Tripoli 1300, Lebanon
* Correspondence: mo368@cornell.edu or marwan.osman@outlook.com; Tel.: +1-607-262-4219

Abstract: *Background and Objectives*: Due to their weakened immune response, hemodialysis (HD) patients with latent tuberculosis infection (LTBI) are at higher risk for active tuberculosis (TB) disease and are more subject to patient-to-patient transmission within dialysis units. Consequently, current guidelines advocate screening these patients for LTBI. To our knowledge, the epidemiology of LTBI in HD patients has never been examined before in Lebanon. In this context, this study aimed to determine LTBI prevalence among patients undergoing regular HD in Northern Lebanon and to identify potential factors associated with this infection. Notably, the study was conducted during the COVID-19 pandemic, which is likely to have catastrophic effects on TB and increase the risk of mortality and hospitalization in HD patients. *Materials and Methods*: A multicenter cross-sectional study was carried out in three hospital dialysis units in Tripoli, North Lebanon. Blood samples and sociodemographic and clinical data were collected from 93 HD patients. To screen for LTBI, all patient samples underwent the fourth-generation QuantiFERON-TB Gold Plus assay (QFT-Plus). Multivariable logistic regression analysis was used to identify the predictors of LTBI status in HD patients. *Results*: Overall, 51 men and 42 women were enrolled. The mean age of the study population was 58.3 ± 12.4 years. Nine HD patients had indeterminate QFT-Plus results and were therefore excluded from subsequent statistical analysis. Among the remaining 84 participants with valid results, QFT-Plus was positive in 16 patients, showing a positivity prevalence of 19% (95% interval for *p*: 11.3%, 29.1%). Multivariable logistic regression analysis showed that LTBI was significantly associated with age [OR = 1.06; 95% CI = 1.01 to 1.13; $p = 0.03$] and a low-income level [OR = 9.29; 95% CI = 1.62 to 178; $p = 0.04$]. *Conclusion*: LTBI was found to be prevalent in one in five HD patients examined in our study. Therefore, effective TB control measures need to be implemented in this vulnerable population, with special attention to elderly patients with low socioeconomic status.

Keywords: latent tuberculosis infection; hemodialysis; QuantiFERON-TB Gold Plus assay; Lebanon

Citation: Ismail, M.B.; Zarriaa, N.; Osman, M.; Helfawi, S.; Kabbara, N.; Chatah, A.N.; Kamaleddine, A.; Alameddine, R.; Dabboussi, F.; Hamze, M. Prevalence of Latent Tuberculosis Infection among Patients Undergoing Regular Hemodialysis in Disenfranchised Communities: A Multicenter Study during COVID-19 Pandemic. *Medicina* **2023**, *59*, 654. https://doi.org/10.3390/medicina59040654

Academic Editors: Yusra Habib Khan, Tauqeer Hussain Mallhi, Tahir Mehmood Khan and Muhammad Salman

Received: 24 February 2023
Revised: 21 March 2023
Accepted: 24 March 2023
Published: 26 March 2023

Copyright: © 2023 by the authors. Licensee MDPI, Basel, Switzerland. This article is an open access article distributed under the terms and conditions of the Creative Commons Attribution (CC BY) license (https://creativecommons.org/licenses/by/4.0/).

1. Introduction

Tuberculosis (TB), caused by the *Mycobacterium tuberculosis* complex (MTBC), is the world's most common cause of death from a single infectious agent next to coronavirus disease 2019 (COVID-19) and one of the leading causes of death from antimicrobial resistance [1,2]. According to the World Health Organization (WHO), a quarter of the world's population has TB infection, a minority of whom will rapidly develop active TB. However, the majority (>90%) of infected individuals develop effective acquired immunity to MTBC, which persists within the human host as latent TB infection (LTBI) [2]. Individuals with LTBI present a persistent immune response to stimulation by mycobacterial antigens without evidence of clinically manifested TB disease. However, they can potentially develop active TB, usually when their immune system becomes weakened. In 2021, there were an estimated 1.6 million deaths from TB worldwide [2]. Notably, COVID-19 is likely to have catastrophic effects on TB. Due to the COVID-19 pandemic, it was predicted that TB deaths in high-TB settings would rise by up to 20% over 5 years [3]. Similarly, TB disease can worsen COVID-19. Indeed, TB was found to be an independent risk factor for increased mortality due to COVID-19 [4,5]. Similarly, the risk of death and percentage recovery in COVID-19 patients with TB were, respectively, 2.17 times higher and 25% lower than in those without TB [6].

Chronic kidney disease (CKD) is a relatively neglected global public health threat, with high morbidity and mortality rates [7]. Indeed, CKD accounts for more than one million deaths yearly, which makes it the 12th leading cause of death worldwide [8]. Advanced renal impairment leads to end-stage renal disease (ESRD), necessitating renal replacement therapy, such as HD [9]. CKD impairs both innate and adaptive host immunity. The coexistence of chronic immune activation and chronic immune suppression is a common implication of uremia, resulting in a weak vaccination response and an increased incidence of cancers and microbial infections [10,11]. The TB reactivation risk is increased by 10–25 times among dialysis patients compared to the general population [12]. The mortality rate of TB in dialysis patients appears to be higher as well [13]. This may be commonly associated with late diagnosis and treatment, which, in turn, is due to the nonspecific symptoms of TB in dialysis patients, whereas the involvement is often extrapulmonary [13,14].

In this context, screening and treatment for LTBI in this population are recommended by the World Health Organization (WHO) to prevent the reactivation of LTBI and the secondary transmission of the infection within dialysis units [15]. While there are numerous available diagnostic assays to detect active TB, the diagnosis of LTBI remains challenging, relying on the detection of an immune response against MTBC antigens. A gold standard for the diagnosis of LTBI is lacking, but screening tests (tuberculin skin test (TST) and interferon-gamma release assays (IGRAs)) are used for this purpose [16]. IGRAs are ex vivo blood tests that measure the T-cell release of IFN-γ following stimulation by antigens specific to the MTBC (with the exception of BCG substrains), i.e., culture filtrate protein 10 (CFP-10) and early secreted antigenic target of 6 kDa protein (ESAT-6).

Lebanon remains a low-TB-burden country, with an estimated incidence of 13 per 100,000 population and a total of 474 notified cases in 2021 [17]. Recently, the estimated prevalence of CKD in Lebanon was 12.5%, which is surprisingly higher than the globally estimated prevalence of 9.1% in 2017. It is worth noting that the burden of dialysis in Lebanon is also among the highest worldwide, with 777 patients per million compared to 410 dialysis patients per million people worldwide [8].

Many studies have confirmed an increased risk (6.9- to 52.5-fold) of TB in dialysis patients compared to the general population [18]. Although several reports investigated the epidemiology of LTBI in HD patients in the Middle East and North Africa (MENA) region [19–21], there is a lack of data regarding LTBI prevalence and infection-associated factors among this vulnerable population in Lebanon. In this context, this study, conducted during the COVID-19 pandemic, aimed to determine LTBI prevalence among HD patients in Northern Lebanon and to identify potential factors associated with this infection.

2. Materials and Methods

2.1. Study Design and Population

This investigation was a multicenter cross-sectional analytic study conducted at two time points in Tripoli, North Lebanon. Between August and October 2020, forty-nine (49) patients attending the dialysis unit at a public hospital (Orange-Nassau Governmental Hospital) were enrolled in the survey. In February 2022, forty-four (44) patients attending the dialysis unit at two private hospitals (Nini Hospital and Dar Al-Chifae Hospital) were added to the survey. Overall, we included 93 patients from the three above-mentioned care centers. The study population corresponds to all eligible HD patients attending the dialysis units within the study period. We excluded patients who (i) were younger than 18 years; (ii) had a history of active TB or had TB symptoms at the time of enrollment; or (iii) were non-Lebanese.

2.2. Data and Sample Collection and Laboratory Examination

Data on sociodemographic factors (e.g., age, sex, educational level, and income level), medical records (e.g., BCG vaccine, previous contact with active TB patients, and TST), clinical characteristics of dialysis conditions (e.g., cause of ESRD, HD duration, frequency of HD session per week, and HCV and HBV infections), behavior (e.g., smoking and alcoholism), and the presence of other additional co-morbidities were recorded in the study population. A total of 5 mL of blood was drawn from each participant into two lithium heparin tubes for further laboratory examination.

LTBI was investigated using the QuantiFERON-TB Gold Plus (QFT-Plus) (Qiagen, Germantown, MD) assay, performed according to the manufacturer's instructions. This assay uses four specialized blood collection tubes: a Nil tube (a negative control to adjust for background IFN-γ), a Mitogen tube (a positive control to confirm baseline immune status), and two antigen tubes, TB1 and TB2, which contain specific M. tuberculosis peptides designed to stimulate both CD4 and CD8 T-cells. TB1 contains peptides from ESAT-6 and CFP-10 mycobacterial antigens to target the cell-mediated responses of CD4 T-cells, while TB2 contains the same CD4 antigenic peptides of TB1 in addition to newly designed peptides that stimulate CD8 T-cells. One milliliter of blood was transferred to each QFT-P tube (Nil, TB1, TB2, and Mitogen). The tubes were labeled, shaken, and incubated at 37 °C ± 1 °C for 16–24 h. They were then centrifuged for 15 min at 2000 to 3000 RCF, and the plasma from each tube was then collected and stored at −20 °C until use. The measurement of IFN-γ via ELISA was subsequently performed, and IFN-γ concentrations were obtained using QFT-Plus Analysis Software, version 2.71.

2.3. Statistical Analysis

Statistical analysis was performed using R software (R Core team, version 4.1.0; R Studio, version 1.4.1106) using several packages (e.g., summarytools, DescTools, prettyR, dplyr, and tidyr), and the obtained findings were illustrated using the ggplot2 R package. The categorical data were described as frequencies and associated proportions. The difference between the proportions of LTBI among different categories was initially compared using Fisher's exact test for categorical covariates and a t-test for continuous covariates. Subsequently, multivariable logistic regression analysis was performed with LTBI as the outcome and age, income level, smoking behavior, and HD due to diabetes mellitus as predictors. We also used a backward stepwise model to identify and confirm the associations of covariates with LTBI. The statistical tests were two-sided, with the type I error set at $\alpha = 0.05$. The code necessary to replicate the analysis is publicly available (http://doi.org/10.6084/m9.figshare.22043252; accessed on 25 March 2023).

3. Results

A total of 93 HD patients, 51 men and 42 women, attending the dialysis units of three hospitals in North Lebanon were enrolled in the study and screened for LTBI. The mean age of the study population was 58.3 ± 12.4 years (age range 26–84 years). Most enrolled patients were from Tripoli (62.4%), came from low-income families (71%), and were overweight (Average Body Mass Index (BMI) = 25.7). Out of all patients, 7.5% had previous contact with a confirmed TB patient, and 39.8% had a history of BCG vaccination. The mean duration of HD was 6.8 ± 4.9 years. Other sociodemographic and clinical characteristics of the study population are summarized in Table 1.

Table 1. Sociodemographic and clinical characteristics of the study population and the prevalence of latent tuberculosis infection.

	Total = 93 Patients	
	n	%
QuantiFERON-TB		
Positive	16	17.2
Negative	68	73.1
Indeterminate	9	9.7
Hospital		
Orange-Nassau Governmental Hospital (Public)	49	52.7
Nini Hospital (Private)	31	33.3
Dar Al-Chifae Hospital (Private)	13	14.0
Sex		
Female	42	45.2
Male	51	54.8
Age (mean [SD; min–max])	58.3 [12.4; 26–84 years]	
Body Mass Index (BMI) (mean [SD; min–max])	25.7 [4.0; 16.6–38.8]	
District		
Tripoli	58	62.4
Miniyeh-Danniyeh	13	14.0
Akkar	12	12.9
Zgharta	6	6.5
Koura	4	4.3
Education		
Illiterate	26	28.0
Literate	67	72.0
Income level		
Low	66	71.0
Middle to high	27	29.0
BCG vaccination		
Yes	37	39.8
No	50	53.8
Unknown	6	6.5

Table 1. *Cont.*

	Total = 93 Patients	
	n	%
Smoking		
Yes	40	43.0
No	53	57.0
Drinking alcohol		
Yes	5	5.4
No	88	94.6
Contact with a tuberculosis patient		
Yes	7	7.5
No	86	92.5
Chronic glomerulonephritis *		
Yes	11	11.8
No	82	88.2
Polycystic kidney disease *		
Yes	5	5.4
No	88	94.6
High blood pressure *		
Yes	29	31.2
No	64	68.8
Diabetes mellitus *		
Yes	12	12.9
No	81	87.1
Nephroangiosclerosis *		
Yes	10	10.8
No	83	89.2
Diabetic nephropathy *		
Yes	14	15.1
No	79	84.9
Kidney transplantation		
Yes	6	6.5
No	87	93.5
Hepatitis B infection		
Yes	2	2.2
No	91	97.8
Hepatitis C infection		
Yes	1	1.1
No	92	98.9

Table 1. *Cont.*

	Total = 93 Patients	
	n	%
Starting hemodialysis in years ago (mean [SD; min–max])	6.8 [4.9; 1–22 years]	
Duration of hemodialysis sessions		
<4 h	39	41.9
≥4 h	54	58.1
Frequency of weekly hemodialysis sessions		
Up to 2 per week	21	22.6
3 per week	72	77.4

* Suggested cause of hemodialysis. Data are presented as mean [standard deviation (SD); min–max] for the continuous variables and as frequency and percentage for categorical variables.

The QFT-Plus results showed that out of 93 HD patients, nine had indeterminate QFT-Plus results and were therefore excluded from subsequent statistical analysis. Among the remaining 84 participants with valid QFT-Plus results, 16 tested positive, reflecting a prevalence of 19% (95% interval for *p*: 11.3%, 29.1%). Among patients who had positive QFT-Plus results, the majority were men (62.5%), smokers (56.25%), and BCG-unvaccinated (68.8%) and had low-income status (93.8%). Regarding HD etiologies, high blood pressure and diabetes mellitus were more common among patients with positive QFT-Plus compared to peers with negative results. Multivariable logistic regression analysis showed that LTBI was significantly associated with age [OR = 1.06; 95% CI = 1.01 to 1.13; *p* = 0.03] and a low-income level [OR = 9.29; 95% CI = 1.62 to 178; *p* = 0.04] (Table 2).

Table 2. Determinants of latent tuberculosis among patients on hemodialysis using univariate analysis and multivariable logistic regression models.

	Univariate Analysis		Multivariable Logistic Regression Models					
			Model 1 [i]			Model 2 [ii]		
Categorical variables	%	*p*	adj. OR	95%CI	*p*	adj. OR	95%CI	*p*
Sex								
Female [1]	16.7							
Male	20.8	0.78						
District								
Tripoli [1]	22.6							
Outside Tripoli	12.9	0.39						
Education								
Illiterate [1]	25.0							
Literate	16.7	0.38						
Income level								
Middle to high [1]	4.2							
Low	25.0	0.03	8.75	1.49–169	0.05	9.29	1.62–178	0.04
BCG vaccination								
Yes [1]	14.7							
No	23.9	0.40						

Table 2. *Cont.*

	Univariate Analysis			Multivariable Logistic Regression Models					
				Model 1 [i]			Model 2 [ii]		
Smoking									
Yes [1]	25.7								
No	14.3		0.26	0.43	0.12–1.44	0.17	0.41	0.12–1.35	0.15
Contact with a tuberculosis patient									
Yes [1]	28.6								
No	18.1		0.61						
High blood pressure *									
Yes [1]	25.9								
No	15.8		0.37						
Diabetes mellitus *									
Yes [1]	36.4								
No	16.4		0.21	0.75	0.17–3.79	0.71			
Kidney transplantation									
Yes	0.0								
No	20.3		0.58						
Duration of hemodialysis sessions									
<4 h	20.0								
≥4 h	18.4		1.00						
Frequency of weekly hemodialysis sessions									
Up to 2 per week	16.7								
3 per week	19.7		1.00						
Continuous variables	Infection	No infection	*p*	adj. OR	95%CI	*p*	adj. OR	95%CI	*p*
Age	64.7	57.6	0.05	1.06	1.01–1.13	0.04	1.06	1.01–1.13	0.03
Body Mass Index (BMI)	25.5	25.8	0.73						
Starting hemodialysis in years ago	5.93	6.97	0.39						

Determinants of latent tuberculosis were predicted using univariate (*t*-test and Fisher's exact test for continuous and categorical variables, respectively) and multivariable analysis (logistic regression models). [i] The variables tested by univariate analysis that had a p value < 0.30 were included in Model 1 (multivariable logistic regression analysis). [ii] In Model 2, a backward logistic regression model was created including only complete cases. [1] Reference group. * Suggested cause of hemodialysis.

4. Discussion

People with ESRD have an increased risk of active TB [22]. This dual public health threat commonly affects low- and middle-income countries the most, as the CKD burden is increasing more rapidly in these countries and their resident households are at a greater risk of contracting TB [23,24]. Due to the lack of effective surveillance systems, the official data on ESRD and TB might underestimate the actual rates of these diseases and consequently prevent the implementation of appropriate preventive measures.

Since late 2019, Lebanon has been facing calamitous economic and political crises, which were further exacerbated by the COVID-19 pandemic and the blast of the Beirut port [25]. Many sectors were severely affected, including the healthcare sector, endangering the ability of healthcare centers to provide life-saving care services. Indeed, unprecedented inflation and its consequent health and socioeconomic results have negatively impacted both HD and TB services. Prices of healthcare consultations and life-saving medicines for serious illnesses have increased dramatically, which precipitously threatens the control and treatment of infectious and non-communicable diseases in the Lebanese community [26]. Moreover, laboratory diagnostic supplies and essential drugs have been widely reported as inaccessible to a large part of the Lebanese population [27,28]. In addition to the prevailing extreme poverty and malnutrition (two of the major social determinants of TB) in the Lebanese community, the Beirut port explosion in August 2020 heavily damaged the national TB program (NTP) premises in the Karantina region of the capital Beirut, where the central unit and main TB center are located [17]. The COVID-19 pandemic has also played a key role in increasing TB cases in Lebanon, where TB control services were significantly altered by the pandemic [17]. Furthermore, there was a threat of dialysis service suspension due to severe shortages in supplies. This fact impacts not only HD patients but also individuals who will not be diagnosed and cases who will not be operated on [29].

To the best of our knowledge, we determined the prevalence of LTBI for the first time in the MENA region with the latest generation of IGRAs—the QFT test (i.e., QFT-Plus). Unlike the previous QFT generations (i.e., QuantiFERON-TB Gold In-Tube (QFT-GIT) and QuantiFERON-TB Gold (QFT-G)), the QFT-Plus assay stimulates both CD4 and CD8 T-cells, which makes it very useful in conditions of immune depression due to CD4 T-cell impairments [30]. Indeed, QFT-Plus is the most relevant available tool for appropriately identifying LTBI in individuals with specific immune disorders, including CKD [31].

Our findings show a relatively low prevalence of LTBI (19%) among HD patients. In comparison with other MENA countries (Table 3), Lebanon has the lowest LTBI prevalence among HD patients according to IGRA tests. Higher percentages of LTBI have been reported in Iran [32], Egypt [33], and Saudi Arabia [34], in which 23.4%, 35.1%, and 45.3% of HD patients were shown to have LTBI, respectively. Notably, the highest percentages of LTBI among HD patients were observed in Turkey, ranging from 39.6% to 61% [19,35–40]. The low LTBI prevalence found in the present study may be explained by the geographical difference in TB incidence and the fact that Lebanon is a low-TB-burden country [41].

Table 3. Prevalence of latent tuberculosis infection among hemodialysis patients in the Middle East and North Africa (MENA) region.

Country	Publication Year	Number of Patients	Prevalence (%)		Ref.
			Tuberculin Skin Test	IGRA *, a, b, c	
Egypt	2014	40	15	20 [c]	[42]
	2016	60	45	31.7 [b]	[43]
	2017	74	13.5	35.1 [c]	[33]
Iran	2008	100	16	ND [!]	[44]
	2012	255	20.8	ND	[45]
	2014	47	43.5	23.4 [b]	[32]
	2022	119	81.5	ND	[21]
Iraq	2016	71	28.6	ND	[46]
Saudi Arabia	2013	133	19	39 [a]	[47]
	2013	200	13	32.5 [c]	[48]
	2015	181	17.4	45.3 [c]	[34]
Tunisia	2002	60	10	ND	[49]

Table 3. *Cont.*

Country	Publication Year	Number of Patients	Prevalence (%)		Ref.
			Tuberculin Skin Test	IGRA *, a, b, c	
Turkey	2009	50	56	ND	[50]
	2009	56	ND	58.9 [c]	[35]
	2010	733	38.6	ND	[51]
	2010	100	34	43 [b]	[36]
	2011	96	43.8	39.6 [c]	[37]
	2011	89	31.5	45 [b]	[38]
	2012	411	39	61 [a]	[39]
	2012	92	30.4	ND	[52]
	2015	50	36.4	54 [c]	[40]
	2016	95	32	41 [c]	[19]

* Interferon-gamma release assay (IGRA) tests performed using T-SPOT.TB [a]; QuantiFERON-TB Gold (QFT-G) [b]; or QuantiFERON-TB Gold In-Tube (QFT-GIT) [c] method. [!] ND, not determined.

The study population and the sensitivity and specificity of the adopted diagnostic tests may also affect the prevalence of infection. In immunocompromised patients, such as those undergoing HD treatment, the TST performs poorly due to an increased possibility of false-negative results [53]. In addition, Hussein et al. [33] demonstrated that the prevalence of LTBI changed significantly according to the adopted diagnostic method, with 13.5% using the TST and 35.1% using QFT-GIT. The results of most studies in Saudi Arabia [34,47,48], Egypt [33,42], and Turkey [19,36,38–40] corroborated that using IGRA tools allows the better detection of LTBI among HD patients. On the other hand, only three studies conducted in Egypt, Iran, and Turkey [32,37,43] showed discordant data, with a higher LTBI prevalence using the TST compared to IGRA tests. To maintain the sensitivity of the QFT-Plus assay in our study population, we collected the samples immediately before the start of the dialysis process. An obvious reduction in IFN-γ production levels in response to TB antigens was detected after the start of the HD process in CKD patients with ESRD [35]; thus, the prior collection of samples was determined to be better to detect LTBI among patients with ESRD.

Patients receiving dialysis are at high risk of developing TB and should be prioritized for LTBI management due to the fact that they present an increased prevalence of MTBC infection and an increased risk of TB reactivation. In this context, current guidelines recommend screening and treating dialysis patients for LTBI [15,54]. In the present study, LTBI was significantly associated with age and a low-income level. A significant association between older age and LTBI was also revealed by Ogawa et al. [55], Shu et al. [56], and Lee et al. [57] in Japan and Taiwan. Low socioeconomic status affects the aspects of both the "exposure-infection-disease-adverse outcome" spectrum and the health of populations in general [58]. On the other hand, other risk factors have been associated with LTBI in other studies. Two studies carried out in Taiwan and Indonesia (Bandiara et al.) showed a significant association between smoking behavior and LTBI [12,56]. Hayuk and colleagues [59] revealed that alcohol consumption was significantly associated with LTBI among HD patients. Moreover, Turkish investigations reported that QFT positivity was more frequent in males compared to females [38] and in patients with previous contact with active TB cases [36].

Our data revealed that 9.7% of HD patients had indeterminate results, which is in agreement with the wide percentage range (2% to 40%) reported in previous studies [36,47,60]. For example, 30% of HD patients had indeterminate QFT-GIT results in Egypt [60]. In contrast, another study using the same diagnostic method showed that only 5.9% of HD patients had indeterminate results [55]. Although an indeterminate QFT-Plus result does not indicate a failed test, it does not provide useful information regarding the likelihood of LTBI. An indeterminate result may be related to immunosuppression associated with older age and underlying diseases or due to some technical errors [61]. The rate of indeterminate results in immunocompromised patients is higher than that observed in immunocompetent individuals [62]. In addition, the indeterminate results determined by QFT-GIT were higher compared with QFT-Plus [62]. Since our samples were transported within the specified time interval and the proper procedure was followed during the specimens' storage and processing, the possibility of a wrong technical practice is potentially excluded. Taken together, the percentage of indeterminate results in our investigation is probably associated with the immunosuppressed state of HD patients.

It is worth bearing in mind that our samples were collected in the period between 2020 and 2022, during which the world was facing the COVID-19 pandemic. Hemodialysis centers were considered high-risk places for COVID-19 transmission, and HD patients represented a group at risk of infection with severe acute respiratory syndrome coronavirus 2 (SARS-CoV-2) due to impaired immunity. Moreover, due to the lockdown and containment measures taken to combat the pandemic, several patients could not access medical care and consequently missed their HD sessions [63–65]. Altogether, these factors reduced the life-saving HD frequency and the weekly duration of HD sessions [63,66] and hindered patients' access to HD units. We may therefore have missed possible cases of HD patients with different clinical conditions whose enrollment may have affected our findings on LTBI prevalence and its associated risk factors in this vulnerable population.

This study had limitations. Due to the cross-sectional design of this study, we were unable to assess the relationship between CKD/ESRD, HD-associated conditions, and LTBI. In parallel, due to logistic reasons, the follow-up of subjects with indeterminate QFT-Plus results has not been performed (i.e., either repeating the IGRA test with a newly obtained blood specimen or administering a TST). Moreover, the low number of enrolled patients at two time points limits the statistical power for tests and consequently the conclusions that can be drawn. Finally, as previously mentioned, our data were collected during the COVID-19 pandemic, which potentially had an impact on our study findings. The epidemiological significance of our findings remains to be confirmed in future studies.

5. Conclusions

To our knowledge, this study represents the first report assessing the prevalence of LTBI in HD patients in Lebanon. Our work showed that 19% of the examined HD patients were positive for LTBI, and infection is significantly associated with age and low-income status. The possibility of TB reactivation with extrapulmonary involvement or spreading must be taken into consideration in order to reduce the morbidity and mortality of TB in these patients. Therefore, there is a paramount need to implement effective TB control strategies among this vulnerable population, with special attention to high-risk patients such as HD and peritoneal dialysis patients. For a better understanding of the local epidemiology of LTBI in Lebanon, further large-scale, nationwide studies are required to explore TB determinants in the community and suggest interventions tackling this issue of global concern.

Author Contributions: Conceptualization, M.B.I. and M.H.; methodology, M.B.I., N.Z., M.O., S.H., N.K., A.N.C., A.K., R.A., F.D. and M.H.; formal analysis, M.B.I., N.Z., M.O. and S.H.; investigation, M.B.I., N.Z., M.O. and S.H.; writing—original draft preparation, M.B.I., N.Z. and M.O.; writing—review and editing, M.B.I., N.Z., M.O., F.D. and M.H.; visualization, M.B.I. and M.O.; supervision, M.B.I.; project administration, M.B.I., F.D. and M.H. All authors have read and agreed to the published version of the manuscript.

Funding: This research was funded by the Lebanese University, Lebanon; project: Mtb Infection in High-Risk Populations by Interferon Gamma Release Assay (MTB-HRP-IGRA).

Institutional Review Board Statement: This study was approved by both the ethics committee of the Doctoral School of Science and Technology/Lebanese University (CE-EDST-11-2019) and the institutional review board (IRB) of Nini Hospital (IRB-F01).

Informed Consent Statement: Written informed consent was obtained from all patients involved in the study.

Data Availability Statement: The database and code necessary to replicate the analysis are publicly available (http://doi.org/10.6084/m9.figshare.22043252; accessed on 25 March 2023).

Acknowledgments: We would like to thank the staff of the dialysis units at Orange-Nassau Governmental Hospital, Nini Hospital, and Dar Al-Chifae Hospital. We also acknowledge the technical assistance of Taha Abdou and Sara Amrieh. M.O. is supported by the Atkinson Postdoctoral Fellowship (Cornell University).

Conflicts of Interest: The authors declare that there is no conflict of interest.

References

1. Murray, C.J.; Ikuta, K.S.; Sharara, F.; Swetschinski, L.; Aguilar, G.R.; Gray, A.; Han, C.; Bisignano, C.; Rao, P.; Wool, E.; et al. Global burden of bacterial antimicrobial resistance in 2019: A systematic analysis. *Lancet* **2022**, *399*, 629–655. [CrossRef] [PubMed]
2. WHO. Global Tuberculosis Report 2022. Available online: https://www.who.int/teams/global-tuberculosis-programme/tb-reports/global-tuberculosis-report-2022 (accessed on 23 February 2023).
3. Trajman, A.; Felker, I.; Alves, L.C.; Coutinho, I.; Osman, M.; Meehan, S.-A.; Singh, U.B.; Schwartz, Y. The COVID-19 and TB syndemic: The way forward. *Int. J. Tuberc. Lung Dis.* **2022**, *26*, 710–719. [CrossRef] [PubMed]
4. Jassat, W.; Cohen, C.; Tempia, S.; Masha, M.; Goldstein, S.; Kufa, T.; Murangandi, P.; Savulescu, D.; Walaza, S.; Bam, J.-L.; et al. Risk factors for COVID-19-related in-hospital mortality in a high HIV and tuberculosis prevalence setting in South Africa: A cohort study. *Lancet HIV* **2021**, *8*, e554–e567. [CrossRef] [PubMed]
5. Western Cape Department of Health in collaboration with the National Institute for Communicable Diseases, South Africa. Risk Factors for Coronavirus Disease 2019 (COVID-19) Death in a Population Cohort Study from the Western Cape Province, South Africa. *Clin. Infect. Dis.* **2021**, *73*, e2005–e2015. [CrossRef] [PubMed]
6. Sy, K.T.L.; Haw, N.J.L.; Uy, J. Previous and active tuberculosis increases risk of death and prolongs recovery in patients with COVID-19. *Infect. Dis.* **2020**, *52*, 902–907. [CrossRef]
7. Jha, V.; Garcia-Garcia, G.; Iseki, K.; Li, Z.; Naicker, S.; Plattner, B.; Saran, R.; Wang, A.Y.-M.; Yang, C.-W. Chronic kidney disease: Global dimension and perspectives. *Lancet* **2013**, *382*, 260–272. [CrossRef]
8. Aoun, M.; Helou, E.; Sleilaty, G.; Zeenny, R.M.; Chelala, D. Cost of illness of chronic kidney disease in Lebanon: From the societal and third-party payer perspectives. *BMC Health Serv. Res.* **2022**, *22*, 586. [CrossRef]
9. Ruzangi, J.; Iwagami, M.; Smeeth, L.; Mangtani, P.; Nitsch, D. The association between chronic kidney disease and tuberculosis; a comparative cohort study in England. *BMC Nephrol.* **2020**, *21*, 420. [CrossRef]
10. Syed-Ahmed, M.; Narayanan, M. Immune Dysfunction and Risk of Infection in Chronic Kidney Disease. *Adv. Chronic Kidney Dis.* **2019**, *26*, 8–15. [CrossRef]
11. Pahl, M.V.; Vaziri, N.D. Chapter 32—Immune Function in Chronic Kidney Disease. In *Chronic Renal Disease*, 2nd ed.; Kimmel, P.L., Rosenberg, M.E., Eds.; Academic Press: Cambridge, MA, USA, 2020; pp. 503–519.
12. Bandiara, R.; Indrasari, A.; Rengganis, A.D.; Sukesi, L.; Afiatin, A.; Santoso, P. Risk factors of latent tuberculosis among chronic kidney disease with routine haemodialysis patients. *J. Clin. Tuberc. Other Mycobact. Dis.* **2022**, *27*, 100302. [CrossRef]
13. Ram, R.; Swarnalatha, G.; Pai, B.S.; Ramesh, V.; Rao, C.S.S.; Naidu, G.D.; Dakshinamurty, K.; Rao, T.M. Tuberculosis in haemodialysis patients: A single centre experience. *Indian J. Nephrol.* **2013**, *23*, 340–345. [CrossRef] [PubMed]
14. El Bardai, G.; Kabbali, N.; Baba, H.; Chouhani, B.A.; Houssaini, T.S. Tuberculosis in Dialysis Patients in the Central Region of Morocco: What Is the Health-Care Delay? *Cureus* **2022**, *14*, e30369. [CrossRef] [PubMed]
15. WHO. WHO Consolidated Guidelines on Tuberculosis. Module 1: Prevention Tuberculosis preventive Treatment. Available online: https://www.who.int/publications-detail-redirect/9789240001503 (accessed on 23 February 2023).
16. Auguste, P.; Tsertsvadze, A.; Pink, J.; Court, R.; McCarthy, N.; Sutcliffe, P.; Clarke, A. Comparing interferon-gamma release assays with tuberculin skin test for identifying latent tuberculosis infection that progresses to active tuberculosis: Systematic review and meta-analysis. *BMC Infect. Dis.* **2017**, *17*, 200. [CrossRef] [PubMed]
17. National Tuberculosis Program Annual Report 2021. Tuberculosis in Lebanon. Available online: https://www.moph.gov.lb/userfiles/files/Prevention/TB%20Program/NTP%20Annual%20Report-2021-1.pdf (accessed on 23 February 2023).
18. Magdi, M.; Hussein, J.M.M.; Roujouleh, H. Tuberculosis and Chronic Renal Disease. *Semin. Dial.* **2003**, 38–44. Available online: https://onlinelibrary.wiley.com/toc/1525139x/2003/16/1 (accessed on 23 February 2023).
19. Seyhan, E.C.; Gunluoglu, M.Z.; Tural, S.; Sokucu, S.; Gunluoglu, G. Predictive value of the tuberculin skin test and QuantiFERON-tuberculosis Gold In-Tube test for development of active tuberculosis in hemodialysis patients. *Ann. Thorac. Med.* **2016**, *11*, 114–120. [CrossRef]

20. Edathodu, J.; Varghese, B.; Alrajhi, A.A.; Shoukri, M.; Nazmi, A.; Elgamal, H.; Aleid, H.; Alrabiah, F.; Ashraff, A.; Mahmoud, I.; et al. Diagnostic potential of interferon-gamma release assay to detect latent tuberculosis infection in kidney transplant recipients. *Transpl. Infect. Dis.* **2017**, *19*, e12675. [CrossRef]
21. Mohtashami, A.Z.; Amiri, A.; Hadian, B.; Nasiri, P. Assessment of the prevalence of latent tuberculosis infection in hemodialysis patients using tuberculin skin test. *J. Ren. Inj. Prev.* **2022**, *11*. [CrossRef]
22. Min, J.; Kil Kwon, S.; Jeong, H.W.; Han, J.-H.; Kim, Y.J.; Kang, M.; Kang, G. End-stage Renal Disease and Risk of Active Tuberculosis: A Nationwide Population-Based Cohort Study. *J. Korean Med. Sci.* **2018**, *33*, e341. [CrossRef]
23. Romanowski, K.; Clark, E.; Levin, A.; Cook, V.J.; Johnston, J.C. Tuberculosis and chronic kidney disease: An emerging global syndemic. *Kidney Int.* **2016**, *90*, 34–40. [CrossRef]
24. Al-Efraij, K.; Mota, L.; Lunny, C.; Schachter, M.; Cook, V.; Johnston, J. Risk of active tuberculosis in chronic kidney disease: A systematic review and meta-analysis. *Int. J. Tuberc. Lung Dis.* **2015**, *19*, 1493–1499. [CrossRef]
25. Osman, M.; Cummings, K.J.; El Omari, K.; Kassem, I.I. Catch-22: War, Refugees, COVID-19, and the Scourge of Antimicrobial Resistance. *Front. Med.* **2022**, *9*, 921921. [CrossRef]
26. Das, M. Lebanon faces critical shortage of drugs. *Lancet Oncol.* **2021**, *22*, 1063. [CrossRef] [PubMed]
27. Osman, M.; Kasir, D.; Kassem, I.I.; Hamze, M. Shortage of appropriate diagnostics for antimicrobial resistance in Lebanese clinical settings: A crisis amplified by COVID-19 and economic collapse. *J. Glob. Antimicrob. Resist.* **2021**, *27*, 72–74. [CrossRef] [PubMed]
28. Kassem, I.I.; Osman, M. A brewing storm: The impact of economic collapse on the access to antimicrobials in Lebanon. *J. Glob. Antimicrob. Resist.* **2022**, *29*, 313–315. [CrossRef] [PubMed]
29. Karam, Z.; Tawil, F. No More Kidney Dialysis? Lebanese Hospitals Issue Warning. Available online: https://apnews.com/article/beirut-middle-east-lebanon-business-health-7ff67b0bc6154b0fc1eaca63c04baa21 (accessed on 23 February 2023).
30. Petruccioli, E.; Chiacchio, T.; Pepponi, I.; Vanini, V.; Urso, R.; Cuzzi, G.; Barcellini, L.; Palmieri, F.; Cirillo, D.M.; Ippolito, G.; et al. Characterization of the CD4 and CD8 T-cell response in the QuantiFERON-TB Gold Plus kit. *Int. J. Mycobacteriol.* **2016**, *5* (Suppl. S1), S25–S26. [CrossRef] [PubMed]
31. Won, D.; Park, J.Y.; Kim, H.-S.; Park, Y. Comparative Results of QuantiFERON-TB Gold In-Tube and QuantiFERON-TB Gold Plus Assays for Detection of Tuberculosis Infection in Clinical Samples. *J. Clin. Microbiol.* **2020**, *58*, e01854-19. [CrossRef] [PubMed]
32. Savaj, S.; Savoj, J.; Ranjbar, M.; Sabzghabaei, F. Interferon-gamma release assay agreement with tuberculin skin test in pretransplant screening for latent tuberculosis in a high-prevalence country. *Iran. J. Kidney Dis.* **2014**, *8*, 329–332.
33. Hussein, M.T.; Yousef, L.M.; Ali, A.T. Detection of latent tuberculosis infection in hemodialysis patients: Comparison between the quantiferon-tuberculosis gold test and the tuberculin skin test. *Egypt. J. Bronchol.* **2017**, *11*, 255–259. [CrossRef]
34. Al Wakeel, J.; Makoshi, Z.; Al Ghonaim, M.; Al Harbi, A.; Al Suwaida, A.; Al Gahtani, F.; Al Hedaithy, M.; Almogairin, S.; Abdullah, S. The use of Quantiferon-TB gold in-tube test in screening latent tuberculosis among Saudi Arabia dialysis patients. *Ann. Thorac. Med.* **2015**, *10*, 284–288. [CrossRef]
35. Hursitoglu, M.; Cikrikcioglu, M.; Tukek, T.; Beycan, I.; Ahmedova, N.; Karacuha, S.; Sansal, M.; Ozkan, O.; Celik, V. Acute effect of low-flux hemodialysis process on the results of the interferon-gamma-based QuantiFERON®-TB Gold In-Tube test in end-stage renal disease patients. *Transpl. Infect. Dis.* **2009**, *11*, 28–32. [CrossRef]
36. Seyhan, E.; Sökücü, S.; Altin, S.; Günlüoğlu, G.; Trablus, S.; Yilmaz, D.; Koksalan, O.K.; Issever, H. Comparison of the QuantiFERON-TB Gold In-Tube test with the tuberculin skin test for detecting latent tuberculosis infection in hemodialysis patients. *Transpl. Infect. Dis.* **2010**, *12*, 98–105. [CrossRef] [PubMed]
37. Maden, E.; Bekci, T.T.; Kesli, R.; Atalay, H.; Teke, T.; Solak, Y.; Turk, S.; Uzun, K.; Koylu, R. Evaluation of performance of quantiferon assay and tuberculin skin test in end stage renal disease patients receiving hemodialysis. *New Microbiol.* **2011**, *34*, 351–356. [PubMed]
38. Sayarlioğlu, H. QuantiFERON-TB Gold test for screening latent tuberculosis infection in hemodialysis patients. *Tuberk. Toraks* **2011**, *59*, 105–110. [CrossRef]
39. Soysal, A.; Toprak, D.; Koc, M.; Arikan, H.; Akoglu, E.; Bakir, M. Diagnosing latent tuberculosis infection in haemodialysis patients: T-cell based assay (T-SPOT.TB) or tuberculin skin test? *Nephrol. Dial. Transplant.* **2012**, *27*, 1645–1650. [CrossRef] [PubMed]
40. Gunluoglu, G.; Seyhan, E.C.; Kazancıoğlu, R.T.; Gunluoglu, Z.; Veske, N.S.; Yazar, E.E.; Altin, S. Diagnosing latent tuberculosis in immunocompromised patients measuring blood IP-10 production capacity: An analysis of chronic renal failure patients. *Intern. Med.* **2015**, *54*, 465–472. [CrossRef] [PubMed]
41. Ismail, M.B.; Rafei, R.; Dabboussi, F.; Hamze, M. Tuberculosis, war, and refugees: Spotlight on the Syrian humanitarian crisis. *PLoS Pathog.* **2018**, *14*, e1007014. [CrossRef] [PubMed]
42. Abdel-Nabi, E.; Eissa, S.; Soliman, Y.; Amin, W. Quantiferon vs. tuberculin testing in detection of latent tuberculous infection among chronic renal failure patients. *Egypt. J. Chest Dis. Tuberc.* **2014**, *63*, 161–165. [CrossRef]
43. Elyazeid, H.; Mohamed, G.; Mostafa, K.; Ahmed, H.; Aly, A. Clinical relevance of interferon-gamma release assay versus tuberculin skin testing for diagnosis of latent tuberculosis in chronic hemodialysis patients. *Int. J. Adv. Res.* **2016**, *4*, 1329–1336. [CrossRef]
44. Sagheb, M.M.; Goodarzi, M.; Roozbeh, J. The booster phenomenon of tuberculin skin testing in patients receiving hemodialysis. *Iran. J. Immunol.* **2008**, *5*, 212–216.

45. Khosroshahi, H.T.; Shojaie, E.A.; Habibzadeh, D.; Hajipour, B. Comparison of 5 IU and 10 IU tuberculin test results in patients on chronic dialysis. *Saudi J. Kidney Dis. Transplant.* **2012**, *23*, 823–826. [CrossRef]
46. Sultan, K.M.; Al Obaidy, M.W.; Hasan, A.M. Prevalence of Latent Tuberculosis in End Stage Renal Disease Patients at Baghdad Teaching Hospital. *Iraqi Sci. J.* **2016**, *15*, 321–327.
47. Hassan, H.A.H.; Shorman, M.; Housawi, A.R.E.L.; Elsammak, M.Y. Detecting Latent Tuberculosis Infection Prior to Kidney Transplantation in a Tertiary Hospital in Saudi Arabia: Comparison of the T-SPOT.TB Test and Tuberculin Test. *Br. Microbiol. Res. J.* **2013**, *3*, 116–127. [CrossRef]
48. Al Jahdali, H.; Ahmed, A.E.; Balkhy, H.H.; Baharoon, S.; Al Hejaili, F.F.; Hajeer, A.; Memish, Z.; Binsalih, S.; Al Sayyari, A.A. Comparison of the tuberculin skin test and Quanti-FERON-TB Gold In-Tube (QFT-G) test for the diagnosis of latent tuberculosis infection in dialysis patients. *J. Infect. Public Health* **2013**, *6*, 166–172. [CrossRef] [PubMed]
49. Hassine, E.; Marniche, K.; Hamida, J.; Hassine, K.; Bouaziz, A.; Ben Mustapha, M.A.; Chabbou, A.; Dhahri, M. Tuberculosis in hemodialysis patients in Tunisia. *Nephrologie* **2002**, *23*, 135–140. [PubMed]
50. Aydoğan, O.; Gürgün, A.; Başoğlu, O.K.; Aşçi, G.; Ertilav, M.; Bacakoğlu, F.; Töz, H.; Güzelant, A.; Sayiner, A. Tuberculin skin test reactivity in patients with chronic renal failure. *Tuberk. Toraks* **2009**, *57*, 268–276.
51. Ates, G.; Yıldız, T.; Danis, R.; Akyildiz, L.; Erturk, B.; Beyazit, H.; Topcu, F. Incidence of tuberculosis disease and latent tuberculosis infection in patients with end stage renal disease in an endemic region. *Ren. Fail.* **2010**, *32*, 91–95. [CrossRef]
52. Altunoren, O.; Kahraman, H.; Sayarlıoğlu, H.; Yavuz, Y.C.; Doğan, E.; Köksal, N. The affecting factors and comparison of tuberculin skin test in peritoneal dialysis and hemodialysis patients. *Ren. Fail.* **2012**, *34*, 304–307. [CrossRef]
53. Redelman-Sidi, G.; Sepkowitz, K.A. IFN-γ IFN-gamma release assays in the diagnosis of latent tuberculosis infection among immunocompromised adults. *Am. J. Respir. Crit. Care Med.* **2013**, *188*, 422–431. [CrossRef]
54. Lebanese Ministry of Public Health. National Guidelines for Tuberculosis Prevention, Care and Elimination in Lebanon-2017. Available online: https://www.moph.gov.lb/en/Pages/2/11570/national-guidelines-for-tuberculosis-prevention-care-and-elimination-in-lebanon-2017 (accessed on 23 February 2023).
55. Ogawa, Y.; Harada, M.; Hashimoto, K.; Kamijo, Y. Prevalence of latent tuberculosis infection and its risk factors in Japanese hemodialysis patients. *Clin. Exp. Nephrol.* **2021**, *25*, 1255–1265. [CrossRef]
56. Shu, C.-C.; Wu, V.-C.; Yang, F.-J.; Pan, S.-C.; Lai, T.-S.; Wang, J.-Y.; Lee, L.-N.; Wang, J.-T. Predictors and prevalence of latent tuberculosis infection in patients receiving long-term hemodialysis and peritoneal dialysis. *PLoS ONE* **2012**, *7*, e42592. [CrossRef]
57. Lee, S.S.-J.; Chou, K.-J.; Dou, H.-Y.; Huang, T.-S.; Ni, Y.-Y.; Fang, H.-C.; Tsai, H.-C.; Sy, C.-L.; Chen, J.-K.; Wu, K.-S.; et al. High prevalence of latent tuberculosis infection in dialysis patients using the interferon-gamma release assay and tuberculin skin test. *Clin. J. Am. Soc. Nephrol.* **2010**, *5*, 1451–1457. [CrossRef] [PubMed]
58. Satyanarayana, S.; Thekkur, P.; Kumar, A.M.V.; Lin, Y.; Dlodlo, R.A.; Khogali, M.; Zachariah, R.; Harries, A.D. An Opportunity to END TB: Using the Sustainable Development Goals for Action on Socio-Economic Determinants of TB in High Burden Countries in WHO South-East Asia and the Western Pacific Regions. *Trop. Med. Infect. Dis.* **2020**, *5*, 101. [CrossRef] [PubMed]
59. Hayuk, P.; Boongird, S.; Pornsuriyasak, P.; Bruminhent, J. Interferon-gamma release assays for diagnosis of latent TB infection in chronic kidney diseases and dialysis patients. *Front. Cell. Infect. Microbiol.* **2022**, *12*, 1046373. [CrossRef] [PubMed]
60. Mohamed, K.H.; Hashem, M.M.; Sharaf, S.M. Role of the QuantiFERON-TB gold in tube in ruling out tuberculosis in end stage renal disease patients receiving hemodialysis. *Egypt. J. Chest Dis. Tuberc.* **2012**, *61*, 135–138. [CrossRef]
61. Pandey, S.; Rattan, A.; Singh, M. Evaluating the Indeterminate Results of the QuantiFERON-TB Gold in-Tube Test. *Curr. Res. Tuberc.* **2011**, *3*, 16–19. [CrossRef]
62. Xu, Y.; Yang, Q.; Zhou, J.; Zhou, F.; Hezhang, Y.; Gao, Y.; Shao, L.; Shi, J.; Ruan, Q.; Zhang, W. Comparison of QuantiFERON-TB Gold In-Tube and QuantiFERON-TB Gold-Plus in the Diagnosis of *Mycobacterium tuberculosis* Infections in Immunocompromised Patients: A Real-World Study. *Microbiol. Spectr.* **2022**, *10*, e0187021. [CrossRef]
63. Prasad, N.; Bhatt, M.; Agarwal, S.K.; Kohli, H.; Gopalakrishnan, N.; Fernando, E.; Sahay, M.; Rajapurkar, M.; Chowdhary, A.R.; Rathi, M.; et al. The adverse effect of COVID pandemic on the care of patients with kidney diseases in India. *Kidney Int. Rep.* **2020**, *5*, 1545–1550. [CrossRef]
64. El Karoui, K.; De Vriese, A.S. COVID-19 in dialysis: Clinical impact, immune response, prevention, and treatment. *Kidney Int.* **2022**, *101*, 883–894. [CrossRef]
65. Tannor, E.K.; Bieber, B.; Aylward, R.; Luyckx, V.; Shah, D.S.; Liew, A.; Evans, R.; Phiri, C.; Guedes, M.; Pisoni, R.; et al. The COVID-19 pandemic identifies significant global inequities in hemodialysis care in low and lower-middle income countries-An ISN/DOPPS survey. *Kidney Int. Rep.* **2022**, *7*, 971–982. [CrossRef]
66. Lodge, M.D.S.; Abeygunaratne, T.; Alderson, H.; Ali, I.; Brown, N.; Chrysochou, C.; Donne, R.; Erekosima, I.; Evans, P.; Flanagan, E.; et al. Safely reducing haemodialysis frequency during the COVID-19 pandemic. *BMC Nephrol.* **2020**, *21*, 532. [CrossRef]

Disclaimer/Publisher's Note: The statements, opinions and data contained in all publications are solely those of the individual author(s) and contributor(s) and not of MDPI and/or the editor(s). MDPI and/or the editor(s) disclaim responsibility for any injury to people or property resulting from any ideas, methods, instructions or products referred to in the content.

medicina

MDPI

Article

Knowledge, Attitudes and Perceptions towards COVID-19 Vaccinations: A Cross-Sectional Survey in Pakistan

Asima Bibi [1], Sameen Abbas [1], Saima Mushtaq [2], Atika Mansoor [3], Ivan R. Green [4], Tauqeer Hussain Mallhi [5], Yusra Habib Khan [5] and Amjad Khan [1,*]

1 Department of Pharmacy, Quaid-i-Azam University, Islamabad 45320, Pakistan
2 Department of Healthcare Biotechnology, Atta-ur-Rahman School of Applied Biosciences, National University of Sciences and Technology, Islamabad 44000, Pakistan
3 Institute of Biomedical and Genetic Engineering (IBGE), KRL Hospital, Islamabad 44000, Pakistan
4 Department of Chemistry and Polymer Science, University of Stellenbosch, Matieland, Stellenbosch 7600, South Africa
5 Department of Clinical Pharmacy, College of Pharmacy, Jouf University, Sakaka 72388, Saudi Arabia
* Correspondence: amjadkhan@qau.edu.pk

Abstract: *Background and Objectives:* Several vaccines have been approved for the prevention of the coronavirus disease, discovered on 31 December in Wuhan, China. Pakistan procured vaccines from various countries. However, the lack of knowledge and reluctance of the general population to embrace the use of the vaccines are considered to be the major determinant of the slow vaccination rate. Hence, it is necessary to evaluate the willingness of the general population about their perception of the COVID-19 vaccination. *Materials and Methods:* A cross sectional survey based on a self-structured questionnaire comprising 18 questions was conducted (from 21 April–21 June) on 400 Pakistani participants to evaluate their knowledge, attitude, and perception towards the COVID-19 vaccination. Chi-square independent t-test and one-way Anova including a multiple step wise linear regression were used to draw conclusions about the results. $p < 0.05$ was considered significant. *Results:* A total of 400 participants responded in the knowledge, attitude, and perception (KAP) survey of which 46.5% were female and 53.5% were male. The mean age of participants was 36.08 years. This survey showed a poor knowledge (50.5%), a fair attitude (75.1%) and a poor perception (58.1%) towards the COVID-19 vaccination. Higher mean knowledge and attitude scores were reported in the age group 21–40, females, and unmarried urban citizens. Regression analysis showed that age, education, residence, and employment status influenced the knowledge and perception score to a considerable extent. *Conclusions:* The findings reflect an inadequate knowledge and perception on the one hand, but a better attitude towards the COVID-19 vaccination. This knowledge attitude and perception (KAP) survey will help in better understanding the opinion of the general population towards vaccination, and will be useful for policy makers and health care authorities aiming to increase the vaccination rate.

Keywords: COVID-19; vaccine; knowledge; attitude; perception; survey; questionnaire

Citation: Bibi, A.; Abbas, S.; Mushtaq, S.; Mansoor, A.; Green, I.R.; Mallhi, T.H.; Khan, Y.H.; Khan, A. Knowledge, Attitudes and Perceptions towards COVID-19 Vaccinations: A Cross-Sectional Survey in Pakistan. *Medicina* **2023**, *59*, 272. https://doi.org/10.3390/medicina59020272

Academic Editor: Gennaro De Pascale

Received: 29 October 2022
Revised: 14 December 2022
Accepted: 15 December 2022
Published: 31 January 2023

Copyright: © 2023 by the authors. Licensee MDPI, Basel, Switzerland. This article is an open access article distributed under the terms and conditions of the Creative Commons Attribution (CC BY) license (https://creativecommons.org/licenses/by/4.0/).

1. Background

After the Severe Acute Respiratory Syndrome (SARS) and Middle East Respiratory Syndrome (MERS) outbreak, a new virus was discovered on 31 December in Wuhan, China, named 2019 n-CoV by the World Health Organization (WHO), and later named SARS-CoV-2 by the International Committee on the taxonomy of viruses [1]. The WHO declared COVID-19 to be the sixth Public Health Emergency of International Concern (PHEIC), and later declared it to be a global pandemic on 11 March 2020 (WHO, 2005). The first COVID-19 case was reported in Pakistan on 26 February 2020 [2]. Since then, the number of cases increased rapidly.

Persons infected with COVID-19 develop the common conditions of fever, cough, shortness of breath, sore throat, nasal congestion, weakness, fatigue, and dyspnea [3–5]. Various risk factors are involved with the complexity of COVID-19. These risk factors are: old age, respiration distress, and various chronic co-morbid conditions [6,7] Other risk factors includes respiratory distress, sepsis, metabolic acidosis, arrhythmia heart failure, kidney failure, and hypoxic encephalopathy [8].

Treatment strategies were initially mainly focused on corticosteroids, blood thinners, and neutralizing antibodies, due to the lack of a specific cure, such as vaccination [9]. After an extensive development phase, vaccination became one of the best treatment strategies recommended by the WHO to generate herd immunity in the general population [10,11]. Despite supply challenges, the Pakistan government acquired 40 million COVID-19 vaccines from China, the WHO, USA, UK and Germany, in order to be able to vaccinate an estimated 70 million people [12–16]. Statistics shared by the Government of Pakistan showed that only 18.2% of the Pakistan population is fully vaccinated [17]. Pakistan has a history of a relatively low vaccination rate for a variety of vaccine preventable diseases, such as HBV and polio [18]. Unless this COVID-19 low vaccination rate is not seriously addressed, it will take an unnecessarily longer time for the general population to return a semblance of normalcy from this pandemic [19].

It is well known that, generally, any new medical intervention has its own acceptability rate among the general population, and thus the acceptance of the COVID-19 vaccine, along with its distribution and proper utilization to every member of society, is also very important. [20]. Previous reported data showed that those reluctant to take the COVID-19 vaccination due to safety concerns totaled, in the USA, 33% of general participants and 50% of health care workers [21]; in Turkey, 45.3% of general participants and 42.2% of health care workers; and in Oman, 23% of general respondents and 40% of healthcare workers [22–26]. In the USA, its acceptance was 50%, in France its acceptance was only 62% [20,27]. While in Italy, acceptance of the COVID-19 vaccination was 59% [28,29]. Similarly, one of China's surveys about COVID-19 vaccination declared that only one half, that is 54% pf the population, was willing to have vaccination [30]. Several important factors, such as health knowledge, serve as being important for the participants in increasing their acceptance, as more knowledge by the general population towards breakouts such as the COVID-19 pandemic, its vaccination and potential benefits, coupled with its precautionary measures, contributes in a better implementation of health system facilities [30,31]. Similarly, attitude and perception are the two primary cognitive factors that play a vital role in the vaccination coverage rate of COVID-19.

Knowledge, attitude, and perception (KAP) surveys mostly help to identify knowledge gaps and behavior patterns of the general population on the basis of their socio-demographics, in order to implement effective public health interventions [32]. This study aimed to determine the knowledge, acceptance, and perception of the COVID-19 vaccine among the Pakistani population.

2. Methodology

2.1. Study Design

Cross sectional studies were performed to assess knowledge, attitude, and perception of the Pakistani population towards the COVID-19 vaccination.

2.2. Study Setting

The study was conducted on the general population of all the provinces (Punjab, Sindh, Khyber Pakhtunkhwa, Balochistan) of Pakistan.

2.3. Study Duration

The study was carried out from April–June 2021 through an online questionnaire, which was distributed on different social media platforms (e.g., Facebook and WhatsApp). During this time duration of April to June (3rd and 4th wave of COVID-19), a community-based national survey was not possible. So, relying on online social media links, the questionnaire was posted/reposted to local people living in different areas of Pakistan. In this online survey, answers to all questions was mandatory for final submission.

2.4. Inclusion and Exclusion Criteria

Participants were 18 years or older and Pakistani residents, having an easy access to the Internet and were voluntary participants. People below the targeted age of 18 years were excluded from this study.

2.5. Sample Size and Sampling Technique

Initially, the convenient sampling technique was used for sample size estimation. In this survey, thousands of participants could be included, however, due to the limited time period, sample size was calculated from the estimated current population of Pakistan by using the Rao-soft calculator to have an idea of the least number of participants that must be included in this survey. The current population of Pakistan is 213,222,917 as per 2017 Census of Pakistan. With a 95% confidence interval, 50% population representation and 5% margin of error, a 385 sample size was calculated by using the Rao-soft calculator. However, data from 400 participants was collected. It was a limited sample size because of the limited time duration of survey during the 3rd and 4th wave.

2.6. Study Tool

A self-structured 18-item questionnaire, along with the appropriate demographics, was prepared and divided into three sections. In addition to demographics, six questions explored knowledge about COVID-19 while eight questions focused on attitude and four questions focused on perception of participants towards the COVID-19 vaccination.

2.7. Questionnaires Development and Validation

A self-structured questionnaire was designed based on a previous literature review. After an extensive literature review, the questionnaire was designed in English [33]. The English version of the questionnaire was translated into Urdu by using a back-to-back translation procedure [34]. This questionnaire was tested for its reliability and internal consistency. The internal consistency of the knowledge, attitude, and perception (KAP) survey questionnaire calculated by Cronbach's alpha was 0.720 for knowledge, 0.642 for attitude, and 0.629 for perception, and found to be in an acceptable range. An initial pilot study was performed among 20 participants to evaluate its acceptability and consistency, but these results were not included in the final study.

2.8. Scoring Criteria and Statistical Analysis

The scoring criteria was based on the original bloom's cut-off point used in previous studies conducted on dengue fever anticipation in male people of the Maldives and Bangkok in 2007, as well as a KAP study performed on COVID-19 among Chronic Disease Patients in Northwest Ethiopia in 2020 [35,36]. Criteria of bloom's cut-off point were 80–100% (good), 60.0–79.0% (fair), and $\leq$59.0% (poor). In statistical analysis categorical variables were represented in form percentages and frequencies and Chi Square Independent was used to analyze significant association between demographics and knowledge, attitude, and perception. Independent t-test (for two groups) and one-way ANOVA (for more than two groups) were used to measure association within groups. Similarly, multiple linear regression model was used to analyze the impact of an independent variable over a dependent variable. The statistical software package for social sciences (IBM SPSS for Windows, Version 21.0. SPSS Inc., Chicago, IL, USA) was used to evaluate the data. *p*-value less than 0.05 are considered significant.

2.9. Ethical Approval

This survey was conducted after ethical approval from the institutional research and ethics forum of Rawalpindi Medical University (Vide letter number: 64/IREF/RMU/2021,

Dated 23 April 2021). Respondents were clearly informed about the purpose of the study and privacy of their data was also assured.

3. Results

3.1. Demographics of Knowledge, Attitude and Perception Study

Age, gender, marital status, employment, education status, and residence of participants are articulated in Table 1. All these were categorical variables to facilitate statistical analysis in the form of frequencies and percentages to be performed. In all, 400 participants completed the survey. Both males 53.5% (n = 214) and females 46.5% (n = 186) participated in the study. The mean age of participants was 36.08 years. (S.D 15.54). The majority of the respondents were from age group 21–40 years. Most of the participants were urban 281 (70.2%) and married citizens 220 (55.0%). In the educational category, 43.22% (n = 172) of the participants had a higher education or below, while those with a graduate level of education were 30.3% (n = 121). Participants having a postgraduate level of education were 26.7% (n = 107). Participants having government jobs account for 20.3% (n = 81), non-government employees were 18.9% (n = 75), unemployed 16.9% (n = 67), retired 9.1% (n = 36), self-employed 8.0% (n = 32) and students 27.3% (n = 109). This classification illustrates a greater number of government employee participation in the study.

Table 1. Demographic characteristics of study participants.

Demographics		Frequency (*n*)	Percentages (%)
Age	<20	39	9.7
	21–40	218	54.5
	41–60	109	27.2
	>61	34	8.5
Gender	Female	186	46.5
	Male	214	53.5
Marital status	Unmarried	180	45
	Married	220	55.0
Education level	High school or below	172	43.2
	Graduate	121	30.3
	Postgraduate	107	26.7
Employment status	Gov. employee	81	20.3
	Non Gov. employee	75	18.9
	Self employed	32	8.0
	Student	109	27.3
	Retired	36	9.0
	Unemployed	67	16.9
Residence	Urban	281	70.2
	Rural	119	29.8

Note: number of participants (n); percentages (%) n = 400.

3.2. Frequency of Response to Knowledge

Knowledge was evaluated by six questions about several aspects of the COVID-19 vaccination, with a corresponding scale ranging from 0–6. Responses were scored as 0 for no/don't know and 1 for yes. Total score was calculated by the sum of six knowledge scores and ranged from 0–6. This led to the finding that 318 (79.5%) know about the COVID-19 vaccination, 250 (62.5%) know about the effectiveness of the vaccination, 177 (44.3%) responded that it is unsafe to use an overdose of vaccination, 302 (75.5%) responded that vaccination cannot cause allergic reactions, while 305 (76.2%) don't know that the vaccine is recommended for pregnant women and 272 (68.0%) of the participants reported that vaccination is available in two doses with an additional booster dose becoming available at a later stage. Figure 1 also shows the response to knowledge.

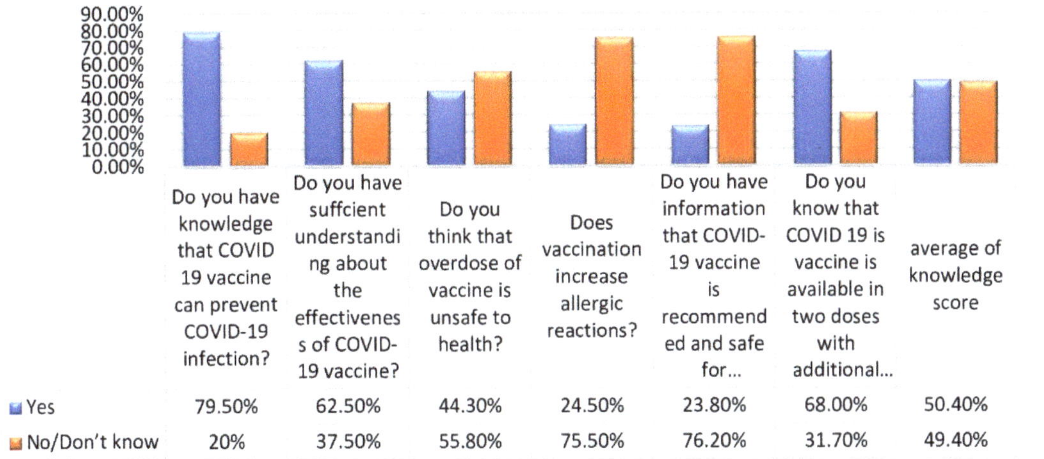

Figure 1. Response to knowledge of the vaccination.

3.3. *Frequency of Response to Attitude*

Attitude was evaluated by eight questions. Each question was scored as disagree, undecided and agree and scaled as 0, 1 and 2 respectively. Scoring scale ranged from 0–16. In these eight questions of attitude assessment, 400 participants responded, out of which: 207 (51.8%) agreed that the vaccine is safe; 310 (77.5%) agreed that the vaccine is essential; 257 (64.3%) agreed that they will take the vaccination when it becomes available in Pakistan; 301 (75.3%) responded that they will encourage their friends, family, and relatives to get vaccinated; 215 (53.8%) agreed to the response that COVID-19 eradication without vaccination is impossible; 325 (81.3%) agreed that the vaccine should be circulated on a priority basis; 206 (51.5%) believed that by taking precautionary measures instead of vaccination COVID-19 could be eradicated; and 317 (79.3%) agreed that vaccination is their social responsibility to control the spread of COVID-19. Similarly, Figure 2 also shows response to attitude.

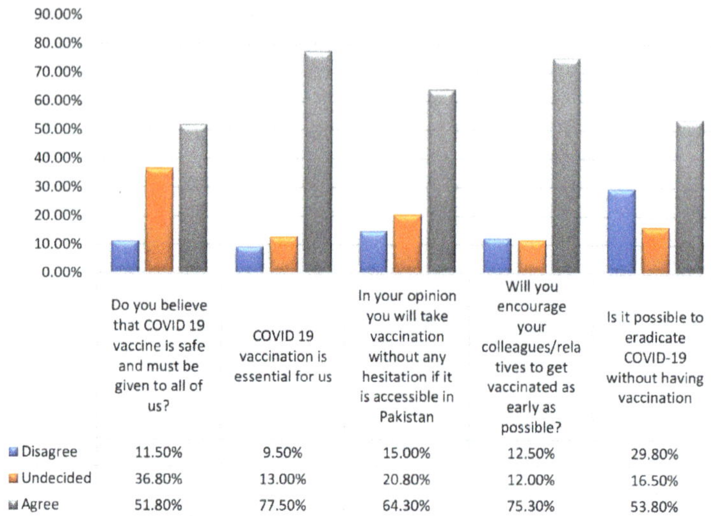

(a) Frequency of response to attitude of 5 questions

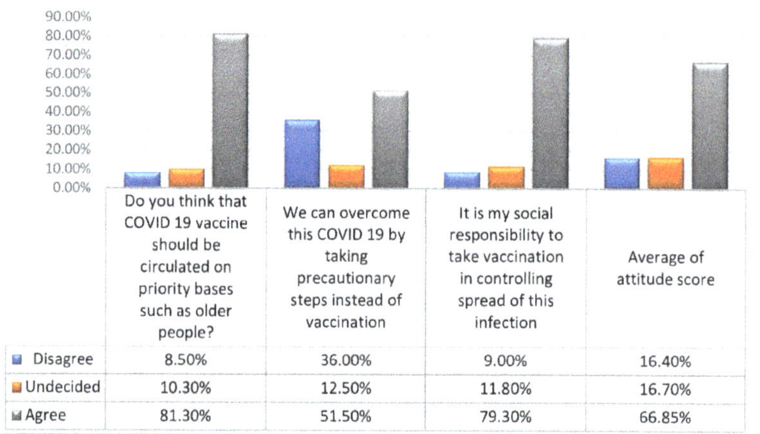

(b) Frequency of response to attitude of 3 questions

Figure 2. Response to attitude of the vaccination.

3.4. Frequency of Response to Perception

Perception was assessed by four questions, which were scored as yes, no, do not know, and scaled as 0, for no/do not know and 1 was for a yes response. Scoring scale ranged from 0–4. Responses of participants showed that: 57.0% (n = 228) indicated that after taking the vaccination they should follow guidelines to combat new variants; 56.0% (n = 224) believe that COVID-19 can be eradicated by taking preventive measures instead of vaccination; 79.5% (n = 318) indicated that they prefer to have the vaccination even if their health is compromised by any other ailment; and 60.0% (n = 240) responded that they could not afford vaccination at their own cost if it was not given free of charge by the state. Figure 3 shows response to perception of the participants towards vaccination.

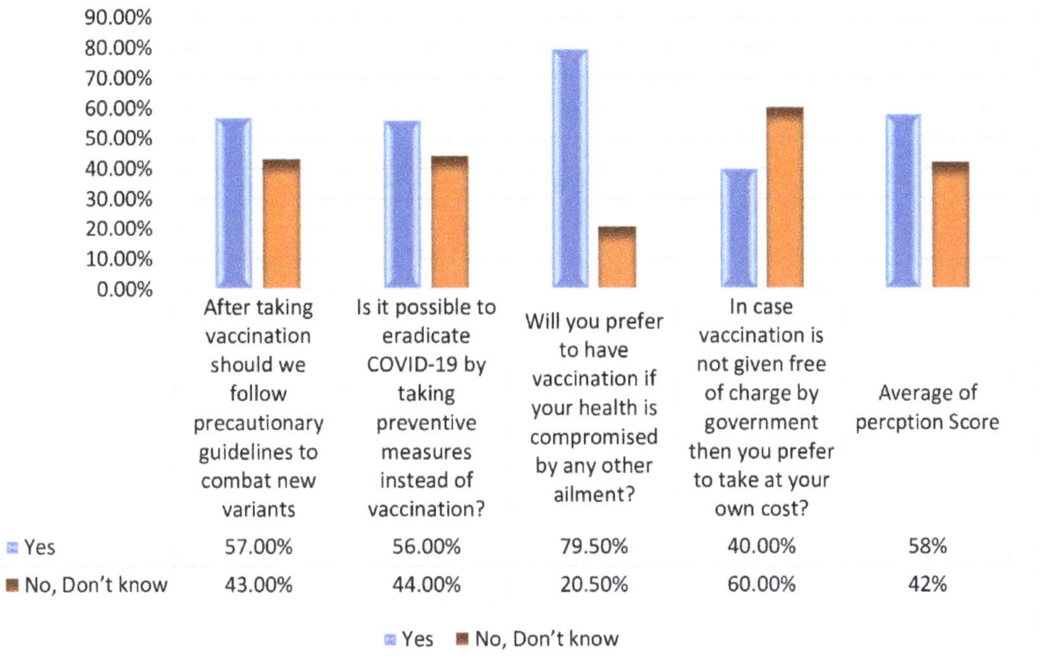

Figure 3. Response to perception of the vaccination.

3.5. Categorization of Participant's Score and Their Association with Demographics

Characterization of the participants' response based on blooms' cut-off points. Criteria of bloom's cut-off point were 80–100% (good), 60.0–79.0% (fair), and ≤59.0% (poor). Similarly for knowledge, this score was determined from scale 0–6, for attitude score, 0–16 and for perception score, 0–4. Responses regarding knowledge, age group of participants and the maximum number of 'fair knowledge' was observed in people of the age group of 21–40 years. In the gender category, both male and female participants had an equal level of 'fair knowledge'. In the marital status group, married people had a high rate of fair knowledge. Students and government employees also had a high rate of fair knowledge. Chi-square analysis was used to find any significant association between demographics and knowledge related questions about COVID-19 vaccination. A significant relationship was found between education, employment, and the residence group.

In responses regarding attitude, participants in the age group of 21–40 years showed a good attitude response. In the gender category, female participants had a high level of 'good attitude score'. In the marital status group, unmarried people had a high rate of good attitude. Students and urban citizens also had a high rate of good attitude. A significant relationship was found between age, education, marital status, employment, and the residence group.

In responses about perception, participants in the age group of 21–40 years showed a fair attitude response. In the gender category, male participants had a high level of 'fair perception'. In the marital status group, married people had a high rate of fair perception. Students and urban citizens also had a high rate of fair perception. No significant association of perception score was noticed with any demographics' variable. Table 2 summarizes the p value obtained.

Table 2. Categorization of participants and association of demographics with knowledge, attitude and perception.

Variables		Knowledge				Attitude				Perception			
		Good	Fair	Poor	*p* Value	Good	Fair	Poor	*p* Value	Good	Fair	Poor	*p* Value
Age	<20	4	25	7	0.347	20	13	3	**0.001**	8	10	18	0.064
	21–40	43	142	29		132	54	28		39	112	63	
	41–60	26	64	15		35	44	26		22	54	29	
	>61	10	15	5		10	10	10		8	16	5	
Gender	Female	32	129	25		103	56	27	0.148	31	96	59	0.077
	Male	51	129	30		96	74	40		54	100	55	
Marital status	Unmarried	40	115	24	0.831	105	49	24	**0.005**	37	80	62	0.088
	Married	44	144	32		94	82	44		49	116	54	
Education level	high school or below	38	100	34	**0.043**	66	72	33	**0.001**	39	82	50	0.577
	graduate	27	83	11		67	34	20		28	63	30	
	postgraduate	19	75	11		66	24	15		19	50	36	
Employment status	Gov. employee	9	62	10	**0.030**	38	32	11	**0.019**	21	40	20	0.615
	non Gov. employee	13	53	9		42	22	11		13	39	23	
	self employed	9	17	4		7	15	8		10	13	7	
	Student	27	63	17		64	25	17		19	55	33	
	Retired	14	15	7		12	14	10		10	17	8	
	Unemployed	12	47	8		34	22	11		13	30	24	
Residence	Urban	48	187	44	**0.015**	149	85	44	0.051	58	141	80	0.755
	Rural	35	69	13		47	46	24		27	54	35	

Note: for knowledge score 4.8–6 considered (Good) 3.6–4.7 (Fair) and ≤3.5 (Poor); for attitude score 12.8–16 considered Good, 9.6–12.7 Fair and ≤9.5 Poor; for perception score 3.2–4 considered good, 2.4–3.16 Fair and ≤2.3 Poor. *p* value < 0.05 compared within groups. Bold *p* values showed significant association.

3.6. Analysis of Mean Knowledge, Attitude and Perception

To estimate association within groups with mean knowledge, an independent *t*-test (for two groups) including one for more than two groups and a one-way ANOVA test was performed. The mean count of knowledge was considerably higher among participants aged 21–40 years. Females, unmarried, graduates or below, students, and urban citizens had a higher mean knowledge score. It was found that the mean knowledge score is significantly associated with age, gender, marital status, residence, and employment status.

The mean score of attitude was appreciably higher among participants in the age group of 21–40 years. In terms of gender, females had a high mean attitude score. The educational level of participants also plays a role since a higher mean score of attitude was found in postgraduates and similarly in unmarried and non-government participants. Urban residents also showed a higher mean score. Mean attitude is significantly related with age, gender, education level, marital status, residence, and employment status.

The mean score of perception was considerably higher among participants aged 21–40 years. In terms of gender, females have a high mean perception score. Educational level is a factor contributing to a higher mean score of perception in graduates, while unmarried and student participants also showed a higher mean perception score, as did urban residents. In this survey, the mean attitude is significantly linked with age, gender, education level, marital status, residence, and employment status. Table 3 below shows association within groups with mean knowledge, mean attitude and mean perception score.

Table 3. Association within groups with mean knowledge, mean attitude and mean perception score.

	Mean Knowledge		Mean Attitude		Mean Perception	
Variables	**Mean (S.D)**	***p* Value**	**Mean (S.D)**	***p* Value**	**Mean (S.D)**	***p* Value**
Age						
<20	0.5602 (0.165)	**0.009**	1.5556 (0.28730)	**0.001**	0.6111 (0.24960)	**0.001**
21–40	0.5964 (0.19568)		1.5736 (0.37016)		0.6752 (0.21860)	
41–60	0.3759 (0.26572)		1.4029 (0.34624)		0.4762 (0.29114)	
>61	0.1944 (0.19615)		1.3375 (0.39000)		0.3750 (0.29906)	
Gender						
Female	0.5658 (0.20926)	**0.001**	1.5390 (0.36552)	**0.066**	0.6452 (0.23052)	**0.017**
Male	0.4525 (0.26746)		1.4705 (0.37266)		0.5226 (0.30705)	
Marital Status						
Unmarried	0.6134 (0.19448)	**0.012**	1.5475(0.37851)	**0.029**	0.6508 (0.23912)	**0.002**
Married	0.4188 (0.25468)		1.4662(0.36106)		0.5239 (0.29792)	
Education Level						
High school or below	0.3777 (0.25744)	**0.001**	1.4523 (0.33256)	0.051	0.4753 (0.29452)	**0.001**
Graduate	0.6074 (0.19467)		1.5289 (0.38587)		0.6426(0.26581)	
Postgraduate	0.5997 (0.19107)		1.5560 (0.40541)		0.6810 (0.20655)	
Employment Status						
Gov. employee	0.5251 (0.20190)	**0.001**	1.5231 (0.29981)	**0.002**	0.5494 (0.30726)	**0.001**
Non Gov. employee	0.5431 (0.23216)		1.5724 (0.33364)		0.5967 (0.25959)	
Self employed	0.2889 (0.25496)		1.2750 (0.40921)		0.5250 (0.33701)	
Student	0.6184(0.19018)		1.5339 (0.39624)		0.6752 (0.21504)	
Retired	0.2269 (0.23622)		1.3819 (0.31756)		0.3750 (0.29580)	
Unemployed	0.5075 (0.24521)		1.5037 (0.41342)		0.5821 (0.26610)	
Residence						
Urban	0.5446 (0.21737)	**0.019**	1.5302 (0.35036)	**0.015**	0.6246 (0.26132)	**0.026**
Rural	0.4074 (0.29152)		1.4306 (0.41015)		0.4722 (0.29503)	

Note: S.D is standard deviation. Statistics: one way ANOVA and independent *t* test; p value < 0.05 compared within groups. Bold *p* values showed significant association.

3.7. Factors Affecting Knowledge, Attitude and Perception Response on the Use of Vaccine

A multiple linear regression model was used to analyze the impact of an independent variable over a dependent variable, as illustrated in Table 4. Age, education, residence, and employment status influenced the knowledge score to a considerable extent. Gender and marital status had no significant impact on the knowledge score. Correlation analyses shows that the relationship between the dependent and independent variable is a reliable factor for further analysis. Perception score was significantly influenced by age, education, and residence.

Table 4. Analysis of factors affecting knowledge, attitude, and perception score.

Independent Variable	Knowledge			Attitude			Perception		
	R Square	**0.316**		**R Square**	**0.063**		**R Square**		**0.224**
	Adjusted R Square	**0.293**		**Adjusted R Square**	**0.031**		**Adjusted R Square**		**0.198**
	Durbin Watson	**1.657**		**Durbin Watson**	**1.938**		**Durbin Watson**		**1.718**
	B	**SE**	***p*-Value**	**B**	**SE**	***p*-Value**	**B**	**SE**	***p*-Value**
(Constant)	0.622	0.057	0.000	1.641	0.090	0.000	0.678	0.066	0.000
Age	−0.070	0.028	**0.013**	−0.073	0.045	0.106	−0.069	0.033	**0.036**
Gender	0.007	0.040	0.869	0.024	0.063	0.704	−0.033	0.046	0.471
Marital status	0.076	0.047	0.110	−0.053	0.076	0.483	0.054	0.055	0.329
Education level	0.077	0.025	**0.002**	0.013	0.040	0.751	0.076	0.029	**0.009**
Employment status	−0.028	0.010	**0.006**	−0.015	0.016	0.349	−0.021	0.012	0.067
Residence	−0.075	0.034	**0.030**	−0.034	0.055	0.533	−0.140	0.040	**0.001**

Note: B = unstandardized regression coefficient; SE = Standard error; p value < 0.05 considered significant. Bold p values showed significant association. Statistics: Multiple linear regression model; p value < 0.05 compared within groups.

4. Discussion

In order to overcome the aftermath of the COVID-19 pandemic, the implementation of COVID-19 vaccination is the best if not the ideal solution. After an extensive development phase and positive responses of clinical trials, various countries approved specific vaccines for further implementation. Although various campaigns have been implemented to increase knowledge about vaccination and previous studies also suggests that COVID-19 vaccines are safe and effective in general, based on the billions of doses administered worldwide and the rare incidence of adverse events only in at-risk group [37]. However, due to the newness of this disease, it poses a serious question for policy-makers regarding the knowledge, attitude, and perceptions of the general population about receiving the COVID-19 vaccination. The present survey has been conducted to assess knowledge, attitude, and perceptions of participants including large demographics factors that influence the knowledge and attitude of the general population [38].

This knowledge-based survey suggest that the people of Pakistan that participated in this study had an average knowledge (50.4%) about the vaccine, its side effects, allergic reactions, and its effect on autoimmune diseases. Knowledge was considerably linked with education, employment status, and residence. This finding is in contrast with the knowledge, attitude, and perception survey conducted in Bangladesh, where knowledge was significantly associated with education, family type, and monthly income of a family [38].

The findings of our survey suggest that the mean knowledge score was found to be higher for female participants, in respondents of the age group 21–40, among graduates, and in unmarried participants. These findings concur with two previous surveys conducted in China and the USA. Data from this survey also indicate that gender and education level could have a constructive impact on the knowledge field of participants [39,40]. In our survey, 76.2% of participants had a lack of knowledge regarding the safety of the COVID-19 vaccination in pregnant women. These findings stress the need to convey effective and updated information for the general population through various social media platforms.

Regarding the attitude domain of this study, a mean attitude score is more associated with females than males. This finding is in line with the results of the studies conducted in Indonesia and Bangladesh [41,42]. We believe this result can be of significant value by appealing to women with a domestic level of education and an encouragement for COVID-19 vaccination could strongly suggest the way to a drastic enhancement in the vaccination program. The findings of a high level of a positive attitude of participants towards the preventive measure of vaccination is also reported globally [42].

Our findings show that 64.3% of the participants were willing to take the COVID-19 vaccination without any hesitation, and 75.3% advised their family, friends, and relatives to also take the COVID-19 vaccination. Findings from our study illustrate the wide scale of variation among countries. A study conducted in France during the pandemic shows that 77% of their participants would agree to take the vaccination [43]. While comparing attitude globally in terms of willingness to take the vaccine, studies show that a high percentage of positive attitude responses come from Panama (87.44%), a lower reaction was from Russia (51.34%), Australia had the highest response (92.88%), while the very lowest response was observed in Egypt (43.55%) for taking the COVID-19 vaccination [44].

An average number of participants (51.8%) in our study agreed that the vaccine is safe. This limited knowledge regarding safety of vaccination may be due to rumors and misinformation related to safety issues of the vaccine. Since the pandemic is generally accepted to have started in December 2019, there was only limited knowledge about the disease, along with rumors and misinformation that affected its perception globally [45].

In the perception domain, 57% of participants believe that COVID-19 vaccination had side effects. This apprehension may be due to misinformation regarding fatal and adverse events associated with the COVID-19 vaccine [46,47].

Overall, in our study, female participants had a better ranking of knowledge, attitude, and perception, as compared to males, which is in agreement with findings of prior studies [48]. Possible reasons identified for this were education and socio-economic factors [49,50].

Equal participation by both genders is important for any social survey. This is because both males and females are equally important for forming an opinion about any critical social issues, such as the COVID-19 vaccination. However, in our study, female participation was found to be less than males, which agrees with a previous knowledge, attitude, and perception survey [51]. These findings suggest that more focused research needs to be conducted to determine the possible barriers that women might be facing in participating in such responses.

In this survey, graduates and postgraduates illustrated high scores towards knowledge, attitude, and perception. This finding suggests that education plays an important role to overcome such pandemics since educated citizens had a greater tendency to analyze the critical situations and consequently behave positively.

Various research studies have been conducted to initiate effective strategies in order to improve the vaccination rate. These studies show that information alone has a limited impact on enhancing the vaccination rate. Acceptance and a willingness of vaccination is still an unparalleled challenge. Data of this survey could strengthen the efforts of health authorities to achieve their targets of high vaccination coverage through effective communication and updated information.

Limitations

This survey was conducted over a short time period with incompetence to reach people residing in far-off, remote locations with no access to the Internet, and therefore the findings obtained in this survey might not express the perspective of the whole general population, and the sample was not generalized to a meaningful population. The general population who do not have Internet access and were not proficient in working with online platforms were difficult to connect with. The study used a virtual self-reporting system that may be exposed to social acceptability and memory biases. There would be a response biasness, too, about being judged on knowledge or on financial situations, that also resulted in low responses being one of the drawbacks of online survey.

5. Conclusions

Until the development of vaccines, the COVID-19 pandemic was a major global threat. Our survey reflects a poor knowledge (50.6%), fair attitude (75.1%), and poor perception (58.1%) towards vaccination. These findings suggest that more educational campaigns and the advertisement of the correct information status could contribute fairly to eradicating the pandemic. Guiding principle makers can take preliminary steps to ensure the distribution of positive information about the attitudes and perceptions towards COVID-19 vaccinations in order to decrease the vaccine timidity and to increase the vaccination rate. However, research should be performed on participants not included in this study, such as immigrants and the elderly, who do not have access to social media and technology.

Author Contributions: Conceptualization: A.B. and A.K.; data curation: A.K. and A.M.; formal analysis: S.M.; investigation: A.B. and A.K.; methodology: A.B. and A.K.; project administration: A.B.; resources: A.M.; supervision: A.K.; visualization: A.M. and Y.H.K.; writing—original draft: A.B.; writing—review and editing: A.K., S.A., T.H.M., and I.R.G. All authors have read and agreed to the published version of the manuscript.

Funding: This research received no external funding.

Institutional Review Board Statement: The study was conducted after ethical approval by the Institutional Review Board (or Ethics Committee) of RAWALPINDI MEDICAL UNIVERSITY (ref. no. 64/IREF/RMU/2021 and date of approval was 23 April 2021).

Informed Consent Statement: Purpose of this survey was clearly explained and written informed consent has been obtained from the participants to publish this paper.

Acknowledgments: We acknowledge all the participants who consented to be a part of this research project.

Conflicts of Interest: The authors declare no conflict of interest.

References

1. Lim, Y.; Ng, Y.; Tam, J.; Liu, D. Human Coronaviruses: A Review of Virus–Host Interactions. *Diseases* **2016**, *4*, 26. [CrossRef] [PubMed]
2. Abid, K.; Bari, Y.A.; Younas, M.; Tahir Javaid, S.; Imran, A. Progress of COVID-19 Epidemic in Pakistan. *Asia-Pac. J. Public Health* **2020**, *32*, 154–156. [CrossRef] [PubMed]
3. Kim, E.S.; Chin, B.S.; Kang, C.K.; Kim, N.J.; Kang, Y.M.; Choi, J.P.; Oh, D.H.; Kim, J.-H.; Koh, B.; Kim, S.E.; et al. Clinical course and outcomes of patients with severe acute respiratory syndrome coronavirus 2 infection: A preliminary report of the first 28 patients from the korean cohort study on COVID-19. *J. Korean Med. Sci.* **2020**, *35*, e142. [CrossRef] [PubMed]
4. Lei, S.; Jiang, F.; Su, W.; Chen, C.; Chen, J.; Mei, W.; Zhan, L.-Y.; Jia, Y.; Zhang, L.; Liu, D.; et al. Clinical characteristics and outcomes of patients undergoing surgeries during the incubation period of COVID-19 infection. *EClinicalMedicine* **2020**, *21*, 100331. [CrossRef] [PubMed]
5. Xie, J.; Tong, Z.; Guan, X.; Du, B.; Qiu, H. Clinical Characteristics of Patients Who Died of Coronavirus Disease 2019 in China. *JAMA Netw Open* **2020**, *3*, e205619. [CrossRef]
6. Gandhi, R.T.; Lynch, J.B.; del Rio, C. Mild or Moderate Covid-19. *N. Engl. J. Med.* **2020**, *383*, 1757–1766. [CrossRef]
7. Fu, L.; Wang, B.; Yuan, T.; Chen, X.; Ao, Y.; Fitzpatrick, T.; Li, P.; Zhou, Y.; Lin, Y.-F.; Duan, Q.; et al. Clinical characteristics of coronavirus disease 2019 (COVID-19) in China: A systematic review and meta-analysis. *J. Infect.* **2020**, *80*, 656–665. [CrossRef]
8. Helmy, Y.A.; Fawzy, M.; Elaswad, A.; Sobieh, A.; Kenney, S.P.; Shehata, A.A. The COVID-19 pandemic: A comprehensive review of taxonomy, genetics, epidemiology, diagnosis, treatment, and control. *J. Clin. Med.* **2020**, *9*, 1225. [CrossRef]
9. Tang, D.; Tou, J.; Wang, J.; Chen, Q.; Wang, W.; Huang, J.; Zhao, H.; Wei, J.; Xu, Z.; Zhao, D.; et al. Prevention and control strategies for emergency, limited-term, and elective operations in pediatric surgery during the epidemic period of COVID-19. *World J. Pediatr. Surg.* **2020**, *3*, e000122. [CrossRef]

10. Chan, J.F.-W.; Yuan, S.; Kok, K.-H.; To, K.K.-W.; Chu, H.; Yang, J.; Xing, F.; Liu, J.; Yip, C.C.-Y.; Poon, R.W.-S.; et al. A familial cluster of pneumonia associated with the 2019 novel coronavirus indicating person to person transmission: A study of a family cluster. *Lancet* **2020**, *395*, 514–523. [CrossRef]
11. Chirwa, G.C. "Who knows more, and why?" Explaining socioeconomic-related inequality in knowledge about HIV in Malawi. *Sci. Afr.* **2020**, *7*, e00213. [CrossRef]
12. UNICEF. Another 1.2 Million Doses of COVID-19 Vaccine Reach Pakistan through COVAX. 2021. Available online: https://www.unicef.org/pakistan/press-releases/another-12-million-doses-covid-19-vaccine-reach-pakistan-through-covax (accessed on 29 July 2021).
13. Farooq, U.; Pakistan to Receive 13 Million Doses of Pfizer Vaccine—Minister. Reuters. *Sec. Asia Pacific.* 2021. Available online: https://www.reuters.com/world/asia-pacific/pakistan-receive-13-mln-doses-pfizer-vaccine-minister-2021-06-22/ (accessed on 31 July 2021).
14. Hussain, S.; Pakistan Set to Procure 30 Million Doses of Coronavirus Vaccine. Yahoo! News. 2021. Available online: https://in.news.yahoo.com/pakistan-set-procure-30-million-120755420.html (accessed on 31 July 2021).
15. Widakuswara, P. US Ships Moderna Vaccine to Pakistan Amid Delta Variant Surge | Voice of America—English. Voice of America. 2021. Available online: https://www.voanews.com/covid-19-pandemic/us-ships-moderna-vaccine-pakistan-amid-delta-variant-surge (accessed on 31 July 2021).
16. Shahzad, A.; Pakistan Commits $1.1 Bln for COVID Vaccine to Cover Eligible Population. Reuters. *Sec. Asia Pacific.* 2021. Available online: https://www.reuters.com/world/asia-pacific/pakistan-administers-10-mln-covid-vaccine-doses-eyes-70-mln-target-2021-06-09/ (accessed on 31 July 2021).
17. Government of Pakistan. Covid-19 Situation. 2021. Available online: https://covid.gov.pk/ (accessed on 31 July 2021).
18. Gavi the Vaccine Alliance. Pakistan Progressing on Immunization Efforts. 2016. Available online: https://www.gavi.org/news/media-room/pakistan-progressing-immunisation-efforts (accessed on 31 July 2021).
19. Khan, M.S.; Improving the Covid-19 Vaccination Rate in Pakistan—A Multipronged Policy Approach. Front. *Public Health 2021.* Available online: https://www.frontiersin.org/article/10.3389/fpubh.2021.729102 (accessed on 29 July 2021).
20. Reiter, P.L.; Pennell, M.L.; Katz, M.L. Acceptability of a COVID-19 vaccine among adults in the United States: How many people would get vaccinated? *Vaccine* **2020**, *38*, 6500–6507. [CrossRef] [PubMed]
21. Akbulut, S.; Gokce, A.; Boz, G.; Saritas, H.; Unsal, S.; Ozer, A.; Akbulut, M.S.; Colak, C. Evaluation of Vaccine Hesitancy and Anxiety Levels among Hospital Cleaning Staff and Caregivers during COVID-19 Pandemic. *Vaccines* **2022**, *10*, 1426. [CrossRef] [PubMed]
22. İkiışık, H.; Akif Sezerol, M.; Taşçı, Y.; Maral, I. COVID-19 vaccine hesitancy: A community-based research in Turkey. *Int. J. Clin. Pract.* **2021**, *75*, e14336. [CrossRef] [PubMed]
23. Khamis, F.; Badahdah, A.; Al Mahyijari, N.; Al Lawati, F.; Al Noamani, J.; Al Salmi, I.; Al Bahrani, M. Attitudes Towards COVID-19 Vaccine: A Survey of Health Care Workers in Oman. *J. Epidemiol. Glob. Health* **2022**, *12*, 1–6. [CrossRef]
24. Malik, A.A.; McFadden, S.A.M.; Elharake, J.; Omer, S.B. Determinants of COVID-19 vaccine acceptance in the US. *EClinicalMedicine* **2020**, *26*, 100495. [CrossRef]
25. Yakut, S.; Karagülle, B.; Atçalı, T.; Öztürk, Y.; Açık, M.N.; Çetinkaya, B. Knowledge, attitudes, practices and some characteristic features of people recovered from COVID-19 in Turkey. *Medicina* **2021**, *57*, 431. [CrossRef]
26. Al-Marshoudi, S.; Al-Balushi, H.; Al-Wahaibi, A.; Al-Khalili, S.; Al-Maani, A.; Al-Farsi, N.; Al-Jahwari, A.; Al-Habsi, Z.; Al-Shaibi, M.; Al-Msharfi, M.; et al. Knowledge, attitudes, and practices (Kap) toward the covid-19 vaccine in oman: A pre-campaign cross-sectional study. *Vaccines* **2021**, *9*, 602. [CrossRef]
27. Neumann-Böhme, S.; Varghese, N.E.; Sabat, I.; Barros, P.P.; Brouwer, W.; van Exel, J.; Stargardt, T. Once we have it, will we use it? A European survey on willingness to be vaccinated against COVID-19. *Eur. J. Health Econ.* **2020**, *21*, 977–982. [CrossRef]
28. Akhu-Zaheya, L.M.; Jagbir, M.T.; Othman, A.; Ahram, M. Media use for seeking health/cancer-related information: Findings from knowledge, attitudes and practices towards cancer prevention and care survey in Jordan. *Int. J. Nurs. Pract.* **2014**, *20*, 608–615. [CrossRef]
29. Gallè, F.; Sabella, E.A.; Roma, P.; Da Molin, G.; Da Molin, G.; Diella, G.; Montagna, M.T.; Ferracuti, S.; Liguori, G.; Orsi, G.B.; et al. Acceptance of covid-19 vaccination in the elderly: A cross-sectional study in Southern Italy. *Vaccines* **2021**, *9*, 1–12. [CrossRef] [PubMed]
30. Lin, Y.; Hu, Z.; Zhao, Q.; Alias, H.; Danaee, M.; Wong, L.P. Understanding COVID-19 vaccine demand and hesitancy: A nationwide online survey in China. *PLoS Negl. Trop. Dis.* **2020**, *14*, e0008961. [CrossRef] [PubMed]
31. Palamenghi, L.; Barello, S.; Boccia, S.; Graffigna, G. Mistrust in biomedical research and vaccine hesitancy: The forefront challenge in the battle against COVID-19 in Italy. *Eur. J. Epidemiol.* **2020**, *35*, 785–788. [CrossRef] [PubMed]
32. MacDonald, N.E.; Smith, J.; Appleton, M. Risk perception, risk management and safety assessment: What can governments do to increase public confidence in their vaccine system? *Biologicals* **2012**, *40*, 384–388. [CrossRef]
33. Papagiannis, D.; Malli, F.; Raptis, D.G.; Papathanasiou, I.V. Assessment of knowledge, attitudes, and practices towards new coronavirus (SARS-CoV-2) of health care professionals in Greece before the outbreak period. *Int. J. Environ. Res. Public Health* **2020**, *17*, 4925. [CrossRef]
34. Harkness, J.A.; Schoua-Glusberg, A. Questionnaires in Translation. *ZUMA-Nachr. Spez.* **1998**, *3*, 87–126. Available online: http://isites.harvard.edu/fs/docs/icb.topic506406.files/znspez3_04_Harkness_Glusberg.pdf (accessed on 22 July 2021).

35. *A Guide To Developing Knowledge, Attitude and Practice Surveys*; WHO: Geneva, Switzerland, 2008.
36. Akalu, Y.; Ayelign, B.; Molla, M.D. Knowledge, attitude and practice towards covid-19 among chronic disease patients at addis zemen hospital, Northwest Ethiopia. *Infect. Drug Resist.* **2020**, *13*, 1949–1960. [CrossRef]
37. Policy, H. The Knowledge and Attitude of the Community from the Aseer Region, Saudi Arabia, Toward COVID-19 and Their Precautionary Measures Against the Disease. *Risk Manag. Healthc. Policy* **2020**, *13*, 1825.
38. Goyal, L.; Zapata, M.; Ajmera, K.; Chaurasia, P.; Pandit, R.; Pandit, T. A Hitchhiker's Guide to Worldwide COVID-19 Vaccinations: A Detailed Review of Monovalent and Bivalent Vaccine Schedules, COVID-19 Vaccine Side Effects, and Effectiveness Against Omicron and Delta Variants. *Cureus* **2022**, *14*, e29837. Available online: http://www.ncbi.nlm.nih.gov/pubmed/36204257%0Ahttp://www.pubmedcentral.nih.gov/articlerender.fcgi?artid=PMC9527088 (accessed on 31 July 2021). [CrossRef]
39. Saiful Islam, M.; Siddique, A.B.; Akter, R.; Tasnim, R.; Safaet, M.; Sujan, H.; Ward, P.R.; Sikder, M.T. Knowledge, attitudes and perceptions towards COVID-19 vaccinations: A cross-sectional community survey in Bangladesh. *BMC Public Health* **2021**, *21*, 1–11. [CrossRef]
40. Fu, C.; Wei, Z.; Pei, S.; Li, S.; Sun, X.; Liu, P. Acceptance and preference for COVID-19 vaccination in health-care workers (HCWs). *medRxiv* **2020**, *548*, 2962.
41. Larson, H.J.; Smith, D.M.D.; Paterson, P.; Cumming, M.; Eckersberger, E.; Freifeld, C.C.; Ghinai, I.; Jarrett, C.; Paushter, L.; Brownstein, J.S.; et al. Measuring vaccine confidence: Analysis of data obtained by a media surveillance system used to analyse public concerns about vaccines. *Lancet Infect. Dis.* **2013**, *13*, 606–613. [CrossRef] [PubMed]
42. Harapan, H.; Anwar, S.; Bustaman, A.; Radiansyah, A.; Angraini, P.; Fasli, R.; Salwiyadi, S.; Bastian, R.A.; Oktiviyari, A.; Akmal, I.; et al. Modifiable determinants of attitude towards dengue vaccination among healthy inhabitants of Aceh, Indonesia: Findings from a community-based survey. *Asian Pac. J. Trop. Med.* **2016**, *9*, 1115–1122. Available online: https://www.sciencedirect.com/science/article/pii/S1995764516303686 (accessed on 29 July 2021). [CrossRef] [PubMed]
43. Ferdous, M.Z.; Islam, M.S.; Sikder, M.T.; Mosaddek, A.S.M.; Zegarra-Valdivia, J.A.; Gozal, D. Knowledge, attitude, and practice regarding COVID-19 outbreak in Bangladesh: An online-based cross-sectional study. *PLoS ONE* **2020**, *15*, e0239254. [CrossRef]
44. Detoc, M.; Bruel, S.; Frappe, P.; Tardy, B.; Botelho-Nevers, E.; Gagneux-Brunon, A. Intention to participate in a COVID-19 vaccine clinical trial and to get vaccinated against COVID-19 in France during the pandemic. *Vaccine* **2020**, *38*, 7002–7006. [CrossRef] [PubMed]
45. Mannan, K.A.; Farhana, K.M. Knowledge, Attitude and Acceptance of a COVID-19 Vaccine: A Global Cross-Sectional Study. *SSRN Electron. J.* **2021**, *6*, 1–23. [CrossRef]
46. Lazarus, J.V.; Ratzan, S.C.; Palayew, A.; Gostin, L.O.; Larson, H.J.; Rabin, K.; Kimball, S.; El-Mohandes, A. A global survey of potential acceptance of a COVID-19 vaccine. *Nat. Med.* **2021**, *27*, 225–228. [CrossRef]
47. Lombardi, A.; Bozzi, G.; Ungaro, R.; Villa, S.; Castelli, V.; Mangioni, D.; Muscatello, A.; Gori, A.; Bandera, A. Mini Review Immunological Consequences of Immunization With COVID-19 mRNA Vaccines: Preliminary Results. *Front. Immunol.* **2021**, *12*, 1–11. [CrossRef]
48. Voysey, M.; Clemens, S.A.C.; Madhi, S.A.; Weckx, L.Y.; Folegatti, P.M.; Aley, P.K.; Angus, B.; Baillie, V.L.; Barnabas, S.L.; Bhorat, Q.E.; et al. Safety and efficacy of the ChAdOx1 nCoV-19 vaccine (AZD1222) against SARS-CoV-2: An interim analysis of four randomised controlled trials in Brazil, South Africa, and the UK. *Lancet* **2021**, *397*, 99–111. [CrossRef]
49. Al-Zalfawi, S.M.; Rabbani, S.I.; Asdaq, S.M.B.; Alamri, A.S.; Alsanie, W.F.; Alhomrani, M.; Mohzari, Y.; Alrashed, A.A.; AlRifdah, A.H.; Almagrabe, T. Public knowledge, attitude, and perception towards COVID-19 vaccination in Saudi Arabia. *Int. J. Environ. Res. Public Health* **2021**, *18*, 10081. [CrossRef]
50. Green, M.S.; Abdullah, R.; Vered, S.; Nitzan, D. A study of ethnic, gender and educational differences in attitudes toward COVID-19 vaccines in Israel—Implications for vaccination implementation policies. *Isr. J. Health Policy Res.* **2021**, *10*, 1–12. [CrossRef] [PubMed]
51. Jabal, K.A.; Ben-Amram, H.; Beiruti, K.; Batheesh, Y.; Sussan, C.; Zarka, S.; Edelstein, M. Impact of age, ethnicity, sex and prior infection status on immunogenicity following a single dose of the BNT162b2 MRNA COVID-19 vaccine: Real-world evidence from healthcare workers, Israel, December 2020 to January 2021. *Eurosurveillance* **2021**, *26*, 2100096. [CrossRef] [PubMed]

Disclaimer/Publisher's Note: The statements, opinions and data contained in all publications are solely those of the individual author(s) and contributor(s) and not of MDPI and/or the editor(s). MDPI and/or the editor(s) disclaim responsibility for any injury to people or property resulting from any ideas, methods, instructions or products referred to in the content.

medicina

MDPI

Article

Comparison of Different Antiviral Regimens in the Treatment of Patients with Severe COVID-19: A Retrospective Cohort

Mohammad E. M. Mahfouz [1], Afrah A. Alharthi [2], Nada M. Alsalmi [2], Ahad A. Alnemari [2], Amjad A. Alwagdani [2], Reem K. Alghamdi [2], Razan A. Almakki [2], Mubarak R. Al Yami [3], Ahmed N. Alghamdi [4], Afaf S. Osman [5], Ahmed S. Abdel-Moneim [4,*] and Dalia Y. Kadry [6,*]

1 Department of Surgery, College of Medicine, Taif University, Taif 21944, Saudi Arabia
2 College of Medicine (Graduate Students), Taif University, Taif 21944, Saudi Arabia
3 King Faisal Medical Center (KFMC) Taif 26514, Saudi Arabia
4 Department of Microbiology, College of Medicine, Taif University, Taif 21944, Saudi Arabia
5 Medical Pharmacology Department, Faculty of Medicine, Cairo University, Cairo 11562, Egypt
6 Department of Microbiology, National Cancer Institute, Cairo University, Cairo 11796, Egypt
* Correspondence: asa@tu.edu.sa (A.S.A.); dy.kadry@nci.cu.edu.eg (D.Y.K.)

Abstract: The severe acute respiratory syndrome coronavirus 2 (SARS-CoV-2) causes respiratory disorders, with disease severity ranging from asymptomatic to critical manifestations. The current retrospective study compared the efficacies of different antiviral regimens used in patients suffering from severe COVID-19 disease from 19 January 2020 to December 2021 in a single center in Saudi Arabia. In total, 188 patients were enrolled in the current study, including 158 patients treated with different antiviral regimens, and 30 who did not receive any antiviral treatment. Different antiviral regimens, including favipiravir, remdesivir, oseltamivir, favipiravir/remdesivir, and favipiravir/oseltamivir were adopted. The effects of using different antivirals and antibiotics on the survival rate were evaluated, as well as the presence of comorbidities. Among all severely affected patients, 39/188 (20.7%) survived. Both age and comorbidities, including diabetes and hypertension, were significantly correlated with high case fatality following SARS-CoV-2 infection. Remdesivir alone and the combination of favipiravir and remdesivir increased the survival rate. Surprisingly, both imipenem and linezolid helped in the deterioration of disease outcome in the patients. A negative correlation was detected between increased mortality and the use of favipiravir and the use of either imipenem or linezolid. Among the compared antiviral regimens used in the treatment of severe COVID-19, remdesivir was found to be an effective antiviral that reduces COVID-19 case fatality. Antibiotic treatment using imipenem and/or linezolid should be carefully re-evaluated.

Keywords: antiviral; clinical outcome; coronavirus; disease severity; COVID-19; SARS-CoV-2; Saudi Arabia

Citation: Mahfouz, M.E.M.; Alharthi, A.A.; Alsalmi, N.M.; Alnemari, A.A.; Alwagdani, A.A.; Alghamdi, R.K.; Almakki, R.A.; Al Yami, M.R.; Alghamdi, A.N.; Osman, A.S.; et al. Comparison of Different Antiviral Regimens in the Treatment of Patients with Severe COVID-19: A Retrospective Cohort. *Medicina* **2023**, *59*, 260. https://doi.org/10.3390/medicina59020260

Academic Editors: Yusra Habib Khan, Tauqeer Hussain Mallhi, Tahir Mehmood Khan and Muhammad Salman

Received: 28 December 2022
Revised: 21 January 2023
Accepted: 26 January 2023
Published: 29 January 2023

Copyright: © 2023 by the authors. Licensee MDPI, Basel, Switzerland. This article is an open access article distributed under the terms and conditions of the Creative Commons Attribution (CC BY) license (https://creativecommons.org/licenses/by/4.0/).

1. Introduction

Coronavirus disease 2019 (COVID-19) is caused by severe acute respiratory syndrome coronavirus 2 (SARS-CoV-2), which is a virus related to the subgenus *Sarbecovirus* and genus *Betacoronavirus* within the family *Coronaviridae* [1]. Globally, COVID-19 has been confirmed in more than 661 million cases, with 6,700,519 fatal cases reported to WHO as of 13 January 2023 [2]. The virus is highly transmissible among humans through both direct and indirect contacts [3].

SARS-CoV-2 has an incubation period of 5–7 days; however, it can take up to 14 days to develop symptoms after being exposed to the virus [4]. COVID-19 can be asymptomatic or symptomatic. In symptomatic cases, the disease severity can be mild, moderate, severe, or critical [5]. Patients who suffer from the severe form of the disease develop a hyperinflammatory state that could lead to a critical condition. The asymptotic cases are characterized by respiratory failure, acute respiratory distress syndrome, septic shock, thromboembolism, and/or multi-organ failure [6]. Acute kidney and cardiac injuries are among the most common impacts [7,8].

Older age, smoking, and underlying diseases such as diabetes, hypertension, cardiac diseases, chronic lung diseases, and cancer have all been identified as risk factors for the development of severe diseases and fatal consequences [9].

Antiviral therapy is used effectively in the treatment of several viral infections. Antiviral drugs help in easing symptoms and shortening the duration of the illness. On 22 October 2020, the FDA approved Veklury (remdesivir) for use in adults and pediatric patients (above 12 years of age). Remdesivir (GS-5734) inhibits the viral RNA-dependent RNA polymerase (RdRp) with in vitro inhibitory activity. It was found to be active against both the severe acute respiratory syndrome coronavirus 1 (SARS-CoV-1) and the Middle East respiratory syndrome (MERS-CoV). Owing to its capability to inhibit SARS-CoV-2 in vitro, it was discovered early as a promising therapeutic candidate for COVID-19 [10].

Lopinavir/ritonavir and favipiravir are antivirals that have been used in the treatment of COVID-19 and are currently being employed in different clinical trials, as previously reviewed [11]. Favipiravir triphosphate is a purine nucleoside analog that inhibits RdRp in a competitive manner. It is effective against influenza viruses, RNA viruses associated with viral hemorrhagic fever, and SARS-CoV-2 [12]. Oseltamivir is a neuraminidase inhibitor that has been successfully used as an antiviral treatment against influenza A and B viruses. Although it is used as a therapeutic option in some studies, its efficiency in COVID-19 treatment remains controversial [13,14].

Repurposed drugs, including chloroquine (CQ), hydroxychloroquine (HCQ), and ivermectin, have also been used in COVID-19 treatment [11]. CQ and HCQ aminoquinolines have been used for treating malaria and chronic inflammatory disorders, such as systemic lupus erythematosus and rheumatoid arthritis. Their efficacy in treating patients with COVID-19 infection is attributable to their antiviral and anti-inflammatory activities [15,16]. Ivermectin is an anthelminthic drug that can bind to the SARS-CoV-2 S protein, human ACE-2, and TMPRSS2 receptors and inhibit virus entry to host cells [17].

Other supportive drugs that are essential in reducing inflammatory responses, including corticosteroids and anti-IL-6 Mab, have also been used in COVID-19 treatment. Corticosteroids work through their anti-inflammatory and immunosuppressive properties to reduce damage in different tissues. Glucocorticoids inhibit nuclear transcription factor-κB signaling and inflammatory factor transcription and translation. Thus, they are used as anti-inflammatory drugs in different medical conditions, such as bacterial or viral pneumonia. Corticosteroids have also been used in the past during SARS-CoV-1 and MERS-CoV outbreaks. Accordingly, the use of corticosteroids in the recent COVID-19 pandemic is based on the genetic similarities of SARS-CoV-2 with SARS-CoV-1 and MERS-CoV [18].

Antibiotics have been widely used as part of a treatment protocol for COVID-19 in many countries. In addition to the struggles related to antibiotic resistance, most of the guidelines recommend treatment with antibiotics. The WHO recommended that antibiotic therapy or prophylaxis should not be used in patients with mild/moderate COVID-19 unless it is justifiable. Azithromycin is recommended for treating respiratory, urogenital, dermal, and other bacterial infections and exerts immunomodulatory effects in chronic inflammatory disorders [19]. The use of these antibiotics has been associated with clinical improvement and even reversal of cytokine storms in some infections caused by RNA viruses [20].

Limited information is available regarding the efficacy of different antivirals used in reducing both disease severity and mortality rate. Accordingly, we aimed to investigate the various treatment regimens used to treat COVID-19 patients and how they influence clinical outcomes.

2. Materials and Methods

2.1. Ethical Approval

This research proposal was approved by No. 353 on 9 May 2021, from IRB of the Research and Studies Section of the Directorate of Health Affairs in Taif, Saudi Arabia.

2.2. Patients

The current retrospective study was conducted at the King Faisal Medical Complex in Taif city, Saudi Arabia. The exclusion criterion included patients who tested negative for COVID-19 or COVID-19-positive patients with mild (no shortness of breath or normal chest X-ray) to moderate illness (lower respiratory distress or imaging with oxygen saturation $\geq$94% on room air). The following were the inclusion criterion: laboratory-confirmed COVID-19 patients who suffered from a severe form of the disease and were admitted to the intensive care unit (ICU). Patients with an oxygen saturation <94% in room air, a respiratory rate >30 breaths/min, or lung infiltration of >50% were considered severe COVID-19 patients and were enrolled in the study [21]. In total, 188 patients, including 69 females and 119 males with an age range of 21 to 93 years, were enrolled in the study. Laboratory diagnosis was conducted using real-time reverse transcription polymerase chain reaction or cobas® SARS-CoV-2, which targets the conserved regions within the ORF 1a/b and E genes (Roche, Basel, Switzerland). The test was conducted in the regional reference laboratories belonging to the Saudi Ministry of Health.

2.3. Clinical Data

Data were collected retrospectively from 19 January 2020 to 31 December 2021. Demographic data, including age and sex; clinical data such as clinical signs, comorbidities (diabetes, hypertension, cardiac diseases, and cancer), and clinical findings (respiratory rate, chest X-ray findings, and high-resolution computed tomography); and treatment regimens (antiviral, antibiotic, corticosteroids, and anti-IL-6) were collected from the patients' files.

2.4. Treatment Regimens

The ICU patients who tested positive for COVID-19 were grouped into the following clusters: (i) patients who received supportive treatment only (no antiviral, but antibiotic, anti-pyretic, anti-histaminic, and/or cortisone therapy); (ii) patients who received remdesivir (a single IV injection of 200 mg on the first day and then 100 mg once daily for 5 days) beginning from 20 November 2020; (iii) patients who received favipiravir (oral administration of 1800 mg twice daily on the 1st day followed by a twice daily dose of 800 mg for 7 days); (iv) patients who received oseltamivir (oral administration of 75 mg twice daily for 5 days); (v) patients who received both remdesivir and favipiravir with the same dose and treatment duration as for groups ii and iii; and (vi) patients who received both favipiravir and oseltamivir with the same dose and treatment duration as for groups iii and iv.

2.5. Statistical Analysis

The results were expressed in numbers and percentages and analyzed by Crosstabs analysis with chi-square and Spearman's analyses using SPSS version 16. A multivariate analysis of variance was used to screen the benefits of administering individual drugs to reduce the mortality rate among the patients.

3. Results

3.1. Demographic and Clinical Data

The case fatality was high (149/188, 79.3%), including 91/119 (76.5%) of male patients and 58/69 (84.1%) of female patients (Table 1). All patients suffered from different degrees of lung lesions, including uni- or bilateral infiltration, glass ground consolidation, pleural effusion, and/or bilateral fibrosis.

Table 1. Significance of age, sex, comorbidities, antiviral use, and supportive treatment on the survival rate of critical COVID-19 patients.

Variable		Non-Fatal Cases (39)	Fatal Cases (149)	Total (188)	Significance *
Sex	Male	28 (23.5%)	91 (76.5%)	119 (63.3%)	$p < 0.149$
	Female	11 (15.9%)	58 (84.1%)	69 (36.7%)	R = −0.09
Age (years)	21–30	4 (100%)	0 (0%)	4 (2.1%)	
	31–40	7 (53.8%)	6 (46.2%)	13 (6.9%)	
	41–50	12 (46.2%)	14 (53.8%)	26 (13.8%)	
	51–60	9 (26.5%)	25 (73.5%)	34 (18.1%)	$p < 0.001$ **
	61–70	5 (10.9%)	41 (89.1%)	46 (24.5%)	R = −0.455
	71–80	0 (0%)	37 (100%)	37 (19.7%)	
	81–93	2 (7.1%)	26 (92.9%)	28 (14.9%)	
Diabetes	YES	16 (13.7%)	101 (86.3%)	117 (62.2%)	R = −0.202
	NO	23 (32.4%)	48 (67.6%)	71 (37.8%)	$p < 0.005$ **
Hypertension	YES	12 (12.8%)	82 (87.2%)	94 (50.0%)	R = −0.203
	NO	27 (28.7%)	67 (71.3%)	94 (50.0%)	$p < 0.005$ **
Cardiac diseases	YES	8 (16.7%)	40 (83.3%)	48 (25.5%)	R = −0.059
	NO	31 (22.1%)	109 (77.9%)	140 (74.5%)	$p < 0.258$
Cancer	YES	0 (0%)	6 (100%)	6 (3.2%)	R = −0.093
	NO	39 (21.4)	143 (78.6%)	182 (96.8%)	$p < 0.243$
Using antivirals	YES	3 (22.1%)	123 (77.8%)	158 (84%)	$p < 0.202$
	NO	4 (13.3%)	26 (86.7%)	30 (16%)	R = 0.08
Treatment with a single antiviral	Remdesivir	17 (85%)	3 (15%)	20 (12.7%)	$p < 0.001$ ** R = 0.547
	Favipiravir	9 (9.3%)	88 (90.7%)	97 (61.4%)	$p < 0.001$ ** R = −0.292
	Oseltamivir	1 (11.1%)	8 (88.9%)	9 (5.7%)	$p < 0.409$ R = −0.053
Treatment with two antivirals	Remdesivir and favipiravir	8 (29.6%)	19 (70.4%)	27 (17.1%)	$p > 0.262$
	Favipiravir and oseltamivir	0 (0.0%)	5 (100%)	5 (3.2%)	R = 0.055
Dexamethasone	YES	32 (19.9%)	129 (80.1%)	161 (85.6%)	R = −0.108
	NO	7 (25.9%)	20 (74.1%)	27 (15.4%)	$p < 0.110$
Anti-IL-6	YES	1 (12.5%)	7 (87.5%)	8 (4.3%)	R = −053
	NO	38 (21.1%)	142 (78.9%)	180 (95.7%)	$p < 0.409$

Statistical analysis was conducted using chi-square and Spearman's correlations. * Statistical analysis was conducted using chi-square and Spearman correlations. ** Variables showed a highly significant p value using chi-square.

The overall results revealed no correlation between sex and mortality rate (R = −0.09) (Table 1). The patient age ranged from 21 to 93 years, and there was a significant variation among age groups in relation to the overall mortality rate. In addition, a highly significant correlation was detected between age and mortality rate (R = −0.455). Both diabetes and hypertension constituted risk factors in the fatal cases ($p < 0.005$) (Table 1).

3.2. *Effect of Different Variables on the Clinical Outcomes of Using Antiviral Regimens in Critically Ill COVID-19 Patients*

The use of remdesivir significantly reduced the mortality rate in the treated patients ($p < 0.001$), and there was a high correlation between using remdesivir and increased recovery rate (R = 0.547). In contrast, the use of neither favipiravir nor oseltamivir improved the survival rate. Surprisingly, there was a negative correlation between the use of favipiravir and the mortality rate (R = −0.292) (Table 1). A combination of two antiviral regimens was adopted in some patients. All five patients who were treated with both oseltamivir and favipiravir showed fatal consequences. Twenty-seven patients were treated with both remdesivir and favipiravir. Although not statistically significant, the latter regimen resulted in an improved survival rate (29.6%) (Table 1).

We screened the effect of different variables using crosstabs with different patient groups that were given different antiviral regimens. Remdesivir use was correlated with an enhanced survival rate in both sexes ($p < 0.001$, R = 0.598) (Table 2). Similarly, the combination of remdesivir and favipiravir enhanced the recovery rate in males ($p < 0.048$, R = −0.318) (Table 2). Antiviral use, in general, significantly reduced the fatal consequences in different age groups ($p = 0.027$); however, no significant correlation was detected (R = −0.132) (Table 2). Age was significantly correlated with the overall fatal cases (Table 1). However, there was no statistical variation among the age groups treated with different antiviral regimens and the recovery rate (Table 2). Diabetes ($p = 0.019$, R = 0.185), hypertension ($p < 0.001$, R = 0.329), and cardiac diseases ($p = 0.033$, R = 0.166) were significant risk factors associated with high mortality rates, especially in patients treated with favipiravir (Table 2). The fatal consequences of antiviral use are not aggravated by diabetes. However, it was found to be a risk factor for the increased mortality rate in the favipiravir-treated group (chi-square $p < 0.001$, R = 0.381) and not in other treated groups. Interestingly, the fatal consequences in the remdesivir-treated group were reduced in the diabetic group ($p < 0.001$, R = 0.581). Similarly, hypertension and cardiac diseases were risk factors that increased the fatality rate in the favipiravir-treated group [($p < 0.011$, R = 0.329) and ($p = 0.033$, R = 0.166) for hypertension and cardiac diseases, respectively]. Accordingly, diabetes, hypertension, and cardiac diseases were risk factors and correlated with the increased mortality rate in the favipiravir-treated group.

3.3. *Impact of Using Supportive Therapy*

Most patients [161 (85.6%)] were treated with dexamethasone, and only 27 (15.4%) patients did not receive dexamethasone; no significant differences were found between the two groups (Table 1). Anti-IL-6 was adopted in only 8 patients, 7 (87.5%) of whom died (Table 1).

3.4. *Using Antibiotic Regimens*

Antibiotics were prescribed in most patients in the current study (185/188). Different antibiotic combinations were used in the COVID-19 patients with secondary bacterial infections. Moxifloxacin was used in most patients (90/188, 47.8%), followed by imipenem (71/188, 37.7%), linezolid (65/188, 34.5%), vancomycin (56/188, 29.7%), and levofloxacin (37/188, 19.6%). Azithromycin was used only in 17 (9%) of the treated patients. Meropenem treatment with favipiravir ($p < 0.016$, R = −0.196), as well as the treatment combining remdesivir and favipiravir ($p < 0.001$, R = 0.423), showed a significant increase in fatal cases. An increased mortality rate was also detected in the group treated with linezolid combined with favipiravir ($p < 0.015$, R = 0.200) and in the group treated with imipenem combined with favipiravir ($p = 0.001$, R = 0.518). A significant increase in mortality rate was also detected in patients treated with a combination of remdesivir, favipiravir, and moxifloxacin (Table 3).

Table 2. Effects of different variables on the clinical outcomes of using antiviral regimens in critical COVID-19 patients.

Variable		No Antivirals (30)		Use of Antivirals (158)		Remdesivir (20)		Favipiravir (97)		Oseltamivir (9)		Remdesivir and Favipiravir (27)		Favipiravir and Oseltamivir (5)		Non-Fatal Outcome (39)	Fatal Outcome (149)	Total (188)
		N [a]	F [b]	N [a]	F [b]	N	F	N	F	N	F	N	F	N	F			
Sex	Male	4	17	24	74	7 *	1	8	50	1	6	8 *	14	0	3	28 (23.5%)	91 (76.5%)	119 (63.3%)
	Female	0	9	11	49	10 *	2	1	38	0	2	0	5	0	2	11 (15.9%)	58 (84.1%)	69 (36.7%)
Age (years)	21–30	0	0	4	0	3	0	1	0	0	0	0	0	0	0	4 (100%)	0 (0%)	4 (2.1%)
	31–40	2	0	5	6	3	0	0	3	0	1	2	2	0	0	7 (53.8%)	6 (46.2%)	13 (6.9%)
	41–50	1	4	11	10	6	0	4	5	0	1	1	3	0	1	12 (46.2%)	14 (53.8%)	26 (13.8%)
	51–60	1	0	8	25	3	0	2	19	0	2	3	1	0	3	9 (26.5%)	25 (73.5%)	34 (18.1%)
	61–70	0	8	5	33	2	2	1	26	1	1	1	4	0	0	5 (10.9%)	41 (89.1%)	46 (24.5%)
	71–80	0	6	0	31	0	0	0	21	0	3	0	6	0	1	0 (0%)	37 (100%)	37 (19.7%)
	81–93	0	8	2	18	0	1	1	14	0	0	1	3	0	0	2 (7.1%)	26 (92.9%)	28 (14.9%)
Diabetes	Yes	1	14	15	87	9 *	3	2	66 *	0	5	4	11	0	2	16 (13.7%)	101 (86.3%)	117 (62.2%)
	No	3	12	20	36	8	0	7	22	1	3	4	8	0	3	23 (32.4%)	48 (67.6%)	71 (37.8%)
Hypertension	Yes	1	6 *	11	76 *	4	3	5	61 *	0	3	2	7	0	2	12 (12.8%)	82 (87.2%)	94 (50.0%)
	No	3	20	24	47	13	0	4	27	1	5	6	12	0	3	27 (28.7%)	67 (71.3%)	94 (50.0%)
Cardiac diseases	Yes	1	3	7	37	2	2	4	29 *	0	2	1	3	0	0	8 (16.6%)	40 (83.0%)	48 (25.5%)
	No	3	23	28	86	15	1	5	58 *	1	6	7	16	0	5	31 (22.1%)	109 (77.9%)	140 (74.5%)
Cancer	Yes	0	3	0	3	0	0	0	1	0	0	0	2	0	0	0 (0%)	6 (100%)	6 (3.2%)
	No	4	23	35	120	17	3	9	87	1	8	8	17	0	5	39 (21.4)	143 (78.6%)	182 (96.8%)
Dexamethasone	Yes	3	16	29 *	113 *	14	3	6	82 *	1	6	8	18	0	4	32 (19.9%)	129 (80.1%)	161 (85.6%)
	No	1	10	6 *	10 *	3	0	3	6	0	2	0	1	0	1	7 (25.9%)	20 (74.1%)	27 (15.4%)
Anti-IL-6	Yes	0	0	1	7	1	0	0	6	0	1	0	0	0	0	1 (12.5%)	7 (87.5%)	8 (4.3%)
	No	4	26	34	116	16	3	9	82	1	7	8	19	0	5	38 (21.1%)	142 (78.9%)	180 (95.7%)
Cumulative		4	26	35	123	17	3	9	88	1	8	8	19	0	5	39 (20.7%)	149 (79.3%)	188

[a] N: Non-fatal, [b] F: Fatal. Sex: Use of remdesivir (non-fatal cases: $p < 0.001$, R = 0.598). Remdesivir and favipiravir (non-fatal cases: $p < 0.048$, R = −0.318). Diabetes: Favipiravir (fatal cases: $p = 0.001$, R = 0.381), remdesivir ($p < 0.001$, R = 0.581). Hypertension: favipiravir (fatal cases: $p < 0.001$, R = 0.329). Cardiac diseases: favipiravir (fatal cases: $p = 0.033$, R = 0.166). Dexamethasone: use of antivirals (fatal cases: $p < 0.007$, R = 0.350; non-fatal cases: $p = 0.007$, R = 0.518), favipiravir (fatal cases: $p < 0.005$, R = 0.233).

Table 3. Antibiotics used in critical COVID-19 patients with different antiviral regimens.

Variable		No Antivirals (n:30)		Remdesivir (n:20)		Favipiravir (n:97)		Oseltamivir (n:9)		Remdesivir and Favipiravir (n:27)		Favipiravir and Oseltamivir (n:5)		Total Use of Antivirals(n:158)		Total (n:188)
		N *	F **	N	F	N	F	N	F	N	F	N	F	N [a]	F [b]	
Antibiotic use	NO	0	0	0	0	0	3	0	0	0	0	0	0	0	3	3 (1.6%)
	YES	4	26	17	3	9	85	1	8	8	19	0	5	35	120	185 (98.4%)
Azithromycin	NO	4	24	16	3	8	83	1	7	6	16	0	3	31	112	171 (90.9%)
	YES	0	2	1	0	1	5	0	1	2	3	0	2	4	11	17 (9%)
Ceftriaxone	NO	4	20	16	3	8	74	1	7	5	11	0	3	30	98	152 (80.8%)
	YES	0	6	1	0	1	14	0	1	3	8	0	2	5	25	36 (19.1%)
Vancomycin	NO	2	18	13	3	6	61	1	6	5	15	0	2	25	87	132 (70.2%)
	YES	2	8	4	0	3	27	0	2	3	4	0	3	10	36	56 (29.7%)
Levofloxacin	NO	3	17	10	3	7	77	1	6	8	16	0	3	26	105	151 (80.3%)
	YES	1	9 [a]	7	0	2	11	0	2	0	3	0	2	9	18 [a]	37 (19.6%)
Tienam	NO	4	25	17	3	9	84	1	7	8	19	0	5	35	118	182 (96.8%)
	YES	0	1	0	0	0	4	0	1	0	0	0	0	0	5	6 (3.1%)
Amikacin	NO	4	26	17	3	8	85	1	8	7	17	0	4	33	117	180 (95.7%)
	YES	0	0	0	0	1	3	0	0	1	2	0	1	2	6	8 (4.2%)
Imipenem	NO	4	13	16	3	5	46 [b]	1	4	7	15	0	3	30	70	117 (94.1%)
	YES	0	13	1	0	4	42 [b]	0	4	1	4	0	2	5	53	71 (37.7%)
Ciprofloxacin	NO	4	23	16	3	9	82	1	8	8	16	0	5	34	114	175 (93%)
	YES	0	3	1	0	0	6	0	0	0	3	0	0	1	9	13 (6.9%)
Cefipime	NO	4	25	17	3	9	83	1	8	8	19	0	4	35	116	180 (95.7%)
	YES	0	1	0	0	0	5	0	0	0	0	0	1	0	7	8 (4.2%)
Meropenem	NO	4	23	14	2	8	76 [c]	1	8	6	7 [d]	0	3	26	96	152 (80.8%)
	YES	0	3	3	1	1	12 [c]	0	0	2	12 [d]	0	2	9	27	36 (19.1%)
Tazocin	NO	4	25	16	3	9	87	1	8	8	18	0	5	34	121	184 (97.8%)
	YES	0	1	1	0	0	1	0	0	0	1	0	0	1	2	4 (2.1%)
Moxifloxacin	NO	3	18	11	2	5	48	1	5	0	5	0	1	17	60	98 (52.1%)
	YES	1	8	6	1	4	40	0	3	8 [e]	14 [e]	0	4	18	63	90 (47.8%)
Linezolid	NO	2	19	16	3	8	46 [f]	1	6	6	13	0	4	31	71	123 (65.4%)
	YES	2	7	1	0	1	42 [f]	0	2	2	6	0	1	4	52	65 (34.5%)
Clindamycin	NO	4	25	17	3	9	85	1	8	8	19	0	5	35	120	184 (97.8%)
	YES	0	1	0	0	0	3	0	0	0	0	0	0	0	3	4 (2.1%)

** F: Fatal cases, * N: No fatal cases. [a] Levofloxacin vs. favipiravir in fatal cases ($p < 0.016$, R = −0.175). [b] Imipenem vs. favipiravir in fatal cases ($p = 0.001$, R = 0.518). [c] Meropenem vs. favipiravir in fatal cases ($p < 0.016$, R = −0.196). [d] Meropenem vs. favipiravir and remdesivir in fatal cases ($p < 0.001$, R = 0.423). [e] Moxifloxacin vs. remdesivir and favipiravir (fatal cases: $p < 0.003$, R = 0.238 and non-fatal cases: $p < 0.001$, R = 0.521). [f] Linezolid vs. favipiravir in fatal cases ($p < 0.015$, R = 0.200).

3.5. Multivariate Analysis of Variance for Determining Significant Variants

A multivariate analysis of variance revealed that age ($p > 0.001$), diabetes ($p < 0.005$), hypertension ($p < 0.005$), remdesivir ($p < 0.001$), favipiravir ($p < 0.001$), imipenem ($p < 0.001$), and linezolid ($p < 0.004$) significantly affected the mortality rate of patients with severe forms of COVID-19 (Table 4). The younger the age, the lower the morality rate, and the older the age, the higher the mortality rate. COVID-19 patients suffering from the comorbidities of diabetes and hypertension were at a higher risk of increased mortality rate. Remdesivir use was associated with a significant reduction in the mortality rate, while favipiravir use was associated with increased mortality among patients with severe COVID-19. Increased mortalities were detected when treating severe COVID-19 patients with imipenem, meropenem, linezolid, and moxifloxacin (Table 3). However, according to the multivariate analysis results, only imipenem ($p < 0.001$) and linezolid ($p < 0.004$) were associated with an increased mortality rate (Table 4).

Table 4. Multivariate test of different variables and their effects on the survival rate in patients with severe forms of COVID-19.

Variables	Type III Sum of Squares	df	Mean Square	F	Sig.
Age	107.580	1	107.580	53.409	0.001
Sex	0.355	1	0.355	1.525	0.218
Diabetes	1.810	1	1.810	7.989	0.005
Hypertension	1.922	1	1.922	7.931	0.005
Cardiac diseases	0.124	1	0.124	0.647	0.422
Cancer	0.050	1	0.050	1.619	0.205
Antiviral	0.048	1	0.048	0.358	0.550
Remdesivir	5.343	1	5.343	79.318	0.001
Favipiravir	4.002	1	4.002	17.332	0.001
Tamiflu	0.024	1	0.024	0.529	0.468
Favipiravir and Tamiflu	0.557	1	0.557	1.340	0.249
Remdesivir and favipiravir	4.655	1	4.655	1.510	0.221
Antibiotics	0.013	1	0.013	0.793	0.374
Azithromycin	0.007	1	0.007	0.087	0.768
Ceftriaxone	0.197	1	0.197	1.268	0.262
Vancomycin	0.005	1	0.005	0.022	0.881
Levofloxacin	0.175	1	0.175	1.101	0.296
Tienam	0.050	1	0.050	1.619	0.205
Amikacin	0.004	1	0.004	0.091	0.763
Imipenem	3.062	1	3.062	13.850	0.001
Ciprofloxacin	0.093	1	0.093	1.443	0.231
Cefipime	0.089	1	0.089	2.189	0.141
Meropenem	0.070	1	0.070	0.447	0.505
Tazocin	0.001	1	0.001	0.045	0.833
Moxifloxacin	0.004	1	0.004	0.014	0.906
Linezolid	1.812	1	1.812	8.278	0.004
Clindamycin	0.022	1	0.022	1.064	0.304
Dexamethasone	0.288	1	0.288	2.211	0.139
Anti-IL6	0.024	1	0.024	0.529	0.468

4. Discussion

To date, four antiviral drugs have been FDA-approved for use in COVID-19 cases: veklury (remdesivir), approved on 22 October 2020; olumiant (baricitinib), approved on 10 May 2022; paxlovid (nirmatrelvir and ritonavir), approved on 22 December 2021; and lagevrio (molnupiravir), approved on 23 December 2021 [22]. Both veklury and olumiant are used in the treatment of severe COVID-19 cases. The former is used for intravenous administration in adults and children with an age of 12 years or higher, and it mainly prevents virus replication by inhibiting SARS-CoV-2 RdRp. Olumiant is an oral pill, which is a repurposed drug that possesses an anti-rheumatoid arthritis effect that reduces inflammation, together with having antiviral activity by preventing virus entry into target cells. In contrast, both paxlovid and lagevrio are used in mild-to-moderate COVID-19 cases. Paxlovid, an oral pill, contains two types of medications: nirmatrelvir (block virus replication) and ritonavir (protease inhibitor). Molnupiravir also inhibits RdRp by acting as a ribonucleoside analog for viral RNA polymerase [22]. Meanwhile, many drugs and potential drugs are available for SARS-CoV-2 treatment. Favipiravir (T-705) is a viral RNA polymerase inhibitor that was approved for marketing in Zhejiang Province, China, on 16 February 2020. Other drugs that were tested for their reactivities to SARS-CoV-2 either in vitro or in vivo included CQ and HCQ, ribavirin, penciclovir, nitazoxanide, and nafamostat [11,23]. Ivermectin, a repurposed drug found to possess antiviral activity against dengue fever [24], was also assumed to possess antiviral potential against SARS-CoV-2 [17,25].

In the current study, we compared different antivirals used in treating patients with severe COVID-19 in a retrospective manner. There was no correlation between the overall case fatality and the sex of the patients. High mortality rates in both sexes were detected in most age groups (41–93 years old), with a highly significant correlation between age and mortality rate. This finding agrees with previous studies in which COVID-19 mortality was found to be strongly dependent on age [26–28].

Remdesivir was the first FDA-approved drug for treating COVID-19 patients. In the current study, remdesivir successfully reduced the mortality rate in COVID-19 patients when used alone or in combination with favipiravir. Similarly, a study found at least a 7% reduction in the mortality rate of patients treated with both remdesivir and dexamethasone. The study tested 1694 individuals as a part of a national cohort [29]. In another study, remdesivir treatment resulted in a recovery rate of 74.4% in treated patients versus 59.0% in the non-treated group [30]. In contrast, a study supported by the WHO reported the lack of benefits of remdesivir compared to a placebo in the mortality rate [31].

Favipiravir is an oral drug that was approved by the Chinese FDA for use in clinical trials of COVID-19 patients in early 2020. It showed promising results, especially in patients with mild-to-moderate disease severity [32,33]. Its use reduced the hospitalization time, as well as the probability of deterioration in patients' diseased conditions by reducing the use of mechanical ventilation [32]. However, our study revealed that favipiravir could not reduce the mortality rate in COVID-19 patients with severe disease conditions. Our results agree with previous studies that confirmed the lack of a significant impact of favipiravir in patients in terms of improving their clinical condition and reducing the requirement of oxygen supplementation [34]. Our results also agree with a previous study that confirmed the lack of a satisfactory effect of favipiravir use on the mortality rate [32]. In the current study, oseltamivir, an antiviral against influenza A and B viruses, was not found to be effective in reducing the mortality rate in COVID-19 patients. Our finding agrees with many studies that confirmed the lack of beneficial effects of using oseltamivir in COVID-19 treatment [14,35–37].

Different antibiotic combinations were used in the COVID-19 patients in the current study. The use of azithromycin was not correlated with a reduced mortality rate in COVID-19 patients. Surprisingly, significantly high mortality rates were found when using either imipenem or linezolid. However, in such patients, no significant correlation was detected in their use along with the administration of antiviral drugs. Indeed, antibiotics can save the lives of critical COVID-19 patients; however, we found that fatal consequences in COVID-19 patients were not alleviated using antibiotics unless there was evidence of a secondary bacterial infection [38]. Accordingly, special care should be taken when using antibiotics to avoid the risk of developing resistant bacterial strains.

Furthermore, corticosteroids were used in the current study in most patients and were found to have a beneficial effect in reducing mortality. The WHO and the CDC recommend against the routine use of corticosteroids in patients with COVID-19-related pneumonia unless they are used for treating comorbidities such as asthma [39–41].

5. Conclusions

The current study confirms the benefit of using remdesivir in increasing the survival rate in severe cases of COVID-19. The finding that the use of certain antibiotics is associated with increased mortality needs further investigation. Although this study confirms the benefit of using remdesivir against COVID-19, it may vary with the cohort, age group, comorbidities, severity score, and initiation of antivirals post-infection.

6. Limitations

The patient groups in the current study were heterogeneous in regard to age, which ranged from 21 to 93 years, and sex (119 males and 69 females). The frequency of favipiravir use was higher in comparison to other antiviral drug regimens. There were some confounding results, especially with regard to missing laboratory or clinical information of some patients.

Author Contributions: Conceptualization, A.S.A.-M., M.E.M.M. and M.R.A.Y.; methodology, A.A.A. (Afrah A. Alharthi), A.S.O., N.M.A., A.A.A. (Ahad A Alnemari), A.A.A. (Amjad A. Alwagdani), R.K.A., R.A.A. and D.Y.K.; validation, M.E.M.M. and M.R.A.Y.; formal analysis, A.N.A., A.S.O. and D.Y.K.; investigation, A.A.A. (Afrah A. Alharthi), A.S.O., N.M.A., A.A.A. (Ahad A Alnemari), A.A.A. (Amjad A. Alwagdani), R.K.A. and R.A.A.; data curation, M.E.M.M., A.S.O. and D.Y.K.; writing—original draft preparation, M.E.M.M., D.Y.K. and A.S.O.; writing—review and editing, A.S.A.-M., supervision, M.R.A.Y., M.E.M.M. and A.S.A.-M.; project administration, M.E.M.M. and M.R.A.Y.; funding acquisition, A.N.A. All authors have read and agreed to the published version of the manuscript.

Funding: Taif University Researchers Supporting Program (TURSP-2020/284), Taif University, Taif 21944, Saudi Arabia.

Institutional Review Board Statement: The proposal was granted an ethical approval from No. 353 on 5 September 2021 from IRB of the Research and Studies Section- Directorate of Health Affairs, Taif, Saudi Arabia.

Informed Consent Statement: All study participants or their guardians have provided individual informed consent.

Data Availability Statement: All data are provided in the manuscript; however, any additional inquiries could be requested from the corresponding author.

Acknowledgments: The authors acknowledge the support by Taif University Researchers Supporting Program (TURSP-2020/284), Taif University, Taif 21944, Saudi Arabia.

Conflicts of Interest: The authors declare no conflict of interest.

References

1. Jiang, S.; Du, L.; Shi, Z. An emerging coronavirus causing pneumonia outbreak in Wuhan, China: Calling for developing therapeutic and prophylactic strategies. *Emerg. Microbes Infect.* **2020**, 9, 275–277. [CrossRef] [PubMed]
2. WHO. Coronavirus (COVID-19) Dashboard. Available online: https://covid19.who.int/ (accessed on 13 January 2023).
3. Somsen, G.A.; van Rijn, C.; Kooij, S.; Bem, R.A.; Bonn, D. Small droplet aerosols in poorly ventilated spaces and SARS-CoV-2 transmission. *Lancet Respir. Med.* **2020**, 8, 658–659. [CrossRef] [PubMed]
4. Kimball, A.; Hatfield, K.M.; Arons, M.; James, A.; Taylor, J.; Spicer, K.; Bardossy, A.C.; Oakley, L.P.; Tanwar, S.; Chisty, Z. Asymptomatic and presymptomatic SARS-CoV-2 infections in residents of a long-term care skilled nursing facility—King County, Washington, March 2020. *Morb. Mortal. Wkly. Rep.* **2020**, 69, 377. [CrossRef] [PubMed]
5. WHO. Living Guidance for Clinical Managment of COVID-19. COVID-19: Clinical Care. World Health Organization. 2021. Available online: https://www.who.int/publications/i/item/WHO-2019-nCoV-clinical-2021-2 (accessed on 23 November 2021).
6. Ciceri, F.; Beretta, L.; Scandroglio, A.M.; Colombo, S.; Landoni, G.; Ruggeri, A.; Peccatori, J.; D'Angelo, A.; De Cobelli, F.; Rovere-Querini, P.; et al. Microvascular COVID-19 lung vessels obstructive thromboinflammatory syndrome (MicroCLOTS): An atypical acute respiratory distress syndrome working hypothesis. *Crit. Care Resusc.* **2020**, 22, 95–97. [CrossRef]

7. Chinese-CDC. The epidemiological characteristics of an outbreak of 2019 novel coronavirus diseases (COVID-19) in China. *Zhonghua Liu Xing Bing Xue Za Zhi* **2020**, *41*, 145–151. [CrossRef]
8. Riphagen, S.; Gomez, X.; Gonzalez-Martinez, C.; Wilkinson, N.; Theocharis, P. Hyperinflammatory shock in children during COVID-19 pandemic. *Lancet* **2020**, *395*, 1607–1608. [CrossRef]
9. Alqahtani, J.S.; Oyelade, T.; Aldhahir, A.M.; Alghamdi, S.M.; Almehmadi, M.; Alqahtani, A.S.; Quaderi, S.; Mandal, S.; Hurst, J.R. Prevalence, severity and mortality associated with copd and smoking in patients with COVID-19: A rapid systematic review and meta-analysis. *PLoS ONE* **2020**, *15*, e0233147. [CrossRef]
10. Beigel, J.H.; Tomashek, K.M.; Dodd, L.E.; Mehta, A.K.; Zingman, B.S.; Kalil, A.C.; Hohmann, E.; Chu, H.Y.; Luetkemeyer, A.; Kline, S.; et al. Remdesivir for the treatment of COVID-19—Final report. *N. Engl. J. Med.* **2020**, *383*, 1813–1826. [CrossRef]
11. Abdel-Moneim, A.S.; Abdelwhab, E.M.; Memish, Z.A. Insights into SARS-CoV-2 evolution, potential antivirals, and vaccines. *Virology* **2021**, *558*, 1–12. [CrossRef]
12. Shrestha, D.B.; Budhathoki, P.; Khadka, S.; Shah, P.B.; Pokharel, N.; Rashmi, P. Favipiravir versus other antiviral or standard of care for COVID-19 treatment: A rapid systematic review and meta-analysis. *Virol. J.* **2020**, *17*, 141. [CrossRef]
13. Zendehdel, A.; Bidkhori, M.; Ansari, M.; Jamalimoghaddamsiyahkali, S.; Asoodeh, A. Efficacy of oseltamivir in the treatment of patients infected with Covid-19. *Ann. Med. Surg.* **2022**, *77*, 103679. [CrossRef] [PubMed]
14. Sanders, J.M.; Monogue, M.L.; Jodlowski, T.Z.; Cutrell, J.B. Pharmacologic treatments for coronavirus disease 2019 (COVID-19): A review. *JAMA* **2020**, *323*, 1824–1836. [CrossRef] [PubMed]
15. Prayuenyong, P.; Kasbekar, A.V.; Baguley, D.M. Clinical implications of chloroquine and hydroxychloroquine ototoxicity for COVID-19 treatment: A mini-review. *Front. Public Health* **2020**, *8*, 252. [CrossRef] [PubMed]
16. Caly, L.; Druce, J.D.; Catton, M.G.; Jans, D.A.; Wagstaff, K.M. The FDA-approved drug ivermectin inhibits the replication of SARS-CoV-2 in vitro. *Antiviral. Res.* **2020**, *178*, 104787. [CrossRef] [PubMed]
17. Eweas, A.F.; Alhossary, A.A.; Abdel-Moneim, A.S. Molecular docking reveals ivermectin and remdesivir as potential repurposed drugs against SARS-COV-2. *Front. Microbiol.* **2020**, *11*, 592908. [CrossRef] [PubMed]
18. Budhathoki, P.; Shrestha, D.B.; Rawal, E.; Khadka, S. Corticosteroids in COVID-19: Is it rational? A systematic review and meta-analysis. *SN Compr. Clin. Med.* **2020**, *2*, 2600–2620. [CrossRef]
19. Parnham, M.J.; Haber, V.E.; Giamarellos-Bourboulis, E.J.; Perletti, G.; Verleden, G.M.; Vos, R. Azithromycin: Mechanisms of action and their relevance for clinical applications. *Pharmacol. Ther.* **2014**, *143*, 225–245. [CrossRef]
20. Wright, A.J. The penicillins. *Mayo Clin. Proc.* **1999**, *74*, 290–307. [CrossRef]
21. NIH. Clinical Spectrum of SARS-CoV-2 Infection. NIH. 2021. Available online: https://www.covid19treatmentguidelines.nih.gov/overview/clinical-spectrum/ (accessed on 19 October 2021).
22. FDA. Coronavirus-COVID-19-Drugs. FDA, USA. 2022. Available online: https://www.fda.gov/drugs/emergency-preparedness-drugs/coronavirus-covid-19-drugs (accessed on 22 December 2022).
23. Wang, M.; Cao, R.; Zhang, L.; Yang, X.; Liu, J.; Xu, M.; Shi, Z.; Hu, Z.; Zhong, W.; Xiao, G. Remdesivir and chloroquine effectively inhibit the recently emerged novel coronavirus (2019-nCoV) in vitro. *Cell Res.* **2020**, *30*, 269–271. [CrossRef]
24. Tay, M.Y.; Fraser, J.E.; Chan, W.K.; Moreland, N.J.; Rathore, A.P.; Wang, C.; Vasudevan, S.G.; Jans, D.A. Nuclear localization of dengue virus (DENV) 1-4 non-structural protein 5; protection against all 4 DENV serotypes by the inhibitor Ivermectin. *Antivir. Res.* **2013**, *99*, 301–306. [CrossRef]
25. Lehrer, S.; Rheinstein, P.H. Ivermectin Docks to the SARS-CoV-2 Spike Receptor-binding Domain Attached to ACE2. *In Vivo* **2020**, *34*, 3023–3026. [CrossRef] [PubMed]
26. Bauer, P.; Brugger, J.; König, F.; Posch, M. An international comparison of age and sex dependency of COVID-19 deaths in 2020: A descriptive analysis. *Sci. Rep.* **2021**, *11*, 19143. [CrossRef] [PubMed]
27. Biswas, M.; Rahaman, S.; Biswas, T.K.; Haque, Z.; Ibrahim, B. Association of sex, age, and comorbidities with mortality in COVID-19 patients: A systematic review and meta-analysis. *Intervirology* **2020**, *64*, 1–12. [CrossRef] [PubMed]
28. Abdelsalam, M.; Althaqafi, R.M.M.; Assiri, S.A.; Althagafi, T.M.; Althagafi, S.M.; Fouda, A.Y.; Ramadan, A.; Rabah, M.; Ahmed, R.M.; Ibrahim, Z.S.; et al. Clinical and laboratory findings of COVID-19 in high-altitude inhabitants of Saudi Arabia. *Front. Med.* **2021**, *8*, 670195. [CrossRef] [PubMed]
29. Benfield, T.; Bodilsen, J.; Brieghel, C.; Harboe, Z.B.; Helleberg, M.; Holm, C.; Israelsen, S.B.; Jensen, J.; Jensen, T.; Johansen, I.S.; et al. Improved survival among hospitalized patients with coronavirus disease 2019 (COVID-19) treated with remdesivir and dexamethasone. A nationwide population-based cohort study. *Clin. Infect. Dis.* **2021**, *73*, 2031–2036. [CrossRef]
30. Olender, S.A.; Perez, K.K.; Go, A.S.; Balani, B.; Price-Haywood, E.G.; Shah, N.S.; Wang, S.; Walunas, T.L.; Swaminathan, S.; Slim, J.; et al. Remdesivir for severe coronavirus disease 2019 (COVID-19) versus a cohort receiving standard of care. *Clin. Infect. Dis.* **2021**, *73*, e4166–e4174. [CrossRef]
31. Pan, H.; Peto, R.; Henao-Restrepo, A.M.; Preziosi, M.P.; Sathiyamoorthy, V.; Abdool Karim, Q.; Alejandria, M.M.; Hernández García, C.; Kieny, M.P.; Malekzadeh, R.; et al. Repurposed antiviral drugs for COVID-19—Interim WHO solidarity trial results. *N. Engl. J. Med.* **2021**, *384*, 497–511. [CrossRef]
32. Alamer, A.; Alrashed, A.A.; Alfaifi, M.; Alosaimi, B.; AlHassar, F.; Almutairi, M.; Howaidi, J.; Almutairi, W.; Mohzari, Y.; Sulaiman, T.; et al. Effectiveness and safety of favipiravir compared to supportive care in moderately to critically ill COVID-19 patients: A retrospective study with propensity score matching sensitivity analysis. *Curr. Med. Res. Opin.* **2021**, *37*, 1085–1097. [CrossRef]

33. Udwadia, Z.F.; Singh, P.; Barkate, H.; Patil, S.; Rangwala, S.; Pendse, A.; Kadam, J.; Wu, W.; Caracta, C.F.; Tandon, M. Efficacy and safety of favipiravir, an oral RNA-dependent RNA polymerase inhibitor, in mild-to-moderate COVID-19: A randomized, comparative, open-label, multicenter, phase 3 clinical trial. *Int. J. Infect. Dis.* **2021**, *103*, 62–71. [CrossRef] [PubMed]
34. Özlüşen, B.; Kozan, Ş.; Akcan, R.E.; Kalender, M.; Yaprak, D.; Peltek, İ.B.; Keske, Ş.; Gönen, M.; Ergönül, Ö. Effectiveness of favipiravir in COVID-19: A live systematic review. *Eur. J. Clin. Microbiol. Infect. Dis.* **2021**, *40*, 2575–2583. [CrossRef]
35. Ramatillah, D.L.; Isnaini, S. Treatment profiles and clinical outcomes of COVID-19 patients at private hospital in Jakarta. *PLoS ONE* **2021**, *16*, e0250147. [CrossRef] [PubMed]
36. WHO. *Clinical Management of Severe Acute Respiratory Infection (SARI) when COVID-19 Disease Is Suspected: Interim Guidance*; World Health Organization: Geneva, Switzerland, 2020.
37. Tobaiqy, M.; Qashqary, M.; Al-Dahery, S.; Mujallad, A.; Hershan, A.A.; Kamal, M.A.; Helmi, N. Therapeutic management of patients with COVID-19: A systematic review. *Infect. Prev. Pract.* **2020**, *2*, 100061. [CrossRef] [PubMed]
38. Popp, M.; Stegemann, M.; Riemer, M.; Metzendorf, M.I.; Romero, C.S.; Mikolajewska, A.; Kranke, P.; Meybohm, P.; Skoetz, N.; Weibel, S. Antibiotics for the treatment of COVID-19. *Cochrane Database Syst. Rev.* **2021**, *10*, Cd015025. [CrossRef] [PubMed]
39. Russell, C.D.; Millar, J.E.; Baillie, J.K. Clinical evidence does not support corticosteroid treatment for 2019-nCoV lung injury. *Lancet* **2020**, *395*, 473–475. [CrossRef]
40. Lamontagne, F.; Rochwerg, B.; Lytvyn, L.; Guyatt, G.H.; Møller, M.H.; Annane, D.; Kho, M.E.; Adhikari, N.K.; Machado, F.; Vandvik, P.O. Corticosteroid therapy for sepsis: A clinical practice guideline. *BMJ* **2018**, *362*, k3284. [CrossRef]
41. Sterne, J.A.C.; Murthy, S.; Diaz, J.V.; Slutsky, A.S.; Villar, J.; Angus, D.C.; Annane, D.; Azevedo, L.C.P.; Berwanger, O.; Cavalcanti, A.B.; et al. Association between administration of systemic corticosteroids and mortality among critically ill patients with COVID-19: A meta-analysis. *JAMA* **2020**, *324*, 1330–1341. [CrossRef]

Disclaimer/Publisher's Note: The statements, opinions and data contained in all publications are solely those of the individual author(s) and contributor(s) and not of MDPI and/or the editor(s). MDPI and/or the editor(s) disclaim responsibility for any injury to people or property resulting from any ideas, methods, instructions or products referred to in the content.

medicina

MDPI

Article

Adherence to the Mediterranean Diet Association with Serum Inflammatory Factors Stress Oxidative and Appetite in COVID-19 Patients

Mahsa Mohajeri [1,*], Reza Mohajery [2] and Arrigo F. G. Cicero [3,4,*]

[1] Digestive Disease Research Center, Ardabil University of Medical Sciences, Ardabil 56189-85991, Iran
[2] Energy Management Research Center, University of Mohaghegh Ardabili, Ardabil 56199-11367, Iran
[3] Medicine and Surgery Sciences Department, Alma Mater Studiorum University of Bologna, 40126 Bologna, Italy
[4] IRCCS AOU S. Orsola-Malpighi University Hospital, 40138 Bologna, Italy
[*] Correspondence: mahsa.mohajeri.93@gmail.com (M.M.); arrigo.cicero@unibo.it (A.F.G.C.); Tel.: +98-9143592794 (M.M.); +39-512142224 (A.F.G.C.)

Abstract: *Background and Objectives:* The Mediterranean diet's bioactive components are suggested to strengthen the immune system and to exert anti-inflammatory actions. This study investigated the association between adherence to the Mediterranean diet with serum inflammatory factors, total antioxidant capacity, appetite, and symptoms of COVID-19 patients. *Materials and Methods:* This cross-sectional study was conducted among 600 Iranian COVID-19 patients selected by a simple random method. The ten-item Mediterranean diet adherence questionnaire was used to assess diet adherence. At the beginning of the study, 5 cc of blood was taken from all patients for measurement of serum interleukin 1β) IL-1β), tumor necrosis factor (TNF-α), malondialdehyde (MDA), high sensitivity C-reactive protein (hs-CRP) and total antioxidant capacity (TAC). A human ELISA kit with serial number 950.090.096 produced by the Diaclone Company was used to test this cytokine using the sandwich ELISA method. *Results:* One hundred and five patients presented a high adherence and 495 patients presented a low adherence to the Mediterranean diet. The incidence of fever, cough, diarrhea, taste changes, and pneumonia severity index were significantly lower in patients who adhered to the Mediterranean diet more than other patients. Serum levels of tumor necrosis factor (5.7 ± 2.1 vs. 6.9 ± 2.8 p = 0.02), interleukin 1 beta (3.2 ± 0.02 vs. 4.9 ± 0.01 p = 0.02), high-sensitivity C-reactive protein (17.08 ± 4.2 vs. 19.8 ± 2.5 p = 0.03), and malondialdehyde (5.7 ± 0.2 vs. 6.2 ± 0.3 p = 0.02) were significantly lower in patients who adhered more to the Mediterranean diet than other patients. *Conclusion:* The Mediterranean diet can improve the symptoms and elevated serum inflammatory factors in COVID-19 patients, so clinical trial studies are suggested to confirm this effect.

Keywords: mediterranean diet; inflammatory factors; stress oxidative; appetite; COVID-19

Citation: Mohajeri, M.; Mohajery, R.; Cicero, A.F.G. Adherence to the Mediterranean Diet Association with Serum Inflammatory Factors Stress Oxidative and Appetite in COVID-19 Patients. *Medicina* **2023**, *59*, 227. https://doi.org/10.3390/medicina59020227

Academic Editors: Yusra Habib Khan, Tauqeer Hussain Mallhi, Tahir Mehmood Khan and Muhammad Salman

Received: 25 December 2022
Revised: 18 January 2023
Accepted: 22 January 2023
Published: 26 January 2023

Copyright: © 2023 by the authors. Licensee MDPI, Basel, Switzerland. This article is an open access article distributed under the terms and conditions of the Creative Commons Attribution (CC BY) license (https://creativecommons.org/licenses/by/4.0/).

1. Introduction

COVID-19 was identified as a pandemic by the World Health Organization on 11 March 2020 [1]. Optimizing] respiratory functioning is the major strategy, particularly in cases where the lower respiratory tract is involved [2,3]. The development of COVID-19 may be greatly influenced by inflammatory responses, according to the last studies' results [4,5]. Rapid SARS-CoV-2 viral multiplication, cellular damage, and inflammatory responses can attract macrophages and monocytes and cause the production of cytokines and chemokines [6–8]. Cytokine storms and aggravations are induced following the attraction of immune cells and activation of immunological responses by these cytokines and chemokines. Several inflammatory indicators can be used to track and identify illness severity and mortality with some degree of accuracy. The high risks of developing severe COVID-19 are strongly associated with inflammatory markers such as procalcitonin

(PCT), serum ferritin, erythrocyte sedimentation rate (ESR), C-reactive protein (CRP), and interleukin-6 (IL-6) [9,10]. Furthermore, it has been demonstrated that elevated serum amyloid A (SAA) levels play a role in the pathogenesis of COVID-19 and may be used as a biomarker to track the course of the illness. However, these findings are still debatable because other studies have not shown a change in the levels of IL-6, SAA, ESR, or CRP [11–14].

The Mediterranean diet (MD) is distinguished by a high intake of fruits, nuts, vegetables, legumes, and cereals (which in the past were largely unrefined), a high intake of olive oil but a low intake of saturated lipids, a moderately high intake of fish (depending on the proximity of the sea), a low-to-moderate intake of dairy products (and then mostly in the form of cheese or yogurt), a low intake of meat and poultry [15,16]. It is because of the preventive impact that the MD exhibits against a variety of chronic illnesses, including a beneficial effect on overall mortality, cardiovascular disease, and certain cancers, that high adherence to it has been associated with a higher health status [17,18]. The MD has also been suggested as one of the factors influencing these populations' lifespans. The metabolic syndrome (MetS), certain of its components, and type 2 diabetes have been demonstrated to be negatively correlated with following a healthy eating pattern such as MD [19–21]. Due to the nutritious nature of this food pattern, it can also be effective in strengthening the immune system and preventing and controlling infectious diseases. An increasing body of research indicates that the MD's anti-inflammatory qualities may contribute, at least in part, to its protective benefits [22–24].

Considering the importance of dietary pattern's role in the prevention and control of COVID-19 complications, this study investigated the relationship between adherence to the Mediterranean diet and dietary inflammatory factors, appetite, and oxidative stress in COVID-19 patients.

2. Materials and Methods

2.1. Study Participants

This cross-sectional study was conducted among 600 COVID-19 patients aged ≥30 years old in Iranian hospitals. Sampling was carried out by a simple random method and using patient file numbers. Six hundred adult patients that met the inclusion criteria out of a total of 670 COVID-19 patients were enrolled in the research (Figure 1). The study included patients who were referred to the COVID-19 outpatient clinics of the Iranian hospital between January 2022 and March, having both calculated tomography (CT) scans of the thorax displaying moderate or severe involvement of the lower respiratory tract (as per radiologist diagnosis), and positive real-time reverse transcriptase–polymerase chain reaction (RT-PCR) tests in oro-nasopharyngeal swab samples. Patients with COVID-19 who had particular diseases, such as chronic liver or kidney diseases, or who were hesitant to participate in the study were excluded. Control patients with chronic diseases other than the skin-ones were also excluded from the study.

The study was conducted according to the guidelines of the Declaration of Helsinki and approved by the Ethics Committee of the Ardabil University of Medicine Sciences on 17 January 2022 (IR.ARUMS.REC.1400.293). Informed consent was obtained from all subjects involved in the study. Written informed consent has been obtained from the patients to publish this paper.

2.2. Biochemical Measurements

At the beginning of the study, 5 cc of blood was taken from all patients for measurement of serum interleukin 1β) IL-1β), tumor necrosis factor (TNF-α), malondialdehyde (MDA), high sensitivity C-reactive protein (hs-CRP) and total antioxidant capacity (TAC). A human ELISA kit with serial number 950.090.096 produced by the Diaclone Company, Besançon, Frane, was used to test this cytokine using the sandwich ELISA method.

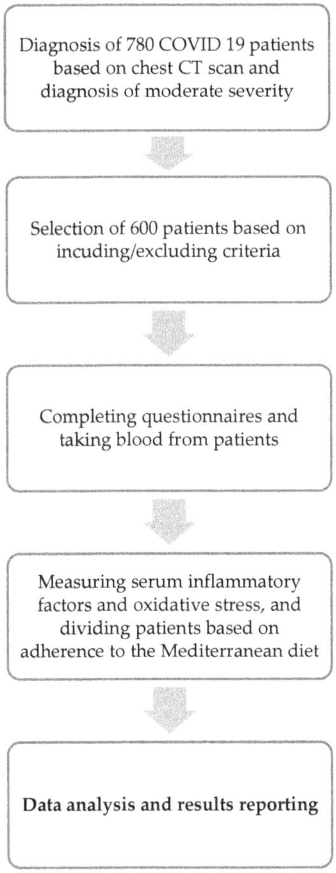

Figure 1. Study flow diagram.

RANDOX's RANSOM kit was utilized by the suggested procedure to assess the total antioxidant capacity employing spectrophotometry on an Abbot auto-analyzer at 600 nm. A particular substrate is incubated with peroxidase and hydrogen peroxide to form a radical substrate cation, which results in a persistent green-blue color that can be detected at a wavelength of 600 nm. This is the foundation for the measurement. The TAC is expressed in mmol/L. Immunoturbidimetric employed the Pars test diagnostic kit to measure the hs-CRP protein. Following the kit's instruction manual, 200 L of reagent 2 comprising mouse monoclonal and goat polyclonal antibodies against human CRP antibody was added after placing 20 L of serum and 200 L of reagent 1 at 37 °C for 5 min. With the Abbot auto-analyzer set to 500 nm in mg/L, absorption was recorded at 30 and 90 s. Using kits from Bender Medical Systems, interleukins 1 were quantified by ELISA (Vienna, Austria).

2.3. *Appetite Assessment*

A subjective assessment and an objective indicator for measuring appetite were taken into consideration in this study. To measure a subject's sensations of hunger, desire to eat, and the likelihood of intake and fullness, a visual analog scale (VAS) was utilized (for subjective parameters). Food greasiness was added to the VAS to gauge the degree of food greasiness. To measure the experience before or after eating, a scale of 0 to 10 was used; the greater the number, the stronger the sensation. The subjects were in charge of their own experience.

2.4. Mediterranean Dietary Pattern Assessment

To calculate adherence to the MD, the ten-item, ten-point MEDAS (Mediterranean Diet Adherence Screener) [25], which has been scientifically verified, was used. With the use of the MEDAS questionnaire, the level of adherence to the MD was scored. Participants in the research were split into two groups based on their MEDAS scores: those who adhered to the MD less frequently (0–9) and those who adhered more frequently (10+). The frequency and proportion of replies that were positive to consuming each food were summed.

2.5. Statistical Analysis

Statistical analyses were performed with STATA Version 14.0 for windows. All continuous variables were reported as the mean ± standard deviation. Inflammatory markers were compared between groups of adherence to the MD. Differences between group means were tested using an independent T-test. The Association between inflammatory markers and adherence to the MD was also assessed using multivariate regression. In all analyses, a p-value, of less than 0.05 was considered statically significant. Due to the difference in the study groups sample sizes, to validate the results of the T-test, the means difference of the variables and the confidence interval of all the variables were checked.

3. Results

Table 1 shows the general characteristics of the participants. None of the enrolled patients was vaccinated before infection. The mean ± SD of study patients was 52.9 ± 6.8 years old. Fifty percent of patients were male and 49% were female.

Table 1. Demographic characteristics of the study patients.

Variables	Mean ± SD	Men N = 305	Women N = 295	p *
Age (y)	52.9 ± 6.8	51.8 ± 3.4	51.6 ± 6.4	0.08
Body mass index (Kg/m^2)	29.5 ± 2.3	30.2 ± 2.8	28.4 ± 3.9	0.02
Smoking (%)	15 (35.83%)	215 (72.88%)	0	0.01 [&]

*: Based on independent T-test [&]: Based on chi-square test.

In Table 2, the results of positive answers to the MEDAS questionnaire are shown. In terms of positive response to the regular consumption of olive oil (97 vs. 67 p = 0.04), fruits (105 vs. 89 p = 0.04), vegetables (103 vs. 94 p = 0.02), legumes (104 vs. 79 p = 0.01), and fish/sea foods (101 vs. 61 p = 0.02), there was a significant difference between people who adhere more to the Mediterranean diet and people with less adherence to the Mediterranean diet.

The status of symptoms and complications of COVID-19 based on the level of adherence to the Mediterranean diet is shown in Table 3.

The incidence of fever [50 (47.6%) vs. 482 (92.5) p = 0.02], cough [38 (36.1%) vs. 380 (76.7), p = 0.01], dyspnea [62 (59.04) vs. 392 (79.1) p = 0.02], diarrhea [44 (41.9) vs. 280 (56.5) p = 0.02], taste changes [23 (21.9) vs. 365 (73.7), p = 0.05], blood pressure and pneumonia severity index [70.4 ± 6.3 vs. 73.4 ± 2.4, p = 0.04] were significantly lower in patients who adhered to the Mediterranean diet more than in patients with less adherence.

The results related to the comparison of appetite in the study patients are shown in Table 4. The amount of desire to eat was higher in patients with more adherence to the Mediterranean diet than in patients with low adherence (60% vs. 23% p = 0.02). About 31% of patients with greater adherence to the Mediterranean diet rarely felt full after eating, while only about 8% of patients with low adherence to the Mediterranean diet tended to eat more food after the main meal.

Table 2. Positive answers to the MEDAS questionnaire.

	Low Adherence to MD (*N* = 495)		High Adherence to MD (*N* = 105)		*p*
Olive oil, the main dressing	68	(13.73%)	98	(93.33%)	0.01
Olive oil, 4 ts/day	67	(13.53%)	97	(92.38%)	0.04
Vegetables, 2 s/day	94	(18.98%)	103	(98.09%)	0.02 *
Fruits, 3 s/day	89	(17.97%)	105	(88.57%)	0.04 *
Red meat, <1 s/day	95	(19.19%)	93	(88.57%)	0.07
Butter, <1 s/day	82	(16.56%)	81	(77.14%)	0.07
Sweet beverage, <1 s/day	89	(17.97%)	104	(99.04%)	0.05 *
Legumes, 3 s/week	79	(15.59%)	104	(99.04%)	0.01 *
Fish and seafood, 3 s/week	61	(12.32%)	101	(96.19%)	0.02
Sweets, <3 s/week	101	(20.40%)	102	(97.14%)	0.06
Nuts, 3/week	88	(17.77%)	104	(99.04%)	0.01 *
White meat over red	102	(20.60%)	104	(99.04%)	0.06

Notes: Positive answers to the MEDAS questionnaire. Data are expressed as numbers and percentages in parenthesis [n (%)] for categorical variables. Vegetables daily serving: 1 medium portion = 200 g; fruit daily serving: 1 serving = 100–150 g portion; red meat/hamburgers/other meat daily serving: 1 medium portion = 100–150 g; butter, margarine, or cream daily serving: 1 medium portion = 12 g; sweet or sugar-sweetened carbonated beverages daily serving: 1 medium portion = 200 mL; legumes weekly serving: 1 portion = 150 g; fish daily serving: 1 medium portion = 100–150 g; seafood daily serving: 1 medium portion = 200 g; nuts weekly serving: 1 portion of dairy product = 30 g. MEDAS: Mediterranean diet adherence screener; MD: Mediterranean diet; s: serving; ts: tablespoon; *: $p < 0.05$.

Table 3. Symptoms of COVID-19 in study participants according to adherence to the MD.

Symptoms	High Adherence *N* = 105 (%)	Low Adherence *N* = 495 (%)	*p* *
Fever	50 (47.6%)	482 (92.5%)	0.02
Cough	38 (36.1%)	380 (76.7%)	0.01
Dyspnea	62 (59.04%)	392 (79.1%)	0.02
Fatigue	98 (93.3%)	421 (85.05%)	0.03
Taste/smell abnormalities	23 (21.9%)	365 (73.7%)	0.05
Diarrhea	44 (41.9%)	280 (56.5%)	0.02
Systolic BP (mmHg) Mean ± SD	102.2 ± 12.1	120.3 ± 10.5	0.04 #
Diastolic BP (mmHg) Mean ± SD	77.3 ± 12.1	81.2 ± 9.8	0.01 #
Heart rate (/min) Mean ± SD	88.6 ± 4.2	87.9 ± 2.3	0.09 #
Respiratory rate (/min) Mean ± SD	18.6 ± 2.9	18.5 ± 2.9	0.8 #
Pneumonia Severity Index Mean ± SD	70.4 ± 6.3	73.4 ± 2.4	0.04 #

*: Based on chi-square test #: based on independent T-test.

The status of serum inflammatory markers in COVID-19 patients according to adherence to the MD has been shown in Table 5. Serum levels of TNF-α (5.7 ± 2.1 vs. 6.9 ± 2.8 $p = 0.02$), interleukin 1 beta (3.2 ± 0.02 vs. 4.9 ± 0.01 $p = 0.02$), hs-CRP (17.08 ± 4.2 vs. 19.8 ± 2.5 $p = 0.03$), and MDA (5.7 ± 0.2 vs. 6.2 ± 0.3 $p = 0.02$) were significantly lower in patients who adhered more to the Mediterranean diet than other patients. The level of serum total antioxidant capacity in patients with greater adherence to the Mediterranean diet (0.8 ± 0.02) was significantly higher than in other patients (0.6 ± 0.04) ($p = 0.04$).

Table 4. Comparison of appetite according to adherence to the MD.

Variables	High Adherence $N = 105$ N (%)	Low Adherence $N = 495$ N (%)	p *
Desire to eat	63 (60%)	114 (23%)	0.02
Satiety time after eating			
After eating a few tablespoons to a third of a plate	35 (33%)	248 (50.10%)	
After eating half of all the food served	30 (25.57%)	206 (41.61%)	
Rarely satiated	40 (30.09%)	41 (8.28%)	0.01
Time of feeling hungry			
Never	18 (3.63%)	283 (51.17%)	
Low and sometimes	49 (65.71%)	104 (21.01%)	0.03
The whole day	38 (36.19%)	108 (21.81%)	
Patients' opinions about the taste of food			
Bad and very bad	14 (13.33%)	264 (53.33%)	
Moderate	28 (26.66%)	181 (36.59%)	0.01
Good and very good	42 (63%)	50 (10.10%)	

*: Based on the chi-square test.

Table 5. Status of serum inflammatory markers in COVID-19 patients according to adherence to the MD.

Adherence to MD (%)	TNF-α pg/mL	Hs-CRP Mg/L	MDA μM/L	TAC Mm/L	Interleukin 1 Beta (pg/mL)
High adherence $N = 105$ (%)	5.7 ± 2.1	17.08 ± 4.2	5.7 ± 0.2	0.8 ± 0.02	3.2 ± 0.02
Low adherence $N = 495$ (%)	6.9 ± 2.8	19.8 ± 2.5	6.2 ± 0.3	0.6 ± 0.04	4.9 ± 0.01
p *	0.02	0.03	0.02	0.04	0.02

*: Based on independent T-test.

Table 6 shows the association of adherence to the MD with inflammatory markers in COVID-19 patients. There was a significant negative association between adherence to the Mediterranean diet and serum inflammatory factors in COVID-19 patients. The serum TNF-α in patients with more adherence to the MD was 1.32 units less than in other patients (coeff. = −1.32, $p = 0.02$). The serum level of hs-CRP in patients who adhered more to the Mediterranean diet was 1.89 units less than in other patients (coeff. = −1.89, $p = 0.01$). More adherence to the Mediterranean diet leads to a decrease of 1.34 units in the serum level of MDA (coeff. = −1.34, $p = 0.04$) and 1.08 units (coeff. = −1.08, $p = 0.04$) in the serum level of interleukin-1 beta in COVID-19 patients. The total antioxidant capacity in patients with greater adherence to the Mediterranean diet was 2.04 units higher than in other patients (coeff. = 2.04, $p = 0.03$).

Table 6. The association of adherence to the MD with inflammatory markers in COVID-19 patients.

Dependent Variables	Coeff.	95% CI	p *
TNF-α	−1.32	−1.28, −1.38	0.02
Hs-CRP	−1.89	−1.76, −1.92	0.01
MDA	−1.34	−1.22, −1.48	0.04
TAC	2.04	1.98, 2.14	0.03
Interleukin 1 beta	−1.08	−1.02, −1.15	0.04

*: Based on multivariate regression, adjusted to age and gender.

Considering the intake of some specific food classes, the adherence of men to the Mediterranean diet is significantly lower than the one of interviewed women ($p \leq 0.05$) (Figure 2). At the same time, the serum levels of the measured inflammatory parameters was significantly higher in men than in women ($p \leq 0.05$), in particular in subjects non-adherent to the Mediterranean diet (Figure 3).

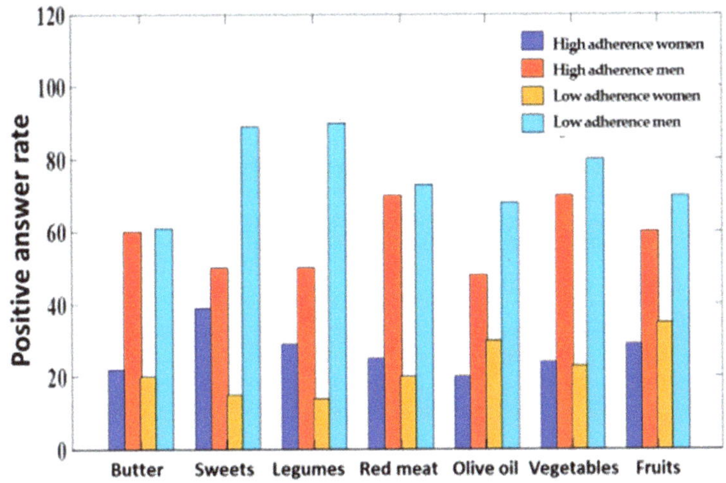

Figure 2. Self-reported dietary food class intake (Mediterranean diet questionnaire) in men and women involved in the study.

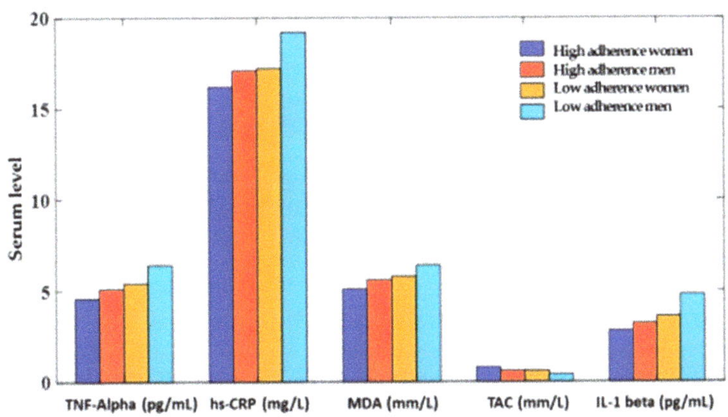

Figure 3. Serum level of inflammatory factors and total antioxidant capacity in study men and women.

4. Discussion

For the first time, this study has shown that adherence to the Mediterranean diet has a significant negative relationship with the symptoms of COVID-19 and serum inflammatory markers among COVID-19 patients. Given the scientific plausibility supporting the positive benefits of an appropriate food intake on the immune system, it is hypothesized that a high-quality dietary pattern may offer protection against COVID-19. However, there is still little information about the association between long-term, sustained good food habits, such as the Mediterranean diet, and the risk of SARS-CoV-2 infection. Barrea et al. [26] pointed out the importance of the Mediterranean diet in improving the health of patients with COVID-19. He pointed out that the presence of olives, olive oil, fruits, and vegetables in this food pattern is one of the important things that affect the recovery process of COVID-19 patients. In another study, Greene et al. [27] examined the association between adherence to a Mediterranean diet and COVID-19 cases and deaths using an ecological study design. They observed that Mediterranean diet adherence was negatively associated with both COVID-19 cases and related deaths across 17 regions in Spain and that the relationship remained when adjusted for factors of well-being. They also observed a negative association between Mediterranean diet adherence and COVID-19-related deaths across 23 countries when adjusted for factors of well-being and physical inactivity. The anti-inflammatory properties of the Mediterranean diet are likely due to the polyphenol content of this diet. The study mentioned that there are confounding factors unrelated to dietary factors driving COVID-19 cases and related deaths. Perez-Araluce et al. [28] indicated that people with intermediate adherence to the Mediterranean diet had less risk of developing COVID-19. Another review study conducted by Anna Lucia Fedullo [29] showed that following the Mediterranean diet before and throughout pregnancy may have a protective impact by lowering gestational diabetes mellitus and gestational weight gain and enhancing the immune system's response to viral infections such as as COVID-19. Inverse relationships have been shown between respiratory disorders, inflammation, and thrombosis with the Mediterranean diet, which includes olive oil, fish, honey, fruits, vegetables, and herbs. It is probable that a phytochemical mixture, such as those found in the Mediterranean diet, has stronger effects than a single molecule. It was indicated that chronic disease patients who follow a Mediterranean diet, as a whole, experience less PAF-induced platelet aggregation. The Mediterranean diet has been mentioned as a possible COVID-19 preventive diet, and it is stated that following this dietary pattern reduces mortality and duration of stay in hospital in patients $\geq$60 years old [30–33].

The increased serum levels of inflammatory factors are one of the important reasons for the COVID-19 incidence. Del Valle et al. [34] found that high serum interleukin-6, interleukin-8, and TNF-α levels at the time of hospitalization were strong and independent predictors of patient survival. While some inflammatory markers measures in this current study are acute phase reactants, some, such as total antioxidant capacity, may represent a chronic baseline state than acute change with a new illness. Yaghoubi et al. [35] reported that total antioxidant capacity levels were considerably lower in COVID-19 patients compared with healthy individuals ($p < 0.05$) and also between patients with mild and severe diseases ($p < 0.05$). Their findings suggest that COVID-19 patients may be susceptible to depleted total antioxidant capacity.

The results of the present study confirmed the negative association between adherence to the Mediterranean diet and serum levels of hs-CRP, TNF-α, and interleukin-1β. Similar to our result, Sureda et al. reported that the high plasmatic inflammatory markers are closely correlated with low adherence to the Mediterranean dietary pattern [36]. Christina Chrysohoou [37] investigated how the Mediterranean diet affected blood levels of C-reactive protein, white blood cell counts, interleukin-6, tumor necrosis factor-α, amyloid A, fibrinogen, and homocysteine. His study results indicated that the levels of coagulation and inflammatory indicators were found to be lower in people who followed a conventional Mediterranean diet. The focus of a typical Mediterranean diet is on fresh, in-season vegetables, fresh salads, tomatoes, eggplant, cucumber, cabbage, rocket, radishes, garlic, onion, spinach, and lettuce are some examples of these. The most significant sources of phenolic compounds (mostly flavonoids) in the Mediterranean diet are vegetables. Vegetables also include dietary fiber, potassium, vitamin A, vitamin C, vitamin K, copper, magnesium, vitamin E, vitamin B6, folate, iron, thiamine, niacin, and choline, etc. [38,39]. Fruits and vegetables, legumes, olives, olive oil, and nuts are all parts of the Mediterranean diet that help blood inflammation reduction [40,41]. A dietary pattern with more fruits and vegetables has an association with low serum inflammatory factor levels. Corinna Koebnick et al. [42] evaluated the relationships of diet, obesity, and adipokine in Mexican

Americans, and indicated that in comparison to those who consumed more fruits and vegetables and less sugar-sweetened beverages, those who had a diet high in sugar-sweetened beverages had greater levels of adiposity, CRP, leptin, and MCP-1 but lower levels of SFRP-5. Dietary patterns with more sugar-sweetened beverages but with fewer fruits and vegetable consumption cause high Adipokine profiles that lead to pro-inflammatory status. Other components of the Mediterranean diet are olive oil and olives. Consumption of these foods is associated with a decrease in inflammatory indicators [43,44]. In general, the results of all studies indicate the anti-inflammatory effect of the Mediterranean diet, so following this dietary pattern is recommended for the prevention and control of infectious diseases, especially COVID-19 [45].

Among other results of this study, there was a significant difference in the symptoms of COVID-19, including fever, cough, diarrhea, pneumonia severity index, and appetite among patients with different adherence to the Mediterranean diet. The incidence of COVID-19 symptoms in patients who adhered more to the Mediterranean diet was lower than in other patients. Consistent with our results, Perez-Araluce et al. [28] assessed the Mediterranean diet association with the risk of COVID-19 in the "Seguimiento Universidad de Navarra" cohort participants. This study results indicated that participants with intermediate adherence to the Mediterranean diet ($3 < \text{MDS} \leq 6$) had significantly lower odds of COVID-19 incidence (multivariable-adjusted OR = 0.50, 95% CI: 0.34–0.73), and those with the highest adherence (MDS > 6) had the lowest risk (multivariable-adjusted OR = 0.36, 95% CI: 0.16–0.84, p for trend < 0.001) as compared with subjects with $\text{MDS} \leq 3$. Angelis et al. [46]. mentioned that adherence to the Mediterranean diet has a main impact on cardiovascular diseases and other cardio-metabolic disorders, like diabetes that predisposes to COVID-19 infection and related outcomes.

This diet is distinguished by a combination of highly complex carbohydrates in fiber (found in cereals, legumes, vegetables, and fruits), polyunsaturated fatty acids with antiatherogenic and anti-inflammatory properties (found in olive oil and nuts), and bioactive substances with antioxidative properties such as flavonoids, phytosterols, terpenes, and polyphenols [37]. A well-balanced intake of micronutrients, such as vitamins and minerals, which are rich in this diet, helps to prevent malnutrition and immune deficiencies [32]. Several chemicals must be consumed together for proper immune system function. Nutrient-rich meals, such as MD, can reduce the elevated serum inflammation factors caused by nutrient-poor and high-calorie diets. Additionally, adhering to MD is associated with the restoration of the microbiota aerobiosis as Bacteroidetes and certain favorable Clostridium groups [47]. Considering that the composition of the intestinal flora indicates health, following a healthy food pattern such as the Mediterranean diet can strengthen the body's immunity by maintaining the proper composition of the intestinal flora. [48] In fact, several nutritional intervention trials based on MD have collected the most important health benefits that this diet creates, including decreases in serum lipid levels; protection against oxidative stress; decreases in inflammation; platelet aggregation; modulation of hormones and growth factors implicated in cancer pathogenesis; and modulation of microbial metabolism, promoting the proper functioning of the host metabolism as well [49]. More research is being carried out now to prevent diseases, including cancer, CVD, metabolic disease, and even viral disorders. Here, we will give an overview of how MD's most important elements affect the immune system's regulation and the gut flora. MD is primarily characterized by its abundance of fruits, as well as by the availability of aromatic plants and spices to season food (dried herbs like oregano, rosemary, and thyme, for example), as well as seeds (cumin, sesame, etc.), olives, and nuts, all of which are high in a variety of polyphenols. Three important phenolic chemicals that are part of the MD are important to mention: hydroxytyrosol (HT), which is found in EVOO, resveratrol (RSV), which is found in red grapes, and quercetin (QUE), which is found in tea [23]. Higher HT concentrations decrease the levels of oxidized LDL and triglycerides and have a small effect on the expression of genes associated with oxidative-stress [50]. In high-fat diet (HFD)-induced obese mouse models, HT is still being investigated as a nutraceutical. It is being used to observe how this particular EVOO component reverses inflammatory parameters (elevated TNF-, IL-1, and IL-6) and inhibits the activation of TLR-4 and NK-kB pathways, which are related to intestinal permeability in obesity. The phenolic components in EVOO, such as HT, also boost the development of Bifidobacteria, which contribute to the anti-inflammatory effects in the gut. In general, it can be concluded that adherence to the Mediterranean diet and consumption of anti-inflammatory foods strengthen the body's immunity and can be effective and important in the prevention, control, and treatment of symptoms and complications of chronic and even infectious diseases, especially COVID-19 [51].

The use of dietary questionnaire data and the cross-sectional design of this study were this study's limitations, even though it was the first study that examined the association between adherence to the Mediterranean diet and inflammatory factors, appetite, and symptoms of COVID-19. An adequately powered, long-term, randomized clinical trial should be carried out to confirm our preliminary observation. Moreover, some inflammatory markers measured in this study are acute phase reactants, so in a next study, other markers like total antioxidant capacity (TAC) may better represent chronic baseline state than acute change with a new illness.

5. Conclusions

There is an inverse relationship between adherence to the Mediterranean diet and the symptoms and complications of COVID-19, and patients who followed the Mediterranean diet more in the past had less fever, cough, diarrhea, and lung infection. There was a negative relationship between adherence to the Mediterranean diet and serum inflammatory factors in COVID-19 patients. Long-term clinical studies among patients suffering from various infectious diseases, especially pneumonia and COVID-19, are needed to prove this relationship.

Author Contributions: A.F.G.C. and M.M. designed the study and wrote the protocol. R.M. collected data, conducted literature searches, and provided summaries of previous research studies. M.M. conducted the statistical analysis. A.F.G.C. and M.M. wrote the first draft of the manuscript. All authors have read and agreed to the published version of the manuscript.

Funding: This research received no external funding.

Institutional Review Board Statement: The study was conducted according to the guidelines of the Declaration of Helsinki and approved by the Ethics Committee of the Ardabil University of Medicine Sciences on 17 January 2022 (IR.ARUMS.REC.1400.293).

Informed Consent Statement: Informed consent was obtained from all subjects involved in the study. Written informed consent has been obtained from the patients to publish this paper.

Data Availability Statement: Data is unavailable due to privacy or ethical restrictions.

Acknowledgments: The authors would like to thank Ardabil University of Medical Sciences, and all patients who participated in this study.

Conflicts of Interest: The authors declare no conflict of interest.

References

1. Ciotti, M.; Ciccozzi, M.; Terrinoni, A.; Jiang, W.-C.; Wang, C.-B.; Bernardini, S. The COVID-19 pandemic. *Crit. Rev. Clin. Lab. Sci.* **2020**, *57*, 365–388. [CrossRef] [PubMed]
2. Calder, P.C.; Carr, A.C.; Gombart, A.F.; Eggersdorfer, M. Optimal nutritional status for a well-functioning immune system is an important factor to protect against viral infections. *Nutrients* **2020**, *12*, 1181. [CrossRef] [PubMed]
3. Polverino, E.; Goeminne, P.C.; McDonnell, M.J.; Aliberti, S.; Marshall, S.E.; Loebinger, M.R.; Murris, M.; Cantón, R.; Torres, A.; Dimakou, K.; et al. European Respiratory Society guidelines for the management of adult bronchiectasis. *Eur. Respir. J.* **2017**, *50*, 1700629. [CrossRef]
4. McElvaney, O.J.; McEvoy, N.L.; McElvaney, O.F.; Carroll, T.P.; Murphy, M.P.; Dunlea, D.M.; Ni Choileain, O.; Clarke, J.; O'Connor, E.; Hogan, G.; et al. Characterization of the inflammatory response to severe COVID-19 illness. *Am. J. Respir. Crit. Care Med.* **2020**, *202*, 812–821. [CrossRef] [PubMed]

5. Merad, M.; Subramanian, A.; Wang, T.T. An aberrant inflammatory response in severe COVID-19. *Cell Host Microbe* **2021**, *29*, 1043–1047. [CrossRef]
6. Jafarzadeh, A.; Chauhan, P.; Saha, B.; Jafarzadeh, S.; Nemati, M. Contribution of monocytes and macrophages to the local tissue inflammation and cytokine storm in COVID-19: Lessons from SARS and MERS, and potential therapeutic interventions. *Life Sci.* **2020**, *257*, 118102. [CrossRef]
7. Bouayad, A. Innate immune evasion by SARS-CoV-2: Comparison with SARS-CoV. *Rev. Med. Virol.* **2020**, *30*, 1–9. [CrossRef]
8. Song, P.; Li, W.; Xie, J.; Hou, Y.; You, C. Cytokine storm induced by SARS-CoV-2. Clin. *Chim. Acta.* **2020**, *509*, 280–287. [CrossRef]
9. Martínez-Colón, G.J.; Ratnasiri, K.; Chen, H.; Jiang, S.; Zanley, E.; Rustagi, A.; Verma, R.; Chen, H.; Andrews, J.R.; Mertz, K.D.; et al. SARS-CoV-2 infection drives an inflammatory response in human adipose tissue through infection of adipocytes and macrophages. *Sci. Transl. Med.* **2022**, *14*, eabm9151. [CrossRef]
10. Akbari, H.; Tabrizi, R.; Lankarani, K.B.; Aria, H.; Vakili, S.; Asadian, F.; Noroozi, S.; Keshavarz, P.; Faramarz, S. The role of cytokine profile and lymphocyte subsets in the severity of coronavirus disease 2019 (COVID-19): A systematic review and meta-analysis. *Life Sci.* **2020**, *258*, 118167. [CrossRef]
11. Pieri, M.; Ciotti, M.; Nuccetelli, M.; Perrone, M.A.; Caliò, M.T.; Lia, M.S.; Minieri, M.; Bernardini, S. Serum Amyloid A Protein as a useful biomarker to predict COVID-19 patients severity and prognosis. *Int. Immunopharmaco.* **2021**, *95*, 107512. [CrossRef]
12. Sorić Hosman, I.; Kos, I.; Lamot, L. Serum amyloid A in inflammatory rheumatic diseases: A compendious review of a renowned biomarker. *Front. Immunol.* **2021**, *11*, 631299. [CrossRef] [PubMed]
13. Tanacan, A.; Yazihan, N.; Erol, S.A.; Anuk, A.T.; Yetiskin, F.D.Y.; Biriken, D.; Ozgu-Erdinc, A.; Keskin, H.L.; Tekin, O.M.; Sahin, D. The impact of COVID-19 infection on the cytokine profile of pregnant women: A prospective case-control study. *Cytokine* **2021**, *140*, 155431. [CrossRef] [PubMed]
14. Ullah, R.; Khan, J.; Basharat, N.; Huo, D.; Ud Din, A.; Wang, G. Evaluation of Cardiac Biomarkers and Expression Analysis of IL-1, IL-6, IL-10, IL-17, and IL-25 among COVID-19 Patients from Pakistan. *Viruses* **2022**, *14*, 2149. [CrossRef]
15. Anania, C.; Perla, F.M.; Olivero, F.; Pacifico, L.; Chiesa, C. Mediterranean diet and nonalcoholic fatty liver disease. *World J. Gastroenterol.* **2018**, *24*, 2083. [CrossRef] [PubMed]
16. Saura-Calixto, F.; Goni, I. Definition of the Mediterranean diet based on bioactive compounds. *Crit. Rev. Food Sci. Nutr.* **2009**, *49*, 145–152. [CrossRef]
17. Trichopoulou, A.; Martínez-González, M.A.; Tong, T.Y.; Forouhi, N.G.; Khandelwal, S.; Prabhakaran, D.; Mozaffarian, D.; de Lorgeril, M. Definitions and potential health benefits of the Mediterranean diet: Views from experts around the world. *BMC Med.* **2014**, *12*, 112. [CrossRef]
18. Martín-Peláez, S.; Fito, M.; Castaner, O. Mediterranean diet effects on type 2 diabetes prevention, disease progression, and related mechanisms. A review. *Nutrients* **2020**, *12*, 2236. [CrossRef]
19. Finicelli, M.; Squillaro, T.; Di Cristo, F.; Di Salle, A.; Melone, M.A.B.; Galderisi, U.; Peluso, G. Metabolic syndrome, Mediterranean diet, and polyphenols: Evidence and perspectives. *J. Cell. Physiol.* **2019**, *234*, 5807–5826. [CrossRef]
20. Veček, N.N.; Mucalo, L.; Dragun, R.; Miličević, T.; Pribisalić, A.; Patarčić, I.; Hayward, C.; Polašek, O.; Kolčić, I. The association between salt taste perception, mediterranean diet and metabolic syndrome: A cross-sectional study. *Nutrients* **2020**, *12*, 1164. [CrossRef]
21. Koopen, A.M.; Almeida, E.L.; Attaye, I.; Witjes, J.J.; Rampanelli, E.; Majait, S.; Kemper, M.; Levels, J.H.M.; Schimmel, A.W.M.; Herrema, H.; et al. Effect of fecal microbiota transplantation combined with Mediterranean diet on insulin sensitivity in subjects with metabolic syndrome. *Front. Microbiol.* **2021**, *12*, 662159. [CrossRef] [PubMed]
22. Finicelli, M.; Di Salle, A.; Galderisi, U.; Peluso, G. The Mediterranean Diet: An Update of the Clinical Trials. *Nutrients* **2022**, *14*, 2956. [CrossRef] [PubMed]
23. Mentella, M.C.; Scaldaferri, F.; Ricci, C.; Gasbarrini, A.; Miggiano, G.A.D. Cancer and Mediterranean diet: A review. *Nutrients* **2019**, *11*, 2059. [CrossRef] [PubMed]
24. Mazzocchi, A.; Leone, L.; Agostoni, C.; Pali-Schöll, I. The secrets of the Mediterranean diet. Does [only] olive oil matter? *Nutrients* **2019**, *11*, 2941. [CrossRef] [PubMed]
25. Schröder, H.; Fitó, M.; Estruch, R.; Martínez-González, M.A.; Corella, D.; Salas-Salvadó, J.; Lamuela-Raventós, R.; Ros, E.; Salaverría, I.; Fiol, M.; et al. A short screener is valid for assessing Mediterranean diet adherence among older Spanish men and women. *J. Nutr.* **2011**, *141*, 1140–1145. [CrossRef] [PubMed]
26. Barrea, L.; Vetrani, C.; Caprio, M.; Cataldi, M.; Ghoch, M.E.; Elce, A.; Camajani, E.; Verde, L.; Savastano, S.; Colao, A.; et al. From the Ketogenic Diet to the Mediterranean Diet: The Potential Dietary Therapy in Patients with Obesity after CoVID-19 Infection (Post CoVID Syndrome). *Curr. Obes. Rep.* **2022**, *11*, 144–165. [CrossRef]
27. Greene, M.W.; Roberts, A.P.; Frugé, A.D. Negative association between Mediterranean diet adherence and COVID-19 cases and related deaths in Spain and 23 OECD countries: An ecological study. *Front. Nutr.* **2021**, *8*, 591964. [CrossRef]
28. Perez-Araluce, R.; Martinez-Gonzalez, M.A.; Fernández-Lázaro, C.I.; Bes-Rastrollo, M.; Gea, A.; Carlos, S. Mediterranean diet and the risk of COVID-19 in the 'Seguimiento Universidad de Navarra' cohort. *Clin. Nutr.* **2021**, *41*, 3061–3068. [CrossRef]
29. Fedullo, A.L.; Schiattarella, A.; Morlando, M.; Raguzzini, A.; Toti, E.; De Franciscis, P.; Peluso, I. Mediterranean Diet for the Prevention of Gestational Diabetes in the Covid-19 Era: Implications of Il-6 In Diabesity. *Int. J. Mol. Sci.* **2021**, *22*, 1213. [CrossRef]
30. Guilleminault, L.; Williams, E.J.; Scott, H.A.; Berthon, B.S.; Jensen, M.; Wood, L.G. Diet and asthma: Is it time to adapt our message? *Nutrients* **2017**, *9*, 1227. [CrossRef]

31. Koloverou, E.; Panagiotakos, D.B.; Pitsavos, C.; Chrysohoou, C.; Georgousopoulou, E.N.; Grekas, A.; Christou, A.; Chatzigeorgiou, M.; Skoumas, I.; Tousoulis, D.; et al. Adherence to Mediterranean diet and 10-year incidence (2002–2012) of diabetes: Correlations with inflammatory and oxidative stress biomarkers in the ATTICA cohort study. *Diabetes Metab. Res. Rev.* **2016**, *32*, 73–81. [CrossRef]
32. Maiorino, M.I.; Bellastella, G.; Longo, M.; Caruso, P.; Esposito, K. Mediterranean diet and COVID-19: Hypothesizing potential benefits in people with diabetes. *Front. Endocrinol.* **2020**, *11*, 574315. [CrossRef] [PubMed]
33. Lampropoulos, C.E.; Konsta, M.; Dradaki, V.; Roumpou, A.; Dri, I.; Papaioannou, I. Effects of Mediterranean diet on hospital length of stay, medical expenses, and mortality in elderly, hospitalized patients: A 2-year observational study. *Nutrition* **2020**, *79*, 110868. [CrossRef] [PubMed]
34. Del Valle, D.M.; Kim-Schulze, S.; Huang, H.H.; Beckmann, N.D.; Nirenberg, S.; Wang, B.; Lavin, Y.; Swartz, T.H.; Madduri, D.; Stock, A.; et al. An inflammatory cytokine signature predicts COVID-19 severity and survival. *Nat. Med.* **2020**, *26*, 1636–1643. [CrossRef] [PubMed]
35. Yaghoubi, N.; Youssefi, M.; Jabbari Azad, F.; Farzad, F.; Yavari, Z.; Zahedi Avval, F. Total antioxidant capacity as a marker of severity of COVID-19 infection: Possible prognostic and therapeutic clinical application. *J. Med. Virol.* **2022**, *94*, 1558–1565. [CrossRef]
36. Sureda, A.; Bibiloni, M.D.; Julibert, A.; Bouzas, C.; Argelich, E.; Llompart, I.; Pons, A.; Tur, J.A. Adherence to the Mediterranean Diet and Inflammatory Markers. *Nutrients* **2018**, *10*, 62. [CrossRef]
37. Chrysohoou, C.; Panagiotakos, D.B.; Pitsavos, C.; Das, U.N.; Stefanadis, C. Adherence to the Mediterranean diet attenuates inflammation and coagulation process in healthy adults: The ATTICA Study. *J. Am. Coll. Cardiol.* **2004**, *44*, 152–158. [CrossRef]
38. Martínez-González, M.A.; Salas-Salvadó, J.; Estruch, R.; Corella, D.; Fitó, M.; Ros, E.; Predimed Investigators. Benefits of the Mediterranean diet: Insights from the PREDIMED study. *Prog. Cardiovasc. Dis.* **2015**, *58*, 50–60. [CrossRef]
39. Davis, C.; Bryan, J.; Hodgson, J.; Murphy, K. Definition of the Mediterranean diet: A literature review. *Nutrients* **2015**, *7*, 9139–9153. [CrossRef]
40. Naureen, Z.; Dhuli, K.; Donato, K.; Aquilanti, B.; Velluti, V.; Matera, G.; Iaconelli, A.; Bertelli, M. Foods of the Mediterranean diet: Tomato, olives, chili pepper, wheat flour and wheat germ. *J. Prev. Med. Hyg.* **2022**, *63* (Suppl. 3), E4.
41. Gantenbein, K.V.; Kanaka-Gantenbein, C. Mediterranean diet as an antioxidant: The impact on metabolic health and overall wellbeing. *Nutrients* **2021**, *13*, 1951. [CrossRef] [PubMed]
42. Koebnick, C.; Black, M.H.; Wu, J.; Shu, Y.-H.; MacKay, A.W.; Watanabe, R.M.; Buchanan, T.A.; Xiang, A.H. A diet high in sugar-sweetened beverage and low in fruits and vegetables is associated with adiposity and a pro-inflammatory adipokine profile. *Br. J. Nutr.* **2018**, *120*, 1230–1239. [CrossRef] [PubMed]
43. Morvaridi, M.; Jafarirad, S.; Seyedian, S.S.; Alavinejad, P.; Cheraghian, B. The effects of extra virgin olive oil and canola oil on inflammatory markers and gastrointestinal symptoms in patients with ulcerative colitis. *Eur. J. Clin. Nutr.* **2020**, *74*, 891–899. [CrossRef] [PubMed]
44. Noce, A.; Marrone, G.; Urciuoli, S.; Di Daniele, F.; Di Lauro, M.; Zaitseva, A.P.; Di Daniele, N.; Romani, A. Usefulness of extra virgin olive oil minor polar compounds in the management of chronic kidney disease patients. *Nutrients* **2021**, *13*, 581. [CrossRef] [PubMed]
45. Angelidi, A.M.; Kokkinos, A.; Katechaki, E.; Ros, E.; Mantzoros, C.S. Mediterranean diet as a nutritional approach for COVID-19. Metab. *Clin. Exp.* **2021**, *114*, 154407.
46. Angelis, A.; Chrysohoou, C.; Tzorovili, E.; Laina, A.; Xydis, P.; Terzis, I.; Ioakeimidis, N.; Aznaouridis, K.; Vlachopoulos, C.; Tsioufis, K. The Mediterranean diet benefit on cardiovascular hemodynamics and erectile function in chronic heart failure male patients by decoding central and peripheral vessel rheology. *Nutrients* **2020**, *13*, 108. [CrossRef]
47. Serra-Majem, L.; Roman-Vinas, B.; Sanchez-Villegas, A.; Guasch-Ferre, M.; Corella, D.; La Vecchia, C. Benefits of the Mediterranean diet: Epidemiological and molecular aspects. *Mol. Asp. Med.* **2019**, *67*, 1–55. [CrossRef]
48. Strasser, B.; Wolters, M.; Weyh, C.; Krüger, K.; Ticinesi, A. The effects of lifestyle and diet on gut microbiota composition, inflammation and muscle performance in our aging society. *Nutrients* **2021**, *13*, 2045. [CrossRef]
49. Baratta, F.; Cammisotto, V.; Tozzi, G.; Coronati, M.; Bartimoccia, S.; Castellani, V.; Nocella, C.; D'Amico, A.; Angelico, F.; Carnevale, R.; et al. High Compliance to Mediterranean Diet Associates with Lower Platelet Activation and Liver Collagen Deposition in Patients with Nonalcoholic Fatty Liver Disease. *Nutrients* **2022**, *14*, 1209. [CrossRef]
50. Nomikos, T.; Fragopoulou, E.; Antonopoulou, S.; Panagiotakos, D.B. Mediterranean diet and platelet-activating factor; a systematic review. *Clin. Biochem.* **2018**, *60*, 1–10. [CrossRef]
51. García-Montero, C.; Fraile-Martínez, O.; Gómez-Lahoz, A.; Pekarek, L.; Castellanos, A.; Noguerales-Fraguas, F.; Coca, S.; Guijarro, L.; García-Honduvilla, N.; Asúnsolo, A.; et al. Nutritional components in Western diet versus Mediterranean diet at the gut microbiota–immune system interplay. Implications for health and disease. *Nutrients* **2021**, *13*, 699. [CrossRef] [PubMed]

Disclaimer/Publisher's Note: The statements, opinions and data contained in all publications are solely those of the individual author(s) and contributor(s) and not of MDPI and/or the editor(s). MDPI and/or the editor(s) disclaim responsibility for any injury to people or property resulting from any ideas, methods, instructions or products referred to in the content.

medicina

MDPI

Article

Identification of Genomic Variants of SARS-CoV-2 Using Nanopore Sequencing

Ionut Dragos Capraru [1,2,3], Mirabela Romanescu [2,4,5], Flavia Medana Anghel [2,4], Cristian Oancea [6], Catalin Marian [4,5], Ioan Ovidiu Sirbu [4,5], Aimee Rodica Chis [4,5,*] and Paula Diana Ciordas [2,4,5]

1 Discipline of Epidemiology, "Victor Babes" University of Medicine and Pharmacy, 300041 Timișoara, Romania
2 Doctoral School, "Victor Babes" University of Medicine and Pharmacy, 300041 Timișoara, Romania
3 Public Health Authority Timiș County, 300029 Timișoara, Romania
4 Discipline of Biochemistry, "Victor Babes" University of Medicine and Pharmacy, 300041 Timișoara, Romania
5 Center for Complex Network Science, "Victor Babes" University of Medicine and Pharmacy, 300041 Timişoara, Romania
6 Discipline of Pulmonology, "Victor Babes" University of Medicine and Pharmacy, 300041 Timișoara, Romania
* Correspondence: chis.aimee@umft.ro

Abstract: *Background and Objectives*: SARS-CoV-2 is the first global threat and life-changing event of the twenty-first century. Although efficient treatments and vaccines have been developed, due to the virus's ability to mutate in key regions of the genome, whole viral genome sequencing is needed for efficient monitoring, evaluation of the spread, and even the adjustment of the molecular diagnostic assays. *Materials and Methods*: In this study, Nanopore and Ion Torrent sequencing technologies were used to detect the main SARS-CoV-2 circulating strains in Timis County, Romania, between February 2021 and May 2022. *Results*: We identified 22 virus lineages belonging to seven clades: 20A, 20I (Alpha, V1), 21B (Kappa), 21I (Delta), 21J (Delta), 21K (Omicron), and 21L (Omicron). *Conclusions*: Results obtained with both methods are comparable, and we confirm the utility of Nanopore sequencing in large-scale epidemiological surveillance due to the lower cost and reduced time for library preparation.

Keywords: SARS-CoV-2; sequencing; Nanopore; MinION; Ion Torrent

Citation: Capraru, I.D.; Romanescu, M.; Anghel, F.M.; Oancea, C.; Marian, C.; Sirbu, I.O.; Chis, A.R.; Ciordas, P.D. Identification of Genomic Variants of SARS-CoV-2 Using Nanopore Sequencing. *Medicina* **2022**, *58*, 1841. https://doi.org/10.3390/medicina58121841

Academic Editors: Yusra Habib Khan, Tauqeer Hussain Mallhi, Tahir Mehmood Khan and Muhammad Salman

Received: 21 November 2022
Accepted: 13 December 2022
Published: 15 December 2022

Publisher's Note: MDPI stays neutral with regard to jurisdictional claims in published maps and institutional affiliations.

Copyright: © 2022 by the authors. Licensee MDPI, Basel, Switzerland. This article is an open access article distributed under the terms and conditions of the Creative Commons Attribution (CC BY) license (https://creativecommons.org/licenses/by/4.0/).

1. Introduction

During the last two years, the COVID-19 pandemic has been the main concern worldwide, causing socio-economical losses at an unanticipated scale [1]. The causative pathogen is the severe acute respiratory syndrome coronavirus 2 (SARS-CoV-2) [2]; it is a single stranded, positive-sense, enveloped RNA virus of the *Coronaviridae* family, *Betacoronavirus* genus. SARS-CoV-2 is the seventh identified coronavirus shown to infect humans [3]. Its genome was sequenced and published in January 2020 by Wu and collaborators [4]; it comprises 29,903 nucleotides (Genbank-MN908947, RefSeq acc.nos.-NC_045512) [4]. This reference genome has been used for the development of rapid and sensitive molecular diagnostic methods, of which the gold standard is a quantitative real-time polymerase chain reaction (RT-qPCR) [5].

SARS-CoV-2 has a high mutation rate; its genome shows ~1.1×10^{-3} substitutions per site each year, which is roughly equivalent to one substitution every 11 days [6]. Consequently, regular viral genome sequencing is needed to obtain information concerning the origin of an infection, the variants circulating in different regions, and the evolution of the spread [2]. Moreover, since these mutations might occur in key regions of the genome, sequencing is needed for the adjustment of the molecular diagnostic assays (primer redesign) and even vaccine development and readjustment [7]. SARS-CoV-2 sequencing could also help in deciphering the link between the mutations occurring and the clinical aspects of the COVID-19 disease [8]. Of note, sequencing proved that reinfections reported shortly after the first infection were caused by a different variant of the virus [9,10].

Today, over 13 million sequences of SARS-CoV-2 have been deposited on GISAID (https://www.gisaid.org/ accessed on 20 November 2022). SARS-CoV-2 sequencing was performed using different approaches: metagenomics, sequence capture or enrichment, and Polymerase Chain Reaction (PCR) amplification using primer/amplicon pools [7,8]. Metagenomics is more appropriate when identifying new, uncharacterized pathogens, without having any knowledge of their genome [11] and is less laborious than other methods. On the other hand, it is relatively expensive, and shows lower depth and coverage for lower viral loads [12]; whole genome sequencing is possible only for samples with a high viral load [11]. In the case of target enrichment sequencing, the knowledge of the genome sequence is essential, because only a predefined region of interest is targeted. These sequences are enriched by hybridization to biotinylated probes or by PCR. Because enrichment occurs even if there is an imperfect complementarity between the samples and the probes, although considered more robust, hybridization is less sensitive to variations in the genome than PCR amplification. Moreover, DNA hybridization enrichment is rather expensive and prone to coverage bias due to competitive binding of the host [11,12]. In both methods, the number of reads depends on the viral load; however, PCR amplification-based methods are better suited in the case of a low viral load or degraded samples [11,13].

In the PCR-tiling amplicon method, one generates pools of amplicons that cover either entirely or partially the viral genome; this can offer sufficient depth and coverage, it is highly specific, and less expensive [8,11]. The approach is not suited to discovering new pathogens, because it requires the knowledge of the sequence, so that the primers can be specifically designed [12]. The major limitation one should consider in PCR methods concerns the primer efficacy, especially when the appearance of new variants is suspected; the interference with the annealing sequences leads to decreased coverage in specific regions or even incomplete assembly.

Short-read sequencing platforms such as Ion Torrent and Illumina are highly accurate and regarded as the current standard [2]. Although long-read sequencing is considered to show lower accuracy, multiple research groups proved that they can be comparable, in terms of coverage and quality of the final sequence, to the short-read sequencing methods [2,8,14,15].

Of the current sequencing technologies available, Oxford Nanopore Technologies (ONT) has gained popularity due to the affordable price and portability of their devices. Nanopore sequencing does not require complex laboratory infrastructure or well-trained personnel, the library preparation procedure is relatively simple, and the results can even be analyzed in real-time [2]. Furthermore, since the Nanopore MinION does not need an internet connection, it can be used for field experiments [12]. The experience with Ebola [16], Zika [17], Lassa fever [18], Yellow fever [19], Influenza [20], and other outbreaks proved that Nanopore rapid sequencing is well-suited not only to epidemic/pandemic surveillance [2], but also transcriptome mapping, identification of new mutations in the viral genome, and characterization of various types of RNA molecules [8].

The ARTIC network (https://artic.network/) has developed a protocol for Nanopore sequencing and data analysis, which was successfully used during Ebola and Zika outbreaks. Shortly after the discovery of the SARS-CoV-2 virus, the protocol was optimized for the identification and characterization of RNA purified directly from nasopharyngeal and oropharyngeal samples. A first pool of primers (V1 primer scheme) was designed to generate 400 bp overlapping amplicons and completely sequence the viral genome. Since then, due to the mutations in the virus's genome, the protocol has undergone several modifications in terms of alternative primer schemes and amplicon size, which have led to improvements in library preparation (shorter time and up to 96-sample multiplexing) [8,14,15]. Starting at the end of 2020 and early 2021, the V3 primer pool was mainly used. However, new mutations emerged, some of them deletions or single nucleotide polymorphisms (SNPs) in the primer binding sites, leading to amplicon drop-out and incomplete coverage. Hence, yet another set of primers (ARTIC V4) has been designed to solve these issues. The main changes were in the 72_Right primer in G142D (Delta), 74_Left primer in 241/243del (Beta), and 76_Left primer in the K417N (Beta) or K417T (Gamma) (https://community.artic.network/t/sars-cov-2-version-4-scheme-release/312) [21].

The objective of the present study was the setup of workflow for identification by Nanopore sequencing (using a MinION MK1C device and the ARTIC protocol) of different variants of SARS-CoV-2 virus circulating in Timis County, Romania between August 2021 and May 2022. Furthermore, we have compared the Nanopore sequencing results obtained using the V3 and V4 primer pools, and evaluated their quality as compared to Ion Torrent sequencing on an S5 instrument.

2. Materials and Methods

2.1. Sample Collection and Processing/Ethics

Nasopharyngeal and oropharyngeal swabs were collected from patients infected with SARS-CoV-2 virus hospitalized at the "Victor Babes" Hospital for Infectious Diseases, Timisoara, Romania. All samples were kept in approximately 3 mL of viral transport medium (Shenzen Dakewe Bio-engineering, Shenzen, China) and delivered within 3 h to the Laboratory of Molecular and Biochemical Diagnostic (LDBM) of "Victor Babes" University of Medicine and Pharmacy (VBUMP). All samples were stored anonymized at −80 °C, until further use. The project obtained the approval of the Ethics Committee of VBUMP, Timisoara, Romania.

2.2. RT-qPCR Confirmation

Viral RNA was extracted using the Maxwell® RSC Viral TNA Kit (Promega, Madison, WI, USA) on a Maxwell RSC automated machine (Promega, Madison, WI, USA), according to the manufacturer's protocol. The viral concentration was quantified using an RNA HS Assay Kit (Thermo Fisher, Waltham, MA, USA) on a Qubit 2.0 instrument (Invitrogen, Waltham, MA, USA). All samples were stored at −80 °C until further use. Probes were tested for the presence of SARS-CoV-2 using a GenomeCov19 Detection Kit (ABM, Richmond, BC, Canada) according to the manufacturer's instructions. All RT-qPCR runs were performed on a Bio-Rad CFX96 instrument (BioRad, Hercules, CA, USA) using a positive and a negative control, targeting N (nucleocapsid) gene, S (spike) gene, and having actin as an internal control. Samples with a Ct over 32 were discarded.

2.3. Library Preparation and Sequencing with MinION Mk1C

We used a shorter, adapted version of the SARS-CoV-2 sequencing protocol (nCoV-2019 sequencing protocol v3 (LoCost) V.3) developed and adapted by the ARTIC Network (https://artic.network/) using the reagent from New England BioLabs (NEB, Ipswich, MA, USA) and Oxford Nanopore Technology (ONT, Oxford, UK). Each sequencing run contained 23 samples and a negative control and was performed using the Ligation Sequencing Kit 109 (SQK-LSK109, ONT, Oxford, UK). For cDNA synthesis, 2 uL of LunaScript RT SuperMix (M3010, NEB, Ipswich, MA, USA) was mixed with 8 uL of viral RNA, incubated 2 min at 25 °C, 10 min at 55 °C, and 1 min at 95 °C for enzyme inactivation, then kept at 4 °C until the next step. Samples with Ct between 12–15 and 15–18 were diluted at 1:100 and 1:10, respectively; samples with Ct values between 18 and 32 were used undiluted.

Next, the overlapping amplicons were generated (~400 bp) by mixing 12.5 uL of Hot Start High Fidelity Master Mix (M0494, NEB, Ipswich, MA, USA), 4 uL of primer pool V3 or V4 (ARTIC nCoV-2019 V3 Panel and ARTIC nCoV-2019 V4 Panel, IDT, Corralville, IA, USA), 6 uL of nuclease free water (NFW, NEB, Ipswich, MA, USA), and 2.5 uL of cDNA. Two separate reactions were performed for each sample, using the two primer pools. The cycling program was the following: initial step 30 s at 98 °C, followed by 15 s at 98 °C, and 5 min at 65 °C, for a cycle number between 25 and 35 and cooling at 4 °C. Samples were then pooled together and diluted in 45 μL of NFW (NEB, Ipswich, MA, USA). For the end preparing, we used NebNext Ultra II End Repair/dA-Tailing module

(NEB, Ipswich, MA, USA), as follows: 1.2 µL of Ultra II End Prep Reaction Buffer (NEB, Ipswich, MA, USA), 0.5 µL Ultra II End Prep Enzyme Mix (NEB, Ipswich, MA, USA), 5 µL of NFW (NEB, Ipswich, MA, USA), and 3.3 diluted samples from the previous step. The reaction mixture was incubated for 15 min at 25 °C, 15 min at 65 °C, and cooled at 4 °C. Samples were barcoded using 1.25 µL of EXP-NBD104 (barcodes 1–12, ONT, Oxford, UK) and EXP-NBD114 (barcodes 13–24, ONT, Oxford, UK), 5 ul of Blunt TA Ligase Master Mix (M0367, NEB, Ipswich, MA, USA), 3 µL of NFW (NEB, Ipswich, MA, USA), and 0.75 uL of reaction mixture from the previous step, then incubated as follows: 20 min at 25 °C, 10 min at 65 °C, and cooling for 1 min at 4 °C. Next, 10 µL of all barcoded samples was pooled together and purified using 0.4 µL of AMPure XP Magnetic Beads (Beckman Coulter, Brea, CA, USA). Samples were quantified using a Qubit 2.0 spectrophotometer (Invitrogen, Waltham, MA, USA) and dsDNA HS Assay Kit (Thermo Fisher, Waltham, MA, USA). For adaptor ligation, about 30 ng of the barcoded samples was mixed with 10 µL NEBNext Quick Ligation Reaction Buffer (NebNext Quick Ligation Module, E6056, NEB, Ipswich, MA, USA), 5 µL of adaptor MIX (AMII, ONT, Oxford, UK), and 5 µL of Quick T4 DNA Ligase (NebNext Quick Ligation Module, E6056, NEB, Ipswich, MA, USA). The mixture was incubated at room temperature for 20 min, followed by purification with AMPure XP Magnetic Beads (Beckman Coulter, Brea, CA, USA) 1:1 and another Qubit quantification. About 15 ng of the library was loaded in a final volume of 75 µL on a primed R9.4.1 flow cell (ONT, Oxford, UK) fitted in a MinION Mk1C (ONT, Oxford, UK) instrument.

Basecalling and demultiplexing were performed with the MinKNOW 20.10 (ONT, Oxford, UK) (having strict parameters to ensure that amplicons had barcodes at both ends) software, which is integrated in MinION Mk1C (ONT, Oxford, UK). A further data analysis was carried out on the Epi2me platform developed by Metrichor Ltd. (Oxford, UK), Version 2022.04.26-13521, which uses Artic, Nextclade, Pangolin sub-sections (Artic + Nextclade + Pangolin-v3.3.1). The Artic software investigates the depth of coverage for each barcoded sample and can be used for exploring individual amplicons that might not have been amplified with the 2 primer pools. Nextclade software identifies the genetic variants compared to the reference genome and provides data concerning quality control [22]. Pangolin reports the sample lineage [23]. The SARS-CoV-2 virus from Wuhan was used as the reference genome (MN908947).

2.4. Ion Torrent Sequencing

The samples were chosen for sequencing based on the quantity and quality of viral RNA (Ct < 32 and minimum 7 ng/µL), and the number of viral copies for each sample was evaluated using the TaqMan 2019-nCoV Assay Kit v1 (Applied Biosystems, Waltham, MA, USA).

The viral RNA was reverse-transcribed using the SuperScript™ VILO™ cDNA Synthesis Kit (Invitrogen, Waltham, MA, USA), according to the protocol provided by the manufacturer. The targets for sequencing were obtained using the Ion AmpliSeq™ SARS-CoV-2 Panel (Thermo Fisher, Waltham, MA, USA). Library preparation was performed with Ion AmpliSeq™ Library Kit Plus (Thermo Fisher, Waltham, MA, USA), on an Ion Chef instrument (ThermoFisher Scientific, Waltham, MA, USA). The samples were sequenced on an Ion Gene Studio S5 instrument (Thermo Fisher Scientific, Waltham, MA, USA), using an Ion Torrent 540 chip (Thermo Fisher Scientific, Waltham, MA, USA). The reads were mapped and assembled using the Iterative Refinement Meta Assembler (IRMA). The alignment, lineage, and clade identification were performed using Nextclade and SARS-CoV-2 as a reference genome (MN908947).

3. Results

3.1. Nanopore Sequencing

With two exceptions (with Ct of 31.6 and 31.9), all samples had Ct values between 11.9 and 29. For all rounds of sequencing, the average quality score (12.025) was well above the default threshold 7, which indicates a very good sequencing run. Out of the 103 samples loaded, we obtained 96 sequences; the remaining 7 samples had more than

3000 ambiguous reads and could not be unambiguously interpreted. We performed six rounds of sequencing experiments; 23 of the samples were sequenced twice using ARTIC nCoV-2019 V3 Panel (round 4) and ARTIC nCoV-2019 V4 Panel (round 5).

Except for sequencing run 2 (with an overall bad quality), the total number of reads analyzed varied between 705,499 and 4,465,541 (Table 1) with a maximum of 19.95% unclassified reads for the first round. The average number of reads obtained for all rounds was 1,646,673, of which an average of 390,414 were unclassified. The very high number of reads obtained after the first round of sequencing was the result of the longer sequencing time/run (24 h) compared to the other sequencing rounds (6 h). On average, the highest number of reads/clade, 164,439, was obtained for 20I (Alpha, V1), and the lowest for 21K (Omicron) with 39,870 and 21B (Kappa) with 3447 (Figure 1).

Table 1. Overview of the nanopore indicators obtained.

	Round 1	Round 2	Round 3	Round 4	Round 5	Round 6
Reads Analyzed	4,465,541	1,765,872	998,468	1,095,194	705,499	849,462
Unclassified Reads	890,927	1,214,457	62,643	74,064	52,421	47,970
Total Yield	2.3 Gbases	920.8 Mbases	513.9 Mbases	533.9 Mbases	393.9 Mbases	434.4 Mbases
Average Quality Score	14.1	11.84	11.73	11.32	11.6	11.56
Average Sequence Length (Bp)	524	521	514	487	558	511

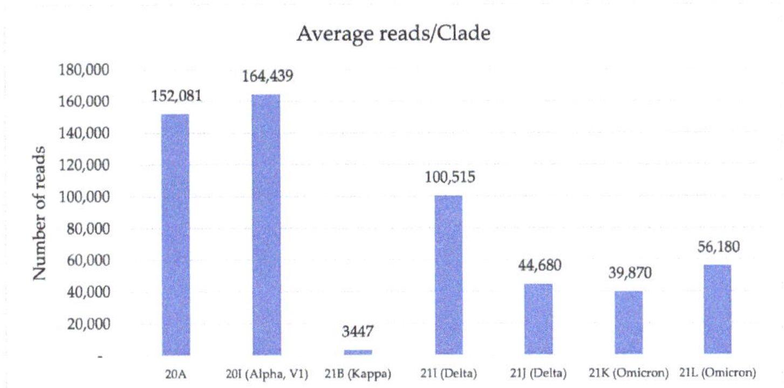

Figure 1. Average read count per each clade.

With respect to the average number of mutations identified, the highest was recorded for 21L (Omicron) clade-59, followed by 21K (Omicron) clade with 47 mutations, 21J (Delta) having 34 mutations, 20I (Alpha, V1) 32, 21J (Delta) with 26 and the lowest for 20A (24 mutations), and only 1 for 21B (Kappa).

For most of the samples, the overall genome coverage was above 250× with an average sequence length of 519.17 bp. Unexpectedly, the 20 k–22 k genomic region of the virus had a lower coverage, possibly due to sequence alteration in the primers' binding sites. In Figure 2, there is an example of the coverage obtained for sample barcode 5 from sequencing round 6, for primer pools A and B.

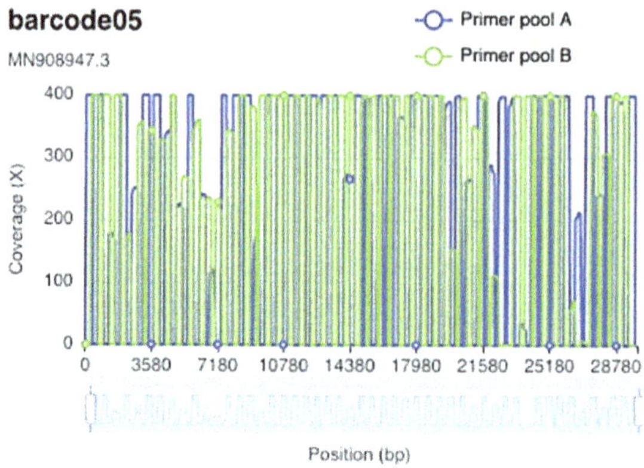

Figure 2. Example of coverage for barcode 5 from round 6.

We identified a total of 22 lineages belonging to 7 clades: 20A, 20I (Alpha, V1), 21B (Kappa), 21I (Delta), 21J (Delta), 21K (Omicron), and 21L (Omicron) (Figure 3). Although not all lineages were identified, the clades were still assigned as follows: the unidentified lineages from the first round belonged to 21J (Delta), 21I (Delta); from the second round to 21J (Delta), 21B (Kappa); from the third round 21J (Delta); and from the fifth round to 21K (Omicron) (Figure 3).

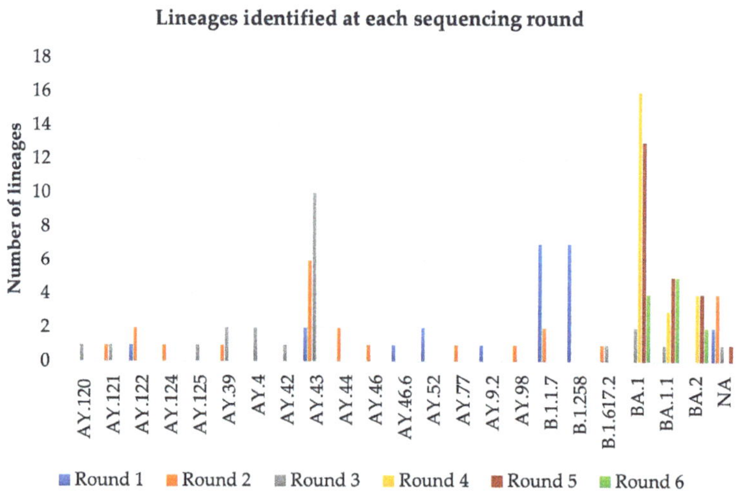

Figure 3. Lineage distribution in the six rounds of Nanopore sequencing.

In the first round of sequencing (performed on 10.12.2021), we identified 20I (Alpha, V1), 20A for the samples collected in February 2021, and Delta for the samples collected in August—September 2021. Except for only two (Delta) samples, Nanopore results (clades) were confirmed by Ion Torrent sequencing on an Ion S5 instrument (Table 2).

Table 2. Comparison of the results generated by Ion Torrent and Nanopore sequencing.

Ion Torrent			Nanopore			No. of Common Mutations	Concordance (%)
Clade	Lineage	Total No. of Mutations	Clade	Lineage	Total No. of Mutations		
20I (Alpha, V1)	B.1.1.7	35	20I (Alpha, V1)	B.1.1.7	35	35	100.0
20A	B.1.258.3	32	20A	B.1.258	28	27	84.4
20A	B.1.258	25	20A	B.1.258	20	19	76.0
20A	B.1.258	30	20A	B.1.258	22	21	70.0
21I (Delta)	B.1.617.2	38	21I (Delta)	AY.52	35	33	86.8
20I (Alpha, V1)	B.1.1.7	36	20I (Alpha, V1)	B.1.1.7	33	32	88.9
20A	B.1.258	29	20A	B.1.258	29	28	96.6
20I (Alpha, V1)	B.1.1.7	30	20I (Alpha, V1)	B.1.1.7	30	30	100.0
20I (Alpha, V1)	B.1.1.7	32	20I (Alpha, V1)	B.1.1.7	31	31	96.9
20I (Alpha, V1)	B.1.1.7	34	20I (Alpha, V1)	B.1.1.7	33	33	97.1
21J (Delta)	AY.122	48	21J (Delta)	AY.122	41	41	85.4
20I (Alpha, V1)	B.1.1.7	36	20I (Alpha, V1)	B.1.1.7	34	34	94.4
20A	B.1.258	25	20A	B.1.258	21	21	84.0
20A	B.1.258	21	20A	B.1.258	19	19	90.5
21I (Delta)	B.1.617.2	39	21J (Delta)	AY.46.6	36	16	41.0
21J (Delta)	AY.43	37	21J (Delta)	AY.43	34	34	91.9
21J (Delta)	AY.43	38	21J (Delta)	AY.43	32	32	84.2
20A	B.1.258	33	20A	B.1.258	30	30	90.9
21I (Delta)	AY.9.2	33	21I (Delta)	AY.9.2	27	26	78.8
21J (Delta)	AY.125	45	21J (Delta)	None	21	21	46.7
21J (Delta)	AY.46.6	40	21I (Delta)	AY.52	34	17	42.5
21I (Delta)	B.1.617.2	40	21I (Delta)	None	12	12	30.0

In the second round of sequencing, performed on 21.01.2022, we used samples from October 2021, and the variants most frequently identified were 21J (Delta) and 21I (Delta); two of the samples were classified as 20I (Alpha, V1). For four samples belonging to 21J (Delta), 21B (Kappa) clades, the lineages could not be identified.

In the third round (performed in 10.03.2022) of sequencing, we used samples from November and December 2021, when Delta (AY.120, AY.121, AY.125, AY.39, AY.4, AY.42, AY.43) was still the main circulating variant. In the January and February 2022 samples, the predominant variant circulating was 21K (Omicron) and 21L (Omicron) (BA.1, BA.1.1, BA.2). These samples were sequenced two times, with the V3 primer set (round 4, 12.03.2022) and V4 primer set (round 5, 14.04.2022). For most of the samples, the same lineages were obtained with both sets of primers; in the case of two samples, the sequencing with the V4 pool of primers offered a refinement, as BA.1.1 was diagnosed instead of BA.1 with V3. Nevertheless, we noticed a better-quality score and higher average sequence length when using the V4 primer set. In the last set of samples sequenced in 12.05.2022 (patients from February until May 2022), only 21K (Omicron) and 21L (Omicron) were identified.

3.2. Ion Torrent Sequencing

For Ion Torrent sequencing, the average loading of Ion Sphere Particles (IPS) was 91%, 99.5% of which contained the actual patient library. The percentage of polyclonal IPS was 28%, low quality products 11.3%, and there were 0% adapter dimers, so the final library IPS was around 60%. The mean read length obtained was 190 bp. A very high percentage of the total reads (98.6%) was aligned against the reference genome. Overall, these indicators show a very good quality of the sequencing run.

The results obtained for 22 samples from the first sequencing run performed on Nanopore and Ion Torrent are presented in Table 2. For most of the samples, the results were concordant in terms of clade (90.90%) and lineage (72.72%) identification. However, with the exception of the 20I (Alpha) clade (on average, 33.8 mutations on Ion Torrent vs. 32.4 on Nanopore), the Ion Torrent consistently identified more mutations compared to Nanopore sequencing: on average 27.9 and 39.8 mutations in the case of Ion Torrent vs. 24.1 and 30.9 in the case of Nanopore, for 20A and 21I+J (Delta), respectively. In terms of concordance between the two methods, the average value was 80% (Table 2). We also noticed that 2 out of 3 samples with the same number of mutations on both methods, had the same substitutions. A representative example is shown in Figure 4.

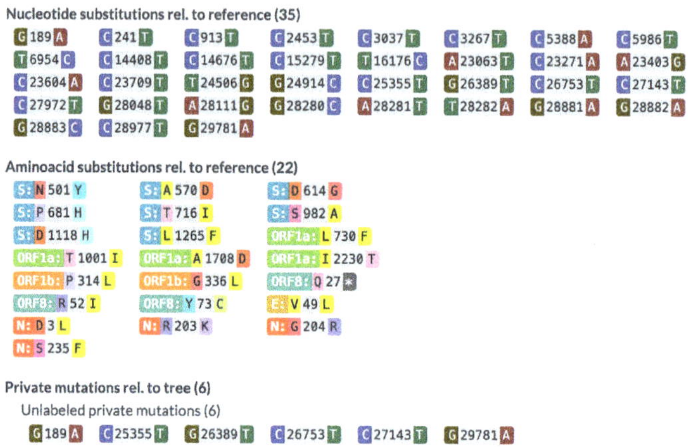

(a)

(b)

Figure 4. Mutations identified in sample 1 using Ion Torrent (**a**) and Nanopore (**b**).

4. Discussion

With each wave, SARS-CoV-2 has become more infectious and more virulent, underlying the importance of understanding its mutation diversity and rate, which are a major source of vaccine evasion [24,25] and treatment resistance [26]. Whole genome sequencing offers important insights on the evolution of the virus [27]; most of these methods are expensive, laborious, and time-consuming, which represent major disadvantages in the case of an epidemic or pandemic. The ideal sequencing method would need to be rapid, affordable, and easy to perform [2,24]; Nanopore sequencing fulfills all these requirements.

Nanopore sequencing is clearly less time-consuming compared to other platforms: ONT sequencing takes less than 20 h compared to Illumina and Ion Torrent (36 h) [28]. Library preparation for ONT sequencing is very easy and requires far less time than other methods. The workflows (using a modified ARTIC protocol) require 8 h or even 5 h using the Rapid Barcoding Kit [14,29]. In our hands, the entire protocol took approximately 10 h for libraries preparation, and 6 h to run the sequencing. In comparison, samples sequenced on Ion Torrent took around 18–20 h only for library preparation, 10 h run on Ion Chef, and another 4 h run time on the S5 instrument.

In terms of costs, Illumina and Ion Torrent sequencing are generally associated with higher costs and more laborious library preparation [15,28]. By using ONT, costs can be reduced significantly [29], and this is a very important aspect in large-scale sequencing. According to Tyson et al. when using the ARTIC LoCost protocol, the material costs for 24 barcodes on MinION can be reduced to GBP 24.91 pounds/sample (even down to GBP 16.85 for LoCost with one wash); when using 96 barcodes, the method becomes even more affordable, GBP 10.49/sample (GBP 8.47 for LoCost with one wash) [30]. Generally, Nanopore sequencing is considered less appropriate due to its lower read-level sequencing accuracy than the short-read gold standard sequencing platforms, Illumina and Ion Torrent [31]. Given the high mutation rate of the SARS-CoV-2 virus, sequencing accuracy is essential. However, Bull et al. proved that regardless of the high error rates, the sensitivity and specificity of ONT methods can be comparable with short-read sequencing (both >99% comparing to Illumina). Single nucleotide variants (SNVs) were detected with high accuracy, and with very high concordance between ONT and Illumina: 99.66% using the *Nanopolish* pipeline, and 98.83% using the *Medaka* pipeline. However, when it came to detecting small indels, ONT performed rather poorly [2].

The potential of Nanopore sequencing was proven by its large-scale use in several outbreaks such as Ebola and Zika [16,17]. Still, despite the advanced Nanopolish pipeline, which significantly reduces the error rate, some groups obtained a lower genome quality with GridION than Illumina MiSeq, possibly due to the diversity of the variants analyzed [28]. Except for the second round, we obtained overall good quality scores. Furthermore, clade (with two exceptions) and lineage (with seven exceptions) analyses performed on MinION were confirmed and are comparable with the Ion Torrent method. However, there were more mutations detected with Ion Torrent, and the concordance between the mutations identified by the two methods was 80%. In the case of ONT sequencing, we had only two samples with unidentified lineages, but known clades.

The ARTIC protocol has been widely adopted, even in laboratories without extensive next generation sequencing (NGS) experience, thanks to its simplicity, low cost, and very good sensitivity [30]. However, due to the frequent SARS-CoV-2 mutations, protocol adjustments, especially the primer sequences, are needed to improve its performance. The V3 primer scheme was the best choice until the Delta variant appeared, which prompted yet another upgrade, to the V4 primer pool [32]. When comparing the performances of V3 and V4 primer pools on a set of 23 samples, we noticed an overall higher quality score and average sequence length when using the V4 primer set. Improvements in the quality, depth, and resolution of the SNPs related to the usage of V4 primers were also reported by other groups. Of note, G142D amino acid substitution might be underrepresented in Delta variants deposited early, since it was not identified with the V3 primer set [21]. Moreover, Lambisia et al. reported that genome recovery was increased in Alpha, Beta, Delta, and Eta variants when the V4 primer set concentration was augmented [32].

Of note, it has been shown that the wastewater surveillance of SARS-CoV-2 by Nanopore sequencing could be a helpful tool as a forewarning system in the case of a new emerging variant [33,34], underlying that continuous, rapid, sensitive, genomic surveillance (and data sharing) is essential in outbreak monitoring [35–37].

5. Conclusions

In conclusion, we showed that Nanopore sequencing is a method that is easy to introduce in practice, even by laboratories with limited experience in NGS. It offers a reliable alternative for the rapid, efficient monitoring of COVID-19 outbreaks, at a level of sensitivity comparable to Ion Torrent, but with major advantages such as the ease of library preparation, real-time data analysis, affordable costs, and high accuracy of the results.

Author Contributions: Conceptualization, I.O.S. and P.D.C.; methodology, P.D.C.; validation, I.D.C. and M.R.; formal analysis, I.D.C. and F.M.A.; investigation, I.D.C. and F.M.A.; resources, C.O. and C.M; data curation, A.R.C. and P.D.C.; writing—original draft preparation, A.R.C.; writing—review and editing, A.R.C., M.R. and I.O.S.; visualization, M.R.; supervision, P.D.C. and I.O.S.; project administration, A.R.C. and I.O.S.; funding acquisition, C.M. and I.O.S. All authors have read and agreed to the published version of the manuscript.

Funding: This research was funded by a grant from the Romanian National Council for Higher Education Funding, CNFIS, grant number CNFIS-FDI-2021-0484, and by the Romanian Ministry of Education and Research, UEFISCDI, grant number PN-III-P2-2.1-SOL-2020-0142.

Institutional Review Board Statement: The study was conducted in accordance with the Declaration of Helsinki, and approved by the Ethics Committee of "Victor Babes" University of Medicine and Pharmacy, Timisoara (Nr. 34/28.07.2020).

Informed Consent Statement: Informed consent was obtained from all subjects involved in the study.

Data Availability Statement: Not applicable.

Acknowledgments: We thank Andrei Lobiuc for the help in optimizing the procedure for SARS-CoV-2 sequencing on Ion Torrent Chef and S5.

Conflicts of Interest: The authors declare no conflict of interest.

References

1. Baker, S.R.; Bloom, N.; Davis, S.J.; Terry, S.J. COVID-Induced Economic Uncertainty (No. w26983). National Bureau of Economic Research. Available online: https://www.policyuncertainty.com/media/COVID-Induced%20Economic%20Uncertainty.pdf (accessed on 13 April 2020).
2. Bull, R.A.; Adikari, T.N.; Ferguson, J.M.; Hammond, J.M.; Stevanovski, I.; Beukers, A.G.; Naing, Z.; Yeang, M.; Verich, A.; Gamaarachchi, H.; et al. Analytical validity of nanopore sequencing for rapid SARS-CoV-2 genome analysis. *Nat. Commun.* **2020**, *11*, 6272. [CrossRef] [PubMed]
3. Hourdel, V.; Kwasiborski, A.; Balière, C.; Matheus, S.; Batéjat, C.F.; Manuguerra, J.C.; Vanhomwegen, J.; Caro, V. Rapid genomic characterization of SARS-CoV-2 by direct amplicon-based sequencing through comparison of MinION and Illumina iSeq100TM system. *Front. Microbiol.* **2020**, *11*, 571328. [CrossRef] [PubMed]
4. Wu, F.; Zhao, S.; Yu, B.; Chen, Y.M.; Wang, W.; Song, Z.G.; Hu, Y.; Tao, Z.W.; Tian, J.H.; Pei, Y.Y.; et al. A new coronavirus associated with human respiratory disease in China. *Nature* **2020**, *579*, 265–269. [CrossRef] [PubMed]
5. van Kasteren, P.B.; van Der Veer, B.; van den Brink, S.; Wijsman, L.; de Jonge, J.; van den Brandt, A.; Molenkamp, R.; Reusken, C.B.; Meijer, A. Comparison of seven commercial RT-PCR diagnostic kits for COVID-19. *J. Clin. Virol.* **2020**, *128*, 104412. [CrossRef]
6. Martin, M.A.; VanInsberghe, D.; Koelle, K. Insights from SARS-CoV-2 sequences. *Science* **2021**, *371*, 466–467. [CrossRef]
7. Pater, A.A.; Bosmeny, M.S.; White, A.A.; Sylvain, R.J.; Eddington, S.B.; Parasrampuria, M.; Ovington, K.N.; Metz, P.E.; Yinusa, A.O.; Barkau, C.L.; et al. High throughput nanopore sequencing of SARS-CoV-2 viral genomes from patient samples. *J. Biol. Methods* **2021**, *8*, e155. [CrossRef]
8. Brejová, B.; Boršová, K.; Hodorová, V.; Čabanová, V.; Gafurov, A.; Fričová, D.; Neboháčová, M.; Vinař, T.; Klempa, B.; Nosek, J. Nanopore sequencing of SARS-CoV-2: Comparison of short and long PCR-tiling amplicon protocols. *PLoS ONE* **2021**, *16*, e0259277. [CrossRef]
9. González-Recio, O.; Gutiérrez-Rivas, M.; Peiró-Pastor, R.; Aguilera-Sepúlveda, P.; Cano-Gómez, C.; Jiménez-Clavero, M.Á.; Fernández-Pinero, J. Sequencing of SARS-CoV-2 genome using different nanopore chemistries. *Appl. Microbiol. Biotechnol.* **2021**, *105*, 3225–3234. [CrossRef]
10. Tillett, R.L.; Sevinsky, J.R.; Hartley, P.D.; Kerwin, H.; Crawford, N.; Gorzalski, A.; Laverdure, C.; Verma, S.C.; Rossetto, C.C.; Jackson, D.; et al. Genomic evidence for reinfection with SARS-CoV-2: A case study. *Lancet Infect. Dis.* **2021**, *21*, 52–58. [CrossRef]
11. Chiara, M.; D'Erchia, A.M.; Gissi, C.; Manzari, C.; Parisi, A.; Resta, N.; Zambelli, F.; Picardi, E.; Pavesi, G.; Horner, D.S.; et al. Next generation sequencing of SARS-CoV-2 genomes: Challenges, applications and opportunities. *Brief. Bioinform.* **2021**, *22*, 616–630. [CrossRef]

12. Quick, J.; Grubaugh, N.D.; Pullan, S.T.; Claro, I.M.; Smith, A.D.; Gangavarapu, K.; Oliveira, G.; Robles-Sikisaka, R.; Rogers, T.F.; Beutler, N.A.; et al. Multiplex PCR method for MinION and Illumina sequencing of Zika and other virus genomes directly from clinical samples. *Nat. Protoc.* **2017**, *12*, 1261–1276. [CrossRef] [PubMed]
13. Thomson, E.; Ip, C.L.; Badhan, A.; Christiansen, M.T.; Adamson, W.; Ansari, M.A.; Bibby, D.; Breuer, J.; Brown, A.; Bowden, R.; et al. Comparison of next-generation sequencing technologies for comprehensive assessment of full-length hepatitis C viral genomes. *J. Clin. Microbiol.* **2016**, *54*, 2470–2484. [CrossRef] [PubMed]
14. Li, J.; Wang, H.; Mao, L.; Yu, H.; Yu, X.; Sun, Z.; Qian, X.; Cheng, S.; Chen, S.; Chen, J.; et al. Rapid genomic characterization of SARS-CoV-2 viruses from clinical specimens using nanopore sequencing. *Sci. Rep.* **2020**, *10*, 17492. [CrossRef]
15. Gohl, D.M.; Garbe, J.; Grady, P.; Daniel, J.; Watson, R.H.; Auch, B.; Nelson, A.; Yohe, S.; Beckman, K.B. A rapid, cost-effective tailed amplicon method for sequencing SARS-CoV-2. *BMC Genom.* **2020**, *21*, 863. [CrossRef] [PubMed]
16. Quick, J.; Loman, N.J.; Duraffour, S.; Simpson, J.T.; Severi, E.; Cowley, L.; Bore, J.A.; Koundouno, R.; Dudas, G.; Mikhail, A.; et al. Real-time, portable genome sequencing for Ebola surveillance. *Nature* **2016**, *530*, 228–232. [CrossRef] [PubMed]
17. Faria, N.R.; Quick, J.; Claro, I.M.; Theze, J.; de Jesus, J.G.; Giovanetti, M.; Kraemer, M.U.; Hill, S.C.; Black, A.; da Costa, A.C.; et al. Establishment and cryptic transmission of Zika virus in Brazil and the Americas. *Nature* **2017**, *546*, 406–410. [CrossRef]
18. Kafetzopoulou, L.E.; Pullan, S.T.; Lemey, P.; Suchard, M.A.; Ehichioya, D.U.; Pahlmann, M.; Thielebein, A.; Hinzmann, J.; Oestereich, L.; Wozniak, D.M.; et al. Metagenomic sequencing at the epicenter of the Nigeria 2018 Lassa fever outbreak. *Science* **2019**, *363*, 74–77. [CrossRef] [PubMed]
19. Giovanetti, M.; de Mendonça, M.C.L.; Fonseca, V.; Mares-Guia, M.A.; Fabri, A.; Xavier, J.; de Jesus, J.G.; Gräf, T.; dos Santos Rodrigues, C.D.; Dos Santos, C.C.; et al. Yellow fever virus reemergence and spread in Southeast Brazil, 2016–2019. *J. Virol.* **2019**, *94*, e01623-19. [CrossRef]
20. Wang, J.; Moore, N.E.; Deng, Y.M.; Eccles, D.A.; Hall, R.J. MinION nanopore sequencing of an influenza genome. *Front. Microbiol.* **2015**, *6*, 766. [CrossRef]
21. Davis, J.J.; Long, S.W.; Christensen, P.A.; Olsen, R.J.; Olson, R.; Shukla, M.; Subedi, S.; Stevens, R.; Musser, J.M. Analysis of the ARTIC version 3 and version 4 SARS-CoV-2 primers and their impact on the detection of the G142D amino acid substitution in the spike protein. *Microbiol. Spectr.* **2021**, *9*, e01803-21. [CrossRef]
22. Aksamentov, I.; Roemer, C.; Hodcroft, E.B.; Neher, R.A. Nextclade: Clade assignment, mutation calling and quality control for viral genomes. *J. Open Source Softw.* **2021**, *6*, 3773. [CrossRef]
23. O'Toole, Á.; Scher, E.; Underwood, A.; Jackson, B.; Hill, V.; McCrone, J.T.; Colquhoun, R.; Ruis, C.; Abu-Dahab, K.; Taylor, B.; et al. Assignment of epidemiological lineages in an emerging pandemic using the pangolin tool. *Virus Evol.* **2021**, *7*, veab064. [CrossRef] [PubMed]
24. Plitnick, J.; Griesemer, S.; Lasek-Nesselquist, E.; Singh, N.; Lamson, D.M.; George, K.S. Whole-genome sequencing of SARS-CoV-2: Assessment of the Ion Torrent AmpliSeq panel and comparison with the Illumina MiSeq ARTIC Protocol. *J. Clin. Microbiol.* **2021**, *59*, e00649-21. [CrossRef] [PubMed]
25. Andeweg, S.P.; Vennema, H.; Veldhuijzen, I.; Smorenburg, N.; Schmitz, D.; Zwagemaker, F.; van Gageldonk-Lafeber, A.B.; Hahné, S.J.; Reusken, C.; Knol, M.J.; et al. Elevated risk of infection with SARS-CoV-2 Beta, Gamma, and Delta variant compared to Alpha variant in vaccinated individuals. *Sci. Transl. Med.* **2022**, eabn4338. [CrossRef]
26. Birnie, E.; Biemond, J.J.; Appelman, B.; de Bree, G.J.; Jonges, M.; Welkers, M.R.; Wiersinga, W.J. Development of resistance-associated mutations after sotrovimab administration in high-risk individuals infected with the SARS-CoV-2 omicron variant. *JAMA* **2022**, *328*, 1104–1107. [CrossRef]
27. Dächert, C.; Muenchhoff, M.; Graf, A.; Autenrieth, H.; Bender, S.; Mairhofer, H.; Wratil, P.R.; Thieme, S.; Krebs, S.; Grzimek-Koschewa, N.; et al. Rapid and sensitive identification of omicron by variant-specific PCR and nanopore sequencing: Paradigm for diagnostics of emerging SARS-CoV-2 variants. *Med. Microbiol. Immunol.* **2022**, *211*, 71–77. [CrossRef]
28. Tshiabuila, D.; Giandhari, J.; Pillay, S.; Ramphal, U.; Ramphal, Y.; Maharaj, A.; Anyaneji, U.J.; Naidoo, Y.; Tegally, H.; San, E.J.; et al. Comparison of SARS-CoV-2 sequencing using the ONT GridION and the Illumina MiSeq. *BMC Genom.* **2022**, *23*, 319. [CrossRef]
29. Freed, N.E.; Vlková, M.; Faisal, M.B.; Silander, O.K. Rapid and inexpensive whole-genome sequencing of SARS-CoV-2 using 1200 bp tiled amplicons and Oxford Nanopore Rapid Barcoding. *Biol. Methods Protoc.* **2020**, *5*, bpaa014. [CrossRef]
30. Tyson, J.R.; James, P.; Stoddart, D.; Sparks, N.; Wickenhagen, A.; Hall, G.; Choi, J.H.; Lapointe, H.; Kamelian, K.; Smith, A.D.; et al. Improvements to the ARTIC multiplex PCR method for SARS-CoV-2 genome sequencing using nanopore. *BioRxiv.* **2020**. [CrossRef]
31. Laver, T.; Harrison, J.; O'neill, P.A.; Moore, K.; Farbos, A.; Paszkiewicz, K.; Studholme, D.J. Assessing the performance of the oxford nanopore technologies minion. *Biomol. Detect. Quantif.* **2015**, *3*, 1–8. [CrossRef]
32. Lambisia, A.W.; Mohammed, K.S.; Makori, T.O.; Ndwiga, L.; Mburu, M.W.; Morobe, J.M.; Moraa, E.O.; Musyoki, J.; Murunga, N.; Mwangi, J.N.; et al. Optimization of the SARS-CoV-2 ARTIC Network V4 Primers and Whole Genome Sequencing Protocol. *Front. Med.* **2022**, *9*, 836728. [CrossRef] [PubMed]
33. Rasmussen, L.D.; Richter, S.R.; Midgley, S.E.; Franck, K.T. Detecting SARS-CoV-2 Omicron B.1.1.529 variant in wastewater samples by using nanopore sequencing. *Emerg. Infect. Dis.* **2022**, *28*, 1296. [CrossRef] [PubMed]
34. Dharmadhikari, T.; Rajput, V.; Yadav, R.; Boargaonkar, R.; Patil, D.; Kale, S.; Kamble, S.P.; Dastager, S.G.; Dharne, M.S. High throughput sequencing based direct detection of SARS-CoV-2 fragments in wastewater of Pune, West India. *Sci. Total Environ.* **2022**, *807*, 151038. [CrossRef] [PubMed]

35. Cheng, V.C.C.; Ip, J.D.; Chu, A.W.H.; Tam, A.R.; Chan, W.M.; Abdullah, S.M.U.; Chan, B.P.C.; Wong, S.C.; Kwan, M.Y.W.; Chua, G.T.; et al. Rapid spread of severe acute respiratory syndrome coronavirus 2 (SARS-CoV-2) Omicron subvariant BA. 2 in a single-source community outbreak. *Clin. Infect. Dis.* **2022**, *75*, e44–e49. [CrossRef] [PubMed]
36. Wang, Y.; Chen, D.; Zhu, C.; Zhao, Z.; Gao, S.; Gou, J.; Guo, Y.; Kong, X. Genetic Surveillance of Five SARS-CoV-2 Clinical Samples in Henan Province Using Nanopore Sequencing. *Front. Immunol.* **2022**, *13*, 814806. [CrossRef]
37. Chen, Z.; Azman, A.S.; Chen, X.; Zou, J.; Tian, Y.; Sun, R.; Xu, X.; Wu, Y.; Lu, W.; Ge, S.; et al. Global landscape of SARS-CoV-2 genomic surveillance and data sharing. *Nat. Genet.* **2022**, *54*, 499–507. [CrossRef]

medicina

MDPI

Article

Effect of the Duration of NSAID Use on COVID-19

Kyeongmi Kim [1], Siyeoung Yoon [2], Junwon Choi [3] and Soonchul Lee [2,*]

[1] Department of Laboratory Medicine, CHA Ilsan Medical Center, School of Medicine, CHA University, 100 Ilsan-ro, Ilsandong-gu, Goyang-si 10444, Republic of Korea
[2] Department of Orthopaedic Surgery, CHA Bundang Medical Center, School of Medicine, CHA University, 335 Pangyo-ro, Bundang-gu, Seongnam-si 13488, Republic of Korea
[3] Department of Molecular Science and Technology, Department of Applied Chemistry and Biological Engineering, Ajou University, 206 World cup-ro, Yeongtong-gu, Suwon-si 16499, Republic of Korea
* Correspondence: lsceline78@gmail.com; Tel.: +82-31-780-5289

Abstract: *Background and Objectives:* Non-steroidal anti-inflammatory drugs (NSAIDs) are commonly used to control pain and fever. However, their effect on COVID-19 infected patients has not been fully studied. In this study, we investigated the effect of the duration of NSAIDs use on COVID-19 infection and clinical outcomes. *Materials and Methods:* In South Korea, 25,739 eligible patients who received COVID-19 testing between 1 January and 31 July 2020, were included in this retrospective observational cohort analysis. Based on the date of the first COVID-19 test for each patient, NSAID prescription dates were used to separate patients into two groups (short-term group: <2 weeks; long-term group: 8–12 weeks). COVID-19 infectivity and clinical outcomes were analyzed. We used the propensity score-matching (PSM) method. *Results:* Of the 580 patients who had taken NSAIDs before the date of COVID-19 test, 534 and 46 patients were grouped in the short- and long-term NSAID-use groups, respectively. We did not find a statistically significant increased risk of COVID-19 infection (adjustment for age and sex, $p = 0.413$; adjustment for age, sex, region of residence, comorbidity, Charlson Comorbidity Index, and current use of medication, $p = 0.259$) or change in clinical outcomes, including conventional oxygen therapy, admission of intensive care unit, artificial ventilation, or death, between the two groups in which the PSM method was applied. *Conclusions:* The duration of NSAIDs use did not have a statistically significant effect on COVID-19 infectivity or clinical outcomes. However, further studies looking at clinical presentation and laboratory test results in a large number of people should be performed.

Keywords: COVID-19; NSAID; duration

Citation: Kim, K.; Yoon, S.; Choi, J.; Lee, S. Effect of the Duration of NSAID Use on COVID-19. *Medicina* **2022**, *58*, 1713. https://doi.org/10.3390/medicina58121713

Academic Editors: Yusra Habib Khan, Tauqeer Hussain Mallhi, Tahir Mehmood Khan and Muhammad Salman

Received: 4 November 2022
Accepted: 22 November 2022
Published: 23 November 2022

Publisher's Note: MDPI stays neutral with regard to jurisdictional claims in published maps and institutional affiliations.

Copyright: © 2022 by the authors. Licensee MDPI, Basel, Switzerland. This article is an open access article distributed under the terms and conditions of the Creative Commons Attribution (CC BY) license (https://creativecommons.org/licenses/by/4.0/).

1. Introduction

In December 2019, the Coronavirus disease 2019 (COVID-19), caused by a novel coronavirus (SARS-CoV-2) that causes viral pneumonia, was first discovered in China [1]. It has rapidly spread globally through close human interactions or the respiratory secretions of infected people. On 11 March 2020, the World Health Organization (WHO) has declared the COVID-19 outbreak as a "pandemic" [2]. The number of infected cases and deaths due to COVID-19 is rapidly increasing, and in August 2022, there were more than 58 hundred million confirmed cases, with over 6,400,000 deaths globally [3]. In Korea, six outbreaks have been recorded, with more than 20 million confirmed cases and over 25,332 deaths [4]. The spread of COVID-19 is affecting economic, social, and racial issues, not only in Korea but also around the world.

In COVID-19-infected patients, non-steroidal anti-inflammatory drugs (NSAIDs) such as ibuprofen, along with acetaminophen, are commonly used to control symptoms such as fever and muscle pain. However, French authorities have warned about the risks of using ibuprofen for COVID-19 infection, and there are reports of serious COVID-19 cases requiring intensive care after exposure to ibuprofen in young patients [5,6]. Our previous study reported that aspirin, a class of NSAIDs, had a negative effect on clinical outcomes in patients with COVID-19 infection [7]. However, according to a meta-analysis by Moore et al., NSAIDs use does not increase the risk of COVID-19 infection, hospital admission, severe COVID-19, or death [8]. In addition, studies on the length of NSAIDs exposure revealed that NSAIDs had no effect on the infection and severity of COVID-19 with various exposure periods, including current or acute exposure [9,10] or within 30 days [11] or 4 months [12]. However, NSAIDs use in COVID-19 patients is still controversial, and there is a lack of sufficient research on the effect of NSAIDs on COVID-19 depending on the duration of use.

This study aimed to evaluate the difference in COVID-19 infection and clinical outcomes according to the duration of NSAIDs use. We analyzed patients by subdividing them according to the duration of NSAID use before the diagnosis of COVID-19 using nationwide Korean COVID-19 data.

2. Materials and Methods

2.1. Data Source

We analyzed the database of Korean National Health Insurance System (NHIS)-COVID-19 cohort, which includes data on all patients tested for COVID-19 in South Korea from 1 January to 31 July 2020 (N = 25,739). The COVID-19 testing date, results, and demographic information were all included in the data. Furthermore, the database contains codes for disease diagnosis, prescription information, outcomes related to COVID-19, and death records. All of the personal information used in this study was de-identified.

2.2. Study Population

The cohort's index date was the first COVID-19 test for each patient. We included all patients aged 20 years and older with a history of taking NSAIDs among patients who tested positive for COVID-19 between 1 January and 31 July 2020 (N = 580). We extracted and combined patient characteristics such as sex, age (20–29, 30–39, 40–49, 50–59, 60–69, 70–79, 80+), and region of residence (Seoul, Gyeonggi, Daegu, Gyeongbuk, etc.). At least two claims were evaluated within a year to confirm the presence of underlying diseases (such as asthma, cerebrovascular disease (CVD), chronic kidney disease (CKD), chronic obstructive pulmonary disease (COPD), diabetes mellitus (DM), hypertension (HTN)) and the Charlson comorbidity index score was calculated using previously reported methods [13]. Systemic steroid use within 30 days of the index date was analyzed using the types and codes obtained from a previous study [14].

2.3. Study Group Classification

We used NHIS-COVID-19 database's inpatient and outpatient prescription records for NSAIDs including both oral and intravenous formulations. We classified 580 patients prescribed NSAIDs according to treatment duration. From the index data, patients who took NSAIDs within 2 weeks were classified into the short-term group, and those who had taken NSAIDs for more than 8 weeks and within 12 weeks were classified into the long-term group.

2.4. Outcomes

The outcomes included composite endpoint 1 and composite endpoint 2. Composite end point 1 contains conventional oxygen therapy, admission of intensive care unit (ICU), artificial ventilation, or death. Composite end point 2 contains admission of ICU, artificial ventilation, or death except for conventional oxygen therapy in composite end point 1.

2.5. Statistis

p-values less than 0.05 were considered significant. Pearson's $\chi 2$ test or Fisher's exact test used data analysis. To reduce potential bias caused by differences in patients' baseline characteristics, we used the propensity score matching (PSM) method. A logistic regression model was used, with adjustments for the variables. We calculated the PSM of the two groups at a 1:1 fixed ratio based on a greedy nearest neighbor algorithm and estimated the predicted probability of short-term versus long-term NSAIDs users. We examined standardized mean differences (SMDs) across groups to detect any remaining imbalance in the matched samples [15]. Data processing and statistical analysis were performed using R software, version 3.6.3 (The R Foundation for Statistical Computing, Vienna, Austria).

3. Results

3.1. Study Subjects

This retrospective analysis was performed on patients enrolled in the NHIS-COVID-19 cohort database due to a positive COVID-19 result via real-time reverse transcription polymerase chain reaction (RT-PCR). Of the 25,739 individuals who tested positive for COVID-19, 580 had taken NSAIDs prior to the positive result. Among them, 534 patients (92.07%) used NSAIDs within 2 weeks and 46 (7.93%) patients used NSAIDs for more than 8 weeks and within 12 weeks before the index date.

3.2. Baseline Characteristics

The baseline patient characteristics are shown in Table 1. Among NSAIDs users, 271 (53.3%) were women and 309 (46.7%) were men. In the short-term group, the age group with the most participants (20.4%) was the 50–59 age group, whereas in the long-term group, the 60–69 age group and 70–79 age group were the most common. Hypertension was the most common comorbidity observed in the two groups. In the long-term group, COPD, DM, and hypertension were also significantly higher than those in the short-term group, but there was no difference in asthma, CKD, and CVD. The Charlson comorbidity index score was significantly higher in the long-term group (Table 1).

Table 1. Baseline characteristics of patients who were used non-steroidal anti-inflammatory drugs (NSAIDs) for short (2 weeks) or long term (8–12 weeks) duration before the COVID-19 index date in the Korean National Health Insurance System (NHIS) COVID-19 database.

Characteristic	Entire Cohort $N = 580$	Short-Term $N = 534$	Long-Term $N = 46$	*p*-Value
Sex, *n* (%)				0.123
Male	271 (46.7)	244 (45.7)	27 (58.7)	
Female	309 (53.3)	290 (54.3)	19 (41.3)	
Age, *n* (%)				0.009
20–29	79 (13.6)	78 (14.6)	1 (2.2)	
30–39	76 (13.1)	73 (13.7)	3 (6.5)	
40–49	80 (13.8)	76 (14.2)	4 (8.7)	
50–59	118 (20.3)	109 (20.4)	9 (19.6)	
60–69	101 (17.4)	91 (17.0)	10 (21.7)	
70–79	71 (12.2)	61 (11.4)	10 (21.7)	
80+	55 (9.5)	46 (8.6)	9 (19.6)	
Region, *n* (%)				0.171
Seoul	79 (13.6)	75 (14.0)	4 (8.7)	
Gyeonggi	69 (11.9)	67 (12.5)	2 (4.3)	
Daegu	163 (28.1)	144 (27.0)	19 (41.3)	
Gyeongbuk	54 (9.3)	50 (9.4)	4 (8.7)	
Other	215 (37.1)	198 (37.1)	17 (37.0)	
Comorbidity, *n* (%)				
Asthma	102 (17.6)	95 (17.8)	7 (15.7)	0.812
CVA	68 (11.7)	58 (10.9)	10 (21.7)	0.05
CKD	32 (5.5)	28 (5.2)	4 (8.7)	0.517
COPD	**40 (6.9)**	**33 (6.2)**	**7 (15.2)**	**0.044**
DM	**134 (23.1)**	**113 (21.2)**	**21 (45.7)**	**<0.001**
HTN	**184 (31.7)**	**159 (29.8)**	**25 (54.3)**	**0.001**

Table 1. *Cont.*

Characteristic	Entire Cohort N = 580	Short-Term N = 534	Long-Term N = 46	p-Value
Charlson Comorbidity Index, n (%)				**0.032**
0	217 (37.4)	207 (38.8)	10 (21.7)	
1	89 (15.3)	83 (15.5)	6 (13.0)	
2 or more	274 (47.2)	244 (45.7)	30 (65.2)	
Current use of medication, n (%)				
Steroid	118 (20.3)	103 (19.3)	15 (32.6)	0.05

3.3. Propensity Score-Matching

Short- and long-term NSAIDs users before COVID-19 diagnosis were individually matched to an equal number of long-term NSAIDs use patients in our PSM cohorts (Table 2). When SMD was used to analyze the demographics and clinical variables in the PSM cohorts, no significant differences were found in either (SMD < 0.25). In the long-term group, the minimally adjusted odds accounting for age and gender via PSM of COVID-19 positivity were 1.5 (95% CI, 0.57–4.05), and the fully adjusted odds accounting for all variables included in this analysis were 2.24 (95% CI, 0.56–9.57). Patients who used NSAIDs for a long time were more likely to be confirmed to have COVID-19, but this was not statistically significant (minimally adjusted, $p = 0.413$; fully adjusted, $p = 0.259$).

Table 2. Propensity score-matched baseline characteristics and positive COVID-19 test result between the short- and long-term NSAIDs-use groups.

Characteristic	Short-Term N = 46	Long-Term N = 46	SMD
Sex, n (%)			0.044
Male	26 (56.5)	27 (58.7)	
Female	20 (43.5)	19 (41.3)	
Age, n (%)			0.068
20–29	2 (4.3)	1 (2.2)	
30–39	3 (6.5)	3 (6.5)	
40–49	3 (6.5)	4 (8.7)	
50–59	11 (23.9)	9 (19.6)	
60–69	8 (17.4)	10 (21.7)	
70–79	11 (23.9)	10 (21.7)	
80+	8 (17.4)	9 (19.6)	
Region, n (%)			0.213
Seoul	10 (21.7)	4 (8.7)	
Gyeonggi	18 (39.1)	2 (4.3)	
Daegu	1 (2.2)	19 (41.3)	
Gyeongbuk	3 (6.5)	4 (8.7)	
Other	14 (30.4)	17 (37.0)	
Comorbidity, n (%)			
Asthma	6 (13.0)	7 (15.7)	0.060
CVA	**10 (21.7)**	**10 (21.7)**	**0.000**
CKD	1 (2.2)	4 (8.7)	0.230
COPD	6 (13.0)	7 (15.2)	0.060
DM	**20 (43.5)**	**21 (45.7)**	**0.043**
HTN	20 (43.5)	25 (54.3)	0.216
Charlson Comorbidity Index, n (%)			0.104
0	8 (17.4)	10 (21.7)	
1	6 (13.0)	6 (13.0)	
2 or more	32 (69.6)	30 (65.2)	

Table 2. *Cont.*

Characteristic	Short-Term N = 46	Long-Term N = 46	SMD
Current use of medication, n (%)			
Steroid	18 (39.1)	15 (32.6)	0.138
COVID-19, n (%)			
Minimally adjusted OR *	1.00 (reference)	1.5 (0.57–4.05)	
Fully adjusted OR #	1.00 (reference)	2.24 (0.56–9.57)	

* Adjustment for age and sex (p-value: 0.413); # Adjustment for age, sex, region of residence, comorbidity, Charlson Comorbidity Index, and current use of medication (p-value: 0.259).

3.4. Clinical Outcome

In Table 3, the endpoints of 13 patients in the short-term group and 17 patients in the long-term group with confirmed clinical outcomes were analyzed. The composite endpoints 1 and 2 were 15.4% (2/13) and 7.7% (1/13) in the short-term group and 47.1% (8/17) and 23.5% (4/17) in the long-term group, respectively. Patients in the long-term group had a higher probability of experiencing severe clinical outcomes, but this was not statistically significant (composite endpoint 1, $p = 0.119$; composite endpoint 2, $p = 0.355$).

Table 3. Clinical outcomes of COVID-19-infected patients between the short- and long-term NSAIDs-use groups.

Variables	Short-Term N = 13	Long-Term N = 17	p-Value *
Composite endpoint1, n (%)			0.119
No	11 (84.6)	9 (52.9)	
Yes	2 (15.4)	8 (47.1)	
Composite endpoint2, n (%)			0.355
No	12 (92.3)	13 (76.5)	
Yes	1 (7.7)	4 (23.5)	

* Fisher's exact test; Composite endpoint 1: conventional oxygen therapy, admission of intensive care unit (ICU), artificial ventilation, or death. Composite endpoint 2: admission of ICU, artificial ventilation, or Death.

4. Discussion

NSAIDs are among the most-prescribed drugs worldwide, constituting 5% of all prescribed drugs [16]. NSAIDs are mostly used to relieve pain, reduce inflammation, and decrease fever, and even used extensively as analgesics [16,17]. NSAIDs exhibit anti-inflammatory properties by decreasing the biosynthesis of prostaglandin (PG) through the inhibition of intracellular cyclo-oxygenase enzymes [18]. NSAIDs are indicated for rheumatoid arthritis, osteoarthritis, fever, headache, and dysmenorrhea and have been shown to prevent Alzheimer's dementia [19]. However, despite the many indications mentioned above, NSAIDs should be used with caution as they may have adverse effects on a variety of organs, including the respiratory tract [19,20].

French officials warned against using ibuprofen, one of the NSAIDs, in patients with COVID-19 symptoms in March 2020 [6]. Initially, the European Medicines Agency, Medicines and Healthcare Products Regulatory Agency in the UK, and the WHO recommended against using ibuprofen [21–23]. Similarly, the Korea Centers for Disease Control and Prevention (KCDC) recommended the use of acetaminophen instead of NSAIDs for symptom relief [24]. The cell entry receptor for SARS-CoV-2 is angiotensin-converting enzyme 2 (ACE2), and previous research has indicated that NSAIDs upregulate this enzyme, thus raising concerns that NSAIDs may increase vulnerability to infection [25,26]. As such, a lower death rate has been reported in patients using ACE inhibitors [26]. There is also a report that NSAIDs use increases the risk of hospital death, ICU admission, artificial ventilation, and sepsis in Korean patients with COVID-19, so that NSAIDs use should be cautioned in COVID-19 patients [27]. Based on the results of these reports, the use of NSAIDs in COVID-19 patients has been questioned in many countries.

However, many studies related to COVID-19 have been conducted, and many have reported that the use of NSAIDs has little effect or positive effects on COVID-19 infection. Chen et al. reported that suppressing COX-2/PGE2 signaling with ibuprofen and meloxicam, two commonly used NSAIDs, had no influence on ACE2 expression, viral entrance, or viral replication [25]. Multi-center studies found that the use of NSAIDs was not correlated with COVID-19. On the contrary, it serves to reduce both the prevalence and severity of COVID-19 infection [10,28]. In addition, exposure to ibuprofen has been reported to be related to a lower risk of hospitalization and artificial ventilation [29]. A meta-analysis of 266 papers mentioning NSAIDs did not confirm that the use of NSAIDs, including ibuprofen, increase the risk of COVID-19 infection, hospital admission, severe COVID-19, or death [8]. Nevertheless, many clinicians and patients are still hesitant to use NSAIDs.

Although the administration of NSAIDs to COVID-19 patients is still controversial, recently published papers support the use of NSAIDs [8,10,28,29]. Accordingly, we attempted to investigate the effect of NSAIDs on COVID-19 using a nationwide Korean cohort to determine whether the duration of NSAIDs use reduced susceptibility to COVID-19. The NHIS-COVID-19 cohort database was created by the Health Insurance Review and Assessment of Korea (HIRA) and the KCDC for use in medical research. We did not observe a statistically significantly higher risk of SARS-CoV-2 infection in the propensity score-matched population with short- and long-term NSAID exposure, which is consistent with the findings of prior research. Furthermore, we found no statistically significant increased risk associated with conventional oxygen therapy, ICU admission, artificial ventilation, or death from COVID-19 between the two groups. Based on several other studies and our analysis, there is currently little scientific data to support the use of NSAIDs increasing the infection rate and severity of clinical outcomes with COVID-19.

However, this study had several limitations. First, many patients who were taking long-term NSAIDs were not included in the analysis (7.9% of 580 patients). Furthermore, the number of patients who had clinically confirmed outcomes was minimal (5.2% of 580 patients). Second, because a comparison with the patient group who did not use NSAIDs was not made, it was not possible to analyze whether the use of NSAIDs affected COVID-19 and not only the period of use. Third, unmeasured factors may have influenced the results, despite our best efforts to account for all confounding factors using PSM analysis. Additionally, clinical presentation, symptoms, clinical course, and laboratory test results could not be included because this study was retrospective and used information from the Korean NHIS. Fourth, even though NSAIDs are over-the-counter medicines in Korea, we only analyzed the data for prescribed NSAIDs use.

Regardless of these drawbacks, the study's information on the effects of NSAID use in Korean COVID-19 patients is reliable. In addition, it is meaningful in that it analyzes how the period of taking NSAIDs affects COVID-19 in Koreans using a large amount of Korean NHIS data, and we used PSM to eliminate the effects of factors other than NSAIDs. However, more large-scale studies of the association between COVID-19 and NSAIDs use are needed, with better control of variables except NSAIDs.

5. Conclusions

The duration of NSAIDs use did not have a statistically significant effect on COVID-19 infectivity or severity of clinical outcomes. Therefore, our study results are expected to help physicians and patients decide whether to take NSAIDs in relation to COVID-19 infection. However, further studies focusing on clinical presentation and laboratory test results in a large number of people should be performed.

Author Contributions: Conceptualization, S.L.; Data curation, K.K. and S.Y.; Formal analysis, K.K. and S.Y.; Funding acquisition, S.L.; Investigation, S.L.; Methodology, S.L.; Project administration, K.K.; Visualization, J.C.; Writing–original draft, K.K. and S.Y.; Writing–review & editing, J.C. and S.L. All authors have read and agreed to the published version of the manuscript.

Funding: This work was supported by the National Research Foundation of Korea (NRF) grant funded by the Korean government (MSIT) (Nos. 2022R1A2C2005916 and 2021R1G1A109434111).

Institutional Review Board Statement: Not applicable.

Informed Consent Statement: Not applicable.

Data Availability Statement: Data are contained within the article.

Acknowledgments: We would like to thank everyone who assisted us with the writing of this article.

Conflicts of Interest: The authors declare no conflict of interest.

References

1. Zhu, N.; Zhang, D.; Wang, W.; Li, X.; Yang, B.; Song, J.; Zhao, X.; Huang, B.; Shi, W.; Lu, R.; et al. A Novel Coronavirus from Patients with Pneumonia in China, 2019. *N. Engl. J. Med.* **2020**, *382*, 727–733. [CrossRef] [PubMed]
2. World Health Organization. Coronavirus Disease (COVID-19) Situation Report—51. Available online: https://apps.who.int/iris/bitstream/handle/10665/331475/nCoVsitrep11Mar2020-eng.pdf?sequence=1&isAllowed=y (accessed on 10 August 2022).
3. World Health Organization. Coronavirus (COVID-19) Dashboard Online. Available online: https://covid19.who.int/?adgroupsurvey=\{adgroupsurvey\}&gclid=EAIaIQobChMIzY_xsoC7-QIV2sKWCh0b9g9iEAAYASABEgIo2PD_BwE (accessed on 10 August 2022).
4. Korea Disease Control and Prevention Agency. Coronavirus (COVID-19), Republic of Korea, Occurrence Status Online. Available online: http://ncov.mohw.go.kr (accessed on 10 August 2022).
5. Micallef, J.; Soeiro, T.; Jonville-Bera, A.P. French Society of Pharmacology Team. Non-steroidal anti-inflammatory drugs, pharmacology, and COVID-19 infection. *Therapie* **2020**, *75*, 355–362. [CrossRef]
6. Moore, N.; Carleton, B.; Blin, P.; Bosco-Levy, P.; Droz, C. Does Ibuprofen Worsen COVID-19? *Drug Saf.* **2020**, *43*, 611–614. [CrossRef] [PubMed]
7. Kim, I.; Yoon, S.; Kim, M.; Lee, H.; Park, S.; Kim, W.; Lee, S. Aspirin is related to worse clinical outcomes of COVID-19. *Medicina* **2021**, *57*, 931. [CrossRef] [PubMed]
8. Moore, N.; Bosco-Levy, P.; Thurin, N.; Blin, P.; Droz-Perroteau, C. NSAIDs and COVID-19: A Systematic Review and Meta-analysis. *Drug Saf.* **2021**, *44*, 929–938. [CrossRef]
9. Chandan, J.S.; Zemedikun, D.T.; Thayakaran, R.; Byne, N.; Dhalla, S.; Acosta-Mena, D.; Gokhale, K.M.; Thomas, T.; Sainsbury, C.; Subramanian, A.; et al. Nonsteroidal Antiinflammatory Drugs and Susceptibility to COVID-19. *Arthritis Rheumatol.* **2021**, *73*, 731–739. [CrossRef]
10. Reese, J.T.; Coleman, B.; Chan, L.; Blau, H.; Callahan, T.J.; Cappelletti, L.; Fontana, T.; Bradwell, K.R.; Harris, N.L.; Casiraghi, E.; et al. NSAID use and clinical outcomes in COVID-19 patients: A 38-center retrospective cohort study. *Virol. J.* **2022**, *19*, 84. [CrossRef]
11. Lund, L.C.; Kristensen, K.B.; Reilev, M.; Blau, H.; Callahan, T.J.; Cappelletti, L.; Fontana, T.; Bradwell, K.R.; Harris, N.L.; Casiraghi, E.; et al. Adverse outcomes and mortality in users of non-steroidal anti-inflammatory drugs who tested positive for SARS-CoV-2: A Danish nationwide cohort study. *PLoS Med.* **2020**, *17*, e1003308. [CrossRef]
12. Wong, A.Y.; MacKenna, B.; Morton, C.E.; Christensen, S.; Thomsen, R.W.; Christiansen, C.F.; Stovring, H.; Johansen, N.B.; Brun, N.; Hallas, J.; et al. Use of non-steroidal anti-inflammatory drugs and risk of death from COVID-19: An OpenSAFELY cohort analysis based on two cohorts. *Ann. Rheum. Dis.* **2021**, *80*, 943–951. [CrossRef]
13. Kim, J.S.; Shin, D.H.; Kim, H.W. Analysis of Major COVID-19 Issues Using Unstructured Big Data. *Knowl. Manag. Res.* **2021**, *22*, 145–165. [CrossRef]
14. Jung, S.Y.; Choi, J.C.; You, S.H.; Kim, W.Y. Association of Renin-angiotensin-aldosterone System Inhibitors With Coronavirus Disease 2019 (COVID-19)- Related Outcomes in Korea: A Nationwide Population-based Cohort Study. *Clin. Infect. Dis.* **2020**, *71*, 2121–2128. [CrossRef] [PubMed]
15. Zhang, Z.; Kim, H.J.; Lonjon, G.; Zhu, Y.; on behalf of AME Big-Data Clinical Trial Collaborative Group. Balance diagnostics after propensity score matching. *Ann. Transl. Med.* **2019**, *7*, 16. [CrossRef] [PubMed]
16. Bindu, S.; Mazumder, S.; Bandyopadhyay, U. Non-steroidal anti-inflammatory drugs (NSAIDs) and organ damage: A current perspective. *Biochem. Pharmacol.* **2020**, *180*, 114147. [CrossRef] [PubMed]
17. Ho, K.Y.; Gwee, K.A.; Cheng, Y.K.; Yoon, K.H.; Hee, H.T.; Omar, A.R. Nonsteroidal anti-inflammatory drugs in chronic pain: Implications of new data for clinical practice. *J. Pain Res.* **2018**, *11*, 1937–1948. [CrossRef]
18. Dwivedi, A.K.; Gurjar, V.; Kumar, S.; Singh, N. Molecular basis for nonspecificity of nonsteroidal anti-inflammatory drugs (NSAIDs). *Drug Discov. Today.* **2015**, *20*, 863–873. [CrossRef]
19. Park, J.S.; Kim, H.Y. Current trend of NSAIDs use. *Korean J. Med.* **2000**, *59*, 491–504.
20. White, A.A.; Stevenson, D.D. Aspirin-Exacerbated Respiratory Disease. *N. Engl. J. Med.* **2018**, *379*, 1060–1070. [CrossRef]
21. European Medicines Agency. EMA Gives Advice on the Use of Non-Steroidal Anti-Infammatories for COVID-19. Available online: https://www.ema.europa.eu/en/news/ema-gives-advice-use-non-steroidal-anti-inflammatories-covid-19 (accessed on 10 August 2022).

22. AFP. Updated: WHO Now Doesn't Recommend Avoiding Ibuprofen For COVID-19 Symptoms. *Science Alert*. Available online: https://www.sciencealert.com/whorecommends-to-avoid-taking-ibuprofen-for-covid-19-symptoms (accessed on 10 August 2022).
23. Torjesen, I. Covid-19: Ibuprofen Can Be Used for Symptoms, Says UK Agency, but Reasons for Change in Advice Are Unclear. *BMJ* **2020**, *369*, m1555. [CrossRef]
24. Korea Disease Control and Prevention Agency. Information about Adverse Events Following Vaccination and What to Expect. Available online: https://ncv.kdca.go.kr/board.es?mid=a20400000000&bid=0038#content (accessed on 10 August 2022).
25. Chen, J.S.; Alfajaro, M.M.; Wei, J.; Chow, R.D.; Filler, R.B.; Eisenbarth, S.C.; Wilen, C.B. Cyclooxgenase-2 is induced by SARS-CoV-2 infection but does not affect viral entry or replication. *bioRxiv* **2020**. *Preprint*. [CrossRef]
26. Fang, L.; Karakiulakis, G.; Roth, M. Are patients with hypertension and diabetes mellitus at increased risk for COVID-19 infection? *Lancet Respir. Med.* **2020**, *8*, e21. [CrossRef]
27. Jeong, H.E.; Lee, H.; Shin, H.J.; Choe, Y.J.; Filion, K.B.; Shin, J.Y. Association Between Nonsteroidal Antiinflammatory Drug Use and Adverse Clinical Outcomes Among Adults Hospitalized With Coronavirus 2019 in South Korea: A Nationwide Study. *Clin. Infect. Dis.* **2021**, *73*, e4179–e4188. [CrossRef] [PubMed]
28. Drake, T.M.; Fairfield, C.J.; Pius, R.; Knight, S.R.; Norman, L.; Girvan, M.; Hardwick, H.E.; Docherty, A.B.; Thwaites, R.S.; Openshaw, P.J.M.; et al. Non-steroidal anti-inflammatory drug use and outcomes of COVID-19 in the ISARIC Clinical Characterisation Protocol UK cohort: A matched, prospective cohort study. *Lancet Rheumatol.* **2021**, *3*, e498–e506. [CrossRef] [PubMed]
29. Castro, V.M.; Ross, R.A.; Cbrode, S.; Perlis, R.H. Brief Report: Identifying common pharmacotherapies associated with reduced COVID-19 morbidity using electronic health records. *medRxiv* **2020**, 20061994. [CrossRef]

medicina

MDPI

Article

The Impact of Antibiotic Use on Mortality in Patients Hospitalized in a COVID-19 Centre from Romania: A Retrospective Study

Maria-Ilinca Iosub [1,*], Elena-Sabina Balan [2], Larisa Pinte [1,3], Ana-Maria Draghici [1], Cristian Baicus [1,3] and Camelia Badea [1,3]

1 Department of Internal Medicine, Colentina Clinical Hospital, 020125 Bucharest, Romania
2 Cardiology Department, Colentina Clinical Hospital, 020125 Bucharest, Romania
3 Faculty of Medicine, Carol Davila University of Medicine and Pharmacy, 050474 Bucharest, Romania
* Correspondence: maria-ilinca.iosub@rez.umfcd.ro

Abstract: *Background and Objectives*: Considering the significant number of patients worldwide that received empirical antibiotic therapy for COVID-19 infection due to their critical condition and the lack of therapeutical guidelines, we wanted to find out the consequences of antibiotic use in our study population. *Materials and Methods*: We conducted a retrospective cohort study including symptomatic patients older than 18 years, hospitalized for SARS-CoV-2 between March and December 2020 in the Internal Medicine and Pneumology Departments of Colentina Clinical Hospital. The elected outcome was death, while independent variables were antibiotic therapy and literature-cited parameters associated with mortality in this disease. *Results*: Out of 198 included patients, 96 (48.48%) patients received antibiotic therapy during hospitalization. Female gender (OR = 2.61, $p = 0.04$), history of neoplasm (OR = 7.147, $p = 0.01$), heart failure (OR = 8.62, $p = 0.002$), and diabetes mellitus (OR = 3.05, $p = 0.02$) were significantly associated with death in multivariate analysis. Antibiotic treatment showed a higher probability of death both in bivariate (OR = 5.333, $p < 0.001$) and multivariate analysis adjusted for the aforementioned prognostic factors (OR = 3.55, $p = 0.01$). *Conclusions*: After adjusting for confounders, in-hospital antibiotic administration did not improve survival in COVID-19 patients.

Keywords: COVID-19; antibiotic therapy; mortality; female gender; neoplasm history; heart failure; diabetes mellitus

Citation: Iosub, M.-I.; Balan, E.-S.; Pinte, L.; Draghici, A.-M.; Baicus, C.; Badea, C. The Impact of Antibiotic Use on Mortality in Patients Hospitalized in a COVID-19 Centre from Romania: A Retrospective Study. *Medicina* **2022**, *58*, 1628. https://doi.org/10.3390/medicina58111628

Academic Editors: Yusra Habib Khan, Tauqeer Hussain Mallhi, Tahir Mehmood Khan and Muhammad Salman

Received: 15 September 2022
Accepted: 9 November 2022
Published: 11 November 2022

Publisher's Note: MDPI stays neutral with regard to jurisdictional claims in published maps and institutional affiliations.

Copyright: © 2022 by the authors. Licensee MDPI, Basel, Switzerland. This article is an open access article distributed under the terms and conditions of the Creative Commons Attribution (CC BY) license (https://creativecommons.org/licenses/by/4.0/).

1. Introduction

The year 2020 was seriously marked by the unforeseeable evolution of the COVID-19 pandemic. The public health system worldwide was constantly suffering from a lack of means in predicting and treating this novel infection. Doctors faced the challenge of having to apply different methods of treatment when the guidelines offered no more answers. An important issue was the extensive prescription of antibiotics even when no bacterial co-infection or secondary infection was involved.

There is a big concern nowadays with multi-resistant bacterial infections that lead to around 700,000 deaths per year, and the number is estimated to reach 10 million deaths by the year 2050 [1]. Having this in mind it is impossible not to worry about the extensive use of antibiotics since the pandemic has started. A literature review about this subject reports that empirical antibiotic therapy was given to even more than 70% of the hospitalized patients for COVID-19 infection [2]. Another retrospective study from a southern European country stated that 21.6% of the hospitalized patients were prescribed no antibiotics, 43.9% were appropriately prescribed antibiotics, and 34.2% were inappropriately prescribed antibiotics [3]. Another literature review that included studies from all over the world showed that 8501 out of 10,329 COVID-19 patients (82.3%) were prescribed antibiotics [4].

An important prospective cohort study from UK pointed out that 85.2% patients with inpatient antimicrobial data received antimicrobial therapy at some point during their admission (the rate was highest for patients in critical care) [5].

On the other hand, as a response to this exponential trend in treating COVID-19 patients, new guidelines appeared concerning the use of antibiotics. WHO guidelines recommend no antibiotic therapy or prophylaxis for patients with a moderate form of COVID-19 unless signs and symptoms of a bacterial infection exist, while for severe forms of the disease, a daily assessment for de-escalation of antibiotics is required. The March 2021 UK National Institute for Health and Care Excellence (NICE) rapid guideline on managing COVID-19 pleads for not using antibiotics in the prevention or treatment of COVID-19 infection and that the only recommendation for antibiotics use is when there is a strong clinical or paraclinical suspicion of bacterial infection [6].

Taking care of hospitalized patients daily, we had witnessed a progressively worsening situation that seemed almost impossible to manage.

The main aim of our study was to unveil the effect of antibiotic therapy on mortality among the patients hospitalized in a COVID-19 centre from Bucharest, Romania and to see if our results corresponded to those published worldwide. We were also interested in finding out other parameters that influenced the prognostic of our patients.

2. Materials and Methods

This is a retrospective study that included symptomatic patients older than 18 years, hospitalized for COVID-19 infection between March and December 2020 at the Internal Medicine and Pneumology Departments of Colentina Clinical Hospital, Bucharest, Romania, confirmed either with a PCR or rapid antigen test. The exclusion criteria were: asymptomatic patients, patients that needed transferred to the ICU, and the ones who could not provide us an exact date for the onset of their symptoms.

Data collection was based on the observational charts of the hospitalized patients. Demographic, clinical, biological, imaging, treatment, and evolution data were analysed. Disease severity was classified as mild—symptomatic, but without dyspnea or abnormal chest imaging, moderate—if evidence of lower respiratory disease is present, but with an oxygen saturation (SpO2) above 94% on room air, or severe—patients that exhibited pulmonary infiltrates on more than 50% of the lung parenchyma accompanied by an SpO2 below 94% [7].

Comorbidities were summarized by the Charlson comorbidity index and obesity was clinician-defined. The sample was divided in two groups, one that received and one that did not receive antibiotic therapy during hospitalization. The identification of bacterial infection was based on blood, urine, sputum, and stool microbiological analysis in patients with a high clinical (presence of fever, purulent cough) and paraclinical likelihood (raised level of procalcitonin, C-reactive protein, consolidation on chest computed tomography).

The outcome was mortality. The independent variables were antibiotic prescription, and the clinical and biological parameters showed by the previous studies as associated with a higher mortality. As the ISARIC score (4C mortality score) [8] was found to be the most valid for prognosis, we used its variables for adjustment. Additionally, this model showed that $\geq$2 comorbidities showed an 80% increase in mortality, and we used this for adjustment too.

The statistical analysis was performed using SPSS Version 20.0. An Internet-based calculator (EBM calculator—Knowledge Translation Program, Toronto, ON, Canada) was used for calculation of relative risk with confidence interval [9].

The variables associated with death with $p < 0.10$ in bivariate analysis were evaluated in a logistic regression model. The variables were selected for logistic regression with the forward conditional method because of the relative low sample size. Hypothesis testing was 2-tailed. Statistical significance was defined by $p < 0.05$.

The design of our study is summarized in the following flowchart (Figure 1). Firstly, we performed bivariate and multivariate analysis on the entire sample. Secondly, because it implies another antibiotic course, as well as increased inflammation and mortality, we excluded patients with a positive *Clostridioides difficile* test, and afterwards we also excluded any other patient with microbiological evidence of a superimposed bacterial infection. On the resulting subgroups we applied the same statistical tests as we did on the initial sample, comparing the retrieved results.

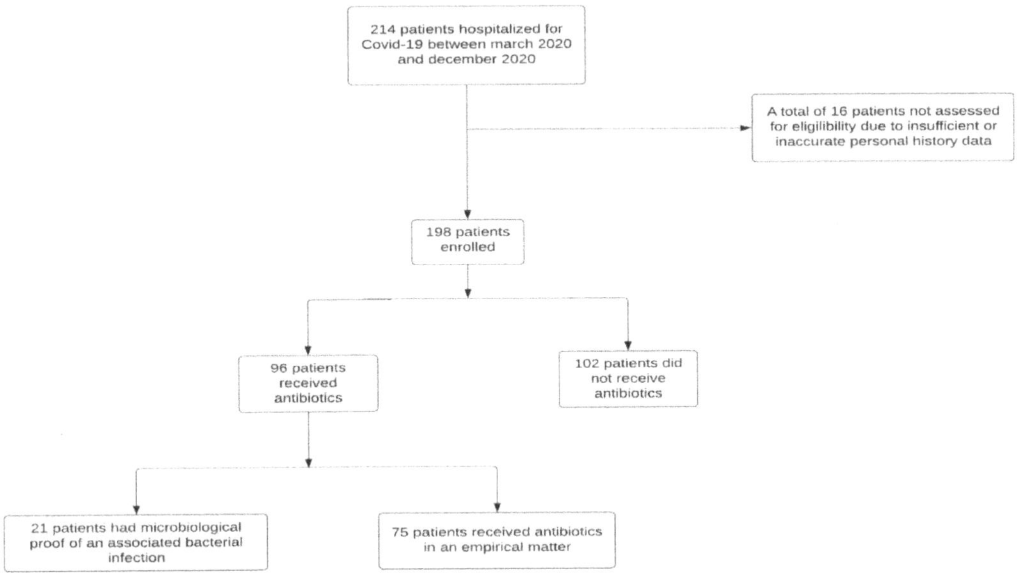

Figure 1. Study design.

3. Results

Following the exclusion criteria, our sample was represented by 198 patients with a slightly male predominance (109/198). The median age was 61 (23–91).

Ten (5.1%) of the patients had a mild form of disease, 91 (45.95%) had a moderate form, while 97 (48.98%) had a severe form of COVID-19.

The overall mortality rate in our sample was 15.15–13.13% with severe disease, and 2.02 % with moderate disease.

Demographic and comorbidity data distribution were summarized in Table 1.

Forty-four (22.22%) out of the 198 patients received antibiotics at home prior to the admission, while 96 (48.48%) of the patients were first administered one or more antibiotic classes during the hospitalization. Out of the patients who were prescribed antibiotics, 2 (2.1%) developed a mild disease, 41 (42.7%) had a moderate disease and 53 (55.2%) a severe form of the disease. The prescribed antibiotic classes during hospitalization were: beta-lactams (penicillins, cephalosporins, carbapenems, beta-lactams inhibitors), glycopeptides (vancomycin), tetracyclins (doxycycline, tygecycline), oxazolidonones (linezolid), macrolides (clarithromycin, azithromycin), and fluoroquinolones (Ciprofloxacin, Levofloxacin, Moxifloxacin). Because of the heterogeneous data that resulted from simultaneous or successive antibiotic regimens, it is very difficult to determine the exact percentage of each prescribed antibiotic class. Twenty-one (10.61%) patients underwent antimicrobial therapy guided by the evidence of a bacterial infection (positive blood, urine or sputum culture or *Clostridioides difficile* stool test). The following bacteria species were isolated: *Klebsiella* spp. (4 cases), *Staphylococcus aureus* (1 case), MDR *E. coli* (2 cases), *Clostridioides difficile* (14 cases). The other 75 received antibiotics in an empirical manner (based on increasing procalcitonin levels, inflammatory biomarkers, and clinical judgement).

Table 1. Medical history data and its impact on mortality.

	Yes	Deceased	Alive	Relative Risk of Death	95% CI	*p*
Antibiotic	96 (48.48%)	24 (25%)	72 (75%)	5.333	[2.072; 13.726]	<0.001
No antibiotic	-	6 (5.88%)	96 (94.11%)	-	-	-
Female gender	89 (44.94%)	19 (21.34%)	70 (78.65%)	2.115	[1.063; 4.208]	0.046
Hypertension	103 (52.02%)	17 (16.51%)	86 (83.49%)	1.206	[0.62; 2.348]	0.723
Dyslipidaemia	24 (12.12%)	4 (16.66%)	20 (83.33%)	1.115	[0.426; 2.92]	0.934
Diabetes mellitus	45 (22.72%)	12 (26.66%)	33 (73.33%)	2.267	[1.183; 4.344]	0.027
Obesity	42 (21.21%)	9 (21.42%)	33 (78.57%)	1.592	[0.788; 3.214]	0.300
Atrial fibrillation	22 (11.11%)	8 (36.36%)	14 (63.63%)	2.909	[1.478; 5.725]	0.009
Chronic coronary syndrome	22 (11.11%)	5 (22.72%)	17 (77.27%)	1.600	[0.683; 3.75]	0.462
Heart failure	13 (6.56%)	9 (69.23%)	4 (30.76%)	6.099	[3.548; 10.484]	<0.001
Chronic hepatitis/cirrhosis	14 (7.07%)	3 (21.42%)	11 (78.57%)	1.460	[0.505; 4.223]	0.770
CKD	11 (5.55%)	2 (18.18%)	9 (81.81%)	1.214	[0.331; 4.452]	0.885
Asthma/COPD	17 (8.58%)	4 (23.52%)	13 (76.47%)	1.638	[0.648 to 4.143]	0.513
Stroke	5 (2.52%)	0(0%)	5 (100%)	0.530	[0.037; 7.683]	0.936
Neoplasm	10 (5.05%)	6 (60%)	4 (40%)	4.700	[2.506; 8.817]	<0.001
Autoimmunity	6 (3.03%)	2 (33.33%)	4 (66.66%)	2.286	[0.701; 7.455]	0.494
IBD/celiac disease	4 (2.02%)	1 (25%)	3 (75%)	1.672	[0.296; 9.436]	0.881
At least 2 comorbidities	141 (71.21%)	29 (20.56%)	112 (79.43%)	11.723	[1.636; 84.03]	0.002
Charlson Index	-	5 (0, 9)	2 (0, 9)	-	-	<0.001

Upon admission, based on the Charlson comorbidity index, we were able to stratify the patients' risk of developing a milder or more severe form of the disease and anticipate what prospects they might have had. It can be regarded as a useful marker, hence its good predictive value of mortality—AUC = 0.784, $p < 0.001$, 95% CI [0.697; 0.872].

Some inflammation biomarkers showed a significantly statistic association between themselves and mortality in the bivariate analysis ($p < 0.005$)—the maximum values of C reactive protein and D-dimer.

ROC curve analysis proves that both the maximum value of the C reactive protein and the maximum value of D-dimer are good predictors of death as shown in Table 2.

Table 2. Biological markers proven as good predictors of death in ROC curve analysis.

	AUC	*p*	95% CI
The maximum value or CRP *	0.850	0.025	[0.723; 0.977]
The maximum value of D-dimers	0.802	<0.001	[0.723; 0.881]

* CRP = C-reactive protein, AUC = area under the curve, 95% CI = confidence interval.

In our sample there was no association between mortality and maximum level of ferritin.

In bivariate analysis we found out that antibiotic treatment shows a higher probability of death, and respectively has an OR of 5.333 with a *p*-value below 0.001. Age ($p < 0.001$), female gender, the history of a neoplasm, heart failure, and diabetes mellitus were the other parameters associated with the outcome of death, as shown in Table 1.

Additionally, the number of comorbid conditions showed a significant statistic association with mortality ($p = 0.009$). Furthermore, we tested an ISARIC score-derived parameter, the presence of at least two comorbidities, which was as well associated with in-hospital mortality ($p = 0.03$).

Multivariate analysis showed that age, neoplasm history, heart failure, and diabetes mellitus had a significant risk of death—Table 3. When adjusted for those conditions and for disease severity, association between antibiotic therapy and mortality did not remain as statistically significant.

Table 3. Antibiotic therapy adjusted for several comorbidities that were highly associated with mortality (logistic regression).

	B	*p*	OR, 95% CI
Antibiotic treatment	0.863	0.122	2.369, [0.795; 7.064]
Age	0.042	0.044	2.530, [1.001; 1087]
Neoplasm	2.006	0.014	7.437, [1.494; 37.016]
Heart failure	1.154	0.039	4.546, [1.080; 19.139]
Diabetes mellitus	1.007	0.056	2.737, [1.171; 7.988]
Female gender	0.928	0.068	2.530, [0.934; 6.855]
Disease severity	1.403	0.006	4.067, [1.506; 10.986]

Since the presence of a significant inflammatory state was also known as a mortality predictor, the maximum values of C reactive protein and D-dimer were added in the logistic regression model. Furthermore, we adjusted the analysis for the patients' preexisting conditions using a more concentrated variable, an ISARIC score derived parameter (the presence of at least two comorbidities). The results are presented below, in Table 4.

Table 4. The association between antibiotic therapy and mortality—logistic regression model after the adjustment for other involved prognostic factors.

	B	*p*	OR, 95% CI
Antibiotic treatment	0.893	0.128	2.443, [0.773; 7.717]
Female gender	0.948	0.059	2.579, [0.965; 6.896]
Age	0.062	0.004	1.064, [1.020; 1.110]
Disease severity	1.374	0.008	3.951, [1.422; 10.981]
Maximal value of D-dimer	0.132	0.003	1.141, [1.044; 1.246]
Maximal value of C reactive protein	0.002	0.564	1.002, [0.996; 1008]
The presence of at least 2 comorbidities	−0.654	0.313	0.520, [0.146; 1.851]

Antibiotic therapy failed to associate with mortality after being adjusted for age, gender, comorbidities, inflammatory markers and disease severity. The latter remained the most important mortality predictor (OR 3.95, $p = 0.008$).

In order to further remove other confounding variables we excluded the patients with a confirmed *Clostridioides difficile* infection, thus resulting in a new subgroup. According to the bivariate analysis patients who were prescribed antibiotics were almost five times more likely to decease (RR = 4.905, [1.957; 12.299], $p < 0.001$). If they had at least two comorbidities they had an eleven fold greater risk of mortality (RR = 11.938, [1.666; 85.563], $p = 0.002$).

Even though in the bivariate analysis there was a statistically significant association, when taking into consideration other prognostic factors, antibiotic therapy did not show a significant association with mortality after the adjustment of the logistic regression model (Table 5).

Table 5. Multivariate analysis in patients without a proven *Clostridioides* infection—adjusted for age, gender, severity, inflammatory markers and the presence of at least 2 comorbidities.

	B	*p*	OR, 95% CI
Antibiotic treatment	0.872	0.174	2.391, [0.680; 8.411]
Female gender	1.048	0.056	2.851, [0.974; 8.344]
Age	0.058	0.020	1.059, [1.009; 1.112]
Disease severity	1.518	0.009	4.565, [1.469; 14.180]
Maximal value of D-dimer	0.178	0.001	1.195, [1.077; 1.327]
Maximal value of C-reactive protein	0.001	0.871	1.001, [0.994; 1.007]
The presence of at least 2 comorbidities	−1.473	0.093	0.229, [0.041; 1.276]

We went further with the exclusion of the patients with any proof of secondary bacterial infection, resulting in a subgroup treated with antibiotics solely in an empirical manner, in which we searched for the association between antibiotic treatment and survival.

Bivariate analysis in patients without any proven bacterial infection showed that patients who received antibiotics had a threefold higher risk of in-hospital death (RR = 3.283, 95% CI [1.358; 7.934], $p < 0.009$). Using the same type of analysis, the presence of at least two comorbidities was associated with an increase in the risk of death by eight times (RR = 8.422, [1.167; 60.801], $p = 0.0015$).

The results obtained from the logistic regression model performed in patients without any documented bacterial infection remained similar to those obtained in the earlier stage of the statistical analysis (before the exclusion of those specific participants). As presented in Table 6, antibiotic therapy failed to associate with a significant increase in mortality. Variables with a significant impact upon mortality were: disease severity, the maximal value of D-dimer, and age.

Table 6. Multivariate analysis concerning patients who received antibiotic therapy solely in an empirical manner—adjusted for age, gender, severity, inflammatory markers, and the presence of at least 2 comorbidities.

	B	*p*	OR, 95% CI
Antibiotic treatment	0.376	0.562	1.456, [0.409; 5.185]
Female gender	0.829	0.137	2.290, [0.767; 6.835]
Age	0.048	0.049	1.049, [1.000; 1.100]
Disease severity	1.159	0.008	4.906, [1.524; 15.789]
Maximal value of D-dimer	0.155	0.001	1.168, [1.062; 1.283]
Maximal value of C-reactive protein	0.002	0.585	1.002, [0.996;1.008]
The presence of at least 2 comorbidities	−1.119	0.171	0.327, [0.066;1.624]

4. Discussion

Some of our results come as a reiteration stated in the studies on this topic [2–5,10–14], which proved that an important percentage of patients hospitalized worldwide for COVID-19 infection received empirical antimicrobial therapy and that this management did not lead to an improved outcome [10,15].

Some biological markers, surrogates of the cytokine storm, have shown a significantly association with the outcome of death in bivariate analysis; furthermore, they have proven themselves as good predictors of mortality in the ROC curve analysis. In this aspect we chose to use the maximum value of C reactive protein, D-dimers and ferritin from all the available values of a patient during his or her hospital stay. Our results concerning the prognostic utility of C-reactive protein correspond to the results stated in other studies [16,17]. We concluded that D-dimer levels were also associated with a higher mortality rate, in the same way that was mentioned in other studies [18–20]. In our sample there was no association between mortality and maximum level of ferritin, unlike the results described in other studies [21,22]. The former can also be stated about the lack of an association between procalcitonin levels and an increase in mortality in our sample.

The ISARIC 4C mortality score was validated in several papers as an efficient prognostic score [8]. Some of its components were already used in the severity stratification of patients (oxygen saturation upon admission, the presence of pulmonary infiltrates, respiratory rate) according to the NIH protocols [23]. Other parameters associated with a significant increase in mortality in the aforementioned score (age, gender, C-reactive protein, and the presence of at least two comorbidities) were used as covariates in the logistic regression model.

As antibiotic therapy is the main cause of the *Clostridioides difficile* infection, we decided to remove the patients that had this particular secondary infection in order to predict more accurately the real effect antibiotics had upon the studied outcome. Furthermore, after removing the patients that had other proof of a microbiological infection, the lack of an association between antibiotic therapy and mortality persisted.

In bivariate analysis the mortality was increased in patients that receive antibiotic therapy because the majority of patients in our group had a moderate or severe form of disease (94.9%) and besides that they also had multiple comorbidities that led to various complications (acute kidney injury, stroke, deep vein thrombosis, acute heart failure).

This therapeutic class, prescribed as a desperate act in a life-threatening situation, did not come to rescue, therefore the survival rate did not improve. Moreover, at first glance it made us think that it was rather harmful, but after careful adjusting to the other known prognostic factors we concluded that the apparent increase in mortality was due to the fact that a significant proportion of the patients were already in an aggravated state rather than the effect of the antibiotic therapy itself.

The main limitations of this study are represented by its observational (retrospective) design, the relatively small sample of patients and the monocentric approach, even though the data were rigorously collected and there were no missing data. It should be acknowledged that the resulting conclusions could not reflect the evolution of all the SARS-CoV-2 variants in relationship with antibiotic prescribing.

An important bias could be the confounding by indication (the patients with the most severe cases were preferentially treated with antibiotic therapy), which, if strong, could not have been reversed by the adjustments for the known prognostic factors. Therefore, only a randomized controlled trial will probably give us a more certain conclusion.

We underline the fact that at the time when our patients were hospitalized, the national and international guidelines were changing in a very rapid manner and also lacked clear answers regarding antibiotic therapy.

5. Conclusions

After adjusting for confounders, in-hospital antibiotic administration did not improve survival in COVID-19 patients.

Thus, taking into account the fact that the unnecessary usage of antibiotics does not come without consequences, the data available in the literature so far, including our study, does not support unjustified antimicrobial agent administration in COVID-19 infection.

Author Contributions: Conceptualization, M.-I.I., E.-S.B., C.B. (Cristian Baicus) and C.B. (Camelia Badea); methodology, M.-I.I., E.-S.B., L.P. and C.B. (Cristian Baicus); software, M.-I.I., E.-S.B. and C.B. (Cristian Baicus); validation, M.-I.I., E.-S.B., C.B. (Camelia Badea) and C.B. (Cristian Baicus); formal analysis, M.-I.I., E.-S.B., L.P. and C.B. (Cristian Baicus); investigation, M.-I.I., E.-S.B. and A.-M.D.; resources, M.-I.I., E.-S.B., A.-M.D. and C.B. (Camelia Badea); data curation, M.-I.I., E.-S.B., A.-M.D. and C.B. (Camelia Badea); writing—original draft preparation, M.-I.I. and E.-S.B.; writing—review and editing, M.-I.I., E.-S.B., L.P., C.B. (Cristian Baicus) and C.B. (Camelia Badea); visualization, M.-I.I., E.-S.B., C.B. (Camelia Badea) and C.B. (Cristian Baicus); supervision, M.-I.I., E.-S.B., C.B. (Cristian Baicus) and C.B. (Camelia Badea); project administration, M.-I.I., E.-S.B., C.B. (Camelia Badea) and C.B. (Cristian Baicus). All authors have read and agreed to the published version of the manuscript.

Funding: This research received no external funding.

Institutional Review Board Statement: The study was conducted according to the guidelines of the Declaration of Helsinki and approved by the Institutional Review Board (or Ethics Committee) of Colentina Clinical Hospital (2/08.02.2021).

Informed Consent Statement: Informed consent was obtained from all the subjects involved in the study. Patients signed a written informed consent during hospital admission that was registered in the medical chart by their treating physician.

Data Availability Statement: The data presented in this study are available on request from the corresponding author.

Conflicts of Interest: The authors declare no conflict of interest.

References

1. Mohammed, A.; Ghebreyesus, T.A.; Chen, J.; Davies, S.; So, A.D. *No Time To Wait: Securing The Future From Drug-Resistant Infections*; The United Nations: New York, NY, USA, 2019.
2. Cherry, W.; Brown, M.; Garner, C. A rapid review of the overuse of antibiotics during the COVID-19 pandemic: Lessons learned and recommendations for the future. *AMRC Open Res.* **2021**, 3, 17. Available online: https://amrcopenresearch.org/articles/3-17 (accessed on 24 November 2021). [CrossRef]
3. Calderón-Parra, J.; Muiño-Miguez, A.; Bendala-Estrada, A.D.; Ramos-Martínez, A.; Muñez-Rubio, E.; Carracedo, E.F.; Montes, J.T.; Rubio-Rivas, M.; Arnalich-Fernandez, F.; Pérez, J.L.B.; et al. Inappropriate antibiotic use in the COVID-19 era: Factors associated with inappropriate prescribing and secondary complications. Analysis of the registry SEMI-COVID. *PLoS ONE* **2021**, *16*, e0251340. Available online: https://journals.plos.org/plosone/article?id=10.1371/journal.pone.0251340 (accessed on 24 November 2021). [CrossRef]
4. Cong, W.; Poudel, A.N.; Aihusein, N.; Wang, H.; Yao, G.; Lambert, H. Antimicrobial use in covid-19 patients in the first phase of the sars-cov-2 pandemic: A scoping review. *Antibiotics* **2021**, *10*, 745. Available online: https://www.mdpi.com/2079-6382/10/6/745/htm (accessed on 24 November 2021). [CrossRef] [PubMed]
5. Russell, C.D.; Fairfield, C.J.; Drake, T.M.; Turtle, L.; Seaton, R.A.; Wootton, D.G.; Sigfrid, L.; Harrison, E.M.; Docherty, A.B.; de Silva, T.I.; et al. Co-infections, secondary infections, and antimicrobial use in patients hospitalised with COVID-19 during the first pandemic wave from the ISARIC WHO CCP-UK study: A multicentre, prospective cohort study. *Lancet Microbe* **2021**, *2*, e354–e365. Available online: http://www.thelancet.com/article/S2666524721000902/fulltext (accessed on 24 November 2021). [CrossRef]
6. Overview | COVID-19 Rapid Guideline: Managing COVID-19 | NICE. Available online: https://www.nice.org.uk/guidance/ng191 (accessed on 24 November 2021).
7. Gandhi, R.T.; Lynch, J.B.; del Rio, C. Mild or Moderate Covid-19. *N. Engl. J. Med.* **2020**, *383*, 1757–1766. Available online: https://www.nejm.org/doi/full/10.1056/nejmcp2009249 (accessed on 10 February 2022). [CrossRef] [PubMed]
8. Lombardi, Y.; Azoyan, L.; Szychowiak, P.; Bellamine, A.; Lemaitre, G.; Bernaux, M.; Daniel, C.; Leblanc, J.; Riller, Q.; Steichen, O.; et al. External validation of prognostic scores for COVID-19: A multicenter cohort study of patients hospitalized in Greater Paris University Hospitals. *Intensive Care Med.* **2021**, *47*, 1426–1439. [CrossRef] [PubMed]
9. Evidence-Based Medicine Toolbox | Prospective Study Calculator. Available online: https://ebm-tools.knowledgetranslation.net/calculator/prospective/ (accessed on 10 February 2022).
10. Bendala Estrada, A.D.; Calderón Parra, J.; Fernández Carracedo, E.; Muiño Míguez, A.; Ramos Martínez, A.; Muñez Rubio, E.; Rubio-Rivas, M.; Agudo, P.; Fernández, F.A.; Perez, V.E.; et al. Inadequate use of antibiotics in the COVID-19 era: Effectiveness of antibiotic therapy. *BMC Infect. Dis.* **2021**, *21*, 1144. Available online: https://bmcinfectdis.biomedcentral.com/articles/10.1186/s12879-021-06821-1 (accessed on 21 September 2022). [CrossRef] [PubMed]
11. Argenzian, M.G.; Bruc, S.L.; Slate, C.L.; Tia, J.R.; Baldwi, M.R.; Barr, R.G.; Chang, B.P.; Chau, K.H.; Choi, J.J.; Gavin, N.; et al. Characterization and clinical course of 1000 patients with coronavirus disease 2019 in New York: Retrospective case series. *BMJ* **2020**, *369*, m1996. Available online: https://www.bmj.com/content/369/bmj.m1996 (accessed on 21 September 2022). [CrossRef] [PubMed]
12. Langford, B.J.; So, M.; Raybardhan, S.; Leung, V.; Westwood, D.; MacFadden, D.R.; Soucy, J.-P.R.; Daneman, N. Bacterial co-infection and secondary infection in patients with COVID-19: A living rapid review and meta-analysis. *Clin. Microbiol. Infect.* **2020**, *26*, 1622–1629. Available online: http://www.clinicalmicrobiologyandinfection.com/article/S1198743X20304237/fulltext (accessed on 21 September 2022). [CrossRef] [PubMed]
13. Pinte, L.; Ceasovschih, A.; Niculae, C.M.; Stoichitoiu, L.E.; Ionescu, R.A.; Balea, M.I.; Cernat, R.C.; Vlad, N.; Padureanu, V.; Purcarea, A.; et al. Antibiotic Prescription and In-Hospital Mortality in COVID-19: A Prospective Multicentre Cohort Study. *J. Pers. Med.* **2022**, *12*, 877. [CrossRef] [PubMed]
14. Stoichitoiu, L.E.; Pinte, L.; Ceasovschih, A.; Cernat, R.C.; Vlad, N.D.; Padureanu, V.; Sorodoc, L.; Hristea, A.; Purcarea, A.; Badea, C.; et al. In-Hospital Antibiotic Use for COVID-19: Facts and Rationales Assessed through a Mixed-Methods Study. *J. Clin. Med.* **2022**, *11*, 3194. [CrossRef] [PubMed]
15. Cong, W.; Stuart, B.; AIhusein, N.; Liu, B.; Tang, Y.; Wang, H.; Wang, Y.; Manchundiya, A.; Lambert, H. Antibiotic Use and Bacterial Infection in COVID-19 Patients in the Second Phase of the SARS-CoV-2 Pandemic: A Scoping Review. *Antibiotic* **2022**, *11*, 991. Available online: https://pubmed.ncbi.nlm.nih.gov/35892381/ (accessed on 21 September 2022). [CrossRef] [PubMed]
16. Lentner, J.; Adams, T.; Knutson, V.; Zeien, S.; Abbas, H.; Moosavi, R.; Manuel, C.; Wallace, T.; Harmon, A.; Waters, R.; et al. C-reactive protein levels associated with COVID-19 outcomes in the United States. *J. Osteopath. Med.* **2021**, *121*, 869–873. Available online: https://pubmed.ncbi.nlm.nih.gov/34592071/ (accessed on 21 September 2022). [CrossRef] [PubMed]
17. Villoteau, A.; Asfar, M.; Otekpo, M.; Loison, J.; Gautier, J.; Annweiler, C. Elevated C-reactive protein in early COVID-19 predicts worse survival among hospitalized geriatric patients. *PLoS ONE* **2021**, *16*, e0256931. Available online: https://pubmed.ncbi.nlm.nih.gov/34506514/ (accessed on 21 September 2022). [CrossRef] [PubMed]
18. Soni, M.; Gopalakrishnan, R.; Vaishya, R.; Prabu, P. D-dimer level is a useful predictor for mortality in patients with COVID-19: Analysis of 483 cases. *Diabetes Metab. Syndr. Clin. Res. Rev.* **2020**, *14*, 2245–2249. Available online: https://www.ncbi.nlm.nih.gov/pmc/articles/PMC7670909/ (accessed on 21 September 2022). [CrossRef] [PubMed]

19. Yao, Y.; Cao, J.; Wang, Q.; Shi, Q.; Liu, K.; Luo, Z.; Chen, X.; Chen, S.; Yu, K.; Huang, Z.; et al. D-dimer as a biomarker for disease severity and mortality in COVID-19 patients: A case control study. *J. Intensive Care* **2020**, *8*, 49. Available online: https://jintensivecare.biomedcentral.com/articles/10.1186/s40560-020-00466-z (accessed on 21 September 2022). [CrossRef] [PubMed]
20. Poudel, A.; Poudel, Y.; Adhikari, A.; Aryal, B.B.; Dangol, D.; Bajracharya, T.; Maharjan, A.; Gautam, R. D-dimer as a biomarker for assessment of COVID-19 prognosis: D-dimer levels on admission and its role in predicting disease outcome in hospitalized patients with COVID-19. *PLoS ONE* **2021**, *16*, e0256744. Available online: https://journals.plos.org/plosone/article?id=10.1371/journal.pone.0256744 (accessed on 21 September 2022). [CrossRef] [PubMed]
21. Alroomi, M.; Rajan, R.; Omar, A.A.; Alsaber, A.; Pan, J.; Fatemi, M.; Zhanna, K.D.; Aboelhassan, W.; Almutairi, F.; Alotaibi, N.; et al. Ferritin level: A predictor of severity and mortality in hospitalized COVID-19 patients. *Immun. Inflamm. Dis.* **2021**, *9*, 1648–1655. Available online: https://pubmed.ncbi.nlm.nih.gov/34438471/ (accessed on 21 September 2022). [CrossRef] [PubMed]
22. Lino, K.; Guimarães, G.M.C.; Alves, L.S.; Oliveira, A.C.; Faustino, R.; Fernandes, C.S.; Tupinambá, G.; Medeiros, T.; da Silva, A.A.; Almeida, J.R.; et al. Serum ferritin at admission in hospitalized COVID-19 patients as a predictor of mortality. *Braz. J. Infect. Dis.* **2021**, *25*. Available online: http://bjid.elsevier.es/en-serum-ferritin-at-admission-in-articulo-S1413867021000386 (accessed on 21 September 2022). [CrossRef] [PubMed]
23. Clinical Spectrum | COVID-19 Treatment Guidelines | NIH. Available online: https://www.covid19treatmentguidelines.nih.gov/overview/clinical-spectrum/ (accessed on 24 October 2022).

medicina

MDPI

Review

Telemedicine in Primary Practice in the Age of the COVID-19 Pandemic—Review

Anna Romaszko-Wojtowicz [1,*], Łukasz Jaśkiewicz [2], Paweł Jurczak [3] and Anna Doboszyńska [1]

1 Department of Pulmonology, School of Public Health, Collegium Medicum, University of Warmia and Mazury in Olsztyn, 10-719 Olsztyn, Poland; anna.doboszynska@wp.pl
2 Department of Human Physiology and Pathophysiology, School of Medicine, Collegium Medicum, University of Warmia and Mazury in Olsztyn, 10-082 Olsztyn, Poland; lukasz.jaskiewicz@uwm.edu.pl
3 Student Scientific Club of Cardiopulmonology and Rare Diseases of the Respiratory System, School of Medicine, Collegium Medicum, University of Warmia and Mazury in Olsztyn, 10-082 Olsztyn, Poland; pawel.jurczak.1@student.uwm.edu.pl
* Correspondence: anna.romaszko@uwm.edu.pl

Abstract: *Background and Objectives*: In the era of the COVID-19 pandemic, telemedicine, so far underestimated, has gained in value. Currently, telemedicine is not only a telephone or chat consultation, but also the possibility of the remote recording of signals (such as ECG, saturation, and heart rate) or even remote auscultation of the lungs. The objective of this review article is to present a potential role for, and disseminate knowledge of, telemedicine during the COVID-19 pandemic. *Material and Methods*: In order to analyze the research material in accordance with PRISMA guidelines, a systematic search of the ScienceDirect, Web of Science, and PubMed databases was conducted. Out of the total number of 363 papers identified, 22 original articles were subjected to analysis. *Results*: This article presents the possibilities of remote patient registration, which contributes to an improvement in remote diagnostics and diagnoses. *Conclusions*: Telemedicine is, although not always and not by everyone, an accepted form of providing medical services. It cannot replace direct patient–doctor contact, but it can undoubtedly contribute to accelerating diagnoses and improving their quality at a distance.

Keywords: COVID-19; telemedicine; primary practice

Citation: Romaszko-Wojtowicz, A.; Jaśkiewicz, Ł.; Jurczak, P.; Doboszyńska, A. Telemedicine in Primary Practice in the Age of the COVID-19 Pandemic—Review. *Medicina* **2023**, *59*, 1541. https://doi.org/10.3390/medicina59091541

Academic Editors: Yusra Habib Khan, Tauqeer Hussain Mallhi, Tahir Mehmood Khan and Muhammad Salman

Received: 14 July 2023
Revised: 18 August 2023
Accepted: 22 August 2023
Published: 25 August 2023

Copyright: © 2023 by the authors. Licensee MDPI, Basel, Switzerland. This article is an open access article distributed under the terms and conditions of the Creative Commons Attribution (CC BY) license (https://creativecommons.org/licenses/by/4.0/).

1. Introduction

Telemedicine, also called telehealth, is the provision of health-related services over a distance using digital communication technologies. The origins of telemedicine date back to the 1950s, when the first mentions of the possibilities of the remote transmission of imaging tests appeared [1]. Telemedicine may take different forms, e.g., it can be in the form of communication between a patient and a doctor such as a doctor's advice via telephone, chat, or videoconference. It may also be associated with more experimental innovations, e.g., telesurgery, where a surgeon remotely manipulates surgical instruments with the aid of a robotic surgical system.

The pandemic caused by the SARS-CoV-2 virus has stimulated the more rapid development of telemedicine. Pursuant to the WHO recommendations, telemedicine was chosen as a key strategy for the provision, maintenance, and enhancement of health-related services which were disrupted by the COVID-19 outbreak [2]. There are many scientific articles dedicated to the use of telemedicine in various specialties (e.g., internal diseases, family medicine, psychiatry, oncology) [3]. According to the report presented by Omboni et al., the most common purpose of using telemedicine (49.7%) was to ensure integrated patient care, including a combination of services with the aim of providing diagnosis, treatment, observation, and rehabilitation [4]. Monitoring patients in their home environment enables doctors to gain a better insight into the social conditions of their patients' health statuses.

Of key importance for the development of telemedicine is the growing accessibility of technologies. In line with the Pew Research Centre's report of 2021, 93% of Americans use the internet [5]. Moreover, 81% of Americans have smartphones, nearly 75% have desktops or laptops, and around 50% have tablets or e-readers [6]. Nowadays, telemedicine does not have to be limited to consulting one's doctor by telephone, but can involve the use of other, more modern methods, e.g., measuring instruments which allow objectivization of symptoms reported by the patients and enable the doctor to make a correct diagnosis, which means that telemedicine can improve significantly. These are instruments such as cameras and video cameras in smartphones, digital stethoscopes, ophthalmoscopes, otoscopes, and various types of biosensors. This form of telemedicine, in which mobile medical devices and technologies are employed in order to collect health data generated by the patient (PGHD—patient-generated health data) and transmitted to health care providers, is referred to in the literature as remote patient monitoring (RPM) [7].

This starts from the simplest solutions, in which medical documentation is stored, monitored, and edited practically from anywhere in the world, to more complex ones related to artificial intelligence. In this way, it is possible, for example, to remotely supervise surgical procedures. Telemedicine is already widely used in emergency medicine systems. ECG transmission, in terms of qualification for invasive treatment, has already become a standard which is possible in most ambulances.

The purpose of this systematic review has been to evaluate telemedicine technologies that were employed during the COVID-19 pandemic, from the viewpoint of optimization of their use in situations of limited direct access to a physician. In particular, we are interested in the issue of using telemedicine techniques used in primary health care, as if creating a telemedicine primary care guide.

2. Material and Methods

The study was conducted according to the Preferred Reporting Items for Systematic Review and Meta-Analysis Protocols (PRISMA) statement [8]. The systematic review of the literature was based on an a priori definition of inclusion and exclusion criteria, which enabled an objective selection of articles dealing with the connections between telemedicine and COVID-19. This approach allowed us to preselect the research material objectively, preventing any subjectivity in our decisions to include some or exclude other studies from the review. The search employed the following terms: "telemedicine, telehealth, lung, respiratory, COVID-19, SARS-CoV-2, diagnosis, symptoms".

The following search sequences were used in the work:

- "telemedicine", "symptoms", "diagnosis", "covid-19", "respiratory", "lung";
- "telehealth", "symptoms", "diagnosis", "covid-19", "respiratory", "lung";
- "telemedicine", "symptoms", "diagnosis", "sars-cov-2", "respiratory", "lung";
- "telehealth", "symptoms", "diagnosis", "sars-cov-2", "respiratory", "lung".

Due to the multitude of available studies and the symptomatology of COVID-19, the study was limited to searches related to the involvement of the respiratory system.

In this way, attempts were made to isolate publications enabling the assessment of the respiratory system, using methods of remote assessment of the general condition of patients, including remote registration. In particular, we wanted to present in the review solutions facilitating the work of a clinician at the level of primary care.

The review of the literature took advantage of the following databases: ScienceDirect, Web of Science, and PubMed. While searching the ScienceDirect database, a filter was activated to exclude meta-analyses, reviews (also systematic reviews), and books, in addition to which the search was limited to studies in medical sciences and that were original publications. The Web of Science database was searched for articles in medical sciences. As for PubMed, the same filters as applied to ScienceDirect were used. Some records were also retrieved via references found in published articles. No limits regarding the date of publication were set. Detailed results of the search are presented in a flow diagram (Figure 1) [9,10]. The search was carried out in the fourth and fifth weeks of March 2023.

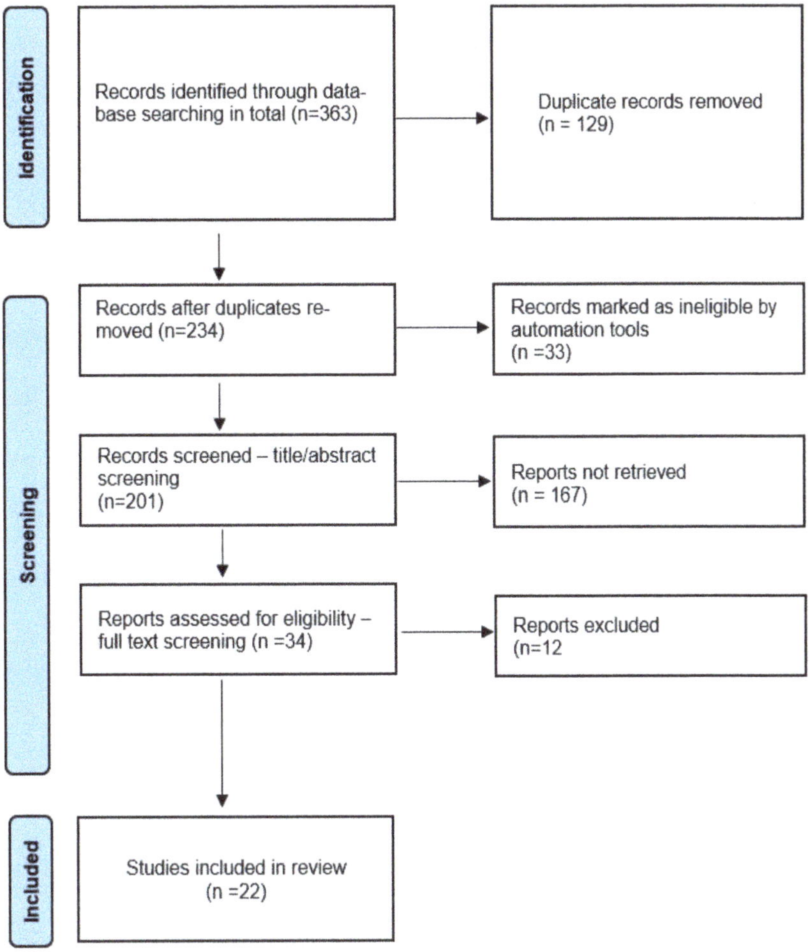

Figure 1. PRISMA flow diagram.

Selection of Studies and Exclusion Criteria

For further preselection of papers, the software Rayyan was employed [11]. Firstly, duplicates were eliminated and records implicated by the software as possibly being duplicates were reviewed. Next, three independent researchers analyzed the abstracts, and those dedicated to telemedicine methods used during the COVID-19 pandemic were selected. Lists of references were searched manually in order to identify further publications suitable for our analysis. Thus, articles were selected compliant with the previously established exclusion and inclusion criteria for a full-text review. Any disputes were resolved by consensus. In total, 234 publications were checked and 34 were chosen for complete analysis. Having analyzed the complete texts, 22 publications were selected for the systematic review.

The inclusion criteria were to choose original articles, published in the English language, with clearly determined measures applied to clinical results. The exclusion criteria were to discard studies with unclear measures applied to clinical results, descriptions of single cases, or series of cases with a sample size <5. The articles selected for the final analysis are collated in Table 1. A forest plot was used to visually depict publication bias (Figure 2).

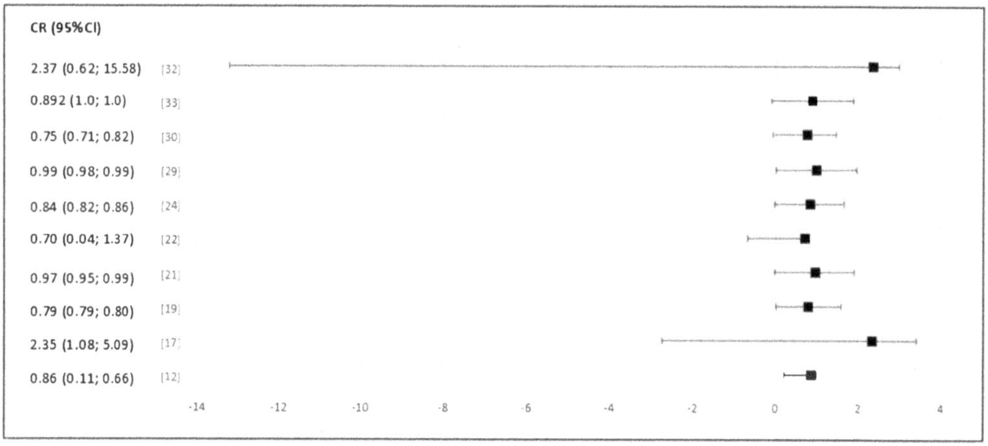

Figure 2. Plots of the proportion of the incidence of symptomatic and asymptomatic acute respiratory tract infection in COVID-19.

Table 1. Detailed breakdown of work selected for analysis.

Authors (Ref.)	Number of Patients	Country	Study Design	Publication Date	Journal
		Telehealth			
		1. Teleconsultations			
Accorsi TAD, et al. [12]	98	Brazil	Randomized controlled trial	May 2022	*Einstein (Sao Paulo)*
Zhang A, et al. [13]	416	Netherlands	Descriptive survey—Case reports	Mar 2022	*Healthc (Amst).*
Baena-Díez JM, et al. [14]	453	Spain	Cohort study	Nov 2021	*Healthcare (Basel)*
Coronado-Vázquez V, et al. [15]	166	Spain	Cohort study	May 2021	*J. Pers. Med.*
Khairat S, et al. [16]	1139	USA	Cross-sectional—descriptive study	Oct 2020	*J. Patient Exp.*
		Artificial intelligence			
		2. Algorithms			
Porter P, et al. [17]	322	Australia	Cohort study	Mar 2021	*Br J Gen Pract.*
Jose T, et al. [18]	765,324	USA	Descriptive survey	Feb 2021	*Mayo Clin Proc Innov Qual Outcomes*
Eythorsson E, et al. [19]	4756	Iceland	Cohort study	Sep 2022	*Diagn Progn Res.*
Tartaglia E, et al. [20]	200–875/day	Italy	Observational study	Dec 2022	*Smart Health (Amst).*
Yoo TK, et al. [21]	339	South Korea	Cross-sectional—analytical study	Oct 2020	*Comput Biol Med.*
Li H, et al. [22]	965	USA, China	Cross-sectional—analytical study	Dec 2022	*Smart Health (Amst).*
		3. Mobile Apps			
Liu L, et al. [23]	4589	China	Cohort study	July 2020	*JMIR Mhealth Uhealth.*
Yang D, et al. [24]	3249	China	Multi-center clinical study	Dec 2022	*Clinical eHealth*
Ahmad M, et al. [25]	185	India	Cross-sectional—analytical study	June 2022	*Diabetes Metab Syndr.*
		Remote Patient Monitoring			

Table 1. *Cont.*

Authors (Ref.)	Number of Patients	Country	Study Design	Publication Date	Journal
		4. Wearable Body Sensors			
Balasubramanian V, et al. [26]	1200	India	Cross-sectional—analytical study	Jan 2022	*Med Biol Eng Comput.*
Al Bassam N, et al. [27]	-	Oman	Cross-sectional—descriptive study	May 2021	*Inform Med Unlocked.*
		5. Stethoscope			
Glangetas A, et al. [28]	1000	Switzerland	Cohort study	Mar 2021	*BMC Pulm Med.*
Zhu H, et al. [29]	172	China	Cohort study	Jan 2022	*Computer Methods and Programs in Biomedicine*
Pancaldi F, et al. [30]	28	Italy	Cross-sectional—analytical study	Mar 2022	*Comput Biol Med.*
Lalouani W, et al. [31]	128	USA	Descriptive survey	Dec 2022	*Smart Health (Amst).*
		6. Ultrasound			
Kirkpatrick AW, et al. [32]	27	Canada, USA	Randomized controlled trial	Dec 2022	*Ultrasound J.*
Kimura BJ, et al. [33]	201	USA	Cross-sectional—analytical study	Oct 2022	*J Am Soc Echocardiogr.*

3. Results

The analyzed studies were published from July 2020 to December 2022. The 22 reviewed articles deal with seven issues, presented in Figure 2: telemedicine (telephone consultations, chats, and video consultations) (n = 5); AI techniques (n = 2) and algorithms (n = 4), that is, the issues related to telehealth and remote registration of patients, and the use of USG (n = 2); stethoscopes (n = 4); mobile applications (n = 3); and the "wearable body sensor network" (n = 2). Most studies were conducted in Europe (n = 7), and the remaining papers originated from Asia (n = 7), North America (n = 6), Australia (n = 1), and South America (n = 1). The most articles about telehealth covering various types of teleconsultations was published in Europe [13–15] and one work in North America [16] and South America [12]. In Asia, all publications concerned AI techniques and remote patient monitoring. It is worth noting that all publications on the use of mobile applications [23–25] and wearables [26,27] were created there. The use of stethoscopes as a tool for remote control of the patient's health was established in Asia [29], Europe [28,30], and North America [31]. The articles on the use of ultrasonography in patient follow-up were exclusively from North America [32,33]. The creation of algorithms useful in medicine based on artificial intelligence has been described in Asia [21], Europe [19,20], North America [18,22], and Australia [17]. These divisions are presented in Figure 3.

The preselected publications focused on the following aspects: providing health-related consultations via telemedicine using applications designed for this purpose, as well as a remote assessment of a patient's condition with the help of the so-called wearable body sensor network, electronic stethoscopes, and a lung USG (Figure 4).

The presented review focuses on the aspects of telemedicine used in the practice of GPs. These methods focus on three main aspects, i.e., telehealth, methods of remote registration of patients, and the use of artificial intelligence methods for their assessment.

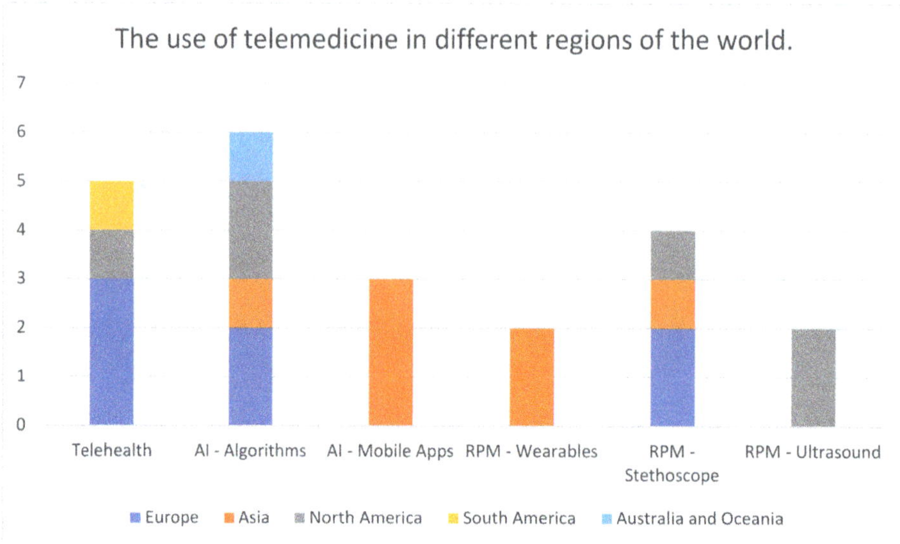

Figure 3. The use of telemedicine in different regions of the world. AI, artificial intelligence; RPM, remote patient monitoring.

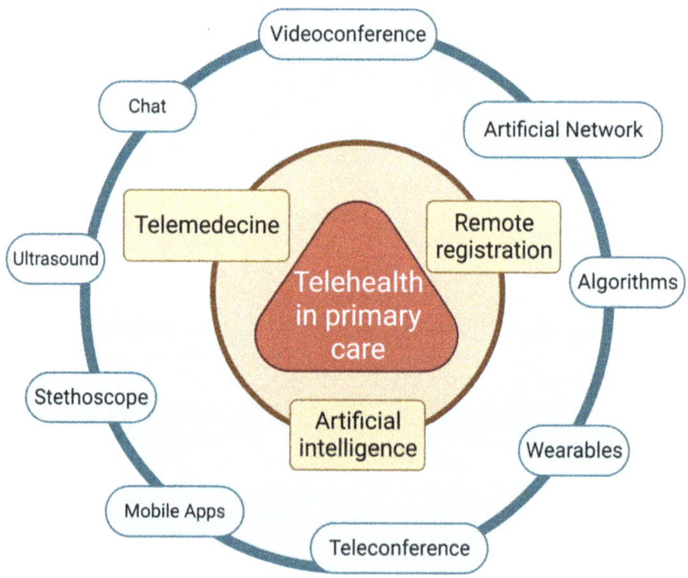

Figure 4. Telemedicine architecture used in the publication. Created with BioRender.com.

3.1. *Telehealth*

Telehealth consultations can be provided through various telemedicine channels, e.g., by telephone advice, chat, or videoconference. Remote consultations can be used both for a full patient interview, as well as to collect screening information enabling further proper triage of patients, which turned out to be particularly important during the COVID-19 pandemic [13]. The content and quality of consultations, regardless of their form (teleconsultation, chat, videoconsultation) are comparable [34].

3.2. Artificial Intelligence

Telemedicine solutions combined with artificial intelligence allow for the creation of algorithms that facilitate decision making or guide patients or doctors through the diagnostic path. These algorithms can be used to assess the general health status and cohort of patients. They can also make the first diagnosis based on the sent image of the throat or the recorded cough sound [21].

3.3. Remote Patient Monitoring

Remote patient registration methods are aimed at obtaining health parameters based on wearable body sensors, mobile apps, stethoscope, or ultrasound. Wearable body sensors, using sensors attached to the body, collect information about heart rate, saturation, respiratory rate, ECG, and body temperature [35]. It is also possible to remotely assess breath sounds and images of the lungs. Wearable body sensors are becoming an increasingly accurate diagnostic tool to help identify and treat diseases [36].

The detailed specifications of the articles, divided according to subject areas, is contained in Table 1.

4. Discussion

Telemedicine, also known as telehealth, involves the use of technologies to facilitate remote patient monitoring. Scientists have developed many different forms of telemedicine systems to fight the pandemic. This literature review is supposed to emphasize the possibilities of telemedicine methods which can be used in primary health care. The COVID-19 pandemic itself led to a significant increase in the number of health-related consultations provided with the help of ICT tools. This has necessitated, in a certain manner, the development of a collaboration between IT and medicine for the best possible objectivization of the health services provided. Monitoring the health status of patients with COVID-19 remotely can take different forms, from giving advice by telephone to using custom-designed teleinformation tools via the internet. Appropriate remote monitoring of the health of patients and chronic conditions can help to reduce the number of patients who need to be hospitalized, and this lowers the costs of medical care [37]. In a paper published in 2023 in JAMA, it was shown that telemedicine advice contributes to significant time and cost savings, including transport costs and the cost of medical visits. Increasing access to a doctor results in a reduction in the number of visits, hospitalizations, and mortality [38].

In our study, we have shown the possible division of telemedicine into three categories: telehealth, AI, and remote patient monitoring. This division has been used in order to easily present the possibilities of remote medical care methods, e.g., in a family doctor's office. Thanks to the extremely rapid progress of technology in the 21st century, medical care provided through telemedicine channels does not have to differ much from direct contact with the patient. Not only that, according to the data presented in Figure 2, the recognition of respiratory tract infections by various methods of telemedicine can be just as effective.

4.1. Telehealth

During the outbreak of the COVID-19 pandemic, teleconsultations served to provide adequate education to patients in order to restrain the spread of the disease. Furthermore, telemedicine gave patients emotional support [13]. However, it soon turned out that teleconsultations were on the front line in effective management and conduct during the COVID-19 pandemic. Telephone history taking in primary health care was effective in detecting pneumonia in patients diagnosed with mild SARS-CoV-2 [16]. Accorsi et al., in their randomized trial, showed that teleconsultation is comparable to an in-patient consultation for patients with a low risk of progressing to a severe course of COVID-19 infection who developed symptoms of acute respiratory tract infection [12].

Truong et al., based on their systematic review, confirmed that teleconsultations show a high level of care and satisfaction of patients [39].

4.2. Artificial Intelligence

An artificial neural network (ANN), or simply a neural network, is a method of supervised learning. The learning process tries to mimic the learning that takes place in the human brain. Artificial intelligence models are employed to create appropriate groups of patients [23]. AI enables researchers to use data collected, for example, in the form of digital diagnostic tests, in order to improve telemedicine consultations.

Artificial intelligence methods based on a convolutional neural network (CNN) were used to evaluate chest X-rays of patients with COVID-19. [25] They served to help diagnose and classify COVID-19 cases, and to distinguish patients with COVID-19 from other patients with (viral or bacterial) pneumonia [40–43]. It was demonstrated that a preliminary evaluation of chest X-rays could be achieved remotely, considerably limiting of person-to-person contact. A deep learning model (CycleGAN) was used by Yoo et al. to detect severe cases of pharyngitis using a smartphone [21]. This approach was employed for screening patients in order to rapidly identify cases of pharyngitis and launch proper diagnostic and treatment procedures.

Algorithms created by artificial intelligence can support the diagnostic and therapeutic process. An example of this can be the management of community-acquired pneumonia, which can be one of the manifestations of COVID-19. Diagnosis of community-acquired pneumonia (CAP) is based on an evaluation of the signs and symptoms of a respiratory tract infection. Its clinical image varies. The manifestations of pneumonia can be divided into two groups: systemic (pyrexia, chills, malaise) and related to the respiratory system (cough, dyspnea, chest pain). The diagnosis of pneumonia in outpatients can be made on the basis of clinical manifestation not necessarily confirmed by laboratory and imaging tests. This option gained particular importance during the COVID-19 pandemic when the isolation of patients and the limitation of direct human contact were most important from the point of view of epidemiology. Porter et al. proved that the mathematical algorithm they tested enabled the accurate identification of patients with CAP of varying severity, excluding an analysis of vital signs and physical and radiological examinations, in addition to which it ensured an immediate result. These Australian researchers built an algorithm on the basis of such symptoms as pyrexia, acute cough <7 days (registered by a smartphone), and age. The algorithm was then used to make a preliminary selection of patients [17].

Coronado-Vázquez et al. carried out telemedicine monitoring of patients with COVID-19, which enabled early detection of complications as well as the monitoring and treatment of concomitant illnesses, thereby contributing to reducing the risk of hospitalization [15]. In turn, Liu et al., who used an online application specially developed for their study, enabled patients to provide in real time all new data regarding the course of the illness, which contributed to gaining a better insight into the disease itself and improved overall evaluation of the health status of a given patient. The above researchers conducted medical consultations using an online application, including a preliminary triage, with the help of a voice conversation, text messaging, photo communication, or a video call. Out of 4589 patients, 310 were referred to the hospital and 301 were recommended to see a doctor in an in-patient setting (e.g., in a hospital) for physical examination. The cited authors demonstrated that telemedicine can facilitate the initial selection of patients, particularly during health crises such as COVID-19 [23].

Telemedicine services provided via another application (nCapp) were presented by Yang et al. [24]. In this case, the mobile tool used served to synchronize and share the data concerning the diagnosis and previous treatment. The aim of this application was to enable early diagnosis of COVID-19 and classification of patients (with a focus on patients with ambiguous or false negative results of RT-PCR tests) to appropriate risk groups. Owing to this application, the remote management of new cases of COVID-19 infections was improved.

Amjad et al., in their systematic review published in January 2023, have summarized the methods of artificial intelligence currently used in medicine. They proved that telehealth based on artificial intelligence can lead to an improvement in the quality of medical practice and also contribute to its modernization [44].

4.3. Remote Patient Monitoring

Monitoring of the health conditions of patients may take different forms, and one option employed nowadays is to use biosensors, which enable making non-invasive measurements. The sensors used in these devices read parameters from the skin or from the movements made by the person being monitored [45,46]. This allows the monitoring of a patient in any circumstances, including at home, remotely. The wearable body sensor network, according to Qureshi et al., is most probably the best solution for the remote monitoring of patients in health care systems. Such sensors as accelerometers, temperature sensors, or ECGs collect information about the health of a patient, acting as a monitoring network. The data are stored in a local server and can be retrieved by a clinician to aid the decision-making process [47].

Bassam et al. described a system that makes use of an online application as an external interface and an Android-based mobile application for the patient [27]. Both interfaces are synchronized with each other in order to gather data on the health of a patient. The system is composed of a device mounted like a bracelet on one of the patient's limbs. It allows recording of the following parameters: body temperature, systolic heart rate, saturation, and cough episodes. It also has a built-in GPS reader.

Similar systems used during the COVID-19 pandemic for remote registration of vital signs have been presented in the literature by Balasubramanian V., Ding X, Romaszko et al. [26,48,49].

It seems that wearable body sensors may solve the monitoring problem, as was shown by Snehi et al. [50].

Telemedicine can play a role in decreasing the costs of health care borne by the patient and by the health care system. Adequate remote monitoring of health conditions and chronic conditions can help patients to avoid expensive visits to hospital emergency wards and even hospitalization. A stethoscope is an inexpensive instrument that is easy to use, but which can considerably facilitate making a preliminary diagnosis. However, its usefulness largely depends on the user's perceptual ability and experience. In recent years, there has been a growing interest in the automation of auscultation, its standardization and digitalization. This trend gained momentum during the COVID-19 pandemic when any form of a remote physical examination helped to make a diagnosis via telemedicine. A team of researchers from Switzerland created an algorithm for the diagnosis and stratification of COVID-19 risk based on lung auscultation [28]. To this aim, an algorithm involving artificial intelligence and deep learning was developed that achieved standardization of lung auscultation. The data for their research were recorded with a digital stethoscope Littmann 3200. It was demonstrated that automated interpretation of lung auscultation can help to improve the accuracy of a physical examination. In turn, Zhu et al. employed artificial intelligence models and showed that an AI-based system can identify correctly different types of irregular murmurs detected during an auscultation examination of the lungs [29].

Pancaldi et al. created an algorithm called VECTOR (Velcro crackles detector) to evaluate Velcro crackles registered with the help of a digital stethoscope [51]. In 2022, these authors used the VECTOR algorithm to identify patients with interstitial pneumonia secondary to SARS-CoV-2 infection [30]. To this aim, a digital stethoscope Littmann 3200 was used to evaluate respiratory crackles in eight auscultation points, i.e., paravertebral lower lobes, axillary lower lobes, paravertebral middle lobes, and paravertebral upper lobes. The automated lung auscultation results proved the potential usefulness of artificial intelligence methods in the near future.

Undoubtedly, the COVID-19 pandemic has contributed to the search for new methods of remote diagnosis. In March 2023, *Diagnostics* published a paper comparing the types of stethoscopes, including electronic stethoscopes. The authors of this article showed many benefits of remote lung auscultation, or even the sound recording itself. They also did not omit the problem related to the use of artificial intelligence to interpret the recorded auscultation phenomena, which primarily result from their possible variability [52].

A group of 27 volunteers was submitted to a study in which a portable USG device and a teleconference on the Zoom platform were used to examine the images of the lungs of patients with COVID-19 [32]. The purpose of the study was to generate an adequate "batwing" image of the pleura interface between two rib shadows at each location on the thorax. The use of ultrasound ensures reliable monitoring and stratification of the risk of developing serious illnesses. These conclusions were confirmed by Kimura et al., in a study including 201 patients, in which the presence of a B line, which is associated with a higher risk of hospitalization of high-risk patients, was detected in the early phase of SARS-CoV-2 infection [33]. Moreover, these researchers confirmed that patients were able to perform a simple lung USG test themselves. Heldeweg et al., based on a systematic review of the literature, proved that ultrasound imaging of the lungs significantly affects clinical decision making, especially in the so-called places for quick diagnostics (e.g., emergency departments) [52].

The usefulness of a remote ultrasound exam has also been verified in cases of abdominal USG tests [53]. However, because of the topic area of this study not pertaining to the subject of our review, this paper was not included in the current systematic review.

Telemedicine is a rapidly developing field of medicine which has already been used widely owing to its usefulness and ability to provide medical services safely during the COVID-19 pandemic. It is obvious that telemedicine, nowadays, cannot replace personal patient care and that not all clinical situations can rely on video consultations alone, but it is also undeniable that in the time of medical staff shortages, telemedicine can help to improve the monitoring of the health status of patients, the functionality of the health care system, as well as the accessibility to medical advice. Not long ago, the only option for remote communication was by letter. Other remote communication channels, not to mention remote medical diagnosis methods, were unknown. The COVID-19 pandemic showed that medical care in the form of telehealth could be the not-so-distant future of medicine. Technological progress, a collaboration between IT and medicine, and the development of pro-health applications, such as 'Apple-health', remote auscultation, or imaging of internal organs, may become commonplace in everyday life.

The variety of methods used in telemedicine allows for almost unlimited possibilities for patients' remote registration. At present, it is possible to conduct a full history-taking using remote methods of communication as well as remote registration and transmission of vital measurements enriched with the possibility of recording auscultatory changes. The analysis of these data using artificial intelligence methods minimizes the risk of medical error.

5. Conclusions

The COVID-19 pandemic has changed the perception of telemedicine. Conducted scientific studies have shown that telemedicine can be highly effective in recognizing upper respiratory tract infections, regardless of the type of method used.

The rapid development of 21st century technology may soon lead to even more efficient methods of telemedicine.

Author Contributions: Conceptualization, A.R.-W.; methodology, A.R.-W., Ł.J., P.J. and A.D.; formal analysis, A.R.-W., Ł.J. and P.J.; investigation, A.R.-W. and Ł.J.; resources, A.R.-W.; data curation, A.R.-W.; writing—original draft preparation, A.R.-W. and Ł.J.; writing—review and editing, A.R.-W., Ł.J., P.J. and A.D.; visualization, A.R.-W.; supervision, A.D.; project administration, A.R.-W. All authors have read and agreed to the published version of the manuscript.

Funding: This research received no external funding.

Institutional Review Board Statement: Not applicable.

Informed Consent Statement: Not applicable.

Data Availability Statement: The data are available in a publicly accessible repository.

Conflicts of Interest: The authors declare no conflict of interest.

References

1. Gershon-Cohen, J.; Cooley, A.G. Telognosis. *Radiology* **1950**, *55*, 582–587. [CrossRef] [PubMed]
2. Available online: https://apps.who.int/iris/handle/10665/336862 (accessed on 10 March 2023).
3. Haleem, A.; Javaid, M.; Singh, R.P.; Suman, R. Telemedicine for healthcare: Capabilities, features, barriers, and applications. *Sens. Int.* **2021**, *2*, 100117. [CrossRef] [PubMed]
4. Omboni, S.; Padwal, R.S.; Alessa, T.; Benczúr, B.; Green, B.B.; Hubbard, I.; Kario, K.; Khan, N.A.; Konradi, A.; Logan, A.G.; et al. The worldwide impact of telemedicine during COVID-19: Current evidence and recommendations for the future. *Connect. Health* **2022**, *1*, 7–35. [CrossRef] [PubMed]
5. Available online: https://www.pewresearch.org/internet/fact-sheet/internet-broadband (accessed on 10 March 2023).
6. Available online: https://www.pewresearch.org/internet/2019/06/13/mobile-technology-and-home-broadband-2019 (accessed on 10 March 2023).
7. Vegesna, A.; Tran, M.; Angelaccio, M.; Arcona, S.; Tabacof, L.; Kellner, C.; Breyman, E.; Dewil, S.; Braren, S.; Nasr, L.; et al. Remote Patient Monitoring via Non-Invasive Digital Technologies: A Systematic Review. *Telemed. e-Health* **2017**, *23*, 3–17. [CrossRef]
8. Sarkis-Onofre, R.; Catalá-López, F.; Aromataris, E.; Lockwood, C. How to properly use the PRISMA Statement. *Syst. Rev.* **2021**, *10*, 117. [CrossRef]
9. Page, M.J.; McKenzie, J.E.; Bossuyt, P.M.; Boutron, I.; Hoffmann, T.C.; Mulrow, C.D.; Shamseer, L.; Tetzlaff, J.M.; Akl, E.A.; Brennan, S.E.; et al. The PRISMA 2020 statement: An updated guideline for reporting systematic reviews. *BMJ* **2021**, *372*, n71. [CrossRef]
10. Uman, L.S. Systematic reviews and meta-analyses. *J. Can. Acad. Child Adolesc. Psychiatry* **2011**, *20*, 57–59.
11. Ouzzani, M.; Hammady, H.; Fedorowicz, Z.; Elmagarmid, A. Rayyan—A web and mobile app for systematic reviews. *Syst. Rev.* **2016**, *5*, 210. [CrossRef]
12. Accorsi, T.A.D.; Moreira, F.T.; Pedrotti, C.H.S.; De Amicis, K.; Correia, R.F.V.; Morbeck, R.A.; Medeiros, F.F.; de Souza, J.L., Jr.; Cordioli, E. Telemedicine diagnosis of acute respiratory tract infection patients is not inferior to face-to-face consultation: A randomized trial. *Einstein* **2022**, *20*, eA06800. [CrossRef]
13. Zhang, A.; GoodSmith, M.; Server, S.; Uddin, S.; McNulty, M.; Sherer, R.; Lio, J. Providing support in a pandemic: A medical student telehealth service for ambulatory patients with COVID-19. *Healthcare* **2022**, *10*, 100612. [CrossRef]
14. Baena-Díez, J.M.; Gonzalez-Casafont, I.; Cordeiro-Coelho, S.; Fernández-González, S.; Rodríguez-Jorge, M.; Pérez-Torres, C.U.F.; Larrañaga-Cabrera, A.; García-Lareo, M.; de la Arada-Acebes, A.; Martín-Jiménez, E.; et al. Effectiveness of Telephone Monitoring in Primary Care to Detect Pneumonia and Associated Risk Factors in Patients with SARS-CoV-2. *Healthcare* **2021**, *9*, 1548. [CrossRef] [PubMed]
15. Coronado-Vázquez, V.; Ramírez-Durán, M.d.V.; Gómez-Salgado, J.; Dorado-Rabaneda, M.S.; Benito-Alonso, E.; Holgado-Juan, M.; Bronchalo-González, C. Evolution of a Cohort of COVID-19 Infection Suspects Followed-Up from Primary Health Care. *J. Pers. Med.* **2021**, *11*, 459. [CrossRef] [PubMed]
16. Khairat, S.; Pillai, M.; Edson, B.; Gianforcaro, R. Evaluating the Telehealth Experience of Patients With COVID-19 Symptoms: Recommendations on Best Practices. *J. Patient Exp.* **2020**, *7*, 665–672. [CrossRef] [PubMed]
17. Porter, P.; Brisbane, J.; Abeyratne, U.; Bear, N.; Wood, J.; Peltonen, V.; Della, P.; Smith, C.; Claxton, S. Diagnosing community-acquired pneumonia via a smartphone-based algorithm: A prospective cohort study in primary and acute-care consultations. *Br. J. Gen. Pract.* **2020**, *71*, e258–e265. [CrossRef]
18. Jose, T.; Warner, D.O.; O'horo, J.C.; Peters, S.G.; Chaudhry, R.; Binnicker, M.J.; Burger, C.D. Digital Health Surveillance Strategies for Management of Coronavirus Disease 2019. *Mayo Clin. Proc. Innov. Qual. Outcomes* **2020**, *5*, 109–117. [CrossRef]
19. Eythorsson, E.; Bjarnadottir, V.; Runolfsdottir, H.L.; Helgason, D.; Ingvarsson, R.F.; Bjornsson, H.K.; Olafsdottir, L.B.; Bjarnadottir, S.; Agustsson, A.S.; Oskarsdottir, K.; et al. Development of a prognostic model of COVID-19 severity: A population-based cohort study in Iceland. *Diagn. Progn. Res.* **2022**, *6*, 17. [CrossRef]
20. Tartaglia, E.; Vozzella, E.A.; Iervolino, A.; Egidio, R.; Buonocore, G.; Perrone, A.; Toscano, G.; Tremante, R.; Cesaro, F.; Sommella, V.; et al. Telemedicine: A cornerstone of healthcare as-sistance during the SARS-Cov2 pandemic outbreak but also a great opportunity for the near future. *Smart Health* **2022**, *26*, 100324. [CrossRef]
21. Yoo, T.K.; Choi, J.Y.; Jang, Y.; Oh, E.; Ryu, I.H. Toward automated severe pharyngitis detection with smartphone camera using deep learning networks. *Comput. Biol. Med.* **2020**, *125*, 103980. [CrossRef]
22. Li, H.; Chen, X.; Qian, X.; Chen, H.; Li, Z.; Bhattacharjee, S.; Zhang, H.; Huang, M.-C.; Xu, W. An explainable COVID-19 detection system based on human sounds. *Smart Health* **2022**, *26*, 100332. [CrossRef]
23. Liu, L.; Gu, J.; Shao, F.; Liang, X.; Yue, L.; Cheng, Q.; Zhang, L. Application and Preliminary Outcomes of Remote Diagnosis and Treatment During the COVID-19 Outbreak: Retrospective Cohort Study. *JMIR mHealth uHealth* **2020**, *8*, e19417. [CrossRef]
24. Yang, D.; Xu, T.; Wang, X.; Chen, D.; Zhang, Z.; Zhang, L.; Liu, J.; Xiao, K.; Bai, L.; Zhang, Y.; et al. A large-scale clinical validation study using nCapp cloud plus terminal by frontline doctors for the rapid diagnosis of COVID-19 and COVID-19 pneumonia in China. *Clin. eHealth* **2022**, *5*, 79–90. [CrossRef]

25. Ahmad, M.; Sadiq, S.; Eshmawi, A.A.; Alluhaidan, A.S.; Umer, M.; Ullah, S.; Nappi, M. Industry 4.0 technologies and their applications in fighting COVID-19 pandemic using deep learning techniques. *Comput. Biol. Med.* **2022**, *145*, 105418. [CrossRef] [PubMed]
26. Balasubramanian, V.; Vivekanandhan, S.; Mahadevan, V. Pandemic tele-smart: A contactless tele-health system for efficient monitoring of remotely located COVID-19 quarantine wards in India using near-field communication and natural language processing system. *Med. Biol. Eng. Comput.* **2022**, *60*, 61–79. [CrossRef]
27. Al Bassam, N.; Hussain, S.A.; Al Qaraghuli, A.; Khan, J.; Sumesh, E.; Lavanya, V. IoT based wearable device to monitor the signs of quarantined remote patients of COVID-19. *Inform. Med. Unlocked* **2021**, *24*, 100588. [CrossRef] [PubMed]
28. Glangetas, A.; Hartley, M.-A.; Cantais, A.; Courvoisier, D.S.; Rivollet, D.; Shama, D.M.; Perez, A.; Spechbach, H.; Trombert, V.; Bourquin, S.; et al. Deep learning diagnostic and risk-stratification pattern detection for COVID-19 in digital lung auscultations: Clinical protocol for a case–control and prospective cohort study. *BMC Pulm. Med.* **2021**, *21*, 103. [CrossRef] [PubMed]
29. Zhu, H.; Lai, J.; Liu, B.; Wen, Z.; Xiong, Y.; Li, H.; Zhou, Y.; Fu, Q.; Yu, G.; Yan, X.; et al. Automatic pulmonary auscultation grading diagnosis of Coronavirus Disease 2019 in China with artificial intelligence algorithms: A cohort study. *Comput. Methods Programs Biomed.* **2022**, *213*, 106500. [CrossRef]
30. Pancaldi, F.; Pezzuto, G.S.; Cassone, G.; Morelli, M.; Manfredi, A.; D'Arienzo, M.; Vacchi, C.; Savorani, F.; Vinci, G.; Barsotti, F.; et al. VECTOR: An algorithm for the detection of COVID-19 pneumonia from velcro-like lung sounds. *Comput. Biol. Med.* **2022**, *142*, 105220. [CrossRef]
31. Lalouani, W.; Younis, M.; Emokpae, R.N.; Emokpae, L.E. Enabling effective breathing sound analysis for automated diagnosis of lung diseases. *Smart Health* **2022**, *26*, 100329. [CrossRef]
32. Kirkpatrick, A.W.; McKee, J.L.; Ball, C.G.; Ma, I.W.Y.; Melniker, L.A. Empowering the willing: The feasibility of tele-mentored self-performed pleural ultrasound assessment for the surveillance of lung health. *Ultrasound J.* **2022**, *14*, 2. [CrossRef]
33. Kimura, B.J.; Resnikoff, P.M.; Tran, E.M.; Bonagiri, P.R.; Spierling Bagsic, S.R. Simplified Lung Ultrasound Examination and Telehealth Feasibility in Early SARS-CoV-2 Infection. *J. Am. Soc. Echocardiogr.* **2022**, *35*, 1047–1054. [CrossRef]
34. Hammersley, V.; Donaghy, E.; Parker, R.; McNeilly, H.; Atherton, H.; Bikker, A.; Campbell, J.; McKinstry, B. Comparing the content and quality of video, telephone, and face-to-face consultations: A non-randomised, quasi-experimental, exploratory study in UK primary care. *Br. J. Gen. Pract.* **2019**, *69*, e595–e604. [CrossRef]
35. Malasinghe, L.P.; Ramzan, N.; Dahal, K. Remote patient monitoring: A comprehensive study. *J. Ambient. Intell. Humaniz. Comput.* **2017**, *10*, 57–76. [CrossRef]
36. Appelboom, G.; Camacho, E.; Abraham, M.E.; Bruce, S.S.; Dumont, E.L.; Zacharia, B.E.; D'amico, R.; Slomian, J.; Reginster, J.Y.; Bruyère, O.; et al. Smart wearable body sensors for patient self-assessment and monitoring. *Arch. Public Health* **2014**, *72*, 28. [CrossRef] [PubMed]
37. Snoswell, C.L.; Taylor, M.L.; Comans, T.A.; Smith, A.C.; Gray, L.C.; Caffery, L.J. Determining if Telehealth Can Reduce Health System Costs: Scoping Review. *J. Med. Internet Res.* **2020**, *22*, e17298. [CrossRef] [PubMed]
38. Patel, K.B.; Turner, K.; Tabriz, A.A.; Gonzalez, B.D.; Oswald, L.B.; Nguyen, O.T.; Hong, Y.-R.; Jim, H.S.L.; Nichols, A.C.; Wang, X.; et al. Estimated Indirect Cost Savings of Using Telehealth Among Nonelderly Patients With Cancer. *JAMA Netw. Open* **2023**, *6*, e2250211. [CrossRef] [PubMed]
39. Truong, M.; Yeganeh, L.; Cook, O.; Crawford, K.; Wong, P.; Allen, J. Using telehealth consultations for healthcare provision to patients from non-Indigenous racial/ethnic minorities: A systematic review. *J. Am. Med. Inform. Assoc.* **2022**, *29*, 970–982. [CrossRef]
40. El Asnaoui, K.; Chawki, Y. Using X-ray images and deep learning for automated detection of coronavirus disease. *J. Biomol. Struct. Dyn.* **2020**, *39*, 3615–3626. [CrossRef]
41. Shi, F.; Wang, J.; Shi, J.; Wu, Z.; Wang, Q.; Tang, Z.; He, K.; Shi, Y.; Shen, D. Review of Artificial Intelligence Techniques in Imaging Data Acquisition, Segmentation, and Diagnosis for COVID-19. *IEEE Rev. Biomed. Eng.* **2021**, *14*, 4–15. [CrossRef]
42. Zhang, J.; Xie, Y.; Pang, G.; Liao, Z.; Verjans, J.; Li, W.; Sun, Z.; He, J.; Li, Y.; Shen, C.; et al. Viral Pneumonia Screening on Chest X-Rays Using Confidence-Aware Anomaly Detection. *IEEE Trans. Med. Imaging* **2020**, *40*, 879–890. [CrossRef]
43. Farooq, M.; Hafeez, A. COVID-ResNet: A Deep Learning Framework for Screening of COVID-19 from Radiographs. *arXiv* **2020**. [CrossRef]
44. Amjad, A.; Kordel, P.; Fernandes, G. A Review on Innovation in Healthcare Sector (Telehealth) through Artificial Intelligence. *Sustainability* **2023**, *15*, 6655. [CrossRef]
45. Pilavaki, E.; Parolo, C.; McKendry, R.; Demosthenous, A. Wireless paper-based biosensor reader for the detection of infectious diseases at the point of care. In Proceedings of the 2016 IEEE SENSORS, Orlando, FL, USA, 30 October–3 November 2016; pp. 1–3. [CrossRef]
46. Kim, J.; Campbell, A.S.; de Ávila, B.E.-F.; Wang, J. Wearable biosensors for healthcare monitoring. *Nat. Biotechnol.* **2019**, *37*, 389–406. [CrossRef] [PubMed]
47. Ren, Y.; Yang, J.; Chuah, M.C.; Chen, Y. Mobile Phone Enabled Social Community Extraction for Controlling of Disease Propagation in Healthcare. In Proceedings of the 2011 IEEE Eighth International Conference on Mobile Ad-Hoc and Sensor Systems, Valencia, Spain, 17–22 October 2011; pp. 646–651.
48. Romaszko-Wojtowicz, A.; Maksymowicz, S.; Jarynowski, A.; Jaśkiewicz, Ł.; Czekaj, Ł.; Doboszyńska, A. Telemonitoring in Long-COVID Patients—Preliminary Findings. *Int. J. Environ. Res. Public Health* **2022**, *19*, 5268. [CrossRef] [PubMed]

49. Ding, X.; Clifton, D.; Ji, N.; Lovell, N.H.; Bonato, P.; Chen, W.; Yu, X.; Xue, Z.; Xiang, T.; Long, X.; et al. Wearable Sensing and Telehealth Technology with Potential Applications in the Coronavirus Pandemic. *IEEE Rev. Biomed. Eng.* **2021**, *14*, 48–70. [CrossRef]
50. Snehi, V.; Verma, H.; Pathak, D. Telemedicine and Biosensors, A Boon in COVID Era: An Update. *Int. J. Res. Rev.* **2022**, *9*, 232–240. [CrossRef]
51. Pancaldi, F.; Sebastiani, M.; Cassone, G.; Luppi, F.; Cerri, S.; Della Casa, G.; Manfredi, A. Analysis of pulmonary sounds for the diagnosis of interstitial lung diseases secondary to rheumatoid arthritis. *Comput. Biol. Med.* **2018**, *96*, 91–97. [CrossRef] [PubMed]
52. Seah, J.J.; Zhao, J.; Wang, D.Y.; Lee, H.P. Review on the Advancements of Stethoscope Types in Chest Auscultation. *Diagnostics* **2023**, *13*, 1545. [CrossRef]
53. Ryu, S.; Kim, S.-C.; Won, D.-O.; Bang, C.S.; Koh, J.-H.; Jeong, I.C. iApp: An Autonomous Inspection, Auscultation, Percussion, and Palpation Platform. *Front. Physiol.* **2022**, *13*, 825612. [CrossRef]

Disclaimer/Publisher's Note: The statements, opinions and data contained in all publications are solely those of the individual author(s) and contributor(s) and not of MDPI and/or the editor(s). MDPI and/or the editor(s) disclaim responsibility for any injury to people or property resulting from any ideas, methods, instructions or products referred to in the content.

medicina MDPI

Review

Coinfections and Superinfections Associated with COVID-19 in Colombia: A Narrative Review

Diana Dueñas [1], Jorge Daza [2] and Yamil Liscano [1,*]

[1] Grupo de Investigación en Salud Integral (GISI), Departamento Facultad de Salud, Universidad Santiago de Cali, Cali 760035, Colombia; diana.duenas00@usc.edu.co
[2] Grupo de Investigación de Salud y Movimiento, Programa de Fisioterapia, Facultad de Salud, Universidad Santiago de Cali, Cali 760035, Colombia; jorge.daza01@usc.edu.co
* Correspondence: yamil.liscano00@usc.edu.co

Abstract: The COVID-19 pandemic has had significant impacts on healthcare systems around the world, including in Latin America. In Colombia, there have been over 23,000 confirmed cases and 100 deaths since 2022, with the highest number of cases occurring in females and the highest number of deaths in males. The elderly and those with comorbidities, such as arterial hypertension, diabetes mellitus, and respiratory diseases, have been particularly affected. Coinfections with other microorganisms, including dengue virus, *Klebsiella pneumoniae*, and *Mycobacterium tuberculosis*, have also been a significant factor in increasing morbidity and mortality rates in COVID-19 patients. It is important for surveillance systems to be improved and protocols to be established for the early detection and management of coinfections in COVID-19. In addition to traditional treatments, alternatives such as zinc supplementation and nanomedicine may have potential in the fight against COVID-19. It is also crucial to consider the social, labor, educational, psychological, and emotional costs of the pandemic and to address issues such as poverty and limited access to potable water in order to better prepare for future pandemics.

Keywords: COVID-19; SARS-CoV-2; coinfections; antimicrobials; Colombia; epidemiology; coinfections; superinfections

Citation: Dueñas, D.; Daza, J.; Liscano, Y. Coinfections and Superinfections Associated with COVID-19 in Colombia: A Narrative Review. *Medicina* **2023**, *59*, 1336. https://doi.org/10.3390/medicina59071336

Academic Editors: Yusra Habib Khan, Tauqeer Hussain Mallhi, Tahir Mehmood Khan and Muhammad Salman

Received: 25 May 2023
Revised: 7 July 2023
Accepted: 17 July 2023
Published: 20 July 2023

Copyright: © 2023 by the authors. Licensee MDPI, Basel, Switzerland. This article is an open access article distributed under the terms and conditions of the Creative Commons Attribution (CC BY) license (https://creativecommons.org/licenses/by/4.0/).

1. Introduction

In December 2019, in Wuhan, China, an unidentified coronavirus emerged, causing a major outbreak in many cities and rapidly spreading globally. This new coronavirus, known as severe acute respiratory syndrome coronavirus (SARS-CoV) 2 (SARS-CoV-2), is a virus containing a genome with 29,903 nucleotides and 29 proteins, belonging to the family Coronaviridae, subfamily Coronavirinae, and is the main cause of severe acute respiratory syndrome, also known as COVID-19 [1–3]. By the end of 2021 and early 2022, COVID-19 had infected 224 million people, and 4.6 million had died globally [4].

In addition, microbial coinfections and superinfections [5] had occurred, influenced by factors such as the potentiation of pathogenesis and the increased risk of morbidity and mortality of patients with COVID-19. Coinfection can be defined as the recovery of other pathogens in a patient with an infection within 48 h of admission [6,7], and superinfection occurs when a patient has clinical signs and symptoms of pneumonia or bacteremia combined with a positive culture of a new pathogen from a lower respiratory tract or blood specimen obtained $\geq$48 h after admission [8]. In other words, coinfection occurs simultaneously with the spread of the microorganism, while superinfection develops after the initial infection [9].

Latin America had been one of the most severely affected regions by the COVID-19 pandemic, accounting for 25% of global infections. Moreover, of the ten countries with the highest mortality rates worldwide, eight were from this region, including Colombia [10]. In a study conducted in Colombia, a high incidence of early mortality associated with

COVID-19 24 h after hospital admission was reported [11]. However, studies related to the incidence of coinfection and superinfection in patients with COVID-19 are generally limited, especially in Latin American countries [5,12,13]. It was observed that severely ill COVID-19 patients, especially those in the intensive care unit (ICU), were more prone to secondary infections, owing to the increased use of prophylactic or therapeutic antibiotics whose task is to ensure the successful eradication of susceptible pathogens [14]. However, antibiotic misuse poses a threat due to the increase in the number of antibiotic-resistant microorganisms; additionally, it has a negative impact on the host microbiota. Clinical evidence suggests that inappropriate empirical use of antimicrobials may be associated with increased morbidity and mortality [9,15,16]. Therefore, the objective of this review is to describe scientific evidence on SARS-CoV-2-related coinfections and superinfections and their relevance in patients with COVID-19 in Colombia.

2. Methodology

A comprehensive literature search was conducted using databases such as PubMed, Scopus, SciELO, and Web of Science. The search was based on keywords related to COVID-19, SARS-CoV-2, coinfections, superinfections, Colombia, and COVID-19 treatments ((SARS-CoV-2 OR COVID-19) AND Colombia AND coinfection AND superinfection AND therapy). Relevant data corresponding to each section of the manuscript, such as definitions, pathophysiology, and treatment of SARS-CoV-2, were extracted. The extracted data were then analyzed to identify common themes, patterns, and trends related to coinfections and superinfections. The findings were organized in a narrative format, highlighting key points, similarities, and differences among the studies.

Definitions included the following:

Coinfections: "Coinfections with other microorganisms such as bacteria, fungi, and other viruses are commonly associated with respiratory viral infections. Coinfections are directly linked to increased rates of morbidity and mortality, thus requiring early diagnosis and specific treatment" [17].

Superinfection: "Superinfection is diagnosed when patients present with clinical signs and symptoms of pneumonia or bacteremia combined with a positive culture of a new pathogen from a lower respiratory tract sample (including sputum, transtracheal aspirates, or bronchoalveolar lavage fluid) or blood samples taken $\geq$48 h after admission" [8].

3. SARS-CoV-2

Coronaviruses are approximately 80–220-nm-diameter enveloped viruses [2]. The viral genome encodes five structural proteins which are encoded within the 3′ end, namely, spike protein (S), envelope (E), membrane (M), nucleocapsid (N), and hemagglutinin esterase (HE) [1–3,18,19]. Protein S is a transmembrane glycoprotein that facilitates viral envelope binding to angiotensin-converting enzyme 2 (ACE-2) receptors expressed on the surface of host cells; it also forms protruding homotrimers on the viral surface, and this protein comprises two functional subunits: receptor binding (S1) and cell membrane fusion (S2) [1,2,18]. The E protein is the smallest protein in the SARS-CoV-2 structure, and its function is not necessary for replication. However, it plays a huge role in pathogenesis since it helps in the assembly and liberation of virions [1,18]. The M protein is the most abundant protein in the virion, and it was suggested that this protein plays a role in RNA packaging and promoting the assembly and budding of viral particles through interaction with N and accessory proteins 3a and 7a [1,2,18]. The N protein packages genetic material and binds to the viral genome in a bead-on-a-string conformation. Consequently, it modifies host-cell RNA processing, alters the TGF-β pathway by blocking apoptosis, and promotes binding of the transcription factor NF-κβ to the COX-2 promoter, leading to an inflammatory response. Notably, it is also involved in RNA replication and immune evasion [2,18]. The HE protein acts as a hemagglutinin, binds to sialic acids on surface glycoproteins, contains acetyl esterase activity, and helps the virus spread through the mucosa [1]. Among these five proteins, the most important ones are protein N and protein S. While the former helps in the development of the capsid, the latter allows the virus to bind to target cells. Meanwhile, the most complex component is the receptor-binding domain (RBD) in the S protein because six RBD amino acids are needed to bind to the ACE-2 receptor and harbor SARS-CoV-2-like coronaviruses [1,2].

The RBDs of SARS-CoV-2 have a stronger attraction or affinity for the ACE-2 receptor compared to the RBDs of SARS-CoV. Furthermore, in the case of SARS-CoV-2, a significant portion of the RBDs is in the bound state, meaning they are attached or bound to the ACE-2 receptor. This binding state leads to a comparable or potentially lower affinity for the receptor when compared to SARS-CoV [3].

SARS-CoV-2 entry into host cells and the release of its genomes depend on a sequence of steps, but it should be noted that four of the structural proteins it possesses (S, N, M, and E) allow it to gain access to target cells. For entry, the virus requires binding of the S protein to ACE-2 on the cell's plasma membrane. However, this protein must be cleaved by the transmembrane serine protease 2 (TMPRSS2) of the cell membrane into the two subunits—S1 containing the RBD to ACE-2 and S2 facilitating viral fusion—although this cleavage can also occur by cathepsin-L in the endosomes, which helps to infect cells without TMPRSS2, but this is a slower process [18,20,21]. The literature suggests that the modified RBD residues of protein S in SARS-CoV-2 contribute to its high pathogenicity and transmissibility compared to SARS-CoV. Moreover, the presence of the polybasic furin cleavage site is not observed in other coronaviruses. Thus, this facilitates efficient cleavage of the S protein by furin and other proteases. Even the "S trimer" exists in a partially open state in highly pathogenic coronaviruses [20]. After the virus enters the target cell cytoplasm, uncoated genomic RNA is translated into polyproteins (pp1a and pp1ab), which are then assembled into replicating or virus-induced double-membrane vesicle transcription complexes. Subsequently, these complexes replicate and synthesize a nested set of genomic RNA by genome transcription, which encodes structural proteins (M, E, and N) and some accessory proteins. The endoplasmic reticulum and the Golgi complex mediate the binding of the newly formed viral particles, then finally, the new virions leave the cell by exocytosis [18].

4. SARS-CoV-2 Immunology

A special feature of SARS-CoV-2 is the inhibition of receptor signaling pathways responsible for triggering antiviral immunity, mainly pattern recognition receptors (PRRs) tasked to recognize molecular patterns associated with pathogens or cellular damage (PAMPs and DAMPs). Figure 1 shows the immunology against SARS-CoV-2. PAMPs are associated with microbial pathogens [22]. The main PRRs for viral recognition are toll-like receptors 3 (TLR3) and 7 (TLR7) in the endosome or the cytosolic sensors retinoic acid-inducible gene 1 (RIG-I) and melanoma differentiation-associated gene 5 (MDA5). Activation of these PRRs is mainly associated with IFN production [22,23]. RGI-I and MDA5 activate the mitochondrial antiviral signaling protein of the downstream adaptor in the mitochondria, followed by activation of TNF receptor-associated protein [23]. SARS-CoV-2 has the ability to suppress the production and function of type 1 IFNs, triggering IFN-stimulated genes [22,23].

Similarly, in response to coronavirus infection, humans produce TCD4+ lymphocytes, TCD8+ lymphocytes, and specific antibodies, which have protective functions against viral infections; however, these functions and their importance vary according to the viral infection. TCD4+ cell responses to primary *SARS-CoV-2* infection are more prominent than those of TCD8+, whereas the presence of specific TCD8+ cells has been associated with better outcomes in COVID-19 [24]. Humoral response to SARS-CoV-2 involves neutralizing antibodies (nAb) specific to viral epitopes. N protein epitopes are conserved among different coronaviruses, prompting the generation of cross-reactive antibodies. However, nAb targets protein S and its RBD region to neutralize the coronavirus. In turn, they protect against future infections [3,24]. Moreover, SARS-CoV-2 infection can lead to a reduction in lymphocytes [23].

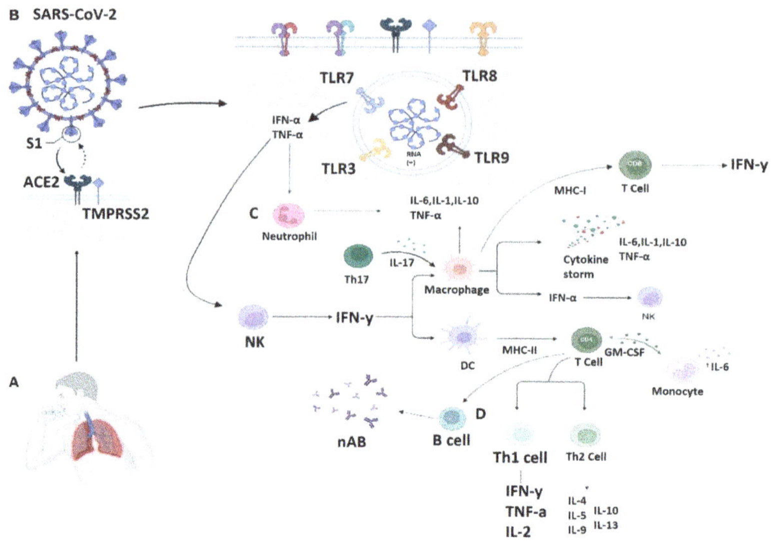

Figure 1. (**A**) Primary mode of transmission of SARS-CoV-2, which is through respiratory droplets. (**B**) SARS-CoV-2 enters via the angiotensin-converting enzyme receptor 2 (ACE-2). It also shows toll-like receptors whose function is to recognize viral RNA in endosomes. (**C**) Activation of the antiviral innate immune response associated with IFN production and activation of proinflammatory cytokines mediated by T lymphocytes causing a cytokine storm. (**D**) Humoral response to SARS-CoV-2 with the use of neutralizing antibodies (nAb). The figure was created with https://app.biorender.com (accessed on 1 June 2023).

It is worth mentioning that the virus has an impact on the mechanisms of cellular stress activation in immunocompetent cells because it causes the activation and apoptosis of lymphocytes and macrophages as well as immunosuppression [22]. The cytokine storm correctly reflects the immune response in patients with COVID-19. The observed elevated IL-6 levels are considerably low. However, there are dynamic changes in the concentration of many cytokines, including IL-6. In addition, kynurenines, molecules related with immunosuppression, are elevated in severe COVID-19 [23].

5. Impact of SARS-CoV-2in Colombia

Nearly two decades after the emergence of SARS-CoV, SARS-CoV-2spread rapidly after the first reported case in December 2019 and became a serious global health crisis [25]. Noticeably, the most affected countries were industrialized ones with strong public health systems and advanced medical facilities that have been severely strained in the course of the pandemic [26]. However, Latin America's health care systems have been significantly disrupted as SARS-CoV-2 spread around the world [27]. These nations opted for strict quarantine and the promotion of self-care, following WHO guidelines, whose objective was to separate potential carriers of the virus from uninfected individuals and thus reduce the spread of the virus, corresponding to epidemiological fences, but the social, labor, educational, psychological, and emotional costs were high [28].

In particular, the pandemic adversely affected the elderly and the disadvantaged the most. While all age groups were susceptible to SARS-CoV-2 infection, older adults suffered a higher risk of mortality [29]. Latin American countries faced an extremely protracted challenge, as factors such as poverty and limited access to potable water, among others, continued to be a critical point in the development of the region. In addition, there was a fundamental lack of preparedness to deal with a pandemic [29].

In early March 2020, the first positive cases in Colombia were reported in the city of Bogota, causing great concern among the people and leading to the implementation of weak measures to mitigate transmission. In turn, the government had to declare mandatory containment on 25 March 2020, which remained in force, totally or partially, until the beginning of 2022 [30–32]. For some authors, the health and security system, the economic sector, the social context, and people's mental health were the most critically impacted by the pandemic in the country, with the health and social security system being most affected due to the rapid chains of transmission [30].

In Colombia, from 3 January 2020 to 5 July 2023 at 4:01 p.m. CEST, there have been 6,373,599 confirmed cases of COVID-19 with 142,836 deaths reported to the WHO. As of 2 June 2023, a total of 90,506,612 vaccine doses have been administered [33].

Colombia had a case fatality rate of 2.5% with an accumulated positivity rate of 22.6%, with the highest number of cases occurring in females (53%) and the highest number of deaths in males (60.7%). Furthermore, the highest frequency of deaths was found among those between 40 and 90 years old with 389,736 deaths, peaking from 70 to 79 years old with 34,924 deaths. Among the comorbidities affecting the deceased, the most frequent were arterial hypertension (6416 deaths), diabetes mellitus (3901 deaths), respiratory diseases (2421 deaths), renal diseases (2226 deaths), obesity (1910 deaths), cardiac diseases (2083 deaths), and cancer (1115 deaths) [34].

Colombia faced six "waves," and their delimitations correlated with the restriction and relaxation of measures such as social distancing [35]. It should be noted that, according to clinical evidence, most of the cases reported in the second, third, and fourth waves were mild to moderate with lower hospital admission requirements and short hospital stays, i.e., there was a higher survival rate from COVID-19, but findings showed a large increase in the number of confirmed cases in those periods. According to the Instituto Nacional de Salud (INS), a total of 5,823,994 symptomatic cases, 488,614 asymptomatic cases, and 141828 deaths have been recorded in the six waves that have occurred in the country. The fourth and fifth waves reported higher numbers of symptomatic COVID-19 cases, with 3 January 2022 (belonging to the fifth wave) being the day with the highest number of confirmed cases (41,474). The second and fourth waves had higher numbers of asymptomatic cases reported in consultation, with 15 June 2021 (belonging to the fourth wave) being the day with the highest number of registered asymptomatic cases (5315). The fourth wave saw the highest number of COVID-19 deaths reported [34].

In addition, the INS reports 22,968 complete genomes sequenced with 267 lineages identified from 25,066 tests. Among the lineages found in the first sampling on 5 September 2021, there was a similar prevalence between the Mu (55%) and Delta (45%) variants. Patiño et al. [36] analyzed the effective reproduction number (Rt) of *SARS-CoV-2*, the virus that causes COVID-19, in Cali, Colombia between April and July 2021. The study found that Rt values were higher during the period of frequent protests compared to the preceding and following months. Genomic analysis revealed the circulation of 16 different lineages of SARS-CoV-2, including variants of concern (VOCs) and variants of interest (VOIs). The study suggests that the spread of highly virulent strains of SARS-CoV-2 in Cali and other parts of Colombia was facilitated by the limited biosecurity strategies during the period of political turmoil and social demonstrations, as well as the movement of large numbers of people into and out of the city. The Mu variant is thought to have been introduced to Cali on two separate occasions, and may have contributed to the 55% increase in the number of reported cases during the protests.

By 2 January 2022, 62% belonged to the delta variant and 38% to the Omicron variant, which later became dominant with 100% in circulation on 13 March 2022. On 8 May 2022, two sublineages of the Omicron strain, BA.2.12.1 (20%) and BA.2.x (80%), were presented. Finally, on the last sampling date of 7 August 2022, two sublineages of the Omicron variant, BA.4 (40%) and BA.5 (60%), were revealed [34]. Finally, until 18 December 2022, the omicron BQ.1.x subvariant was reported with 90% prevalence in Colombia and the XBB variant with 10%, the latter being the most transmissible variant [37].

6. Coinfections Associated with SARS-CoV-2 in Colombia

Coinfections with microbial pathogens have played an important role in increasing the morbidity and mortality rate in pandemics, and SARS-CoV-2 is no exception [38]. Coinfection between other microorganisms and this new coronavirus is an important factor to take into account in COVID-19, as it may increase the difficulties in diagnosis, management, and prognosis, and even worsen symptoms and mortality [12]. It should be noted that a wide spectrum of atypical presentations were found to be associated with COVID-19, which complicated critically ill immunocompromised patients [39]. Table 1 lists the most frequent coinfections; however, bacterial and viral coinfections were most frequently reported in patients with COVID-19 and had proportions as high as 50% among non-survivors. However, severe cases of COVID-19 related to fungal infections were documented, especially representing a major threat to life in ICU patients [16,38,40,41]. Mechanical ventilators and catheters are risk factors for nosocomial infections [14,40].

The source and specific nature of these infections have not yet been fully explored, but there is evidence to suggest that multidrug-resistant bacteria, such as *Staphylococcus aureus*, *Streptococcus pneumoniae*, *Klebsiella pneumoniae*, and *Escherichia coli*, are among the pathogens believed to be causative agents. *Acinetobacter* spp., *Enterobacter* spp., *Enterococcus* spp., and *Pseudomonas* spp. are also associated with hospital-acquired infections. Similarly, several studies have indicated that coinfection with fungi such as *Aspergillus* spp. and *Candida* spp. can increase mortality rates [14,41,42]. In addition, coinfections with SARS-CoV-2 and other respiratory viruses are unusual. They have been observed from 3.2% to 22.4% of the time, with rhinovirus–enterovirus (6.9%) and respiratory syncytial virus (5.2%) being the most commonly reported [43].

Table 1. Coinfections with *SARS-CoV-2* worldwide. HIV: Human Immunodeficiency Virus; MRSA: Methicillin-Resistant Staphylococcus Aureus.

Author	Coinfection	Country
García-Vidal et al., 2021 [5]	Influenza A Influenza B *Virus sincitial respiratorio* *Streptococcus pneumoniae* *Staphylococcus aureus* *Haemophilus influenzae* *Moraxella catarrhalis*	Spain
Acosta-Pérez et al., 2022 [13]	Dengue	Colombia
Motta et al., 2022 [43]	Adenovirus	Colombia
Forero-Peña et al., 2022 [44]	Malaria	Venezuela
Jeong et al., 2022 [45]	*Acinetobacter baumannii* *Pseudomonas aeruginosa* *Staphylococcus aureus* *Klebsiella pneumoniae* *Escherichia coli* *Bocavirus* *Influenza B*	South Korea
Palou et al., 2021 [46]	Rhizopus spp.	Honduras
Schulte et al., 2021 [47]	Dengue	Brazil
Almeida et al., 2021 [48]	*Candida auris*	
Santana et al., 2020 [49]	*Aspergillus penicillioides*	

Table 1. *Cont.*

Author	Coinfection	Country
Torres-Serrano et al., 2021 [50]	*Cryptococcus neoformans*	Colombia
Ortiz-Martínez et al., 2021 [51]	*Mycobacterium tuberculosis*	
Martínez-Montalvo et al., 2021 [52]	*Pneumocystis jirovecii.*	
Álzate- Ángel et al., 2020 [53]	VIH	
Mejía- Parra et al., 2021 [54]	Dengue	Peru
Fernandes-Matano et al., 2021 [55]	*Coronavirus 229E* *Virus sincitial respiratorio* *Influenza A* *Parainfluenza*	Mexico
Hazra et al., 2020 [56]	*Adenovirus* *Coronavirus NL63* *Human metapneumovirus* *Influenza A* *Parainfluenza*	USA
Hirotsu et al., 2020 [57]	*Rinovirus-enterovirus* *Metapneumovirus* *Coronavirus 229E* *Coronavirus OC43* *Adenovirus* *Virus sincitial respiratorio* *Coronavirus NL63*	Japan
Leuzinger et al., 2020 [58]	*Rinovirus* *Virus parainfluenza* *Influenza A* *Adenovirus* *Virus sincitial respiratorio*	Switzerland
Intra et al., 2020 [59]	*Candida albicans* *Candida glabrata* *Aspergillus fumigatus* *Staphylococcus aureus* *Streptococcus pyogenes* *Escherichia coli*	Italy
Nasir et al., 2020 [60]	*Klebsiella pneumoniae* *Pseudomonas aeruginosa* *Acinetobacter baumannii* *Staphylococcus aureus (MRSA)*	Pakistan
Lv et al., 2020 [61]	*Acinetobacter baumannii* *Escherichia coli* *Staphylococcus haemolyticus* *Pseudomonas aeruginosa* *Mycoplasma pneumoniae* *Stenotrophomonas maltophilia* *Enterococcus faecium* *Candida albicans* *Candida tropicalis* *Candida parapsilosis* *Candida lusitaniae*	China
Messina et al., 2020 [62]	*Histoplasma capsulatum*	Argentina

Molina et al. [63], who conducted a study in eight hospitals in Colombia, reported the most frequently seen microorganisms in coinfections in the ICU as follows: *Staphylococcus aureus*, *Streptococcus agalactiae*, and *Klebsiella pneumoniae* [63].

The most common coinfections with SARS-CoV2 in Colombia, as shown in Table 2, were dengue virus (DENV), *Klebsiella pneumoniae*, *Mycobacterium tuberculosis* (MTB), *Pneumocystis jirovecii* (*P. jirovecii*), *Cryptococcus neoformans*, *rhinovirus–enterovirus*, *adenovirus*, *human immunodeficiency virus* (HIV), and *Trypanosoma cruzi.*

Table 2. Coinfections with *SARS-CoV-2* in Colombia.

Author	Coinfection	City/State
Algarín-Lara et al., 2021 [39]	*Pneumocystis jirovecii*	Barranquilla
Motta et al., 2022 [43]	*Adenovirus*	Bogota
Torres-Serrano et al., 2021 [50]	*Cryptococcus neoformans*	Bogota
Ortiz-Martínez et al., 2021 [51]	*Mycobacterium tuberculosis*	Bucaramanga
Angel et al., 2020 [53]	VIH	Santiago de Cali
Cardona-Ospina et al., 2021 [64]	Dengue	Valle del Cauca
Agudelo Rojas et al., 2020 [65]	Dengue	Cali
Restrepo et al., 2021 [66]	*Cryptococcus neoformans*	Bogota
León et al., 2022 [67]	*Trypanosoma cruzi*	Bucaramanga
Villamil-Gómez et al., 2021 [68]	*Trypanosoma cruzi*	Sincelejo
Medina-Ahumada et al., 2022 [69]	*Aspergillus fumigatus*	Cartagena
Molina et al., 2022 [63]	*Enterobacter cloacae* *Haemophilus influenzae* *Klebsiella pneumoniae* *Klebsiella oxytoca* *Pseudomonas aeruginosa* *Streptococcus agalactiae* *Staphylococcus aureus* *Streptococcus pneumoniae*	Medellin
Pinzón et al., 2021 [70]	*Mycoplasma pneumoniae* *Salmonella* spp. *Mycobacterium tuberculosis* *Pneumococcus* *Influenza* *Bordetella* spp.	Antioquia
Molano et al., 2021 [71]	*Klebsiella pneumoniae*	Bogota
García-Posada et al., 2021 [72]	*Klebsiella pneumoniae* *Pseudomonas aeruginosa* *Staphylococcus aureus* *Enterobacter cloacae* *Rhinovirus-enterovirus*	Cordoba
Orozco-Hernandez et al., 2020 [73]	*Rinovirus-enterovirus*	Cartago
Contreras-Acosta et al., 2020 [74]	*Influenza H1N1*	Barranquilla

7. SARS-CoV-2, and Dengue Coinfection

Initial differentiation between dengue and COVID-19 is a challenge as both infections have similar symptoms, such as fever, diarrhea, myalgia, and headache, and these overlap [64,65]. However, studies suggested that SARS-CoV-2 and DENV coinfection had less severe symptoms compared to isolated monoinfection [13]. Tropical countries, especially those with endemic DENV, approached a syndemic state, because multiple patients were coinfected with both SARS-CoV-2 and DENV. COVID-19 can be misdiagnosed with dengue. This situation complicates matters, so it can be difficult to distinguish between early infections and coinfections, generating an important risk for the population and demanding greater attention from health systems, because both viruses can cause serious complications, mainly through the cytokine storm in lung tissue caused by macrophage hyperactivation [13,27,64].

Diagnosing coinfection requires a combination of tests for the direct detection of the virus and indirect techniques that measure the immune response [65]. It is important to take into account the clinical and epidemiological particularities of both infections [13,65].

In 2020, 28,068 cases of dengue were reported in the department of Valle del Cauca, of which a case fatality rate of 6.6% was reported for severe dengue. It should be noted that from weeks 1 to 36, the cases were higher than expected, but from weeks 37 to 52, they were within the limit according to their historical behavior between 2013 and 2017 [63]. Likewise, in 2021, 8141 cases of dengue were reported, with 23 probable deaths due to severe dengue, although the number of cases was within the expected range [75]. However, a rebound peak of dengue was observed due to the replenishment of susceptible individuals with low exposure to infection. In addition, the number of patients requiring intensive care and mechanical ventilation increased. Therefore, regions such as Valle del Cauca should consider intensified preparedness for such scenarios, and further studies should be conducted to address this critical issue promptly to reduce the potential overload on the national health system [64].

8. Coinfections with Bacteria

Klebsiella pneumoniae is a Gram-negative species that can reside in the gastrointestinal tract [76]. In immunocompromised patients, it can cause serious infections, including urinary tract infections, respiratory infections, soft tissue infections, peritonitis, and sepsis [45,68]. Lipopolysaccharide and cell wall protein receptors are responsible for pathogenicity and determine the process of binding to host cells and provide protection against the human immune system response [76]. Mechanical ventilation, exposure to carbapenems and β-lactamase/β-lactamase inhibitors, renal replacement therapy, transfusions, and prolonged hospital stay are risk factors for coinfection with *Klebsiella pneumoniae* [77]. Patients with COVID-19, in whom immune mechanisms appear to be weakened by this viral infection, should follow rational antibiotic therapy with the aim of preventing bacterial resistance [76].

Mycobacterium tuberculosis (MTB) is an acid-fast bacterium and is the main causative agent of human tuberculosis. Evidence suggests a twofold increased mortality risk in patients with COVID-19 and tuberculosis [27]. For example, a systematic review reported an increased risk of mortality in patients with coinfection of these two microorganisms, although MTB and SARS-CoV-2 coinfections are poorly understood. On the other hand, a meta-analysis and systematic case study of SARS-CoV-2 coinfection with drug-resistant tuberculosis failed to show the same. In both cases, the evidence was inconsistent, and more high-quality studies are needed to better understand the causal association [51]. However, another study reported that active or latent tuberculosis increased susceptibility to *SARS-CoV-2* and disease severity [27].

9. Coinfections with Fungi

One of the underestimated microorganisms in patients with coronavirus disease 2019 is *Pneumocystis jirovecii*, an opportunistic infection that mainly affects immunosuppressed patients [52]. It occurs due to an imbalance between T lymphocyte subtypes, mainly due to the absence of $CD4^+$ T cells, causing a deficiency in the immune response and generating a predominance of TCD8+, causing epithelial damage secondary to an excessive inflammatory state. In severe infections, 50% of patients may require hospitalization in the ICU, with a mortality rate of up to 40–60% [39,52]. SARS-CoV-2 infection can cause a state of immunodeficiency that may allow the appearance of this opportunistic fungus. At the same time, *P. jirovecii* and SARS-CoV-2 infections presented as joint processes, primarily in immunocompromised patients. It presents acutely with severe hypoxemia and the rapid deterioration of respiratory function, requiring invasive mechanical ventilation. It was found that the (1,3)-β-D-glucan detection technique is of potential use for the detection of *P. jirovecii* in patients with acute SARS-CoV-2 coinfection [39].

Cryptococcus neoformans is an encapsulated yeast-like fungus that is considered an opportunistic and rare pathogen in transplant recipients [50] and can cause cryptococcosis in immunocompromised patients. The most frequent and severe form of presentation is infection of the central nervous system, manifesting as subacute or chronic meningitis and characterized by headache, nausea, vomiting, fever, and altered consciousness; pulmonary, skin, lymph node, or other organ involvement may also occur to a lesser extent [66]. COVID-19 has been observed to increase infection by other rare pathogens in immunocompetent patients, such as that caused by *Aspergillus* spp., and studies have reported that patients required ICU stay and invasive mechanical ventilation secondary to infection by COVID-19, without a history of immunosuppression. Therefore, it can be said that coinfection with SARS-CoV-2 and Cryptococcus is rare. For example, in 2021, among 293 patients in a case study conducted in China, there was only one case reported [50,66]. However, it should be taken into account that SARS-CoV-2 infection may be an etiology for fungal infection by *Cryptococcus neoformans* due to the great multisystemic impact and the multiorgan dysfunction established by the viral agent, as the main cause of immunosuppression predisposing to infections by this microorganism. At the same time, management with glucocorticoids (dexamethasone) may favor immunological compromise [66].

10. Coinfection with Virus

Rhinoviruses (*RVH*) and *enteroviruses* (*EVH*) belong to the *Picornaviridae* family and are the main cause of infections worldwide. They are characterized as small with a single-stranded RNA genome in an icosahedral capsid. In a study by Kim et al. [78], it was observed that 9.5% of 1217 patients with respiratory symptoms tested positive for SARS-CoV-2 and 318 for another microorganism. Of the group positive for SARS-CoV-2, 20.7% were positive for one or more pathogens, with *RVH* and EVH being the most frequent [78,79]. Regarding concomitant SARS-CoV-2 and *rhinovirus–enterovirus* infection, it is recommended that the multiplex PCR respiratory panel be performed only for severe patients and those in whom a positive result requires modification of treatment to prevent disease progression and even death [79].

Adenoviruses are icosahedral viruses that possess a double-stranded DNA genome, belonging to the *Adenoviridae* family. They cause only respiratory, ocular, and enteric disease in humans. Cases of coinfection with SARS-CoV-2 and respiratory viruses are poorly documented; for example, by 2020, only two patients with *adenovirus* coinfection had been documented. The pathogenesis of coinfection is not clearly explained, although there are hypotheses about the low presentation of SARS-CoV-2 without a predisposing risk factor. In addition, it has been documented that there is a higher proportion of coinfection in patients with acute respiratory distress syndrome and septic shock and requiring ICU admission [43].

HIV, which belongs to the *Retroviridae* family, is characterized by attacking the immune system and thus generating a state of immunodeficiency. People living with HIV (PLHIV) should not consider themselves protected against SARS-CoV-2, as people with low $CD4^+$ T-cell counts may have worse outcomes than people with normal immunity [27,51]. Moreover, poorer COVID-related outcomes were observed in patients with HIV than those without the infection, especially in those with multimorbidity and advanced age [51]. A recent prospective cohort study reported that 8% of PLHIV infected with *SARS-CoV-2* required admission to the ICU. It should be noted that clinical manifestations, disease severity, and mortality are independent of HIV or antiretroviral-related factors.

There are possible similarities between HIV-*1* and SARS-CoV-2 proteins. At the same time, it has not been identified as a common comorbidity in patients with COVID-19. In addition, there are differences between the receptors through which HIV and other pathogenic *coronaviruses* enter target cells, the ways of assembly, and their encapsulation. In the case of HIV, it does so near the cytoplasmic membrane, and in the case of *coronavirus*, the process takes place in the endoplasmic reticulum, which may suggest that there is no synergistic or cooperative pathogenesis [53].

11. Coinfections with Parasites

The protozoan parasite, *Trypanosoma cruzi*, is the main infectious agent of Chagas disease. This disease causes cardiac and gastrointestinal complications, among others, and is endemic in Latin America [80]. The intense inflammatory process of COVID-19 in immunocompromised patients could potentially influence the evolution of the disease and latently trigger reactivation of Chagas disease due to viral interference of the infection. It is important to highlight that different clinical and epidemiological scenarios may increase susceptibility to SARS-CoV-2 infection, because the new *coronavirus* disease has a significant impact on the heart. Likewise, the pandemic influences access to treatment for people with acute and chronic indeterminate Chagas disease [68].

In patients with SARS-CoV-2 pneumonia and immunosuppression, antibiotic treatment should be initiated in order to address opportunistic pulmonary infections. However, there are infections that are not covered by first-line antibiotics [39]. An example is *P. jirovecii*, where the first choice is the use of trimethoprim–sulfamethoxazole, a broad-spectrum antibiotic for bacterial and fungal germs [39,52]. Another case is *Klebsiella pneumoniae*, which has a very low sensitivity profile to most categories of antibiotics [14,38,45,76,77] and is very difficult to treat, but the drug combinations aztreonam and ceftazidime/avibactam or meropenem/vaborbactam show universal coverage against beta-lactamase-producing *Enterobacteriaceae*, including those with extensive drug resistance [76].

However, concerns about coinfections have led to significant antimicrobial use in up to 80% of critically ill patients with COVID-19, and their overuse could lead to antimicrobial resistance [38,63,81]. The rate of antimicrobial resistance ranged from 33.3% to 90.0%, depending on the infecting species [45]. The use of antibiotics over the last 50 years has exerted selective pressure on susceptible bacteria and may have favored the survival of resistant strains [15]. Of concern is that there is clinical evidence suggesting that inappropriate empirical use of antibiotics and other broad-spectrum antimicrobials may be associated with increased mortality [16]. One of the main aspects that needs to be evaluated in the prevalence of coinfections is the application of empirical antimicrobial treatment in patients with SARS-CoV-2 infection [38]. In addition, it is important to know more information about the prevalence of coinfections in the community [82], and hospital-acquired or healthcare-associated infections need to be continuously monitored and controlled. These should not only focus on minimizing the spread of SARS-CoV-2 infection but also on reducing bacterial cross-transmission, particularly of multidrug-resistant organisms [76]. Therefore, strategies should be established to improve antimicrobial stewardship in patients with COVID-19.

12. SARS-CoV-2—Associated Superinfections in Colombia

SARS-CoV-2 superinfections increase difficulties in the prognosis, diagnosis, and treatment of patients [83]. According to the U.S. Centers for Disease Control and Prevention, "a superinfection is an infection that follows a previous infection, especially when caused by pathogens that are resistant or have become resistant to previously used antibiotics" [6,84]. The mechanisms of superinfections include virus-induced damage to the respiratory system, decreased mucociliary clearance, and damage to the immune system. The decrease in lymphocytes and host immune function is the main reason that facilitates superinfection [83]. It should also be noted that clinical deterioration, elevated inflammatory markers, and bilateral radiological infiltrates may lead to misperception regarding the presence of a co-pathogen and should be used as an impetus to initiate comprehensive diagnostic workup with sampling, rather than as an indicator of underlying superinfection [84].

Superinfection in hospitalized patients with COVID-19 is associated with disease progression and poor prognosis. This situation increases antimicrobial treatment and mortality. They have even been related mainly to ICU admission, especially with the use of mechanical ventilation and catheters, and patients with comorbidities. In addition to having a higher prevalence, they also have a higher risk of death than in other patients [5,6,83]. The study by Clancy et al., (2021) [85] described several common risk factors, including being older than 60 years, male, ICU admission, mechanical ventilation, renal failure requiring hemodialysis, arterial hypertension, diabetes mellitus, and cancer [5,8,83].

Similarly, Paparoupa et al. [84] reported that 45% of invasively mechanically ventilated patients with COVID-19 pneumonia had bacterial, viral, or fungal respiratory superinfection in at least one of the sequential study periods. Therefore, the frequency of hospital-acquired superinfections remained low despite the fact that many patients received treatment that resulted in severe immunosuppression.

Factors such as the empirical use of antibiotics, isolation measures, or the host macrophage activation explain this. At the same time, the lack of additional microbiological testing after SARS-CoV-2 was detected may have also contributed. Further studies will be needed to elucidate the role of each measure in reducing superinfections [5]. Table 3 lists the most frequent superinfections. *Acinetobacter* spp. has been identified as a common infection in ventilated patients. It is more frequent in patients with superinfection [6].

Table 3. Superinfections with SARS-CoV-2.

Author	Superinfection	Country
García-Vidal et al., 2021 [5]	*Staphylococcus aureus* *Stenotrophomonas maltophilia* *Pseudomonas aeruginosa* *Klebsiella pneumoniae*	Spain
Musuuza et al., 2021 [6]	*Acinetobacter* spp. *Pseudomonas* spp. *Escherichia coli* *Rhinovirus* *Candida* spp.	USA
Nag et al., 2021 [8]	*Klebsiella pneumoniae* *Pseudomonas aeruginosa* *Serratia marcescens* *Enterobacter cloacae* *Acinetobacter baumannii* *Escherichia coli* *Staphylococcus aureus* *Bacillus cereus* *Aspergillus flavus* *Aspergillus fumigatus* *Candida albicans* *Candida glabrata*	India
Al-Tawfiq et al., 2021 [86]	*Mucorales*	
Arcangeletti et al., 2022 [87]	*Influenza A H3*	Italy
Vaseghi et al., 2022 [88]	*Candida auris*	Iran
Wertheim et al., 2022 [89]	Alpha and Epsilon del SARS-CoV-2	USA
Pickens et al., 2021 [90]	*Methicillin-susceptible* *Staphylococcus aureus (MSSA)* *Streptococcus agalactiae* *Stenotrophomonas maltophilia* *Methicillin-resistant* *Staphylococcus aureus (MRSA)* *Pneumocystis* spp. *Haemophilus influenzae*	
Awada et al., 2021 [91]	*Candida duobushaemulonii*	Lebanon
Lamballerie et al., 2020 [92]	*Aspergillus* spp.	France
Nieuwenhuis MB et al., 2020 [93]	*Staphylococcus aureus* *Pseudomonas aeruginosa*	Netherlands

The superinfections with SARS-CoV-2 documented so far in Colombia, shown in Table 4, are bacterial in nature, with *Raoultella planticola* and *Pandoraea pnomenusa* standing out.

Table 4. Superinfections with SARS-CoV-2 in Colombia.

Author	Superinfection	City/State
Castaño-Correa et al., 2021 [83]	*Klebsiella pneumoniae* *Staphylococcus aureus* *Enterobacter cloacae* *Enterobacter aerogenes* *Pseudomonas aeruginosa* *Serratia marcescens* *Haemophilus influenzae* *Escherichia coli*	Medellin
Montalvo et al., 2022 [94]	*Raoultella planticola*	Bogota
Cubides-Diaz et al., 2022 [95]	*Pandoraea pnomenusa*	Cundinamarca

R. planticola is a bacterium of the *Enterobacteriaceae* family that can be found in soil and water, and is associated with seafood consumption, biliary tract diseases, malignancy, diabetes mellitus, trauma, immunosuppression, and nosocomial infection. Initially considered harmless, the number of cases has increased in recent years, mainly consisting of cystitis, bacteremia, and pneumonia. Most strains of *R. planticola* are usually multisensitive and treatment is effective with second and third generation cephalosporins, aminoglycosides, and fluoroquinolones. With respect to *R. planticola* infection as a complication of SARS-CoV-2 infection, there is a paucity of cases reported in the literature. However, an infection by this microorganism has been reported as a complication of pulmonary bulla, a rare complication of COVID-19 affecting only 1% of patients, secondary to SARS-CoV-2 infection [94].

Pandoraea pnomenusa is a bacterium belonging to the *Pandoraea* genus. It should be noted that its usual presentation is the colonization of structurally abnormal airways. Infection generated by this microorganism occurs rarely, but its mortality rate is high, reaching up to 60%. It usually presents with multiple antimicrobial resistance. It presents an intrinsic ß-lactamase of the OXA type and a gyrB gene [95].

Bacterial superinfection in hospitalized patients with COVID-19 is associated with disease progression and poor prognosis. For example, in March 2020, a case of pneumonia caused by *Staphylococcus aureus* secreting leukocidin toxin in a man with mechanical ventilation was reported and treated with piperacillin–tazobactam, linezolid, meropenem, and gentamicin; however, the patient died 17 days after admission [8].

Antimicrobial stewardship will continue to be a priority because antimicrobial use in SARS-CoV-2 -infected patients remains higher than in superinfections [14]. Antimicrobial stewardship principles help guide the appropriate use of antibiotics [8]. Paparoupa et al. [84] demonstrated extensive use of broad-spectrum antibacterials in more than 70% of COVID-19 cases.

It is important that centers collect and publish their clinical, microbiological, and antimicrobial prescribing data. Further research is also needed on current infection control guidelines [8].

13. Therapeutic against COVID-19 in Colombia

In the context of COVID-19, antibiotics are primarily used to treat secondary bacterial infections that may occur as complications of the viral disease. These bacterial infections can manifest as secondary bacterial pneumonia, respiratory tract infections, or urinary tract infections, among others. The use of antibiotics in these cases aims to treat concurrent bacterial infections or prevent their occurrence in patients with compromised immune systems, particularly those who are in a severe condition [83]. In their study on antibiotic resistance during COVID-19 in Valle del Cauca, Colombia, Hurtado et al. [4] analyzed data from 31 hospitals and compared antibiotic resistance and consumption before (March 2018 to July 2019) and during (March 2020 to July 2021) the pandemic. The results showed an increase in the total number of bacterial isolates during the pandemic, accompanied by a significant decrease in resistance for four bug–drug combinations. However, there was a noticeable rise in vancomycin resistance among *Enterococcus faecium*. Overall, antibiotic consumption increased, except for meropenem in ICU settings. These findings suggest that the COVID-19 pandemic contributed to an increase in community-acquired infections, resulting in changes in antibiotic resistance patterns. Monitoring the increasing resistance of *E. faecium* to vancomycin and implementing effective infection control measures is crucial.

In a study conducted by Valladales-Restrepo et al., (2023) in Colombia, a descriptive cross-sectional study was carried out to examine the utilization of systemic antibiotics among patients diagnosed with COVID-19 between 2020 and 2022. The study involved eight clinics and included a total of 10,916 predominantly male patients with a median age of 57 years. Approximately 57.5% of the patients received antibiotics, with ampicillin/sulbactam and clarithromycin being the most frequently prescribed ones. Based on the WHO AWaRe classification, the majority of prescribed antibiotics belonged to the Watch category, followed by access and reserve categories. Several factors were found to be associated with a higher likelihood of receiving systemic antibiotics, such as male gender, older age, presence of dyspnea, rheumatoid arthritis, high blood pressure, in-hospital treatment, or ICU admission, and the use of systemic glucocorticoids, vasopressors, or invasive mechanical ventilation. Despite the low prevalence of bacterial coinfections, a significant proportion of COVID-19 patients received antibiotics, with a noticeable dominance of Watch antibiotics, which deviates from the recommendations provided by the World Health Organization [96].

In Colombia, various treatments have been used to combat COVID-19, including Remdesivir, Molnupiravir, Tocilizumab, and Convalescent Plasma Therapy. Remdesivir works by inhibiting the replication of the virus in the body and has been used in hospitalized patients with severe illness. Its emergency use authorization has made it available for those in need during the pandemic [97–99]. Molnupiravir is an antiviral medication that has shown activity against SARS-CoV-2 and has been authorized for emergency use in the treatment of COVID-19 by the Colombian regulatory agency, the National Institute for Surveillance of Drugs and Food (INVIMA) [100]. Preclinical studies have shown that Molnupiravir has the potential to significantly reduce viral load and decrease virus transmission in animal models. Additionally, early findings from clinical trials and systematic reviews have demonstrated promising results, indicating a reduction in hospitalization and mortality rates among patients with mild to moderate COVID-19. Molnupiravir presents a new ray of hope in combating the pandemic and could play a crucial role in the treatment of this disease [101–103].

Tocilizumab, on the other hand, is an immunosuppressive medication used in severe cases of COVID-19. This drug works by blocking interleukin-6 (IL-6), an inflammatory protein involved in the exaggerated immune response that can lead to severe complications in COVID-19 patients. Tocilizumab is administered via intravenous infusion and has been used in patients exhibiting excessive inflammatory response, such as cytokine release syndrome [104–106].

Convalescent Plasma Therapy is another treatment option used in Colombia for patients with COVID-19. It involves transfusing blood plasma from individuals who have recovered from the disease and have developed antibodies against the virus. It is believed that these antibodies can help fight the infection and improve symptoms in sick patients. However, it is important to note that the effectiveness of this therapy is still being investigated, and more scientific evidence is needed to support its widespread use [107,108].

14. Therapeutic Alternatives against COVID-19

The COVID-19 pandemic predisposes patients to potentially life-threatening infections in the ICU, hindering proper diagnosis and treatment [109]. Thus, specific therapy for

COVID-19 should take into account coverage of local endemic pathogens that may occur in a similar manner, particularly while confirmation of SARS-CoV-2 infection is pending [17].

On the other hand, the WHO treatment guideline recommends empirically prescribed broad-spectrum antibiotics to treat possible coinfections. However, the effect of this respiratory disease on antimicrobial resistance is a dimension that requires necessary attention, since 15% to 50% of bacterial isolates are resistant to at least one antimicrobial group [109]. Therefore, antimicrobial therapy should be evaluated against a patient's host factors and local epidemiology on a daily basis [17].

It has been documented that systemic glucocorticoids improve survival when administered to moderate or severe COVID patients. Its use is associated with reduced oxygen therapy and decreased risk of invasive mechanical ventilation among patients receiving supplemental oxygen [98,110]. However, treatment with corticosteroids was associated with a higher risk of progression of hospital stay and it is not clear if there is an increased risk of superinfection in non-severe COVID patients [110]. There are currently drugs or vaccines available to inhibit the new *coronavirus*. Although current vaccines effectively prevent serious complications and deaths, treatment options are still under validation, especially for immunocompromised patients [111]. Therefore, to avoid viral exposure, it is important to adhere to the following measures: maintaining social distancing, wearing face coverings, practicing frequent hand washing, using alcohol-based hand sanitizers when necessary, and avoiding touching the face. However, it is important to note that not all of these measures should be grouped together. While the effectiveness of alcohol-based hand sanitizers has been highlighted [17], it is also worth mentioning that the effectiveness of face coverings, such as masks, has been extensively studied. Additionally, it is crucial to be mindful of the potential contribution of these practices to the threat of antimicrobial resistance. Therefore, alternatives such as supplementation and the development of nanomedicine should be considered.

Zinc (Zn) is involved in several biological processes as a cofactor and signaling molecule in the immune system. Additionally, it is an important component of the hormone thymulin, whose function is in T-cell differentiation, maturation, and NK actions [17]. Zn deficiency causes IL-10 dysregulation that alters Th1 cell response and macrophage functions [112]. Zn deficiency is associated with the risk and extreme progression of COVID-19 [17]. On the other hand, it has been shown that Zn ions can inhibit *coronavirus* RNA polymerase activity by reducing replication [112]. Thus, Zn supplementation may be associated with a lower mortality rate in patients with COVID-19, although more research is needed to understand the intimate mechanisms of antiviral activity [17].

Nanotechnology allows the manipulation and evaluation of individual molecules, and nanotechnology applied to medicine, also called nanomedicine, has been used to improve care in neurological, cardiovascular, and infectious diseases, and cancer [17]. Nanotechnology-based targets should be harnessed to aid in the fight against COVID-19, as well as any future pandemics, including the use of biosensors, virus inhibition by nanosystems, new vaccines and drugs, superfine filters for face masks or blood filters, and improvements to contact-tracing instruments, as it provides significant benefits and early-stage disease detection. In addition, established methods do not require specialized instrumentation, which provides a pathway to simple integral answers [113,114].

Another alternative is the use of REGEN-COV for patients who are at high risk of progressing to severe COVID-19 and who are not fully vaccinated or are not expected to develop a complete immune response [98]. This combination of monoclonal antibodies has been shown to reduce the viral load in symptomatic outpatient patients and the number of medical visits. It also has in vitro activity against current strains and reduces the risk of hospitalization or death. However, it may be associated with worse outcomes when given to patients who require high-flow oxygen or mechanical ventilation [98,115].

15. Conclusions

The COVID-19 pandemic has had a significant impact on Latin America, particularly on countries with weaker healthcare systems. The disease has disproportionately affected the elderly and disadvantaged, and has been exacerbated by comorbidities such as hypertension, diabetes, and respiratory diseases. Coinfections with other microorganisms, such as bacteria, viruses, and fungi, have also contributed to the morbidity and mortality rates of COVID-19 in the region. In Colombia, dengue virus, *Klebsiella pneumoniae, Mycobacterium tuberculosis, Pneumocystis jirovecii, Cryptococcus neoformans,* and *rhinovirus–enterovirus* have been reported as common coinfections with SARS-CoV-2. There is a need to improve surveillance systems and establish protocols for the early detection and management of coinfections in COVID-19 to reduce the burden on healthcare systems. While current vaccines have been effective in preventing serious complications and deaths, there is a lack of specific treatment options for COVID-19, especially for immunocompromised patients. Alternative approaches, such as zinc supplementation and the use of nanomedicine, have been proposed as potential therapies, but more research is needed to fully understand their effectiveness.

Author Contributions: D.D.; investigation, D.D.; writing—original draft preparation, Y.L. and J.D.; writing—review and editing, D.D., J.D. and Y.L.; visualization, Y.L.; supervision, Y.L.; project administration. The corresponding author attests that all listed authors meet authorship criteria and that no others meeting the criteria have been omitted. All authors have read and agreed to the published version of the manuscript.

Funding: This review was funded by the General Direction of Research of the Universidad Santiago de Cali convocatoria Interna No. 02–2023.

Institutional Review Board Statement: Not applicable.

Informed Consent Statement: Not applicable.

Data Availability Statement: Not applicable.

Acknowledgments: To the General Direction of Research of the Universidad Santiago de Cali.

Conflicts of Interest: The authors declare no conflict of interest.

Abbreviations

SARS-CoV-2	Severe Acute Respiratory Syndrome Coronavirus 2
ICU	Intensive Care Unit
COVID-19	Coronavirus Disease 2019
WHO	World Health Organization
INVIMA	National Institute for Surveillance of Drugs and Food (Instituto Nacional de Vigilancia de Medicamentos y Alimentos)
IL-6	Interleukin-6
NK	Natural Killer
Zn	Zinc
RNA	Ribonucleic Acid
Th1	T-helper 1
REGEN-COV	Regeneron Antibody Cocktail
DENV	Dengue virus
MTB	*Mycobacterium tuberculosis*

References

1. Arandia-Guzmán, J.; Antezana-Llaveta, G. SARS-CoV-2: Estructura, replicación y mecanismos fisiopatológicos relacionados con COVID-19. *Gac. Médica Boliv.* **2020**, *43*, 170–178.
2. Argüello, H.F.; Martínez, A.H.; Moncada, D.L.; Bohórquez, D.F.G.; Rivero, J.E.F. Caracterización y fisiopatología del SARS-CoV-2, Revisión de la literatura actual. *Rev. Médicas UIS* **2021**, *34*, 61–75.

3. SARS-COV-2 Variants: Differences and Potential of Immune Evasion—PMC. Available online: https://www.ncbi.nlm.nih.gov/pmc/articles/PMC8805732/ (accessed on 11 June 2022).
4. Hurtado, I.C.; Hurtado, J.S.; Valencia, S.L.; Pinzón, E.M.; Guzmán, A.R.; Lesmes, M.C. Reinfection by SARS CoV2 in Valle Del Cauca, Colombia: A Descriptive Retrospective Study. *Inquiry* **2022**, *59*, 00469580221096528. [CrossRef] [PubMed]
5. Garcia-Vidal, C.; Sanjuan, G.; Moreno-García, E.; Puerta-Alcalde, P.; Garcia-Pouton, N.; Chumbita, M.; Fernandez-Pittol, M.; Pitart, C.; Inciarte, A.; Bodro, M.; et al. Incidence of Co-Infections and Superinfections in Hospitalized Patients with COVID-19: A Retrospective Cohort Study. *Clin. Microbiol. Infect.* **2021**, *27*, 83–88. [CrossRef]
6. Musuuza, J.S.; Watson, L.; Parmasad, V.; Putman-Buehler, N.; Christensen, L.; Safdar, N. Prevalence and Outcomes of Co-Infection and Superinfection with SARS-CoV-2 and Other Pathogens: A Systematic Review and Meta-Analysis. *PLoS ONE* **2021**, *16*, e0251170. [CrossRef]
7. Wang, L.; Amin, A.K.; Khanna, P.; Aali, A.; McGregor, A.; Bassett, P.; Gopal Rao, G. An Observational Cohort Study of Bacterial Co-Infection and Implications for Empirical Antibiotic Therapy in Patients Presenting with COVID-19 to Hospitals in North West London. *J. Antimicrob. Chemother.* **2021**, *76*, 796–803. [CrossRef]
8. Nag, V.L.; Kaur, N. Superinfections in COVID-19 Patients: Role of Antimicrobials. *DMJ* **2021**, *4*, 117–126. [CrossRef]
9. Del Pozo, J.L. Respiratory Co-and Superinfections in COVID-19. *Rev. Esp. Quim.* **2021**, *34*, 69–71. [CrossRef]
10. The Lancet COVID-19 in Latin America—Emergency and Opportunity. *Lancet* **2021**, *398*, 93. [CrossRef]
11. Viana-Cárdenas, E.; Triana, A.; Mendoza, H.; Buendia, E.; Viasus, D. Epidemiology of 4963 Deaths Associated with COVID-19 during Three Pandemic Waves in a Latin American City with a High Mortality Rate, 2020–2021. *Trop. Med. Int. Health* **2022**, *27*, 158–164. [CrossRef]
12. Quiñones-Laveriano, D.M.; Soto, A.; Quilca-Barrera, L.; Quiñones-Laveriano, D.M.; Soto, A.; Quilca-Barrera, L. Frecuencia de Coinfección Por Patógenos Respiratorios y Su Impacto En El Pronóstico de Pacientes Con COVID-19. *Rev. Fac. Med. Humana* **2021**, *21*, 610–622. [CrossRef]
13. Acosta-Pérez, T.; Rodríguez-Yánez, T.; Almanza-Hurtado, A.; Martínez-Ávila, M.C.; Dueñas-Castell, C. Dynamics of Dengue and SARS-CoV-2 Co-Infection in an Endemic Area of Colombia. *Trop. Dis. Travel. Med. Vaccines* **2022**, *8*, 12. [CrossRef]
14. Bazaid, A.S.; Barnawi, H.; Qanash, H.; Alsaif, G.; Aldarhami, A.; Gattan, H.; Alharbi, B.; Alrashidi, A.; Al-Soud, W.A.; Moussa, S.; et al. Bacterial Coinfection and Antibiotic Resistance Profiles among Hospitalised COVID-19 Patients. *Microorganisms* **2022**, *10*, 495. [CrossRef]
15. Cabrera Morales, G.C.; Urquizo Ayala, G.; Cabrera Morales, G.C.; Urquizo Ayala, G. Terapia Antimicrobiana Empirica En Pacientes Con Coinfeccion Bacteriana Asociada A Covid 19. *Rev. Médica La. Paz.* **2021**, *27*, 80–86.
16. Bengoechea, J.A.; Bamford, C.G. SARS-CoV-2, Bacterial Co-infections, and AMR: The Deadly Trio in COVID-19? *EMBO Mol. Med.* **2020**, *12*, e12560. [CrossRef]
17. Goel, N.; Ahmad, R.; Fatima, H.; Khare, S.K. New Threatening of SARS-CoV-2 Coinfection and Strategies to Fight the Current Pandemic. *Med. Drug Discov.* **2021**, *10*, 100089. [CrossRef]
18. Mohamadian, M.; Chiti, H.; Shoghli, A.; Biglari, S.; Parsamanesh, N.; Esmaeilzadeh, A. COVID-19: Virology, Biology and Novel Laboratory Diagnosis. *J. Gene Med.* **2021**, *23*, e3303. [CrossRef]
19. Peña López, B.O.; Rincón Orozco, B.; Castillo León, J.J. SARS-CoV-2: Generalidades bioquímicas y métodos de diagnóstico. *Nova* **2020**, *18*, 11–33. [CrossRef]
20. Ochani, R.K.; Asad, A.; Yasmin, F.; Shaikh, S.; Khalid, H.; Batra, S.; Sohail, M.R.; Mahmood, S.F.; Ochani, R.; Arshad, M.H.; et al. COVID-19 Pandemic: From Origins to Outcomes. A Comprehensive Review of Viral Pathogenesis, Clinical Manifestations, Diagnostic Evaluation, and Management. *Infez. Med.* **2021**, *29*, 20–36.
21. Bedoya-Sommerkamp, M.; Medina-Ranilla, J.; Chau-Rodríguez, V.; Li-Soldevilla, R.; Vera-Albújar, Á.; García, P.J. Variantes del SARS-CoV-2: Epidemiología, fisiopatología y la importancia de las vacunas. *Rev. Peru. Med. Exp. Salud Publica* **2021**, *38*, 442–451. [CrossRef]
22. Gusev, E.; Sarapultsev, A.; Solomatina, L.; Chereshnev, V. SARS-CoV-2-Specific Immune Response and the Pathogenesis of COVID-19. *Int. J. Mol. Sci.* **2022**, *23*, 1716. [CrossRef] [PubMed]
23. Schultze, J.L.; Aschenbrenner, A.C. COVID-19 and the Human Innate Immune System. *Cell* **2021**, *184*, 1671–1692. [CrossRef] [PubMed]
24. Sette, A.; Crotty, S. Adaptive Immunity to SARS-CoV-2 and COVID-19. *Cell* **2021**, *184*, 861–880. [CrossRef] [PubMed]
25. Ramírez, J.D.; Muñoz, M.; Hernández, C.; Flórez, C.; Gomez, S.; Rico, A.; Pardo, L.; Barros, E.C.; Paniz-Mondolfi, A.E. Genetic Diversity Among SARS-CoV2 Strains in South America May Impact Performance of Molecular Detection. *Pathogens* **2020**, *9*, 580. [CrossRef] [PubMed]
26. Ramírez, J.D.; Florez, C.; Muñoz, M.; Hernández, C.; Castillo, A.; Gomez, S.; Rico, A.; Pardo, L.; Barros, E.C.; Castañeda, S.; et al. The Arrival and Spread of SARS-CoV-2 in Colombia. *J. Med. Virol.* **2021**, *93*, 1158–1163. [CrossRef]
27. Pérez-Herrera, L.C.; Ordoñez-Cerón, S.; Moreno-López, S.; Peñaranda, D.; García, E.; Peñaranda, A. Impact of the COVID-19 National Lockdown in the Allergic Rhinitis Symptoms in Patients Treated with Immunotherapy at Two Allergy Referral Centers in Bogotá, Colombia. *Laryngoscope Investig. Otolaryngol.* **2022**, *7*, 305–315. [CrossRef]
28. Flórez, J.F.M.; de Cali, U.S.; Isaza, I.; Osorio, J.D. Efectos psicológicos inmediatos y autocuidado en la cuarentena por SARS-CoV-2 en el suroccidente colombiano. *Pensam. Psicológico* **2021**, *19*, 12.

29. Ibanez, A.; Santamaria-Garcia, H.; Guerrero Barragan, A.; Kornhuber, A.; Ton, A.M.M.; Slachevsky, A.; Teixeira, A.L.; Mar Meza, B.M.; Serrano, C.M.; Cano, C.; et al. The Impact of SARS-CoV-2 in Dementia across Latin America: A Call for an Urgent Regional Plan and Coordinated Response. *Alzheimers Dement.* **2020**, *6*, e12092. [CrossRef]
30. Almeida-Espinosa, A.; Sarmiento-Ardila, J.A.; Almeida-Espinosa, A.; Sarmiento-Ardila, J.A. COVID-19: Implications of SARS-CoV-2 in Colombia. *Gac. Médica México* **2020**, *156*, 330–334. [CrossRef]
31. Pertuz-Cruz, S.L.; Molina-Montes, E.; Rodríguez-Pérez, C.; Guerra-Hernández, E.J.; Cobos de Rangel, O.P.; Artacho, R.; Verardo, V.; Ruiz-Lopez, M.D.; García-Villanova, B. Exploring Dietary Behavior Changes Due to the COVID-19 Confinement in Colombia: A National and Regional Survey Study. *Front. Nutr.* **2021**, *8*, 644800. [CrossRef]
32. Elías-Cuartas, D.; Arango-Londoño, D.; Guzmán-Escarria, G.; Muñoz, E.; Caicedo, D.; Ortega-Lenis, D.; Fandiño-Losada, A.; Mena, J.; Torres, M.; Barrera, L.; et al. Análisis espacio-temporal del SARS-CoV-2 en Cali, Colombia. *Rev. Salud Pública* **2020**, *22*, 138–143. [CrossRef]
33. Colombia: WHO Coronavirus Disease (COVID-19) Dashboard with Vaccination Data. Available online: https://covid19.who.int (accessed on 6 July 2023).
34. Instituto Nacional de Salud Coronavirus Colombia. Available online: https://www.ins.gov.co/Noticias/paginas/coronavirus.aspx (accessed on 10 August 2022).
35. Zawbaa, H.M.; Osama, H.; El-Gendy, A.; Saeed, H.; Harb, H.S.; Madney, Y.M.; Abdelrahman, M.; Mohsen, M.; Ali, A.M.A.; Nicola, M.; et al. Effect of Mutation and Vaccination on Spread, Severity, and Mortality of COVID-19 Disease. *J. Med. Virol.* **2022**, *94*, 197–204. [CrossRef] [PubMed]
36. Patiño, L.H.; Castañeda, S.; Muñoz, M.; Ballesteros, N.; Ramirez, A.L.; Luna, N.; Guerrero-Araya, E.; Pérez, J.; Correa-Cárdenas, C.A.; Duque, M.C.; et al. Epidemiological Dynamics of SARS-CoV-2 Variants During Social Protests in Cali, Colombia. *Front. Med.* **2022**, *9*, 863911. [CrossRef] [PubMed]
37. Miller, J.; Hachmann, N.P.; Collier, A.Y.; Lasrado, N.; Mazurek, C.R.; Patio, R.C.; Powers, O.; Surve, N.; Theiler, J.; Korber, B.; et al. Substantial Neutralization Escape by SARS-CoV-2 Omicron Variants BQ.1.1 and XBB.1. *N. Engl. J. Med.* **2023**, *388*, 662–664. [CrossRef] [PubMed]
38. Pakzad, R.; Malekifar, P.; Shateri, Z.; Zandi, M.; Akhavan Rezayat, S.; Soleymani, M.; Karimi, M.R.; Ahmadi, S.E.; Shahbahrami, R.; Pakzad, I.; et al. Worldwide Prevalence of Microbial Agents' Coinfection among COVID-19 Patients: A Comprehensive Updated Systematic Review and Meta-analysis. *J. Clin. Lab. Anal.* **2021**, *36*, e24151. [CrossRef]
39. Algarín-Lara, H.; Osorio-Rodríguez, E.; Patiño-Patiño, J.; Mendoza-Morales, I.; Rodado-Villa, R. Neumonía por SARS-CoV-2 asociado a coinfección por Pneumocystis jirovecii en paciente inmunocomprometido: A propósito de un caso y revisión de la literatura. *Acta Colomb Cuid. Intensivo* **2021**, *22*, S106–S113. [CrossRef]
40. Sreenath, K.; Batra, P.; Vinayaraj, E.V.; Bhatia, R.; SaiKiran, K.; Singh, V.; Singh, S.; Verma, N.; Singh, U.B.; Mohan, A.; et al. Coinfections with Other Respiratory Pathogens among Patients with COVID-19. *Microbiol. Spectr.* **2021**, *9*, e00163-21. [CrossRef]
41. Soltani, S.; Zandi, M.; Faramarzi, S.; Shahbahrami, R.; Vali, M.; Rezayat, S.A.; Pakzad, R.; Malekifar, P.; Pakzad, I.; Jahandoost, N.; et al. Worldwide Prevalence of Fungal Coinfections among COVID-19 Patients: A Comprehensive Systematic Review and Meta-Analysis. *Osong Public. Health Res. Perspect.* **2022**, *13*, 15–23. [CrossRef]
42. Mirzaei, R.; Goodarzi, P.; Asadi, M.; Soltani, A.; Aljanabi, H.A.A.; Jeda, A.S.; Dashtbin, S.; Jalalifar, S.; Mohammadzadeh, R.; Teimoori, A.; et al. Bacterial Co-infections with SARS-CoV-2. *IUBMB Life* **2020**, *72*, 2097–2111. [CrossRef]
43. Motta, J.C.; Gómez, C.C. Adenovirus and Novel Coronavirus (SARS-CoV2) Coinfection: A Case Report. *IDCases* **2020**, *22*, e00936. [CrossRef]
44. Forero-Peña, D.; Carrión-Nessi, F. Malaria En Tiempos de La COVID-19 En Venezuela: Una Sindemia Incomprendida. *Acta Cient. Estud.* **2022**, *14*, 78–81.
45. Jeong, S.; Lee, N.; Park, Y.; Kim, J.; Jeon, K.; Park, M.-J.; Song, W. Prevalence and Clinical Impact of Coinfection in Patients with Coronavirus Disease 2019 in Korea. *Viruses* **2022**, *14*, 446. [CrossRef]
46. Palou, E.Y.; Ramos, M.A.; Cherenfant, E.; Duarte, A.; Fuentes-Barahona, I.C.; Zambrano, L.I.; Muñoz-Lara, F.; Montoya-Ramirez, S.A.; Cardona-Ortiz, A.F.; Valle-Reconco, J.A.; et al. COVID-19 Associated Rhino-Orbital Mucormycosis Complicated by Gangrenous and Bone Necrosis—A Case Report from Honduras. *Vaccines* **2021**, *9*, 826. [CrossRef]
47. Schulte, H.L.; Brito-Sousa, J.D.; Lacerda, M.V.G.; Naves, L.A.; de Gois, E.T.; Fernandes, M.S.; Lima, V.P.; Rassi, C.H.R.E.; de Siracusa, C.C.; Sasaki, L.M.P.; et al. SARS-CoV-2/DENV Co-Infection: A Series of Cases from the Federal District, Midwestern Brazil. *BMC Infect. Dis.* **2021**, *21*, 727. [CrossRef]
48. De Almeida, J.N.; Francisco, E.C.; Hagen, F.; Brandão, I.B.; Pereira, F.M.; Presta Dias, P.H.; de Miranda Costa, M.M.; de Souza Jordão, R.T.; de Groot, T.; Colombo, A.L. Emergence of Candida Auris in Brazil in a COVID-19 Intensive Care Unit. *J. Fungi* **2021**, *7*, 220. [CrossRef]
49. Santana, M.F.; Pivoto, G.; Alexandre, M.A.A.; Baía-da-Silva, D.C.; Borba, M.G. da S.; Val, F.A.; Brito-Sousa, J.D.; Melo, G.C.; Monteiro, W.M.; Souza, J.V.B.; et al. Confirmed Invasive Pulmonary Aspergillosis and COVID-19: The Value of *Postmortem* Findings to Support *Antemortem* Management. *Rev. Soc. Bras. Med. Trop.* **2020**, *53*, e20200401. [CrossRef]
50. Serrano, R.E.T.; Martin, C.R.S.; Algarin, O.O.; Gonzalez, S.A.; Ayerbe, M.P.C.; Zuñiga, V.E.C. Co-Infección por Cryptococcus neoformans en paciente trasplantado renal con COVID-19. Reporte de caso. *Rev. Colomb. Nefrol.* **2021**, *8*, e521. [CrossRef]
51. Ortiz-Martínez, Y.; Mogollón-Vargas, J.M.; López-Rodríguez, M.; Rodriguez-Morales, A.J. A Fatal Case of Triple Coinfection: COVID-19, HIV and Tuberculosis. *Travel. Med. Infect. Dis.* **2021**, *43*, 102129. [CrossRef]

52. Martínez Montalvo, C.M.; Perez, M.A.; Fuentes-Lacouture, M.C.; Bravo Mena, K.; Leal Bernal, S.F.; Velasco, Y.M.; Charria Caicedo, M.; Estrada Serrano, N.; Martínez Montalvo, C.M.; Perez, M.A.; et al. Neumonía Por Coinfección de Aspergillus Fumigatus y Pneumocystis Jirovecii En Un Paciente No VIH: Reporte de Caso. *Acta Médica Peru.* **2021**, *38*, 313–318. [CrossRef]
53. Angel, J.C.A.; Martínez-Buitrago, E.; Posada-Vergara, M.P. COVID-19 and HIV. *Colomb. Médica* **2020**, *51*, e-4327. [CrossRef]
54. Mejía-Parra, J.L.; Aguilar-Martinez, S.; Fernández-Mogollón, J.L.; Luna, C.; Bonilla-Aldana, D.K.; Rodriguez-Morales, A.J.; Díaz-Vélez, C. Characteristics of Patients Coinfected with Severe Acute Respiratory Syndrome Coronavirus 2 and Dengue Virus, Lambayeque, Peru, May–August 2020: A Retrospective Analysis. *Travel Med. Infect. Dis.* **2021**, *43*, 102132. [CrossRef] [PubMed]
55. Fernandes-Matano, L.; Monroy-Muñoz, I.E.; Uribe-Noguez, L.A.; Sarquiz-Martínez, B.; Pardavé-Alejandre, H.D.; Coy-Arechavaleta, A.S.; Elías, J.; Rojas-Mendoza, T.; Santacruz-Tinoco, C.E.; Grajales-Muñiz, C.; et al. Coinfections by SARS-CoV-2 and other respiratory viruses and their clinical outcome. *Rev. Med. Inst. Mex. Seguro Soc.* **2021**, *59*, 482–489. [PubMed]
56. Hazra, A.; Collison, M.; Pisano, J.; Kumar, M.; Oehler, C.; Ridgway, J.P. Coinfections with SARS-CoV-2 and Other Respiratory Pathogens. *Infect. Control Hosp. Epidemiol.* **2020**, *41*, 1228–1229. [CrossRef] [PubMed]
57. Hirotsu, Y.; Maejima, M.; Shibusawa, M.; Amemiya, K.; Nagakubo, Y.; Hosaka, K.; Sueki, H.; Mochizuki, H.; Tsutsui, T.; Kakizaki, Y.; et al. Analysis of COVID-19 and Non-COVID-19 Viruses, Including Influenza Viruses, to Determine the Influence of Intensive Preventive Measures in Japan. *J. Clin. Virol.* **2020**, *129*, 104543. [CrossRef] [PubMed]
58. Leuzinger, K.; Roloff, T.; Gosert, R.; Sogaard, K.; Naegele, K.; Rentsch, K.; Bingisser, R.; Nickel, C.H.; Pargger, H.; Bassetti, S.; et al. Epidemiology of Severe Acute Respiratory Syndrome Coronavirus 2 Emergence Amidst Community-Acquired Respiratory Viruses. *J. Infect. Dis.* **2020**, *222*, 1270–1279. [CrossRef]
59. Intra, J.; Sarto, C.; Beck, E.; Tiberti, N.; Leoni, V.; Brambilla, P. Bacterial and Fungal Colonization of the Respiratory Tract in COVID-19 Patients Should Not Be Neglected. *Am. J. Infect. Control* **2020**, *48*, 1130–1131. [CrossRef]
60. Nasir, N.; Farooqi, J.; Mahmood, S.F.; Jabeen, K. COVID-19 Associated Pulmonary Aspergillosis (CAPA) in Patients Admitted with Severe COVID-19 Pneumonia: An Observational Study from Pakistan. *Mycoses* **2020**, *63*, 766–770. [CrossRef]
61. Lv, Z.; Cheng, S.; Le, J.; Huang, J.; Feng, L.; Zhang, B.; Li, Y. Clinical Characteristics and Co-Infections of 354 Hospitalized Patients with COVID-19 in Wuhan, China: A Retrospective Cohort Study. *Microbes Infect.* **2020**, *22*, 195–199. [CrossRef]
62. Messina, F.A.; Marin, E.; Caceres, D.H.; Romero, M.; Depardo, R.; Priarone, M.M.; Rey, L.; Vázquez, M.; Verweij, P.E.; Chiller, T.M.; et al. Coronavirus Disease 2019 (COVID-19) in a Patient with Disseminated Histoplasmosis and HIV—A Case Report from Argentina and Literature Review. *J. Fungi* **2020**, *6*, 275. [CrossRef]
63. Molina, F.J.; Botero, L.E.; Isaza, J.P.; Cano, L.E.; López, L.; Tamayo, L.; Torres, A. Diagnostic Concordance between BioFire® FilmArray® Pneumonia Panel and Culture in Patients with COVID-19 Pneumonia Admitted to Intensive Care Units: The Experience of the Third Wave in Eight Hospitals in Colombia. *Crit. Care* **2022**, *26*, 130. [CrossRef]
64. Cardona-Ospina, J.A.; Arteaga-Livias, K.; Villamil-Gómez, W.E.; Pérez-Díaz, C.E.; Katterine Bonilla-Aldana, D.; Mondragon-Cardona, Á.; Solarte-Portilla, M.; Martinez, E.; Millan-Oñate, J.; López-Medina, E.; et al. Dengue and COVID-19, Overlapping Epidemics? An Analysis from Colombia. *J. Med. Virol.* **2021**, *93*, 522–527. [CrossRef]
65. Agudelo Rojas, O.L.; Tello-Cajiao, M.E.; Rosso, F. Challenges of Dengue and Coronavirus Disease 2019 Coinfection: Two Case Reports. *J. Med. Case Rep.* **2021**, *15*, 439. [CrossRef]
66. Restrepo, H.F.; Lara, C.G.; Alvarez, M.M. Criptococosis diseminada en paciente positivo para COVID-19. *Rev. Repert. Med. Y Cirugía* **2021**, *30*, 56–60. [CrossRef]
67. León, J.S.T.; Delgado, M.C.; Garcia, G.N.P.; Meriño, Y.M.; Badillo, L.Y.E.; Caballero, H.V.; Brilla, M.F.G. Coinfección chagas e infección por covid 19 en una paciente indígena. *Cienc. Lat. Rev. Científica Multidiscip.* **2022**, *6*, 4278–4286. [CrossRef]
68. Villamil-Gómez, W.E.; Rodriguez-Morales, A.J. Cocirculación y Coinfección de COVID-19 y Patógenos Tropicales Endémicos de América Latina: Enfermedad de Chagas. *Rev. Peru. Investig. En. Salud* **2021**, *5*, 57–58. [CrossRef]
69. Ahumada, P.M.; Borre-Naranjo, D.; Duran, A.Y.M.; Herrera, S.; Castro-Mendoza, W.; Baños, I. Aspergilosis pulmonar asociada a COVID-19: Reporte de caso. *Rev. Colomb. Neumol.* **2022**, *34*, 39–45. [CrossRef]
70. Pinzón, M.A.; Cardona Arango, D.; Betancur, J.F.; Ortiz, S.; Holguín, H.; Arias Arias, C.; Muñoz Palacio, B.J.; Amarillo, M.; Llano, J.F.; Montoya, P. Clinical Outcome of Patients with COVID-19 Pneumonia Treated with Corticosteroids and Colchicine in Colombia. *Ann. Clin. Microbiol. Antimicrob.* **2021**, *20*, 66. [CrossRef]
71. Daniel, M.F.; Albert, V.; Victor, N.; Ivan, R.; Daniela, O.-P.; Daniela, R. Spontaneous Pneumothorax and Pneumomediastinum in COVID 19: Case Series. *Int. J. Anesthesiol. Res.* **2021**, *9*, 8–14. [CrossRef]
72. García-Posada, M.; Aruachan-Vesga, S.; Mestra, D.; Humánez, K.; Serrano-Coll, H.; Cabrales, H.; Faccini, Á.; Mattar, S. Clinical Outcomes of Patients Hospitalized for COVID-19 and Evidence-Based on the Pharmacological Management Reduce Mortality in a Region of the Colombian Caribbean. *J. Infect. Public. Health* **2021**, *14*, 696–701. [CrossRef]
73. SARS-CoV-2 and Rhinovirus/Enterovirus Co-Infection in a Critically Ill Young Adult Patient in Colombia. Available online: http://www.scielo.org.co/scielo.php?pid=S0120-41572020000600034&script=sci_abstract&tlng=en (accessed on 22 June 2022).
74. Contreras Acosta, R.; Cueto Chaparro, M.; Zuluaga de León, I. de J.; Rebolledo Maldonado, C.E.; Morales Vergara, C.J.; Tarad Ayub, R.; Vélez-Verbel, M.; Contreras Acosta, R.; Cueto Chaparro, M.; Zuluaga de León, I. de J.; et al. Presentaciones atípicas de COVID-19: Serie de casos. *Rev. Colomb. Nefrol.* **2020**, *7*, 343–353. [CrossRef]
75. Gobernación del Valle del Cauca. Gobierno Del Valle Pide a IPS Poner En Marcha Planes de Contingencia Para Atender Fiestas de Fin de Año. Available online: https://www.valledelcauca.gov.co/publicaciones/73571/gobierno-del-valle-pide-a-ips-poner-en-marcha-planes-de-contingencia-para-atender-fiestas-de-fin-de-ano/ (accessed on 6 July 2023).

76. Mędrzycka-Dąbrowska, W.; Lange, S.; Zorena, K.; Dąbrowski, S.; Ozga, D.; Tomaszek, L. Carbapenem-Resistant Klebsiella Pneumoniae Infections in ICU COVID-19 Patients—A Scoping Review. *J. Clin. Med.* **2021**, *10*, 2067. [CrossRef] [PubMed]
77. Guzek, A.; Rybicki, Z.; Woźniak-Kosek, A.; Tomaszewski, D. The Clinical Manifestation of SARS-CoV-2 in Critically Ill Patients with Klebsiella Pneumoniae NDM Hospitalized in the ICU of a Modular Hospital during the Third Wave of the Pandemic in Poland—An Observational Cohort Study. *Diagnostics* **2022**, *12*, 1118. [CrossRef] [PubMed]
78. Kim, D.; Quinn, J.; Pinsky, B.; Shah, N.H.; Brown, I. Rates of Co-Infection Between SARS-CoV-2 and Other Respiratory Pathogens. *JAMA* **2020**, *323*, 2085–2086. [CrossRef] [PubMed]
79. Orozco-Hernández, J.P.; Montoya-Martínez, J.J.; Pacheco-Gallego, M.C.; Céspedes-Roncancio, M.; Porras-Hurtado, G.L. Coinfección por SARS-CoV-2 y rinovirus-enterovirus en una paciente adulta joven críticamente enferma en Colombia. *Biomedica* **2020**, *40*, 34–43. [CrossRef] [PubMed]
80. Zaidel, E.J.; Forsyth, C.J.; Novick, G.; Marcus, R.; Ribeiro, A.L.P.; Pinazo, M.-J.; Morillo, C.A.; Echeverría, L.E.; Shikanai-Yasuda, M.A.; Buekens, P.; et al. COVID-19: Implications for People with Chagas Disease. *Glob. Heart* **2020**, *15*, 69. [CrossRef]
81. Sathyakamala, R.; Peace, A.R.; Shanmugam, P. A Comparative Study on Bacterial Co-Infections and Prevalence of Multidrug Resistant Organisms among Patients in COVID and Non-COVID Intensive Care Units. *J. Prev. Med. Hyg.* **2022**, *63*, E19–E26. [CrossRef]
82. Vaughn, V.M.; Gandhi, T.N.; Petty, L.A.; Patel, P.K.; Prescott, H.C.; Malani, A.N.; Ratz, D.; McLaughlin, E.; Chopra, V.; Flanders, S.A. Empiric Antibacterial Therapy and Community-Onset Bacterial Coinfection in Patients Hospitalized With Coronavirus Disease 2019 (COVID-19): A Multi-Hospital Cohort Study. *Clin. Infect. Dis.* **2020**, *72*, e533–e541. [CrossRef]
83. Cataño-Correa, J.C.; Cardona-Arias, J.A.; Porras Mancilla, J.P.; García, M.T. Bacterial Superinfection in Adults with COVID-19 Hospitalized in Two Clinics in Medellín-Colombia, 2020. *PLoS ONE* **2021**, *16*, e0254671. [CrossRef]
84. Paparoupa, M.; Aldemyati, R.; Roggenkamp, H.; Berinson, B.; Nörz, D.; Olearo, F.; Kluge, S.; Roedl, K.; de Heer, G.; Wichmann, D. The Prevalence of Early- and Late-Onset Bacterial, Viral, and Fungal Respiratory Superinfections in Invasively Ventilated COVID-19 Patients. *J. Med. Virol.* **2022**, *94*, 1920–1925. [CrossRef]
85. Clancy, C.J.; Schwartz, I.S.; Kula, B.; Nguyen, M.H. Bacterial Superinfections Among Persons With Coronavirus Disease 2019: A Comprehensive Review of Data From Postmortem Studies. *Open Forum Infect. Dis.* **2021**, *8*, ofab065. [CrossRef]
86. Al-Tawfiq, J.A.; Alhumaid, S.; Alshukairi, A.N.; Temsah, M.-H.; Barry, M.; Al Mutair, A.; Rabaan, A.A.; Al-Omari, A.; Tirupathi, R.; AlQahtani, M.; et al. COVID-19 and Mucormycosis Superinfection: The Perfect Storm. *Infection* **2021**, *49*, 833–853. [CrossRef]
87. Arcangeletti, M.-C.; De Conto, F.; Montecchini, S.; Buttrini, M.; Maccari, C.; Chezzi, C.; Calderaro, A. A Rare Case Of SARS-CoV-2 And Influenza A Virus Super-Infection. *Diagn. Microbiol. Infect. Dis.* **2022**, *140*, 115743. [CrossRef]
88. Vaseghi, N.; Sharifisooraki, J.; Khodadadi, H.; Nami, S.; Safari, F.; Ahangarkani, F.; Meis, J.F.; Badali, H.; Morovati, H. Global Prevalence and Subgroup Analyses of Coronavirus Disease (COVID-19) Associated Candida Auris Infections (CACa): A Systematic Review and Meta-Analysis. *Mycoses* **2022**, *65*, 683–703. [CrossRef]
89. Wertheim, J.O.; Wang, J.C.; Leelawong, M.; Martin, D.P.; Havens, J.L.; Chowdhury, M.A.; Pekar, J.E.; Amin, H.; Arroyo, A.; Awandare, G.A.; et al. Detection of SARS-CoV-2 Intra-Host Recombination during Superinfection with Alpha and Epsilon Variants in New York City. *Nat. Commun.* **2022**, *13*, 3645. [CrossRef]
90. Pickens, C.O.; Gao, C.A.; Cuttica, M.J.; Smith, S.B.; Pesce, L.L.; Grant, R.A.; Kang, M.; Morales-Nebreda, L.; Bavishi, A.A.; Arnold, J.M.; et al. Bacterial Superinfection Pneumonia in Patients Mechanically Ventilated for COVID-19 Pneumonia. *Am. J. Respir. Crit. Care Med.* **2021**, *204*, 921–932. [CrossRef]
91. Awada, B.; Alam, W.; Chalfoun, M.; Araj, G.; Bizri, A.R. COVID-19 and Candida Duobushaemulonii Superinfection: A Case Report. *J. Med. Mycol.* **2021**, *31*, 101168. [CrossRef]
92. Nicolas de Lamballerie, C.; Pizzorno, A.; Fouret, J.; Szpiro, L.; Padey, B.; Dubois, J.; Julien, T.; Traversier, A.; Dulière, V.; Brun, P.; et al. Transcriptional Profiling of Immune and Inflammatory Responses in the Context of SARS-CoV-2 Fungal Superinfection in a Human Airway Epithelial Model. *Microorganisms* **2020**, *8*, 1974. [CrossRef]
93. Nieuwenhuis, M.B.; Van Biesen, S.; Juffermans, N.P. Response to "Co-Infections in COVID-19 Critically Ill and Antibiotic Management: A Prospective Cohort Analysis". *Crit. Care* **2020**, *24*, 591. [CrossRef]
94. Montalvo, C.M.M.; Kozhakin, D.V.R.; Forero, M.A.V.; Giraldo, M.R.; Vargas, J.G.M.; Cabal, N. Raoultella Planticola Pneumonia in a Patient with Critical COVID-19. *Acta Medica Peru.* **2022**, *39*. [CrossRef]
95. Cubides-Diaz, D.A.; Muñoz Angulo, N.; Martin Arsanios, D.A.; Ovalle Monroy, A.L.; Perdomo-Rodriguez, D.R.; Del-Portillo, M.P. Pandoraea Pnomenusa Superinfection in a Patient with SARS-CoV-2 Pneumonia: First Case in the Literature. *Infect. Dis. Rep.* **2022**, *14*, 205–212. [CrossRef]
96. Valladales-Restrepo, L.F.; Constain-Mosquera, C.A.; Hoyos-Guapacha, M.A.; Hoyos-Guapacha, K.L.; Gaviria-Mendoza, A.; Machado-Duque, M.E.; Machado-Alba, J.E. Indicación y prescripción de macrólidos en una población colombiana. *Biomedica* **2022**, *42*, 302–314. [CrossRef] [PubMed]
97. Al-Abdouh, A.; Bizanti, A.; Barbarawi, M.; Jabri, A.; Kumar, A.; Fashanu, O.E.; Khan, S.U.; Zhao, D.; Antar, A.A.R.; Michos, E.D. Remdesivir for the Treatment of COVID-19: A Systematic Review and Meta-Analysis of Randomized Controlled Trials. *Contemp. Clin. Trials* **2021**, *101*, 106272. [CrossRef] [PubMed]
98. Patil, D.S.; Narwade, G.; Gondhali, G. Treatment Options Used in COVID-19 Disease: Steroids, Anticoagulants, Remdesivir and/or Antibiotics—Which Worked Better or Combo Was the Right Choice? *J. Appl. Sci. Res.* **2022**.

99. Gottlieb, R.L.; Vaca, C.E.; Paredes, R.; Mera, J.; Webb, B.J.; Perez, G.; Oguchi, G.; Ryan, P.; Nielsen, B.U.; Brown, M.; et al. Early Remdesivir to Prevent Progression to Severe Covid-19 in Outpatients. *N. Engl. J. Med.* **2022**, *386*, 305–315. [CrossRef]
100. El Uso de Molnupiravir Para Tratar Covid-19—Instituto Nacional de Vigilancia de Medicamentos y Alimentos. Available online: https://www.invima.gov.co/el-uso-de-molnupiravir-para-tratar-covid-19 (accessed on 6 July 2023).
101. Gao, Y.; Liu, M.; Li, Z.; Xu, J.; Zhang, J.; Tian, J. Molnupiravir for Treatment of Adults with Mild or Moderate COVID-19: A Systematic Review and Meta-Analysis of Randomized Controlled Trials. *Clin. Microbiol. Infect.* **2023**, S1198743X23001854. [CrossRef] [PubMed]
102. Jayk Bernal, A.; Gomes Da Silva, M.M.; Musungaie, D.B.; Kovalchuk, E.; Gonzalez, A.; Delos Reyes, V.; Martín-Quirós, A.; Caraco, Y.; Williams-Diaz, A.; Brown, M.L.; et al. Molnupiravir for Oral Treatment of Covid-19 in Nonhospitalized Patients. *N. Engl. J. Med.* **2022**, *386*, 509–520. [CrossRef]
103. Malin, J.J.; Weibel, S.; Gruell, H.; Kreuzberger, N.; Stegemann, M.; Skoetz, N. Efficacy and Safety of Molnupiravir for the Treatment of SARS-CoV-2 Infection: A Systematic Review and Meta-Analysis. *J. Antimicrob. Chemother.* **2023**, *78*, 1586–1598. [CrossRef]
104. Maraolo, A.E.; Crispo, A.; Piezzo, M.; Di Gennaro, P.; Vitale, M.G.; Mallardo, D.; Ametrano, L.; Celentano, E.; Cuomo, A.; Ascierto, P.A.; et al. The Use of Tocilizumab in Patients with COVID-19: A Systematic Review, Meta-Analysis and Trial Sequential Analysis of Randomized Controlled Studies. *JCM* **2021**, *10*, 4935. [CrossRef]
105. Petrelli, F.; Cherri, S.; Ghidini, M.; Perego, G.; Ghidini, A.; Zaniboni, A. Tocilizumab as Treatment for COVID-19: A Systematic Review and Meta-Analysis. *WJM* **2021**, *11*, 95–109. [CrossRef]
106. Wei, Q.; Lin, H.; Wei, R.-G.; Chen, N.; He, F.; Zou, D.-H.; Wei, J.-R. Tocilizumab Treatment for COVID-19 Patients: A Systematic Review and Meta-Analysis. *Infect. Dis. Poverty* **2021**, *10*, 71. [CrossRef]
107. Filippatos, C.; Ntanasis-Stathopoulos, I.; Sekeri, K.; Ntanasis-Stathopoulos, A.; Gavriatopoulou, M.; Psaltopoulou, T.; Dounias, G.; Sergentanis, T.N.; Terpos, E. Convalescent Plasma Therapy for COVID-19: A Systematic Review and Meta-Analysis on Randomized Controlled Trials. *Viruses* **2023**, *15*, 765. [CrossRef]
108. Klassen, S.A.; Senefeld, J.W.; Senese, K.A.; Johnson, P.W.; Wiggins, C.C.; Baker, S.E.; Van Helmond, N.; Bruno, K.A.; Pirofski, L.; Shoham, S.; et al. Convalescent Plasma Therapy for COVID-19: A Graphical Mosaic of the Worldwide Evidence. *Front. Med.* **2021**, *8*, 684151. [CrossRef]
109. Dománi, M.; Bányai, K. COVID-19-Associated Fungal Infections: An Urgent Need for Alternative Therapeutic Approach? *Front. Microbiol.* **2022**, *13*, 919501. [CrossRef]
110. Chatterjee, K.; Wu, C.-P.; Bhardwaj, A.; Siuba, M. Steroids in COVID-19: An Overview. *Clevel. Clin. J. Med.* **2020**. [CrossRef]
111. Saha, S.; Yeom, G.S.; Nimse, S.B.; Pal, D. Combination Therapy of Ledipasvir and Itraconazole in the Treatment of COVID-19 Patients Coinfected with Black Fungus: An In Silico Statement. *Biomed. Res. Int.* **2022**, *2022*, 5904261. [CrossRef]
112. Tabatabaeizadeh, S.-A. Zinc Supplementation and COVID-19 Mortality: A Meta-Analysis. *Eur. J. Med. Res.* **2022**, *27*, 70. [CrossRef]
113. Weiss, C.; Carriere, M.; Fusco, L.; Capua, I.; Regla-Nava, J.A.; Pasquali, M.; Scott, J.A.; Vitale, F.; Unal, M.A.; Mattevi, C.; et al. Toward Nanotechnology-Enabled Approaches against the COVID-19 Pandemic. *ACS Nano* **2020**, *14*, 6383–6406. [CrossRef]
114. Palestino, G.; García-Silva, I.; González-Ortega, O.; Rosales-Mendoza, S. Can Nanotechnology Help in the Fight against COVID-19? *Expert. Rev. Anti-Infect. Ther.* **2020**, *18*, 849–864. [CrossRef]
115. REGEN-COV Antibody Combination and Outcomes in Outpatients with COVID-19—PubMed. Available online: https://pubmed.ncbi.nlm.nih.gov/34587383/ (accessed on 5 December 2022).

Disclaimer/Publisher's Note: The statements, opinions and data contained in all publications are solely those of the individual author(s) and contributor(s) and not of MDPI and/or the editor(s). MDPI and/or the editor(s) disclaim responsibility for any injury to people or property resulting from any ideas, methods, instructions or products referred to in the content.

medicina MDPI

Review

Variants of SARS-CoV-2: Influences on the Vaccines' Effectiveness and Possible Strategies to Overcome Their Consequences

Ali A. Rabaan [1,2,3,*], Shamsah H. Al-Ahmed [4], Hawra Albayat [5], Sara Alwarthan [6], Mashael Alhajri [6], Mustafa A. Najim [7], Bashayer M. AlShehail [8], Wasl Al-Adsani [9,10], Ali Alghadeer [11], Wesam A. Abduljabbar [12], Nouf Alotaibi [13], Jameela Alsalman [14], Ali H. Gorab [15], Reem S. Almaghrabi [16], Ali A. Zaidan [17], Sahar Aldossary [18], Mohammed Alissa [19], Lamees M. Alburaiky [20], Fatimah Mustafa Alsalim [21], Nanamika Thakur [22,*], Geetika Verma [23] and Manish Dhawan [24,25,*]

1 Molecular Diagnostic Laboratory, Johns Hopkins Aramco Healthcare, Dhahran 31311, Saudi Arabia
2 College of Medicine, Alfaisal University, Riyadh 11533, Saudi Arabia
3 Department of Public Health and Nutrition, The University of Haripur, Haripur 22610, Pakistan
4 Specialty Paediatric Medicine, Qatif Central Hospital, Qatif 32654, Saudi Arabia
5 Infectious Disease Department, King Saud Medical City, Riyadh 7790, Saudi Arabia
6 Department of Internal Medicine, College of Medicine, Imam Abdulrahman Bin Faisal University, Dammam 34212, Saudi Arabia
7 Department of Medical Laboratories Technology, College of Applied Medical Sciences, Taibah University, Madinah 41411, Saudi Arabia
8 Pharmacy Practice Department, College of Clinical Pharmacy, Imam Abdulrahman Bin Faisal University, Dammam 31441, Saudi Arabia
9 Department of Medicine, Infectious Diseases Hospital, Kuwait City 63537, Kuwait
10 Department of Infectious Diseases, Hampton Veterans Administration Medical Center, Hampton, VA 23667, USA
11 Department of Anesthesia, Dammam Medical Complex, Dammam 32245, Saudi Arabia
12 Department of Medical Laboratory Sciences, Fakeeh College for Medical Science, Jeddah 21134, Saudi Arabia
13 Clinical Pharmacy Department, College of Pharmacy, Umm Al-Qura University, Makkah 21955, Saudi Arabia
14 Infection Disease Unit, Department of Internal Medicine, Salmaniya Medical Complex, Ministry of Health, Kingdom of Bahrain, Manama 435, Bahrain
15 Al Kuzama Primary Health Care Center, Al Khobar Health Network, Eastern Health Cluster, Al Khobar 34446, Saudi Arabia
16 Organ Transplant Center of Excellence, King Faisal Specialist Hospital and Research Center, Riyadh 11211, Saudi Arabia
17 Gastroenterology Department, King Fahad Armed Forces Hospital, Jeddah 23831, Saudi Arabia
18 Pediatric Infectious Diseases, Women and Children's Health Institute, Johns Hopkins Aramco Healthcare, Dhahran 31311, Saudi Arabia
19 Department of Medical Laboratory Sciences, College of Applied Medical Sciences, Prince Sattam bin Abdulaziz University, Al-Kharj 11942, Saudi Arabia
20 Pediatric Department, Safwa General Hospital, Eastern Health Cluster, Safwa 31921, Saudi Arabia
21 Department of Family Medicine, Primary Health Care, Qatif Health Cluster, Qatif 32434, Saudi Arabia
22 University Institute of Biotechnology, Department of Biotechnology, Chandigarh University, Mohali 140413, India
23 Department of Experimental Medicine and Biotechnology, Post Graduate Institute of Medical Education and Research (PGIMER), Chandigarh 160012, India
24 Department of Microbiology, Punjab Agricultural University, Ludhiana 141004, India
25 Trafford College, Altrincham, Manchester WA14 5PQ, UK
* Correspondence: arabaan@gmail.com (A.A.R.); nanamika.e13132@cumail.in (N.T.); dhawanmanish501@gmail.com (M.D.)

Citation: Rabaan, A.A.; Al-Ahmed, S.H.; Albayat, H.; Alwarthan, S.; Alhajri, M.; Najim, M.A.; AlShehail, B.M.; Al-Adsani, W.; Alghadeer, A.; Abduljabbar, W.A.; et al. Variants of SARS-CoV-2: Influences on the Vaccines' Effectiveness and Possible Strategies to Overcome Their Consequences. *Medicina* **2023**, *59*, 507. https://doi.org/10.3390/medicina59030507

Academic Editors: Yusra Habib Khan, Tauqeer Hussain Mallhi, Tahir Mehmood Khan and Muhammad Salman

Received: 6 February 2023
Revised: 27 February 2023
Accepted: 3 March 2023
Published: 5 March 2023

Copyright: © 2023 by the authors. Licensee MDPI, Basel, Switzerland. This article is an open access article distributed under the terms and conditions of the Creative Commons Attribution (CC BY) license (https://creativecommons.org/licenses/by/4.0/).

Abstract: The immune response elicited by the current COVID-19 vaccinations declines with time, especially among the immunocompromised population. Furthermore, the emergence of novel SARS-CoV-2 variants, particularly the Omicron variant, has raised serious concerns about the efficacy of currently available vaccines in protecting the most vulnerable people. Several studies have reported that vaccinated people get breakthrough infections amid COVID-19 cases. So far, five variants of concern (VOCs) have been reported, resulting in successive waves of infection. These variants have shown a variable amount of resistance towards the neutralising antibodies (nAbs) elicited either through natural infection or the vaccination. The spike (S) protein, membrane (M) protein, and envelope (E) protein on the viral surface envelope and the N-nucleocapsid protein in the core of the ribonucleoprotein are the major structural vaccine target proteins against COVID-19. Among these targets, S Protein has been extensively exploited to generate effective vaccines against COVID-19. Hence, amid the emergence of novel variants of SARS-CoV-2, we have discussed their impact on currently available vaccines. We have also discussed the potential roles of S Protein in the development of novel vaccination approaches to contain the negative consequences of the variants' emergence and acquisition of mutations in the S Protein of SARS-CoV-2. Moreover, the implications of SARS-CoV-2's structural proteins were also discussed in terms of their variable potential to elicit an effective amount of immune response.

Keywords: SARS-CoV-2; COVID-19; breakthrough infections; neutralizing antibodies (NAbs); Omicron; vaccines; variants

1. Introduction

Safe and effective vaccination has been critical in the ongoing battle against Severe Acute Respiratory Syndrome Coronavirus 2 (SARS-CoV-2). The development of precise vaccine platforms in such a short period is a testament to global scientific prowess, and, as of 9 June, 2021, more than 2,156,550,767 doses of the COVID-19 vaccine have been given across the five continents [1]. Unfortunately, reports on variants of SARS-CoV-2 brought about by mutations with enhanced virulence, pathogenicity, and the ability to detrimentally affect host immune systems, especially the antibodies produced after COVID-19 vaccination, is a matter of concern and scientific deliberation.

However, the available published data divulge that the current vaccines could still be effective in preventing severe infection and death in people infected with the recent variants of SARS-CoV-2, such as Omicron and Delta [2–6]. Multiple studies have shown several advantages of the numerous mutations of the Omicron variant of the SARS-CoV-2 virus [7–9]. The Omicron variant and its subvariants evolved by evolutionary processes that may lead to a number of significant modifications in the virus's characteristics, such as immunological escape from the nAbs produced by the administration of the vaccines [10–12]. The high frequency of mutations has also been linked to improved proteolytic priming with transmembrane serine protease 2 (TMPRSS2) and the increased binding capacities of S Protein to the angiotensin converting enzyme 2 (ACE2) receptor [9,10,13–15]. The higher number of mutations in the Omicron variant have also been associated with improved resistance to endosomal restriction factors, specifically IFITM proteins, which enables the variant's more effective cellular invasion via the endocytic route [16]. Additionally, the modifications may make it more likely for spike protomers to adopt an up configuration to interact with ACE2, and may increase the stability of a down configuration to prevent contact with nAbs [12,17,18].

A variant can be defined as an isolate whose genome sequence differs from that of the reference virus. Thus, the variants share an identical inherited set of distinct mutations and are classified based on a lineage, i.e., the type of mutations that resulted in the origination of a new lineage of SARS-CoV-2. From this perspective, it is crucial to understand the mutational dynamics of SARS-CoV-2 and its effects on the vaccines that are currently available [19]. Studies have deciphered that a typical SARS-CoV-2 virus accrues, on average, one or two single-nucleotide genomic mutations in a period of 30 days [3,4]. This is just 50% of the rate of the mutational dynamics of influenza and 25% of the AIDS human immunodeficiency virus (HIV). The retarded mutational dynamics of SARS-CoV-2 could perhaps be credited to the specific exoribonuclease (ExoN) present in the genome of coronaviruses (CoVs), since inactivation of this ExoN has demonstrated a twenty-fold increase in the mutation rates [4,5].

Effects of Mutations on Variants' Characteristics

Some significant mutations documented in SARS-CoV-2 include the 'N501Y', in which the spike protein (S Protein) 501st amino acid is swapped from N (asparagine) to Y (tyrosine) and assists the virus to attach more rigidly to human cells. Substitution of histidine at 681 positions instead of proline results in a change in an amino acid on the stem region of the spike of SARS-CoV-2 that triggers infected host cells to give rise to new spike proteins. 'H69-V70' is yet another mutation caused by the deletion in the 69th and 70th position of the a/a in spike protein, and it changes the shape of the spike, facilitating the virus to escape from some antibodies [4,20,21].

The 'Y144/145' mutation caused by the elimination of the 144th or 145th amino acids (tyrosine, Y) in the S Protein area challenges the effectual attachment of antibodies with the SARS-CoV-2 virus. 'ORF8 Q27stop' is another important mutation that involves the ORF8, a 121 amino acid protein whose function is yet to be completely deciphered. The 'D614 G' mutation has a moderate documented impact on transmissibility brought about by the alteration in the spike protein, where G (glycine) is substituted by D (aspartic acid). 'E484K', often referred to as the "escape mutation," brought about by a swap wherein the glutamic acid (E) is substituted by lysine (K) at position 484, shields the virus from at least one type of monoclonal antibody. 'L452R', initially detected in Denmark, is yet another mutation that has been detected in various lineages [4,22,23]. Moreover, the presence of mutations such as H69/V70 deletions, the substitution of lysine instead of threonine (T478K), and the insertion of alanine at 484 positions instead of glutamic acid (E484A) in already reported variants of concern (VOC-) have been associated to the variants' enhanced capacity to evade the defense mechanism of the body [21]. The higher ACE2 receptor binding capacity of the S Protein has been linked to the N501Y mutation. Furthermore, the S Protein's capacity to attach to the ACE2 receptor was markedly enhanced by the Q498R mutation with N501Y. These modifications make it simple for the Omicron variant to penetrate the host cell [10].

Important mutations in the Omicron variant [7] include A76V, Y145del, G339D, N440K, G446S, E484A, Q493R, G496S, Q498R, Y505H, T547K, H655Y, N679K, N764K, D796Y, N856K, Q954H, N969K, and L981F [7]. It is interesting to note that similar changes have been observed in other types, albeit with varying effects. Moreover, the Omicron variant acquired new mutations that increased its ability to spread [24,25]. Key amino acid alterations in the RBD of the S Protein [7] include G339D, S371L, S373P, S375F, K417N, N440K, G446S, S477N, T478K, E484A, Q493R, G496S, Q498R, N501Y, and Y505H [7,24,25]. Such alterations may also be linked to elevated affinities of the S Protein for the ACE2 receptor [26]. The crucial step in obtaining access into the host cell is the binding of the ACE2 receptor to the S Protein of the SARS-CoV-2 [27]. Human transmembrane protease serine 2 (TMPRSS2) cleaves the S Protein after it interacts with ACE2 receptors on the cell membrane. The S Protein is split up into its S1 and S2 subunits by TMPRSS2, which in turn makes the RBD on the S1 subunit available for interactions [28–30]. Consecutively, the S2 domain undergoes structural modifications that assist in the union of viral and cellular membranes [31,32]. It is noteworthy that according to studies using electron microscopy, the SARS-CoV-2 S Protein has a binding affinity to ACE2 that is around 10–20 times larger than that of the S proteins from other SARS-CoVs [30,33].

The S Protein of SARS-CoV-2 must be split at the S1-S2 and S2 locations in order to enter host cells [7]. Furin24, type II transmembrane serine protease (TMPRSS2), or cathepsin L are the enzymes responsible for this cleavage [34,35]. The TMPRSS2 and cathepsin L breakdown at the S2 site facilitate two distinct SARS-CoV-2 entry pathways [7]. However, mutations in certain variants are considered plausible reasons behind the changes in such entry pathways [7]. Due to it being expressed on the cell membrane, TMPRSS2 promotes the invasion via the plasma membrane as opposed to cathepsin L in the endosome, which favors the endosomal pathway [35,36]. Six different mutations in the subunit 2 (S2) of the S Protein of the Omicron variant, notably N764K, D796Y, N856K, Q954H, N969K, and L981F, were linked to variations in viral entrance into the cellular machinery and modes of transmission [37–39]. Recent investigations have shown that the Omicron variant favors the endosomal entry pathway over the plasma membrane entrance route [40]. Infection by the Omicron spike pseudotyped virus was likewise shown to be restricted in cells that express the transcription factor TMPRSS2 but increased in cells that support an endosomal route for entry [7,40].

Recent findings suggest that genetic alterations to the Omicron S protein non-RBD may alter the mode of viral entry into host cells, which is associated with a shift in cellular tropism away from TMPRSS2-expressing cells. These findings also demonstrate why, in contrast to other VOCs, such as the Alpha, Beta, and Delta variants, Omicron replicates more rapidly in the upper respiratory system than in the lower respiratory tract [40–43]. It seems that the Omicron variety also has three significant mutations, including P681H, H655Y, and N679K, in the furin cleavage region. It is known that changes such as P681H at the polybasic cleavage site (PBCS), which are also present in other VOCs such as Alpha and Gamma, make it easier for the S protein to be digested by furin and may thus make the organism more pathogenic [44]. Hence, altogether, this information suggests that the mutations or alterations in the viral genome led to drastic changes in the characteristics of their nature to infect and disseminate among populations. As per the mutations and their impacts on the pathogenicity and transmission, many government bodies have classified the variants of SARS-CoV-2 into various categories. The following section will highlight the same.

2. Classification of Variants of SARS-CoV-2

SARS-CoV-2 variants could be classified into four different groups, i.e., variants of interest (VOIs), variants of high consequence (VOHCs), variants under monitoring (VUMs), and variants of concern (VOCs) by the US Department of Health and Human Services [17–19], and all five VOCs have been further categorized as α, β, γ, δ, and Omicron variants by the World Health Organization (WHO). The Omicron variant has quickly competed with other VOCs and spread across the world [10] [Table 1].

2.1. Variants of Interest (VOIs)

VOI is a variant that has genetic markers specifically linked with changes to host receptor binding, exhibiting reduced antibody neutralization production versus a previous infection by the reference virus or vaccination, and showing a reduced response to hitherto effective treatments, causing a potential diagnostic impediment, and carrying on it a label of predictive upsurge in infection. These include the B.1.525 lineage brought about by the spike protein (S protein) substitutions 69del, 144del, 70del, A67V, D614G, E484K, F888L, andQ677H, which was first detected in the United Kingdom and Nigeria in December 2020; the B.1.526 lineage brought about by spike protein substitutions A701V, D253G, D614G, E484K, L5F, T95I, and S477N, which was first detected in the United States in November 2020; the B.1.526.1 lineage brought about by spike protein (S protein) substitutions D80G, D614G, D950H, 144del, F157S, L452R, T791I, and T859N, which was first detected in the United States in October 2020; the B.1.617 lineage, brought about by spike protein (S protein) substitutions D614G, L452R, and E484Q, which was first noticed in India in February 2021; the B.1.617.1 lineage, brought about by spike protein (S protein) substitutions, i.e., D614G, E484Q, E154K, G142D, L452R, P681R, Q1071H, and T95I, which was first identified in India in December 2020; B.1.617.3 lineage, brought about by spike protein (S protein) substitutions D614G, D950N, E484Q, G142D, L452R, P681R, and T19R, which was first spotted in India in October 2020; and the P.2 lineage, brought about by spike protein (S protein) substitutions D614G, E484K, F565L, andV1176F, which was first identified in Brazil in April 2020 [45–51].

Table 1. Showing the various categories of the variants of SARS-CoV-2 with their clades and origin information.

Categories	WHO Label	Pango Lineage	GISAID Clade	Nextstrain Clade	Area of Documentation	Time of Documentation
Variants of Interest (VOIs)	Epsilon	B.1.427/B.1.429	GH/452R.V1	20C/S.452R	United states of America	March-2020
	Zeta	P.2	GR	20B/S.484K	Brazil	April-2020
	Eta	B.1.525	G/484K.V3	20A/S484K	Not defined	December-2020
	Theta	P.3	GR	20B/S:265C	Philippines	January-2021
	Iota	B.1.526	GH	20C/S:484K	United states of America	November-2020
	Kappa	B.1.617.1	G/452R.V3	21A/S:154K	India	October-2020
Variants of Concern (VOCs)	Alpha	B.1.1.7	GRY	20I (V1)	United Kingdom	September-2020
	Beta	B.1.351	GH/501Y.V2	20H (V2)	South Africa	May-2020
	Gamma	P.1	GR/501Y.V3	20J (V3)	Brazil	November-2020
	Delta	B.1.617.2	G/478K.V1	21A, 21I, 21J	India,	October-2020
	Omicron	B.1.1.529	GR/484A	21K, 21L, 21M, 22A, 22B, 22C, 22D	First lineage reported in South Africa	November-2021
Variants of High Consequence (VOHCs)	None of variant of high consequence has been recorded					

2.2. Variants of Concern (VOCs)

A variant for concern (VOC) is a variant that has strong evidence of an intensified transmissibility; severity of the disease symptoms, including a higher number of hospitalizations and deaths; shows a significant decrease in neutralization by post-vaccination and convalescent sera; displays the significant reduction in the efficacy of existing treatments and vaccines; and poses notable diagnostic challenges, which lead to insufficiency in the diagnosis of the variant. Up to this point, the WHO has identified five VOC variants, including α, β, γ, δ, and Omicron. The Omicron variant has quickly spread around the globe and fought against all the VOCs. According to the most recent information [10], the Omicron variant (B.1.1.529) contains >30 mutations in the S Protein compared to other VOCs such as α (B.1.1.7), β (B.1.351) and δ (B.1.617.2). Significant changes to the N-terminal domain (NTD) and receptor-binding domain (RBD) of the S Protein have been linked to greater resistance to nAbs and transmission [10]. Interestingly, these VOCs could necessitate serious emergency public health engagements, including immediate notification of the detected variant to the World Health Organisation (WHO) under the regulation of International Health to CDC, and the regional and governmental authorities to control and end the spread.

These variants could also compel improved testing and investigation of the efficacy of pre-existing vaccines and treatments as well as force the deployment of newer diagnostics and the modification or production of suitable vaccines/therapeutics. These include the B.1.1.7 lineage, brought about by S Protein substitutions deletion at 69, 70, 144, N501Y, E484K, A570D, P681H, S982A, K1191N, S494P, D1118H, D614G, and T716I, which was first detected in the United Kingdom [52,53]; the B.1.351 lineage, brought about by spike protein substitutions D2, 241del, 243del, D614G, D80A, E484K, 15G, 242del, K417N, N501Y, and A701V, which was first found in South Africa [52–54]; the B.1.427 lineage, brought about by spike protein substitutions L452R and D614G, and observed for the first time in California, USA; the B.1.429 lineage, first observed in California, USA, due to substitutions such as L452R, S13I, W152C, and D614G in the spike protein [54–56]; the B.1.617.2 lineage (Delta), brought about by spike protein substitutions T19R, P681R, G142D, D614G, R158G, L452R, T478K, 156del, 157del, and D950N, which was first detected in India in December 2020 [41]; and the P.1 lineage, due to substitution in spike protein (L18F, D138Y, T20N, E484K, D614G, P26S, R190S, T1027I, K417T, N501Y, H655Y), which was first detected in Japan and Brazil [57–67].

2.3. *Variants of High Consequence (VOHCs)*

A variant of high consequence is explained as a variant for which there is absolute evidence that its prevalence has significantly decreased the effectiveness of medical countermeasures (MCMs) and preventive measures compared to the previously circulating variants. A variant of high consequence can also cause the established failure of diagnostic protocols and severe reduction in efficiency of the currently available vaccines and jeopardize the (EUA) Emergency Use Authorization and approved therapeutics, perhaps with harsher clinical manifestations and a higher number of hospitalizations. To this date, none of the variants of high consequence have been recorded [68].

3. Influence of Variants' Emergence on Vaccine Effectiveness

VOCs, especially the Delta variant, may affect the neutralising activity of vaccine-elicited Abs and MAbs, which might result in a mild-to-significant decrease in efficiency for COVID-19 vaccines and immunotherapeutic treatment [69,70]. The existing vaccination strategies failed to prevent the outbreak of Omicron variants [59,62,66,71–73]. NAbs in sera from those who received a 2-dose Ad26.COV2.S (Johnson & Johnson) vaccine were considerably less efficient against the Omicron variant than the primary strain of SARS-CoV-2. A luciferase-based pseudo virus neutralisation experiment revealed a dramatic decline in the antibody-mediated immune response, 20 × 102, when compared to the original strain, which was 184 × 103 on the eighth day following vaccination [46]. Similar researchers, however, have shown that cellular immunity produced by existing vaccines against SARS-CoV-2 is largely conserved to the SARS-CoV-2 Omicron spike protein [46]. Vaccination with Ad26.COV2.S or BNT162b2 resulted in substantial spike-specific CD8+ and CD4+ T cell responses as well as significant cross-reactivity against both the Delta and Omicron variants in both the central and effector memory cell subpopulations [46].The serum neutralizing ability of individuals receiving BNT162b2 (Pfizer/BioNTech) was diminished 35-fold against BA.1 compared to D614G variant [62,66,74]. Additionally, it was not effective against BA.2 and BA.3 [75]. However, the booster doses of vaccines proved beneficial in increasing the efficacy of serum-neutralizing titers against Omicron [62,71,76].

A Phase III trial of Covaxin (BBV152), an inactivated SARS-CoV-2 vaccine, established by Bharat Biotech, India, confirmed its potential effectiveness against symptomatic cases (77.8%) and the Delta variant (68.2%) [77]. However, the convalescent serum of recipients of BBV152 was not able to neutralise the P.1 lineage [78].

Studies have shown that ChAdOx1 nCoV-19 (AZD1222) is effective against Alpha (74.5%), Delta (67%) [79], and Gamma (77.9%) [80]; however, not against Beta (10.4%) [5]. Further, this vaccine was associated with some cases of thrombosis and thrombocytopenia syndrome (TTS), blood clot events, and deaths, causing the suspension of the use of this vaccine in many European and Asian countries [81].

A renowned mRNA-based vaccine BNT162b2 was created by Pfizer and is often utilized in the immunization programs of nations. Two booster doses of this vaccine give a similar level of protection against Delta, but recent comparative studies have cast doubt on the vaccine's effectiveness [76,82]. The efficacy of the BNT162b2 and ChAdOx1 nCoV-9 vaccinations was shown to be lower in those who had the Delta variation of the virus than in those who had the other VOCs. It is critical to keep in mind that these outcomes were attained in patients who received only one dose of the vaccine [70].

Further investigation with two doses of the vaccination has demonstrated the apparent efficiency of the primary vaccines against the δ variant. Two doses of the BNT162b2 vaccination were effective in persons with the Alpha version, and 88% in those with the Delta version. Two doses of the ChAdOx1 nCoV-19 vaccine were shown to be 74.5% effective in those with the Alpha form and 67.0% effective among individuals with the δ variant. Upon receiving the two vaccine doses, minor changes in vaccine efficacy were observed between the δ and α variants. Absolute disparities in vaccination effectiveness become more evident after the first dose. This outcome will aid the efforts to increase vaccination uptake among a vulnerable subset of individuals through the administration of two doses [79]. According to several investigations, three doses of BNT162b2 mRNA seem to be necessary to protect against Omicron-driven COVID-19 [83–85]. Surprisingly, Gao et al. proposed that pre-existing SARS-CoV-2 spike-specific CD8+ and CD4+ T cell responses are usually intact against Omicron, especially after BNT162b2 vaccination [86].

Additional research revealed that two doses of the BNT162b2 or ChAdOx1 nCoV-19 vaccination only partially protected against the omicron variant. Upon receiving a BNT162b2 or mRNA-1273 vaccine booster shots, the protection from the BNT162b2 or ChAdOx1 nCoV-19 primary vaccination increased but ultimately wore out [87].

However, the serum from individuals administered triple doses of ChAdOx1 (Oxford/AstraZeneca) or BNT162b2 showed a decreased efficacy against BA.4/5, contrary to BA.1 and BA.2 [88]. Recent research by Zou et al. 2022 found that following the complete dosage of the SARS-CoV-2 vaccine, the immune protection diminishes with time against the Omicron variant.

The Omicron form could not be neutralised by more than half of the mRNA-1273 recipients' plasma, leading to GMTs that were 43 times lower [60]. According to Pajon et al., neutralisation titers against the Omicron version of the mRNA-1273 vaccination were 35 times lower than those against the D614G variant after the first two doses of the vaccine. On the other hand, neutralisation titers against the Omicron variant were 20 times greater following the booster dose of the mRNA-1273 immunisation than following the second dosage, indicating that the risk of relapse is significantly reduced. Six months following the booster injection, neutralisation titers against the Omicron variant decreased [61].

The effectiveness of the serum from people who received an mRNA vaccination against Omicron was evaluated by Edara et al.: using a live viral experiment, they noticed a 30-fold decrease in neutralising activity against the Omicron 2–4 weeks after receiving a primary batch of immunisations, but six months after the first two vaccination doses, no neutralising activity against the Omicron was found, and, in addition, they found that following a booster injection (third dosage), naive individuals' neutralising activity against Omicron decreased fourteen-fold [62]. This implies that the vaccination's effectiveness has been compromised by the appearance of variations, which calls for the administration of booster doses of the vaccine at progressively longer intervals.

4. The SARS-CoV-2 Structural Proteins and their Inference in the Vaccine's Development

S Protein, M-protein, E-protein, and N-nucleocapsid protein (ribonucleoprotein core) are the main structural vaccine target proteins for COVID-19 [63,64]. Sixteen non-structural proteins (nsp1–16) and nine accessory proteins encoded by the virus are additional targets [65]. S Proteins help viruses perceive host cellular receptors and enter [Figure 1]. Hence, the S Protein is the main target of SARS-CoV-2 vaccines, and it exists as a homotrimer in the viral envelope with its membrane-distal S1 and S2 subunits (which are membrane-proximal). S1's receptor-binding domain modulates receptor recognition [66,67,89]. It is imperative to mention here that the N-terminal domain (NTD) of the subunit S1 could also serve as a receptor-interacting domain, as in the case of the mouse hepatitis virus [90–92]. The S2 subunit facilitates membrane fusion during host entry and comprises the fusion peptide, connecting region HR1 and HR2 (heptad repeats) as a 'helix-turn-helix' construct around a central helix [93].

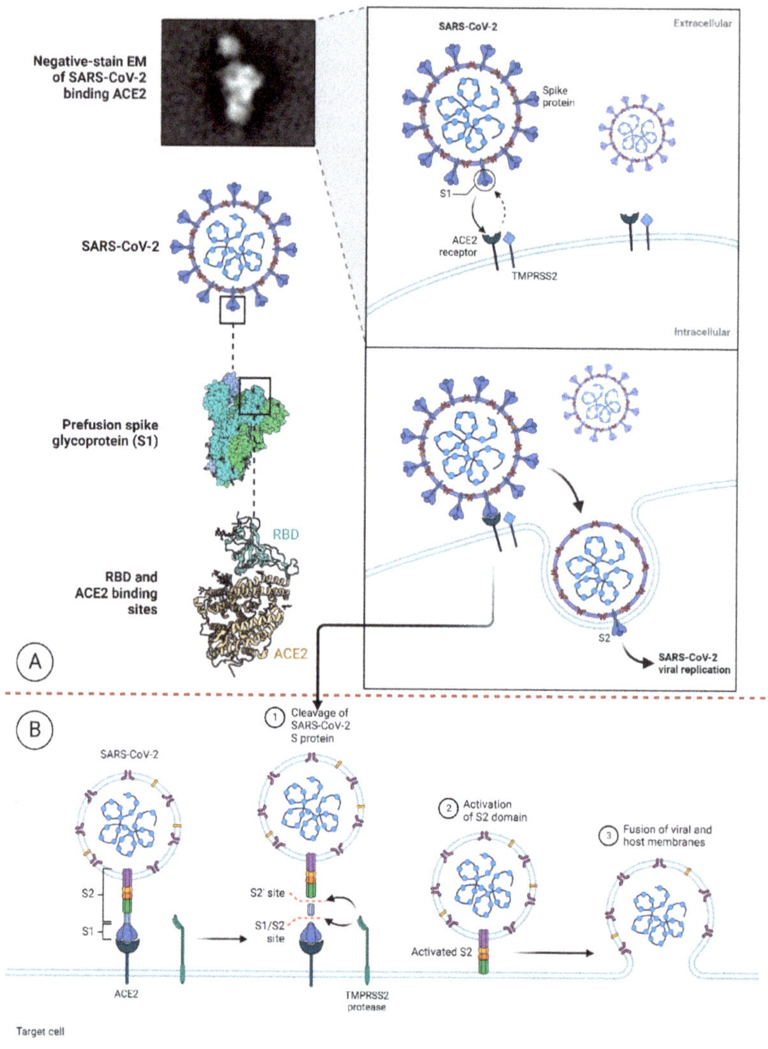

Figure 1. The schematic representation of the SARS-CoV-2 entry into the host cell. (**A**) Representation of the S Protein and its various regions such as receptor binding domain (RBD); (**B**) Binding of the S Protein with the ACE2 receptor of the host cell. After binding of the S Protein with the ACE2 receptor, there is cleavage of the S Protein into S1 and S2 sites. Activated S2 domain helps in the fusion of the viral particle with the cell membrane. [The figure was created with the templates available in BioRender.com, accessed on 25 January 2023].

Recent molecular evidence of this structure has advocated a paradigm where there occurs a rearrangement of this S Protein subsequent to the identification of the host cell receptor [94,95]. Recent research has shown that upon the RBD's interaction with ACE2, the S1 subunit dissociates while the S2 subunit simultaneously refolds, allowing the FP to protrude for effective membrane fusion. The S2 subunit then folds and enters a long helical bundle post-fusion conformation after the FP is inserted into the host cell membrane [60].

More recently, research has focused on strategies that aim to keep the spike-protein in its pre-fusion form, especially in the wake of studies on two proline substitutions at the top of the central helix, HR1 of MERS-CoV and SARS-CoV, and HKU1 that can keep the S Proteins in the pre-fusion conformation [96]. Studies have further shown that this hybrid antigen 'S-2P' could produce higher NAb titres than the S protein. Thus, the S-2P hybrid strategy is a potential vaccine target against SARS-CoV-2. The S-2P has further facilitated the generation of a new S protein ectodomain, 'HexaPro', consisting of six proline substitutions, with the inclusion of the two from S-2P positioned at the N termini of helices or flexible loops in the CR, FP, and HR1 [97]. Such positioning has been shown to promote limiting the reorganization of the S2 subunit structure, stabilizing the pre-fusion spike protein and producing a tenfold increase in the titre expression than S-2P [97]. Hence, stratagems to fix the S-protein to the pre-fusion conformation are a promising avenue.

Interestingly, NAbs have been found capable of targeting the S Protein at various stages of the viral entry, and RBD has been the major target of these Nabs, thwarting the viral receptor binding in the host [31,98,99], whilst almost all NAbs from the vaccines versus the SARS-CoV-2 have RBD as their target [32,100–111]. Many of the NAbs for SARS-CoV-2 have been observed to append to the RBD, thereby blocking the interaction of the RBD with hACE2 and thwarting the virus-host attachment during an infection episode [112]. Thus, the RBD is an alluring vaccine target with a guaranteed evocation of robust antibodies without any hazards of antibody-dependent enhancement of infection typically arbitrated by faint NAbs [113–117]. Further, RBD has also been shown to have T-cell response epitopes [118–123]. However, the petite molecular dimension and the probable existence of the same as multiple complexes, such as monomers or dimers, impose definite limits for the utilization of RBD as an effectual target. Various manoeuvres are being attempted now to trounce these disadvantages, such as magnifying the size of the antigen by fusion of the RBD with a fragment crystallizable region (Fc) [124–128] and multiplication of copies of the RBD (multimerization) [129–131]. A more recent study has suggested a dimeric design of the beta-CoV antigen RBDs that can be employed against SARS-CoV-2, since the RBDs have been shown to form dimers in solution naturally [132–136]. Studies have also demonstrated the possibility of homogeneous RBD-dimers as single chain repeats that would induce a ten-to-hundred-fold amplification of NAbs titres than the RBD-monomer [132,137].

Recent studies have demonstrated that the NAbs could also target the NTD, as stated previously [137], and the S1 protein-NTD has been shown to have Coronavirus NAbs epitopes [138,139]. Studies have shown that though the NAbs that target the NTD could not block the binding of the receptor directly, they could hinder the binding of the receptor binding [138,139] and curtail the previously discussed conformational modifications that occur during the process of pre-fusion to post-fusion alteration in the S-protein during infection. Though the NAbs that target NTD have been established to only display diminutive neutralizing efficacy compared to RBD-NAbs [49], NTD protein has been revealed to elicit definitive NTD-NAbs and T-cell responses with a decrease in lung-related abnormalities during infection [140].

The peptides of major interest in the S2 subunit capable of thwarting a viral fusion with target cells during infection are those elicited by HR1 or HR2 of the S2 subunit. Studies have established the effectual neutralization of the S2 of SARS-CoV-2 with NAbs [141–143], despite the expansive N-glycan shielding of the subunit S2 that renders it a difficult target for immune detection with lower NAb titers compared to the S1 and the RBD [144–146]. It is true that the subunit S2 as a sole entity might not be an operative humoral response target, but relative sequence conservation of the subunit S2 amongst various species of the virus makes it a candidate for recognition by CD4+ T cells and cross-reactive antibodies that can detect SARS-CoV-2 and various other human coronaviruses [147,148].

There has been little exploratory focus on the M, E, or N proteins in contrast to S. The M and E proteins have seldom displayed strong immunogenic elicitation of humoral responses, perhaps due to their petite ectodomains and molecular dimensions that are insufficient for immune recognition [149]. Yet, the relative sequence conservation of the M and E proteins amongst various species of the virus, i.e., SARS-CoV, SARS-CoV-2, and MERS-CoV, makes it a candidate for recognition by CD4+ T cells and cross-reactive antibodies [150]. The N protein, on the other hand, has been shown to be amply immunogenic during previous Corona episodes with established T cell epitopes [151]. Even though they failed against the SARS-CoV-2, N-target antibodies have been indicated to be effective in the mouse Hepatitis virus, which is another Coronavirus [152,153]. N protein has been demonstrated to elicit good T-cell immune responses (CD4+ and CD8+) [154]. T cell (CD8+) epitopes-specific to N protein in chicken IBV infection [155], and the Venezuelan Equine Encephalitis Virus replicon particles with a CD4+ T cell epitope specific to N have been shown to be fully effectual and immunologically protective for SARS-CoV infection [156]. Due to the conserved protein sequences between viruses, these virus replicon particles also provide some cross-protection against MERS-CoV, resulting in a decreased viral load [156]. Since previous vaccine studies on SARS-CoV expressing the N protein have reported infection-induced pneumonia due to enhanced Pulmonary Eosinophil Infiltration and Th-2 cell responses [157,158], causing a risk of Enhanced Respiratory Syncytial Virus Disease (ERD), vaccines based on the N protein have received little or no attention against SARS-CoV-2 [137,159].

5. Recent Strategies in the Vaccine Developments

A 'Pan-corona Vaccine', or at least a Pan-SARS-CoV-2 vaccine that will serve as a booster vaccine, seems to be the global stratagem now. In January 2021, Moderna began researching the SARS-CoV-2 B.1.351 variant, first discovered in South Africa [140,141]. Three vaccine candidates expressing the S Protein are entering Phase III clinical studies. The vaccine proposal from China is based on human adenovirus type 5 (Adn5). In contrast, the vaccine candidates from the United Kingdom are based on a recombinant chimpanzee adenovirus (AdnV), ChAdOx1, and the vaccine approach from Russia is based on recombinant human Ad26 and Ad5 [146]. RBD-based vaccines employ a protein sub-unit method [117], whereas the vaccine ARCoV encodes the RBD of the SARS-CoV-2 delivered via lipid nanoparticles (NPS) [147] [Figure 2].

Inactivated vaccines have already gained a lot of interest due to their ability to trigger immune responses comparable to those seen when viruses are exposed [160]. Given the absence of active genetic material, these vaccines include complete virus particles with no replication capabilities. Such vaccines are made utilizing viral inactivation techniques, including chemical agents such as formaldehyde, phenol, and glutaraldehyde; radiations such as UV, Xray, and Gamma; and physical means such as heat, pressure, and pH [160,161].

Nucleic acid-based vaccines, which include RNA vaccines, are novel forms of vaccinations [162]. These vaccinations include an mRNA strand that codes for a particular antigen/protein. When transported into living organisms, they may be translated into viral proteins. The viral protein might be displayed on the cell surface, where it is detected by immune system elements to elicit an immunological response [162]. RNA-based vaccines for viral illnesses such as influenza and rabies have already been investigated [161,162]. There are primarily two categories of viral vector-based vaccinations. Non-replicating vector vaccines do not manufacture any new viral particles; they only produce the vaccine protein. At the same time, replicating vector vaccines could create new virus particles and also infect cells. The SARS-CoV-2 vaccines currently under research employ non-replicating viral vectors [52,53].

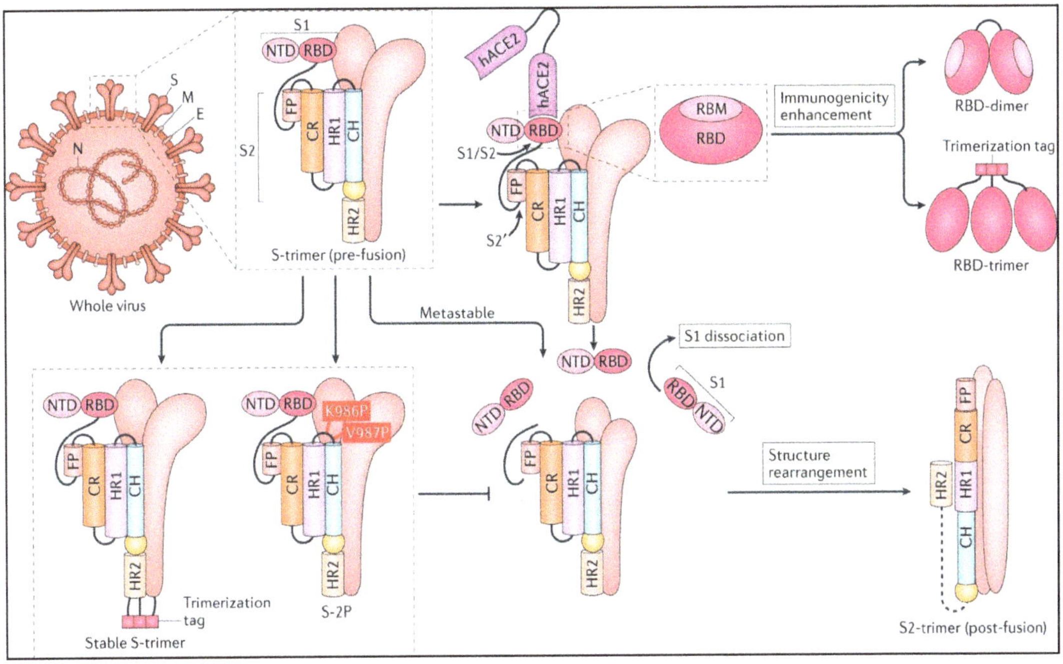

Figure 2. The principal targets of candidates for the COVID-19 vaccination; Source: [137].

Furthermore, Virus-like particles (VLPs) have gained much attention recently as they elicit a substantial amount of immune response as compared to conventional vaccines. In order to explain their strong immunogenicity and the initiation of both antibody-mediated immune response and cell-mediated immune responses, VLPs are artificially created nanoparticles made of a subset of viral components that roughly resemble the structure, size, and surface composition of natural viruses [54,163]. VLPs have been created using a variety of expression platforms, comprising mammalian cell lines, bacterial cell lines, insect cell lines, yeast, and plant cells [55]. VLPs are non-infectious due to the absence of core genetic material, suggesting that they are a safer vaccination platform than several other types of vaccine. They are also a safe and relevant model for conducting viral molecular investigations under BSL-2 circumstances without biosafety protection [161]. VLP vaccines offer the benefits of multivalency, inhaled vaccination possibility, self-adjuvant characteristics, scalable manufacture, and readily maintained temperatures throughout the supply chain, in addition to being safe and effective [56]. The FDA has authorized commercially accessible VLP vaccinations against the human papillomavirus (HPV) and hepatitis B [164] and other VLP vaccines, including those for COVID-19 that are presently under development [161].

An 'S-protein' expressing DNA vaccine capable of effectively eliciting NAbs and spike-protein-specific T-cell responses has completed phase-II clinical trials [165]. A native-like trimeric spike protein subunit vaccine candidate has been testified that uses the spike protein fused to the C-terminal area of Iα collagen (human type) to construct a disulfide-bonded homotrimer [166]. The S-trimer, together with another AS03 adjuvant or CpG 1018 agonist adjuvant, is also under active phase-I clinical trials. An mRNA vaccine, BNT162b1 from BioNTech/Pfizer, expressing an RBD-trimer stabilized by the fold on a trimerization domain has been observed to elicit high NAbs and TH1 cell-based responses as well as the protein subunit vaccine-ZF2001, which comprises the RBD-dimer, as the target [117]. SARS-CoV-2 S-2P, which contains proline substitution at K986 and V987 residues, is used as the target antigen in the mRNA vaccines produced by Moderna/National Institute of Allergy and Infectious Diseases (NIAID), BioNTech/Pfizer, and a recombinant Ad26 vaccine produced by Janssen [117,150]. The S-2P in the Janssen Ad26-vectored vaccine (Ad26.COV2.S) and the Novavax protein-based vaccine (NVX-CoV2373) employ this tactic because it has been demonstrated that additional mutations at the S1-S2 polybasic cleavage site from RRAR to SRAG or QQAQ make it resistant to a protease that stabilizes the S-protein more in its pre-fusion conformation [151,152], and Ad26 expressing S-2P has been shown to elicit elevated NAb titers [167]. The mRNA vaccines BNT162b2 from BioNTech/Pfizer and mRNA1273 from Modera/NIAID as well as the protein subunit vaccine NVX-CoV2373 have been found to elicit better T-cell responses in addition to high titers [117,153], indicating that the method of stabilizing the spike protein in its pre-fusion state could be a promising area for the production of the SARS-CoV-2 vaccine [154]. Efforts are in place to utilize the specific exoribonuclease (ExoN) present in the genome of coronaviruses to arrest the mutations, since inactivation of this ExoN has demonstrated a twenty-fold increase in the mutation rates [4,5].

Aside from COVAXIN from Bharath Biotech, other inactivated viral vaccine candidates are currently in phase-III clinical trials and one is in the phase I/II stages of trial. Using the "Whole-Virion Inactivated Vero Cell" derived platform technology, Bharat Biotech developed COVAXIN®, India's indigenous COVID-19 vaccine, also in collaboration with the Indian Council of Medical Research (ICMR) and National Institute of Virology (NIV). The two-dose, ready-to-use liquid presentation vaccination regimen administered at 28-day intervals requires no reconstitution or storage below 0 °C temperature. It is also stable between 2 and 8 °C temperature. This vaccine candidate has the unique benefit that, in the same Phase-I research that produced outstanding safety data, vaccination-induced neutralizing antibody titers were seen with two distinct SARS-CoV-2 strains. The Phase-II/III study has also shown adequate safety sequels and better humoral/cell-mediated immune outcomes. The inactivated vaccine candidate has been shown to elicit excellent NAbs titers with no induction of TH1 or TH2 cell-linked cytokines after vaccination [168,169]. Live-attenuated virus vaccines for SARS-CoV-2 have received little research attention [137]. A new adenovirus vectored intra-nasal vaccine, BBV154, that elicits a wide-ranging immune response, reacting effectively with IgG, mucosal IgA, and T cells in the nasal mucosa, is currently under active investigation at Bharath Biotech. The nasal route is the primary portal of entry, and the nasal mucosa is the most vulnerable infective domain for the SARS-CoV-2 virus. The vaccine candidate BBV154 is, furthermore, non-invasive, needle-free, and carries with it the merit of an effortless ease of administration and no needle-associated risk of injuries and infections [170,171].

6. Implications of Changing Patterns of Mutations

Undoubtedly, the existing vaccines have been effective in containing the deleterious consequences of COVID-19. Still, the emerging variants of the SARS-CoV-2 have raised concerns regarding the extent of efficacy of these available vaccines to elicit an efficient immune response. This is more germane after the most recent published reports on 'Vaccine Breakthrough Infections' with SARS-CoV-2 strains that denote a potential risk of infection with a viral variant virus, even after successful vaccination. Recent studies amongst a cohort who had taken the two doses of BNT162b2 produced by Pfizer–BioNTech or mRNA-1273 prepared by Moderna have reported two women with a vaccine breakthrough infection [172]. These individuals had developed a variant infection despite proven immunogenicity against SARS-CoV-2. Furthermore, the incidence of a breakthrough infection also showed variability among different vaccinated persons who received different mRNA-based vaccines as a preventive measure against COVID-19 infection [173–179]. A study conducted on 192,123 participants who got two doses of the mRNA-Moderna-1273 vaccine was complemented with an equal number of control individuals, exposed to two doses of the BioNTech-162b2 vaccine, were observed to develop 878 and 1262 breakthrough COVID-19 infections, respectively [174]. Out of the recorded breakthrough infections, seven proceeded to severe COVID-19 conditions but none to other critical diseases, and one to death in the case of BNT162b2. In contrast, in another cohort, only three cases proceeded to acute-care hospitalization, but none led to death or other severe systemic health conditions [174].

The above findings indicate the higher efficacy of the Moderna mRNA-1273 vaccine. They are observed to be associated with a small incidence of Severe Acquired Respiratory Syndrome-CoV-2 breakthrough infection as compared to the Pfizer BioNTech162b2 mRNA vaccine due to their differences in neutralizing antibody titers [180]. A study published by Tang and colleagues on native residents of Qatar indicates the effectiveness of the BNT162b2 vaccine up to 93.4% (95% CI, 85.4–97.0%) against δ variant-induced fatal, critical, or severe disease, which was comparatively lower than the Moderna mRNA-1273 vaccine, i.e., 96.1% (95% CI, 71.6–99.5%) on ≥14 d after the administration of the vaccine's second dose [178]. Such differences in the efficacy of the abovementioned two nucleoside modified mRNA vaccines could be a product of several factors. There are variations in the formulation and vaccination regime. In contrast to BNT162b2, which is administered at a rate of 30 mg/0.3 mL (100 mg/mL), mRNA-1273 is injected at a dose of 100 mg/0.5 mL (200 mg/mL) 28 days apart. This means that the dose of the Moderna mRNA-1273 vaccine provides three times more copies of the spike protein mRNA compared to BNT162b2, which may enhance immune responses [152,168–170]. Further, to enhance in vivo functionality, cellular uptake, and stable delivery systems, lipid nanoparticle (LNP) is rapidly used to coat nucleic acid vaccines. In the Moderna-based mRNA-1273 COVID-19 vaccine, DSPC, SM-102, PEG-DMG, and cholesterol are utilized as LNP, while Pfizer-BioNtech-162b2 is made up of DSPC, ALC-0315, cholesterol, and ALC0159 [171]. The mRNA-LNP vaccination will stop the mRNA from prematurely degrading and will make it easier for antigen-presenting cells (APCs), such as dendritic cells (DCs), to receive it in their cytoplasm [181]. The choice of LNP, however, affects the mRNA stability and durability, which determines the outcome of the immunological response. Heterogeneous variances in immune responses may result from disparities in lipid properties and lipid concentrations [171], despite the reality that both types of vaccine are known to give their recipients a potent immune response against symptomatic COVID-19 infection, compared to acute hospitalizations and death in the unprotected group.

It is interesting to note that research on mRNA-LNP structures suggests that water, ionizable cationic lipids, and mRNA are all found in the core of LNPs. This prompts crucial queries concerning the mRNA's potential protection against water [182]. For instance, it is not known if or how the LNP's ionizable cationic lipids interact with the mRNA. To validate the suggested structure and comprehend the effects, further research must be performed. For instance, it has been determined that it is crucial to research the pH within the LNPs in connection to stability [171,182]. The exact type(s) of degradation that mRNA molecules go through in their final formulation should also be thoroughly examined, as should the possibility that strand integrity might be preserved by sequence change [182]. While there are hints that certain folded configurations are more stable, this might also be connected to the analysis and improvement of the secondary and tertiary structure of mRNA [8,171,181,182].

Since most of the vaccines target the spike protein and the variants have emerged from the same gene S, a big question mark has emerged on the efficacy of these available vaccines to elicit an effectual immune response on these variants, apart from a compulsion to improve the diagnostics and accuracy of the sequencing. The P.1 variant brought about by Spike Protein Substitutions P26S, L18F, T20N, K417T, D138Y, D614G, R190S, E484K, N501Y, H655Y, and T1027I [Figure 3], first noticed in Brazil and Japan, is yet another example of a COVID-19 variant displaying decreased neutralization by post-vaccination and convalescent sera, apart from B.1.1.7, B.1.351, B.1.427, and B.1.429, ruled out by the CDC as variants of concern. The variability in such major mutations has shown an inconsistent trend in the past years; interestingly, the D614G mutation has been reported as an important mutation in the VOCs [Figure 3].

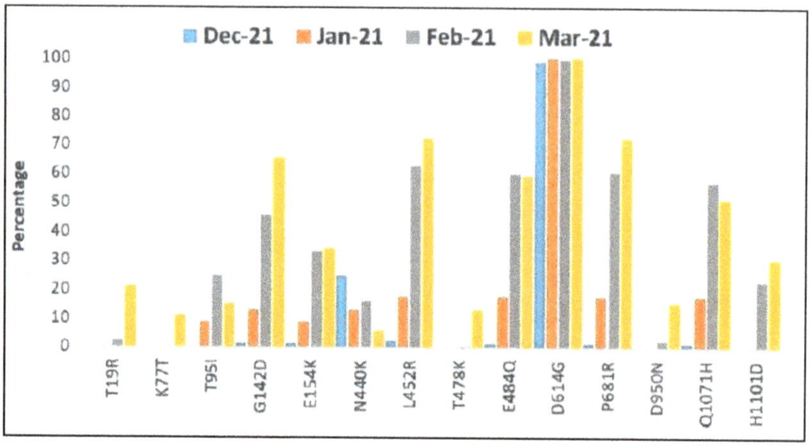

Figure 3. Trend of major mutations in the spike protein from December 2020 to March 2021. [Source: https://www.news-medical.net/news/20210427/Triple-mutation-in-SARS-CoV-2-seen-in-second-wave-of-COVID-19-in-India.aspx, accessed on 15 January 2023].

The city of New York, NY, USA, has documented a manifold increase in the cases of variants, especially the B.1.1.7. It is important to consider the factors such as availability of medical care facilities, diagnostic facilities, misdiagnosis, and delay in detection of the disease in asymptomatic patients in determining the vaccine efficacy and difference of fatality rate among different nations [183,184]. The capability of these variants to escape the vaccine-elicited immune response, thereby causing asymptomatic and symptomatic infection spread, is a public health complication of grave concern [172].

However, a very recent (March 2021) study has shown that an inactivated Severe Acquired Respiratory Syndrome-CoV-2 vaccine, BBV152/COVAXIN, can neutralize B.1.1.7 variant considerably [185]. Though the variant has 17 mutations in the genome, 8 of them are located in the spike (S)-RBD that facilitates the binding of the virus to the ACE2 receptor in the host. The study has elucidated that the mutation N501Y, at position 501, with a tyrosine replacement instead of asparagine, upsurges the binding capacity of SARS-CoV-2 to human Angiotensin Converting Enzyme 2, and since many vaccine candidates solely target just one epitope of the original D614G ancestral spike sequence, it is feasible that they are unable to stimulate an immune reaction against the subsequent versions. As a consequence, the study adopted a strategy that involved painstakingly isolating and sequencing the hCoV-19/India/20203522 SARS-CoV-2 (VOC) 202 012/01 from UK returnees to India, which comprised all signature mutations of the UK variant (VOC 202012/01 hallmarks belong to the GR clade of the viral isolates recovered from the UK returnees).

The SARS-CoV-2 strain, i.e., NIV-2020-770, retrieved from tourists arriving in India, has been used for the development of the BBV152 COVAXIN vaccine. The "Vero CCL-81" cells were used for the viral isolation, and the genome sequence was deposited in the GISAID (EPI ISL 420545). The Asp614Gly mutation, which causes glycine to shift from aspartic acid at the 614 amino acid (AA) spike protein position, is present in the BBV152 vaccine candidate strain, which belongs to the G clade and was used for the study's PRNT50 experiment. Previous studies by the same team have also reported the incapacitated whole-virion SARS-CoV-2 vaccine BBV152, which could elicit a significant neutralizing antibody titre in Phase-I clinical trials against hCoV-19/India/2020770 (homologous) and two heterologous strains from an uncategorized cluster i.e., hCoV-19/India/2020Q111 and hCoV-19/India/2020Q100 that comprise the L3606F mutation. The vaccine has been shown to display significant results for PRNT50 assay (Plaque Reduction Neutralization Test) with 98.6% seroconversion rates for NAbs in Phase-II clinical trial, subsequent to a two-dose immunization plan (0 and 28 days) with a six to eight micrograms antigen with TLR7/TLR8 agonist imidazoquinoline adsorbed on aluminium hydroxide gel.

The NAb titres obtained by PRNT50 of the sera collected 28 days after day 28 of the second dose from 38 recipients of the BBV152 vaccine candidate in Phase-II trial has evidently recognized the efficacy of the BBV152 vaccine against the SARS-CoV-2 UK variant, with (VOC) 202 012/01 hallmarks belonging to GR clade and strain hCoV-19/India/2020770 belonging to G clade. Additional PRNT50 test assay evaluation of 20 representative serum samples from vaccine recipients against the heterologous strains hCoV-19/India/2020Q111 (unclassified cluster) revealed uniform equivalent NAbs titres to the homologous strain hCoV-19/India/2020770 and two heterologous strains, including the distinctive N501Y substitution of the UK variant, hCoV-19/India/20203522 (UK strain), and the hCoV-19/India/2020Q111 as well (for all the samples). These sample sera showed NAbs titre that were equal to the hCoV-19/India/2020770 homologous strain and two heterologous strains, including the hCoV-19/India/20203522 (UK strain) and the hCoV-19/India/2020Q111, both of which had the distinctive N501Y substitution of the UK variety. When compared to the mutant hCoV-19/India/20203522 (UK variation), the median ratio of 50% neutralisation of sera was 0.8, and when compared to hCoV-19/India/2020Q111, it was 0.9 [185,186].

Amid reports of poor neutralization of the UK variant (with E484K substitution) by high NAbs in convalescent plasma, raising a serious question on the global COVID-19 vaccination initiatives, the study has lucidly demonstrated palpable evidence of neutralization of a variant by the vaccinated sera. The most significant aspect of the study is that the vaccinated sera could neutralize the heterologous strains, to, with equal efficacy. Similar studies to evaluate the neutralizing competence of the sera immunized with the mRNA-1273 vaccine have also reported an efficacious neutralizing response against the B.1.1.7 variant [64,186].

7. Conclusion and Future Prospectives

The variants of COVID-19 have not only compounded the risk of the infection further but also complicated the diagnostic and therapeutic aspect of the pandemic with reports on 'Vaccine Breakthrough Infections'. Every vaccine candidate against SARS-CoV-2 is a product of an extraordinary human effort amidst an unprecedented raging pandemic in a short period. Each vaccine candidate carries with it a merit of its own. A conventionally defined ideal candidate vaccine elicits high titers of Nabs and diminishes the production of non-NAbs, thereby reducing the potential of ADE incidence, producing good TH1 cell-responses yet low TH2 cell- responses, reducing enhanced respiratory disease, prompting an enduring immunological memory, and also possesses cross-protection capabilities. Though it is good to conceive and work on a vaccine target cocktail and several other stratagems, several million people are invested in vaccine research across the world, and every vaccine rollout is time-bound, with every rollout going through several stages of cumbersome clinical trials and patient safety protocols. Thus, every vaccine breakthrough infection is quite significant and a considerable challenge to vaccination programs. This is more so in third-world economies.

Thus, the variant challenge mandates more precise and quicker diagnostic tools as well as rapid therapeutic responses to effectively arrest the further spread of infection by the variant. Experience with COVAXIN® and other inactivated vaccine candidates shows us that inactivated whole virus vaccines that could be constructed with little or no complex molecular interventions or alterations in a short period could be an effective manoeuvre to tackle the variants. In fact, these vaccines could be administered as booster shots after the initial vaccination program in regions that have already completed the vaccination for the reference virus. The intranasal vaccine is another promising avenue that confers immunity at the nasal mucosal domain, a vital arena in the infection episode of Severe Acquired Respiratory Syndrome-CoV-2 and additional respiratory viruses with ease of administration of the vaccine.

Author Contributions: Conceptualization, A.A.R. and M.D.; investigation and resources, A.A.R., M.D., S.H.A.-A., H.A., S.A. (Sara Alwarthan), M.A. (Mashael Alhajri), M.A.N., B.M.A., W.A.-A., A.A., W.A.A., N.A., J.A., A.H.G., R.S.A., A.A.Z., N.T. and G.V.; writing—original draft preparation, A.A.R., N.T. and M.D., writing—review and editing, A.A.R., M.D., R.S.A., S.A. (Sahar Aldossary), W.A.A., A.A.Z., M.A. (Mohammed Alissa), L.M.A., F.M.A., M.A.N. and B.M.A.; visualization and supervision, M.D., A.A.R. and N.T.; project administration, M.D. and A.A.R. All authors have read and agreed to the published version of the manuscript.

Funding: This study is supported via funding from Prince Sattam bin Abdulaziz University project number (PSAU/2023/R/1444).

Institutional Review Board Statement: Not applicable.

Informed Consent Statement: Not applicable.

Data Availability Statement: All data are available in this manuscript.

Acknowledgments: All the authors acknowledge and thank their respective Universities and Institutes.

Conflicts of Interest: The authors declare no conflict of interest.

Abbreviations

ACE2	angiotensin converting enzyme 2
APCs	antigen-presenting cells
BCR	B cell receptor
BALF	bronchoalveolar lavage fluid
COVID-19	coronavirus disease 19
mAbs	monoclonal antibodies
NAbs	neutralising antibodies
NTD	N-terminal domain
RBD	Receptor binding domain
TH1	T helper 1
TH2	T helper 2

References

1. COVAX. Available online: https://www.who.int/initiatives/act-accelerator/covax (accessed on 8 January 2023).
2. Fontanet, A.; Autran, B.; Lina, B.; Kieny, M.P.; Karim, S.S.A.; Sridhar, D. SARS-CoV-2 Variants and Ending the COVID-19 Pandemic. *Lancet* **2021**, *397*, 952. [CrossRef] [PubMed]
3. Wang, Z.; Schmidt, F.; Weisblum, Y.; Muecksch, F.; Barnes, C.O.; Finkin, S.; Schaefer-Babajew, D.; Cipolla, M.; Gaebler, C.; Lieberman, J.A.; et al. MRNA Vaccine-Elicited Antibodies to SARS-CoV-2 and Circulating Variants. *Nature* **2021**, *592*, 616–622. [CrossRef]
4. Moore, J.P.; Offit, P.A. SARS-CoV-2 Vaccines and the Growing Threat of Viral Variants. *JAMA* **2021**, *325*, 821–822. [CrossRef]
5. Madhi, S.A.; Baillie, V.; Cutland, C.L.; Voysey, M.; Koen, A.L.; Fairlie, L.; Padayachee, S.D.; Dheda, K.; Barnabas, S.L.; Bhorat, Q.E.; et al. Efficacy of the ChAdOx1 NCoV-19 COVID-19 Vaccine against the B.1.351 Variant. *N. Engl. J. Med.* **2021**, *384*, 1885–1898. [CrossRef] [PubMed]
6. Wibmer, C.K.; Ayres, F.; Hermanus, T.; Madzivhandila, M.; Kgagudi, P.; Oosthuysen, B.; Lambson, B.E.; de Oliveira, T.; Vermeulen, M.; van der Berg, K.; et al. SARS-CoV-2 501Y.V2 Escapes Neutralization by South African COVID-19 Donor Plasma. *Nat. Med.* **2021**, *27*, 622–625. [CrossRef]
7. Fan, Y.; Li, X.; Zhang, L.; Wan, S.; Zhang, L.; Zhou, F. SARS-CoV-2 Omicron Variant: Recent Progress and Future Perspectives. *Signal Transduct. Target. Ther.* **2022**, *7*, 141. [CrossRef]
8. Chavda, V.P.; Balar, P.; Vaghela, D.; Solanki, H.K.; Vaishnav, A.; Hala, V.; Vora, L. Omicron Variant of SARS-CoV-2: An Indian Perspective of Vaccination and Management. *Vaccines* **2023**, *11*, 160. [CrossRef]
9. Ren, S.-Y.; Wang, W.-B.; Gao, R.-D.; Zhou, A.-M. Omicron Variant (B.1.1.529) of SARS-CoV-2: Mutation, Infectivity, Transmission, and Vaccine Resistance. *World J. Clin. Cases* **2022**, *10*, 1–11. [CrossRef]
10. Dhawan, M.; Saied, A.R.A.; Mitra, S.; Alhumaydhi, F.A.; Emran, T.B.; Wilairatana, P. Omicron Variant (B.1.1.529) and Its Sublineages: What Do We Know so Far amid the Emergence of Recombinant Variants of SARS-CoV-2? *Biomed. Pharmacother.* **2022**, *154*, 113522. [CrossRef] [PubMed]
11. Cameroni, E.; Bowen, J.E.; Rosen, L.E.; Saliba, C.; Zepeda, S.K.; Culap, K.; Pinto, D.; VanBlargan, L.A.; De Marco, A.; di Iulio, J.; et al. Broadly Neutralizing Antibodies Overcome SARS-CoV-2 Omicron Antigenic Shift. *Nature* **2022**, *602*, 664–670. [CrossRef]

12. Gobeil, S.M.C.; Henderson, R.; Stalls, V.; Janowska, K.; Huang, X.; May, A.; Speakman, M.; Beaudoin, E.; Manne, K.; Li, D.; et al. Structural Diversity of the SARS-CoV-2 Omicron Spike. *Mol. Cell* **2022**, *82*, 2050. [CrossRef] [PubMed]
13. Dhawan, M.; Rabaan, A.A.; Fawarah, M.M.A.; Almuthree, S.A.; Alsubki, R.A.; Alfaraj, A.H.; Mashraqi, M.M.; Alshamrani, S.A.; Abduljabbar, W.A.; Alwashmi, A.S.S.; et al. Updated Insights into the T Cell-Mediated Immune Response against SARS-CoV-2: A Step towards Efficient and Reliable Vaccines. *Vaccines* **2023**, *11*, 101. [CrossRef]
14. Sheinin, M.; Jeong, B.; Paidi, R.K.; Pahan, K. Regression of Lung Cancer in Mice by Intranasal Administration of SARS-CoV-2 Spike S1. *Cancers* **2022**, *14*, 5648. [CrossRef]
15. Paidi, R.K.; Jana, M.; Mishra, R.K.; Dutta, D.; Raha, S.; Pahan, K. ACE-2-Interacting Domain of SARS-CoV-2 (AIDS) Peptide Suppresses Inflammation to Reduce Fever and Protect Lungs and Heart in Mice: Implications for COVID-19 Therapy. *J. Neuroimmune Pharmacol.* **2021**, *16*, 59. [CrossRef] [PubMed]
16. Zimmerman, M.I.; Porter, J.R.; Ward, M.D.; Singh, S.; Vithani, N.; Meller, A.; Mallimadugula, U.L.; Kuhn, C.E.; Borowsky, J.H.; Wiewiora, R.P.; et al. SARS-CoV-2 Simulations Go Exascale to Predict Dramatic Spike Opening and Cryptic Pockets across the Proteome. *Nat. Chem.* **2021**, *13*, 651–659. [CrossRef]
17. Miller, N.L.; Clark, T.; Raman, R.; Sasisekharan, R. Insights on the Mutational Landscape of the SARS-CoV-2 Omicron Variant Receptor-Binding Domain. *Cell Reports Med.* **2022**, *3*, 100527. [CrossRef]
18. Dhawan, M.; Priyanka; Choudhary, O.P. Emergence of Omicron Sub-Variant BA.2: Is It a Matter of Concern amid the COVID-19 Pandemic? *Int. J. Surg.* **2022**, *99*, 106581. [CrossRef] [PubMed]
19. Abulsoud, A.I.; El-Husseiny, H.M.; El-Husseiny, A.A.; El-Mahdy, H.A.; Ismail, A.; Elkhawaga, S.Y.; Khidr, E.G.; Fathi, D.; Mady, E.A.; Najda, A.; et al. Mutations in SARS-CoV-2: Insights on Structure, Variants, Vaccines, and Biomedical Interventions. *Biomed. Pharmacother.* **2023**, *157*, 113977. [CrossRef]
20. Lemieux, J.E.; Siddle, K.J.; Shaw, B.M.; Loreth, C.; Schaffner, S.F.; Gladden-Young, A.; Adams, G.; Fink, T.; Tomkins-Tinch, C.H.; Krasilnikova, L.A.; et al. Phylogenetic Analysis of SARS-CoV-2 in Boston Highlights the Impact of Superspreading Events. *Science* **2021**, *371*, eabe3261. [CrossRef]
21. Starr, T.N.; Greaney, A.J.; Hilton, S.K.; Ellis, D.; Crawford, K.H.D.; Dingens, A.S.; Navarro, M.J.; Bowen, J.E.; Tortorici, M.A.; Walls, A.C.; et al. Deep Mutational Scanning of SARS-CoV-2 Receptor Binding Domain Reveals Constraints on Folding and ACE2 Binding. *Cell* **2020**, *182*, 1295–1310.e20. [CrossRef]
22. Korber, B.; Fischer, W.M.; Gnanakaran, S.; Yoon, H.; Theiler, J.; Abfalterer, W.; Hengartner, N.; Giorgi, E.E.; Bhattacharya, T.; Foley, B.; et al. Tracking Changes in SARS-CoV-2 Spike: Evidence That D614G Increases Infectivity of the COVID-19 Virus. *Cell* **2020**, *182*, 812–827.e19. [CrossRef]
23. Tan, H.W.; Xu, Y.M.; Lau, A.T.Y. Angiotensin-Converting Enzyme 2: The Old Door for New Severe Acute Respiratory Syndrome Coronavirus 2 Infection. *Rev. Med. Virol.* **2020**, *30*, e2122. [CrossRef]
24. Wang, L.; Cheng, G. Sequence Analysis of the Emerging SARS-CoV-2 Variant Omicron in South Africa. *J. Med. Virol.* **2022**, *94*, 1728–1733. [CrossRef]
25. Kannan, S.R.; Spratt, A.N.; Sharma, K.; Chand, H.S.; Byrareddy, S.N.; Singh, K. Omicron SARS-CoV-2 Variant: Unique Features and Their Impact on Pre-Existing Antibodies. *J. Autoimmun.* **2022**, *126*, 102779. [CrossRef]
26. Harvey, W.T.; Carabelli, A.M.; Jackson, B.; Gupta, R.K.; Thomson, E.C.; Harrison, E.M.; Ludden, C.; Reeve, R.; Rambaut, A.; Peacock, S.J.; et al. SARS-CoV-2 Variants, Spike Mutations and Immune Escape. *Nat. Rev. Microbiol. 2021 197* **2021**, *19*, 409–424. [CrossRef] [PubMed]
27. Behl, T.; Kaur, I.; Sehgal, A.; Singh, S.; Sharma, N.; Anwer, M.K.; Makeen, H.A.; Albratty, M.; Alhazmi, H.A.; Bhatia, S.; et al. There Is Nothing Exempt from the Peril of Mutation—The Omicron Spike. *Biomed. Pharmacother.* **2022**, *148*, 112756. [CrossRef]
28. V'kovski, P.; Kratzel, A.; Steiner, S.; Stalder, H.; Thiel, V. Coronavirus Biology and Replication: Implications for SARS-CoV-2. *Nat. Rev. Microbiol.* **2020**, *19*, 155–170. [CrossRef] [PubMed]
29. Sahu, U.; Biswas, D.; Singh, A.K.; Khare, P. Mechanism Involved in the Pathogenesis and Immune Response against SARS-CoV-2 Infection. *VirusDisease* **2021**, *32*, 211–219. [CrossRef]
30. Bergmann, C.C.; Lane, T.E.; Stohlman, S.A. Coronavirus Infection of the Central Nervous System: Host-Virus Stand-Off. *Nat. Rev. Microbiol.* **2006**, *4*, 121–132. [CrossRef]
31. Yuan, M.; Liu, H.; Wu, N.C.; Wilson, I.A. Recognition of the SARS-CoV-2 Receptor Binding Domain by Neutralizing Antibodies. *Biochem. Biophys. Res. Commun.* **2021**, *538*, 192. [CrossRef] [PubMed]
32. Robbiani, D.F.; Gaebler, C.; Muecksch, F.; Lorenzi, J.C.C.; Wang, Z.; Cho, A.; Agudelo, M.; Barnes, C.O.; Gazumyan, A.; Finkin, S.; et al. Convergent Antibody Responses to SARS-CoV-2 in Convalescent Individuals. *Nature* **2020**, *584*, 437–442. [CrossRef] [PubMed]
33. Latifi-Pupovci, H. Molecular Mechanisms Involved in Pathogenicity of SARS-CoV-2: Immune Evasion and Implications for Therapeutic Strategies. *Biomed. Pharmacother.* **2022**, *153*, 113368. [CrossRef]
34. Simmons, G.; Gosalia, D.N.; Rennekamp, A.J.; Reeves, J.D.; Diamond, S.L.; Bates, P. Inhibitors of Cathepsin L Prevent Severe Acute Respiratory Syndrome Coronavirus Entry. *Proc. Natl. Acad. Sci. USA* **2005**, *102*, 11876–11881. [CrossRef]
35. Sun, G.; Sui, Y.; Zhou, Y.; Ya, J.; Yuan, C.; Jiang, L.; Huang, M. Structural Basis of Covalent Inhibitory Mechanism of TMPRSS2-Related Serine Proteases by Camostat. *J. Virol.* **2021**, *95*, JVI0086121. [CrossRef]

36. Teixeira, L.M.C.; Coimbra, J.T.S.; Ramos, M.J.; Fernandes, P.A. Transmembrane Protease Serine 2 Proteolytic Cleavage of the SARS-CoV-2 Spike Protein: A Mechanistic Quantum Mechanics/Molecular Mechanics Study to Inspire the Design of New Drugs to Fight the COVID-19 Pandemic. *J. Chem. Inf. Model.* **2022**, *62*, 2510–2521. [CrossRef] [PubMed]
37. Meng, B.; Abdullahi, A.; Ferreira, I.A.T.M.; Goonawardane, N.; Saito, A.; Kimura, I.; Yamasoba, D.; Gerber, P.P.; Fatihi, S.; Rathore, S.; et al. Altered TMPRSS2 Usage by SARS-CoV-2 Omicron Impacts Infectivity and Fusogenicity. *Nature* **2022**, *603*, 706–714. [CrossRef] [PubMed]
38. Sun, C.; Xie, C.; Bu, G.L.; Zhong, L.Y.; Zeng, M.S. Molecular Characteristics, Immune Evasion, and Impact of SARS-CoV-2 Variants. *Signal Transduct. Target. Ther.* **2022**, *7*, 202. [CrossRef]
39. Pia, L.; Rowland-Jones, S. Omicron Entry Route. *Nat. Rev. Immunol.* **2022**, *22*, 144. [CrossRef]
40. Zhao, H.; Lu, L.; Peng, Z.; Chen, L.L.; Meng, X.; Zhang, C.; Ip, J.D.; Chan, W.M.; Chu, A.W.H.; Chan, K.H.; et al. SARS-CoV-2 Omicron Variant Shows Less Efficient Replication and Fusion Activity When Compared with Delta Variant in TMPRSS2-Expressed Cells. *Emerg. Microbes Infect.* **2022**, *11*, 277. [CrossRef]
41. Metzdorf, K.; Jacobsen, H.; Greweling-Pils, M.C.; Hoffmann, M.; Lüddecke, T.; Miller, F.; Melcher, L.; Kempf, A.M.; Nehlmeier, I.; Bruder, D.; et al. TMPRSS2 Is Essential for SARS-CoV-2 Beta and Omicron Infection. *Viruses* **2023**, *15*, 271. [CrossRef]
42. Shuai, H.; Chan, J.F.W.; Hu, B.; Chai, Y.; Yuen, T.T.T.; Yin, F.; Huang, X.; Yoon, C.; Hu, J.C.; Liu, H.; et al. Attenuated Replication and Pathogenicity of SARS-CoV-2 B.1.1.529 Omicron. *Nature* **2022**, *603*, 693–699. [CrossRef]
43. Hui, K.P.Y.; Ho, J.C.W.; Cheung, M.C.; Ng, K.-c.; Ching, R.H.H.; Lai, K.-l.; Kam, T.T.; Gu, H.; Sit, K.Y.; Hsin, M.K.Y.; et al. SARS-CoV-2 Omicron Variant Replication in Human Bronchus and Lung Ex Vivo. *Nature* **2022**, *603*, 715–720. [CrossRef]
44. Peacock, T.P.; Goldhill, D.H.; Zhou, J.; Baillon, L.; Frise, R.; Swann, O.C.; Kugathasan, R.; Penn, R.; Brown, J.C.; Sanchez-David, R.Y.; et al. The Furin Cleavage Site in the SARS-CoV-2 Spike Protein Is Required for Transmission in Ferrets. *Nat. Microbiol.* **2021**, *6*, 899–909. [CrossRef] [PubMed]
45. Fact Sheet for Health Care Providers Emergency Use Authorization (EUA) OF REGEN-COV® (Casirivimab and Imdevimab). 2022. Available at Regeneron EUA HCP Fact Sheet 01242022 (fda.gov); accessed on 20 January 2023. 20 January.
46. Deng, X.; Garcia-Knight, M.A.; Khalid, M.M.; Servellita, V.; Wang, C.; Morris, M.K.; Sotomayor-González, A.; Glasner, D.R.; Reyes, K.R.; Gliwa, A.S.; et al. Transmission, Infectivity, and Antibody Neutralization of an Emerging SARS-CoV-2 Variant in California Carrying a L452R Spike Protein Mutation. *medRxiv* **2021**. [CrossRef]
47. Jangra, S.; Ye, C.; Rathnasinghe, R.; Stadlbauer, D.; Alshammary, H.; Amoako, A.A.; Awawda, M.H.; Beach, K.F.; Bermúdez-González, M.C.; Chernet, R.L.; et al. SARS-CoV-2 Spike E484K Mutation Reduces Antibody Neutralisation. *Lancet. Microbe* **2021**, *2*, e283–e284. [CrossRef]
48. Garcia-Beltran, W.F.; Lam, E.C.; St. Denis, K.; Nitido, A.D.; Garcia, Z.H.; Hauser, B.M.; Feldman, J.; Pavlovic, M.N.; Gregory, D.J.; Poznansky, M.C.; et al. Multiple SARS-CoV-2 Variants Escape Neutralization by Vaccine-Induced Humoral Immunity. *Cell* **2021**, *184*, 2372–2383.e9. [CrossRef]
49. Annavajhala, M.K.; Mohri, H.; Zucker, J.E.; Sheng, Z.; Wang, P.; Gomez-Simmonds, A.; Ho, D.D.; Uhlemann, A.-C. A Novel SARS-CoV-2 Variant of Concern, B.1.526, Identified in New York. *medRxiv* **2021**. [CrossRef]
50. Yadav, P.D.; Sapkal, G.N.; Abraham, P.; Ella, R.; Deshpande, G.; Patil, D.Y.; Nyayanit, D.A.; Gupta, N.; Sahay, R.R.; Shete, A.M.; et al. Neutralization of Variant under Investigation B.1.617 with Sera of BBV152 Vaccinees. *bioRxiv* **2021**. [CrossRef]
51. Greaney, A.J.; Loes, A.N.; Crawford, K.H.D.; Starr, T.N.; Malone, K.D.; Chu, H.Y.; Bloom, J.D. Comprehensive Mapping of Mutations in the SARS-CoV-2 Receptor-Binding Domain That Affect Recognition by Polyclonal Human Plasma Antibodies. *Cell Host Microbe* **2021**, *29*, 463–476.e6. [CrossRef]
52. Ura, T.; Okuda, K.; Shimada, M. Developments in Viral Vector-Based Vaccines. *Vaccines* **2014**, *2*, 624–641. [CrossRef] [PubMed]
53. Khalaj-Hedayati, A. Protective Immunity against SARS Subunit Vaccine Candidates Based on Spike Protein: Lessons for Coronavirus Vaccine Development. *J. Immunol. Res.* **2020**, *2020*, 7201752. [CrossRef] [PubMed]
54. Mohsen, M.O.; Zha, L.; Cabral-Miranda, G.; Bachmann, M.F. Major Findings and Recent Advances in Virus–like Particle (VLP)-Based Vaccines. *Semin. Immunol.* **2017**, *34*, 123–132. [CrossRef]
55. Xu, R.; Shi, M.; Li, J.; Song, P.; Li, N. Construction of SARS-CoV-2 Virus-Like Particles by Mammalian Expression System. *Front. Bioeng. Biotechnol.* **2020**, *8*, 862. [CrossRef]
56. Gomes, A.C.; Mohsen, M.; Bachmann, M.F. Harnessing Nanoparticles for Immunomodulation and Vaccines. *Vaccines* **2017**, *5*, 6. [CrossRef] [PubMed]
57. Davies, N.G.; Abbott, S.; Barnard, R.C.; Jarvis, C.I.; Kucharski, A.J.; Munday, J.D.; Pearson, C.A.B.; Russell, T.W.; Tully, D.C.; Washburne, A.D.; et al. Estimated Transmissibility and Impact of SARS-CoV-2 Lineage B.1.1.7 in England. *Science* **2021**, *372*, eabg3055. [CrossRef]
58. Horby, P.; Bell, I.; Breuer, J.; Cevik, M.; Challen, R.; Davies, N.; Dabrera, G.; Edmunds, J.; Ferguson, N.; Funk, S.; et al. Update Note on B.1.1.7 Severity.
59. Pearson, C.A.; Russell, T.; Davies, N.; Kucharski, A.; CMMID COVID-19 Working Group; Edmunds, J.; Eggo, R.M. Estimates of Severity and Transmissibility of Novel SARS-CoV-2 Variant 501Y.V2 in South Africa | CMMID Repository. Available online: https://cmmid.github.io/topics/covid19/sa-novel-variant.html (accessed on 8 January 2023).
60. Wang, P.; Casner, R.G.; Nair, M.S.; Wang, M.; Yu, J.; Cerutti, G.; Liu, L.; Kwong, P.D.; Huang, Y.; Shapiro, L.; et al. Increased Resistance of SARS-CoV-2 Variant P.1 to Antibody Neutralization. *bioRxiv* **2021**. [CrossRef]

61. Shen, X.; Tang, H.; McDanal, C.; Wagh, K.; Fischer, W.; Theiler, J.; Yoon, H.; Li, D.; Haynes, B.F.; Sanders, K.O.; et al. SARS-CoV-2 Variant B.1.1.7 Is Susceptible to Neutralizing Antibodies Elicited by Ancestral Spike Vaccines. *bioRxiv* **2021**. [CrossRef]
62. Edara, V.V.; Floyd, K.; Lai, L.; Gardner, M.; Hudson, W.; Piantadosi, A.; Waggoner, J.J.; Babiker, A.; Ahmed, R.; Xie, X.; et al. Infection and MRNA-1273 Vaccine Antibodies Neutralize SARS-CoV-2 UK Variant. *medRxiv* **2021**. [CrossRef]
63. Collier, D.A.; De Marco, A.; Ferreira, I.A.; Meng, B.; Datir, R.; Walls, A.C.; Bassi, J.; Pinto, D.; Fregni, C.S.; Bianchi, S.; et al. SARS-CoV-2 B.1.1.7 Sensitivity to MRNA Vaccine-Elicited, Convalescent and Monoclonal Antibodies. *medRxiv* **2021**. [CrossRef]
64. Wu, K.; Werner, A.P.; Moliva, J.I.; Koch, M.; Choi, A.; Stewart-Jones, G.B.E.; Bennett, H.; Boyoglu-Barnum, S.; Shi, W.; Graham, B.S.; et al. MRNA-1273 Vaccine Induces Neutralizing Antibodies against Spike Mutants from Global SARS-CoV-2 Variants. *bioRxiv* **2021**. [CrossRef]
65. Emary, K.R.W.; Golubchik, T.; Aley, P.K.; Ariani, C.V.; Angus, B.J.; Bibi, S.; Blane, B.; Bonsall, D.; Cicconi, P.; Charlton, S.; et al. Efficacy of ChAdOx1 NCoV-19 (AZD1222) Vaccine Against SARS-CoV-2 VOC 202012/01 (B.1.1.7). *SSRN Electron. J.* **2021**. [CrossRef]
66. Liu, Y.; Liu, J.; Xia, H.; Zhang, X.; Fontes-Garfias, C.R.; Swanson, K.A.; Cai, H.; Sarkar, R.; Chen, W.; Cutler, M.; et al. Neutralizing Activity of BNT162b2-Elicited Serum. *N. Engl. J. Med.* **2021**, *384*, 1466–1468. [CrossRef] [PubMed]
67. Lai, L.; Sahoo, M.K.; Floyd, K.; Sibai, M.; Solis, D.; Flowers, M.W.; Hussaini, L.; Rose Ciric, C.; Bechnack, S.; Stephens, K.; et al. Infection and Vaccine-Induced Neutralizing Antibody Responses to the SARS-CoV-2 B.1.617.1 1 Variant 2 3 Venkata-Viswanadh Edara. *bioRxiv* **2021**. [CrossRef]
68. Variants of the Virus | CDC. Available online: https://www.cdc.gov/coronavirus/2019-ncov/variants/index.html (accessed on 8 January 2023).
69. Wahid, M.; Jawed, A.; Mandal, R.K.; Dailah, H.G.; Janahi, E.M.; Dhama, K.; Somvanshi, P.; Haque, S. Variants of SARS-CoV-2, Their Effects on Infection, Transmission and Neutralization by Vaccine-Induced Antibodies. *Eur. Rev. Med. Pharmacol. Sci.* **2021**, *25*, 5857–5864. [CrossRef]
70. Dhawan, M.; Sharma, A.; Priyanka; Thakur, N.; Rajkhowa, T.K.; Choudhary, O.P. Delta Variant (B.1.617.2) of SARS-CoV-2: Mutations, Impact, Challenges and Possible Solutions. *Hum. Vaccines Immunother.* **2022**, *18*, 2068883. [CrossRef] [PubMed]
71. Novavax Investor Relations—Press Releases & Statements. Available online: https://ir.novavax.com/2021-01-28-Novavax-COVID-19-Vaccine-Demonstrates-89-3-Efficacy-in-UK-Phase-3-Trial (accessed on 8 January 2023).
72. SARS-CoV-2 Variant Classifications and Definitions, Available at SARS-CoV-2 Variant Classifications and Definitions (cdc.gov); accessed on 2 February 2023. 2 February.
73. Wang, P.; Liu, L.; Iketani, S.; Luo, Y.; Guo, Y.; Wang, M.; Yu, J.; Zhang, B.; Kwong, P.D.; Graham, B.S.; et al. Increased Resistance of SARS-CoV-2 Variants B.1.351 and B.1.1.7 to Antibody Neutralization. *bioRxiv* **2021**. [CrossRef]
74. Lu, L.; Mok, B.W.Y.; Chen, L.L.; Chan, J.M.C.; Tsang, O.T.Y.; Lam, B.H.S.; Chuang, V.W.M.; Chu, A.W.H.; Chan, W.M.; Ip, J.D.; et al. Neutralization of Severe Acute Respiratory Syndrome Coronavirus 2 Omicron Variant by Sera from BNT162b2 or CoronaVac Vaccine Recipients. *Clin. Infect. Dis.* **2022**, *75*, e822–e826. [CrossRef]
75. Ai, J.; Wang, X.; He, X.; Zhao, X.; Zhang, Y.; Jiang, Y.; Li, M.; Cui, Y.; Chen, Y.; Qiao, R.; et al. Antibody Evasion of SARS-CoV-2 Omicron BA.1, BA.1.1, BA.2, and BA.3 Sub-Lineages. *Cell Host Microbe* **2022**, *30*, 1077. [CrossRef]
76. Liu, J.; Chandrashekar, A.; Sellers, D.; Barrett, J.; Jacob-Dolan, C.; Lifton, M.; McMahan, K.; Sciacca, M.; VanWyk, H.; Wu, C.; et al. Vaccines Elicit Highly Conserved Cellular Immunity to SARS-CoV-2 Omicron. *Nature* **2022**, *603*, 493–496. [CrossRef]
77. Ella, R.; Reddy, S.; Blackwelder, W.; Potdar, V.; Yadav, P.; Sarangi, V.; Aileni, V.K.; Kanungo, S.; Rai, S.; Reddy, P.; et al. Efficacy, Safety, and Lot-to-Lot Immunogenicity of an Inactivated SARS-CoV-2 Vaccine (BBV152): Interim Results of a Randomised, Double-Blind, Controlled, Phase 3 Trial. *Lancet* **2021**, *398*, 2173–2184. [CrossRef]
78. Medigeshi, G.R.; Batra, G.; Murugesan, D.R.; Thiruvengadam, R.; Chattopadhyay, S.; Das, B.; Gosain, M.; Ayushi; Singh, J.; Anbalagan, A.; et al. Sub-Optimal Neutralisation of Omicron (B.1.1.529) Variant by Antibodies Induced by Vaccine Alone or SARS-CoV-2 Infection plus Vaccine (Hybrid Immunity) Post 6-Months. *eBioMedicine* **2022**, *78*, 103938. [CrossRef] [PubMed]
79. Lopez Bernal, J.; Andrews, N.; Gower, C.; Gallagher, E.; Simmons, R.; Thelwall, S.; Stowe, J.; Tessier, E.; Groves, N.; Dabrera, G.; et al. Effectiveness of COVID-19 Vaccines against the B.1.617.2 (Delta) Variant. *N. Engl. J. Med.* **2021**, *385*, 585–594. [CrossRef]
80. Hitchings, M.D.T.; Ranzani, O.T.; Dorion, M.; D'Agostini, T.L.; de Paula, R.C.; de Paula, O.F.P.; de Moura Villela, E.F.; Torres, M.S.S.; de Oliveira, S.B.; Schulz, W.; et al. Effectiveness of the ChAdOx1 Vaccine in the Elderly during SARS-CoV-2 Gamma Variant Transmission in Brazil. *medRxiv* **2021**. [CrossRef]
81. Hadj Hassine, I. COVID-19 Vaccines and Variants of Concern: A Review. *Rev. Med. Virol.* **2022**, *32*, e2313. [CrossRef]
82. Bian, L.; Gao, Q.; Gao, F.; Wang, Q.; He, Q.; Wu, X.; Mao, Q.; Xu, M.; Liang, Z. Impact of the Delta Variant on Vaccine Efficacy and Response Strategies. *Expert Rev. Vaccines* **2021**, *20*, 1201–1209. [CrossRef] [PubMed]
83. Nemet, I.; Kliker, L.; Lustig, Y.; Zuckerman, N.; Erster, O.; Cohen, C.; Kreiss, Y.; Alroy-Preis, S.; Regev-Yochay, G.; Mendelson, E.; et al. Third BNT162b2 Vaccination Neutralization of SARS-CoV-2 Omicron Infection. *N. Engl. J. Med.* **2022**, *386*, 492–494. [CrossRef] [PubMed]
84. Muik, A.; Wallisch, A.K.; Sänger, B.; Swanson, K.A.; Mühl, J.; Chen, W.; Cai, H.; Maurus, D.; Sarkar, R.; Türeci, Ö.; et al. Neutralization of SARS-CoV-2 Lineage B.1.1.7 Pseudovirus by BNT162b2 Vaccine–Elicited Human Sera. *Science* **2021**, *371*, 1152. [CrossRef]

85. Carreño, J.M.; Alshammary, H.; Tcheou, J.; Singh, G.; Raskin, A.J.; Kawabata, H.; Sominsky, L.A.; Clark, J.J.; Adelsberg, D.C.; Bielak, D.A.; et al. Activity of Convalescent and Vaccine Serum against SARS-CoV-2 Omicron. *Nature* **2022**, *602*, 682–688. [CrossRef]
86. Gao, Y.; Cai, C.; Grifoni, A.; Müller, T.R.; Niessl, J.; Olofsson, A.; Humbert, M.; Hansson, L.; Österborg, A.; Bergman, P.; et al. Ancestral SARS-CoV-2-Specific T Cells Cross-Recognize the Omicron Variant. *Nat. Med. 2022 283* **2022**, *28*, 472–476. [CrossRef]
87. Andrews, N.; Stowe, J.; Kirsebom, F.; Toffa, S.; Rickeard, T.; Gallagher, E.; Gower, C.; Kall, M.; Groves, N.; O'Connell, A.-M.; et al. COVID-19 Vaccine Effectiveness against the Omicron (B.1.1.529) Variant. *N. Engl. J. Med.* **2022**, *386*, 1532–1546. [CrossRef]
88. Tuekprakhon, A.; Nutalai, R.; Dijokaite-Guraliuc, A.; Zhou, D.; Ginn, H.M.; Selvaraj, M.; Liu, C.; Mentzer, A.J.; Supasa, P.; Duyvesteyn, H.M.E.; et al. Antibody Escape of SARS-CoV-2 Omicron BA.4 and BA.5 from Vaccine and BA.1 Serum. *Cell* **2022**, *185*, 2422–2433.e13. [CrossRef]
89. Nejat, R.; Torshizi, M.F.; Najafi, D.J. S Protein, ACE2 and Host Cell Proteases in SARS-CoV-2 Cell Entry and Infectivity; Is Soluble ACE2 a Two Blade Sword? A Narrative Review. *Vaccines* **2023**, *11*, 204. [CrossRef] [PubMed]
90. Chi, X.; Yan, R.; Zhang, J.; Zhang, G.; Zhang, Y.; Hao, M.; Zhang, Z.; Fan, P.; Dong, Y.; Yang, Y.; et al. A Neutralizing Human Antibody Binds to the N-Terminal Domain of the Spike Protein of SARS-CoV-2. *Science* **2020**, *369*, 650–655. [CrossRef] [PubMed]
91. Lu, G.; Wang, Q.; Gao, G.F. Bat-to-Human: Spike Features Determining "host Jump" of Coronaviruses SARS-CoV, MERS-CoV, and Beyond. *Trends Microbiol.* **2015**, *23*, 468–478. [CrossRef]
92. Li, F. Receptor Recognition Mechanisms of Coronaviruses: A Decade of Structural Studies. *J. Virol.* **2015**, *89*, 1954–1964. [CrossRef] [PubMed]
93. Paidi, R.K.; Jana, M.; Mishra, R.K.; Dutta, D.; Pahan, K. Selective Inhibition of the Interaction between SARS-CoV-2 Spike S1 and ACE2 by SPIDAR Peptide Induces Anti-Inflammatory Therapeutic Responses. *J. Immunol.* **2021**, *207*, 2521–2533. [CrossRef]
94. Cai, Y.; Zhang, J.; Xiao, T.; Peng, H.; Sterling, S.M.; Walsh, R.M.; Rawson, S.; Rits-Volloch, S.; Chen, B. Distinct Conformational States of SARS-CoV-2 Spike Protein. *Science (80-.)* **2020**, *369*, 1586–1592. [CrossRef]
95. Gao, G.F. Peptide Inhibitors Targeting Virus-Cell Fusion in Class I Enveloped Viruses. In *Combating the Threat of Pandemic Influenza: Drug Discovery Approaches*; Wiley: Hoboken, NJ, USA, 2007; pp. 226–246.
96. Pallesen, J.; Wang, N.; Corbett, K.S.; Wrapp, D.; Kirchdoerfer, R.N.; Turner, H.L.; Cottrell, C.A.; Becker, M.M.; Wang, L.; Shi, W.; et al. Immunogenicity and Structures of a Rationally Designed Prefusion MERS-CoV Spike Antigen. *Proc. Natl. Acad. Sci. USA* **2017**, *114*, E7348–E7357. [CrossRef]
97. Hsieh, C.L.; Goldsmith, J.A.; Schaub, J.M.; DiVenere, A.M.; Kuo, H.C.; Javanmardi, K.; Le, K.C.; Wrapp, D.; Lee, A.G.; Liu, Y.; et al. Structure-Based Design of Prefusion-Stabilized SARS-CoV-2 Spikes. *Science* **2020**, *369*, 1501–1505. [CrossRef]
98. Premkumar, L.; Segovia-Chumbez, B.; Jadi, R.; Martinez, D.R.; Raut, R.; Markmann, A.J.; Cornaby, C.; Bartelt, L.; Weiss, S.; Park, Y.; et al. The Receptor Binding Domain of the Viral Spike Protein Is an Immunodominant and Highly Specific Target of Antibodies in SARS-CoV-2 Patients. *Sci. Immunol.* **2020**, *5*, eabc8413. [CrossRef]
99. Wan, J.; Xing, S.; Ding, L.; Wang, Y.; Gu, C.; Wu, Y.; Rong, B.; Li, C.; Wang, S.; Chen, K.; et al. Human-IgG-Neutralizing Monoclonal Antibodies Block the SARS-CoV-2 Infection. *Cell Rep.* **2020**, *32*, 107918. [CrossRef] [PubMed]
100. Ju, B.; Zhang, Q.; Ge, J.; Wang, R.; Sun, J.; Ge, X.; Yu, J.; Shan, S.; Zhou, B.; Song, S.; et al. Human Neutralizing Antibodies Elicited by SARS-CoV-2 Infection. *Nat. 2020 5847819* **2020**, *584*, 115–119. [CrossRef]
101. Guo, Z.D.; Wang, Z.Y.; Zhang, S.F.; Li, X.; Li, L.; Li, C.; Cui, Y.; Fu, R.B.; Dong, Y.Z.; Chi, X.Y.; et al. Aerosol and Surface Distribution of Severe Acute Respiratory Syndrome Coronavirus 2 in Hospital Wards, Wuhan, China, 2020. *Emerg. Infect. Dis.* **2020**, *26*, 1586–1591. [CrossRef]
102. Barnes, C.O.; West, A.P.; Huey-Tubman, K.E.; Hoffmann, M.A.G.; Sharaf, N.G.; Hoffman, P.R.; Koranda, N.; Gristick, H.B.; Gaebler, C.; Muecksch, F.; et al. Structures of Human Antibodies Bound to SARS-CoV-2 Spike Reveal Common Epitopes and Recurrent Features of Antibodies. *Cell* **2020**, *182*, 828–842.e16. [CrossRef]
103. Cao, Y.; Su, B.; Guo, X.; Sun, W.; Deng, Y.; Bao, L.; Zhu, Q.; Zhang, X.; Zheng, Y.; Geng, C.; et al. Potent Neutralizing Antibodies against SARS-CoV-2 Identified by High-Throughput Single-Cell Sequencing of Convalescent Patients' B Cells. *Cell* **2020**, *182*, 73–84. [CrossRef]
104. Shi, R.; Shan, C.; Duan, X.; Chen, Z.; Liu, P.; Song, J.; Song, T.; Bi, X.; Han, C.; Wu, L.; et al. A Human Neutralizing Antibody Targets the Receptor-Binding Site of SARS-CoV-2. *Nat. 2020 5847819* **2020**, *584*, 120–124. [CrossRef] [PubMed]
105. Du, S.; Cao, Y.; Zhu, Q.; Yu, P.; Qi, F.; Wang, G.; Du, X.; Bao, L.; Deng, W.; Zhu, H.; et al. Structurally Resolved SARS-CoV-2 Antibody Shows High Efficacy in Severely Infected Hamsters and Provides a Potent Cocktail Pairing Strategy. *Cell* **2020**, *183*, 1013–1023.e13. [CrossRef]
106. Zost, S.J.; Gilchuk, P.; Case, J.B.; Binshtein, E.; Chen, R.E.; Nkolola, J.P.; Schäfer, A.; Reidy, J.X.; Trivette, A.; Nargi, R.S.; et al. Potently Neutralizing and Protective Human Antibodies against SARS-CoV-2. *Nature* **2020**, *584*, 443–449. [CrossRef] [PubMed]
107. Wu, Y.; Wang, F.; Shen, C.; Peng, W.; Li, D.; Zhao, C.; Li, Z.; Li, S.; Bi, Y.; Yang, Y.; et al. A Noncompeting Pair of Human Neutralizing Antibodies Block COVID-19 Virus Binding to Its Receptor ACE2. *Science* **2020**, *368*, 1274–1278. [CrossRef]
108. Brouwer, P.J.M.; Caniels, T.G.; van der Straten, K.; Snitselaar, J.L.; Aldon, Y.; Bangaru, S.; Torres, J.L.; Okba, N.M.A.; Claireaux, M.; Kerster, G.; et al. Potent Neutralizing Antibodies from COVID-19 Patients Define Multiple Targets of Vulnerability. *Science* **2020**, *369*, 643–650. [CrossRef]

109. Wec, A.Z.; Wrapp, D.; Herbert, A.S.; Maurer, D.P.; Haslwanter, D.; Sakharkar, M.; Jangra, R.K.; Eugenia Dieterle, M.; Lilov, A.; Huang, D.; et al. Broad Neutralization of SARS-Related Viruses by Human Monoclonal Antibodies. *Science* **2020**, *369*, 731–736. [CrossRef] [PubMed]
110. Rogers, T.F.; Zhao, F.; Huang, D.; Beutler, N.; Burns, A.; He, W.T.; Limbo, O.; Smith, C.; Song, G.; Woehl, J.; et al. Isolation of Potent SARS-CoV-2 Neutralizing Antibodies and Protection from Disease in a Small Animal Model. *Science* **2020**, *369*, 956–963. [CrossRef]
111. Hansen, J.; Baum, A.; Pascal, K.E.; Russo, V.; Giordano, S.; Wloga, E.; Fulton, B.O.; Yan, Y.; Koon, K.; Patel, K.; et al. Studies in Humanized Mice and Convalescent Humans Yield a SARS-CoV-2 Antibody Cocktail. *Science* **2020**, *369*, 1010–1014. [CrossRef] [PubMed]
112. Liu, L.; Wang, P.; Nair, M.S.; Yu, J.; Rapp, M.; Wang, Q.; Luo, Y.; Chan, J.F.W.; Sahi, V.; Figueroa, A.; et al. Potent Neutralizing Antibodies against Multiple Epitopes on SARS-CoV-2 Spike. *Nature* **2020**, *584*, 450–456. [CrossRef]
113. Weiss, R.C.; Scott, F.W. Antibody-Mediated Enhancement of Disease in Feline Infectious Peritonitis: Comparisons with Dengue Hemorrhagic Fever. *Comp. Immunol. Microbiol. Infect. Dis.* **1981**, *4*, 175–189. [CrossRef]
114. Su, S.; Du, L.; Jiang, S. Learning from the Past: Development of Safe and Effective COVID-19 Vaccines. *Nat. Rev. Microbiol.* **2020**, *19*, 211–219. [CrossRef] [PubMed]
115. Rey, F.A.; Stiasny, K.; Vaney, M.; Dellarole, M.; Heinz, F.X. The Bright and the Dark Side of Human Antibody Responses to Flaviviruses: Lessons for Vaccine Design. *EMBO Rep.* **2018**, *19*, 206–224. [CrossRef]
116. Hohdatsu, T.; Nakamura, M.; Ishizuka, Y.; Yamada, H.; Koyama, H. A Study on the Mechanism of Antibody-Dependent Enhancement of Feline Infectious Peritonitis Virus Infection in Feline Macrophages by Monoclonal Antibodies. *Arch. Virol.* **1991**, *120*, 207. [CrossRef]
117. Wang, Q.; Zhang, L.; Kuwahara, K.; Li, L.; Liu, Z.; Li, T.; Zhu, H.; Liu, J.; Xu, Y.; Xie, J.; et al. Immunodominant SARS Coronavirus Epitopes in Humans Elicited Both Enhancing and Neutralizing Effects on Infection in Non-Human Primates. *ACS Infect. Dis.* **2016**, *2*, 361–376. [CrossRef]
118. Zhang, N.N.; Li, X.F.; Deng, Y.Q.; Zhao, H.; Huang, Y.J.; Yang, G.; Huang, W.J.; Gao, P.; Zhou, C.; Zhang, R.R.; et al. A Thermostable MRNA Vaccine against COVID-19. *Cell* **2020**, *182*, 1271–1283.e16. [CrossRef]
119. Yang, J.; Wang, W.; Chen, Z.; Lu, S.; Yang, F.; Bi, Z.; Bao, L.; Mo, F.; Li, X.; Huang, Y.; et al. A Vaccine Targeting the RBD of the S Protein of SARS-CoV-2 Induces Protective Immunity. *Nature* **2020**, *586*, 572–577. [CrossRef]
120. Zhou, M.; Xu, D.; Li, X.; Li, H.; Shan, M.; Tang, J.; Wang, M.; Wang, F.-S.; Zhu, X.; Tao, H.; et al. Screening and Identification of Severe Acute Respiratory Syndrome-Associated Coronavirus-Specific CTL Epitopes. *J. Immunol.* **2006**, *177*, 2138–2145. [CrossRef] [PubMed]
121. Jiang, S.; Bottazzi, M.E.; Du, L.; Lustigman, S.; Tseng, C.T.K.; Curti, E.; Jones, K.; Zhan, B.; Hotez, P.J. Roadmap to Developing a Recombinant Coronavirus S Protein Receptor-Binding Domain Vaccine for Severe Acute Respiratory Syndrome. *Expert Rev. Vaccines* **2012**, *11*, 1405–1413. [CrossRef]
122. Wang, C.B. [Analysis of Low Positive Rate of Nucleic Acid Detection Method Used for Diagnosis of Novel Coronavirus Pneumonia]. *Zhonghua Yi Xue Za Zhi* **2020**, *100*, 961–964. [CrossRef] [PubMed]
123. Zhou, Y.; Yang, Y.; Huang, J.; Jiang, S.; Du, L. Advances in MERS-CoV Vaccines and Therapeutics Based on the Receptor-Binding Domain. *Viruses* **2019**, *11*, 60. [CrossRef] [PubMed]
124. Gu, H.; Chen, Q.; Yang, G.; He, L.; Fan, H.; Deng, Y.Q.; Wang, Y.; Teng, Y.; Zhao, Z.; Cui, Y.; et al. Adaptation of SARS-CoV-2 in BALB/c Mice for Testing Vaccine Efficacy. *Science* **2020**, *369*, 1603–1607. [CrossRef]
125. Du, L.; Zhao, G.; He, Y.; Guo, Y.; Zheng, B.J.; Jiang, S.; Zhou, Y. Receptor-Binding Domain of SARS-CoV Spike Protein Induces Long-Term Protective Immunity in an Animal Model. *Vaccine* **2007**, *25*, 2832–2838. [CrossRef]
126. Du, L.; Kou, Z.; Ma, C.; Tao, X.; Wang, L.; Zhao, G.; Chen, Y.; Yu, F.; Tseng, C.T.K.; Zhou, Y.; et al. A Truncated Receptor-Binding Domain of MERS-CoV Spike Protein Potently Inhibits MERS-CoV Infection and Induces Strong Neutralizing Antibody Responses: Implication for Developing Therapeutics and Vaccines. *PLoS ONE* **2013**, *8*, e0278474. [CrossRef]
127. Ma, C.; Wang, L.; Tao, X.; Zhang, N.; Yang, Y.; Tseng, C.T.K.; Li, F.; Zhou, Y.; Jiang, S.; Du, L. Searching for an Ideal Vaccine Candidate among Different MERS Coronavirus Receptor-Binding Fragments–the Importance of Immunofocusing in Subunit Vaccine Design. *Vaccine* **2014**, *32*, 6170–6176. [CrossRef]
128. He, Y.; Zhou, Y.; Liu, S.; Kou, Z.; Li, W.; Farzan, M.; Jiang, S. Receptor-Binding Domain of SARS-CoV Spike Protein Induces Highly Potent Neutralizing Antibodies: Implication for Developing Subunit Vaccine. *Biochem. Biophys. Res. Commun.* **2004**, *324*, 773–781. [CrossRef]
129. Wang, C.; Zheng, X.; Gai, W.; Wong, G.; Wang, H.; Jin, H.; Feng, N.; Zhao, Y.; Zhang, W.; Li, N.; et al. Novel Chimeric Virus-like Particles Vaccine Displaying MERS-CoV Receptor-Binding Domain Induce Specific Humoral and Cellular Immune Response in Mice. *Antiviral Res.* **2017**, *140*, 55–61. [CrossRef] [PubMed]
130. Kim, Y.S.; Son, A.; Kim, J.; Kwon, S.B.; Kim, M.H.; Kim, P.; Kim, J.; Byun, Y.H.; Sung, J.; Lee, J.; et al. Chaperna-Mediated Assembly of Ferritin-Based Middle East Respiratory Syndrome-Coronavirus Nanoparticles. *Front. Immunol.* **2018**, *9*, 1093. [CrossRef]
131. Walls, A.C.; Fiala, B.; Schäfer, A.; Wrenn, S.; Pham, M.N.; Murphy, M.; Tse, L.V.; Shehata, L.; O'Connor, M.A.; Chen, C.; et al. Elicitation of Potent Neutralizing Antibody Responses by Designed Protein Nanoparticle Vaccines for SARS-CoV-2. *Cell* **2020**, *183*, 1367–1382.e17. [CrossRef] [PubMed]

132. Dai, L.; Zheng, T.; Xu, K.; Han, Y.; Xu, L.; Huang, E.; An, Y.; Cheng, Y.; Li, S.; Liu, M.; et al. A Universal Design of Betacoronavirus Vaccines against COVID-19, MERS, and SARS. *Cell* **2020**, *182*, 722–733.e11. [CrossRef]
133. Hwang, W.C.; Lin, Y.; Santelli, E.; Sui, J.; Jaroszewski, L.; Stec, B.; Farzan, M.; Marasco, W.A.; Liddington, R.C. Structural Basis of Neutralization by a Human Anti-Severe Acute Respiratory Syndrome Spike Protein Antibody, 80R. *J. Biol. Chem.* **2006**, *281*, 34610–34616. [CrossRef] [PubMed]
134. Lan, J.; Ge, J.; Yu, J.; Shan, S.; Zhou, H.; Fan, S.; Zhang, Q.; Shi, X.; Wang, Q.; Zhang, L.; et al. Structure of the SARS-CoV-2 Spike Receptor-Binding Domain Bound to the ACE2 Receptor. *Nature* **2020**, *581*, 215–220. [CrossRef] [PubMed]
135. Zhang, S.; Zhou, P.; Wang, P.; Li, Y.; Jiang, L.; Jia, W.; Wang, H.; Fan, A.; Wang, D.; Shi, X.; et al. Structural Definition of a Unique Neutralization Epitope on the Receptor-Binding Domain of MERS-CoV Spike Glycoprotein. *Cell Rep.* **2018**, *24*, 441–452. [CrossRef]
136. Xiao, X.; Feng, Y.; Chakraborti, S.; Dimitrov, D.S. Oligomerization of the SARS-CoV S Glycoprotein: Dimerization of the N-Terminus and Trimerization of the Ectodomain. *Biochem. Biophys. Res. Commun.* **2004**, *322*, 93–99. [CrossRef]
137. Dai, L.; Gao, G.F. Viral Targets for Vaccines against COVID-19. *Nat. Rev. Immunol. 2020 212* **2020**, *21*, 73–82. [CrossRef] [PubMed]
138. Wang, N.; Rosen, O.; Wang, L.; Turner, H.L.; Stevens, L.J.; Corbett, K.S.; Bowman, C.A.; Pallesen, J.; Shi, W.; Zhang, Y.; et al. Structural Definition of a Neutralization-Sensitive Epitope on the MERS-CoV S1-NTD. *Cell Rep.* **2019**, *28*, 3395–3405.e6. [CrossRef]
139. Zhou, H.; Chen, Y.; Zhang, S.; Niu, P.; Qin, K.; Jia, W.; Huang, B.; Zhang, S.; Lan, J.; Zhang, L.; et al. Structural Definition of a Neutralization Epitope on the N-Terminal Domain of MERS-CoV Spike Glycoprotein. *Nat. Commun.* **2019**, *10*, 3068. [CrossRef]
140. Jiaming, L.; Yanfeng, Y.; Yao, D.; Yawei, H.; Linlin, B.; Baoying, H.; Jinghua, Y.; Gao, G.F.; Chuan, Q.; Wenjie, T. The Recombinant N-Terminal Domain of Spike Proteins Is a Potential Vaccine against Middle East Respiratory Syndrome Coronavirus (MERS-CoV) Infection. *Vaccine* **2017**, *35*, 10–18. [CrossRef]
141. Huang, Y.; Yang, C.; Xu, X.F.; Xu, W.; Liu, S. wen Structural and Functional Properties of SARS-CoV-2 Spike Protein: Potential Antivirus Drug Development for COVID-19. *Acta Pharmacol. Sin.* **2020**, *41*, 1141–1149. [CrossRef]
142. Song, G.; He, W.; Callaghan, S.; Anzanello, F.; Huang, D.; Ricketts, J.; Torres, J.L.; Beutler, N.; Peng, L.; Vargas, S.; et al. Cross-Reactive Serum and Memory B Cell Responses to Spike Protein in SARS-CoV-2 and Endemic Coronavirus Infection. *bioRxiv* **2020**. [CrossRef] [PubMed]
143. Ng, K.W.; Faulkner, N.; Cornish, G.H.; Rosa, A.; Harvey, R.; Hussain, S.; Ulferts, R.; Earl, C.; Wrobel, A.G.; Benton, D.J.; et al. Preexisting and de Novo Humoral Immunity to SARS-CoV-2 in Humans. *Science* **2020**, *370*, 1339–1343. [CrossRef] [PubMed]
144. Watanabe, Y.; Allen, J.D.; Wrapp, D.; McLellan, J.S.; Crispin, M. Site-Specific Glycan Analysis of the SARS-CoV-2 Spike. *Science* **2020**, *369*, 330–333. [CrossRef] [PubMed]
145. Ravichandran, S.; Coyle, E.M.; Klenow, L.; Tang, J.; Grubbs, G.; Liu, S.; Wang, T.; Golding, H.; Khurana, S. Antibody Signature Induced by SARS-CoV-2 Spike Protein Immunogens in Rabbits. *Sci. Transl. Med.* **2020**, *12*, eabc3539. [CrossRef]
146. Walls, A.C.; Park, Y.J.; Tortorici, M.A.; Wall, A.; McGuire, A.T.; Veesler, D. Structure, Function, and Antigenicity of the SARS-CoV-2 Spike Glycoprotein. *Cell* **2020**, *181*, 281–292.e6. [CrossRef]
147. Jeyanathan, M.; Afkhami, S.; Smaill, F.; Miller, M.S.; Lichty, B.D.; Xing, Z. Immunological Considerations for COVID-19 Vaccine Strategies. *Nat. Rev. Immunol. 2020 2010* **2020**, *20*, 615–632. [CrossRef]
148. Braun, J.; Loyal, L.; Frentsch, M.; Wendisch, D.; Georg, P.; Kurth, F.; Hippenstiel, S.; Dingeldey, M.; Kruse, B.; Fauchere, F.; et al. SARS-CoV-2-Reactive T Cells in Healthy Donors and Patients with COVID-19. *Nature* **2020**, *587*, 270–274. [CrossRef]
149. Du, L.; He, Y.; Jiang, S.; Zheng, B.J. Development of Subunit Vaccines against Severe Acute Respiratory Syndrome. *Drugs Today* **2008**, *44*, 63–73. [CrossRef]
150. Liu, W.J.; Zhao, M.; Liu, K.; Xu, K.; Wong, G.; Tan, W.; Gao, G.F. T-Cell Immunity of SARS-CoV: Implications for Vaccine Development against MERS-CoV. *Antiviral Res.* **2017**, *137*, 82. [CrossRef]
151. Sariol, A.; Perlman, S. Lessons for COVID-19 Immunity from Other Coronavirus Infections. *Immunity* **2020**, *53*, 248. [CrossRef]
152. Nakanaga, K.; Yamanouchi, K.; Fujiwara, K. Protective Effect of Monoclonal Antibodies on Lethal Mouse Hepatitis Virus Infection in Mice. *J. Virol.* **1986**, *59*, 168. [CrossRef]
153. Lecomte, J.; Cainelli-Gebara, V.; Mercier, G.; Mansour, S.; Talbot, P.J.; Lussier, G.; Oth, D. Protection from Mouse Hepatitis Virus Type 3-Induced Acute Disease by an Anti-Nucleoprotein Monoclonal Antibody. *Arch. Virol.* **1987**, *97*, 123. [CrossRef] [PubMed]
154. Liu, S.J.; Leng, C.H.; Lien, S.P.; Chi, H.Y.; Huang, C.Y.; Lin, C.L.; Lian, W.C.; Chen, C.J.; Hsieh, S.L.; Chong, P. Immunological Characterizations of the Nucleocapsid Protein Based SARS Vaccine Candidates. *Vaccine* **2006**, *24*, 3100. [CrossRef] [PubMed]
155. Collisson, E.W.; Pei, J.; Dzielawa, J.; Seo, S.H. Cytotoxic T Lymphocytes Are Critical in the Control of Infectious Bronchitis Virus in Poultry. *Dev. Comp. Immunol.* **2000**, *24*, 187–200. [CrossRef] [PubMed]
156. Zhao, J.; Zhao, J.; Mangalam, A.K.; Channappanavar, R.; Fett, C.; Meyerholz, D.K.; Agnihothram, S.; Baric, R.S.; David, C.S.; Perlman, S. Airway Memory CD4+ T Cells Mediate Protective Immunity against Emerging Respiratory Coronaviruses. *Immunity* **2016**, *44*, 1379. [CrossRef]
157. Deming, D.; Sheahan, T.; Heise, M.; Yount, B.; Davis, N.; Sims, A.; Suthar, M.; Harkema, J.; Whitmore, A.; Pickles, R.; et al. Vaccine Efficacy in Senescent Mice Challenged with Recombinant SARS-CoV Bearing Epidemic and Zoonotic Spike Variants. *PLoS Med.* **2006**, *3*, 2359–2375. [CrossRef] [PubMed]
158. Yasui, F.; Kai, C.; Kitabatake, M.; Inoue, S.; Yoneda, M.; Yokochi, S.; Kase, R.; Sekiguchi, S.; Morita, K.; Hishima, T.; et al. Prior Immunization with Severe Acute Respiratory Syndrome (SARS)-Associated Coronavirus (SARS-CoV) Nucleocapsid Protein Causes Severe Pneumonia in Mice Infected with SARS-CoV. *J. Immunol.* **2008**, *181*, 6337–6348. [CrossRef]

159. Kyriakidis, N.C.; López-Cortés, A.; González, E.V.; Grimaldos, A.B.; Prado, E.O. SARS-CoV-2 Vaccines Strategies: A Comprehensive Review of Phase 3 Candidates. *Npj Vaccines* **2021**, *6*, 28. [CrossRef] [PubMed]
160. Sanders, B.; Koldijk, M.; Schuitemaker, H. Inactivated Viral Vaccines. In *Vaccine Analysis: Strategies, Principles, and Control*; Springer: Berlin/Heidelberg, Germany, 2015; pp. 45–80. [CrossRef]
161. Sadeghalvad, M.; Mansourabadi, A.H.; Noori, M.; Nejadghaderi, S.A.; Masoomikarimi, M.; Alimohammadi, M.; Rezaei, N. Recent Developments in SARS-CoV-2 Vaccines: A Systematic Review of the Current Studies. *Rev. Med. Virol.* **2023**, *33*, e2359. [CrossRef] [PubMed]
162. Pardi, N.; Hogan, M.J.; Porter, F.W.; Weissman, D. MRNA Vaccines—A New Era in Vaccinology. *Nat. Rev. Drug Discov.* **2018**, *17*, 261–279. [CrossRef]
163. Bezbaruah, R.; Chavda, V.P.; Nongrang, L.; Alom, S.; Deka, K.; Kalita, T.; Ali, F.; Bhattacharjee, B.; Vora, L. Nanoparticle-Based Delivery Systems for Vaccines. *Vaccines* **2022**, *10*, 1946. [CrossRef] [PubMed]
164. Donaldson, B.; Lateef, Z.; Walker, G.F.; Young, S.L.; Ward, V.K. Virus-like Particle Vaccines: Immunology and Formulation for Clinical Translation. *Expert Rev. Vaccines* **2018**, *17*, 833. [CrossRef]
165. Ma, J.; Su, D.; Huang, X.; Liang, Y.; Ma, Y.; Liang, P.; Zheng, S. Cryo-EM Structure of S-Trimer, a Subunit Vaccine Candidate for COVID-19. *bioRxiv* **2020**. [CrossRef]
166. Mercado, N.B.; Zahn, R.; Wegmann, F.; Loos, C.; Chandrashekar, A.; Yu, J.; Liu, J.; Peter, L.; McMahan, K.; Tostanoski, L.H.; et al. Single-Shot Ad26 Vaccine Protects against SARS-CoV-2 in Rhesus Macaques. *Nature* **2020**, *586*, 583–588. [CrossRef] [PubMed]
167. Pfizer and BioNTech Announce Vaccine Candidate Against COVID-19 Achieved Success in First Interim Analysis from Phase 3 Study | Pfizer. Available online: https://www.pfizer.com/news/press-release/press-release-detail/pfizer-and-biontech-announce-vaccine-candidate-against (accessed on 11 January 2023).
168. Thiagarajan, K. What Do We Know about India's Covaxin Vaccine? *BMJ* **2021**, *373*, n997. [CrossRef]
169. Safety and Immunogenicity of an Intranasal SARS-CoV-2 Vaccine (BBV154) for COVID-19—Full Text View—ClinicalTrials.Gov. Available online: https://clinicaltrials.gov/ct2/show/NCT04751682 (accessed on 11 January 2023).
170. INCOVACC—Intranasal Vaccine for COVID-19 | Bharat Biotech. Available online: https://www.bharatbiotech.com/intranasal-vaccine.html (accessed on 11 January 2023).
171. Hacisuleyman, E.; Hale, C.; Saito, Y.; Blachere, N.E.; Bergh, M.; Conlon, E.G.; Schaefer-Babajew, D.J.; DaSilva, J.; Muecksch, F.; Gaebler, C.; et al. Vaccine Breakthrough Infections with SARS-CoV-2 Variants. *N. Engl. J. Med.* **2021**, *384*, 2212–2218. [CrossRef] [PubMed]
172. Sapkal, G.N.; Yadav, P.D.; Ella, R.; Deshpande, G.R.; Sahay, R.R.; Gupta, N.; Vadrevu, K.M.; Abraham, P.; Panda, S.; Bhargava, B. Inactivated COVID-19 Vaccine BBV152/COVAXIN Effectively Neutralizes Recently Emerged B 1.1.7 Variant of SARS-CoV-2. *J. Travel Med.* **2021**, *28*, taab051. [CrossRef]
173. Abu-Raddad, L.J.; Chemaitelly, H.; Ayoub, H.H.; Yassine, H.M.; Benslimane, F.M.; Al Khatib, H.A.; Tang, P.; Hasan, M.R.; Coyle, P.; Al Kanaani, Z.; et al. Association of Prior SARS-CoV-2 Infection with Risk of Breakthrough Infection Following MRNA Vaccination in Qatar. *JAMA* **2021**, *326*, 1930–1939. [CrossRef]
174. Abu-Raddad, L.J.; Chemaitelly, H.; Bertollini, R. Effectiveness of MRNA-1273 and BNT162b2 Vaccines in Qatar. *N. Engl. J. Med.* **2022**, *386*, 799–800. [CrossRef] [PubMed]
175. Rotshild, V.; Hirsh-Raccah, B.; Miskin, I.; Muszkat, M.; Matok, I. Comparing the Clinical Efficacy of COVID-19 Vaccines: A Systematic Review and Network Meta-Analysis. *Sci. Rep.* **2021**, *11*, 22777. [CrossRef] [PubMed]
176. Chemaitelly, H.; Tang, P.; Hasan, M.R.; AlMukdad, S.; Yassine, H.M.; Benslimane, F.M.; Khatib, H.A.A.; Coyle, P.; Ayoub, H.H.; Al Kanaani, Z.; et al. Waning of BNT162b2 Vaccine Protection against SARS-CoV-2 Infection in Qatar. *N. Engl. J. Med.* **2021**, *385*, e83. [CrossRef] [PubMed]
177. Dickerman, B.A.; Gerlovin, H.; Madenci, A.L.; Kurgansky, K.E.; Ferolito, B.R.; Muñiz, M.J.F.; Gagnon, D.R.; Gaziano, J.M.; Cho, K.; Casas, J.P.; et al. Comparative Effectiveness of BNT162b2 and MRNA-1273 Vaccines in U.S. Veterans. *N. Engl. J. Med.* **2022**, *386*, 105–115. [CrossRef]
178. Tang, P.; Hasan, M.R.; Chemaitelly, H.; Yassine, H.M.; Benslimane, F.M.; Al Khatib, H.A.; AlMukdad, S.; Coyle, P.; Ayoub, H.H.; Al Kanaani, Z.; et al. BNT162b2 and MRNA-1273 COVID-19 Vaccine Effectiveness against the Delta (B.1.617.2) Variant in Qatar. *medRxiv* **2021**. [CrossRef]
179. Puranik, A.; Lenehan, P.J.; Silvert, E.; Niesen, M.J.M.; Corchado-Garcia, J.; O'Horo, J.C.; Virk, A.; Swift, M.D.; Gordon, J.E.; Speicher, L.L.; et al. Comparative Effectiveness of MRNA-1273 and BNT162b2 against Symptomatic SARS-CoV-2 Infection. *Med* **2022**, *3*, 28. [CrossRef]
180. Khoury, D.S.; Cromer, D.; Reynaldi, A.; Schlub, T.E.; Wheatley, A.K.; Juno, J.A.; Subbarao, K.; Kent, S.J.; Triccas, J.A.; Davenport, M.P. Neutralizing Antibody Levels Are Highly Predictive of Immune Protection from Symptomatic SARS-CoV-2 Infection. *Nat. Med. 2021 277* **2021**, *27*, 1205–1211. [CrossRef]
181. Chavda, V.P.; Jogi, G.; Dave, S.; Patel, B.M.; Nalla, L.V.; Koradia, K. MRNA-Based Vaccine for COVID-19: They Are New but Not Unknown! *Vaccines* **2023**, *11*, 507. [CrossRef]
182. Pereira De Sousa, F.; Valente, J.; Gao, Y.; Liu, X.; Chen, N.; Yang, X.; Tang, F. Recent Advance of Liposome Nanoparticles for Nucleic Acid Therapy. *Pharmaceutics* **2023**, *15*, 178. [CrossRef]
183. CountryWatch Global Coronavirus Alert. Available online: https://www.countrywatch.com/home/coronavirus (accessed on 13 January 2023).

184. Cascella, M.; Rajnik, M.; Cuomo, A.; Dulebohn, S.C.; Di Napoli, R. *Features, Evaluation, and Treatment of Coronavirus (COVID-19)*; StatPearls: Tampa, FL, USA, 2022.
185. Sapkal, G.; Yadav, P.D.; Ella, R.; Abraham, P.; Patil, D.Y.; Gupta, N.; Panda, S.; Mohan, V.K.; Bhargava, B. Neutralization of VUI B.1.1.28 P2 Variant with Sera of COVID-19 Recovered Cases and Recipients of Covaxin an Inactivated COVID-19 Vaccine. *J. Travel Med.* **2021**, *28*, taab077. [CrossRef] [PubMed]
186. Padron-Regalado, E. Vaccines for SARS-CoV-2: Lessons from Other Coronavirus Strains. *Infect. Dis. Ther.* **2020**, *9*, 255. [CrossRef] [PubMed]

Disclaimer/Publisher's Note: The statements, opinions and data contained in all publications are solely those of the individual author(s) and contributor(s) and not of MDPI and/or the editor(s). MDPI and/or the editor(s) disclaim responsibility for any injury to people or property resulting from any ideas, methods, instructions or products referred to in the content.

medicina

MDPI

Systematic Review

The Impact of Therapeutic Plasma Exchange on Inflammatory Markers and Acute Phase Reactants in Patients with Severe SARS-CoV-2 Infection

Tamara Mirela Porosnicu [1,2], Ioan Ovidiu Sirbu [3], Cristian Oancea [4], Dorel Sandesc [5], Felix Bratosin [6], Ovidiu Rosca [6], Daniel Jipa [2], Estera Boeriu [7,*], Satya Sai Sri Bandi [8] and Marius Pricop [9]

1 Doctoral School, "Victor Babes" University of Medicine and Pharmacy Timisoara, Eftimie Murgu Square 2, 300041 Timisoara, Romania
2 Intensive Care Unit, "Pius Brinzeu" Emergency Clinical County Hospital, 300723 Timisoara, Romania
3 Center for Complex Network Sciences, "Victor Babes" University of Medicine and Pharmacy Timisoara, Eftimie Murgu Square 2, 300041 Timisoara, Romania
4 Center for Research and Innovation in Precision Medicine of Respiratory Disease, "Victor Babes" University of Medicine and Pharmacy Timisoara, Eftimie Murgu Square 2, 300041 Timisoara, Romania
5 Department of Anesthesia and Intensive Care, "Victor Babes" University of Medicine and Pharmacy Timisoara, Eftimie Murgu Square 2, 300041 Timisoara, Romania
6 Department XIII, Discipline of Infectious Disease, "Victor Babes" University of Medicine and Pharmacy Timisoara, Eftimie Murgu Square 2, 300041 Timisoara, Romania
7 Department of Pediatrics, Discipline of Pediatric Oncology and Hematology, "Victor Babes" University of Medicine and Pharmacy Timisoara, Eftimie Murgu Square 2, 300041 Timisoara, Romania
8 Malla Reddy Institute of Medical Sciences, Suraram Main Road 138, Hyderabad 500055, India
9 Discipline of Oral and Maxillo-Facial Surgery, Faculty of Dental Medicine, "Victor Babes" University of Medicine and Pharmacy Timisoara, Eftimie Murgu Square 2, 300041 Timisoara, Romania
* Correspondence: estera.boeriu@umft.ro

Citation: Porosnicu, T.M.; Sirbu, I.O.; Oancea, C.; Sandesc, D.; Bratosin, F.; Rosca, O.; Jipa, D.; Boeriu, E.; Bandi, S.S.S.; Pricop, M. The Impact of Therapeutic Plasma Exchange on Inflammatory Markers and Acute Phase Reactants in Patients with Severe SARS-CoV-2 Infection. *Medicina* **2023**, *59*, 867. https://doi.org/10.3390/medicina59050867

Academic Editors: Yusra Habib Khan, Tauqeer Hussain Mallhi, Tahir Mehmood Khan and Muhammad Salman

Received: 19 January 2023
Revised: 21 April 2023
Accepted: 27 April 2023
Published: 29 April 2023

Copyright: © 2023 by the authors. Licensee MDPI, Basel, Switzerland. This article is an open access article distributed under the terms and conditions of the Creative Commons Attribution (CC BY) license (https://creativecommons.org/licenses/by/4.0/).

Abstract: *Background and Objectives:* Due to the poor prognosis and the very high mortality rate associated with severe SARS-CoV-2 infections, various regimens have been tried to stop the evolution of the inflammatory cascade, such as immunomodulatory therapy and plasma clearance of the acute phase reactants involved. Therefore, the objective of this review was to analyze the effects of using therapeutic plasma exchange (TPE), also known as plasmapheresis, on the inflammatory markers of critically ill COVID-19 patients admitted to the intensive care unit (ICU). *Materials and Methods:* A thorough scientific database search was performed, and it included a review of articles published on PubMed, Cochrane Database, Scopus, and Web of Science from the beginning of the COVID-19 pandemic in March 2020 until September 2022 that focused on the treatment of SARS-CoV-2 infections using plasma exchange for patients admitted to the ICU. The current study included original articles, reviews, editorials, and short or special communications regarding the topic of interest. *Results:* A total of 13 articles were selected after satisfying the inclusion criterion of three or more patients enrolled with clinically severe COVID-19 that were eligible for TPE. From the included articles, it was observed that TPE was used as a last-resort salvage therapy that can be regarded as an alternative treatment method when the standard management for these patients fails. TPE significantly decreased the inflammatory status as measured by Interleukin-6 (IL-6), C-reactive protein (CRP), lymphocyte count, and D-dimers, as well as improving the clinical status measured with PaO_2/FiO_2 and duration of hospitalization. The pooled mortality risk reduction after TPE was 20%. *Conclusions:* There are sufficient studies and evidence to show that TPE reduces inflammatory mediators and improves coagulation function and the clinical/paraclinical status. Nevertheless, although it was shown that TPE decreases the severe inflammatory status without significant complications, the improvement of survival rate remains unclear.

Keywords: inflammatory markers; therapeutic plasma exchange; plasmapheresis; SARS-CoV-2; COVID-19

1. Introduction

The new coronavirus SARS-CoV-2, unlike the other two viruses, MERS (Middle East respiratory syndrome) and SARS (severe acute respiratory syndrome), was a real challenge for the entire global health system due to the many cases that required hospitalization in a short period of time, causing a global crisis in the health system [1–5]. Regarding biological inflammatory markers, increased values of lactate dehydrogenase (LDH), ferritin, fibrinogen, interleukin-6 (IL-6), C reactive protein, D-dimers, and a reduced number of lymphocytes were described in multiple studies [6,7]. Many of the abnormalities identified in hospitalized cases were caused by a "cytokine storm", characterized by an exaggerated host response to the virus with similar characteristics to bacterial septic shock and negative fulminant evolution that is usually fatal. In other words, the leading causes of death in patients with COVID-19 infection are ARDS and cytokine storm syndrome, which lead to multisystemic organ failure [8,9].

Depending on a population's features and its associated risk factors, the mortality rate of severe COVID-19 cases continues to be significant. Despite the fact that several potentially useful therapeutic approaches have been investigated and tried, only a few of them have been shown to be successful, and only in particular circumstances [10,11]. For example, therapeutic plasma exchange (TPE), or plasmapheresis, is a medical procedure in which the patient's plasma is removed from the morphotic components of their blood and then replaced with either an albumin solution or fresh frozen plasma (FFP) [12]. The primary objective of TPE is the removal of morbid components, such as pathogenic antibodies and inflammatory proteins [13,14].

Because a cytokine storm-mediated immune response is what causes organ damage, it stands to reason that removing damaging antibodies and cytokines might reduce the severity of the illness. The use of TPE in COVID-19 patients is based on the rationale that by removing the excess of proinflammatory cytokines, such as IL-6, tumor necrosis factor-alpha (TNF-α), and interleukin-1β (IL-1β), TPE can attenuate the cytokine storm and prevent the subsequent multiorgan failure and acute respiratory distress syndrome (ARDS) that are often observed in severe cases. The elimination of other fibrin breakdown products, such as D-dimers, might also contribute to an improvement in the hemostatic equilibrium [15,16]. In light of these considerations, TPE has lately been brought up as a potential supportive therapy option for severe SARS-CoV-2 infections.

However, despite the growing interest in TPE as a potential therapy for severe COVID-19, the impact of TPE on the inflammatory markers and acute phase reactants in patients with SARS-CoV-2 infection remains inadequately studied. Therefore, the objective of this systematic review was to present the role of plasma exchange therapy in lowering inflammation markers and acute phase reactants in critically ill COVID-19 patients and finding the optimal treatment protocol to improve patients' survival.

2. Materials and Methods

2.1. Study Design and Search Protocol

All relevant scientific papers discussing the use of TPE in severe SARS-CoV-2 infection were included in the analysis by using a structured and methodical search approach, which was carried out in accordance with the PRISMA criteria and PROSPERO guidelines [17]. The current systematic review was registered to the Open-Science Framework (OSF) platform. The search period was considered from the beginning of the COVID-19 pandemic in January 2020 until September 2022, focusing on the epidemiology, pathogenesis, diagnosis, COVID-19 treatment management, and immunopathology of the inflammatory markers in association with our topic of interest.

Reference lists from the retrieved articles were manually examined for relevant information. PubMed, Cochrane Database, Scopus, and Web of Science were filtered using specific keywords, including {COVID-19}, {SARS-COV-2}, {severe inflammation}, {C-reactive protein}, {plasmapheresis}, {therapeutic plasma exchange}, {cytokine storm}, and {fibrinogen}. We used a combination of the following keywords: "therapeutic plasma exchange + COVID-19 + cytokine storm"; "plasmapheresis + COVID-19 + Cytokine storm"; "therapeutic plasma exchange + COVID-19 + critical care"; "therapeutic plasma exchange + COVID-19 + ICU".

In this systematic review, our primary objectives were to address two key questions related to the management of severe SARS-CoV-2 infection. First, we sought to determine the optimal treatment protocol for utilizing Therapeutic Plasma Exchange (TPE) in patients with severe COVID-19. Second, we aimed to identify the inflammatory markers that are most commonly influenced by the use of TPE in this patient population.

2.2. Inclusion and Exclusion Criteria

The inclusion criteria comprised the following: (1) original studies, reviews, editorials, case series with three or more patients, and short or special communications that focused on the management of severe SARS-CoV-2 infection; (2) hospitalized patients with SARS-CoV-2 infection older than 18 years; (3) having a positive polymerase chain reaction (PCR) for SARS-CoV-2 infection; (4) use of a controlled design for the administration of TPE.

The exclusion criteria comprised the following: (1) studies involving animal experiments; (2) publications that were not written in English; (3) case reports; (4) duplicate studies. The selected studies were evaluated by two different investigators independently, and complete texts were obtained only if both of them decided that the paper should be included. A third researcher was involved in case of divergent opinions.

2.3. Data Extraction and Quality Assessment

For the purpose of our analysis, we retrieved the following information from the studies that were included: authors, year of publication, type of study, patient characteristics, concomitant therapies, time of TPE initiation and cessation, dose of TPE, type of replacement fluids, adverse effects associated with TPE, inflammatory markers, and outcomes.

All information was gathered from the articles' text, tables, figures, and online supplemental resources. The selection procedure comprised the elimination of duplicate entries, abstract screening, and full-text screening. Initial results from the search returned 242 matching entries, of which 31 were duplicates. Figure 1 shows that 13 reports were included in the systematic review after abstract and title screening eliminated 177 studies, whereas full-text reading eliminated 23 studies.

Following the NHLBI-published Study Quality Assessment Tools, two researchers evaluated information from existing articles and reported results individually. The tools are unique to research designs and screen for any methodological or operational problems. The Quality Assessment Tool for Observational Cohort and Cross-Sectional Investigations was used for the remaining studies [18]. For each of the 14 questions for study evaluation, "Yes" replies were worth 1 point, whereas "No" and "Other" responses were worth 0 points. The final quality score was then calculated. Therefore, investigations with a rating from 0 to 4 were deemed to be of low quality, research with a grade between 5 and 9 was deemed to be of acceptable quality, and investigations with a score of 10 or more were deemed to be of good quality.

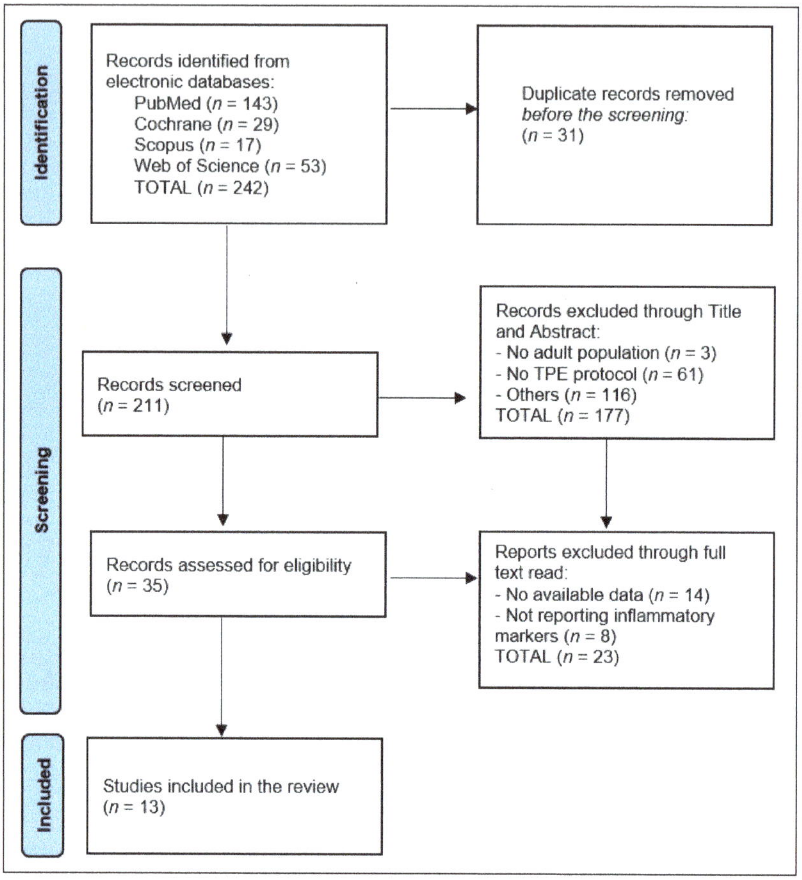

Figure 1. PRISMA flowchart.

3. Results

After filtering the matching studies, we included in this systematic review 13 articles that used TPE as treatment in adult patients with severe COVID-19 [19–31]. The included articles are summarized in Table 1. The main outcomes extracted from the studied papers observed a total of 485 severely ill patients treated with TPE, with a mortality rate of 18.1% (72 patients). However, the mortality rate is arguably lower than in patients without TPE treatment because only six studies had a control group for comparison [19,22,27–31], and their results were not always statistically significant. However, the duration of ICU admission was reported as significantly lower than in control groups, averaging six days compared with fourteen days among controls.

TPE was usually performed multiple times, averaging three times during hospitalization and ranging from one to seven times. The main component of replacement fluid was fresh frozen plasma in all 13 studies, or FFP with a combination of citrate dextrose solution [19], human albumin and normal saline [21], normal saline only [22,29], or 5% human albumin only [23–27,30]. Regarding the safety of TPE, only one study reported one patient with associated hypotension [19], whereas another study reported femoral artery puncture in one patient and thrombophlebitis of the femoral vein in another patient [22].

Some key observations from the included studies comprise reduced inflammatory markers [19,21,22,24], reductions in SOFA scores [19,23], and the conclusion of better results in critically ill patients when TPA is used early after disease onset [19,22,26,29]. Another important finding is improved oxygenation after plasmapheresis, which was reported in five of the analyzed studies [20,21,23,25,28].

Regarding the change in inflammatory markers observed in patients with severe COVID-19, it was observed in all studies that reported a change in variation that inflammatory markers significantly decreased after undergoing TPE. The highest reduction of inflammatory markers was observed in a study by Khamis [19], which reported a 336 mg/mL decrease of CRP. A study by Zaid [26] reported a 574 pg/mL decrease in IL-6 levels post-TPE. However, data is inconsistent regarding the timing of serum marker measurement, or how long after TPE the measurements were taken. As seen in Table 2 and Figure 2, most of the patients were men (66.7%) who had an age range between 48–75 years and a median age of 57 years. The average IL-6 reduction after TPE was 193.5 pg/mL; CRP decreased by an average of 145.9 mg/L, whereas D-dimers decreased by 111.2 ng/mL. Lymphocyte count was also significantly lower after TPE with a 41.7 × 10^9/L decrease. The length of hospitalization, however, was very long; studies reported an average of 25.2 days of admission. The mortality rate varied significantly, which is probably due to the severity of patients involved, from 0.0% in some of the studies [24–26,28] up to 60.0% in the study described by Matsushita et al. [20] and an overall average of 18.1%. Lastly, only four studies reported the odds ratio for improvement after TPE compared with a control group [21,27,29–31], but data showed a significant improvement in clinical and inflammatory status of the patients from 17% to 32%.

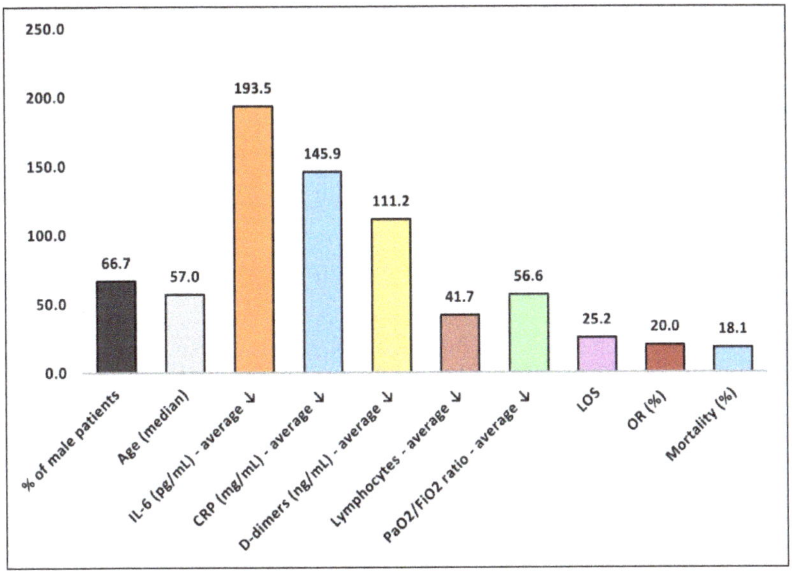

Figure 2. Summary of findings representing the average values of variables reported in the included studies, and the average decrease (down arrow) of inflammatory markers after TPE procedure; IL-6—Interleukin-6; CRP—C-reactive protein; PaO_2—Partial pressure of oxygen; FiO_2—Fraction of inspired oxygen; LOS—length of stay in hospital (days); OS—Overall survival.

Table 1. Literature review of researched articles.

First Author, Country	Type of Study	Number of Patients	Number of TPE Treatment	Replacement Fluid	TPE Safety	Special Observations/Conclusions
F. Kharmis, Oman [19]	Case–control series	11 TPE 20 Control group	5	FFP, citrate dextrose solution	Hypotension (1 patient)	Reduced inflammatory markers and SOFA scores. TPE should be utilized earlier in critically ill patients within 7–14 days of illness onset.
Y. Matsushita, Japan [20]	Retrospective study	5	3–7	FFP	Not reported	Positive evolution in 40% of patients. Decrease in CRP and improvement in PaO2/FiO$_2$ ratio in all cases.
S. M. Hashemian, Iran [21]	Single group case series study	15	3	5% human albumin solution and 0.9% saline. FFP from with positive detection anti-SARS COV-2 IgG and IgM (4 patients).	Not reported	Improvement in oxygenation status. Reduced inflammatory mediators $p < 0.001$. Improvement in hepatic functions. TPE offers safety and efficacy in removing inflammatory cytokine and acute phase proteins.
S. M. Kamran, Pakistan [22]	Retrospective observational study	45 TPE 45 control group	1–5	FFP and normal saline 2:1	Femoral artery puncture (1 patient) Thrombophlebitis of the femoral vein (1 patient)	Decreased duration of hospitalization. Reduced inflammatory markers. Better results of TPE when used closer (within 12 days) to onset of symptoms.
F. Faqihi, Saudi Arabia [23]	Prospective study	10	5–7	FFP or human albumin 5%	None	Significantly reduced inflammatory markers and improved PaO2/FiO$_2$ ratios and SOFA scores.
J. Fernandez, Spain [24]	Single center case series study	4	2–6	Human albumin 5%	None	Reduced inflammatory markers. Effective rescue therapy in critically ill patients. Improved survival in very severe COVID-19 therapy. Decreased in severity scores.
W. L. Gluck, USA [25]	Single center case series study	10	4–5	FFP or human albumin 5%	None	Reduction in inflammatory markers. Improved oxygenation parameters. 4/4 of patients were liberated from supplemental oxygen. 2/6 patients were extubated within 14 days.
I. Zaid, Marocco [26]	Retrospective case series study	7	3–5	FFP	None	Significant reduction in inflammatory markers. TPE should be used earlier in critically ill patients.
F. Faqihi, Saudi Arabia [27]	Randomized controlled clinical trial study	43 TPE 44 control group	1–5	FFP or human albumin 5%	None	Decrease in inflammatory markers. Increased lymphocytes and ADAMTS-13 activity. Duration of hospitalization in ICU was reduced in the TPE group. Faster clinical recovery decreased the SOFA score for TPE patients.
M. Hassaniazad, Iran [28]	Retrospective clinical study	22 TPE 22 control group	3	Human albumin 5%, normal saline, FFP	None	TPE can effectively improve clinical symptoms and reduce inflammatory markers.
Z. Jamil, Saudi Arabia [29]	Retrospective cohort study	81 TPE 81 control group	5	FFP, normal saline	None	Reduction of inflammatory markers. Improved PaO2/FiO$_2$ ratio. Days of mechanical ventilation were reduced compared with the control group. Higher rate of survival in TPE group.

Table 1. *Cont.*

First Author, Country	Type of Study	Number of Patients	Number of TPE Treatment	Replacement Fluid	TPE Safety	Special Observations/Conclusions
L. Cegolan, Iran [30]	A retrospective observational controlled study	43 TPE 30 control group	1–5	50% FFP + 50% human albumin 5%	None	Reduction of inflammatory markers. Mortality was lower in the TPE group due to the lower severity of patients with COVID-19.
CJ. Diskin, USA [31]	Prospective observational	42 TPE 147 controls	5	FFP, convalescent plasma	2 patients with "minor reactions"	Reduction of inflammatory markers. Higher rate of survival in TPE group. PaO_2/FiO_2 ratio in all cases.

TPE—Therapeutic Plasma Exchange; FFP—Fresh Frozen Plasma; SOFA—Sequential Organ Failure Assessment; ICU—Intensive Care Unit; PaO2/FiO2 ratio—The ratio of arterial oxygen partial pressure (PaO2 in mmHg) to fractional inspired oxygen; CRP—C-reactive protein

Table 2. Patients' outcomes identified in the studied articles.

No.	Quality Assessment	Male%	Age *	IL-6 (pg/mL)	CRP (mg/L)	D-dimer (ng/mL)	Ly ($\times 10^9$/L)	PaO2/FiO2	LOS	OR%	Mortality
1 [19]	Acceptable	100	50	334	336	23	60	15	19.0	NR	9.1%
2 [20]	Low	80.0	75	NR	NR	NR	NR	NR	31.6	NR	60.0%
3 [21]	Acceptable	60.0	57	26	188	NR	NR	40	9.6 (ICU)	17%	40.0%
4 [22]	Low	92.0	60	17	250	150	54	NR	15.0	NR	17.9%
5 [23]	Good	70.0	51	128	58	65	55	23	15.0 (ICU)	NR	10.0%
6 [24]	Low	100	57	20	66	81	NR	40	41.2	NR	0.0%
7 [25]	Low	30.0	52	26	123	NR	NR	43	NR	NR	0.0%
8 [26]	Low	57.1	57	574	133	NR	42	20	20.2	NR	0.0%
9 [27]	Good	82.8	48	423	201	40	50	165	19.0 (ICU)	19%	20.9%
10 [28]	Acceptable	50.0	61	NR	180	N	21	76	NR	NR	0.0%
11 [29]	Good	24.7	56	NR	24	308	10	69	NR	19%	19.8%
12 [30]	Acceptable	50.0	NR	NR	146	NR	NR	22	NR	32%	14%
13 [31]	Good	70.7%	60	NR	46	NR	NR	110	24.1	13%	43.9%

* Data reported as medians, unless specified differently; IL-6—interleukin-6; LOS—length of stay in hospital (days); Ly—Lymphocytes ($\times 10^9$/L); OR—Odds Ratio for exposure to TPE (% of increased survival after TPE). Laboratory markers reported as the difference between pre-treatment and post-treatment with TPE; PaO2/FiO2 ratio—The ratio of arterial oxygen partial pressure (PaO2 in mmHg) to fractional inspired oxygen; NR—Not reported; ICU—Intensive care unit; CRP—C-reactive protein.

4. Discussion

4.1. Supporting Literature for the Safety and Efficacy of TPE

In our study, we investigated the impact of TPE on various inflammatory markers, including CRP, IL-6, ferritin, and lymphocyte counts. The significant reduction in these inflammatory markers after TPE suggests that this treatment effectively mitigates the cytokine storm, which is a major contributing factor to the severe manifestations of COVID-19. The cytokine storm is characterized by an excessive and uncontrolled release of pro-inflammatory cytokines, leading to acute respiratory distress syndrome (ARDS), multi-organ failure, and ultimately, death. The TPE treatment's ability to suppress this excessive inflammatory response may explain the observed improvement in clinical outcomes, such as oxygenation and SOFA scores, among the treated patients [32–34].

Fahad Faqihi et al. noted that patients receiving TPE showed marked and sustained increases in lymphocyte count and significant decreases in CRP, LDH, ferritin, D-dimers, and IL-6. This study demonstrates that TPE reduces inflammatory markers and improves oxygenation and the clinical status of patients with life-threatening forms of COVID-19. However, it does not significantly affect mortality at 35 days [27]. The observed increase in lymphocyte counts following TPE treatment is particularly notable in the context of COVID-19, as lymphopenia has been identified as a common laboratory abnormality in patients with severe disease. Lymphocytes play a crucial role in the immune response to viral infections, and their depletion in COVID-19 patients is associated with a higher risk of severe outcomes. By increasing lymphocyte counts, TPE may contribute to enhancing the immune response against SARS-CoV-2 and facilitating recovery.

Similarly, Khamis et al. observed a significant decrease in inflammatory markers and an increase in lymphocyte count after TPE. As a result, patients receiving TPE had an improved clinical course compared to patients in the control group in terms of extubation and mortality rates. Patients receiving TPE were also less likely to develop severe pneumonia by comparison to those in the control group [19]. In addition, a case series study by Zaid et al. proved the effectiveness of plasma exchange therapy by lowering pro-inflammatory cytokines and ameliorating the cytokine storm [26], as all patients had increased inflammatory markers before TPE and presented good clinical and biological courses afterward. According to the authors, the improved evolution was due to prompt TPE initiation (on the first day of the "cytokine storm") before intubation, and mechanical ventilation was needed.

Molecules with a molecular weight of less than 1000 kDa, such as interleukins, can be filtered through TPE. All of the inflammatory markers and acute phase reactants mentioned in this paper have a molecular weight low enough to be effectively eliminated through TPE, decreasing the inflammatory burden and suppressing cytokine release syndrome. Lu et al. observed much higher serum values of IL-1beta in the blood of COVID-19 patients compared to non-COVID patients, but they also noted higher cytokine values in general in patients admitted to the ICU [34].

According to other studies, IL-1 plays a key role in inducing the cytokine storm that appears in severe COVID-19 cases [23]. This cytokine storm can lead to acute lung injury (ALI), systemic inflammatory response syndrome (SIRS), or ARDS. IL-1 also promotes bronchial and alveolar inflammatory responses in patients with pulmonary tissue damage. In addition, it can stimulate hepatocytes to produce acute phase reactants. Several studies have shown that IL-1 controls the biosynthesis of IL-6, which is known to be one of the major negative prognostic factors in COVID-19 [35]. Thus, uncontrolled production of IL-1beta may be an underlying factor in acute lung injury and cytokine storm in SARS-CoV-2-infected patients. In view of this, the inhibition or purging of IL-1 may be extremely beneficial in the treatment of cytokine storm syndromes.

Even from the beginning of the new coronavirus pandemic, IL-6 has been a prognostic biomarker with important clinical value that has distinguished between mild, moderate, and severe forms of the disease, raising the important question of whether controlling IL-6 could prevent the severity of SARS-CoV-2 infection. In many studies, attempts were made to control IL-6 by keeping it within normal limits through various medical procedures. One of the procedures was using therapeutic plasma exchange, which significantly reduced IL-6 levels [24,36–39].

Recent literature data show that IL-6 is one of the biomarkers involved in severe inflammatory syndrome, but a more detailed analysis shows that its value is lower in bacterial septic shock [40]. In severe inflammatory syndrome from coronavirus type 2 infection, the clear impact of interleukin-6 on mortality and morbidity has been demonstrated; basically, the multiple system organ failure in the clinical picture is caused by severe inflammatory syndrome and not by direct action of the virus. In a retrospective longitudinal cohort study conducted by Manson et al., an increase in IL-6 was associated with an increase in oxygen demand and an increase in noninvasive and invasive mechanical ventilation support, resulting in increased mortality [38]. In a study conducted in the USA on 289 patients, Ashrafzadeh-Kian et al. showed the usefulness of IL-6, being the most reliable biomarker as a disease severity predictor in COVID-19, as it was correlated with the hospitalization duration, disease severity, and prognosis. The author pointed out that the test can be used in the triage of infected patients [39].

In the context of SARS-CoV-2 infection, elevated CRP values have been associated with tissue destruction, poor prognosis, and, implicitly, increased mortality [40]. Elevated CRP levels in the early stages of COVID-19 have been associated with lung destruction and disease severity. According to lung investigations using computed tomography corroborated with the laboratory analyses, the increase in CRP level was found before the appearance of lung lesions; thus, it was considered that CRP has a predictive value on disease severity [41].

According to a study conducted in China by Ling et al., there is a strong correlation between the CRP and albumin ratio, sequential organ failure assessment (SOFA) score, and the length of hospitalization in surviving COVID-19 patients. In the acute inflammatory stage, there is an increase in CRP and a decrease in albumin values. These changes are not only an indicator of the disease severity but even mortality risk factors in patients with severe COVID-19, as they indicate the cytokine storm's debut [42,43]. Another study conducted in Spain suggests that a CRP value above the threshold of 9.1 mg/dl and a SOFA score higher than 2 in COVID-19 patients at the time of admission are independent predictors (with a sensitivity and specificity of 77%) of admission to the ICU [44].

Studies show that plasma exchange is more likely to alter pathogenic immunological drivers than antibody-mediated immune responses in severely ill COVID-19 patients. This might lower D-dimer levels depending on their molecular weight, suggesting a contrived reduction rather than a genuine recovery in the patient's illness. Moreover, the findings presented are consistent with those of other studies, in which the authors demonstrated a beneficial effect of plasma exchange by demonstrating decreased fatality rates in patients with D-dimers greater than or equal to 2 mg/L on plasma exchange therapy compared to patients with D-dimers >2 mg/L without plasma exchange [45]. Despite the severity of the illness, these findings additionally reinforce the hypothesis that TPE improves survival by demonstrating a 30-day death rate of 32.1% in TPE-treated patients compared to 57.1% in patients receiving conventional therapy.

Fibrinogen is a large molecule with a molecular weight of approximately 340 kDa that plays an important role in blood clotting, inflammatory response, cellular interactions, wound healing, and neoplasia. It is considered an acute phase reactant present in many clinical syndromes with procoagulant status, such as severe bacterial infections, various neoplasms, and almost all moderate and severe forms of COVID-19. A study by Kuluöztürk M. et al. described the correlation between fibrinogen and albumin ratio, lung damage, and C-reactive protein values, concluding that a fibrinogen/albumin ratio of over 144.59 may be an early prognostic marker and may predict admission to ICU [46].

One of the major challenges in the therapeutic management of COVID-19 patients (especially in the ICU) is the clogging of filters, plasma filters, cytokine filters, and ECMO systems. This has been attributed to a procoagulant status found in patients with SARS-

CoV2 infection. Compared with the literature, Zarbock et al. showed the importance of using citrate anticoagulation during dialysis sessions, concluding that filters have a longer lifespan if citrate is used rather than heparin [47]. In another study conducted last year by Sui et al., which included 119 COVID-19 patients with high fibrinogen values, fibrinogen is shown to be closely correlated with several biological abnormalities such as elevated inflammatory markers, multiple organ dysfunction, intensive care admission, and higher mortality [48].

Erythrocyte sedimentation rate (ESR) was recognized as an acute phase reactant used to indicate systemic inflammation. Although the increase in ESR in COVID-19 patients cannot be fully explained, it is suspected to be due to changes in erythrocyte forms and plasmatic changes [49]. Mahat et al. performed a meta-analysis on the dynamics of the inflammatory markers in COVID-19, which included 83 patients. It was observed that the severe group of patients had higher ESR values compared to the mild/moderate group, thereby being associated with the severity of the disease [50]. This increase in ESR in severe cases of COVID-19 reflects a profound inflammatory response and a strong expression of acute phase proteins.

An interesting link between ESR and coagulation is described by Al-Samkari et al. in a study on 400 hospitalized COVID-19 patients. The authors showed that patients with thrombotic complications or bleeding had higher ESR values than patients without thrombotic complications or bleeding. It was concluded that elevated ESR values at admission are predictive of thrombotic complications during hospitalization [51]. In addition, elevated ESR values at admission were predictive of both severe disease and mortality. The authors concluded that high values of ESR and other inflammatory markers correlate with the disease severity and the risk of death.

LDH is considered an inflammatory marker that indicates acute or chronic tissue destruction. An increase in serum LDH has also been reported in acute lung injury caused by interstitial lung disease and severe respiratory failure [52,53]. In addition, it is considered to be one of the strongest biomarkers associated with mortality in ARDS. LDH is independently associated with one-month mortality in elderly patients with COVID-19 and is also a respiratory failure predictor in hospitalized, SARS-CoV-2-infected patients [54,55]. In a pooled analysis by Henry et al. containing nine studies with 1532 patients, it was found that elevated LDH values were associated with a sixfold increased risk of developing severe COVID-19 and a 16-fold increase in mortality rate [56]. According to Masumoto et al., serum LDH values > 355U/L at admission were associated with an increased risk of death in patients with COVID-19 and cardiac comorbidities [57].

Elevated LDH levels may reflect the destruction of pneumocytes, myocardial cells, and other organs. According to a study by Hachim et al. on 541 patients, it was observed that patients with severe or critical forms of COVID-19 had much higher LDH values compared to patients with mild or moderate forms, and patients admitted to the ICU had higher LDH values compared to those treated in non-critical wards; non-survivors also had elevated serum LDH values compared to survivors, and higher LDH values were found in patients with ARDS compared to patients without ARDS [58]. Zheng et al. conducted a retrospective study comparing computerized tomography scans and biological investigations of 231 COVID-19 patients. The results suggest that the severity of the lung damage found on CT scans correlates positively with age and plasma values of ESR, D-dimers, LDH, and CRP [59]. Similarly, a study involving approximately 400 COVID-19 patients observed that elevated LDH values were found in deceased patients compared to survivors (median 702 vs. 498 U/L, $p < 0.001$), concluding that LDH values higher than 400 IU/L are associated with increased mortality in COVID-19 patients [60].

During the COVID-19 pandemic, abnormally elevated levels of ferritin were observed in patients with SARS-CoV-2 infections, bringing into question the correlation between the value of ferritin and their prognosis. The common connection between hyperferritinemia syndrome and the aforementioned complications is the combination of elevated ferritin levels and life-threatening inflammation, which will eventually lead to multiple organ failures. Although the exact link between COVID-19 and ferritin is not known at the cellular level, the literature shows many links between the severity of the disease and ferritin [61]. Ferritin levels were higher in non-surviving patients than in survivors as well as in those admitted to the intensive care units (ICU) who needed mechanical ventilation as opposed to those treated in other medical stations and those who did not require mechanical ventilation [62].

In a study by Carubbi et al., ferritin percentiles were calculated, and it was concluded that patients with ferritin values above the 25th percentile were more common in men and had higher fibrinogen, LDH, and procalcitonin levels in comparison with those who had ferritin values below the 25th percentile [63]. It should also be noted that lung damage, prevalence of septal thickening, and enlargement of the mediastinal lymph nodes were more pronounced in patients with elevated ferritin values, and functional impairment ($PaO2/FiO2$) was also more severe. Ferritin levels above the 25th percentile were also associated with the involvement of all five lung lobes, the presence of septal thickening, and the presence of mediastinal lymphadenopathy, regardless of age and sex [64]. In Pakistan, 78% of COVID-19 patients included in a study had elevated ferritin values, showing that the mean values of ferritin, D-dimers, CRP, and LDH were higher in patients with severe symptoms than in patients with mild or moderate symptoms. Patients with mild symptoms showed a mean value of 732.73 ng/mL, patients with moderate symptoms, 801.96 ng/mL, and patients with severe symptoms, 819.85 ng/mL [64].

4.2. Study Limitations

A limitation of our paper is that only the usual inflammatory markers involved in the cytokine storm were analyzed, limiting the complete evaluation of the inflammation profile. Five of the included articles were case series, which often provide positive results; hence, there is a substantial publication bias, and the aforementioned investigations should be evaluated with care. However, the total number of patients that underwent TPE was 485, which contributes to the overall significance of the observed findings. In addition, the COVID-19 diagnosis and treatment protocol were not standardized throughout all studies. The included studies are not homogenous regarding clinical indications, timing of TPE initiation, number of sessions, time intervals between sessions, and type of replacement fluid differed amongst trials; thus, additional data regarding these factors would be necessary for future research. Therefore, the studies included in the present systematic review did not allow us to adequately provide an optimum TPE therapy regimen.

5. Conclusions

TPE could be regarded as an alternative therapy complementary to standard treatment in severely ill COVID-19 patients. Most studies describe a reduction in inflammatory mediators and improvement of coagulation function, as well as clinical status, compared with admission features after three to five TPE sessions. However, the described studies are not standardized, and the results show inconsistency between them; the majority report no significant improvement after TPE in comparison with a control group. In addition, some studies suggest that TPE improves survival rate by correcting the inflammatory status of the patients without significant side effects, although it is not yet statistically proven in trials with a higher number of patients to offer reliability. Thus, it is important to emphasize the need for more well-designed randomized controlled trials with larger sample sizes and standardized protocols to determine the true efficacy, safety, and optimal treatment protocol for TPE in the management of critically ill COVID-19 patients. This will help provide more robust and reliable evidence for the clinical application of TPE in this patient population.

Author Contributions: Conceptualization, T.M.P. and D.J.; methodology, I.O.S., O.R. and F.B.; data curation, E.B. and F.B.; writing—original draft preparation, T.M.P. and D.J.; writing—review and editing, O.R., C.O., S.S.S.B. and M.P.; visualization, D.S., E.B. and M.P.; supervision, C.O. and I.O.S. All authors have read and agreed to the published version of the manuscript.

Funding: This research received no external funding.

Institutional Review Board Statement: Not applicable.

Informed Consent Statement: Not applicable.

Data Availability Statement: Not applicable.

Conflicts of Interest: The authors declare no conflict of interest.

References

1. Lorini, F.L.; Matteo, D.M.; Gritti, P.; Grazioli, L.; Benigni, A.; Zacchetti, L. Coagulopathy and COVID-19. *Eur. Heart J. Suppl.* **2020**, *23*, 95–98. [CrossRef] [PubMed]
2. Manolescu, D.; Timar, B.; Bratosin, F.; Rosca, O.; Citu, C.; Oancea, C. Predictors for COVID-19 Complete Remission with HRCT Pattern Evolution: A Monocentric, Prospective Study. *Diagnostics* **2022**, *12*, 1397. [CrossRef] [PubMed]
3. Papava, I.; Dehelean, L.; Romosan, R.S.; Bondrescu, M.; Dimeny, C.Z.; Domuta, E.M.; Bratosin, F.; Bogdan, I.; Grigoras, M.L.; Tigmeanu, C.V.; et al. The Impact of Hyper-Acute Inflammatory Response on Stress Adaptation and Psychological Symptoms of COVID-19 Patients. *Int. J. Environ. Res. Public Health* **2022**, *19*, 6501. [CrossRef] [PubMed]
4. Batah, S.S.; Fabro, A.T. Pulmonary pathology of ARDS in COVID-19: A pathological review for clinicians. *Respir. Med.* **2021**, *176*, 106239. [CrossRef]
5. Broască, L.; Trușculescu, A.A.; Ancușa, V.M.; Ciocârlie, H.; Oancea, C.-I.; Stoicescu, E.-R.; Manolescu, D.L. A Novel Method for Lung Image Processing Using Complex Networks. *Tomography* **2022**, *8*, 1928–1946. [CrossRef]
6. Zodpey, S.P.; Negandhi, H.; Kamal, V.K.; Bhatnagar, T.; Ganeshkumar, P.; Athavale, A. Determinants of severity among hospitalised COVID-19 patients: Hospital-based case-control study, India, 2020. *PLoS ONE* **2021**, *16*, e0261529. [CrossRef]
7. Citu, C.; Burlea, B.; Gorun, F.; Motoc, A.; Gorun, O.M.; Malita, D.; Ratiu, A.; Margan, R.; Grigoras, M.L.; Bratosin, F.; et al. Predictive Value of Blood Coagulation Parameters in Poor Outcomes in COVID-19 Patients: A Retrospective Observational Study in Romania. *J. Clin. Med.* **2022**, *11*, 2831. [CrossRef]
8. Fericean, R.M.; Citu, C.; Manolescu, D.; Rosca, O.; Bratosin, F.; Tudorache, E.; Oancea, C. Characterization and Outcomes of SARS-CoV-2 Infection in Overweight and Obese Patients: A Dynamic Comparison of COVID-19 Pandemic Waves. *J. Clin. Med.* **2022**, *11*, 2916. [CrossRef]
9. Ragab, D.; Salah, E.H.; Taeimah, M.; Khatta, R.; Salem, R. The COVID-19 Cytokine Storm; What We Know So Far. *Front. Immunol.* **2020**, *11*, 1446. [CrossRef]
10. Tanase, A.; Manea, A.; Scurtu, A.D.; Bratu, L.M.; Chioran, D.; Dolghi, A.; Alexoi, I.; Abed, H.; Lazureanu, V.; Dehelean, C.A. The "Invisible Enemy" SARS-CoV-2: Viral Spread and Drug Treatment. *Medicina* **2022**, *58*, 261. [CrossRef]
11. Tirnea, L.; Bratosin, F.; Vidican, I.; Cerbu, B.; Turaiche, M.; Timircan, M.; Margan, M.-M.; Marincu, I. The Efficacy of Convalescent Plasma Use in Critically Ill COVID-19 Patients. *Medicina* **2021**, *57*, 257. [CrossRef]
12. Mungmungpuntipantip, R.; Wiwanitkit, V. Antithrombin, COVID-19, and Fresh Frozen Plasma Treatment. *Turk. J. Haematol.* **2021**, *38*, 157–159. [CrossRef]
13. Clark, W.; Huang, S. Introduction to therapeutic plasma exchange. *Transfus. Apher. Sci.* **2019**, *58*, 228–229. [CrossRef]
14. Padmanabhan, A.; Connelly-Smith, L.; Aqui, N.; Balogun, R.A.; Klingel, R.; Meyer, E.; Pham, H.P.; Schneiderman, J.; Witt, V.; Wu, Y.; et al. Guidelines on the Use of Therapeutic Apheresis in Clinical Practice—Evidence-Based Approach from the Writing Committee of the American Society for Apheresis: The Eighth Special Issue. *J. Clin. Apher.* **2019**, *34*, 171–354. [CrossRef]
15. Gucyetmez, B.; Atalan, H.K.; Sertdemir, I.; Cakir, U.; Telci, L.; COVID-19 Study Group. Therapeutic plasma exchange in patients with COVID-19 pneumonia in intensive care unit: A retrospective study. *Crit. Care* **2020**, *24*, 492. [CrossRef]
16. Cerbu, B.; Grigoras, M.L.; Bratosin, F.; Bogdan, I.; Citu, C.; Bota, A.V.; Timircan, M.; Bratu, M.L.; Levai, M.C.; Marincu, I. Laboratory Profile of COVID-19 Patients with Hepatitis C-Related Liver Cirrhosis. *J. Clin. Med.* **2022**, *11*, 652. [CrossRef]
17. Liberati, A.; Altman, D.G.; Tetzlaff, J.; Mulrow, C.; Gøtzsche, P.C.; Ioannidis, J.P.A.; Clarke, M.; Devereaux, P.J.; Kleijnen, J.; Moher, D. The PRISMA statement for reporting systematic reviews and meta-analyses of studies that evaluate healthcare interventions: Explanation and elaboration. *BMJ* **2009**, *339*, b2700. [CrossRef]
18. Tran, L.; Tam, D.N.H.; Elshafay, A.; Dang, T.; Hirayama, K.; Huy, N.T. Quality assessment tools used in systematic reviews of in vitro studies: A systematic review. *BMC Med. Res. Methodol.* **2021**, *21*, 101. [CrossRef]
19. Khamis, F.; Al-Zakwani, I.; Al Hashmi, S.; Al Dowaiki, S.; Al Bahrani, M.; Pandak, N.; Khalili, H.; Memish, Z. Therapeutic plasma exchange in adults with severe COVID-19 infection. *Int. J. Infect. Dis.* **2020**, *99*, 214–218. [CrossRef]
20. Matsushita, Y.; Kusaoi, M.; Hiki, M.; Murayama, G.; Abe, Y.; Nozawa, K.; Takahashi, K.; Yamaji, K.; Tamura, N.; Naito, T. Combination therapy with plasma exchange and glucocorticoid may be effective for severe COVID-19 infection: A retrospective observational study. *Ther. Apher. Dial.* **2021**, *25*, 33887110. [CrossRef]
21. Hashemian, S.M.R.; Shafigh, N.; Afzal, G.; Jamaati, H.; Tabarsi, P.; Marjani, M.; Malekmohammad, M.; Mortazavi, S.M.; Khoundabi, B.; Mansouri, D. Plasmapheresis reduces cytokine and immune cell levels in COVID-19 patients with acute respiratory distress syndrome (ARDS). *Pulmonology* **2021**, *27*, 486–492. [CrossRef] [PubMed]

22. Kamran, S.M.; Mirza, Z.-E.H.; Naseem, A.; Liaqat, J.; Fazal, I.; Alamgir, W.; Saeed, F.; Saleem, S.; Nisar, S.; Yousaf, M.A.; et al. Therapeutic plasma exchange for coronavirus disease-2019 triggered cytokine release syndrome; A retrospective propensity matched control study. *PLoS ONE* **2021**, *16*, e0244853. [CrossRef] [PubMed]
23. Faqihi, F.; Alharthy, A.; Alodat, M.; Kutsogiannis, D.J.; Brindley, P.G.; Karakitsos, D. Therapeutic plasma exchange in adult critically ill patients with life-treathening SARS-CoV-2 disease: A pilot study. *J. Crit. Care* **2020**, *60*, 328–333. [CrossRef] [PubMed]
24. Fernandez, J.; Gratacos-Ginès, J.; Olivas, P.; Costa, M.; Nieto, S.; Mateo, D.; Sanchez, M.B.; Aguillar, F.; Bassegoda, O.; Ruiz, P.; et al. Plasma exchange: An effective rescue therapy in critically ILL patients with coronavirus disease 2019 infection. *Crit. Care Med.* **2020**, *48*, e1350–e1355. [CrossRef]
25. Gluck, W.L.; Callahan, S.P.; Brevetta, R.A.; Stenbit, A.E.; Smith, W.M.; Martin, J.C.; Blenda, A.V.; Arce, S.; Edenfield, W.J. Efficacy of therapeutic plasma exchange in the treatment of penn class 3 and 4 cytokine release syndrome complicating COVID-19. *Respir. Med.* **2020**, *175*, 106188. [CrossRef]
26. Zaid, I.; Essaad, O.; Al Aidouni, G.; Aabdi, M.; Berrichi, S.; Taouihar, S.; Marbouh, M.; Bkiyer, H.; Abda, N.; Housni, B. Therapeutic plasma exchange in patients with COVID-19 pneumonia in intensive care unit: Cases series. *Ann. Med. Surg.* **2021**, *71*, 102920. [CrossRef]
27. Faqihi, F.; Alharthy, A.; Abdulaziz, S.; Balhamar, A.; Alomari, A.; Al Aseri, Z.; Tamim, H.; Alqahtani, S.A.; Ktsogiannis, D.J.; Brindley, P.G.; et al. Therapeutic plasma exchange in patients with life- treathening COVID-19: A randomized control clinical trial. *Int. J. Antimicrob. Agents* **2021**, *57*, 106334. [CrossRef]
28. Hassaniazad, M.; Vahedi, S.M.; Samimagham, R.H.; Gharibzadeh, A.; Beyranvand, S.; Abbasi, H.; Nikpoor, A.R. Improvement of clinical outcome, laboratory findings and inflammatory cytokines levels using plasmapheresis therapy in severe COVID-19 cases. *Respir. Med.* **2021**, *189*, 106669. [CrossRef]
29. Jamil, Z.; Khan, A.A.; Yousuf, H.; Khalid, K.; Abbasi, S.M.; Waheed, Y. Role of Therapeutic Plasmapheresis in SARS-CoV-2 Induced Cytokine Release Syndrome: A Retrospective Cohort Study on COVID-19 Patients. *Int. J. Gen. Med.* **2022**, *15*, 4907–4916. [CrossRef]
30. Cegolon, L.; Einollahi, B.; Panahi, Y.; Imanizadeh, S.; Rezapour, M.; Javanbakht, M.; Nikpouraghdam, M.; Abolghasemi, H.; Mastrangelo, G. On Therapeutic Plasma Exchange Against Severe COVID-19- Associated Pneumonia: An Observational Clinical Study. *Front. Nutr.* **2022**, *9*, 809823. [CrossRef]
31. Diskin, C.J.; Maldonado, R.; Leon, J.; Dansby, L.M.; Carter, T.B.; Radcliff, L.; Diskin, C.D. How effective is rescue therapeutic plasma exchange in treatment of SARS-Coronavirus-2? *Ther. Apher. Dial.* **2023**, *27*, 170–176. [CrossRef]
32. Tabibi, S.; Tabibi, T.; Conic, R.R.; Banisaeed, N.; Streiff, M.B. Therapeutic Plasma Exchange: A potential Management Strategy for Critically Ill COVID-19 Patients. *J. Intensive Care Med.* **2020**, *35*, 827–835. [CrossRef]
33. Balagholi, S.; Dabbaghi, R.; Eshghi, P.; Mousavi, S.A.; Heshmati, F.; Mohammadi, S. Potential of therapeutic plasmapheresis in treatment of COVID-19 patients: Immunopathogenesis and coagulopathy. *Transfus. Apher. Sci.* **2020**, *59*, 102993. [CrossRef]
34. Lu, Q.; Zhu, Z.; Tan, C.; Zhou, H.; Hu, Y.; Shen, G. Changes of serum IL-10, IL-1β, IL-6, MCP-1, TNF-α, IP-10 and IL-4 in COVID-19 patients. *Int. J. Clin. Pract.* **2021**, *75*, e14462. [CrossRef]
35. Mardi, A.; Meidaninikjeh, S.; Nikfarjam, S.; Majidi Zolbanin, N.; Jafari, R. Interleukin-1 in COVID-19 Infection: Immunopathogenesis and Possible Therapeutic Perspective. *Viral Immunol.* **2021**, *34*, 679–688. [CrossRef]
36. Tanaka, T.; Narazaki, M.; Kishimoto, T. Interleukin (IL-6) immunotherapy. *Cold Spring Harb. Perspect. Biol.* **2018**, *10*, 1101. [CrossRef]
37. Arthur, T.; Snow, C.; Saleem, N.; Ambler, G.; Nastouli, E. Tocilizumab in COVID-19: A meta-analysis, trial sequential analysis, and meta-regression of randomized-controlled trials. *Intensive Care Med.* **2021**, *47*, 641–652.
38. Manson, J.J.; Naja, M.B.B.S.M.; Ledlie, A.; Goulden, M.B.B.S.B.; Khan, E.; Mehta, M.B.B.S.P. COVID-19-associated hyperinflammation and escalation of patient care: A retrospective longitudinal cohort study. *Lancet Rheumatol.* **2020**, *2*, e594–e602. [CrossRef]
39. Ashrafzadeh-Kian, S.; Campbell, M.R.; Jara Aguirre, J.C.; Walsh, J.; Kumanovics, A.; Jenkinson, G. Role of immune mediators in predicting hospitalization of SARS-CoV-2 positive patients. *Cytokine* **2022**, *150*, 155790. [CrossRef]
40. Mosquera-Sulbaran, J.A.; Pedreañez, A.; Carrero, Y.; Callejas, D. C-reactive protein as an effector molecule in COVID-19 pathogenesis. *Rev. Med. Virol.* **2021**, *31*, e2221. [CrossRef]
41. Lentner, J.; Adams, T.; Knutson, V.; Zeien, S.; Abbas, H.; Moosavi, R. C-reactive protein levels associated with COVID-19 outcomes in the United States. *J. Osteopath. Med.* **2021**, *121*, 869–873. [CrossRef] [PubMed]
42. Li, Y.; Li, H.; Song, C.; Lu, R.; Zhao, Y.; Lin, F. Early Prediction of Disease Progression in Patients with Severe COVID-19 Using C-Reactive Protein to Albumin Ratio. *Dis. Markers* **2021**, *2021*, 6304189. [CrossRef]
43. Gao, Y.D.; Ding, M.; Dong, X.; Zhang, J.J.; Kursat, A.A.; Azkur, D. Risk factors for severe and critically ill COVID-19 patients: A review. *Eur. Allergy* **2021**, *76*, 428–455. [CrossRef] [PubMed]
44. Vaquero-Roncero, L.; Sánchez-Barrado, E.; Escobar-Macias, D.; Arribas-Pérez, P.; González de Castro, R.; González-Porras, J. C-Reactive protein and SOFA scale: A simple score as early predictor of critical care requirement in patients with COVID-19 pneumonia in Spain. *Rev. Esp. Anestesiol. Reanim.* **2021**, *68*, 513–522. [CrossRef] [PubMed]
45. Nusshag, C.; Morath, C.; Speer, C.; Kaelble, F.; Zeier, M.; Boxberger, M.; Schulze-Schleithoff, E.; Fiedler, M.O.; Weigand, M.A.; Merle, U. Plasma Exchange in Patients with Severe Coronavirus Disease 2019: A Single-Center Experience. *Crit. Care Explor.* **2021**, *3*, e0517. [CrossRef]

46. Kuluöztürk, M.; Deveci, F.; Turgut, T.; Öner, Ö. The Glasgow Prognostic Score and fibrinogen to albumin ratio as prognostic factors in hospitalized patients with COVID-19. *Expert Rev. Respir. Med.* **2021**, *15*, 1061–1068. [CrossRef]
47. Zarbock, A.; Küllmar, M.; Kindgen-Milles, D.; Wempe, C.; Gerss, J.; Brandenburger, T. Effect of Regional Citrate Anticoagulation vs Systemic Heparin Anticoagulation During Continuous Kidney Replacement Therapy on Dialysis Filter Life Span and Mortality Among Critically Ill Patients with Acute Kidney Injury a Randomized Clinical Trial. *JAMA* **2020**, *324*, 1629–1639. [CrossRef]
48. Sui, J.; Noubouossie, D.F.; Gandotra, S.; Cao, L. Elevated Plasma Fibrinogen Is Associated with Excessive Inflammation and Disease Severity in COVID-19 Patients. *Front. Cell Infect. Microbiol.* **2021**, *11*, 73405. [CrossRef]
49. Sayit, A.T.; Elmali, M.; Deveci, A.; Gedikli, O. Relationship between acute phase reactants and prognosis in patients with or without COVID-19 pneumonia. *Rev. Inst. Med. Trop. Sao Paulo* **2021**, *63*, e51. [CrossRef]
50. Mahat, R.K.; Panda, S.; Rathore, V.; Swain, S.; Yadav, L.; Sah, S.P. The dynamics of inflammatory markers in coronavirus disease-2019 (COVID-19) patients: A systematic review and meta-analysis. *Clin. Epidemiol. Glob. Health* **2021**, *11*, 100727. [CrossRef]
51. Al-Samkari, H.; Karp Leaf, R.S.; Dzik, W.H.; Carlson, J.C.T.; Fogerty, A.E.; Waheed, A.; Goodarzi, K.; Bendapudi, P.K.; Bornikova, L.; Gupta, S.; et al. COVID-19 and coagulation: Bleeding and thrombotic manifestations of SARS-CoV-2 infection. *Blood* **2020**, *136*, 489–500. [CrossRef] [PubMed]
52. Glick, J.H. Serum lactate dehydrogenase isoenzyme and total lactate dehydrogenase values in healt and disease, and clinical evaluation of these tests by means of discriminant analysis. *Am. J. Clin. Pthol.* **2016**, *52*, 320–328.
53. Hoeboer, S.H.; Straaten, H.O.; Van, M.; Groeneveld, J.B.J. Albumin rather than C-reactive Protein may be valuable in predicting and monitoring the severity and course of acute respiratory distress syndrome in critically ill patients with or at risk for the syndrome after new onset fever. *BMC Pulm. Med.* **2015**, *15*, 22. [CrossRef] [PubMed]
54. Bousquet, G.; Falgarone, G.; Deutsch, D.; Derolez, S.; Lopez-Sublet, M.; Goudot, F.X.; Amari, K.; Uzunhan, Y.; Bouchaud, O.; Pamoukdjian, F. ADL-dependency, D-Dimers, LDH and absence of anticoagulation are independently associated with one-month mortality in older inpatients with COVID-19. *Aging* **2020**, *12*, 11306–11313. [CrossRef] [PubMed]
55. Poggiali, E.; Zaino, D.; Immovilli, P.; Rovero, L.; Losi, G.; Dacrema, A.; Nuccetelli, M.; Vadacca, G.B.; Guidetti, D.; Vercelli, A.; et al. Lactate dehydrogenase and C-reactive Protein as predictors of respiratory failure in COVID-19 patients. *Clin. Chim. Acta.* **2020**, *509*, 135–138. [CrossRef]
56. Henry, B.M.; Aggarwal, G.; Wong, J.; Benoit, S.; Vikse, J.; Plebani, M.; Lippi, G. Lactate dehydrogenase levels predict coronavirus disease 2019 (COVID-19) severity and mortality: A pooled analysis. *Am. J. Emerg. Med.* **2020**, *38*, 1722–1726. [CrossRef]
57. Masumoto, A.; Kitai, T.; Matsumoto, S.; Kuroda, S.; Kohsaka, S.; Tachikawa, R.; Seo, R.; Doi, A.; Tomji, K.; Yonetsu, T.; et al. Impact of serum lactate dehydrogenase on the short-term prognosis of COVID-19 with pre-existing cardiovascular diseases. *J. Cardiol.* **2022**, *79*, 501–508. [CrossRef]
58. Hachim, I.Y.; Hachim, M.Y.; Hannawi, H.; Naeem, K.; Salah, A.; Hannawi, S. The inflammatory biomarkers profile of hospitalized patients with COVID-19 and its association with patient's outcome: A single centered study. *PLoS ONE* **2021**, *16*, e0260537. [CrossRef]
59. Zheng, T.; Ren, H.; Wu, Y.; Wang, J. Association between clinical characteristics and CT findings in patients with coronavirus disease-2019. *Medicine* **2021**, *100*, e27435. [CrossRef]
60. Yousaf, M.N.; Sarwar, S.; Tarique, S.; Ahmed, M.; Tahir, H. Mortality in Patients of COVID-19 Infection: Biochemical Markers and its Cut-off Values for Predicting Outcome. *J. Coll. Physicians Surg. Pak.* **2022**, *32*, 37–41.
61. Mahroum, N.; Alghory, A.; Kiyak, Z.; Alwani, A.; Seida, R.; Alrais, M. Ferritin -from iron, through inflammation and autoimmunity, to COVID-19. *J. Autoimmun.* **2022**, *126*, 102778. [CrossRef]
62. Kaushal, K.; Kaur, H.; Sarma, P.; Bhattacharyya, A.; Sharma, D.J.; Prajapat, M. Serum ferritin as a predictive biomarker in COVID-19. A systematic review, meta-analysis and meta-regression analysis. *J. Crit. Care* **2022**, *67*, 172–181. [CrossRef]
63. Carubbi, F.; Salvati, L.; Alunno, A.; Maggi, F.; Borghi, E.; Mariani, R. Ferritin is associated with the severity of lung involvement but not with worse prognosis in patients with COVID-19: Data from two Italian COVID-19 units. *Sci. Rep.* **2021**, *11*, 4863. [CrossRef]
64. Hassan Shah, S.S.T.; Naeem, I.; Wahid, B. Analyzing Correlation of Clinical Severity of COVID-19 with Other Biochemical Parameters: A Retrospective Study from Pakistan. *Tohoku J. Exp. Med.* **2021**, *255*, 315–323. [CrossRef]

Disclaimer/Publisher's Note: The statements, opinions and data contained in all publications are solely those of the individual author(s) and contributor(s) and not of MDPI and/or the editor(s). MDPI and/or the editor(s) disclaim responsibility for any injury to people or property resulting from any ideas, methods, instructions or products referred to in the content.

medicina

MDPI

Case Report

Epidural Abscesses as a Complication of Interleukin-6 Inhibitor and Dexamethasone Treatment in a Patient with COVID-19 Pneumonia: A Case Report

Valdis Ģībietis [1,2]

[1] Pauls Stradiņš Clinical University Hospital, 13 Pilsoņu iela, LV-1002 Riga, Latvia; valdis.gibietis@rsu.lv
[2] Department of Internal Diseases, Riga Stradiņš University, 16 Dzirciema iela, LV-1007 Riga, Latvia

Abstract: A 66-year-old female patient was hospitalized with severe COVID-19 pneumonia, which led to hypoxia requiring oxygen support with high-flow nasal cannulae. She received anti-inflammatory treatment with a 10-day dexamethasone 6 mg PO course and a single infusion of IL-6 monoclonal antibody tocilizumab 640 mg IV. Treatment led to gradual reduction of oxygen support. However, on Day 10, she was found to have *Staphylococcus aureus* bacteremia with epidural, psoas, and paravertebral abscesses as the source. Targeted history taking revealed a dental procedure for periodontitis 4 weeks prior to hospitalization as the probable source. She received an 11-week antibiotic treatment, which led to resolution of the abscesses. This case report highlights the importance of individual infection risk assessment before the initiation of immunosuppressive treatment for COVID-19 pneumonia.

Keywords: COVID-19; dexamethasone; tocilizumab; epidural abscess; bacteremia

Citation: Ģībietis, V. Epidural Abscesses as a Complication of Interleukin-6 Inhibitor and Dexamethasone Treatment in a Patient with COVID-19 Pneumonia: A Case Report. *Medicina* **2023**, *59*, 771. https://doi.org/10.3390/medicina59040771

Academic Editor: Nicola Luigi Bragazzi

Received: 9 March 2023
Revised: 5 April 2023
Accepted: 14 April 2023
Published: 16 April 2023

Copyright: © 2023 by the author. Licensee MDPI, Basel, Switzerland. This article is an open access article distributed under the terms and conditions of the Creative Commons Attribution (CC BY) license (https://creativecommons.org/licenses/by/4.0/).

1. Introduction

The interleukin-6 (IL-6) receptor monoclonal antibody tocilizumab is included in the international guidelines for the treatment of COVID-19, as the RECOVERY [1] and REMAP-CAP [2] trials observed that the use of tocilizumab in combination with dexamethasone moderately improves mortality in COVID-19 patients with a severe disease course, worsening condition, increased oxygen demand, and significant inflammatory response [3]. Conflicting data suggest an association of tocilizumab with an increased risk of bacterial infection [4]. This case report discusses a patient with severe COVID-19 pneumonia, who experienced a significant bacterial infection as a complication during treatment.

2. Case Report Description

A 66-year-old female patient was acutely hospitalized by the emergency medicine service to a university hospital in Latvia. She complained of persisting fever with body temperature reaching 39 °C for 13 days, fatigue, and progressive dyspnea. Medical history included symptoms of bronchitis with suspicion of asthma during the prior 3 months, grade 2 systemic hypertension, and recently diagnosed type 2 diabetes (glycated hemoglobin 6.8% three months prior). She had been taking perindopril, amlodipine, indapamide, metformin, and inhaled bronchodilators. She reported a history of allergic drug reactions to penicillin group, tetracycline, and gentamycin (angioedema) that had occurred more than a decade earlier. The patient was not vaccinated against COVID-19. The patient was a non-smoker, reported rare alcohol consumption, denied recreational drug use, had no occupational risk factors, and HIV testing was negative.

Objective findings revealed peripheral oxygen saturation (SpO_2) of 80% in room air, rising to 94% with non-rebreather oxygen mask at flow rate of 12 L per minute. Her respiratory rate was 20 breaths per minute on supplemental oxygen, heart rate 78 beats per minute, and systemic blood pressure 154/78 mmHg. At this point, arterial pO_2 was

68 mmHg, SaO_2—96.5%. Nasopharyngeal and oropharyngeal swab was positive for SARS-CoV-2 RNA in PCR testing. Native computed tomography imaging of the thorax revealed signs of advanced bilateral atypical pneumonia in organizing stage consistent with COVID-19 pneumonia (Figure 1). The patient's body mass index was 33.9 kg/m^2.

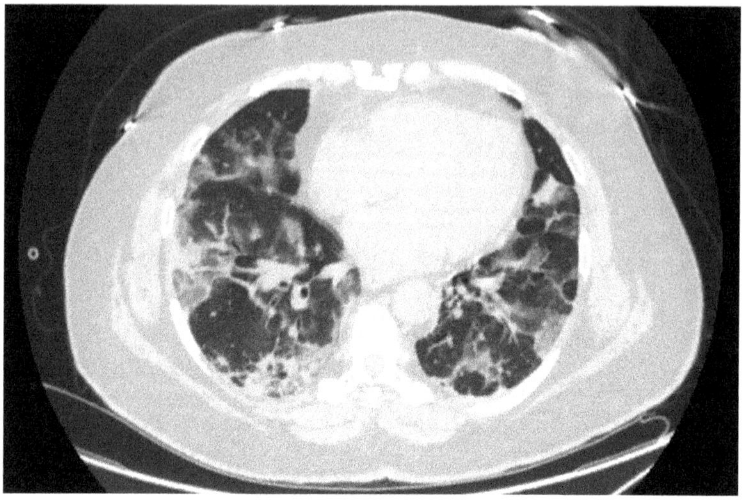

Figure 1. Axial computed tomography image of the lungs on the first day in the hospital.

According to the local protocols, based on the United States National Institutes of Health (NIH) guidelines [3], the patient started a 10-day course of dexamethasone 6 mg PO once daily as well as prophylactic dose low-molecular-weight heparin. The patient was hospitalized in respiratory isolation ward in a monitored room. On Day 1, the oxygen support was increased to high-flow nasal cannulae (HFNC), and during Day 2, it was up-titrated to the maximum flow of FiO_2 100% at 60 L per minute, which produced SpO_2 of 86 to 94% depending on the body position. Due to unsatisfactory saturation, additional oxygen support with non-rebreather oxygen mask at 15 L of oxygen per minute was added over the HFNC, sustaining SpO_2 of 94%. Arterial blood gas analysis showed pO_2 of 59 mmHg (PaO_2/FiO_2 ratio of 59) and SaO_2 of 92.9%, which fit into the target range of 92–96% for COVID-19 patients [3]; therefore, the oxygen support was not escalated to non-invasive ventilation.

In accordance with local criteria—rapidly worsening COVID-19 pneumonia requiring oxygen support, less than 72 h spent in the hospital, and C-reactive protein (CRP) above 40 mg/L—the patient received a weight-adjusted infusion of 640 mg of IV tocilizumab in a single dose. The criteria were based on RECOVERY [1] and REMAP-CAP [2] trials and NIH guidelines [3]. On Day 3, the patient noted a significant improvement of her subjective state and a decrease in dyspnea. Her body temperature had normalized. She remained on oxygen support through HFNC. The oxygen support was reduced to a simple oxygen mask on Day 10 and gradually decreased until discontinuation on Day 15.

On Day 5, the patient complained of new onset back pain at the level of the 12th thoracic vertebra (Th12) of sharp quality during movements with intensity of 4 to 5 out of 10, which was managed with non-opioid analgesics. On Days 8 and 9, the patient had repeated episodes of febrile body temperature, accompanied by leukocytosis in full blood count on Day 7, although her CRP had dropped from 141.8 to 6.6. mg/L (see Table 1). Due to unexplained febrility and leukocytosis, blood cultures through two peripheral sites were performed on Day 10, with subsequently positive result showing methicillin-sensitive *Staphylococcus aureus* (MSSA) bacteremia (resistant to penicillin G, moderately susceptible to ciprofloxacin, and susceptible to erythromycin, clindamycin, tetracycline, chloramphenicol, linezolid, rifampicin, trimethoprim/sulfamethoxazole, and gentamycin). Because of previously reported allergic reactions to penicillin group antibiotics, the patient started a second-choice treatment with an IV course of vancomycin 1500 mg BID with subsequent serum trough concentration monitoring with a target range of 15 to 20 mcg/mL. Due to back pain associated with unexplained bacteremia, the patient underwent magnetic resonance imaging (MRI) of her thoracic and lumbar spine, which revealed small epidural abscesses within the dorsal epidural space at Th9 to 12 (Figure 2), as well as epidural fat infiltration of 0.4 × 0.8 × 2.2 cm at lumbar vertebra 4–5 (L4–5) and psoas sinister muscle 1.3 × 1.4 × 2.8 cm abscess at L5 level and smaller abscesses in paravertebral muscles at L4–5 level. The patient also had lumbar spondylarthritis, mainly at L4-S1 level, with foraminal stenoses. Testing for alternative causative agents for epidural abscesses, e.g., *Mycobacterium tuberculosis*, was not performed because MSSA was already established as the cause due to positive blood cultures.

Table 1. Laboratory findings.

Marker	Day 1	Day 7	Day 15	Unit	Reference Range
Blood leukocytes	6.3	19.6	7.8	$\times 10^9$/L	4–10
Serum C-reactive protein	141.8	6.6	6.8	mg/L	0–5

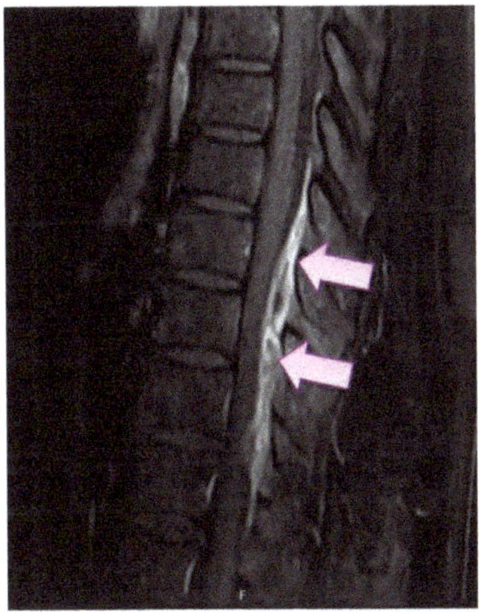

Figure 2. Sagittal magnetic resonance image showing dorsal epidural infiltration with small abscesses from the upper border of Th9 to Th12 (arrows).

Upon a targeted repeated history taking, the patient recalled a dental procedure approximately four weeks prior to hospitalization due to periodontitis. A multidisciplinary decision was made to manage the patient's spinal infection conservatively without surgical treatment. The patient had no immunologic or vascular phenomena associated with endocarditis. Transesophageal echocardiography did not visualize any bacterial vegetations on heart valves. Due to higher theoretical efficacy of beta-lactam, e.g., oxacillin, nafcillin, rather than vancomycin [5,6], on Day 15, after a directly observed successful slow infusion of oxacillin without any adverse effects, the patient continued treatment with oxacillin 2 g IV every 4 h. The IV antibacterial treatment lasted for a total of 4 weeks, with an additional 7 weeks of outpatient treatment with trimethoprim/sulfamethoxazole 960 mg PO every 8 h. The choice of oral antibiotic was based on the antibiogram described above. At Week 8, a repeated MRI of the spine demonstrated no remaining abscesses and diminished inflammatory changes with remaining edema in paraspinal muscles around the left L4–5 joint. The back pain gradually disappeared. No elevation in body temperature, leukocyte count or CRP was seen. The patient discontinued the antibiotics after 11 weeks of treatment without adverse sequelae.

3. Discussion

The presented clinical case occurred during autumn 2021, which, in Latvia, marked the wave of the highest mortality for patients infected with COVID-19 during the pandemic. The mortality peaked at 52 COVID-19-related deaths per 100,000 inhabitants in November 2021, reaching the third highest mortality rate among European Union countries, following Bulgaria and Romania during that month. The higher disease severity of the Delta variant coupled with a low vaccination coverage in the country were important factors to blame for the surge of severely ill hospitalized patients.

This case report demonstrates a patient with severe COVID-19 [3]. RNA sequencing to determine the SARS-CoV-2 variant was not performed in this patient but can be assumed to be Delta because of the 100% Delta (B.1.617.2.) variant prevalence in the Latvian reference laboratory during the period when the patient was diagnosed [7]. The patient had rapid clinical deterioration on Day 13 of illness, which led to hospitalization. The comorbidity of the alleged subacute bronchitis and asthma discouraged her from seeking earlier medical help, as she interpreted the early symptoms as a mere exacerbation, leading to an acute admission at a state of severe hypoxia.

The treatment of hospitalized adults who require supplemental oxygen is based on therapies that directly target SARS-CoV-2 in the early stages and immunosuppressive/anti-inflammatory therapies in later stages to counter the effects of a dysregulated immune/inflammatory response to SARS-CoV-2 leading to tissue damage. In most hospitalized patients who require conventional oxygen, dexamethasone with remdesivir is recommended by the guidelines of NIH [3]. This recommendation is backed by several randomized trials, including ACTT-1 [8] and CATCO [9]. However, in the presented case, the patient was on Day 13 of her illness upon presentation. Remdesivir is not recommended for immunocompetent patients symptomatic for >7 days [10] and was not used. Dexamethasone targets the inflammatory response initiated by SARS-CoV-2 and is recommended in patients with COVID-19 who need supplemental oxygen to meet their prescribed oxygen saturation levels. This recommendation is supported by a meta-analysis of seven randomized trials [11]. The patient received a 10-day course in the standard dose of 6 mg orally.

By the end of Day 1 of hospital stay, the patient was escalated to HFNC oxygen. In such patients, NIH guidelines recommend initiating combined immunomodulator treatment with dexamethasone and oral baricitinib or with dexamethasone and intravenous tocilizumab [3]. Tocilizumab was available at our institution and was administered according to the recommended weight-adjusted dosage. Tocilizumab is a recombinant humanized monoclonal antibody targeted at interleukin-6 (IL-6) receptor. It is approved by the FDA and UK for use in patients with rheumatologic disorders and cytokine release syndrome induced by chimeric antigen receptor T cell therapy [3]. The beneficial effects of this treatment are largely based on the results of the two largest randomized trials—RECOVERY [1] and REMAP-CAP [2]—that demonstrated mortality benefit, including patients who exhibited rapid respiratory decompensation associated with an inflammatory response. The rationale for the use of tocilizumab is its inhibitory effect on interleukin-6, which is one of the key pro-inflammatory cytokines driving the acute inflammatory pneumonic process. The local criteria for administration of tocilizumab in COVID-19 patients also included several contraindications—known hypersensitivity, any other severe infection in addition to COVID-19, hepatic transaminases over 5 times the upper limit of normal, thrombocytopenia $< 50 \times 10^9/L$, neutropenia $< 2 \times 10^9/L$, and ongoing active immunosuppressive treatment. At the moment of administration, the patient did not have any data on the existence of these contraindications.

The patient received a combined treatment of two immunomodulatory drugs—dexamethasone and tocilizumab. She demonstrated a gradual clinical improvement and a steady reduction of oxygen support. On Day 7 of the hospital stay, she had an increase in blood leukocyte count with neutrophil predominance, which, at that point, was attributed to corticosteroid treatment; however, on Day 8, she had a repeated episode of febrile body temperature, which was later proven to be due to MSSA bacteremia with epidural and paravertebral abscesses as the source. At presentation, an important anamnestic event was overlooked and not reported by the patient—a dental procedure for periodontitis. Although it had been performed approximately 4 weeks prior to hospitalization, it is a probable source of bacteremia, with spinal infection as a complication exacerbated by the combined immunomodulatory treatment in the context of a severe COVID-19, which may also act as an immunosuppressive factor by itself, reducing the patient's ability to naturally clear the bacteremia. Diabetes is another well-known risk factor for spinal infections [12].

The duration of antibiotic therapy for epidural abscesses is not well defined. Sources cite 4 to 12 weeks as adequate durations [13]. A relatively long antibiotic duration was chosen in this patient to reduce the risk of recurrence because she was managed conservatively with no drainage of the abscesses [14].

Talamonti et al. [15] reported a case series of six COVID-19 patients with spinal epidural abscesses, indicating an unusually high incidence of this disease in this patient group. Most of the patients did not have typical risk factors for spinal infection, five of them were hypertensive, two were obese, and one had diabetes. The authors hypothesize that the infections may have been caused by the coexistence of an initially asymptomatic bacterial contamination along with COVID-19-induced endotheliitis. Interestingly, three of the patients had received tocilizumab for COVID-19. Sampogna et al. [16] also reported two patients with COVID-19 with respiratory failure requiring mechanical ventilation who acquired spinal epidural abscesses with MSSA and *Enterococcus faecalis* as the causative agents. Both had received tocilizumab, supporting the role of both COVID-19-related and drug-induced immunosuppression along with preexisting clinical factors as the reasons for secondary bacterial infection. Mohamed Ramlee et al. [17] reported three cases of delayed spinal infections following a recent SARS-CoV-2 infection up to three months before the diagnosis. It was not reported whether the patients received any immunosuppressive COVID-19 treatment. Choudhury et al. [18] reported a patient with recurrent and persistent MSSA bacteremia and osteomyelitis, complicated by a spinal epidural abscess, bioprosthetic valve endocarditis, and aortic root abscess despite antibiotic treatment while having tested positive for SARS-CoV-2 infection, implying a COVID-19-induced immunocompromised state with functional exhaustion of CD4 and CD8 T-cells as the potential underlying mechanism for the persistence of such infections. In a report by Chu et al. [19], a 60-year-old patient with diabetes and gingivitis developed *Streptococcus oralis* spinal infection with paraspinal, psoas, and epidural abscesses one week after recovery from a mild COVID-19 infection. The patient had not received any immunosuppressive treatment but did have risk factors for spinal infection—gingivitis and diabetes—similar to the case presented in this report. Our case further strengthens the idea that there is an interplay among initially asymptomatic bacteremia, comorbidities, immune, and endothelial effects of COVID-19 itself along with immunosuppressive treatment, which may explain the development of secondary bacterial infection, particularly spinal epidural abscesses, in such patients.

Similarly, there have been numerous studies and reports on influenza as a predisposing factor for secondary bacterial infection summarized by Radovanovic et al. [20] It is hypothesized that multiple immunological mechanisms may play a role, e.g., damage of the tracheobronchial epithelial layer causing local immunologic response suppression and promotion of bacterial adherence and translocation [21]. As a similar respiratory viral pathogen, SARS-CoV-2 may induce analogous mechanisms for secondary infection.

There is a lack of high-quality trialsthat specifically assess infection risk during treatment with dexamethasone and tocilizumab in COVID-19 patients. In a literature review of 36 studies, Koritala et al. [4] showed mixed results with variable significance for the association of IL-6 inhibitors with risk of infections in patients with COVID-19. Some studies observed an increase in infection risk, mainly bacteremia, while others showed no difference or even a decrease. In a recent retrospective study by Sandhu et al., patients with severe COVID-19 pneumonia treated with tocilizumab experienced high rates of secondary infection—45.5% versus 24.5% in controls [22]. Interestingly, in a study by Kooistra et al. on patients with COVID-19, it was shown that immunomodulatory treatment with dexamethasone and tocilizumab considerably reduced the value of procalcitonin and CRP for detection of secondary infections in COVID-19 patients [23]. This finding may explain why even during and after the onset of back pain and fever, the CRP value remained low while leukocytosis increased in the presented case.

Overall, a careful risk-benefit assessment with thorough history taking is important before initiating a combined immunomodulatory/immunosuppressive treatment in a severe COVID-19 patient to prevent serious adverse effects of the treatment, mainly secondary bacterial infection. The chosen treatment was indicated for the presented patient according to trial data and international guidelines; however, the history of a recent dental procedure due to an oral infection might be a reason to consider alternative approach or a possible dose reduction of the IL-6 inhibitor. Further studies regarding secondary bacterial infection risk in COVID-19 patients treated with immunosuppressive drugs are needed.

4. Conclusions

High-flow oxygen therapy and anti-inflammatory therapy with dexamethasone and the IL-6 inhibitor tocilizumab in a patient with severe COVID-19 pneumonia effectively promoted recovery. However, the patient experienced an infectious complication—abscesses in the epidural space and paravertebral muscles. Individual infection risk assessment is required for patients when initiating treatment with immunosuppressive drugs, as both COVID-19 along with immunomodulatory medication may provoke secondary bacterial infection.

Funding: This research received no external funding.

Institutional Review Board Statement: Ethical review and approval were waived for this paper because it is a retrospective report that involves an individual patient and is not considered a research.

Informed Consent Statement: Informed consent was obtained from the patient involved in the case report.

Data Availability Statement: Not applicable.

Conflicts of Interest: The author declares no conflict of interest.

References

1. Abani, O.; Abbas, A.; Abbas, F.; Abbas, M.; Abbasi, S.; Abbass, H.; Abbott, A.; Abdallah, N.; Abdelaziz, A.; Abdelfattah, M.; et al. Tocilizumab in patients admitted to hospital with COVID-19 (RECOVERY): A randomised, controlled, open-label, platform trial. *Lancet* **2021**, *397*, 1637–1645. [CrossRef]
2. Gordon, A.C.; Mouncey, P.R.; Al-Beidh, F.; Rowan, K.M.; Nichol, A.D.; Arabi, Y.M.; Annane, D.; Beane, A.; Van Bentum-Puijk, W.; Berry, L.R.; et al. Interleukin-6 Receptor Antagonists in Critically Ill Patients with COVID-19. *N. Engl. J. Med.* **2021**, *384*, 1491–1502. [CrossRef] [PubMed]
3. National Institutes of Health. COVID-19 Treatment Guidelines Panel. Coronavirus Disease 2019 (COVID-19) Treatment Guidelines. Available online: https://www.covid19treatmentguidelines.nih.gov/ (accessed on 5 April 2023).
4. Infection risk with the use of interleukin inhibitors in hospitalized patients with COVID-19: A narrative review. *Infez. Med.* **2021**, *29*, 495–503. [CrossRef]
5. Chang, F.-Y.; Peacock, J.E.; Musher, D.M.; Triplett, P.; MacDonald, B.B.; Mylotte, J.M.; O'Donnell, A.; Wagener, M.M.; Yu, V.L. Staphylococcus aureus Bacteremia. *Medicine* **2003**, *82*, 333–339. [CrossRef] [PubMed]
6. Fowler, J.V.G.; Kong, L.K.; Corey, G.R.; Gottlieb, G.S.; McClelland, R.S.; Sexton, D.J.; Gesty-Palmer, D.; Harrell, L.J. Recurrent *Staphylococcus aureus* Bacteremia: Pulsed-Field Gel Electrophoresis Findings in 29 Patients. *J. Infect. Dis.* **1999**, *179*, 1157–1161. [CrossRef] [PubMed]
7. COVID-19 Statistika Slimību Profilakses un Kontroles Centrs. Available online: https://www.spkc.gov.lv/lv/covid-19-statistika (accessed on 5 April 2023).
8. Beigel, J.H.; Tomashek, K.M.; Dodd, L.E.; Mehta, A.K.; Zingman, B.S.; Kalil, A.C.; Hohmann, E.; Chu, H.Y.; Luetkemeyer, A.; Kline, S.; et al. Remdesivir for the Treatment of COVID-19—Final Report. *N. Engl. J. Med.* **2020**, *383*, 1813–1826. [CrossRef] [PubMed]

9. Ali, K.; Azher, T.; Baqi, M.; Binnie, A.; Borgia, S.; Carrier, F.M.; Cavayas, Y.A.; Chagnon, N.; Cheng, M.P.; Conly, J.; et al. Remdesivir for the treatment of patients in hospital with COVID-19 in Canada: A randomized controlled trial. *Can. Med. Assoc. J.* **2022**, *194*, E242–E251. [CrossRef] [PubMed]
10. Ader, F.; Bouscambert-Duchamp, M.; Hites, M.; Peiffer-Smadja, N.; Poissy, J.; Belhadi, D.; Diallo, A.; Lê, M.-P.; Peytavin, G.; Staub, T.; et al. Remdesivir plus standard of care versus standard of care alone for the treatment of patients admitted to hospital with COVID-19 (DisCoVeRy): A phase 3, randomised, controlled, open-label trial. *Lancet Infect. Dis.* **2021**, *22*, 209–221. [CrossRef] [PubMed]
11. WHO TEAM. *Corticosteroids for COVID-19. Living Guidance*; WHO: Geneva, Switzerland, 2 September 2020.
12. Tsantes, A.G.; Papadopoulos, D.V.; Vrioni, G.; Sioutis, S.; Sapkas, G.; Benzakour, A.; Benzakour, T.; Angelini, A.; Ruggieri, P.; Mavrogenis, A.F.; et al. Spinal Infections: An Update. *Microorganisms* **2020**, *8*, 476. [CrossRef] [PubMed]
13. Campioli, C.C.; Go, J.R.; Abu Saleh, O.; Challener, D.; Yetmar, Z.; Osmon, D.R. Antistaphylococcal Penicillin vs Cefazolin for the Treatment of Methicillin-Susceptible *Staphylococcus aureus* Spinal Epidural Abscesses. *Open Forum Infect. Dis.* **2021**, *8*, ofab071. [CrossRef] [PubMed]
14. Lener, S.; Hartmann, S.; Barbagallo, G.M.V.; Certo, F.; Thomé, C.; Tschugg, A. Management of spinal infection: A review of the literature. *Acta Neurochir.* **2018**, *160*, 487–496. [CrossRef] [PubMed]
15. Talamonti, G.; Colistra, D.; Crisà, F.; Cenzato, M.; Giorgi, P.; D'Aliberti, G. Spinal epidural abscess in COVID-19 patients. *J. Neurol.* **2020**, *268*, 2320–2326. [CrossRef] [PubMed]
16. Sampogna, G.; Tessitore, N.; Bianconi, T.; Leo, A.; Zarbo, M.; Montanari, E.; Spinelli, M. Spinal cord dysfunction after COVID-19 infection. *Spinal Cord Ser. Cases* **2020**, *6*, 92. [CrossRef] [PubMed]
17. Ramlee, F.A.M.; Bin Harun, M.H.; Nagaretnam, V.; Lim, T.S.; Aris, H.F.; Tan, C.N. A Case Series of Spinal Infections Following COVID-19: A Delayed Complication. *Cureus* **2022**, *14*, e29272. [CrossRef]
18. Choudhury, I.; Han, H.; Manthani, K.; Gandhi, S.; Dabhi, R. COVID-19 as a Possible Cause of Functional Exhaustion of CD4 and CD8 T-cells and Persistent Cause of Methicillin-Sensitive Staphylococcus aureus Bacteremia. *Cureus* **2020**, *12*, e9000. [CrossRef] [PubMed]
19. Chu, E.C.-P.; Trager, R.J.; Chen, A.T.C.; Shum, J.S.F. A 60-Year-Old Man with Gingivitis and Poorly Controlled Diabetes Developing Low Back Pain 1 Week Following Recovery from COVID-19 Diagnosed with Spinal Abscess Due to Streptococcus oralis. *Am. J. Case Rep.* **2022**, *23*, e937517-1. [CrossRef] [PubMed]
20. Radovanovic, M.; Petrovic, M.; Barsoum, M.K.; Nordstrom, C.W.; Calvin, A.D.; Dumic, I.; Jevtic, D.; Hanna, R.D. Influenza Myopericarditis and Pericarditis: A Literature Review. *J. Clin. Med.* **2022**, *11*, 4123. [CrossRef] [PubMed]
21. Manna, S.; Baindara, P.; Mandal, S.M. Molecular pathogenesis of secondary bacterial infection associated to viral infections including SARS-CoV-2. *J. Infect. Public Health* **2020**, *13*, 1397–1404. [CrossRef] [PubMed]
22. Sandhu, G.; Piraino, S.T.B.; Piticaru, J. Secondary Infection Risk in Patients With Severe COVID-19 Pneumonia Treated With Tocilizumab. *Am. J. Ther.* **2022**, *29*, e275–e278. [CrossRef] [PubMed]
23. Kooistra, E.J.; van Berkel, M.; van Kempen, N.F.; van Latum, C.R.M.; Bruse, N.; Frenzel, T.; Berg, M.J.W.V.D.; Schouten, J.A.; Kox, M.; Pickkers, P. Dexamethasone and tocilizumab treatment considerably reduces the value of C-reactive protein and procalcitonin to detect secondary bacterial infections in COVID-19 patients. *Crit. Care* **2021**, *25*, 281. [CrossRef] [PubMed]

Disclaimer/Publisher's Note: The statements, opinions and data contained in all publications are solely those of the individual author(s) and contributor(s) and not of MDPI and/or the editor(s). MDPI and/or the editor(s) disclaim responsibility for any injury to people or property resulting from any ideas, methods, instructions or products referred to in the content.

medicina

MDPI

Case Report

Multifocal Tuberculosis Verrucosa Cutis: Case Report and Review of the Literature

Niki Ntavari [1], Vasiliki Syrmou [2], Konstantinos Tourlakopoulos [3], Foteini Malli [3,4,*], Irini Gerogianni [3], Angeliki-Viktoria Roussaki [1], Efterpi Zafiriou [1], Maria Ioannou [5], Eirini Tziastoudi [5], Konstantinos I. Gourgoulianis [3] and Ioannis Pantazopoulos [3,6]

1 Department of Dermatology, Faculty of Medicine, University of Thessaly, 41500 Larissa, Greece; nikintavari@gmail.com (N.N.); roussaki@med.uth.gr (A.-V.R.); zafevi@o365.uth.gr (E.Z.)
2 Department of Rheumatology and Clinical Immunology, University of Thessaly, 41500 Larissa, Greece; syrmouvicky@yahoo.gr
3 Department of Respiratory Medicine, Faculty of Medicine, University of Thessaly, 41500 Larissa, Greece; kntourlakopoulos@gmail.com (K.T.); igerogianni@yahoo.gr (I.G.); kgourg@med.uth.gr (K.I.G.); pantazopoulosioannis@yahoo.com (I.P.)
4 Respiratory Disorders Lab, Faculty of Nursing, University of Thessaly, 41500 Larissa, Greece
5 Department of Pathology, Faculty of Medicine, University of Thessaly, 41334 Larissa, Greece; mioan@med.uth.gr (M.I.); etziastoudi@gmail.com (E.T.)
6 Department of Emergency Medicine, Faculty of Medicine, University of Thessaly, 41334 Larissa, Greece
* Correspondence: mallifoteini@yahoo.gr; Tel.: +30-2413508296

Abstract: Cutaneous tuberculosis (TB) is still a major public health problem worldwide. Tuberculosis verrucosa cutis (TBVC) is a cutaneous form of exogenous TB caused by exogenous reinfection in previously sensitized individuals. TBVC typically presents as a unifocal condition. Multifocal cutaneous lesions without any other tubercular foci are extremely rare in exogenous TB and few cases are reported in the literature. We describe the first case of multifocal TBVC in an 81-year-old Greek man. In total, 14 cases of multifocal TBVC have been reported in the literature (8 males and 6 females), with mean age 47.64 years (SD = 20.75) and mean time to diagnosis of 9.69 years (SD = 15.31). Most cases (11/12) responded rapidly to treatment, implying the accuracy of diagnosis, while no one was reported to be immunocompromised. Finally, in 10 cases (71.4%), history of skin microtrauma was reported (related either to daily life habits or to professional praxis), confirming it as the main risk factor. The tuberculin skin test was positive in 10 cases and tissue culture for mycobacteria was negative in all cases. TBVC can present with multiple lesions, even in countries where TB prevalence is not high, especially in patients with history of skin abrasions. Prompt specialist assessment can expedite the establishment of diagnosis.

Keywords: tuberculosis verrucosa cutis (TBVC); multifocal; infectious diseases; tuberculosis

Citation: Ntavari, N.; Syrmou, V.; Tourlakopoulos, K.; Malli, F.; Gerogianni, I.; Roussaki, A.-V.; Zafiriou, E.; Ioannou, M.; Tziastoudi, E.; Gourgoulianis, K.I.; et al. Multifocal Tuberculosis Verrucosa Cutis: Case Report and Review of the Literature. *Medicina* **2023**, *59*, 1758. https://doi.org/10.3390/medicina59101758

Academic Editor: Nicola Luigi Bragazzi

Received: 30 July 2023
Revised: 21 September 2023
Accepted: 28 September 2023
Published: 2 October 2023

Copyright: © 2023 by the authors. Licensee MDPI, Basel, Switzerland. This article is an open access article distributed under the terms and conditions of the Creative Commons Attribution (CC BY) license (https://creativecommons.org/licenses/by/4.0/).

1. Introduction

Cutaneous tuberculosis (TB) is frequently seen among dermatology outpatient departments in India [1]. On the other hand, it is uncommon in developed countries, although it has an increasing incidence among minorities of Indian and African origin. Cutaneous TB can be acquired from hematogenous or lymphatic dissemination of a pulmonary focus, being in many cases multifocal (endogenous cutaneous TB) and otherwise arising through direct inoculation with a more local predominance (exogenous cutaneous TB) [2]. Tuberculosis verrucosa cutis (TBVC) represents the most common form of exogenous TB. Multifocal cutaneous lesions without any other tubercular focus are extremely rare in exogenous TB.

Herein, we report a case of multifocal TBVC presenting with different types of skin rashes depending on the affected site, obstructing easy diagnosis of cutaneous TB. Furthermore, we summarize and compare the available literature on multifocal TBVC. Written and informed permission for publication was obtained from the patient.

2. Detailed Case Description

An 81-year-old, male, a former lawyer, was referred to our outpatient dermatology department with a 4-month-long, polymorphic, multifocal skin rash on the scalp, back, and upper and lower limbs. The patient complained of intense pruritus on the scalp and lower limb pain upon the lesions. He did not report a cough, hemoptysis, fever, night sweats, or weight loss. There was no history of smoking or alcohol abuse. He was not aware of preceding TB infection, and he could not recall any exposure to a known TB case. In terms of past medical history, he reported insulin-dependent type 2 diabetes mellitus, percutaneous transluminal coronary angioplasty, atrial fibrillation, and angiodysplasia of the gastrointestinal tract. He had been vaccinated with the Bacille Calmette–Guerin (BCG) vaccine at the age of 18.

On physical examination, multiple crusted, scaly lesions with marginal erythema and erosions were observed on the scalp. He reported that the lesions were present for several months, but he noticed a sharp growth and the presence of erosions during the last month. A second rash was observed on the patient's back and was characterized by tender, erythematous papules, and small plaques with an arciform pattern, similar to those of Sweet Syndrome (Figure 1a). One of the lesions demonstrated central crusting. In addition, painful, erythematous, subcutaneous nodules with a diameter of 1–2 cm and small scaly plaques were palpable on the patient's lower limbs. The patient mentioned that they were present for a 4-month period (Figure 1b). The nodules were located on the anterior aspect of the patient's calves and shins. The lesions started as painless small skin lesions before progressively enlarging and ulcerating. On the left lower limb, the inflammation overlying the nodules merged, developing a large erythematous lesion without ulceration. In contrast, the nodules showed ulceration with mixed purulent/sanguineous discharge. Left ankle swelling was also observed. On the right shin, there were fewer lesions, and more importantly, a larger less painful ulcerated nodule with central crusting. The patient's most recent rash emerged on the upper limbs 15 days prior to their visit (Figure 1c). No regional or generalized lymphadenopathy was observed. The differential diagnosis included tuberculosis verrucosa cutis, multiple tuberculous abscess, nontuberculous mycobacterial infection, and deep fungal infection.

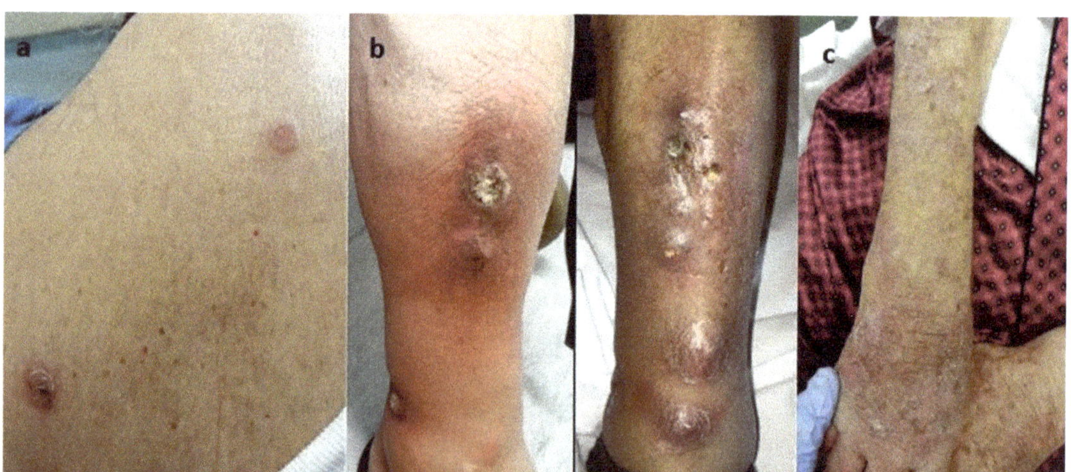

Figure 1. (**a**) Erythematous papules and small plaques with an arciform pattern in the patients' back, (**b**) erythematous, subcutaneous nodules and small scaly plaques in the calves, (**c**) rash on the upper limbs.

Routine blood tests revealed leukocytosis. The patient had a total leukocyte count of 17,700 cells/mm^3 with a differential count of 70% neutrophils, 3% eosinophils, 10% lymphocytes, and an erythrocyte sedimentation rate of 40 mm in the 1st hour. Biochemistry test results and autoimmune markers (including antinuclear antibodies, p- and c-antineutrophil cytoplasmic antibodies, and anti-proteinase 3 anti-myeloperoxidase antibodies) were unremarkable. Thyroid function tests were normal and serum electrophoresis revealed no monoclonal component. VDRL and HIV tests were non-reactive. Chest X-ray revealed no evidence of tuberculosis or any other abnormality. The tuberculin skin test (TST) (SPAN's tuberculin) was 20 mm. Although the patient did not present with fever, the possibility of "Sweet Syndrome" was considered and chest and abdominal computed tomography were conducted without any abnormal findings. Examination of pus and skin scraping with Ziehl Nielsen staining failed to identify any acid-fast bacilli. Scraping was performed on the margin of the lesions on the legs and the back, and a pathology slide was prepared with 10% KOH. The result was negative for mycelia/spores.

A 4 mm punch biopsy specimen was taken from the lesions of the back and upper and lower limbs. Histopathology revealed hyperkeratosis, acanthosis with pseudoepitheliomatous hyperplasia of the epidermis, and diffuse lymphocytic and neutrophilic inflammatory infiltrates (Figure 2). Tuberculoid granulomatous inflammation in the dermis was also observed. A culture for mycobacterium TB was negative. Periodic acid Schiff staining did not reveal fungal elements. Based on the above-mentioned histology findings, the diagnosis of TBVC was made and the patient was started on a six-month antitubercular regimen with rifampicin, isoniazid, pyrazinamide, and ethambutol. On a follow-up visit 2 months later, the nodules had flattened out and the ulcers had disappeared (Figure 3).

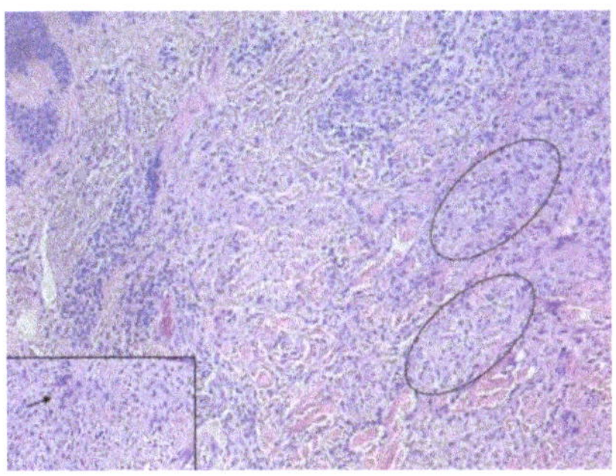

Figure 2. Histology shows a granulomatous inflammation composed of epithelioid histiocytes with sporadic multinucleated giant cells (as present in the rectangle insert) and lymphocytes (hematoxylin and eosin). Hematoxylin and Eosin staining, original magnification ×4. Insert original magnification ×40.

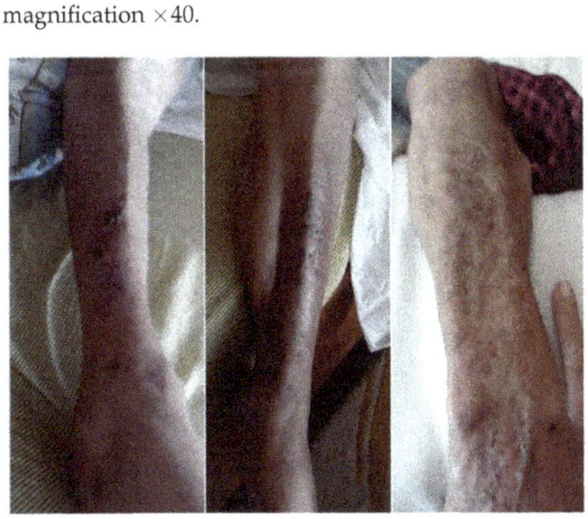

Figure 3. Improvement of the nodules and ulcers after 2 months of antituberculous treatment.

3. Discussion

Cutaneous tuberculosis spans a spectrum, ranging from lupus vulgaris and TBVC at one end to scrofuloderma and tuberculosis cutis orificialis at the other end [3]. The progression along this spectrum is associated with a decline in cell-mediated immunity [3]. TBVC can be acquired via exogenous direct skin inoculation of M. tuberculosis and M. bovis through abrasions in a previously sensitized patient with a moderate to high degree of immunity to mycobacterium TB infection [4]. Thus, it is found predominately in anatomical regions prone to trauma such as the soles, the dorsum of the hands and feet, the fingers, and the toes [2]. Typically, this form of cutaneous TB is observed as a single lesion in one anatomical site. Multifocal TBVC is quite rare and, in our literature search, only 13 published cases were identified (Table 1). Herein, we report the first case of multifocal TBVC in a Greek man, where multiple lesions were identified in the scalp, back, and upper and lower limbs. In our patient, chronic generalized pruritus, most possibly related to type 2 diabetes mellitus, is believed to have been the cause of itching, leading to microtrauma to the skin. Moreover, the patient was self-injecting with insulin and was measuring his glucose blood capillary level at least twice daily, causing micro-needle injuries on the fingertips and abdominal wall.

In Greece, the BCG vaccine was included in the national vaccination schedule until 2016 and this patient was vaccinated. Despite vaccination, he had probably been infected by and successfully cleared the bacillus during his lifetime, acquiring a stronger degree of immunity against the pathogen. This, in turn, at a later phase, led to TBVC, following an exogenous inoculation of the pathogen in the microlesions of the skin. This is not a common phenomenon in Greece; it can, however, be explained by the fact that TB has not been completely eradicated according to authorities. Interestingly, nearly all published cases were noted in Indian patients, except for one patient from the Republic of North Macedonia [5] and one from Bangladesh [6]. Since the development of TBVC requires previous immunity against TB, it is expected to be more common in endemic countries where the prevalence of TB is higher. Moreover, it represents a form of locally secluded bacilli lesion, managed by the body with the formation of a granuloma, which confines the disease to this specific point. For this reason, it is not common to have multiple inoculations in the same person on different body parts. It is noteworthy that although TBVC is reported to be more frequent in children living in endemic countries and walking barefoot on ground contaminated with tuberculous sputum, only two cases of multifocal TBVC have been reported in children aged below 18 years (one in a 17- and one in a 12-year-old child) [6,7].

The long timespan from lesion manifestation till TBVC diagnosis is partially explained by the lack of systemic symptoms that would prompt the patient to seek medical advice early. In countries with paucity of proper primary healthcare services and with the health system prioritizing more severe public health problems, patients with mild skin lesions that do not pose immediate threat to life or do not cause significant disability can go undiagnosed for years. TBVC lesions run an asymptomatic course in most cases and start as small papules that slowly progress to verrucous ones over several months to years later [2]. For this reason, they usually run a prolonged course before being diagnosed. The longest period described in the literature was 60 years, in a 65-year-old patient from the Republic of North Macedonia with multifocal TBVC. The average duration for the diagnosis of multifocal TBVC is nearly 10 years, further indicating the long course of the disease before diagnosis [5]. In our case, the patient had small subcutaneous nodules of 1–2 cm diameter, and small scaly plaques at the lower limbs for a 4-month period. Early referral to a highly specialized unit can explain the timely diagnosis and treatment. Another interesting finding in our case was that not all the lesions appeared with the same macroscopic morphology. According to the other published multifocal TBVC cases, the initial lesion of TBVC appears as a small, painless papule with an inflammatory border progressing to the hyperkeratotic plaque with peripheral extension [2]. The center of the lesion may remain hyperkeratotic, with a white atrophic scar, or may exude pus [2].

Table 1. Brief presentation of the published studies on multifocal TBVC.

First Author/Year	Age/Sex	Country	Duration	Immunosuppression/ Cause	Site	Culture TB/Mantoux	Histology	Response to Therapy
Damevska K/2013 [4]	65, F	Republic of North Macedonia	60 y	Immunocompetent/ N.A.	Bilateral upper limbs and right lower limb	Negative/(+)	Granulomatous inflamma-tion in the dermis, with small foci of caseation necrosis	Damevska K/2013 [4]
Rahman MH/2020 [5]	12, M	Bangladesh	2 y	Immunocompetent/ bare-footed child	Bilateral extremities	N.A./(+) 17 mm	Hypertrophy of the epidermis and mid-dermalgranuloma with Langhans giant cells	At 6 months, complete resolution of the lesions
Rajan J/2011 [6]	17, M	India	2 y	Immunocompetent/ cattleherd	Left foot	N.A./(+) 17 mm	Hypertrophy of the epidermis and mid-dermal granulomata with Langhans giant cells	At 6 months, all the lesions were completely resolved
Vora RV/2016 [7]	60, F	India	12 y	Immunocompetent/ a thorn prick over her right big toe	Right lower limb	N.A./(−)	Hyperkeratosis, acanthosis of the epidermis. Below the epidermis, multiple granulomas, comprised epithelioid cells with Langhans	At 3 months, improvement of the lesions
Sudarshan R/2016 [8]	69, F	India	14 y	Immunocompetent/ farmer handling cattle occasionally	Right upperlimb, lower limbs, face and nape	Negative/(−)	Hyperplasia, hyperkeratosis and hypergranulosis. Dermis epithelioid cell granulomas with many Langhans giant cells and lymphoplasmacytic infiltrate	Incomplete response after 1 year of therapy

Table 1. *Cont.*

First Author/Year	Age/Sex	Country	Duration	Immunosuppression/ Cause	Site	Culture TB/Mantoux	Histology	Response to Therapy
Chahar M/2015 [9]	48, M	India	15 y	Immunocompetent/ walking barefoot	Bilateral buttocks and feet	Negative/(+)	Hyperkeratosis, acanthosis, papillomatosis. Upper dermis mononuclear infiltrate and mid-dermis. Epithelioid cell granulomas comprising Langhans giant cells	At 6 months, complete resolution of the lesions
Verma R/2014 [10]	30, M	India	3 y	Immunocompetent/ farmer	Right lower limb	Negative/(+)	Pseudoepitheliomatous hyperplasia with irregular acanthosis. Dermis epithelioid cell granulomas with Langhans giant cells and neutrophilic microabscesses	At 6 months, resolution of the lesions
Rasineni N/2014 [11]	42, F	India	4 m	N.A./N.A.	Left sole and left index finger	Negative/ (+) 20 mm	Hyperkeratosis along with numerous lymphocytes, epithelioid cells, and Langhans giant cells in the dermis	At 5 months, complete clearance
Manjumeena D/2018 [12]	52, F	India	20 y	Immunocompetent/ trauma while cutting wood	Left leg and foot	Negative/(+)	Hyperkeratosis, acanthosis, papillomatosis, granulomas composed of lymphocytes, neutrophils, giant cells with central caseous necrosis	At 6 months, regression of the lesions

Table 1. *Cont.*

First Author/Year	Age/Sex	Country	Duration	Immunosuppression/ Cause	Site	Culture TB/Mantoux	Histology	Response to Therapy
Sehgal VN/2017 [13]	78, M	India	1 y	N.A/N.A	upper and lower extremities	N.A./(−)	Epithelial hyperplasia, papillomatosis, and perivascular inflammation in dermis. Epithelioid cell granuloma	At 6 months, complete regression of the lesions
Rani S/2020 [14]	29, M	India	2 y	Immunocompetent/ farmer	Heel, antero-posterior and medial side of leg	Negative/ (+) 20 mm	Hyperkeratosis, acanthosis, dermal infiltration with epithelioid cell granulomas with Langhans giant cells and occasional central necrosis	At 5 months, improvement of the lesions
Prasad PVS/2002 [15]	35, M	India	2 y	Immunocompetent	Left hand and left foot	Negative/(−)	Hyperkeratosis, acanthosis, and mid-dermal tuberculoid granulomas	-
Padmaprasad MK/2013 [16]	49, F	India	2 y	Immunocompetent/ butcher	Right shoulder, right breast, lower limbs and buttocks	Negative/ (+) 22 mm	Pseudoepitheliomatous hyperplasia, dense infiltration of plasma cells and giant cells, and caseation necrosis	N.A.

TBVC develops in patients with an intact immune system [17], previously exposed and sensitized to the mycobacterium. A robust immune response seems to be a prerequisite for this form of TB. This is expected as the individual should be sensitized against the pathogen, with effective clearance already performed. In these patients, skin reaction to seclude bacilli leads to the typical tuberculoid granuloma formation.

As TBVC is caused by accidental inoculation through open wounds or abrasions, certain professional groups are at higher risk of becoming infected [18]. As evident in Table 1, most patients with multifocal TBVC were farmers, butchers, or cattle ranchers. Interestingly, our patient was a lawyer without any obvious inoculation site, but with history of pruritus, itching, and regular insulin injections. Multifocal TBVC mainly affects the lower limbs, but it can also affect the buttocks, the upper limbs, and even the head, as seen in our case.

The diagnosis of TBVC is challenging and is mainly based on the correlation of the medical and disease course history, the physical findings (i.e., the characteristic lesions, etc.), and evidence of TB infection (i.e., the culture of the biopsy specimens, positive TST, etc.), while the most important diagnostic tool is the histopathological examination [19]. The lesions are characterized by pseudoepitheliomatous hyperplasia of the epidermis with hyperkeratosis and dense inflammatory cell infiltrates comprising of neutrophils, lymphocytes, and Langhans giant cells [19]. Moreover, tuberculous granulomas with caseous necrosis of moderate intensity can be found in the dermis [19]. However, caseous necrosis in the dermis may not always be evident, as seen in some of the cases presented in Table 1.

TST is typically positive, representing a delayed hypersensitivity reaction, engaging CD4+ T cells sensitized by prior infection [20]. However, as seen in our results, there have been cases of multifocal TBVC with negative TST. For this reason, TST should be performed in all cases, but clinicians should not exclude the diagnosis in the event of a negative result. Tissue mycobacterial culture, although helpful in making a diagnosis, is usually negative (paucibacillary form) as a result of the strong immune response against the bacilli [21]. No positive culture for mycobacterium TB has been reported in patients with multifocal TBVC (Table 1). Molecular tests, when available, such as mycobacterial DNA isolation, can confirm the diagnosis. Nucleic acid amplification (NAA) techniques in tissue specimens can be useful as they can provide early evidence of infection (within 2 h) and information regarding genes associated with drug resistance [8]. Regarding paucibacillary forms, the results are controversial [9,10]. However, in cases where tissue culture and histopathologic stains are both negative, they can assist in the establishment of the diagnosis [10].

TBVC is treated as per the recommendations of therapy for pulmonary TB and the therapeutic response represents a valuable diagnostic criterion [11]. Multifocal TBVC responds to antituberculous treatment within three to six months, as observed in most cases mentioned in Table 1. Response to treatment indirectly confirms the diagnosis, as pathogen isolation is not possible in several instances. Only one case reported a minimal response after one year of treatment [12]. Surgical excision, cryotherapy, and electrocautery can be useful in the treatment of localized lesions in addition to systemic treatment.

After an extensive literature review, we identified 13 cases of multifocal TBVC (Table 1). Including our case, eight patients were males and six were females, giving a male-to-female ratio of 1.33. The mean age was 47.64 ± 20.75 years and the mean time from symptom onset to diagnosis was 9.69 ± 15.31 years. In two cases, information was not provided regarding immunosuppression, but all other cases were described in immunocompetent patients. Eleven individuals were of Asian origin (ten from India and one from Bangladesh) and two came from the Balkan peninsula (one from Greece and one from the Republic of North Macedonia). Ten cases had positive TST (76.9%). Tissue culture for mycobacteria was performed in 11 cases and was negative in all cases, while for the other 3 cases, information was unavailable. In terms of treatment outcome, information was not provided for 2 cases, whereas, in the remaining 12 cases, the lesions persisted one year after initiation of treatment only in 1 woman. Most cases (11/12, 91.6%) had a significant response to treatment within six months. Finally, in 10 cases (71.4%), history of skin microtrauma was provided, indicating it as the main risk factor.

Tuberculosis comprises a major burden for public health worldwide despite the tremendous progress in technology, biomedical research, and pharmacology. This phenomenon is believed to exist due to socioeconomic differences, the global financial crisis, public healthcare services' incompetence, antibiotic resistance, and recently, the SARS-CoV-2 pandemic (delayed diagnosis, limited financial sources, limited access to healthcare services).

4. Conclusions

In conclusion, cutaneous TB, as part of the TB spectrum, can still comprise a challenge for clinicians worldwide. Compatible skin lesions and histology should support the decision to initiate treatment. Quick response to treatment provides the most valuable evidence of an accurate diagnosis. The present case report highlights the importance of considering multifocal TBVC even when various types of skin rashes appear at different sites.

Author Contributions: Conceptualization, N.N. and I.P.; investigation, V.S., K.T., I.G., A.-V.R., E.Z. and K.I.G.; data curation, N.N. and I.P.; resources, E.T. and M.I.; writing—original draft preparation, N.N.; writing—review and editing, I.P. and F.M.; supervision, I.P., K.I.G. and A.-V.R. All authors have read and agreed to the published version of the manuscript.

Funding: This research received no external funding.

Institutional Review Board Statement: Ethical review and approval were waived for this study due to the design of the study (case report and literature review).

Informed Consent Statement: Written informed consent was obtained from the patient to publish this paper.

Data Availability Statement: Not applicable.

Conflicts of Interest: The authors declare no conflict of interest.

References

1. Kumar, B.; Kaur, S. Pattern of Cutaneous Tuberculosis in North India. *Indian J. Dermatol. Venereol. Leprol.* **1986**, *52*, 203–207. [PubMed]
2. Santos, J.B.D.; Figueiredo, A.R.; Ferraz, C.E.; de Oliveira, M.H.; da Silva, P.G.; de Medeiros, V.L.S. Cutaneous tuberculosis: Epidemiologic, etiopathogenic and clinical aspects—Part I. *An. Bras. Dermatol.* **2014**, *89*, 219–228. [CrossRef] [PubMed]
3. Charifa, A.; Mangat, R.; Oakley, A.M. *Cutaneous Tuberculosis*; StatPearls Publishing: Treasure Island, FL, USA, 2023.
4. Sehgal, V.N.; Sehgal, R.; Bajaj, P.; Sriviastava, G.; Bhattacharya, S. Tuberculosis verrucosa cutis (TBVC). *J. Eur. Acad. Dermatol. Venereol. JEADV* **2000**, *14*, 319–321. [CrossRef]
5. Damevska, K.; Gocev, G. Multifocal tuberculosis verrucosa cutis of 60 years duration. *Int. J. Infect. Dis. IJID Off. Publ. Int. Soc. Infect. Dis.* **2013**, *17*, e1266–e1267. [CrossRef]
6. Rahman, M.H.; Ansari, N.P. Extensive multifocal tuberculosis verrucosa cutis in a young child. *Med. Pract. Rev.* **2011**, *2*, 60–65.
7. Rajan, J.; Mathai, A.T.; Prasad, P.V.S.; Kaviarasan, P.K. Multifocal tuberculosis verrucosa cutis. *Indian J. Dermatol.* **2011**, *56*, 332–334. [CrossRef] [PubMed]
8. Acharya, B.; Acharya, A.; Gautam, S.; Ghimire, S.P.; Mishra, G.; Parajuli, N.; Sapkota, B. Advances in diagnosis of Tuberculosis: An update into molecular diagnosis of Mycobacterium tuberculosis. *Mol. Biol. Rep.* **2020**, *47*, 4065–4075. [CrossRef] [PubMed]
9. Tan, S.H.; Tan, B.H.; Goh, C.L.; Tan, K.C.; Tan, M.F.; Ng, W.C.; Tan, W.C. Detection of Mycobacterium tuberculosis DNA using polymerase chain reaction in cutaneous tuberculosis and tuberculids. *Int. J. Dermatol.* **1999**, *38*, 122–127. [CrossRef] [PubMed]
10. Hsiao, P.-F.; Tzen, C.-Y.; Chen, H.-C.; Su, H.-Y. Polymerase chain reaction based detection of Mycobacterium tuberculosis in tissues showing granulomatous inflammation without demonstrable acid-fast bacilli. *Int. J. Dermatol.* **2003**, *42*, 281–286. [CrossRef] [PubMed]
11. Pebriany, D.; Anwar, A.I.; Djamaludin, W.; Adriani, A.; Amin, S. Successful diagnosis and management of tuberculosis verrucosa cutis using antituberculosis therapy trial approach. *Pan Afr. Med. J.* **2020**, *37*, 216. [CrossRef] [PubMed]
12. Sudarshan, R.; Nayak, K.; Kumar, P.; Kadilkar, U. Rare Case of Multifocal Cutaneous Tuberculosis Verrucosa Cutis: Posing Clinical and Histopathological Diagnostic Dilemma. *J. Adv. Med. Med. Res.* **2016**, *16*, 1–5. [CrossRef] [PubMed]
13. Sehgal, V.N.; Verma, P.; Bhattacharya, S.N.; Sharma, S.; Singh, N. Multifocal Tuberculosis Verrucosa Cutis: A Manifestation Extraordinary of Reactivation Secondary Tuberculosis. *Skinmed* **2017**, *15*, 145–147. [PubMed]
14. Rani, S.; Bansal, P.; Ahuja, A.; Agrawal, D. Varied Presentation of Cutaneous Tuberculosis in a Patient. *Indian J. Derm. Diagn Dermatol.* **2020**, *7*, 36–37. [CrossRef]

15. Prasad, P.V.S.; Ambujam, S.; Paul, E.K.; Krishnasamy, B.; Veliath, A.J. Multifocal Tuberculous Verrucosa Cutis: An Unusual Clinical Presentation. *Indian J. Tuberc.* **2002**, *49*, 229–230.
16. Padmaprasad, M.K. Case report: Tuberculosis verrucosa cutis. *J. Evol. Med. Dent. Sci.* **2013**, *2*, 8274.
17. Vora, R.V.; Diwan, N.G.; Rathod, K.J. Tuberculosis verrucosa cutis with multifocal involvement. *Indian Dermatol. Online J.* **2016**, *7*, 60–62. [CrossRef] [PubMed]
18. van Zyl, L.; du Plessis, J.; Viljoen, J. Cutaneous tuberculosis overview and current treatment regimens. *Tuberculosis* **2015**, *95*, 629–638. [CrossRef] [PubMed]
19. dos Santos, J.B.; Figueiredo, A.R.; Ferraz, C.E.; de Oliveira, M.H.; da Silva, P.G.; de Medeiros, V.L.S. Cutaneous tuberculosis: Diagnosis, histopathology and treatment—Part II. *An. Bras. Dermatol.* **2014**, *89*, 545–555. [CrossRef] [PubMed]
20. Cutaneous Tuberculosis: A Clinico-Morphological Study—PubMed. Available online: https://pubmed.ncbi.nlm.nih.gov/27688538/ (accessed on 24 July 2023).
21. Frankel, A.; Penrose, C.; Emer, J. Cutaneous tuberculosis: A practical case report and review for the dermatologist. *J. Clin. Aesthet. Dermatol.* **2009**, *2*, 19–27. [PubMed]

Disclaimer/Publisher's Note: The statements, opinions and data contained in all publications are solely those of the individual author(s) and contributor(s) and not of MDPI and/or the editor(s). MDPI and/or the editor(s) disclaim responsibility for any injury to people or property resulting from any ideas, methods, instructions or products referred to in the content.

medicina

Review

Monkeypox Outbreak in Peru

Max Carlos Ramírez-Soto [1,2]

[1] Centro de Investigación en Salud Pública, Facultad de Medicina Humana, Universidad de San Martín de Porres, Lima 15011, Peru; maxcrs22@gmail.com or c20330@utp.edu.pe

[2] Facultad de Ciencias de la Salud, Universidad Tecnológica del Peru, Lima 15046, Peru

Abstract: Monkeypox (Mpox) is a zoonotic disease caused by the *Orthopoxvirus* monkeypox virus (MPXV). Since 1970, outbreaks of MPXV have occurred in several Sub-Saharan African countries. However, from May 2022 to April 2023, recent outbreaks of Mpox occurred in several countries outside of Africa, and these cases quickly spread to over 100 non-endemic countries on all continents. Most of these cases were found in the region of the Americas and the Europe region. In Latin America, the highest all-age Mpox rates per million inhabitants were in Peru, Colombia, Chile, and Brazil. Given its global impact, Mpox was declared as an international Public Health Emergency by WHO in July 2022. MPXV infection disproportionately affects men who have sex with men and members of the HIV-infected population. Vaccination is the current strategy for controlling and preventing Mpox in high-risk groups. In this context, Peru has the fourth-highest number of Mpox cases in Latin America and faces significant challenges in disease control. Because of this, in this review, we discuss the epidemiology, public health indicators, and prevention of Mpox in the 2022 Peru outbreak so that health authorities can join forces to control MPXV transmission.

Keywords: monkeypox outbreak; public health; emergency; Peru

Citation: Ramírez-Soto, M.C. Monkeypox Outbreak in Peru. *Medicina* **2023**, *59*, 1096. https://doi.org/10.3390/medicina59061096

Academic Editors: Yusra Habib Khan, Tauqeer Hussain Mallhi, Tahir Mehmood Khan and Muhammad Salman

Received: 3 May 2023
Revised: 28 May 2023
Accepted: 5 June 2023
Published: 6 June 2023

Copyright: © 2023 by the author. Licensee MDPI, Basel, Switzerland. This article is an open access article distributed under the terms and conditions of the Creative Commons Attribution (CC BY) license (https://creativecommons.org/licenses/by/4.0/).

1. Introduction

Mpox virus (MPXV) is a zoonotic infection belonging to the genus *Orthopoxviruses*, family *Poxviridae*. It is transmitted via droplet exposure and/or direct contact with contagious materials [1,2]. Since 1970, outbreaks of Mpox have occurred in several Sub-Saharan African countries, primarily in the Democratic Republic of Congo (DRC), Cameroon, the Central African Republic (CAR), Liberia, the Republic of Congo (ROC), and Nigeria. Since then, MPXV has been restricted to these countries [3,4]. However, recent outbreaks of MPXV have occurred in countries outside of Africa, and a high number of cases have quickly spread to almost every continent [2,5,6]. Most cases occur in young men, with a significant proportion of them being men who have sex with men (MSM) and other high-risk groups, whose transmission mainly occurs by close human-to-human contact and sexual contact. [7,8]. In this review, we discuss the epidemiology, transmission and population at risk, public health indicators, and prevention of Mpox in the 2022 Peru outbreak.

2. COVID-19 Pandemic in Peru

Despite the early implementation of a national lockdown and other restraint measures to prevent SARS-CoV-2 transmission, the COVID-19 pandemic severely impacted the Peruvian population, resulting in a high death rate and COVID-19 incidence, excess COVID-19 deaths, and an excess of death from all causes [9–11]. Possible explanations for the poor outcomes of the COVID-19 pandemic are a fragmented healthcare system, a lack of specialized human resources to tackle the pandemic, gaps in infrastructure, a lack of molecular tests (first wave), a lack of intensive care unit beds, a lack of essential drugs, the use of medications without evidence of their efficacy, a lack of leadership from health authorities, and a pandemic response that was directed toward hospitals and not primary healthcare [12,13]. These factors contributed to exacerbating the problem. The Peruvian health system was severely affected, and its health facilities were overfilled with COVID-19 patients. In addition, an urgent need for improvement became evident since non-COVID-19 patients could not access regular healthcare services, which had an indirect impact on the population's health [13]. Peru was severely affected by the COVID-19 pandemic, with more than 4,500,000 cases and 220,000 deaths reported as of 21 April 2023 [14]. However, after the implementation of a vaccination program to combat COVID-19, the burden of disease and death has decreased considerably.

3. Epidemiology

The first case of human Mpox was reported in 1970 in the DRC. Since then, it has spread to West and Central Africa, and the number of cases has been on the rise [15–17]. From 2000 to 2015, there were outbreaks reported in the DRC and Nigeria [3]. The case fatality rate (CFR) in these outbreaks was 8.7%. For the Central African clade and West African clade, the CFR was 10.6 and 3.6%, respectively [3]. Since 2003, the spread outside of Africa has been related to import and travel to endemic countries, which occasionally resulted in outbreaks [18–20]. According to the WHO, Mpox in 2022 was considered endemic in several African countries [21]. In the current global outbreak, the first case of Mpox was reported in May 2022 in the United Kingdom [22]. Since then, MPXV has spread to 111 countries around the world. Given its global impact, Mpox was declared as an international Public Health Emergency by WHO in July 2022 [6].

In terms of cumulative number, from 1 January 2022 to 25 April 2023, there were a total of 87,113 reported cases of Mpox in 111 countries worldwide, including a total of 130 deaths [22]. Most of these cases were found in the region of the Americas (59,220 cases) and the Europe region (25,881 cases) (Figure 1). In Latin America, Peru is the country with the fourth most reported cases, after Mexico, Colombia, and Brazil. In Europe, Spain and France are the countries with the most reported cases (Figure 2) [22].

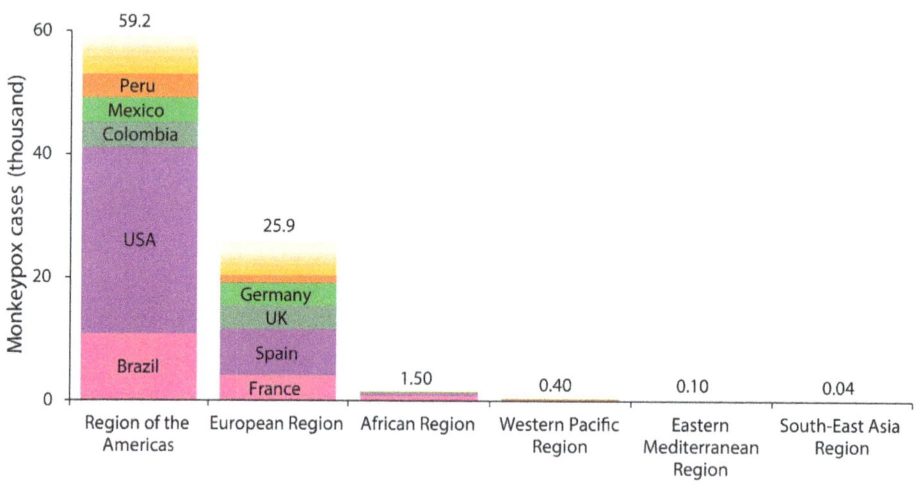

Figure 1. Stacked bar chart of regional distribution of Mpox cases for 2022–2023 (Source: Mpox, WHO) [22]. This figure was built using the cases of Mpox data from the WHO.

To date (27 April 2023), seventeen countries had an all-age cumulative rate of Mpox cases > 50 cases per million inhabitants, including Gibraltar, Spain, Peru, Portugal, the United States of America, Luxembourg, Colombia, Chile, Netherlands, Belgium, Malta, Puerto Rico, Switzerland, France, the United Kingdom, Brazil, and Panama (Figure 3).

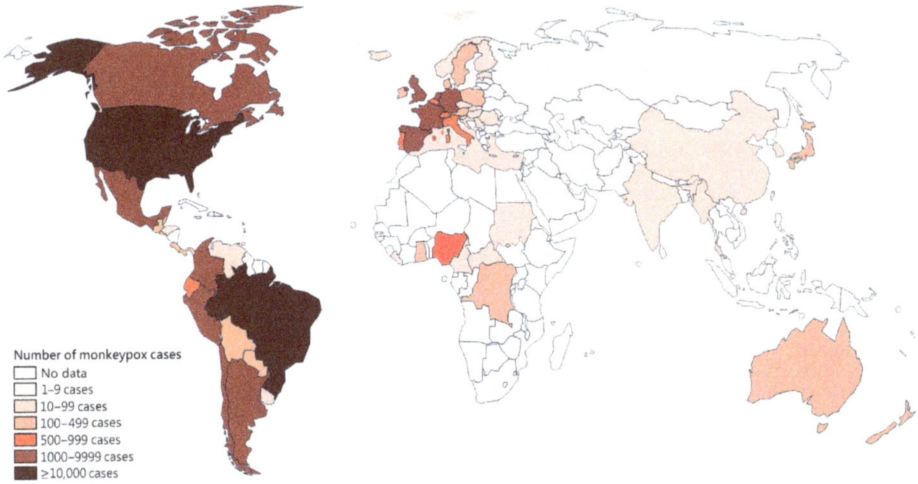

Figure 2. Global distribution of Mpox cases for the period 2022–2023. This figure was built using the cases of Mpox data from the WHO (Source: Monkeypox outbreak—WHO; accessed on 25 April 2023) [22].

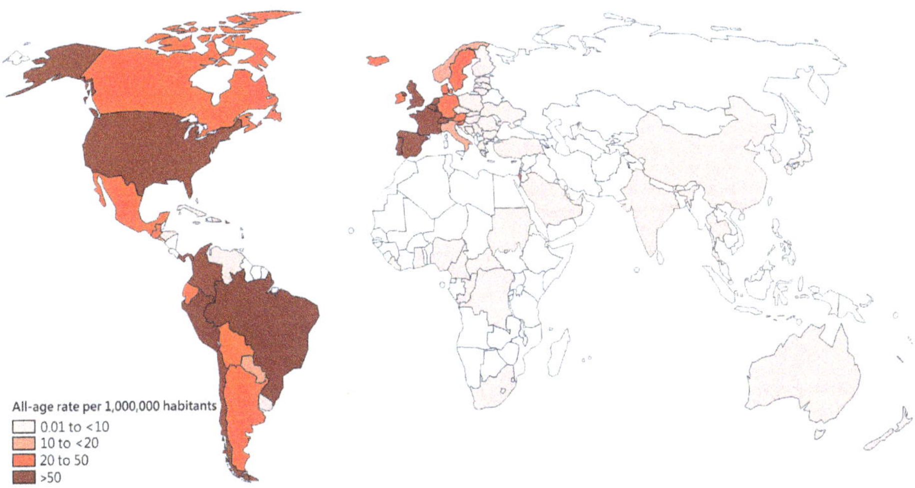

Figure 3. Global distribution of estimated Mpox rate for the cumulative period 2022–2023. Calculated rate by the number of cases reported for the cumulative period 2022–2023 (≥5 cases) in a certain country [22] divided by the total population of that country of that same year as reported by https://data.worldbank.org/indicator/SP.POP.TOTL (accessed on 25 April 2023).

In Latin America, the highest all-age Mpox rates were in Peru (113.9 cases per million inhabitants), Colombia (79.8 cases per million inhabitants), Chile (74.9 cases per million inhabitants), and Brazil (50.9 cases per million inhabitants) (Figure 3).

4. Transmission and Population at Risk

While the animal reservoirs of the MPXV are little known, transmission can occur from animal to human (zoonotic transmission) and from human to human [2,4,21]. During the 2022 Mpox outbreak, it was reported that person-to-person transmission occurred by several routes including respiratory secretions, such as droplets generated when an infected person coughs or sneezes; contact with infected fluids or skin lesions of an MPXV-infected person; percutaneous transmission (such as cuts, abrasions, or puncture wounds); or indirect contact through fomites [7,8,22]. The risk factors for acquiring the MPXV include high-risk sexual behavior (multiple sexual partners or anonymous sexual partners) in the Americas and European countries and living in forested areas in African countries [7,8,18,21,23]. This outbreak affected primarily gays, bisexuals, and MSM [7,8,22]. Although women were the least-affected population in the 2022 outbreak, a global case series found that between cis women, including non-binary individuals and trans women, 61% and 89% of them acquired Mpox through sexual contact [24].

5. Sexually Transmitted Infections Concomitant

Reports indicate that people with Mpox may also have concomitant sexually transmitted infections (STIs). In the current global outbreak of human Mpox, high rates of HIV infection [22] and other STIs were reported among individuals with Mpox [7,8,22]. In previous Mpox outbreaks in Nigeria, there were also concurrent HIV infections [25,26]. In eight USA jurisdictions, the HIV prevalence in Mpox-infected people was 38%, and 41% were diagnosed with one or more other STIs. These STIs included *N. gonorrhoeae, C. trachomatis,* and syphilis in the Mpox patients with and without a diagnosis of HIV infection [27]. In Spain, herpes simplex virus I/II, *N. gonorrhoeae, C. trachomatis,* and syphilis were detected in Mpox patients [28]. In Italy, STIs more frequent were *N. gonorrhoeae* and *M. genitalium* [29]. In Germany, *N. gonorrhoeae, C. trachomatis,* syphilis, and *Mycoplasma* were reported [30]. In Mexico, HIV, syphilis, and some cases of chronic hepatitis C were also identified in patients with Mpox [31]. In Latin America, HIV, syphilis, genital herpes, chlamydia, and gonorrhea were reported in Brazil [32], while in Peru, only HIV and syphilis were reported in patients with Mpox infection [33,34].

6. MPXV Outbreak in Peru

Soon after the first descriptions of Mpox outbreaks in several countries around the world, on 26 May 2022, the Centro Nacional de Epidemiología, Prevencion y Control de Enfermedades (CDC Peru), Peruvian Ministry of Health issued a health alert to health establishments about the risk of imported Mpox cases in the national territory [35]. Subsequently, the government began implementing its control plan for the Mpox outbreak on 7 June, which included health establishments preparing and responding to possible cases [36]. Despite the implementation of a control plan for the Mpox outbreak, we knew that the introduction of MPXV was imminent because of the large numbers of national and international travelers, combined with problems in the Peruvian health system.

Peru's first Mpox case was diagnosed on June 15 in the department of Lima. By mid-July, community transmission was occurring, and the country had neither a sufficient response nor the contact-tracing capacity to contain MPXV. Because of this, on 30 September 2022, the Peruvian Ministry of Health published a new version of the technical health standard for the prevention and management of patients affected by MPXV. This rule aims to protect the population at high risk or affected by MPXV (probable or confirmed cases), including guidelines for community preventive measures and care in health facilities. Despite the implementation of a control plan against Mpox, the disease was almost certain to spread rapidly in Peru because of the same factors that influenced poor outcomes during the COVID-19 pandemic.

Since the first case of Mpox infection was found in Peru (15 June 2022), community transmission was occurring. Beginning on week 36, 2022, the cases have decreased by week 12, 2023 (Figure 4A). Up to 25 April, 3800 human Mpox cases and ten deaths were reported by the CDC Peru [34]. As in other countries [7,8,27,32], most of these cases occurred in young men (96.1%) and MSM (56%). The most-affected population is people living with HIV (55%) and those who receive antiretroviral therapy (85%) (Figure 4B) [34]. According to the WHO (to 19 October 2022), among Mpox cases, 25,718 cases were reported in MSM [22]. This shows that the current spread of MPXV has disproportionately affected MSM, suggesting the amplification of transmission through sexual networks. Although the Mpox outbreak has predominately affected gay men, Mpox is not a "gay disease" [37]. Likewise, the WHO reports that among Mpox cases, approximately 50% of cases are HIV-positive people [22]. As in Peru, several reports in Europe, the United States, and Brazil describe a high rate of HIV infection among Mpox cases [7,27–33,38,39]. Given the transmission route, MPXV could still find other transmission networks, and it could also start to spread among sex workers, their clients, and other population groups [37].

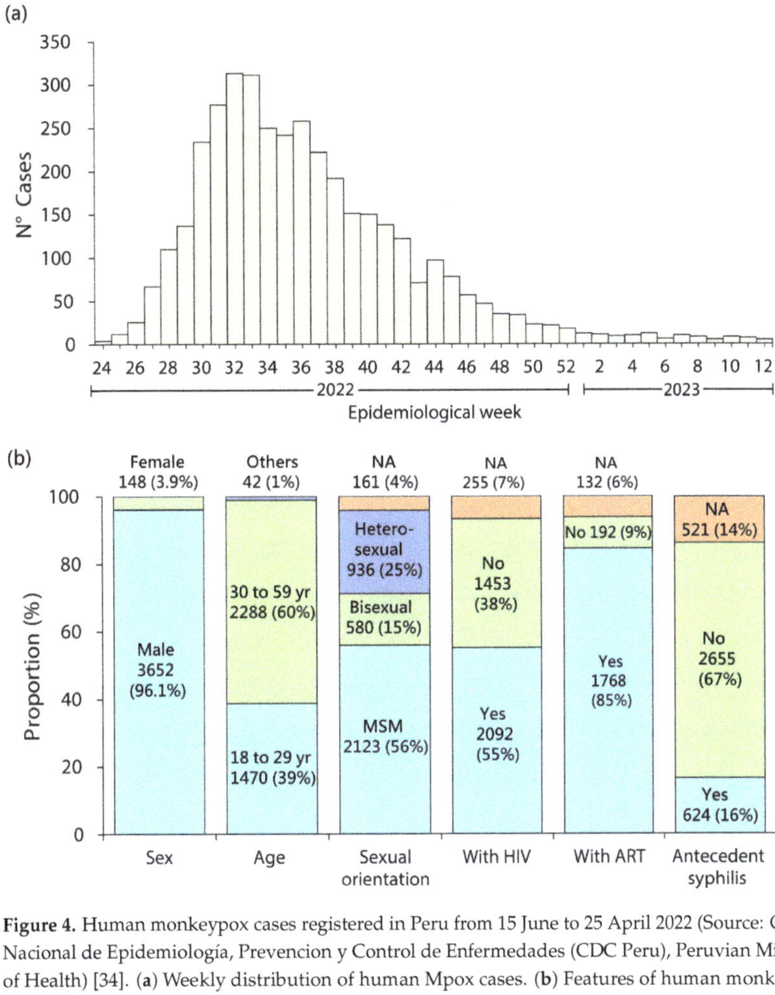

Figure 4. Human monkeypox cases registered in Peru from 15 June to 25 April 2022 (Source: Centro Nacional de Epidemiología, Prevencion y Control de Enfermedades (CDC Peru), Peruvian Ministry of Health) [34]. (**a**) Weekly distribution of human Mpox cases. (**b**) Features of human monkeypox cases. NA: not available; MSM: men who have sex with men; ART: antiretroviral therapy. These figures were built using the cases of Mpox data from the CDC Peru, Peruvian Ministry of Health.

Most cases and the highest rates were recorded in large cities, such as Lima, Callao, La Libertad, and Arequipa (Figure 5A,B) [34]. Figure 5C shows the number of infections by province, which allows us to understand the spread of infections between cities, and how the Mpox cases spread from the province of Lima, where the first cases were reported, to the various provinces over time. With this information can better understand the progression and dynamics of the Mpox outbreak and identify high-risk areas.

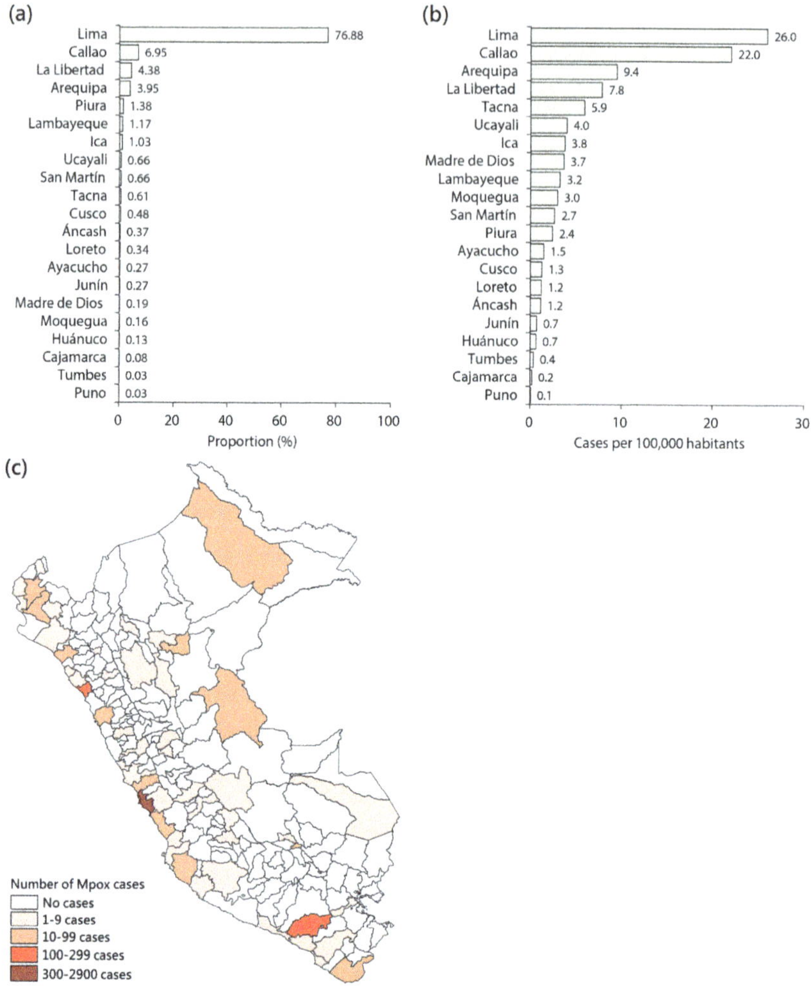

Figure 5. Distribution of Mpox cases in Peru from 15 June 2022 to 23 April 2023 (Source: Centro Nacional de Epidemiología, Prevencion y Control de Enfermedades (CDC Peru), Peruvian Ministry of Health) [34]. (**a**) Proportion of Mpox cases by department. (**b**) Mpox rate by department. (**c**) Number of Mpox cases by province. These figures were built using the cases of Mpox data from the CDC Peru, Peruvian Ministry of Health. Mpox rate was estimated between the number of Mpox cases for the cumulative period 2022–2023 in a certain region [34] divided by the total population of that region per 100,000 inhabitants.

In the late 1970s, smallpox was eradicated through vaccination, and in Peru, as in other countries, the resurgence of MPXV is likely due to smallpox vaccines being phased out over the last four decades, as well as population growth and densely overpopulated areas, which facilitate virus spread [6]. Because of this, numerous individuals are now susceptible to MPXV. The current outbreak of Mpox in Peru also might be driven by changes in human behavior, such as the relaxation of the COVID-19 pandemic prevention measures, including the resumption of international and national travel. Sexual interactions are also associated with social events and large gatherings. In this context, we are currently bearing witness to a monkeypox outbreak in Peru, with the fourth-highest number of cases of Mpox infection in Latin America [22].

7. Mpox Outbreak and Global Health Security Index

The Global Health Security (GHS) indicators may also help explain the current outbreak in Peru. The GHS Index is a tool developed by the Johns Hopkins Center for Health Security and the Nuclear Threat Initiative, in collaboration with the Economist Intelligence Unit. It assesses 195 countries' capabilities in detecting, preventing, and responding to epidemics and pandemics [40]. The GHS Index evaluates various factors such as detection, prevention, reporting, health system, rapid response, international norms compliance, and risk environment. The GHS Index aims to identify gaps in preparedness and encourage countries to strengthen their health security capacities [40]. According to the 2021 GHS Index report, all countries, including Peru, are unprepared for future threats such as epidemics and pandemics; 38.9 is the average overall score in the 2021 GHS Index [40]. The United States is the country with the highest score on the 2021 GHS Index (75.9), and Somalia is the country with the lowest score (16.0) [40]. Peru has a 54.9 Index score (32/195 rank), with low indicators for prevention, detection, response, health, norms, and risks (Figure 6) [40]. Therefore, Peru remains vulnerable to future outbreaks due to failures in quarantine and isolation policies and disease control. During the COVID-19 pandemic, some studies showed that the overall GHS Index was correlated with SARS-CoV-2 infections and COVID-19 deaths [41,42]. In the same vein, countries in the Americas region with different GHS Index scores have different rates of Mpox cases. For example, Peru, the United States, Colombia, Chile, and Brazil are the countries with the highest overall GHS indicators, and they have the highest case rates of Mpox cases in the region (Figure 7). Even the improved GHS indicators regarding the capability to detect, prevent, and respond to epidemics and pandemics cannot guarantee success in controlling the Mpox outbreak; however, these indicators can help contextualize the Mpox outbreak in Latin America and Peru.

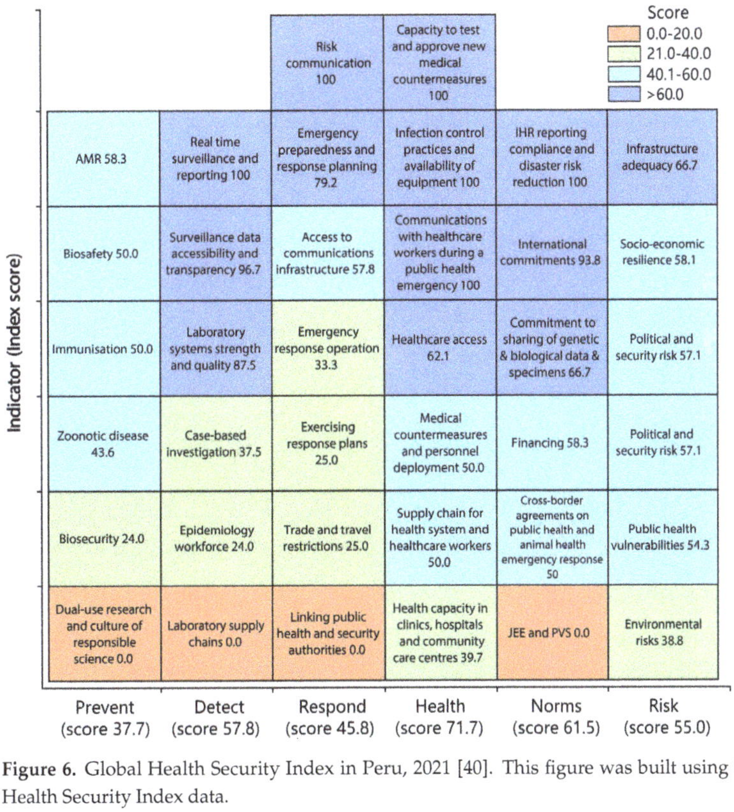

Figure 6. Global Health Security Index in Peru, 2021 [40]. This figure was built using the Global Health Security Index data.

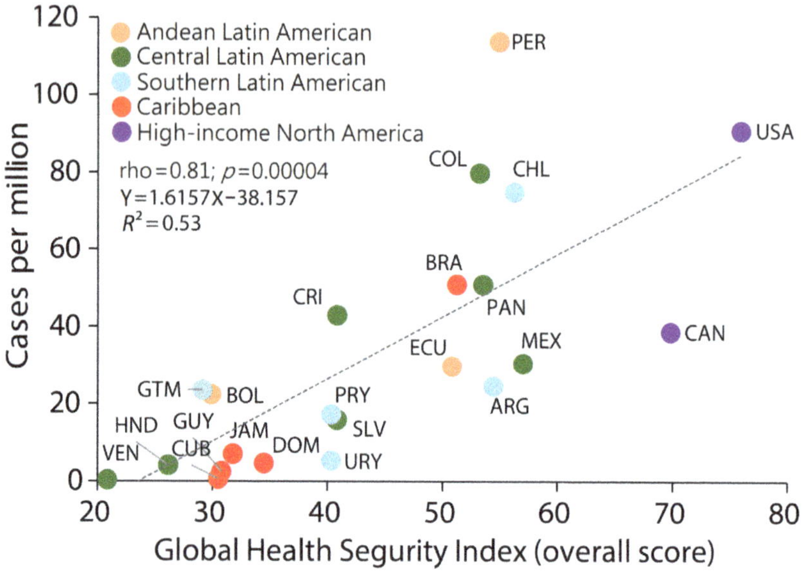

Figure 7. Relationship between Global Health Security (GHS) Index score [40] and Mpox cases in Americas region (data updated to 25 April 2023) [22]. This figure was built using the Global Health Security Index data. Spearman's analysis shows countries with higher GHS Index had higher Mpox case rates per million inhabitants.

8. MPXV Vaccination

We currently have vaccines that offer protection against MPXV, but their availability is limited in some countries [43]. Despite this, mass vaccination is not recommended for Mpox. The WHO provides many interim recommendations on vaccination and immunization against Mpox to prevent the spread of human-to-human MPXV infection, mainly in groups at high risk of exposure [44]. Primary preventive vaccination (pre-exposure) is recommended for the groups that have a high-risk of exposure to MPXV, including bisexuals, gays, MSM, sex workers, laboratory professionals who work with viruses of the genus *Orthopoxviruses*, etc. [44]. Additionally, there is a recommendation for the post-exposure preventive vaccination for contacts of Mpox cases. It is advised to administer the Mpox vaccine within four days of the first exposure. In the absence of symptoms, post-exposure vaccination can be given up to 2 weeks after the initial exposure [44]. In the United States and the United Kingdom, the JYNNEOS vaccine (also known as IMVAMUNE), produced by Bavarian Nordic, is used in high-risk groups to prevent Mpox [43,45], but this vaccine was not available in Peru. This vaccine is administered subcutaneously to individuals 18 years of age or older (two doses with intervals of 4 weeks). It can be used pre-exposure to prevent infection in high-risk exposure groups, or also post-exposure (ideally up to 4 days after exposure) [46,47].

In the current Mpox outbreak, vaccination programs against Mpox are focused on high-risk exposure groups. Globally, the Mpox vaccine is being administered in European countries, the United States, and Latin America, while African countries have limited access to vaccines. [21]. The Peruvian government announced its first batch of an MPXV vaccine in October 2022. These were 5600 of a total of 9800 doses acquired by the country. In the second delivery, 4200 doses arrived in November 2022 [48]. The Mpox vaccination process initiated two phases. The first phase is in people with HIV, and the second phase is in vulnerable populations such as MSM, bisexuals, transgender women, and workers and sex workers [49]. In that sense, the government should work to ensure timely access to vaccines for high-risk groups, including vulnerable populations such as MSM, bisexual men, and HIV-positive people in areas with a high number of Mpox cases and a high amount of risk contact.

9. Reflections and Recommendations

There are several lessons to be learned from outbreaks and previous pandemics in response to the global Mpox outbreak. First, the investment in healthcare capacity and science is essential to building robust and timely responses [6,50]. Second, the implementation of screening policies, contact tracing, and increased awareness of Mpox in the general population can help in the early detection of cases and disease control. Third, the preparedness for new outbreaks and pandemics should be focused on planning and long-term investments in public health. This includes strengthening surveillance systems, establishing early warning systems, and enhancing laboratory capabilities for the rapid and accurate diagnosis of new pathogens. Additionally, capacity building is important, including training healthcare professionals, scientists, and emergency responders. Finally, the findings of the CDC Peru show that some risk groups are disproportionately affected. Thus, to contain the outbreak, special attention should be placed on MSM, people with HIV, and other groups at elevated risk levels, and Mpox vaccination programs should target these high-risk groups. Even if more vaccines do arrive in Peru, behavioral changes will be needed in groups with a high-risk of exposure to MPXV.

Funding: This Review received no funding.

Institutional Review Board Statement: Not applicable.

Informed Consent Statement: Not applicable.

Data Availability Statement: Not applicable.

Conflicts of Interest: The author declares no conflict of interest.

References

1. McCollum, A.M.; Damon, I.K. Human monkeypox. *Clin. Infect. Dis.* **2014**, *58*, 260–267, Erratum in *Clin. Infect. Dis.* **2014**, *58*, 1792. [CrossRef] [PubMed]
2. Lum, F.M.; Torres-Ruesta, A.; Tay, M.Z.; Lin, R.T.P.; Lye, D.C.; Rénia, L.; Ng, L.F.P. Monkeypox: Disease epidemiology, host immunity and clinical interventions. *Nat. Rev. Immunol.* **2022**, *22*, 597–613. [CrossRef] [PubMed]
3. Bunge, E.M.; Hoet, B.; Chen, L.; Lienert, F.; Weidenthaler, H.; Baer, L.R.; Steffen, R. The changing epidemiology of human monkeypox-A potential threat? A systematic review. *PLoS Negl. Trop. Dis.* **2022**, *16*, e0010141. [CrossRef] [PubMed]
4. Ejaz, H.; Junaid, K.; Younas, S.; Abdalla, A.E.; Bukhari, S.N.A.; Abosalif, K.O.A.; Ahmad, N.; Ahmed, Z.; Hamza, M.A.; Anwar, N. Emergence and dissemination of monkeypox, an intimidating global public health problem. *J. Infect. Public Health* **2022**, *15*, 1156–1165. [CrossRef]
5. Velavan, T.P.; Meyer, C.G. Monkeypox 2022 outbreak: An update. *Trop. Med. Int. Health* **2022**, *27*, 604–605. [CrossRef]
6. Damaso, C.R. The 2022 monkeypox outbreak alert: Who is carrying the burden of emerging infectious disease outbreaks? *Lancet Reg. Health Am.* **2022**, *13*, 100315. [CrossRef]
7. Thornhill, J.P.; Barkati, S.; Walmsley, S.; Rockstroh, J.; Antinori, A.; Harrison, L.B.; Palich, R.; Nori, A.; Reeves, I.; Habibi, M.S.; et al. Monkeypox Virus Infection in Humans across 16 Countries—April-June 2022. *N. Engl. J. Med.* **2022**, *387*, 679–691. [CrossRef]
8. Mitjà, O.; Alemany, A.; Marks, M.; Mora, J.I.L.; Rodríguez-Aldama, J.C.; Silva, M.S.T.; Herrera, E.A.C.; Crabtree-Ramirez, B.; Blanco, J.L.; Girometti, N.; et al. Mpox in people with advanced HIV infection: A global case series. *Lancet* **2023**, *401*, 939–949. [CrossRef]
9. World Health Organization. WHO Coronavirus (COVID-19) Dashboard. Peru. WHO: Geneva. 2022. Available online: https://covid19.who.int/region/amro/country/pe (accessed on 25 April 2023).
10. COVID-19 Excess Mortality Collaborators. Estimating excess mortality due to the COVID-19 pandemic: A systematic analysis of COVID-19-related mortality, 2020–2021. *Lancet* **2022**, *399*, 1513–1536. [CrossRef]
11. Ramírez-Soto, M.C.; Ortega-Cáceres, G.; Arroyo-Hernández, H. Excess all-cause deaths stratified by sex and age in Peru: A time series analysis during the COVID-19 pandemic. *BMJ Open* **2022**, *12*, e057056. [CrossRef]
12. Herrera-Añazco, P.; Uyen-Cateriano, A.; Mezones-Holguin, E.; Taype-Rondan, A.; Mayta-Tristan, P.; Malaga, G.; Hernandez, A.V. Some lessons that Peru did not learn before the second wave of COVID-19. *Int. J. Health Plan. Manag.* **2021**, *36*, 995–998. [CrossRef] [PubMed]
13. Schwalb, A.; Seas, C. The COVID-19 Pandemic in Peru: What Went Wrong? *Am. J. Trop. Med. Hyg.* **2021**, *104*, 1176–1178. [CrossRef] [PubMed]

14. Ministry of Health, Peru (MINSA). Situation of COVID-19 Peru. Lima: MINSA. 2022. Available online: https://covid19.minsa.gob.pe/sala_situacional.asp (accessed on 25 April 2023).
15. US Centers for Disease Control and Prevention. Human monkeypox—Kasai Oriental, Democratic Republic of Congo, February 1996–October 1997. *Morb. Mortal. Wkly. Rep.* **1997**, *46*, 1168–1171.
16. Heymann, D.L.; Szczeniowski, M.; Esteves, K. Re-emergence of monkeypox in Africa: A review of the past six years. *Br. Med. Bull.* **1998**, *54*, 693–702. [CrossRef]
17. Jezek, Z.; Szczeniowski, M.; Paluku, K.M.; Mutombo, M. Human monkeypox: Clinical features of 282 patients. *J. Infect. Dis.* **1987**, *156*, 293–298. [CrossRef] [PubMed]
18. Rimoin, A.W.; Mulembakani, P.M.; Johnston, S.C.; Lloyd Smith, J.O.; Kisalu, N.K.; Kinkela, T.L.; Blumberg, S.; Thomassen, H.A.; Pike, B.L.; Fair, J.N.; et al. Major increase in human monkeypox incidence 30 years after smallpox vaccination campaigns cease in the Democratic Republic of Congo. *Proc. Natl. Acad. Sci. USA* **2010**, *107*, 16262–16267. [CrossRef]
19. Mandja, B.A.M.; Brembilla, A.; Handschumacher, P.; Bompangue, D.; Gonzalez, J.P.; Muyembe, J.J.; Mauny, F. Temporal and spatial dynamics of monkeypox in Democratic Republic of Congo, 2000–2015. *EcoHealth* **2019**, *16*, 476–487. [CrossRef]
20. Yinka-Ogunleye, A.; Aruna, O.; Dalhat, M.; Ogoina, D.; McCollum, A.; Disu, Y.; Mamadu, I.; Akinpelu, A.; Ahmad, A.; Burga, J.; et al. Outbreak of human monkeypox in Nigeria in 2017–18: A clinical and epidemiological report. *Lancet Infect. Dis.* **2019**, *19*, 872–879. [CrossRef]
21. Mitjà, O.; Ogoina, D.; Titanji, B.K.; Galvan, C.; Muyembe, J.J.; Marks, M.; Orkin, C.M. Monkeypox. *Lancet* **2023**, *401*, 60–74. [CrossRef]
22. World Health Organization (WHO). WHO Health Emergency Dashboard. Monkeypox. Geneva: WHO 2022. Available online: https://worldhealthorg.shinyapps.io/mpx_global/ (accessed on 25 April 2023).
23. Fuller, T.; Thomassen, H.A.; Mulembakani, P.M.; Johnston, S.C.; Lloyd-Smith, J.O.; Kisalu, N.K.; Lutete, T.K.; Blumberg, S.; Fair, J.N.; Wolfe, N.D.; et al. Using remote sensing to map the risk of human monkeypox virus in the Congo Basin. *EcoHealth* **2011**, *8*, 14–25. [CrossRef]
24. Thornhill, J.P.; Palich, R.; Ghosn, J.; Walmsley, S.; Moschese, D.; Cortes, C.P.; Galliez, R.M.; Garlin, A.B.; Nozza, S.; Mitja, O.; et al. Human monkeypox virus infection in women and non-binary individuals during the 2022 outbreaks: A global case series. *Lancet* **2022**, *400*, 1953–1965. [CrossRef] [PubMed]
25. Ogoina, D.; Iroezindu, M.; James, H.I.; Oladokun, R.; Yinka-Ogunleye, A.; Wakama, P.; Otike-Odibi, B.; Usman, L.M.; Obazee, E.; Aruna, O.; et al. Clinical Course and Outcome of Human Monkeypox in Nigeria. *Clin. Infect. Dis.* **2020**, *71*, e210–e214. [CrossRef] [PubMed]
26. Ogoina, D.; Yinka-Ogunleye, A. Sexual history of human monkeypox patients seen at a tertiary hospital in Bayelsa, Nigeria. *Int. J. STD AIDS* **2022**, *33*, 928–932. [CrossRef] [PubMed]
27. Curran, K.G.; Eberly, K.; Russell, O.O.; Snyder, R.E.; Phillips, E.K.; Tang, E.C.; Peters, P.J.; Sanchez, M.A.; Hsu, L.; Cohen, S.E.; et al. HIV and Sexually Transmitted Infections Among Persons with Monkeypox—Eight U.S. Jurisdictions, May 17–July 22, 2022. *Morb. Mortal. Wkly. Rep.* **2022**, *71*, 1141–1147. [CrossRef] [PubMed]
28. Maldonado-Barrueco, A.; Sanz-González, C.; Gutiérrez-Arroyo, A.; Grandioso-Vas, D.; Roces-Álvarez, P.; Sendagorta-Cudos, E.; Falces-Romero, I.; Mingorance, J.; García-Rodríguez, J.; Quiles-Melero, I. Sexually transmitted infections and clinical features in monkeypox (mpox) patients in Madrid, Spain. *Travel Med. Infect. Dis.* **2023**, *52*, 102544. [CrossRef] [PubMed]
29. Rizzo, A.; Pozza, G.; Salari, F.; Giacomelli, A.; Mileto, D.; Cossu, M.V.; Mancon, A.; Gagliardi, G.; Micol, B.; Micheli, V.; et al. Concomitant diagnosis of sexually transmitted infections and human monkeypox in patients attending a sexual health clinic in Milan, Italy. *J. Med. Virol.* **2023**, *95*, e28328. [CrossRef]
30. Hoffmann, C.; Jessen, H.; Boesecke, C. Monkeypox in Germany. *Dtsch. Arztebl. Int.* **2022**, *119*, 551–557. [CrossRef]
31. Núñez, I.; García-Grimshaw, M.; Ceballos-Liceaga, S.E.; Toledo-Salinas, C.; Carbajal-Sandoval, G.; Sosa-Laso, L.; García-Rodríguez, G.; Cortés-Alcalá, R.; de la Torre, A.; Fragoso-Saavedra, S.; et al. Epidemiological and clinical characteristics of patients with human monkeypox infection in Mexico: A nationwide observational study. *Lancet Reg. Health Am.* **2023**, *17*, 100392. [CrossRef]
32. Pascom, A.R.P.; Souza, I.N.; Krummenauer, A.; Duarte, M.M.S.; Sallas, J.; Rohlfs, D.B.; Pereira, G.M.; Medeiros, A.C.; Miranda, A.E. Epidemiological and clinical characteristics of monkeypox cases in Brazil in 2022: A cross-sectional study. *Epidemiol. Serv. Saude* **2022**, *31*, e2022851. [CrossRef]
33. Sihuincha Maldonado, M.; Lucchetti, A.J.; Paredes Pacheco, R.A.; Martínez Cevallos, L.C.; Zumaeta Saavedra, E.U.; Ponce Zapata, L.R.; Lizarbe Huayta, F.A.; Matos Prado, E.D. Epidemiologic characteristics and clinical features of patients with monkeypox virus infection from a hospital in Peru between July and September 2022. *Int. J. Infect. Dis.* **2023**, *129*, 175–180. [CrossRef]
34. Center for Diseases Control (CDC), Ministry of Health, Peru. Monkeypox Situational Room. Lima: CDC. 2022. Available online: https://www.dge.gob.pe/sala-monkeypox/#an%C3%A1lisis-descriptivo (accessed on 25 April 2023).
35. Center for Diseases Control (CDC), Ministry of Health, Peru. Epidemiological Alert. Code: AE 012-2022. Lima: CDC-Peru. 2022. Available online: https://www.dge.gob.pe/epipublic/uploads/alertas/alertas_202212_26_143419.pdf (accessed on 25 April 2023).
36. Ministry of Health, Peru (MINSA). Technical Document: Monkeypox Preparedness and Response Plan. Lima: MINSA. 2022. Available online: https://www.gob.pe/institucion/minsa/normas-legales/3114429-421-2022-minsa (accessed on 25 April 2023).
37. Kai, K. Why monkeypox is mostly hitting men who have sex with men. *Science* **2022**, *376*, 1364–1365.

38. Angelo, K.M.; Smith, T.; Camprubí-Ferrer, D.; Balerdi-Sarasola, L.; Menéndez, M.D.; Servera-Negre, G.; Barkati, S.; Duvignaud, A.; Huber, K.L.; Chakravarti, A.; et al. Epidemiological and clinical characteristics of patients with monkeypox in the GeoSentinel Network: A cross-sectional study. *Lancet Infect. Dis.* **2022**, *23*, 196–206. [CrossRef] [PubMed]
39. Hoffmann, C.; Jessen, H.; Wyen, C.; Grunwald, S.; Noe, S.; Teichmann, J.; Krauss, A.S.; Kolarikal, H.; Scholten, S.; Schuler, C.; et al. Clinical characteristics of monkeypox virus infections among men with and without HIV: A large outbreak cohort in Germany. *HIV Med.* **2022**, *24*, 389–397. [CrossRef] [PubMed]
40. Nuclear Threat Initiative, Johns Hopkins Center for Health Security, The Economist Intelligence Unit. The Global Health Security Index [Internet]. GHS Index. Available online: https://www.ghsindex.org/ (accessed on 5 August 2022).
41. Ji, Y.; Shao, J.; Tao, B.; Song, H.; Li, Z.; Wang, J. Are we ready to deal with a global COVID-19 pandemic? Rethinking countries' capacity based on the Global Health Security Index. *Int. J. Infect. Dis.* **2021**, *106*, 289–294. [CrossRef]
42. Leichtweis, B.G.; de Faria Silva, L.; da Silva, F.L.; Peternelli, L.A. How the global health security index and environment factor influence the spread of COVID-19: A country level analysis. *One Health* **2021**, *12*, 100235. [CrossRef]
43. Rizk, J.G.; Lippi, G.; Henry, B.M.; Forthal, D.N.; Rizk, Y. Prevention and Treatment of Monkeypox. *Drugs* **2022**, *82*, 957–963. [CrossRef]
44. Wolrd Health Organization (WHO). Vaccines and Immunization for Monkeypox. Interim Guidance. WHO: Geneva. Available online: https://www.who.int/publications/i/item/WHO-MPX-Immunization (accessed on 25 April 2023).
45. The Centers for Disease Control and Prevention (CDC). JYNNEOS Vaccine. Atlanta: CDC. 2022. Available online: https://www.cdc.gov/poxvirus/monkeypox/interim-considerations/jynneos-vaccine.html (accessed on 26 December 2021).
46. Pittman, P.R.; Hahn, M.; Lee, H.S.; Koca, C.; Samy, N.; Schmidt, D.; Hornung, J.; Weidenthaler, H.; Heery, C.R.; Meyer, T.P.; et al. Phase 3 efficacy trial of modified vaccinia Ankara as a vaccine against smallpox. *N. Engl. J. Med.* **2019**, *381*, 1897–1908. [CrossRef]
47. US Food & Drug Administration. Monkeypox Update: FDA Authorizes Emergency Use of Jynneos Vaccine to Increase Vaccine Supply. 9 August 2022. Available online: https://www.fda.gov/news-events/press-announcements/monkeypox-update-fda-authorizes-emergency-use-jynneos-vaccine-increase-vaccine-supply (accessed on 30 April 2023).
48. Ministry of Health, Peru (MINSA). Press Release No. 1132. Lima: MINSA. 2022. Available online: https://www.gob.pe/institucion/minsa/noticias/659167-minsa-anuncia-la-llegada-del-primer-lote-de-vacunas-contra-la-viruela-del-mono-comunicado-de-prensa-n-1132 (accessed on 25 April 2023).
49. Ministry of Health (MINSA), Peru. Vaccination against Monkeypox. MINSA: Lima. 2022. Available online: https://www.gob.pe/31021-vacunacion-contra-la-viruela-del-mono (accessed on 25 April 2023).
50. Zumla, A.; Valdoleiros, S.R.; Haider, N.; Asogun, D.; Ntoumi, F.; Petersen, E.; Kock, R. Monkeypox outbreaks outside endemic regions: Scientific and social priorities. *Lancet Infect. Dis.* **2022**, *22*, 929–931. [CrossRef]

Disclaimer/Publisher's Note: The statements, opinions and data contained in all publications are solely those of the individual author(s) and contributor(s) and not of MDPI and/or the editor(s). MDPI and/or the editor(s) disclaim responsibility for any injury to people or property resulting from any ideas, methods, instructions or products referred to in the content.

medicina

MDPI

Article

Knowledge about HPV Infection and the HPV Vaccine among Parents in Southeastern Serbia

Natasa K. Rancic [1,2,*], Predrag M. Miljkovic [3], Zorana M. Deljanin [2], Emilija M. Marinkov-Zivkovic [1,4], Bojana N. Stamenkovic [1,4], Mila R. Bojanovic [1,4], Marko M. Jovanovic [2], Dusan P. Miljkovic [4], Sandra M. Stankovic [1,4] and Suzana A. Otasevic [1,2]

1 Faculty of Medicine, University of Nis, 18000 Nis, Serbia
2 Public Health Institute, 18000 Nis, Serbia
3 Healthcare Center, 18000 Nis, Serbia
4 Clinical Center, 18000 Nis, Serbia
* Correspondence: drrancicnatasa@gmail.com; Tel.: +381-631-581-489

Abstract: *Background and Objectives*: The vaccine against human papilloma virus (HPV) infection is recommended, according to the Serbian National Immunization Program, for children and adolescents aged 9–19 years. Three doses are given keeping in mind the recommendation that the second dose should be administered at least one month after the first dose, and the third at least three months after the second dose. No children who participated in this first study received the third dose because they did not meet these criteria. The study explored parents' knowledge about HPV infection and their awareness of the HPV vaccine. *Materials and Methods*: A cross-sectional questionnaire-based study was carried out in the city of Nis, in southeastern Serbia. According to the 2011 population census, the sample of children aged 9 to 19 was 850, and during the observed period, 631 children received the vaccine. A total of 615 fully completed questionnaires filled out by parents were included in the study. The study was carried out from 6 June 2022 to 7 October 2022. Multivariable logistic regression analysis was used. The odds ratio (OR) and 95% confidence intervals (CI) were calculated. The statistical significance was $p < 0.05$. *Results*: A total of 615 children were included in the study (499 were vaccinated with the first dose and 116 with the second). Out of 499 children vaccinated with the first dose, 398 (79.6%) were girls, which is significantly higher than the rate for boys (101). The independent variable sex was statistically significant at the level of $p = 0.84$, OR = 2.664 (95% CI from 0.879 to 7.954). Boys are 164% less likely to be vaccinated with the HPV vaccine than girls. We determined that the independent variable place of residence was significant at the level of $p = 0.041$, (OR = 3.809, 95% CI from 1.702 to 8.525). Based on these findings, we determined that parents who came from rural areas were 82% less likely to know about HPV infection and HPV vaccination. Children under 15 years of age were significantly more vaccinated than those $\geq$15 years (OR = 3.698, 95% CI from 1.354 to 12.598). The independent variable parental education was significant at the level of OR = 0.494, 95% CI from 0.301 to 0.791. Parents who had medical education showed significantly higher awareness about the infection caused by HPV and about the HPV vaccine ($p = 0.004$) than parents with no medical education. The possibility that a parent would decide to vaccinate a child significantly increased upon a pediatrician's recommendation, $p = 0.000$ with OR = 0.250 (95% CI from 0.127 to 0.707). Health insurance coverage of HPV vaccination for children aged 9–19 years significantly increased the probability of a positive parental decision to vaccinate a child, $p = 0.001$ with OR = 3.034 (95% CI from 1.063 to 8.662). *Conclusion*: We identified several significant factors that were important for HPV vaccination such as: children under 15 years, female sex, urban place of residence, medical education of parents, pediatrician's recommendation of the HPV vaccination, and HPV vaccination free of charge. Health education and the promotion of HPV vaccination as well as healthy sexual behavior are important factors in the preservation and improvement of the health of the whole population.

Keywords: parental knowledge; HPV infection; HPV vaccine; children; adolescents

Citation: Rancic, N.K.; Miljkovic, P.M.; Deljanin, Z.M.; Marinkov-Zivkovic, E.M.; Stamenkovic, B.N.; Bojanovic, M.R.; Jovanovic, M.M.; Miljkovic, D.P.; Stankovic, S.M.; Otasevic, S.A. Knowledge about HPV Infection and the HPV Vaccine among Parents in Southeastern Serbia. *Medicina* **2022**, *58*, 1697. https://doi.org/10.3390/medicina58121697

Academic Editors: Yusra Habib Khan, Tauqeer Hussain Mallhi, Tahir Mehmood Khan and Muhammad Salman

Received: 20 September 2022
Accepted: 14 November 2022
Published: 22 November 2022

Publisher's Note: MDPI stays neutral with regard to jurisdictional claims in published maps and institutional affiliations.

Copyright: © 2022 by the authors. Licensee MDPI, Basel, Switzerland. This article is an open access article distributed under the terms and conditions of the Creative Commons Attribution (CC BY) license (https://creativecommons.org/licenses/by/4.0/).

1. Background

The most common viral infection, which is predominantly sexually transmitted, is caused by human papillomavirus (HPV) [1]. This infection is highly associated with cervical cancer in low- and middle-income regions of the world and mostly with the oropharyngeal cancers in developed regions of the world [1,2]. Cervical cancer is one of the most common malignant tumors among women. It has the fourth highest incidence and mortality rates among women worldwide, with 604,000 new cases and 342,000 deaths in 2020 [1]. The highest prevalence of HPV infection is registered in sub-Saharan Africa (24.0%), Latin America and the Caribbean (16.1%), Eastern Europe (14.2%), and Southeast Asia (14.0%) [3]. In European countries, the prevalence of HPV infection ranges from 2.0% in Spain to 12.0% in Belgium and France [3,4]. About 6.2 million of new HPV infections in females aged 14–44 years are registered in the United States of America (USA) each year [5]. The highest prevalence by age is among nonvaccinated sexually active adolescents [6,7] and among young women under 25 years of age [8–10].

Chronic HPV infection, together with other risk factors for cervical cancer, plays an important role in the development of this cancer as well. The most significant risk factors are smoking, immunodeficiency, long-term use of oral contraceptives, promiscuous behavior, and having more than two pregnancies. Other risk factors include a family history of cervical cancer and other descriptive characteristics, obesity, and poor diet [6–11]. Cervical cancer is still the second most common malignant tumor in females from 15 to 44 years of age [11]. In most countries, the highest incidence and mortality rates of cervical cancer are registered among younger women under 45 years of age [12], which indicates that this cancer is age-related and mostly affects women in the fertile period. Cervical cancer has a slow progression [13], and if it is discovered at an early stage, it is a highly preventable and highly treatable malignant tumor [14]. It takes more than 10 years after the first exposure to HPV infection to develop some malignant changes in the cervical mucosa [15,16].

There are more than 207 HPV genotypes [16] among which 20 are oncogenic and high-risk HPV types that show high associations with HPV-related cancers, especially with invasive cervical cancer [17]. According to the findings of the first population study of HPV prevalence in women by Kovacevic et al., (2019), the most frequent HPV types in Serbia are type 16 and type 31 [18].

An HPV vaccine was established in order to enable the primary prevention of HPV infection and cervical cancer. Three HPV vaccines exist today: the bivalent (2vHPV) vaccine for girls licensed in 2006, the quadrivalent (4vHPV) HPV vaccine for boys licensed in 2009, and the 9-valent HPV vaccine (9vHPV) licensed for both girls and boys in 2014. The most common World Health Organization (WHO) recommendations regarding routine vaccination are related to children age 9–14 because the HPV vaccine is the most effective if it received before recipients become sexually active, i.e., before they are exposed to HPV infection [19]. The vaccine is also recommended for adolescents, primarily girls and younger women from age 15 to 25 [20]. The CDC recommendations regarding HPV vaccination are somewhat different. Namely, the vaccine is recommended for children aged 11 or 12, but it can also start at the age of nine and is recommended up to the age of 26 [21].

In 2007, Australia became one of the first countries to introduce the HPV vaccine [22,23], and in 2020, the HPV vaccine was introduced in more than half of the WHO member countries. For example, the HPV vaccine has been introduced in 85% of the countries in North America and 77% of the countries in Europe [23].

The three HPV vaccines do not provide complete protection against all oncogenic HPV types, and immunity is not lifelong [24]. That is why cervical cancer screening is an important preventive measure regardless of vaccine status. There is the well-known Pap smear screening method, which is widely available and inexpensive and has good specificity for the detection of precancerous lesions with a proven impact in reducing cervical cancer prevalence and mortality rates [25]. Additionally, the viral DNA of the high-risk strains of HPV viruses can be easily detected in exfoliated cervical cells using commercially available tests. The HP-DNA test represents a convenient, highly sensitive screening tool and is showing a pattern of becoming the main screening method. However, it has an important flaw reflected in its lower specificity [25].

Organized cervical cancer screening has been conducted in the Republic of Serbia since 2012. The screening is mandatory for women aged 25 to 69 [25], and the HPV vaccine is available. However, cervical cancer remains one of the most prevalent cancers among women [26]. According to the data from the population cancer registry of Central Serbia, cervical cancer was the fourth most common cancer in women in 2020, with 1087 new cases and 453 deaths registered [27]. The age-standardized cervical cancer mortality rates in Serbia are still the highest of all the Balkan countries [4].

In the Republic of Serbia, vaccination against HPV infection is not part of the mandatory national immunization program. It is recommended for children aged 9, before the first sexual intercourse, and primarily for children in the seventh grade of primary school (age 13) [28]. HPV vaccination of children was introduced in Serbia according to the WHO recommendations. Children aged 15–19 may also receive the HPV vaccine free of charge. Until now, organized vaccination against HPV infection has not been conducted among children, adolescents, and young adults in Serbia. This year, the focus is on the vaccination of children and adolescents from the age group 9–19 years. Some factors that impact the coverage of HPV vaccination have been determined in the countries that have been conducting the vaccination for over a decade. These include insufficient population awareness about the HPV infection and its consequences, insufficient recommendations from pediatricians or unclear emphasis on the importance of vaccination, and insufficient parental knowledge. The level of knowledge that parents and adolescents have about HPV infection and vaccination was the subject of a large number of studies in the countries of the European Union (EU). In all countries where the immunization process has started, health policy makers have emphasized that raising the awareness of the population, especially health workers and parents, about the importance of preventing these diseases is crucial in order to better implement vaccination [6,13,17,24]. Having in mind that Serbia is not a member of the EU and that this year is the first time the HPV vaccine is being administered on a more organized and mass basis, the objective of this study was to explore parents' knowledge about HPV infection and the HPV vaccine. These are the first data about HPV vaccination of children and adolescents 9 through 19 years of age in the city of Nis.

2. Material and Methods

2.1. Study Design and Study Population

We conducted a cross-sectional study involving the parents of children aged 9–19 years. The period of observation lasted from 6 June 2022 to 7 October 2022. The study took place at the primary clinic at the Healthcare Center Nis at the Counseling Center for Healthy School Children. The Healthcare Center Nis is the largest health care institution of its kind in the Republic of Serbia. The city of Nis is the largest city in southeastern Serbia. An anonymous questionnaire was distributed only to parents of children who came for vaccination. If the parent was not present, which was often the case with children aged $\geq$ 15, the child did not fill out the questionnaire. Some of the children this age were accompanied by parents because the HPV vaccine is being widely administered for the first time this year, and the children only signed the consent form, which they are legally allowed to do [28].

Activities of Pediatricians and Epidemiologists before the Start of Vaccination

Since the beginning of 2022, the promotion of vaccination against HPV infection among parents has been carried out at the counseling center. Certain pediatricians from the Nis health center and an immunization coordinator/epidemiologist from the Nis Institute for Public Health went to Belgrade (the capital of Serbia), where they received basic instructions about the vaccine and were also trained on how to encourage parents and other pediatricians. The results of good preparation were reflected in a great number of parents who brought their children for vaccination in June as well as in unreserved support from all pediatricians for giving this vaccine to as many children as possible.

The state helped by introducing significant relief by making vaccination free for children aged 9–19 years. According to the 2011 population census, the sample of children aged 9 to 19 was 850. In the observed period, 631 children received the vaccine. This study included 615 fully completed questionnaires, which were filled out by parents, and incomplete questionnaires were excluded.

Before vaccine administration, a visit to the pediatrician at the Counseling Center for Healthy School Children was mandatory as well as signing the consent form. According to expert methodological instructions for the application of Gardasil 9 vaccine in Serbia, consent for children up to 15 years of age had to be signed by parents or guardians. Children over 15 years of age could sign their own consent for vaccination with Gardasil 9 [28].

Inclusion criteria were: children born between 2003 and 2013 and signed consent for the vaccination. Exclusion criteria were younger or older children and no signed consent.

Approval by the Ethics Committee of the Public Healthcare Center Nis was not necessary because according to the Serbian National Immunization Laws, signature or written consent of the parent or of the adolescent (if they are aged 15 years or above) is mandatory for the application of each recommended vaccine [28].

The questionnaires were administered to parents at the Counseling Center for Healthy School Children. Participation in the study was voluntary. Signed consent forms were obtained from all participants. The parents filled out the short questionnaire during a visit to the pediatrician for the child's vaccination.

2.2. Data Collection

Data were collected using a short semi-structured questionnaire that consisted of two sections (Supplementary File S1).

Section one: The first section explored participations' sociodemographic characteristics, including sex, age, education, place of residence, and pediatrician recommendation. It consisted of 5 items (Table 1).

Table 1. The most important socio-descriptive characteristics of the participants.

Characteristics		n	%
Age of children	9–14 years	280	56.1
	15–19 years	219	44.7
Sex of children < 15 years	9–14 M	69	24.6
	9–14 F	211	75.4
Sex of children $\geq$ 15 years	15–19 M	32	9.6
	15–19 F	187	90.4
Place of residence	Urban area	450	90.2
	Rural area	49	9.8
Education of parents	Medical education	299	59.9
	Non-medical education	205	40.1

Section two: The second section consisted of 15 items divided into three subsections (knowledge about HPV infection, awareness of HPV vaccine, and HPV vaccination knowledge). Knowledge was evaluated with a composite score estimated using a total of 13 items regarding risk and protective factors, preventive measures, and the outcome of HPV infection. Participants had three possible options regarding the proposed factors and correct answers were coded with two points. As for the rest of the questions, the given options were yes, no, and I do not know and correct answers were given two points. The total number of points represented the participants' HPV infection knowledge score (KS), with higher scores meaning better knowledge. The maximum number of points was 30. The results of all answers are shown in Table 2. Awareness of the HPV vaccine was determined based on whether or not the participants had heard about the vaccine. Participants who had heard about the vaccine answered six more questions about the vaccine (Table 3).

Table 2. Parents' knowledge about HPV infection.

Question Number	Question	Percentage %
6	How can you get infected with HPV	76.0%
7	What are the main ways of transmission?	78.0%
8	Who is at higher risk of HPV infection?	56.0%
9	Are the HPV infections and malignant diseases connected?	92.0%
10	Does HPV infection always lead to clinical manifestation of the disease?	48.0%
11	Do you know what is a Pap smear test?	89.0%
12	What factors increase the risk of developing cervical cancer?	68.0%
13	How can HPV infection be prevented?	82.0%

%—percentage of correct answers.

Table 3. Parental knowledge and awareness about HPV vaccine.

Knowledge about HPV Vaccine	N	% of Correct Answers
1. Is there a vaccine against HPV infection?	499	100%
2. Is it available in Serbia?	499	100%
3. At what age is it best to administer the vaccine?	499	100%
4. In how many doses is it administered?	390	78.2%
5. What are the most common side effects?	321	64.3%
6. How long does immunity last after vaccination?	380	76.2%

N-number of parents who participated; %—percentage of correct answers.

2.3. The Nine-Valent (9vHPVvaccine)-Legislative Regulations in the Republic of Serbia

The 9vHPV vaccination in Serbia is recommended for children aged nine and up, before the first sexual intercourse, and primarily for children in the seventh grade of primary school (13 years of age). Active immunization against HPV infection is carried out with the required number of doses (two or three), which is recommended by the WHO depending on the type of vaccine and age [28]. Three doses are given to children aged 9 to 19 keeping in mind the recommendation that the second dose should be administered at least one month after the first dose, and the third at least 3 months after the second dose. All three doses should be administered within one year. All children who participated in this first study did not receive the third dose because they did not meet these criteria. The 9vHPV (6, 11, 16, 18, 31, 33, 45, 52, 58) HPV vaccine, Gardasil 9 is registered for use in females aged 9 to <46 years and males aged 9 to <27 years [22,23]. It gives effective prevention against some premalignant lesions and cancers of the cervix, vulva, vagina, and anus caused by vaccine HPV types and genital warts (Condyloma acuminata) caused by specific HPV types [20].

2.4. Statistical Analysis

An Excel database was created for all collected data. Data are presented as the mean and standard deviation (SD) or as frequencies and proportions. Percentages were used to describe the demographic status and the frequency of parents' responses to the questions in the questionnaire. All analyses were performed using SPSS software version 22.0. Multivariate analysis was used to determine the factors that had an impact on the parents' decision to vaccinate a child. The p-value was set at $p < 0.05$.

3. Results

Out of the 615 children, 499 received the first dose of HPV vaccine, and 116 received the second dose. Out of the original 499 children (398 girls and 101 boys), there were significantly more girls, 79.6%, than boys. That is, there were 3.9 times more vaccinated girls than boys on average.

The total number of children aged 9–14 years who were vaccinated with the first dose of HPV vaccine was 280 (56.1%). In the age group 15–19, there were 219 children (43.9%) who received the first dose of the HPV vaccine ($p < 0.001$).

Table 1 shows the socio-descriptive characteristics of the research participants.

In the age groups 9–14 and 15–19, 3.1 times more girls were vaccinated than boys. There were significantly more children and parents from urban areas than from rural areas, 90.2% vs. 9.8%, respectively, and there were 1.5 times more parents with medical education than non-medically educated parents (Table 1).

The results presented in Table 2 show the percentages of correct answers given by parents about HPV infection where 78.0% correctly listed all the ways of HPV transmission, 68.0% correctly listed the factors that increase the risk of developing cervical cancer, 56.0% correctly answered who is at higher risk of HPV infection, and 82% of parents correctly answered about prevention of HPV infection. Question 10 had the smallest percentage of correct answers, only 48% (Table 2).

All parents of children who received the first dose of the vaccine knew that the vaccine exists, that it was available in Serbia, and the best age to receive it. The smallest number of parents answered correctly about the number of vaccine doses and the duration of immunity. The question regarding the most common side effects had the fewest correct answers (Table 3).

The results of a multivariate regression analysis are presented in Table 4.

Table 4. The significant factors associated with the parental decision to vaccinate children against HPV infection.

Variable		B	95% CI	*p*	OR
Sex	Boys / Girls	0.972	0.879–7.954	0.84	2.664
Place of residence	Urban / Rural	1.337	1.702–8.525	0.041	3.809
Child's age	<15 / ≥15	−0.056	1.354–12.598	0.024	3.698
Parental education	Medical education / Non-medical	−0.705	0.301–0.791	0.004	0.494
Pediatrician recommendation	Yes / No	−1.386	0.127–0.707	0.000	0.250
Health insurance coverage of HPV vaccination	Yes / No	1.110	1.063–8.662	0.082	3.034

B–coefficient of regression; CI–Standard Error; *p*-possibility; OR—Odds Ratio.

The independent variable sex was statistically significant at the level of $p = 0.84$, OR = 2.664 (95% CI from 0.879 to 7.954). Boys are 164% less likely to be vaccinated with HPV vaccine than girls.

We determined that the independent variable place of residence was significant at the level of $p = 0.041$, OR = 3.809, (95% CI from 1.702 to 8.525). Based on these findings, we determined that parents who came from rural areas were 82% less likely to know about HPV infection and HPV vaccination. Children under 15 years of age were significantly more vaccinated than those $\geq$ 15 years, OR = 3.698 (95% CI from 1.354 to 12.598). The independent variable parental education was significant, OR = 0.494 (95% CI from 0.301 to 0.791). Parents who had medical education showed significantly higher awareness about the infection caused by HPV and about the HPV vaccine (p = 0.004), OR = 0.494 (95% CI from 0.301 to 0.791) than non-medically educated parents. A pediatrician's recommendation had a significant effect on the vaccination rate, OR = 0.250 (95% CI from 0.127 to 0.707). Health insurance coverage of HPV vaccination for children aged 9–19 years significantly increased the probability of a positive parental decision to vaccinate a child, p = 0.001 with OR = 3.034 (95% CI from 1.063 to 8.662) (Table 4).

4. Discussion

This is the first organized immunization of children aged 9–19 with the 9-valent HPV vaccine in Serbia. Our cross-sectional questionnaire-based study was conducted with the aim of exploring parents' knowledge about HPV infection and their awareness of the HPV vaccine. According to the Serbian National Immunization Program, the HPV vaccine is recommended for children and adolescents aged 9–19 years, and for this age group, it is free of charge. In addition to the unexpectedly high response to vaccination against HPV infection, we identified several significant factors that were important for positive parental decisions to vaccinate children with the HPV vaccine: children under age 15, female sex of children, urban residence, medical education of parents, pediatrician recommendation of the HPV vaccination, and health insurance coverage of HPV vaccination.

In general, parents showed good knowledge about HPV infection and the HPV vaccine, which was expected because the majority of parents had medical education. However, we also observed a lack of parental knowledge about whether HPV infection always leads to clinical manifestation of the disease and about who was at higher risk of HPV infection. In terms of knowledge about the HPV vaccine, the questions with the fewest correct answers were those regarding the number of doses, the duration of immunity, and the most common side effects. The results of our study are in agreement with similar studies conducted in Europe and the rest of the world [6,11,29–33].

The most common concerns indicated by parents in our study were related to vaccine safety, side effects of the vaccine, and lifelong protection after vaccination. Our results are in accordance with similar studies. Parents in other studies worried more about post-vaccination sexual promiscuity, moral problems related to sexuality, and conservative and religious views, and there was denial that children are at risk [29,34,35].

Our results showed that there were nearly four times more vaccinated girls than boys. This difference in our study is greater than in the literature, where the difference is mostly twofold. Results of meta-analyses showed that there were two times more vaccinated girls than boys [36,37]. The disparities in uptake of the HPV vaccine by sex of child can be a result of the later approval and recommendation of HPV vaccination for boys than for girls, but despite that, many national immunization programs still do not include vaccination of boys. According to the findings of Radisic et al. [38], HPV vaccine uptake among male adolescents is suboptimal. There is a need to address the predictors of uptake by educating parents about boys' high susceptibility to infection and the benefits of vaccination to reduce the perceived barriers. Data from similar studies show low knowledge about HPV infections and vaccination in the population of adolescents and their parents in both developing and developed regions of the world [6–8,10,28,35,36]. In Greece, the HPV vaccine has been part of the national immunization program since 2008, and it is administered for free to girls from 11 up to 26 years of age [10]. The adolescents had insufficient knowledge about HPV infection and about protection measures, as well as about the association between HPV infection and cervical cancer [35].

In our results, there were nearly 3 times more vaccinated children aged 9–14 than adolescents aged $\geq$15 years, particularly among boys. Parents of children aged 15 years and over were not very well informed about HPV infection and the HPV vaccine. Our findings are in agreement with the findings of other similar studies [20]. Results mainly from systematic analyses available in the literature show that the number of vaccinated children younger than 15 is greater than children older than 15 [37,38].

There are different findings in the available literature. In a systematic meta-analysis by Holman et al., the authors stated that the age of a child was a common reason for refusing or delaying HPV vaccination, and older girls were more likely to be vaccinated than younger girls. In only two studies did age not predict any intention of parents to vaccinate their children [34,35].

The state of parental knowledge has an essential influence on the immunization of children [31]. Newman et al., (2018) presented the results of a meta-analysis in which vaccination was positively impacted by parents' medical education, knowledge and awareness about the relationship between cervical cancer and HPV knowledge ($r = 0.04$ (95% CI from 0.04 to 0.13)), and some socio-descriptive variables such as urban versus rural residence ($r = 0.10$ (95% CI from 0.06 to 0.14)). Fishman et al., found that mothers with more knowledge about HPV were not willing to vaccinate themselves or their daughters [30]. A study of parental knowledge conducted in Poland in 2022 showed that the only factors that really affect attitudes to vaccination are the knowledge and education of parents [17]. The remaining characteristics of parents do not significantly affect the attitude toward vaccination.

As vaccination progressed in the city of Nis, more parents heard about it but when vaccination began, some parents with children under 15 years of age were away on vacation. Children over 15 were still going to school (high school vacation started on 24 June 2022) and that is why there was initially a greater response from parents with children over 15.

Compared with our study, the literature contains fewer recorded vaccination differences among girls and boys. The results of studies showed that there were two times more vaccinated girls than boys [31,32]. The disparities in uptake of the HPV vaccine by sex can be a result of the later approval and recommendation of HPV vaccination for boys than for girls, but despite that, many national immunization programs still do not include the vaccination of boys [19–21]. Our results suggest that it might be more effective to advocate and educate on the HPV vaccination and to strongly promote it to both parents and children.

In undeveloped regions such as Nigeria and Kenya [36,37] and in rural areas and suburban regions, there is resistance towards the HPV vaccination [30]. Surprisingly, in many studies, parents from rural areas were worried about the sexual behavior of their children after the vaccination and did not vaccinate their sons because they were not aware of the direct benefits of HPV vaccination [29,36,37]. This means that socioeconomic status in association with medical education, knowledge, and higher awareness among parents in urban areas might explain their positive decision on the HPV vaccination of children and adolescents. The results of a study from Greece showed that parents' education level plays a major role in teenagers' attitudes and beliefs towards the HPV vaccine [10]. In a study conducted in Poland by Smolarczyk et al., (2022), the significant influencing factors in Poland were lack of recommendations and financing of HPV vaccination by the National Health Fund [17].

The findings of 62 studies showed that a significant predictor of successful HPV vaccination was physician's recommendation ($r = 0.46$ (95% CI from 0.34 to 0.56)). It had the highest impact on parents' positive decision, followed by worry about HPV vaccine safety ($r = -0.31$ (95% CI from -0.41 to -0.16)), preventive examination of children during one year ($r = 0.22$ (95% CI from 0.11 to 0.33)), and parents' health beliefs towards vaccines ($r = 0.19$ (95% CI from 0.08 to 0.29) [39].

In Serbia, the HPV vaccine is expensive, and the government's approval at the beginning of this year to cover the HPV vaccination for children aged 9–19 with health insurance was important for the success of the vaccination effort. In our results, both pediatrician recommendation and health insurance coverage of HPV vaccination were independently associated with positive decision of parents towards the vaccine.

Some studies have shown that a pediatrician recommendation was the most significant predictor of HPV vaccination [8,10,17]. According to meta-analysis, health insurance coverage of HPV vaccination (r = 0.16 (95% CI from 0.04 to 0.29)) or lower out-of-pocket cost (r = −0.15 (95% CI from −0.22 to −0.07)) were significant factors for the vaccination [40].

5. Conclusions

We here presented the results of the first organized vaccination of children and adolescents against HPV infection, and we also showed the results of the first research on parental knowledge about HPV infection and HPV vaccine in southeastern Serbia. Significant factors for positive parental decisions about HPV vaccination for their children were children under 15 years, female children, urban residence, parents' medical education, pediatrician recommendation of vaccination, and free vaccination. The vaccination of boys aged 15 years and over was significantly lower compared with girls from the same age group. In accordance with the results of our study, when it comes to the decision to get the HPV vaccine, personal contact with a pediatrician could be very useful both for parents and children, especially for boys. In order to preserve and improve the health of the whole population as well as of groups of individuals at higher risk, the promotion of HPV vaccination, health education measures, the promotion of healthy sexual behavior, and the support of the government are also important.

5.1. Strengths of Our Study

This study presented the first results of the organized immunization of children aged 9–19 years with the recommended HPV vaccine. Our findings indicated what factors are associated with positive parental decisions to pursue HPV vaccination for their children. We noted extremely high interest among parents for the first dose of HPV vaccine, and no side effects were reported. This study was created as a longitudinal study, and all vaccinated children and adolescents will be followed up for a minimum of 10 years after the vaccination.

5.2. Limitations of Our Study

We could not include all the parents we wanted in the survey.

Supplementary Materials: The following supporting information can be downloaded at: https://www.mdpi.com/article/10.3390/medicina58121697/s1, File S1: Anonymous questionnaire about knowledge about HPV infection and the HPV vaccine.

Author Contributions: N.K.R.—Study design, wrote the manuscript, acted as the corresponding author, P.M.M.—investigation, created the database, Z.M.D.—Methodology; E.M.M.-Z.—critically evaluated the text of the manuscript, B.N.S.—Formal analysis; M.R.B.–Formal analysis; M.M.J.—investigation, D.P.M.—investigation, S.M.S.—software, S.A.O.—revised the manuscript and gave final approval of the manuscript version to submit. All authors have read and agreed to the published version of the manuscript.

Funding: This research received no external funding.

Institutional Review Board Statement: The study was conducted in accordance with the Declaration of Helsinki.

Informed Consent Statement: Written informed consent has been obtained from the patients to publish this paper.

Data Availability Statement: The original data can be obtained by contacting the corresponding author.

Acknowledgments: The authors thank all pediatricians at the Healthcare Center Nis for their contribution to HPV vaccination.

Conflicts of Interest: The authors declare no conflict of interest.

Abbreviations

HPV	Human papillomavirus
STI	Sexually transmitted infection
HR-HPV	high-risk HPV
LR-HPV	low-risk HPV
USA	the United States of America
2vHPV	the bivalent HPV vaccine
4vHPV	quadrivalent HPV vaccine
v9Vhpv	nine-valent HPV vaccine
Gardasil 9	nine-valent HPV vaccine
NIP	National Immunization Program
SD	Standard deviation
CI	Confidence Intervals

References

1. Kombe Kombe, A.J.; Li, B.; Zahid, A.; Mengist, H.M.; Bounda, G.A.; Zhou, Y.; Jin, T. Epidemiology and Burden of Humman papillomavirus and Related diseases, Molecular Pathogenesis, and vaccine Evaluation. *Front. Public Health* **2021**, *8*, 552028. [CrossRef] [PubMed]
2. Gargano, J.; Meites, E.; Watson, M.; Unger, E.; Markowitz, L. Chapter 5: Human Papillomavirus (HPV). In *Manual for the Surveillance of Vaccine-Preventable Diseases*; Centers for Disease Control and Prevention: Atlanta, GA, USA, 2017.
3. Kapamadjija, A. (Ed.) *Prevention of Infections Caused by Human Papilloma Virusess*; Monograph, Number 110; University of Novi Sad, Medical Faculty: Novi Sad, Serbia, 2015.
4. Bruni, L.; Diaz, M.; Castellsagué, X.; Ferrer, E.; Bosch, F.X.; de Sanjosé, S. Cervical Human Papillomavirus Prevalence in 5 Continents: Meta-Analysis of 1 Million Women with Normal Cytological Findings. *J. Infect. Dis.* **2010**, *202*, 1789–1799. [CrossRef] [PubMed]
5. Hariri, S.; Unger, E.; Sternberg, M.; Dunne, E.F.; Swan, D.; Patel, S.; Markowitz, L.E. Prevalence of Genital Human Papillomavirus Among Females in the United States, the National Health and Nutrition Examination Survey, 2003–2006. *J. Infect. Dis.* **2011**, *204*, 566–573. [CrossRef] [PubMed]
6. Markowitz, L.E.; Gee, J.; Chesson, H.; Stokley, S. Ten Years of Human Papillomavirus Vaccination in the United States. *Acad. Pediatr.* **2018**, *18*, S3–S10. [CrossRef] [PubMed]
7. Ma, G.X.; Zhu, L.; Tan, Y.; Zhai, S.; Lin, T.R.; Zambrano, C.; Siu, P.; Lai, S.; Wang, M.Q. A Multilevel Intervention to Increase HPV Vaccination among Asian American Adolescents Grace. *J. Community Health* **2022**, *47*, 9–16. [CrossRef]
8. Salvadori, M.I. Human papillomavirus vaccine for children and adolescents. *Paediatr. Child Health* **2018**, *23*, 262–265. [CrossRef]
9. Cosmas, N.T.; Nimzing, L.; Egah, D.; Famooto, A.; Adebamowo, S.N.; Adebamowo, C.A. Prevalence of vaginal HPV infection among adolescent and early adult girls in Jos, North-Central Nigeria. *BMC Infect. Dis.* **2022**, *22*, 340. [CrossRef]
10. Iliadou, M.; Sahini, K.; Sakellari, E.; Daglas, M.; Orovou, E.; Iatrakis, G.; Antoniou, E. What do Young People Think About HPV and HPV Vaccination? The Role of Health Education Interventions and Health Professionals. *Mater. Socio-Med.* **2021**, *33*, 219–224. [CrossRef]
11. IARC. World Cancer Report 2020: International Agency for Research on Cancer; GLOBOCAN. 2020. Available online: https://gco.iarc.fr/today (accessed on 26 April 2022).
12. Seppä, K.; Pitkäniemi, J.; Malila, N.; Hakama, M. Age-related incidence of cervical cancer supports two aetiological components: A population-based register study. *BJOG* **2016**, *123*, 772–778. [CrossRef]
13. Bruni, L.; Albero, G.; Serrano, B.; Mena, M.; Gómez, D.; Muñoz, J.; Bosch, F.X.; de Sanjosé, S.; Human Papillomavirus and Related Diseases in Europe. ICO/IARC Information Centre on HPV and Cancer (HPV Information Centre). *Human Papillomavirus and Related Diseases in the World. Summary Report 22 October 2021.* Available online: https://hpvcentre.net/statistics/reports/XEX.pdf (accessed on 1 January 2022).
14. Siegel, R.L.; Miller, K.D.; Jemal, A. Cancer statistics 2019. *CA Cancer J. Clin.* **2019**, *69*, 7–34. [CrossRef]
15. Lei, J.; Ploner, A.; Elfström, K.M.; Wang, J.; Roth, A.; Fang, F.; Sundström, K.; Dillner, J.; Sparén, P. HPV Vaccination and the Risk of Invasive Cervical Cancer. *N. Engl. J. Med.* **2020**, *383*, 1340–1348. [CrossRef]
16. IARC Working Group. Biological agents. Volume 100 B. A review of human carcinogens. *IARC Monogr. Eval. Carcinog. Risks Hum.* **2012**, *100 pt B*, 1–441.
17. Smolarczyk, K.; Duszewska, A.; Drozd, S.; Majewski, S. Parents' Knowledge and Attitude towards HPV and HPV Vaccination in Poland. *Vaccines* **2022**, *10*, 228. [CrossRef]
18. Kovacevic, G.; Milosevic, V.; Knezevic, P.; Knezevic, A.; Knezevic, I.; Radovanov, J.; Nikolic, N.; Patric, A.; Petrovic, V.; Cvjetkovic, I.H.; et al. Prevalence of oncogenic human papillomavirus and genetic diversity in the L1 gene of HPV16 HPV 18 HPV31 and HPV33 found in women from Vojvodina Province Serbia. *Biologicals* **2019**, *58*, 57–63. [CrossRef]
19. World Health Organization. Human papillomavirus vaccines: WHO position paper, May 2017-Recommendations. *Vaccine* **2017**, *35*, 5753–5755. [CrossRef]

20. World Health Organization. *Global Vaccine Action Plan 2011–2020*; World Health Organization: Geneva, Switzerland, 2013.
21. Centers for Disease Control and Prevention (CDC). Recommendations on the use of quadrivalent human papillomavirus vaccine in males—Advisory Committee on Immunizations Practices (ACIP), 2011. *MMWR Morb. Mortal. Wkly. Rep.* **2011**, *60*, 1705–1708.
22. Human Papillomavirus (HPV) | The Australian Immunisation Handbook. (Cited 6 February 2022). Available online: https://immunisationhandbook.health.gov.au/vaccine-preventable-diseases/human-papillomavirus-hpv (accessed on 20 September 2022).
23. Human Papillomavirus (HPV) Vaccines—National Cancer Institute (Cited 6 February 2022). Available online: https://www.cancer.gov/about-cancer/causes-prevention/risk/infectious-agents/hpv-vaccine-fact-sheet (accessed on 20 September 2022).
24. Cheng, L.; Wang, Y.; Du, J. Papillomavirus Vaccines: An Updated Review. *Vaccines* **2020**, *8*, 391. [CrossRef]
25. Chrysostomou, A.C.; Stylianou, D.C.; Constantinidou, A.; Kostrikis, G.L. Cervical Cancer Screening Programs in Europe: The Transition Towards HPV Vaccination and Population-Based HPV Testing. *Viruses* **2018**, *10*, 729. [CrossRef]
26. Jovanovic, V.; Jovanovic, A.M.; Kocic, S.; MVasiljevic, M.; Krasic, V. Knowledge about cervical cancer, Pap test, and barriers to women's participation in screening in Belgrade, Serbia. *Eur. J. Gynaecol. Oncol.* **2017**, *38*, 69–75.
27. Malignant Tumors In Republic of Serbia 2020. Serbian Cancer Registry. Department for Prevention and Control of Non-communicable Diseases. Institute of Public Health of Serbia "Dr Milan Jovanović Batut". Belgrade. 2022. Available online: http://www.batut.org.rs/index.php?content=2096 (accessed on 25 September 2022).
28. Ministry of Health of the Republic Serbia. The Rulebook on the Program of Mandatory and Recommended Immunization against Certain Infectious Diseases. Official Gazette of RS, No. 65/2020. 30 September 2017.
29. Degarege, A.; Krupp, K.; Fennie, K.; Srinivas, V.; Li, T.; Stephens, D.; Marlow, L.; Arun, A.; Madhivanan, P. Human Papillomavirus Vaccine Acceptability among Parents of Adolescent Girls in a Rural Area, Mysore, India. *J. Pediatr. Adolesc. Gynecol.* **2018**, *31*, 583–591. [CrossRef]
30. Fishman, J.; Taylor, L.; Kooker, P.; Frank, I. Parent and Adolescent Knowledge of HPV and Subsequent Vaccination. *Pediatrics* **2014**, *134*, e1049–e1056. [CrossRef] [PubMed]
31. Pederson, H.A. Understanding the Implications of HPV Infection: Does Parental Education Impact HPV Vaccination Completion rates? Master's Thesis, Minnesota State University, Mankato, MN, USA, 26 April 2021. Available online: https://cornerstone.lib.mnsu.edu/etds/1100/ (accessed on 26 April 2022).
32. Gamble, H.L.; Klosky, J.L.; Parra, G.R.; Randolph, M.E. Factors Influencing Familial Decision-Making Regarding Human Papillomavirus Vaccination. *J. Pediatr. Psychol.* **2009**, *35*, 704–715. [CrossRef] [PubMed]
33. Sonawane, K.; Zhu, Y.; Montealegre, J.R.; Lairson, D.R.; Bauer, C.; McGee, L.U.; Giuliano, A.R.; Deshmukh, A.A. Parental intent to initiate and complete the human papillomavirus vaccine series in the USA: A nationwide, cross-sectional survey. *Lancet Public Health* **2020**, *5*, e484–e492. [CrossRef]
34. Bacopoulou, F.; Karakitsos, P.; Kottaridi, C.; Stefanaki, C.; Deligeoroglou, E.; Theodoridou, K.; Chrousos, G.P.; Michos, A. Genital HPV in Children and Adolescents: Does Sexual Activity Make a Difference? *J. Pediatr. Adolesc. Gynecol.* **2016**, *29*, 228–233. [CrossRef] [PubMed]
35. Vaidakis, D.; Moustaki, I.; Zervas, I.; Barbouni, A.; Merakou, K.; Chrysi, S.M.; Creatsa, G.; Panoskaltsis, T. Knowledge of Greek adolescents on human papilloma virus (HPV) and vaccination: A national epidemiologic study. *Medicine* **2017**, *96*, e5287. [CrossRef]
36. Rabiu, K.A.; Alausa, T.G.; Akinlusi, F.M.; Davies, N.O.; Shittu, K.A.; Akinola, O.I. Parental acceptance of human papillomavirus vaccination for adolescent girls in Lagos, Nigeria. *J. Fam. Med. Prim. Care* **2020**, *9*, 2950–2957. [CrossRef]
37. Kolek, C.O.; Opanga, S.O.; Okalebo, F.; Birichi, A.; Kurdi, A.; Brian Godman, B.; Meyer, J.C. Impact of Parental Knowledge and Beliefs on HPV Vaccine Hesitancy in Kenya—Findings and Implications. *Vaccines* **2022**, *10*, 1185. [CrossRef]
38. Radisic, G.; Chapman, J.; Flight, I.; Wilson, C. Factors associated with parents' attitudes to the HPV vaccination of their adolescent sons: A systematic review. *Prev. Med.* **2016**, *95*, 26–37. [CrossRef]
39. Garcini, L.; Galvan, T.; Barnack-Tavlaris, J. The study of human papillomavirus (HPV) vaccine uptake from a parental perspective: A systematic review of observational studies in the United States. *Vaccine* **2012**, *30*, 4588–4595. [CrossRef]
40. Newman, P.A.; Logie, C.H.; Lacombe-Duncan, A.; Baiden, P.; Tepjan, S.; Rubincam, C.; Doukas, N.; Asey, F. Parents' uptake of human papillomavirus vaccines for their children: A systematic review and meta-analysis of observational studies. *BMJ Open* **2018**, *8*, e019206. [CrossRef]

medicina

MDPI

Article

Ophthalmological Manifestations in People with HIV from Northeastern Romania

Mihaela Cobaschi [1,2], Isabela Ioana Loghin [3,4,*], Victor Daniel Dorobăț [1,5], George Silvaș [4], Șerban Alin Rusu [4], Vlad Hârtie [3,6] and Victoria Aramă [1,2]

1 Faculty of Medicine/Clinical II Department, "Carol Davila" University of Medicine and Pharmacy, 050474 Bucharest, Romania; cobaschimihaela@gmail.com (M.C.); victordorobat@yahoo.com (V.D.D.); dr.arama@mateibals.ro (V.A.)
2 National Institute for Infectious Diseases "Prof. Dr. Matei Balș", 021105 Bucharest, Romania
3 Department of Infectious Diseases, "Grigore T. Popa" University of Medicine and Pharmacy, 700115 Iasi, Romania; vladhartie@yahoo.com
4 Department of Infectious Diseases, "St. Parascheva" Clinical Hospital of Infectious Diseases, 700116 Iasi, Romania; silvas.george@gmail.com (G.S.); rususerbanalin@yahoo.com (Ș.A.R.)
5 Department of Intensive Care, University Hospital of Emergency, 050098 Bucharest, Romania
6 Department of Intensive Care, Clinical Hospital of Emergency "Prof. Dr. Nicolae Oblu", 700309 Iasi, Romania
* Correspondence: isabelabegezsan@yahoo.com; Tel.: +40-745672347

Abstract: *Background and Objectives*: Although ocular disorders can occasionally impact people with HIV over the course of their illness, HIV/AIDS is unmistakably a multisystem disorder. A physician can rule out a wide range of ophthalmic problems with the assistance of an ophthalmologist, from adnexal disorders to posterior segment diseases, including those affecting the optic tract and optic nerve. *Materials and Methods*: Based on patient medical data from the "St. Parascheva" Clinical Hospital of Infectious Diseases in Iasi, we carried out a retrospective clinical investigation on patients with HIV/AIDS and ophthalmological conditions who were hospitalized in northeastern Romania. We seek to draw attention to the characteristics and ophthalmological comorbidities of HIV/AIDS patients. The studied period was between 1 January 1991 and 31 December 2022. *Results*: There were a total of 38 recorded cases of ophthalmological manifestations in the HIV-infected patients. The research group's average age was 37.31 years old (standard deviation 9.5693917). Males were primarily impacted, having lower total CD4+ T-lymphocyte levels based on sex and CD4+ T-lymphocyte levels overall. The HIV viral load was 999 268.13 copies/mL on average (standard deviation 1,653,722.9). Of all the patients, we found out that 17 had congenital eye diseases (44.73%) and the others (21, 55.26%) developed ophthalmological diseases. CMV Retinitis was found most frequently, in eight patients (21.05%), followed by Myopia in seven patients (18.42%). *Conclusions*: The key to the management of HIV-positive patients is a multidisciplinary approach and access to antiretroviral therapy. Anyone who is HIV-positive and experiences ocular symptoms at any time should be directed to seek professional ophthalmologic treatment as soon as feasible. A therapeutic holdup could result in irreversible vision loss. Long-term coordination is required to combat this disease, improving communication between the ophthalmology and infectious disease fields.

Keywords: ophthalmological diseases; HIV infection; CMV retinitis

Citation: Cobaschi, M.; Loghin, I.I.; Dorobăț, V.D.; Silvaș, G.; Rusu, Ș.A.; Hârtie, V.; Aramă, V. Ophthalmological Manifestations in People with HIV from Northeastern Romania. *Medicina* **2023**, *59*, 1605. https://doi.org/10.3390/medicina59091605

Academic Editors: Yusra Habib Khan, Tauqeer Hussain Mallhi, Tahir Mehmood Khan and Muhammad Salman

Received: 13 July 2023
Revised: 26 August 2023
Accepted: 30 August 2023
Published: 6 September 2023

Copyright: © 2023 by the authors. Licensee MDPI, Basel, Switzerland. This article is an open access article distributed under the terms and conditions of the Creative Commons Attribution (CC BY) license (https://creativecommons.org/licenses/by/4.0/).

1. Introduction

The immune system is the target of the human immunodeficiency virus (HIV) infection. Acquired immunodeficiency syndrome (AIDS) is one of the illness's most severe manifestations. HIV weakens the immune system by targeting the body's CD4 T lymphocytes. This makes contracting illnesses such as tuberculosis, infections, and some malignancies easier [1,2].

HIV/AIDS is clearly a multisystem disorder, but ophthalmic diseases do sometimes affect HIV-positive individuals throughout the natural course of their disease. HIV may damage the eye either directly or indirectly through a number of opportunistic illnesses. Herpes zoster ophthalmicus, cotton wool patches in the retina (the most frequent ophthalmoscopic finding in HIV-infected people), and molluscum contagiosum affecting the eyelids are ocular symptoms indicating towards an HIV infection in an undiagnosed and otherwise asymptomatic patient [3,4]. With the help of an ophthalmologist, a doctor can rule out a variety of ocular issues before starting antiretroviral treatment (ART), from adnexal illnesses to posterior segment diseases, including those affecting the optic tract and optic nerve [5,6].

Adnexa diseases include exfoliative dermatitis, such as Steven–Johnson syndrome, conjunctival molluscum contagiosum, and Herpes Zoster ophthalmicus. Syphilis, uveitis, Herpes keratitis, and candidal keratitis are among the anterior segment illnesses. The non-infectious posterior segment symptoms of HIV include cotton wool patches, hemorrhages, telangiectasias, and optic disc atrophy [7,8].

Acute retinal necrosis, Candida endophthalmitis, tubercular choroiditis, Cryptococcal or Pneumocystis choroiditis, and Cytomegalovirus ocular disease are some of the infectious posterior eye segment diseases [9,10].

In contrast to adults with a lower incidence of CMV retinitis, children are more prone to experiencing neurodevelopmental delays, keratitis sicca, and ocular toxoplasmosis [11]. The presence of blue sclera, hypertelorism, many palpebral fissures, and downward obliquity of the eyes are additional indicators of fetal AIDS-related embryopathy [12]

Ophthalmologists can help with the diagnosis and treatment of other eye diseases associated with HIV infection, such as the implantation of an intraocular ganciclovir implant, which can deliver higher intraocular ganciclovir levels than systemic therapy alone and lowers the risk of a CMV ocular disease relapse. Furthermore, surgically reattaching a retinal detachment caused by CMV can partially restore the eyesight in HIV-positive patients. Today, this condition's prevalence has decreased due to the introduction of antiretroviral medication [13,14].

Adverse effects from drugs can also affect the eyes. Rifabutin is one such medication that might cause uveitis, especially when coupled with azole antifungal medications. The antiviral cidofovir, used in some cases of CMV retinitis, is also linked to uveitis and a drop in intraocular pressure [15].

Immune reconstitution inflammatory syndrome must be understood by ophthalmologists today, since it might result in uveitis after the start of ART. Fundoscopy is essential for the follow-up evaluation of patients using ART, since this condition affects the vitreous, macula, and optic nerve and sporadically causes cataracts and epiretinal membranes [16].

When people with HIV complain of any visual issue, it is strongly advised that they be referred to an ophthalmologist. The eyes of patients with HIV should undergo a thorough examination. Health education about the problems and visual symptoms associated with HIV will raise awareness and lower morbidity. The early detection and rapid treatment of these ocular symptoms will help to avoid or lessen the effects of subsequent vision deterioration [17,18].

Ocular symptoms should be ruled out for people with HIV in a discussion between an infectious disease physician and an ophthalmologist. Untreated ophthalmic issues spread quickly and have poor prognoses. Because of vision loss and opportunistic infections of the retina, all HIV-positive patients should be advised to undergo a baseline ophthalmologic examination. To avoid permanent vision loss, all HIV-infected individuals who have ocular symptoms must receive ophthalmologic care as soon as possible [19,20].

2. Materials and Methods

2.1. Study Design and Database Information

On the foundation of hospital medical data, we carried out a retrospective clinical investigation of patients diagnosed with HIV/AIDS in the northeastern region of Romania, hospitalized in "Sf. Parascheva" Clinical Hospital of Infectious Diseases in Iasi, aiming to emphasize the profile and ophthalmological-associated comorbidities of HIV/AIDS cases. The studied period was between 1 January 1991 and 31 December 2022.

Patients over the age of 18 who were hospitalized at our Regional HIV/AIDS Center in northeastern Romania and tested as HIV-positive via an enzyme-linked immunosorbent assay (ELISA) test, confirmed to have the disease by Western blot (WB), were chosen for inclusion. The HIV plasma viral load and CD4+ T cell counts were also assessed in the patients who tested positive for HIV/AIDS. In our study group, 38 patients were included.

2.2. Ethical Approval

The "St. Parascheva" Clinical Hospital of Infectious Diseases in Iasi, Romania, gave the study its clearance. (May 2023; Approval No. 4/17). At the time of admission, every individual signed a waiver of informed consent.

2.3. Study Variables

Age- and gender-specific demographic information, personal pathological histories, clinical traits, blood tests (viro-immunological testing), assessments of potential opportunistic infections, patient staging, the start of antiretroviral treatment, and the course and outlook of the patients with HIV/AIDS infection were all included in the data collection.

According to the Center for Disease Control and Prevention (CDC), Atlanta, the HIV infection stage was determined using an age-specific CD4+ T-lymphocyte count or the CD4+ T-lymphocyte percentage of the total CD4 T-lymphocyte cells level. HIV infection and AIDS are classified into three stages: stage 1, when CD4+ T-lymphocyte levels are above 500 cells/μL; stage 2, when they are between 200 and 499 cells/μL; and stage 3, when they are below 200 cells/μL. HIV infection is represented by stages 1 and 2, while AIDS is represented by stage 3 [4,6].

Two ELISA tests were used to serologically assess those suspected of having HIV, and a Western blot test was used to confirm the diagnosis. The regional public health management network's epidemiologists carried out all of this work, after which, the patients were sent to the local HIV/AIDS facility.

2.4. Study Setting

The "St. Parascheva" Clinical Hospital of Infectious Disease, Iasi, is a primary referral medical facility for the Moldova region of Romania, with a capacity of 300 beds. It is divided into six pavilions. Pavilion V includes a compartment of Infectious Disease and the HIV/AIDS Regional Center. The Regional Center has a capacity of 12 beds, where patients are periodically evaluated based on the CDC and EACS recommendations.

The hospital's central laboratory completed all the blood tests, and the molecular biology lab measured the patients' CD4+ T cell counts and HIV plasmatic viral loads. RT-PCR HIV 1 was utilized with Cepheid's GeneXpert® as a tool for measuring the viral load levels and determining the HIV viremia. If the viral load was less than 40 copies/mL, it was deemed to be undetectable, and when it was greater than 40 copies/mL, it was deemed to be detectable.

Periodically, the clinical and biological status of every newly diagnosed PWH (person living with HIV) was assessed for metabolic syndrome and liver enzymes. The laboratory reference values were within 5–31 UI/L for AST (aspartate trans-aminase) and ALT (alanine transaminase), within 7–32 UI/L for GGT (gamma-glutamyl transferase), within 122–200 mg/dL for COL (cholesterol), within 30–159 mg/dL for LDL-COL (low-density lipoprotein cholesterol), 40–66 mg/dL for HDL-COL (high-density lipoprotein cholesterol), and 30–150 mg/dL for TG (triglycerides), with no differences between sexes.

The Regional HIV/AIDS Center, Iasi, has a total of 1692 patients in its active records. They are periodically evaluated every six months to ensure their adherence and compliance with the antiretroviral treatment. Each patient has a medical file that mentions their associated diseases, blood test values, level of CD4 T lymphocytes, and HIV viral load, as well as the ART schemes they followed. The data in this study were collected from the paper charts of the patients of our center.

2.5. Statistical Analysis

The Pearson test in the XLSTAT version 2019 program was used to determine the correlation between the demographic characteristics, clinical data, and results. Kendall's Tau correlation coefficients were established [11]. The Statistical Software for Excel (XLSTAT) version 2019 was used to conduct the statistical analysis.

3. Results

In the northeastern part of Romania, from a total of 1692 patients in the active records, there were a total of 38 recorded cases of ophthalmological manifestations in HIV-infected patients. Men were the ones who experienced these most frequently (21 cases, 55.26%) compared to women (17 cases, 44.74%). In total, 17 HIV-infected patients had congenital eye diseases and the other 21 developed ophthalmological diseases (Figure 1).

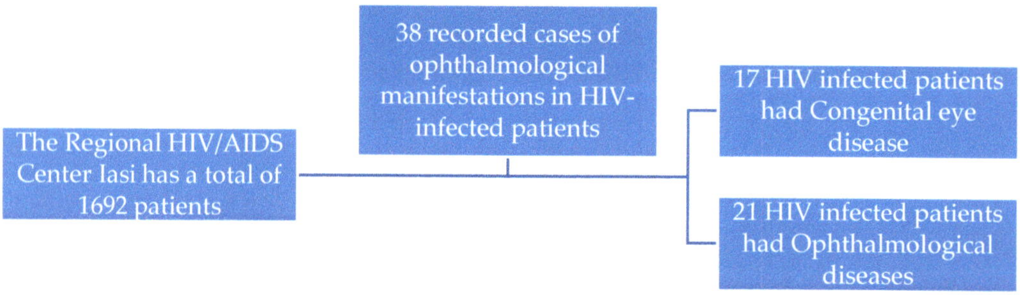

Figure 1. Study case findings.

Most of the instances involved young adults, aged between 30 and 39 years old—28 patients (73.68%), next, the age group of 40–49 had 4 patients (10.53%), 50–59 years—2 patients (5.26%), over 60 years old—2 patients (5.26%), 0–19 years—1 patient (2.63%), and 20–29 years—1 patient (2.63%) (Table 1). The study group's median age was 37.31 years old.

Table 1. Age distribution of HIV/AIDS cases.

Age (Years)	n (38)	%
0–19	1	2.63
20–29	1	2.63
30–39	28	73.68
40–49	4	10.53
50–59	2	5.26
Over 60	2	5.26

Nearly half of the patients in our research group were from Iasi, according to the distribution of the group by county (17 cases, 44.74%), next, Suceava (7 cases, 18.42%), Botosani (5 cases, 13.16%), Neamt (3 cases, 7.89%), Bacau (3 cases, 7.89%), and Vaslui (3 cases, 7.89%), (Figure 2). There were 26 patients who came from the urban region of northeast Romania (68.42%), and the other 66 cases (31.58%) were rural residents.

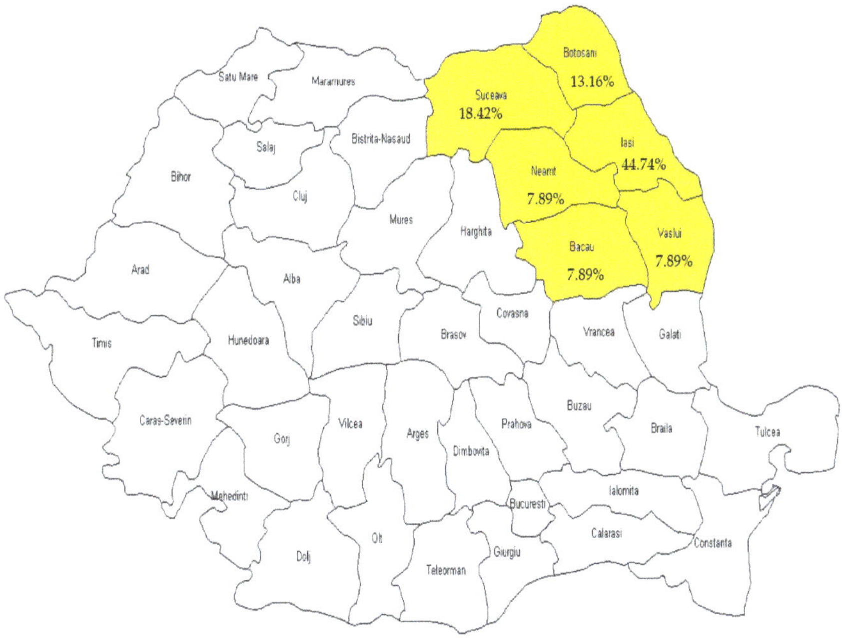

Figure 2. Romania's northeast counties' caseload distribution. The yellow color refers exactly to the Romania's northeast counties.

Given the route of transmission, each case indicated a potential cause. The most common was the perinatal route, with a total of 24 cases (63.16%).

The most afflicted group in terms of the sexual method of transmission (heterosexual and MSM/men having sex with men—34.21% instances) was young adult males (aged 21–40) with a medium level of education (graduated high school). Drug usage administered intravenously was noted in 2.63% of patients.

The virological and immunological status of the study group of patients from the Iasi HIV/AIDS Regional Center was assessed. With an average CD4+ T-lymphocyte level of 372.34 cells/μL (standard deviation 292.60658), it was seen that 36.84% of cases had a CD4+ T-lymphocyte level of 1–199 cells/μL, 31.58% of cases had a CD4+ T-lymphocyte value of 200–499 cells/μL, and 31.58% of cases had a CD4+ T-lymphocyte value over 500 cells/μL (Table 2, Figure 3). Males were primarily impacted, having lower total CD4+ T-lymphocyte levels based on sex and CD4+ T-lymphocyte levels. The HIV viral load was assessed to be 999,268.13 copies/mL on average (standard deviation 1653722.9).

Table 2. Case distribution according to sex and CD4+ T-lymphocyte count at time of diagnosis.

CD4+ T-lymphocytes Level	**Male**		**Female**		**Total**	
$p = 0.137$	**n (21)**	**%**	**n (17)**	**%**	**n (38)**	**%**
0–199 cells/μL	7	18.42	7	18.42	14	36.84
200–499 cells/μL	8	21.05	4	10.53	12	31.58
>500 cells/μL	6	15.79	6	15.79	12	31.58

The following findings were obtained using the CDC (Center for Disease Control and Prevention) phases of HIV/AIDS: according to our data, 12 patients (31.58%) had a stage 1

HIV infection, 12 patients (31.58%) had a stage 2 HIV infection, and 14 patients (36.84%) had a stage 3 HIV infection.

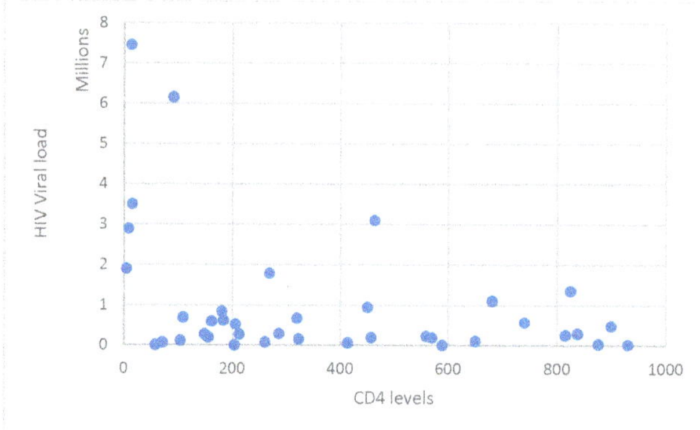

Figure 3. Distribution of cases by HIV viral load and CD4+ T-lymphocyte count.

In the research group, it was found that nearly a third of the males (18.42%) and less than a third (13.15%) of the females (13.15%) had abnormal ALT and AST values, correspondingly. In terms of metabolic profile, the triglyceride levels were abnormal in a third of the participants in the study group, impacting nearly equally each sex (21.05% men and 18.42% females), and the blood cholesterol levels were elevated in a little over half of the sample, independently of sex (26.31% males and 13.15% females). (Table 3). Regarding the metabolic and liver panels, further studies need to focus more on the impact of enzymes on eye manifestations in people with HIV or AIDS.

Table 3. Distribution of cases according to sex, metabolic disorder, and liver enzyme levels.

Laboratory Marker	Value	Male		Female		Total	
		n (21)	%	n (17)	%	n (38)	%
ALT	normal (5–31 UI/L)	14	36.84	12	31.57	26	68.43
	abnormal (>31 UI/L)	7	18.42	5	13.15	12	31.57
AST	normal (5–31 UI/L)	14	36.84	12	31.57	26	68.43
	abnormal (>31 UI/L)	7	18.42	5	13.15	12	31.57
GGT	normal (7–32 UI/L)	12	31.57	11	28.94	23	60.51
	abnormal (>32 UI/L)	9	23.68	6	15.78	15	39.46
Cholesterol	normal (122–200 mg/dL)	11	28.94	12	31.57	23	60.54
	abnormal (>200 mg/dL)	10	26.31	5	13.15	15	39.46
HDL-COL	normal (40–66 mg/dL)	12	31.57	14	36.84	26	68.43
	abnormal (>66 mg/dL)	9	23.68	3	7.89	12	31.57
LDL-COL	normal (30–159 mg/dL)	11	28.94	12	31.57	23	60.54
	abnormal (>159 mg/dL)	10	26.31	5	13.15	15	39.46
Triglycerides	normal (30–150 mg/dL)	13	34.21	10	26.31	23	60.54
	abnormal (>150 mg/dL)	8	21.05	7	18.42	15	39.46

The research group underwent testing for the most prevalent co-infections linked to HIV/AIDS. The findings revealed that various opportunistic infections affected more than half (55.26%) of the patients admitted to our clinic throughout the study period. When the

CD4 T-lymphocyte count fell below 500 cells/µL in stages 2 and 3 of infection (15.79% and 31.58%, respectively), several opportunistic infections were discovered. (Table 4).

Table 4. Opportunistic infections distribution in research sample according to CDC stage.

	Stage 1		Stage 2		Stage 3		Total	
HIV/AIDS Status	**n (12)**	**%**	**n (12)**	**%**	**n (14)**	**%**	**n (38)**	**%**
No opportunistic infections	9	23.68	6	15.79	2	5.26	17	44.74
Opportunistic infections	3	7.89	6	15.79	12	31.58	21	55.26

The findings revealed that hepatitis B co-infections were the most common (21.05% of patients), *Cytomegalic virus* (CMV) (18.42% of patients), followed by hepatitis C (5.26% of patients) and toxoplasmosis (5.26% of patients). Males had a greater incidence of co-infections than females, making them more afflicted. The Pearson test in the XLSTAT version 2019 program was used to determine a p-value of 0.048 (Table 5).

Table 5. HIV/AIDS cases by co-infections distribution.

Co-Infections	**Men**		**Women**		**Total**	
$p = 0.048$	**n (12)**	**%**	**n (7)**	**%**	**n (19)**	**%**
HBV	5	13.16	3	7.89	8	21.05
HCV	2	5.26	0	0	2	5.26
Toxoplasmosis	1	2.63	1	2.63	2	5.26
CMV	4	10.53	3	7.89	7	18.42

In all the patients, we found out that 17 had congenital eye diseases (44.73%) and the others (21, 55.26%) developed ophthalmological diseases (Table 6). CMV Retinitis was found in eight patients (21.05%), Myopia in seven patients (18.42%), Convergent strabismus in three patients (7.89%), Astigmatism in four patients (10.52%), and cataracts in five patients (13.15%) (Table 7). Other diseases such as retinal detachment (3 patients, 7.89%), Molluscum contagiosum infection of the eyelids (2 patients, 5.26%), periorbital abscesses (2 patients, 5.26%), and acute conjunctivitis (4, 10.52%) were found in 11 patients (28.94%).

Table 6. Type of ophthalmologic diseases found in our study group.

Type of Disease	**n (38)**	**%**
Congenital eye disease	17	44.73
Ophthalmological disease	21	55.26

Table 7. Ophthalmologic diseases found in our study patients.

Type of Ophthalmological Disease	**n (38)**	**%**
CMV Retinitis	8	21.05
Myopia	7	18.42
Convergent strabismus	3	7.89
Astigmatism	4	10.52
Cataract	5	13.15
Others	11	28.94

The specific treatment of the ophthalmological conditions identified in the study patients was instituted in collaboration with an ophthalmologist. It should be mentioned that an antiviral treatment with Gancyclovir 5 gm/kgc bid IV for 3 weeks was used in cases of CMV retinitis, in accordance with the specialist guidelines. In total, 28.94% benefited from optical correction and for those with cataracts, surgical treatment was used.

Antiretroviral therapy (ART) was prescribed to every patient at the Iasi HIV/AIDS Regional Center who were confirmed. Therefore, in 18.42% of cases, a single drug was administered, and in the remaining 81.57% of cases, a medication regimen that addressed the patient's comorbidities was prescribed. The period of time between diagnosis and ART initiation ranged between 72 h and 14 days, according to the severity of the cases, in order to avoid IRIS (immune reconstruction inflammatory syndrome) also following www.hiv-druginteractions.org (accessed on 1 January 2022).

The most used antiretroviral regimen was protease inhibitors (17 patients, 44.73%), then a regimen based on nucleoside reverse transcriptase inhibitors (NRTIs) with non-nucleoside reverse transcriptase inhibitors (NNRTIs) being used for 10 patients (26.31%), and lastly, a regimen based on integrase inhibitors (9 patients, 23.68%). Other antiretroviral regimens included CCR5 inhibitors used for two patients (5.26%) (Table 8).

Table 8. HIV/AIDS cases by ART regimen.

ART Regimen	n (38)	%
Integrase inhibitors+ 2 NNRTI	9	23.68
Protease inhibitors+ 2 NNRTI	17	44.73
NRTI+ 2 NNRTI	10	26.31
Other	2	5.26

Following a one-month evaluation of the patients, the viro-immunological state revealed an elevated level of CD4+ T cells and marked decline in HIV viremia. Due to this, 15 patients (39.47%) had a CD4 value between 200 and 499 cells/µL, 8 patients (21.05%) had a value under 200 cells/µL, and 15 patients (39.47%) had a value over 500 cells/L. Most patients of both sexes had a CD4+ T-lymphocyte count of 200–499 or more cells/µL (Table 9).

Table 9. Distribution by sex and the level of CD4+ T-lymphocytes after a month of ART.

CD4 Levels $p = 0.053$	Male		Female		Total	
	n (21)	%	n (17)	%	n (38)	%
0–200 cells/µL	4	10.53	4	10.53	8	21.05
200–499 cells/µL	9	23.68	6	15.79	15	39.47
>500 cells/µL	8	21.05	7	18.42	15	39.47

The patients were assessed at the time of diagnosis and again a month after beginning ART. After beginning antiretroviral medication, the HIV viral load significantly decreased, with viral suppression occurring in 55.26% of cases (21 instances). The patients who were undetectable at the initial assessment were either transferred from a different regional HIV/AIDS center or diagnosed abroad and had already started ART when first evaluated at our Regional HIV/AIDS Center (Table 10).

Table 10. HIV viral loads status distribution at baseline and one month following ART.

HIV Viral Load ($p < 0.05$)	Initial Assessment		One Month after ART	
	n (38)	%	n (38)	%
Undetectable (<40 copies/mL)	9	23.68	21	55.26
Detectable (>40 copies/mL)	29	76.32	17	44.74

4. Discussion

According to the Infectious Disease Society of America, people with HIV who have a CD4 level under 50 cells are recommended to receive ophthalmological care.

This study evaluated the frequency of eye conditions in HAART-treated people with HIV. The participants' ages ranged from 18 to 70 years old, with a mean age of 38.64 years and an SD of 12.84 years. In total, 71% of the participants were between the ages of 26 and 55. In total, 40% of the patients were female and 60% were male. The ratio of men to women was 1.5.

Bekele S. et al. found that the prevalence of ocular symptoms was 25.3% overall within 348 patients (175 were on antiretroviral therapy and 173 were not on therapy). Keratoconjunctivitis sicca (11.3%) was the most prevalent ocular manifestation, followed by blepharitis (3.2%), molluscum contagiosum (2.6%), conjunctival squamous cell carcinoma (2.3%), conjunctival micro vasculopathy (2.3%), cranial nerve palsies (2%), herpes zoster ophthalmicus (HZO) (1.2%), and HIV retinopathy (0.6%). Patients with a CD4+ level of less than 200 cells/L frequently developed HIV retinopathy and conjunctival micro vasculopathy, whereas patients with a CD4+ count of 200–499 cells/L frequently developed HZO and molluscum contagiosum. Patients on HAART had a higher prevalence of ocular manifestations (32.6%) than non-HAART patients (17.9%) [21]. Our study found more cases with a CD4 level of 200–499 cells/mL who already had ophthalmic congenital diseases or developed other infectious eye diseases. CMV retinitis was found in cases with a CD4 level of <200/mL.

Li W. et al. found 667 (8%) individuals with ocular disorders among the 8743 hospitalized HIV/AIDS patients (15 116 cases) that were enrolled in their study. Ocular injuries were found in 65 (2%) of the 2902 patients who underwent a non-professional inspection, 46 (2%) of the 1621 patients who underwent an on-demand inspection, and 556 (13%) of the 3553 patients who underwent a routine check. The majority of HIV/AIDS ocular manifestations (354 [53%] of 667 patients) were caused by infectious diseases. Most infections affected the cornea, conjunctiva (152 [43%] of 354 patients), and retina (145 [41%] of 354 patients), respectively. Retinopathy and retinitis were strongly linked with CD4-positive counts of fewer than 200 cells/mL [22]. Our study found that, besides infectious eye diseases, many patients had chronic congenital ophthalmic diseases such as astigmatism, myopia, and convergent strabismus.

Gurung S. et al. investigated 54 children and 60 adults, which made up 114 cases, and 24.9% of the children and 61.9% of the adults showed ocular signs. Disorders of the anterior segment and external ocular system made up 21% of the cases in this research. Herpes simplex blepharoconjunctivitis (11.1%) was found in seven children, and dry eye (8.3%) and herpes zoster ophthalmicus (2.6%) were observed in adults, and were the most prevalent findings. Adult instances of posterior segment symptoms (HIV retinopathy 13.5%, CMV retinitis 10.8%, retinal detachment 8.1%, multifocal choroiditis 2.7%, and ocular toxoplasmosis 2.7%) made up 34% of the patients in this study [23]. In our study, we did not include children with infectious eye diseases, but we had similar results in terms of adult cases.

Hothi H. et al. observed that, in patients with HIV who were taking HAART, the prevalence of ocular manifestations was 39%. Adnexal involvement, anterior segment involvement, posterior segment involvement, neuro-ophthalmic abnormalities, and orbital involvement all occurred in 20%, 28%, 33%, and 4% of these cases, respectively. In total, 51% of patients had CD4+ T cell counts under 200 cells/L, and 76% were in the WHO clinical stages 2 and 3 [24]. We observed that infectious eye diseases were more frequent in cases with CD4 levels of <200/mL and 201–499/mL.

Rekha K.R. et al. observed that the overall prevalence of ocular manifestations was 23%, 9.3% of which involved the anterior segment and 26.6% involved the posterior region [25]. We found that the prevalence of anterior segment diseases was more frequent (42.10%), followed by posterior segment manifestations (28.94%) and adnexa diseases (28.98%).

In HIV/AIDS patients, Di Y. et al. observed that CMVR was the most prevalent ocular complication, followed by uveitis and HIV retinopathy. The percentage of patients who had CMVR and HIV retinopathy remained constant over time, however, the percentage of patients who had uveitis showed a clear upward trend (from 1.14% to 19.32%) [26]. The most frequent disease in our study was CMV retinitis (8, 21.05%), followed by myopia (7, 18.42%).

Mustapha J et al. studied a total of 103 patients with HIV. A total of 51.5% of the research participants reported impaired visual acuity in at least one eye, and 44.7% had at least one ocular problem. The most prevalent disorders were toxoplasmic retinochoroiditis (3.9%), posterior vitreous detachment (2.9%), blepharitis (10.7%), nucleosclerosis (6.8%), conjunctivitis (5.8%), pinguecula (5.8%), and dry eye (21.4%) [27].

According to Becker et al., postmortem investigations indicate that the rates of ocular findings are closer to 90%, and that between 50 and 70 percent of people with HIV eventually acquire ocular manifestations. CMV retinitis and retinal microvasculopathy are the two visual signs of AIDS that occur most often, although there are numerous additional problems that might result in vision loss. In order to minimize HIV replication, HAART employs a mix of antiretroviral medications; as a result, the CD4+ helper T-cell population typically recovers, leading to a decrease in opportunistic infections, an improvement in quality of life, and decreases in morbidity and death. This has been demonstrated by a 50% or greater decline in the incidence rates of CMV retinitis and other ocular diseases linked to HIV/AIDS [28]. Besides HAART therapy, patients need frequent ophthalmological evaluations to ensure an increased quality of life, furthermore if they have associated eye diseases.

Yuan TH et al. stated that metabolism, oxidative stress, and inflammation are only a few of the pathways that illustrate the intimate relationship between the liver and the eye. Future research on the connection between the liver and the eye will help us to better understand the communication mechanism between the two organs, which will improve our understanding of the pathogenesis and progression of these liver or eye diseases and help us to develop new therapeutic targets and more effective clinical treatments [29].

This study has potential limitations. The model is based on the retrospective observational nature of the study. The limitations of this paper include its small sample size and retrospective nature. In addition, it is possible that other patients were admitted for territorial ophthalmological care.

Nevertheless, HIV is still a serious public health concern. Infected people can experience the virus's rapid mutation. Due to this ability, HIV has been able to evolve a variety of defenses against the body's immunological responses and antiviral treatment. However, it is hoped that ongoing research may result in newer, low-toxicity anti-HIV drugs that more efficiently lower the viral loads of infected patients and stop them from spreading the illness to other people. By collaborating with other physicians in primary care and lending support to international organizations that promote HIV testing for patients at risk, offer pre-test counseling, and enhance access to low-cost antiretroviral treatment, ophthalmologists can help to prolong the lives of infected patients and reduce the risk of virus transmission.

It is important to ensure the long-term follow-up of HIV-infected patients who present ophthalmic manifestations at the national level, so that we can diagnose and ensure rapid treatment in order to increase quality of life.

5. Conclusions

Despite adequate antiretroviral coverage, HIV infection is still identified in our country after a considerable amount of time. Priority must be given to encouraging voluntary testing, especially among those most at risk for infection (men who have sex with other men, people who use drugs, young adults under 24 years old, sex workers, and those from impoverished backgrounds) [30].

Additionally, anyone with HIV who experiences ocular symptoms should seek specialized ophthalmologic treatment as soon as possible. Any therapeutic holdup could result in irreversible vision loss. Long-term coordination is required to combat this terrible disease, improving communication between the ophthalmology and infectious disease fields [31].

The longevity of patients with HIV is expanding due to the widespread use of HAART and development of better drugs. Additionally, they are more likely to experience sight loss and more likely to acquire ocular symptoms. A multidisciplinary team is best suited to addressing HIV, because it affects numerous organs. When individuals with HIV complain of any visual issue, it is strongly advised that they be referred to an ophthalmologist. The eyes of those with HIV should undergo a thorough examination [32].

Author Contributions: Conceptualization, M.C., I.I.L. and V.A.; data curation, I.I.L., M.C. and G.S.; formal analysis, G.S. and Ș.A.R.; investigation, M.C. and I.I.L.; methodology, I.I.L. and V.D.D.; resources, G.S., Ș.A.R. and V.H.; software, V.D.D. and V.H.; supervision, V.A.; validation, M.C., I.I.L. and V.A.; visualization, M.C., I.I.L. and V.A.; writing—original draft, M.C., I.I.L. and G.S.; writing—review and editing, I.I.L. and M.C. All authors have read and agreed to the published version of the manuscript.

Funding: This research received no external funding.

Institutional Review Board Statement: The study was conducted in accordance with the Declaration of Helsinki and approved by the Ethics Committee of the "St. Parascheva" Clinical Hospital of Infectious Diseases, Iasi, Romania. (Approval No. 4 from 17 May 2023).

Informed Consent Statement: This was a retrospective study, and written informed consent had been obtained from the patients when they were admitted to our hospital, according to the hospital policy.

Data Availability Statement: All data generated or analyzed during this study are included in this published article.

Conflicts of Interest: The authors declare no conflict of interest.

References

1. Govender, R.D.; Hashim, M.J.; Khan, M.A.; Mustafa, H.; Khan, G. Global Epidemiology of HIV/AIDS: A Resurgence in North America and Europe. *J. Epidemiol. Glob. Health* **2021**, *11*, 296–301. [CrossRef] [PubMed]
2. Justiz Vaillant, A.A.; Gulick, P.G. HIV Disease Current Practice. In *StatPearls [Internet]*; StatPearls Publishing: Treasure Island, FL, USA, 2023.
3. Davis, J.L.; Feldman, B.H.; Davis, J.L.; Palestine, A.; Shantha, J.; Larochelle, M. *Ocular Involvement in HIV/AIDS*; American Academy of Ophthalmology: San Francisco, CA, USA, 2022.
4. Goldberg, D.E.; Smithen, L.M.; Angelilli, A.; Freeman, W.R. HIV-associated retinopathy in the HAART era. *Retina* **2005**, *25*, 633–683. [PubMed]
5. Luo, J.; Jing, D.; Kozak, I.; Huiming, Z.; Siying, C.; Yezhen, Y.; Xin, Q.; Luosheng, T.; Adelman, R.A.; Forster, S.H. Prevalence of ocular manifestations of HIV/AIDS in the highly active antiretroviral therapy (HAART) era: A different spectrum in Central South China. *Ophthalmic Epidemiol.* **2013**, *20*, 170–175. [CrossRef]
6. Sudharshan, S.; Nair, N.; Curi, A.; Banker, A.; Kempen, J.H. Human immunodeficiency virus and intraocular inflammation in the highly active anti-retroviral therapy era—An update. *Indian J. Ophthalmol.* **2020**, *68*, 1787. [CrossRef] [PubMed]
7. Kunavisarut, P.; Sirirungsi, W.; Pathanapitoon, K.; Rothova, A. Clinical manifestations of human immunodeficiency virus-induced uveitis. *Ophthalmology* **2012**, *119*, 1455–1459. [CrossRef]
8. Biswas, J. Anterior segment manifestations of HIV/AIDS. *Indian J. Ophthalmol.* **2008**, *56*, 363–375. [CrossRef]
9. Banker, A. Posterior segment manifestations of HIV/AIDS. *Indian J. Ophthalmol.* **2008**, *56*, 377–383. [CrossRef]
10. Feroze, K.B.; Wang, J. Ocular Manifestations of HIV. In *StatPearls [Internet]*; StatPearls Publishing: Treasure Island, FL, USA, 2022.
11. Ikoona, E.; Kalyesubula, I.; Kawuma, M. Ocular manifestations in paediatric HIV/AIDS patients in Mulago Hospital, Uganda. *Afr. Health Sci.* **2003**, *3*, 83–86.

12. Almeida, F.P.P.; Paula, J.S.; Martins, M.C.; Sena, D.F.; Cervi, M.C.; Rodrigues, M.L.V. Ocular manifestations in pediatric patients with HIV infection in the post-HAART era in southern Brazil. *Eye* **2007**, *21*, 1017–1018. [CrossRef] [PubMed]
13. Munro, M.; Yadavalli, T.; Fonteh, C.; Arfeen, S.; Lobo-Chan, A.M. Cytomegalovirus Retinitis in HIV and Non-HIV Individuals. *Microorganisms* **2019**, *8*, 55. [CrossRef]
14. Tang, Y.; Sun, J.; He, T.; Shen, Y.; Liu, L.; Steinhart, C.R.; Chen, J.; Qi, T.; Wang, Z.; Song, W.; et al. Clinical Features of Cytomegalovirus Retinitis in HIV Infected Patients. *Front. Cell Infect. Microbiol.* **2020**, *10*, 136. [CrossRef] [PubMed]
15. Murray, J.; Hilbig, A.; Soe, T.T.; Ei, W.L.S.S.; Soe, K.P.; Ciglenecki, I. Treating HIV-associated cytomegalovirus retinitis with oral valganciclovir and intra-ocular ganciclovir by primary HIV clinicians in southern Myanmar: A retrospective analysis of routinely collected data. *BMC Infect Dis* **2020**, *20*, 842. [CrossRef] [PubMed]
16. Soman, R. Human immunodeficiency virus and the ophthalmologist. *Indian J. Ophthalmol.* **2008**, *56*, 355–356. [CrossRef] [PubMed]
17. Venkatesh, K. Impact of highly active antiretroviral therapy on ophthalmic manifestations in HIV/AIDS. *Indian J. Ophthalmol.* **2008**, *56*, 391–393. [PubMed]
18. Saini, N.; Hasija, S.; Kaur, P.; Kaur, M.; Pathania, V.; Singh, A. Study of the prevalence of ocular manifestations in HIV-positive patients. *Nepal. J. Ophthalmol.* **2019**, *11*, 11–18. [CrossRef]
19. Tasiopoulou, A.; Urzua, C.A.; Lightman, S. Successful treatment of cytomegalovirus retinitis with oral/intravitreal antivirals in HIV-negative patients with lymphoma. *Eye* **2023**, *37*, 1895–1903. [CrossRef]
20. Ghate, M.; Gogate, P.; Phadke, S.; Shaikh, G.; Shidhaye, P.; Gurav, S.; Gadhe, K.; Bhusnawar, M.; Mane, A.; Panda, S. Ocular manifestations and refractive errors among people living with HIV in Pune, India: A cross-sectional study. *J. Int. Med. Res.* **2021**, *49*, 03000605211026814. [CrossRef]
21. Bekele, S.; Gelaw, Y.; Tessema, F. Ocular manifestation of HIV/AIDS and correlation with CD4+ cells count among adult HIV/AIDS patients in Jimma town, Ethiopia: A cross sectional study. *BMC Ophthalmol.* **2013**, *13*, 20. [CrossRef]
22. Li, W.; Wang, X.; Zhao, L.; Lin, D.; Liu, Z.; Wu, X.; Wang, J.; Zhang, X.; Yang, Y.; Wang, R.; et al. Ocular manifestation in patients with HIV/AIDS: A hospital-based retrospective study. *Lancet* **2019**, *394* (Suppl. 1), S92. [CrossRef]
23. Gurung, S.; Shah, D.N.; Sharma, A.K.; Shrestha, L.; Thapa, M.; Godar, M. Ocular Manifestations of HIV/AIDS in Children and Adults. *Investig. Ophthalmol. Vis. Sci.* **2017**, *58*, 2156.
24. Hothi, H.S.; Gohil, N.R.; Parekh, N.V.; Patel, S.S. A prevalence study of ocular manifestations in HIV positive patients on highly active antiretroviral therapy. *Int. J. Community Med. Public Health* **2019**, *6*, 2950–2954. [CrossRef]
25. Rekha, K.R. Evaluation of correlation between ocular manifestations with CD4+ count in HIV patients: A cross-sectional study. HIV & AIDS Review. *Int. J. HIV-Relat. Probl.* **2021**, *20*, 264–269.
26. Di, Y.; Yu, W.; Ye, J. Temporal trends in ocular manifestations of HIV/AIDS patients in the past 18 years in a tertiary hospital in China. *Graefes Arch. Clin. Exp. Ophthalmol.* **2022**, *260*, 2807–2818. [CrossRef] [PubMed]
27. Mustapha, J.; Namanga, E.S.; Idriss, B.; Sesay, D.; Jiba, D.F.; Russell, J.B.W.; Vandy, M.J.; Deen, G.F.; Yendewa, G.A., Lakoh, S. Ophthalmic Manifestations among HIV Patients at the Main Tertiary Hospital in Freetown, Sierra Leone: A Cross-Sectional Study. *Venereology* **2022**, *1*, 161–169. [CrossRef]
28. Becker, K.N.; Becker, N.M. Ocular manifestations seen in HIV. *Disease-a-Month* **2014**, *60*, 268–275. [CrossRef] [PubMed]
29. Yuan, T.H.; Yue, Z.S.; Zhang, G.H.; Wang, L.; Dou, G.R. Beyond the Liver: Liver-Eye Communication in Clinical and Experimental Aspects. *Front. Mol. Biosci.* **2021**, *8*, 823277. [CrossRef]
30. Loghin, I.I.; Vâţă, A.; Mihai, I.F.; Silvaş, G.; Rusu, Ş.A.; Luca, C.M.; Dorobăţ, C.M. Profile of Newly Diagnosed Patients with HIV Infection in North-Eastern Romania. *Medicina* **2023**, *59*, 440. [CrossRef]
31. Linzerová, D.; Stepanov, A.; Němčanský, J. Ocular Manifestations in Patients with HIV infection. *Cesk. Slov. Oftalmol.* **2019**, *74*, 234–239. [CrossRef]
32. Rubens, B. The ophthalmologist and the global impact of the AIDS epidemic LV Edward Jackson Memorial Lecture. *Am. J. Ophthalmol.* **2000**, *129*, 1–8.

Disclaimer/Publisher's Note: The statements, opinions and data contained in all publications are solely those of the individual author(s) and contributor(s) and not of MDPI and/or the editor(s). MDPI and/or the editor(s) disclaim responsibility for any injury to people or property resulting from any ideas, methods, instructions or products referred to in the content.

MDPI
St. Alban-Anlage 66
4052 Basel
Switzerland
www.mdpi.com

Medicina Editorial Office
E-mail: medicina@mdpi.com
www.mdpi.com/journal/medicina

Disclaimer/Publisher's Note: The statements, opinions and data contained in all publications are solely those of the individual author(s) and contributor(s) and not of MDPI and/or the editor(s). MDPI and/or the editor(s) disclaim responsibility for any injury to people or property resulting from any ideas, methods, instructions or products referred to in the content.

www.ingramcontent.com/pod-product-compliance
Lightning Source LLC
Chambersburg PA
CBHW040809250926
51850CB00007BA/1121
9783036594682